A Guide to the History of Brazil, 1500–1822

A Guide to the History of Brazil, 1500–1822

The Literature in English

Francis A. Dutra

ABC-Clio
Santa Barbara, California
Oxford, England

Library of Congress Cataloging in Publication Data

Dutra, Francis A 1938–
A guide to the history of Brazil, 1500–1822.

Includes indexes.
1. Brazil—History To 1821—Bibliography.
I. Title.
Z1686.D87 [F2508] 016.981 80-10933
ISBN 0-87436-263-6

ABC-Clio, Inc.
Riviera Campus
2040 Alameda Padre Serra, Box 4397
Santa Barbara, California 93103

Clio Press, Ltd.
Woodside House, Hinksey Hill
Oxford, OX1 5BE, England

Manufactured in the United States of America

1 2 3 4 5 6 7 8 9

To
Carleton Sprague Smith
Bailey W. Diffie
Harry Bernstein
Manoel Cardozo
John E. Fagg
with affection and gratitude and
in recognition of their efforts in promoting
the study of Brazilian history in the
United States.

Contents

Preface

A Guide to the History of Brazil, 1500–1822: The Literature in English had its origins in 1972, when I served as secretary, and Professors Joseph Love of the University of Illinois and Emília Viotti da Costa of Yale University served as chairpersons, of the Brazilianists of the Conference on Latin American History. Our aim was to prepare a bibliography that would be of use to the great majority of students who took courses on Brazilian and Latin American history, art and literature and who knew only English. There was no bibliography in English on colonial Brazil and books that contained bibliographic references to Brazil frequently either had the majority of their entries on works in Portuguese, Spanish or French or had little or no annotation. This guide includes not only books on Brazil but articles and doctoral dissertations as well. Because of the economic difficulties many publishers in the United States—including university presses—were experiencing and what was thought to be too limited a readership for studies on colonial Brazil, a number of excellent dissertations on the first three and one-quarter centuries of Portuguese American history were not being published. Although many dissertations completed during the past two and one-half decades have been available from Xerox University Microfilms, Ann Arbor, Michigan, it has not been until recently that the increasingly high cost of trade books has made the acquisition of photocopies of some of these dissertations both economical and practical for library and class use. Dissertations available from Xerox University Microfilms have been noted by the volume and page number of the official abstract in *Dissertation Abstracts International*.

It also seemed desirable to have more than the customary twenty-five to thirty-five words of comment that grace most bibliographies.

Since the useful *Historical Abstracts* (until 1974) only contained articles that dealt with the period after 1775, there was a need for a combination abstract-narrative summary with annotation regarding the item's value. At the same time, it seemed appropriate to pay special attention to the surprisingly large number of contemporary narratives that either originally appeared in English or were later translated into that language. I have included the most representative excerpts from these. Wherever possible, I have tried not to repeat identical comments when several people have written similarly about their visits to the same place. In addition, each section has been arranged topically and chronologically, so that the reader following the items in consecutive order can get a coherent picture of what happened in colonial Brazil and what has been written in English regarding a certain topic or time period. In the absence of a textbook on the history of the Portuguese in America, 1500–1822, a reading of this guide from cover to cover will provide a historical survey.

History has been taken in its broad sense and every effort has been made to include books, articles, and dissertations on art, literature, geography, sociology, anthropology and archaeology when they were of interest and value to the historian. More recent articles and those that appeared in journals other than the major ones in English of interest to students of colonial Brazil—the *Hispanic American Historical Review, The Americas,* and the *Luso-Brazilian Review*—were often given more detailed descriptions since a number of these journals are more difficult for students and the general reader to obtain. Therefore, there is no necessary correlation between the length of the annotation and the importance of the article or book. In addition, because of a growing interest in audiovisual materials, articles with a large number of excellent plates have been included, even when the historical value of the accompanying text is not of as high quality as the illustrations.

I wish to thank the Conference on Latin American History for the financial aid they gave me to obtain photocopies of many of the items in this guide. Thanks are also due University Microfilms International, Ann Arbor, Michigan. I also wish to express thanks to Walter Brem, Dwight E. Petersen, and Joseph Dorsey, three of my graduate students, for calling attention to several items on colonial Brazil they encountered in their reading and research. I owe a special debt of gratitude and appreciation to Mary Ann Macintosh, my research assistant, who not only aided me in tracing down numerous books and articles but also helped abstract many of the doctoral dissertations. In addition, she pointed out a number of "stylistic infelicities" in the early drafts of this guide and offered suggestions on how to improve the text.

How to Use This Guide

The summaries and excerpts may be read continuously or individual items may be found topically in the table of contents of the *Guide* or by author, editor, translator, or illustrator in the index. There is also a biographical index as well as one which refers to nineteenth- and twentieth-century authors who are cited but not abstracted. Since the citation of Portuguese names in indices and catalogues has frequently varied from index to index and from catalogue to catalogue, I have tried to include several variations in my indices and provided the same item references with each name.

Spelling, capitalization, and punctuation have been left as printed in the original. Where errors in the original might lead to confusion, brackets have been used for clarification. Names of Portuguese who remained in Portugal or who are known better as Portuguese than Brazilians are accented according to Portuguese usage. The important orthographic changes of the early 1940s have resulted in a variety of spellings that have defied attempts to achieve consistency. Titles and quotations from works published before these changes appear as printed.

Chronology

1415 Capture of Ceuta in North Africa by the Portuguese.

1452 Bull of Pope Nicholas V, *Dum Diversas,* gives Afonso V of Portugal "general and indefinite powers to search out and conquer all pagans, enslave them and appropriate their lands and goods."

1455 Bull of Pope Nicholas V, *Romanus Pontifex,* confirms earlier bull and temporarily settles conflict of Castile and Portugal over Africa.

1456 Bull of Pope Calixtus III, *Inter Caetera,* confers on the Portuguese military order of Christ, of which Henry "the Navigator" was governor, control over the church in all matters except those of faith and morals in "all the lands acquired and to be acquired from Capes Bojador and Nam through the whole of Guinea and beyond its southern shore as far as to the Indians."

1460 Death of Prince Henry.

1479 Ratification of the Treaty of Alcáçovas between Castile and Portugal. Portugal cedes to Castile the Canary Islands. Castile promises to stay away from Portuguese Africa and the Azores, Madeiras and Cape Verde Islands.

1481 João II succeeds his father Afonso V as king of Portugal.

1492 Columbus arrives in America.

1493 Four pro-Spanish bulls are issued by Pope Alexander VI. Several are antedated. Two are entitled *Inter Caetera,* the second of which draws a line of demarcation, one hundred leagues west of the Cape Verde Islands, and gives Castile "the exclusive right to acquire territorial possessions and to trade in all the lands west of that line." Another of the Alexandrine bulls, *Dudum Siquidem,* revokes "all the earlier papal grants to Portugal which might seem to give her a claim to lands not already possessed by her."

1494 Two Treaties of Tordesillas. The first of these determines that "all lands lying east of a meridian located 370 leagues west of the Cape Verde Islands, and discovered by Portugal, were to pertain to that country and all lands west of the line, discovered by Spain, were to pertain to Spain."

1495 Death of João II. He is succeeded by the Duke of Beja, who becomes Manuel I.

1498 Vicente Yañez Pinzon sails along the Brazilian coast and explores the mouth of the Amazon river.

1500 Pedro Alvares Cabral, on his way to India, touches Brazil and claims it for Portugal. Pero Vaz Caminha writes his famous letter to King Manuel and describes Brazil.

1501 Additional Portuguese expeditions explore the coast of Brazil.

1502 Fernão de Loronha [Noronha] receives a contract from Manuel I to export brazilwood from Portuguese America.

1504 The French ship *L'Espoir,* captained by Binot Paulmier de Gonneville, visits Brazil.

1511 Voyage of the ship *Bretoa* to Cabo Frio in its search for brazilwood.

1515 Juan Dias de Solis, a Portuguese in Spanish service, explores the coastline of Brazil from Cabo Santo Agostinho to the Rio de la Plata.

1516 The Portuguese under the leadership of Cristovão Jacques establish a trading post in Pernambuco and explore the coast of Brazil to the Rio de la Plata.

1519 Ferdinand Magellan, a Portuguese in Spanish service, visits Guanabara Bay on his voyage around the world.

1521 Death of Manuel I. He is succeeded by João III.

1524 Aleixo Garcia, a Portuguese who had accompanied Juan Dias de Solis on his expedition to the Plata region, reaches the borders of the Inca empire and sends back silver samples.

1526 Sebastian Cabot, in the service of Spain, begins to explore the Plata region.

1530 William Hawkins, father of Richard Hawkins, leads the first English voyage to Brazil.

1532 Martim Afonso de Sousa founds the town of São Vicente near present-day Santos.

1533 Brazil is placed under the ecclesiastical jurisdiction of the bishopric of Funchal in the Madeiras.

1534 Portuguese America is divided into captaincies or colonies and divided among lord-proprietors *(donatários)*.

1535 Duarte Coelho, lord-proprietor of Pernambuco, eventually to be the most prosperous of the donatarial captaincies of Brazil, arrives in Pernambuco.

1540 Alvar Nuñez Cabeza de Vaca travels from Santa Catarina in southern Brazil to Asunción, Paraguay. On his way he passes Iguassú Falls.

1541 Francisco de Orellana begins his voyage down the Amazon, beginning at the Napo River in present-day Ecuador.

1543 Founding of the town of Santos by Braz Cubas.

1548 The administration of Brazil is put in the hands of a governor-general. Certain powers of the lords-proprietor are withdrawn.

1549 Arrival in Brazil of Tomé de Sousa, the first governor-general of Portuguese America. He is accompanied by nine Jesuits headed by Padre Manuel de Nóbrega. The city of Salvador is founded.

1551 Portuguese America's first bishopric is established at Bahia.

1552 Brazil's first bishop, Dom Pedro Fernandes Sardinha, arrives in America. Tomé de Sousa begins his inspection of the captaincies south of Bahia.

1553 Duarte da Costa, Brazil's second governor-general, arrives in Bahia. In his company is young José de Anchieta, the future Jesuit "Apostle of Brazil."

1554 Padre Manuel da Nóbrega founds the Jesuit colégio of São Paulo.

1555 The Frenchman, Nicolas Durand de Villegagnon, establishes the colony, Antarctique France, on Guanabara Bay.

1556 Brazil's first Bishop (Sardinha) eaten by Indians after shipwreck.

1557 Death of João III. Young Sebastião I becomes king under the regency of his grandmother, Catarina of Austria, sister of Charles V.

Mém de Sá, third governor-general of Brazil, arrives in Salvador.

An account of the adventures in Brazil of Hans Staden, a German mercenary in Portuguese service, is published in Europe. The same year also saw the publication of Friar André Thevet's book on Antarctique France.

1558 The Portuguese, Henrique Garcês, discovers mercury in Peru.

1559 A royal *alvará* of this year facilitates the importation of African slaves by Brazilian sugar mill owners.

1560 The Portuguese capture and occupy the French colony of Antarctique France. Duarte Coelho de Albuquerque, the second lord-proprietor of Pernambuco, and his younger brother Jorge de Albuquerque return to Brazil from Lisbon.

1562 Cardinal-Infante Henrique succeeds Catarina as regent.

1565 Estácio de Sá founds the city of São Sabastião do Rio de Janeiro. Jorge de Albuquerque leaves Brazil for the last time. His trouble-filled return voyage to Portugal on the nau *Santo Antônio* becomes one of the most famous of the *Naufrágios.*

1567 The French are definitively ousted from the region around Rio de Janeiro.

1568 Sebastião I reaches his majority.

1570 *Carta régia* of Sebastião I guaranteeing freedom to the Brazilian Indians.

1572 Portuguese America is divided into two administrative sections: one is centered at Bahia under the governorship of Luis de Brito e Almeida; the other is located in Rio de Janeiro under Governor Antônio Salema.

1573 The Jesuit *colégio* of São Sebastião is founded by Padre Manuel da Nóbrega.

1574 Sebastião I makes his first expedition to North Africa.

1576 Pero Magalhães Gandavo's *História da Provincia de Santa Cruz* is published in Lisbon.

1577 Portuguese America is again unified under one governor-general. This time Lourenço da Veiga receives the post.

1578 Sebastião I killed at the battle of Alcacer-Quibir in North Africa. Cardinal-Infante Henrique becomes king of Portugal.

Jean de Lery's *Histoire d'un voyage fait en la terre du Bresil* is published.

1580 Before dying, King Henrique names Philip of Spain as his successor.

Spanish troops occupy Portugal. Philip II of Spain becomes

also Philip I of Portugal as the sixty-year union of Iberian crowns under the Habsburg monarchy begins.

1581 The Cortes held at the Portuguese town of Tomar legalizes Philip II's position as king of Portugal.

The English ship *Minion* arrives in Brazil from London.

1583 The English ship *Royal Merchant* arrives in Brazil.

1584 Paraiba is conquered by the Portuguese.

1586 Expedition of Englishman Thomas Cavendish to Brazil. A combined Spanish-Portuguese force fails to dislodge French from Paraiba in the Brazilian Northeast.

1587 Gabriel Soares de Sousa composes his *Tratado Descritivo do Brasil,* one of the most important descriptions of Portuguese America in the last quarter of the sixteenth century.

1591 Royal prohibition against foreign shipping stopping in Brazil without special licenses. Thomas Cavendish attacks São Vicente. The Inquisitor Heitor Furtado de Mendonça arrives in Bahia, where he will remain until 1593.

1593 The Inquisitor Heitor Furtado de Mendonça leaves Bahia for Pernambuco, where he remains until 1595.

1595 Englishman James Lancaster attacks Recife. Philip II (I of Portugal) prohibits enslavement of Brazilian Indians.

1596 English establish trading posts in the Amazon region.

1598 Death of Philip II (I of Portugal) and the accession to power of Philip III (II of Portugal).

1599 Jerónimo de Albuquerque pacifies the Petiguara Indians of Paraiba and founds the town of Natal.

1601 Diogo Botelho, eighth governor-general of Brazil, remains in Pernambuco instead of Salvador, the capital of Portuguese America.

1602 Appearance of Dutch traders in the Amazon region.

1603 Crown establishes whaling monoply in Brazil.

1609 Beginning of the Twelve-Year Truce between the Dutch and the Spanish.

First Judges of the Relacão (High Court) arrive in Brazil.

1612 Martim Soares Moreno establishes a fort in Ceará near the site of the future city of Fortaleza. The French found a post at São Luis do Maranhão.

1614 French in Maranhão are defeated by a combined Spanish-Portuguese force at the battle of Guaxenduba. Claude de Abbeville's *Histoire des Peres Capucins en l'Isle de Maragnan et terres circonvoisines* is published in Paris.

1615 Jerónimo de Albuquerque, Alexandre de Moura and Francisco Caldeira lead forces that capture French stronghold of São Luis. The French are permanently ousted from Maranhão. The account of Yves d'Evreux, *Suite de l'Histoire des choses memorables advenues en Maragnan es anes 1613 et 1614*, is published.

1616 Francisco Caldeira founds the town of Santa Maria de Belém on the banks of the Pará river.

1619 Philip III of Spain (II of Portugal) visits Lisbon.

1620 Matias de Albuquerque arrives as governor of Pernambuco.

1621 End of Twelve-Year Truce between the Dutch and the Spanish. The Dutch West India Company is founded. Philip III (II of Portugal) dies and is succeeded by Philip IV (III of Portugal). The State of Maranhão is created and includes Maranhão, Pará and Ceará. It is given its own governor and separated from the jurisdiction of the governor-general in Bahia.

1624 The Dutch capture Bahia. The State of Maranhão is divided into captaincies.

1625 A combined Spanish-Portuguese armada under Dom Fadrique de Toledo drives out the Dutch from Bahia. Dutch and English positions in the Amazon region are destroyed by the Portuguese.

1627 Piet Heyn attacks the Brazilian coast.

1628 Piet Heyn captures the Spanish silver fleet at Matanzas Bay, Cuba.

1630 The Dutch attack and capture Recife and Olinda in Pernambuco.

1637 Johan Maurits of Nassau becomes governor of Dutch Brazil. The Dutch capture Mina in Portuguese Africa. Anti-Spanish riots in Evora, Portugal.

1638 Pedro Teixeira reaches Quito via the Amazon and its tributaries. The armada of the Conde da Torre leaves for Brazil.

1640 The Conde da Torre's armada is defeated by the Dutch off the coast of Itamaracá, north of the captaincy of Pernambuco. The Marquis of Montalvão is named viceroy of Brazil. There are riots in Rio de Janeiro, Santos and São Paulo over the publication of Pope Urban VIII's *Commissum nobis* (1638) on the freedom of the Amerindian. The Portuguese revolt against Spanish dominion. Philip IV (III of Portugal) is overthrown and the Duke of Bragança is proclaimed João IV of Portugal.

1641 João IV is proclaimed in Brazil. Ten-Year Truce signed by the Dutch and the Portuguese. Before it goes into effect, the Dutch capture Luanda in Angola and Sergipe and Maranhão in Brazil.

Guaraní Indians armed by Spanish Jesuits defeat *bandeirantes* at Mbororé.

1642 Inhabitants of Rio de Janeiro given the same privileges as those of Porto in Portugal. The Portuguese crown decrees that tobacco is a royal monopoly.

1643 Johan Maurits of Nassau's town of Mauricia (Recife) is completed.

1644 Salvador Correa de Sá is named general of the Brazilian fleets. Matias de Albuquerque leads Portuguese troops to important victory over Spaniards at the battle of Montijo

(Spain). Johan Maurits of Nassau returns to Europe, after administering Dutch Brazil since 1637.

1645 Luso-Brazilians of Pernambuco rise up against the Dutch. The inhabitants of São Luis do Maranhão also are given the privileges of those of Porto.

1648 Francisco Barreto defeats the Dutch at the First Battle of Guararapes. Founding of the town of Paranagua.

1649 Dutch defeated at the Second Battle of Guararapes. Companhia Geral do Comércio do Brazil is founded. Its first fleet leaves Lisbon for Brazil.

1652 The Relação (High Court) of Bahia is reinstated in Brazil, after being suppressed in 1626.

1654 The Dutch, besieged by Luso-Brazilian troops, surrender Recife and leave Brazil.

1658 The town of São Francisco do Sul is founded. The Portuguese crown proclaims salt to be a royal monopoly.

1661 The Dutch sign treaty of peace with Portugal, officially recognizing their loss of Brazil.

1668 Town of Curitiba founded.

1674 The emerald-searching expedition of Fernão Dias Pais leaves São Paulo.

1676 Bahia is raised to the status of an archdiocese. Two new dioceses are created. Olinda (Pernambuco) and Rio de Janeiro, the latter including all of southern Brazil.

1677 Diocese of Maranhão established and made a suffragan see of Lisbon.

1680 D. Manuel Lobo founds Colônia do Sacramento on the banks of the Rio de la Plata. It is captured and destroyed by the Spaniards later this year.

1681 São Paulo is named the center of a captaincy of the same name.

1682 The Companhia do Comércio do Maranhão is founded.

1684 Beckman revolt in Maranhão.

1686 Regimento for the Missions published.

1695 Zumbi, head of the *quilombo* of Palmares, is defeated and killed by the troops of Domingos Jorge Velho and Bernardo Vieira de Melo.

1706 Spaniards capture Colônia do Sacramento.

1708 Emboabas in Minas Gerais name Manuel Nunes Viana, governor of all the mines.

1709 Captaincy of São Paulo and Minas Gerais is established.

1710 Antônio de Albuquerque is named governor of the captaincy of São Paulo and Minas. Recife is raised to the status of a town (*vila*). War of the Mascates breaks out between Olinda and Recife. The Frenchman Duclerc and his forces attack Rio de Janeiro. Duclerc is captured and the French are defeated.

1711 The French under Duguay-Trouin sack Rio de Janeiro. The Academia Científica is founded in Rio de Janeiro.

1716 The captaincy of Pernambuco reverts to the crown.

1719 Diocese of Belém is created.

1720 *Carta régia* separates the Captaincy of Minas Gerais from that of São Paulo. The Companhia do Comércio of Brazil is suppressed.

1722 Gold is discovered in Goiás and Cuiabá.

1724 Spaniards found Montevideo on the banks of the Rio de la Plata after expelling Portuguese from the area. The Brazilian Academy of the *Esquecidos* is founded.

1727 Governor Rodrigo Cesar founds the town of Cuiabá.

1729 Diamonds are discovered in Serra Frio.

1731 Diamonds become a crown monopoly.

1733 Gomes Freire de Andrada becomes governor and captain-general of Rio de Janeiro.

1735 Spaniards attack Colônia do Sacramento. Gomes Freire de Andrada is named administrator of Minas Gerais.

1737 The colonization of Rio Grande do Sul is begun.

1742 Martim Felix de Lima navigates the Guaporé, Madeira and Amazon rivers and reaches Belém do Pará.

1748 Gomes Freire de Andrada is named administrator of the captaincies of Goiás, Cuiabá and Mato Grosso.

1750 Treaty of Madrid signed between Spain and Portugal. Using the principle of *uti possidetis*, Portuguese settlement south and west of the line of the 1494 Treaty of Tordesillas is recognized by Spain. João V dies and is succeeded by José I. Sebastião José de Carvalho e Melo (the future Marquis of Pombal) becomes chief minister of the Portuguese monarch.

1751 A second tribunal of the Relação (High Court) is established in Brazil, this time in Rio de Janeiro.

1752 Rio Grande do Sul is settled by almost two hundred families from the Azores. Pombal begins the process by which the donatarial captaincies of Cameta, Ilha de Joannes, Caeté, Cuma, Itamaracá, Itaparica, Ilheus, Paraiba do Sul and São Vicente become crown colonies.

1754 The Academy of the Renascidos is founded in Bahia.

1755 The captaincy of São José do Rio Negro is founded. The Companhia Geral do Comércio do Grão Pará e Maranhão is founded.

1756 The first fleet of the Companhia Geral do Comércio do Grão Pará and Maranhão leaves Lisbon for Brazil.

1759 The Jesuits are expelled from Brazil. The donatarial captaincy of Porto Seguro becomes a crown colony. The Companhia Geral do Comércio de Pernambuco e Paraiba is founded.

1760 The cultivation of cotton is intensified in Maranhão.

1761 Vila Bela becomes the administrative center for Mato Grosso.

1762 Colônia do Sacramento surrenders to Pedro de Cevallos and the Spaniards.

1763 Pedro de Cevallos captures the town of Rio Grande. Rio de Janeiro becomes the capital of Brazil, replacing Salvador. Brazil is raised to the status of a viceroyalty. Gomes Freire de Andrada dies in Rio de Janeiro.

1766 The cultivation of rice is introduced in Maranhão.

1769 Publication of José Basilio da Gama's epic poem *O Uruguay*.

1772 Royal decree creates the State of Maranhão and Piauí. Pará is administratively tied to the captaincy of Rio Negro.

1776 Portuguese retake the town of Rio Grande from the Spaniards.

1777 Death of José I and the disgrace of the Marquis of Pombal. Maria I becomes queen of Portugal. Treaty of San Ildefonso is signed. It confirms, with alterations, the aborted Treaty of Madrid (1750). The Companhia de Comércio do Grão Pará and Maranhão is dissolved.

1781 The poem *Caramurú* by Frei José de Santa Maria Durão is published.

1789 Minas Conspiracy denounced.

1792 Tiradentes is sentenced to death for his role in the Inconfidência Mineira. Others involved are exiled.

1798 Bahian conspiracy discovered. Four conspirators are hung. The royal whaling monopoly is abolished.

1801 Royal salt monopoly abolished.

1808 Court arrives in Brazil. Ports are opened to the commerce of all friendly nations.

1815 Brazil is raised to the status of a kingdom equal with Portugal.

1822 Brazilian independence is proclaimed. Pedro I is named emperor.

I. Bibliographies [Nos. 1–26]

More than two dozen bibliographical guides in English are of special importance for students of colonial Brazil. For publications appearing during the last four decades, the most comprehensive bibliography is the *Handbook for Latin American Studies* **[1]**, especially its sections on Brazilian history and art. For articles published since the 1950s on colonial Brazil, *Historical Abstracts* **[2]** and *Recently Published Articles* **[3]** are most helpful, the former with a section on Brazil, the latter with one on colonial Latin America. *Latin America. A Guide to the Historical Literature* **[4]** has some valuable sections, though most of the works cited for Brazil are not in English. Robin A. Humphreys's *Latin American History. A Guide to the Literature in English* **[5]** is excellent for books, articles, and contemporary narratives about colonial Brazil published before 1957. The Brazilian sections in Humphreys can be supplemented by E. Bradford Burns's bibliography **[6]**, published in 1965, and A. Curtis Wilgus, *Latin America, Spain and Portugal. A Selected and Annotated Bibliographical Guide to Books Published in the United States, 1954-1974* **[7]**, though the latter, as the title indicates, is limited to titles published in the United States.

Some special topics given bibliographic attention are Trask, Meyer, and Trask's *A Bibliography of United States–Latin American Relations Since 1910* **[8]**; Robert Conrad's *Brazilian Slavery: An Annotated Research Bibliography* **[9]**; Robert C. Smith and Elizabeth Wilder, *A Guide to the Art of Latin America* **[10]**; and James E. Hogan, "Antônio Francisco Lisboa, 'O Aleijadinho': An Annotated Bibliography" **[11]**.

The increasing number of excellent doctoral dissertations on colonial Brazil have been listed by several compilers. The broadest effort has been by Carl A. Hanson **[12]** and **[13]** in his two-part article in *The Americas* and his monumental *Dissertations on Iberian and Latin American History* **[17]**, the latter published in 1975. More recent dissertations as well as earlier ones microfilmed by University Microfilms can be found in *Dissertation Abstracts International* **[18]**. Catalogues of these dissertations dealing with Latin America have been published by University Microfilms **[15]** and **[16]**, in 1974 and 1978, respectively. Titles of dissertations on Latin America not included in *Dissertation Abstracts International* can be found in the compilation of Kidder and Bushong **[14]**.

Bibliographical references to contemporary narratives can be found in Obadiah Rich, *Bibliotheca Americana Nova* **[19]**; Rubens Borba de Moraes *Bibliographia Brasiliana* **[20]**; Alicia V. Tjarks, "Brazil: Travel and Description, 1800–1899. A Selected Bibliography" **[21]**; A. Curtis Wilgus, *Latin America in the Nineteenth Century* **[22]**; Bernard Naylor, *Accounts of Nineteenth-Century South America* **[23]**; P. Lee Phillips, *A List of Books, Magazine Articles, and Maps Relating to Brazil . . . 1800–1900* **[24]**; and George M. Asher, *A Bibliographical and Historical Essay on the Dutch Books and Pamphlets Relating to New-Netherland and to Possessions in Brazil, Angola, etc.* **[25]**.

Robert M. Levine's *Historical Dictionary of Brazil* **[26]**, though weak on the colonial period, contains an unannotated bibliography of over 900 items in English on Brazilian civilization.

[1] *Handbook for Latin American Studies.* v. 1–13. Cambridge, Massachusetts: Harvard University Press, 1936–1951. v. 14–40. Gainesville: University of Florida Press, 1951–1979. In Progress. [An index, covering the first 28 volumes (1936–1966), was published in 1968 by the University of Florida Press.]

This is the chief bibliographical resource for Latin American Studies. The first volume had the subtitle *A Guide to the Material Published in 1935 on Anthropology: Archaeology, Economics, Geography, History, Law and Literature.* The second volume expanded the fields covered to include Art, Education, Folklore, Government, International Relations and Language. Volumes 4–11 included Archives and Libraries, the latter also being found in volume 12. The topics Music and Philosophy were permanently added to the fields covered with volume 5. Labor and Social Welfare were included for the first time in volume 7 and continued through volume 21. Social Welfare appeared an additional time in volume 24. Sociology was added, beginning with volume 18. With volume 19, the *Handbook for Latin American Studies* discontinued the subtitle *A Guide to the Material Published in . . . .* From then on, volumes included "all the important publications seen for the first time by the Handbook office staff and the contributing editors during the year since the preparation of the last volume, regardless of their imprint date." The field of Statistics was added to volume 21, but discontinued in the following volume. The topic Travel appeared for the first time in volume 21. It was continued in volumes 22 and 24, appearing for the last time in volume 25. Volumes 24–26 have an introductory section entitled "Latin America as a Whole." With volume 27 this was replaced by a similar section with the title "Bibliography and General Works." Each of the first 25 volumes of the *Handbook* contained a survey of the entire field of Latin American Studies. With volume 26 (published in 1965) a division was established between Humanities and Social Science, with the former appearing in the even-numbered volumes. Humanities included Art, History, Latin American Language, Literature, Music and Philosophy. Social Science initially encompassed Anthropology, Economics, Education, Geography, Government and International Relations, Law and Sociology. Law, after appearing in volumes 27 and 29, was discontinued. Beginning with volume 35, the field of Government was broadened to Government and Politics. Volumes 38, 39 and 40 included the topic Film. Coverage of studies on Brazilian art in colonial Brazil in English begins with volume 3. Robert C. Smith edited the sections on Brazilian art in volumes 3 (1938), 4 (1939), 5 (1940), 6 (1941), 7 (1942), 8 (1943), 9 (1946), 10 (1947), 15 (1952), 16 (1953), 17 (1954), 18 (1955), 19 (1957), 20 (1958), 21 (1959), 22 (1960), 23 (1961), and 24 (1962). Hanna Deinhard edited the sections on Brazil in volumes 12 (1949) and 14 (1951). Mario Barata was responsible for the sections on Brazil in volumes 25 (1963), 26 (1964), 28 (1966), 30 (1968), and 34 (1972). However, his discussion of the works included is in Portuguese, as is that of José Neistein who edited the section on Brazilian art in volumes 36 (1974), 38 (1976) and 40 (1978). The latter volume, however, is in English. The sections on Brazilian history were edited by Percy Alvin Martin in volumes 1 (1936), 2 (1937), 3 (1938), 4 (1939), and 5 (1940); by Alexander Marchant in volumes 6 (1941), 7 (1942), 8 (1943), 9 (1946), 10 (1947), 11 (1948), and 12 (1949); by Manoel Cardozo in volumes 13 (1950), 14 (1951), 15 (1952), 16 (1953), 17 (1954), 18 (1955), and 19 (1957). The latter was also edited by George Boehrer, who was responsible for volumes 20 (1958), 21 (1959), 22 (1960), 23 (1961), 24 (1962), 25 (1963), 26 (1964), and 28 (1966). Boehrer was aided by Stanley Stein in volume 25 and Mathias Kiemen, O.F.M. in volume 26. Richard Graham edited the Brazilian history section in volume 30 (1968) and 32 (1970). The same task was filled by E. Bradford Burns and Colin Maclachlan in volumes 34 (1972), 36 (1974), 38 (1976). In volume 40 (1978) the section on Brazilian history was edited by Maclachlan and Jean A. and Roderick J. Barman.

[2] *Historical Abstracts.* Ed. Eric H. Boehm. v. 1–4 New York, 1955–1958; v. 5–   Santa Barbara, California, 1959–   . In Progress. Beginning with volume 17 (1971), two parts were issued each year. Part A covered 1775–1914; Part B included the years 1914 to the date of publication. In

1973, volume 19 part A expanded to include the years 1450–1914. Beginning in 1980 with volume 31, *Historical Abstracts* includes citations of books and dissertations as well.

Next to the *Handbook for Latin American Studies* **[1]**, the *Historical Abstracts* provides the most useful information for those interested in the bibliography of colonial Brazil. *Historical Abstracts* not only provides relevant bibliographical data on the scholarly articles published on Brazil. It also includes 50–150 word abstracts of each article's contents along with a description of the documentation, the number of notes, and whether there are tables, graphs, maps, appendices and bibliographies. Though confined to periodical literature, the value of the *Historical Abstracts* for those interested in colonial Brazil has been enhanced by the expansion of coverage from 1450 to 1775, beginning in 1973 with volume 19A.

[3] *Recently Published Articles*. 4 volumes to date. Washington, D. C.: The American Historical Association, 1976–1979.

Published by the American Historical Association, this useful compilation appears three times a year—February, June and October. The section on Latin America is edited by Donald C. Worcester and includes five categories: 1) General; 2) Latin America: Colonial Period; 3) Latin America: National Period. North and Central America and the Caribbean; 4) Latin America: National Period. South America; and 5) Latin America: Bibliography, Historiography, and Archival Guides. As the title indicates, this publication only lists articles. There is no annotation. Before being published separately beginning in 1976, it was included in many of the quarterly issues of the *American Historical Review*. There is also a section for Spain and Portugal.

[4] Charles C. Griffin, ed. *Latin America. A Guide to the Historical Literature*. Austin, Texas: University of Texas Press, 1971. xxx, 700 pp.

Mathias C. Kiemen wrote the introduction and was responsible for the annotations for the colonial period (pp. 296–309), while Dauril Alden prepared the introduction and provided the excellent annotations for the history of Brazil from 1808–1822 (pp. 350–361). The section dealing with bibliographies on Brazil (pp. 18–21) was compiled by Solena V. Bryant. Some general works on Brazil, annotated by a number of scholars, are found on pp. 73–79. Charles E. Nowell's section on discovery and exploration (pp. 170–188), though it contains little in English on Brazil, is helpful in putting the early voyages to Portuguese

America in perspective. Charles Julian Bishko (pp. 148–169) offers some valuable annotations on works dealing with European and African antecedents, but most of the works listed are in languages other than English. The great majority of works on Brazil cited in the above-mentioned sections are not in English.

[5] Robin A. Humphreys. *Latin American History. A Guide to the Literature in English.* London: Oxford University Press, 1958. xiii, 197 pp.

Very thorough but brief. This guide contains judicious statements about books, articles and contemporary narratives on Brazil, published before 1957. The historical period prior to 1808 is handled in Chapter VIII, "The Portuguese in Brazil," pages 65–68. The years from the arrival of the Portuguese Court in Rio de Janeiro in 1808 to the abdication of Pedro I in 1831 are treated in Chapter X, "The Foundations of the Empire of Brazil," pages 90–91.

[6] E. Bradford Burns. "A Working Bibliography for the Study of Brazilian History," *The Americas* 22:1 (July 1965), pp. 54–88.

Although not annotated, this is a useful listing of many important items (mostly in English and Portuguese) for students of Brazilian history.

[7] A. Curtis Wilgus. *Latin America, Spain and Portugal. A Selected and Annotated Bibliographical Guide to Books Published in the United States, 1954–1974.* Metuchen, New Jersey, and London: The Scarecrow Press, 1977. xv, 910 pp.

A handy guide on a variety of topics to many of the books in English on Portugal, Portuguese expansion and colonial Brazil. Wilgus provides helpful twenty-five- to forty-word descriptions along with pertinent bibliographical data for each of the books listed. Brazil (pp. 260–294), from pre-Cabralian times to the present, is divided into a) Archaeology; Anthropology; b) Description; Travel; Geography; c) History; d) Government; Politics; e) Foreign Relations; Diplomacy; f) The Economy; g) The Society; h) The Culture; i) Biographies; Autobiographies; Memoirs; j) Bibliographies; Research Guides. Portugal and Portuguese expansion are covered on pages 684–694 under the following divisions: a) Description; Travel; Geography; b) History, Government; Foreign Relations; c) Economy; Society; Culture; d) Biographies, Autobiographies; Memoirs. There are also the sections "Iberia in General" (pp. 694–699) and "Related European Background" (pp. 699-709). As to be expected, considerable overlapping occurs. Though there is no cross-listing of books, there is an index of names.

[8] David F. Trask, Michael C. Meyer, and Roger R. Trask, eds. *A Bibliography of United States-Latin American Relations Since 1910. A Selected List of Eleven Thousand Published References.* Lincoln, Nebraska: University of Nebraska Press, 1968. 441 pp.

Chapter XXIV, "The United States and Brazil" (pp. 372–383), is divided into five section: A. United States-Brazilian Relations: General Works and Special Studies; B. The United States and Brazilian Independence; C. United States-Brazilian Relations, 1824–1889; D. United States-Brazilian Relations, 1890–1930; E. United States-Brazilian Relations Since 1930. Under the general heading of Guides and Aids, there is also a section on Brazil (pp. 45–46). Chapter III, "The United States and the Period of Latin American Independence" (pp. 66–75), contains several works that deal extensively with Portuguese America. This is a very useful compilation. A few of the works listed are annotated.

[9] Robert Conrad. *Brazilian Slavery: An Annotated Research Bibliography.* Boston: G. K. Hall, 1977. xvi, 163 pp.

Excellent and comprehensive bibliography describing 994 books, articles and doctoral dissertations, most of them in English, Portuguese, French, German and Spanish. Items are listed alphabetically and there are four sections: 1) Bibliographies and Research Aids; 2) Slave Trade and Its Suppression; 3) Slavery; 4) Abolition. The bibliography includes articles and doctoral dissertations as well as monographs and travel accounts. There is an author index. The compiler usually is specific regarding the type of information contained in each entry. For example: slave markets, runaways, punishment, manumission, role of freedmen, slave trade, plantation life, racial composition, race relations, disease, acculturation, slave families, living and working conditions, demographic factors, etc.

[10] Robert C. Smith and Elizabeth Wilder, eds. *A Guide to the Art of Latin America.* Washington, D.C.: Library of Congress, 1948. 480 pp.

Useful, well-annotated guide with a large number of references to works of interest to historians. Colonial Brazil is covered on pages 139–168 and subdivided into General Works, Architecture, Graphic Arts, Minor Arts, Painting and Sculpture. Works dealing with nineteenth-century Brazil are found on pages 274–294 and are subdivided into General Works, Architecture, Education and Institutions, Graphic Arts, Minor Arts, Painting, and Sculpture. Though the *Guide* was published in 1948, the material included does not go beyond 1942. An overview of works on art in Brazil is found on pages 10–12.

[11] James E. Hogan. "Antônio Francisco Lisboa, 'O Aleijadinho': An Annotated Bibliography," *Latin American Research Review* 9:2 (Summer 1974), pp. 83–94.

Sketches the history of Minas Gerais in the eighteenth century and briefly discusses the life and artistry of Aleijadinho, the famed sculptor of colonial Brazil. Hogan provides an annotated list of 112 books and articles (mostly in Portuguese, English, French and Spanish) on Antônio Francisco Lisboa that have appeared since the early 1940s. Three notes.

[12] Carl A. Hanson. "Dissertations on Luso-Brazilian Topics: A Bibliography of Dissertations Completed in the United States, Great Britain and Canada, 1892–1970. Part I," *The Americas* 30:2 (October 1973), pp. 251–267.

Part I of this compilation contains a list of doctoral dissertations on Portugal and Portugal Overseas, including colonial Brazil. Under Portugal, there are categories for general Portuguese history, Medieval Portugal (to ca. 1500), Imperial Portugal, ca. 1500–1800, and Nineteenth and Twentieth Century Portugal. The Portuguese Empire is divided into Portuguese Africa, the Portuguese in Asia, and colonial Brazil, with an additional section on the Rio de la Plata region (to ca. 1850). Hanson lists author, dissertation title, university awarding the degree, the date of the doctorate, and if and where the dissertation is abstracted. Part I includes 236 items, which are frequently cross-listed.

[13] Carl A. Hanson. "Dissertations on Luso-Brazilian Topics: A Bibliography of Dissertations Completed in the United States, Great Britain and Canada, 1892–1970. Part II, with Addendum," *The Americas* 30:3 (January 1974), pp. 373–403.

Continuation of **[12]**. Includes Royalty in Brazil, 1808–1889 and Republican Brazil, 1889–1945. Under the heading "Brazil since World War II" there are sections on Anthropology, Archaeology and Indigenous Languages; Business Administration; Economics; Education;

Geography; History; Journalism and Mass Communications; Language and Literature; Music; Political Science; Religion; and Social Psychology, Social Work and Sociology. The addendum includes information on seventy-four more dissertations, all but five of them completed in 1971. There is also a bibliography of works that were of assistance in the compilation.

[14] Frederick Elwyn Kidder and Allen David Bushong. *Theses on Pan American Topics Prepared by Candidates for Doctoral Degrees in Universities and Colleges in the United States and Canada.* Washington, D.C.: Pan American Union, 1962. vi, 124 pp.

Useful for discovering history-related dissertations on Brazil which were never included in *Dissertation Abstracts International* **[18]** or compilations based on that work **[15]** and **[16]**. Each item contains the name of the author, the university awarding the degree and the date the doctorate was awarded, the title of the dissertation, and the date of publication (including microfilming). There is an alphabetical index (pp. 99–124) as well as the "Index to Theses by Institution" (pp. 91–98).

[15] *Latin America: A Catalog of Dissertations.* Ann Arbor, Michigan: University Microfilms, 1974. vii, 70 pp.

Twenty-two doctoral dissertations on the history of Brazil before 1825 are covered on pages 32–34. Though the listings contain the volume, issue and page number where a description of the thesis can be found in *Dissertation Abstracts International,* the number of pages in the original dissertation is not included. There is an author index. Superseded by [**16**].

[16] Carl W. Deal, ed. *Latin America and the Caribbean: A Dissertation Bibliography.* Ann Arbor, Michigan: University Microfilms International, 1978. x, 164 pp.

Pages 71–72 list 46 doctoral dissertations on the history of Brazil prior to 1825. Author, title, institution awarding the degree, date of doctorate and the number of pages in the dissertation are included, as well as the volume, issue, and page number where a description of the thesis can be found in *Dissertation Abstracts International.* There is an author index. Dissertations that fit into more than one category are frequently cross-indexed.

[17] Carl A. Hanson. *Dissertations on Iberian and Latin American History.* Troy, New York: Whitson Publishing Company, 1975. v, 400 pp.

Lists 3,564 dissertations alphabetically by last name, title of thesis, institution awarding the degree and the date the doctorate was awarded. Colonial Brazil and the Plata region to 1808 are covered on pp. 84–85. Dissertations on nineteenth-century Brazil from 1808 are found on pp. 269-272. Theses are frequently cross-referenced and there is an interesting introduction on the evolution of doctoral research on Iberian and Latin American history since the late nineteenth century. Includes bibliographical references and index.

[18] *Dissertation Abstracts International.* 39 v. to date. Ann Arbor, Michigan: University Microfilms, 1938 to the present.

The title varies. Volumes 1–11 (1938–1951) were called *Microfilm Abstracts.* Volumes 12–29 (1952–1969) were entitled *Dissertation Abstracts.* Beginning with volume 30 (1970), the title became *Dissertation Abstracts International.* With the July, 1966 issue (volume 27), *Dissertation Abstracts* were issued in two sections, with Section A covering the Humanities and the Social Sciences. Section C (International) became a separate number in the Autumn of 1976 (volume 37).

[19] Obadiah Rich. *Bibliotheca Americana Nova. A Catalogue of Books in Various Languages, Relating to America Printed Since the Year 1700 Including Voyages to the Pacific and Round the World and Collections of Voyages and Travels Compiled Principally from the Works Themselves.* 2 v. London: Rich and Sons, 1835–1846. 424 pp.; 412 pp. [Reprinted. New York: Burt Franklin, 1969.]

Useful compilation often neglected by students of colonial Brazil. In volume I Obadiah Rich lists chronologically many books referring to Brazil published from 1701 to 1800 inclusive, includes full bibliographical information and often provides some annotation. Volume II contains books published from 1801–1844, inclusive. There is an index to volume II, but none for volume I. In the Burt Franklin reprint of volume II there are three appendices: "Books Relating to America, 1493–1700" (16 pp.); "Books Relating to America, 1493–1700. Supplement" (8 pp.); and "Catalogue of Books Relating to North & South America, Including also Voyages Round the World, Collections of Voyages and Travels, &c., Being the Duplicates of Mr. Rich's American Collection" (48 pp.).

[20] Rubens Borba de Moraes. *Bibliographia Brasiliana: A Bibliographical Essay on Rare Books about Brazil Published from 1504 to 1900 and Works of Brazilian Authors Published Abroad Before the Independence of Brazil in 1822.* 2 v. Rio de Janeiro and Amsterdam: Colibris Editora, 1958. 427 pp.; 448 pp.

These two volumes are indispensable for those interested in colonial and early nineteenth-century Brazil. The author describes and comments on printed works by colonial figures as well as by foreigners who wrote about Brazil. In the case of travel accounts, Borba de Moraes gives the dates the visitors were in Brazil, the parts of Portuguese America they visited and described, and, where possible, biographical data about the visitors themselves. There is also detailed bibliographical information on each of the printed works. These well-illustrated volumes are further enhanced by a useful introduction.

[21] Alicia V. Tjarks. "Brazil: Travel and Description, 1800–1899. A Selected Bibliography," *Revista de Historia de America* 83 (January-June 1977), pp. 209–247.

The author provides a short introduction, followed by 396 items (actually there are only 394 entries since nos. 76 and 77 are identical to nos. 311 and 103, respectively). She concludes with a helpful bibliography of bibliographies. As the author points out, "the majority of the accounts are by naturalists, geologists, anthropologists, diplomats, missionaries, journalists, artists or travellers, all of them foreigners, who recorded their observations of the country in books or artistic representations." The bibliography does not contain histories, immigration pamphlets or manuscripts. Furthermore, it only includes those works available in the United States. The list includes not only the titles of the original works but those of their translations as well. The bibliography is arranged in alphabetical order with author, dates of birth and death when known, title, place and date of publication and the number of pages. It is not annotated.

[22] A. Curtis Wilgus. *Latin America in the Nineteenth Century: A Selected Bibliography of Books of Travel and Description Published in English.* Metuchen, New Jersey, and London: The Scarecrow Press, 1973. x. 174 pp.

Included in this list of books published in English during the nineteenth century and focusing on Latin America are 132 books on Brazil. Twenty-three of these touch on the period before independence. All books are listed alphabetically by author. There are no subdivisions by country. Though this sometimes makes the bibliography difficult to use, there is a geographical index which helps the reader find books by travellers who visited or authors who wrote about more than one country. The index for Brazil, with the dates for each entry in parentheses, is found on pages 138–139.

[23] Bernard Naylor. *Accounts of Nineteenth-Century South America: An Annotated Checklist of Works by British and United States Observers.* London: Published for the Institute of Latin American Studies by The Athlone Press, 1969. 80 pp.

Brazil before 1830 is covered on pages 3–17. English translations of the accounts of foreign travellers, some of whom visited Brazil, are found on pages 71–75. In spite of the subtitle *An Annotated Checklist,* many entries lack annotation, while others have only a sentence. A number of observers listed for other parts of Latin America (especially the Plata region) also visited Brazil. There is an author index.

[24] P. Lee Phillips. *A List of Books, Magazine Articles, and Maps Relating to Brazil. 1800–1900.* Washington, D.C.: Government Printing Office, 1901. 145 pp.

This compilation is a useful supplement to Borba de Moraes [**20**]. The books are mostly in Portuguese, English, German, French and Latin. They are listed alphabetically by author (pages 5–84). The section "Articles in Periodicals" is arranged by combining author and subject matter in alphabetical order (pages 85–104). The magazine articles include a number of important book reviews on many of the important nineteenth-century travel accounts. There is also a valuable section on maps of Brazil published in the nineteenth century (pages 105–145). The maps are listed chronologically.

[25] George M. Asher. *A Bibliographical and Historical Essay on the Dutch Books and Pamphlets Relating to New-Netherland and to Possessions in Brazil, Angola, etc.* Amsterdam: Frederik Muller, 1854–1867. lii, 234 pp. [A facsimile edition was published in 1960 by N. Israel/Amsterdam.]

There is a useful fifty-two page introduction on the founding of the Dutch West India Company and its role in the western hemisphere. Though most of the works cited are in Dutch, the annotations are in English. The fascimile edition also contains Asher's *A List of the Maps and Charts of New-Netherland, and of the Views of New Amsterdam,* which was published in 1855.

[26] Robert M. Levine. *Historical Dictionary of Brazil.* Metuchen, New Jersey, and London: The Scarecrow Press, 1979. xi, 297.

The historical dictionary is on pp. 1–228. Most of the references, however, are to the nineteenth and twentieth centuries. Though the author includes several dozen brief biographical sketches of figures involved in the history of colonial Brazil, terms in use during the period before independence are frequently given only nineteenth- or twentieth-century definitions. There is also an unannotated bibliography of over 900 items in English on Brazilian civilization. The section on the history of the colonial period, 1500–1808, (IV), however, lists only 41 books and articles. In addition, scattered references to Brazil before independence can be found in section III, "Travel and Contemporary Accounts," where 20 of the 75 entries deal with the period before 1822. There are also useful sections on bibliography, historiography, and research aids (I), general treatments of Brazilian history and culture (II), and slavery and race relations (VII).

II. The Portuguese Background [Nos. 27–63]

A. The History of Portugal [Nos. 27–41]

1. General Accounts [Nos. 27–38]

To date, the best history of the Iberian Peninsula in any language is Stanley Payne's two-volume study, *A History of Spain and Portugal* **[27]**. An earlier, one-volume account was prepared by William C. Atkinson **[28]**. There are several histories of Portugal that provide useful information for the student of colonial Brazil. António H. de Oliveira Marques **[29]**, with a topical approach and an emphasis on socioeconomic factors, probably has produced the best study of Portugal in English. His work contains an extensive treatment of colonial Brazil. Also of use is Harold V. Livermore's *A History of Portugal* **[30]**, which is more detailed than his later *A New History of Portugal* **[31]** and **[32]**. Livermore also authored *Portugal, A Short History* **[33]**, which provides a greater emphasis on social and economic factors than his earlier histories. All four of Livermore's accounts discuss events in colonial Brazil. H. Morse Stephen's *Portugal* **[34]**, though published in 1891, still has much to offer. Briefer accounts are found in Charles E. Nowell's two histories of Portugal **[35]** and **[36]**, the former paying greater attention to Brazil and Portuguese expansion than the latter. J. B. Trend **[37]** focuses mainly on Portugal before 1500. In his account Richard Pattee **[38]** is more interested in contemporary Portugal. He does, however, devote a substantial amount of material to events in Portugal and its empire before 1826.

[27] Stanley G. Payne. *A History of Spain and Portugal.* 2 v. Madison: The University of Wisconsin Press, 1973. 712 pp.

Based on the latest scholarship, these two volumes provide the best history to date of the Iberian Peninsula. Though both Spain and Portugal are given individual treatments, the author frequently ties together the loose strands of the histories of the two countries with his thoughtful comparisons. Chapter 6, "The Emergence of Portugal," traces the story of Portugal's past through the death of João of Avis in 1433. "The Expansion" (chapter 10) views commerce, the early discoveries and conquest from a peninsula perspective. By the beginning of the fifteenth century, as Payne perceptively points out, Portugal, "though its population was no more than one and a half million, . . . had achieved strongly institutionalized government, a sense of national unity, a basis for modest economic development, commercial and maritime forces eager for a more expansive role in the world, a reorganized military aristocracy seeking new fields of adventure, and firm, calculating leadership able to guide the energies of its followers into major enterprises abroad." "Sixteenth-Century Portugal" emphasizes the restoration of strong central authority under João II and the decline of the Portuguese Cortes. The remainder of chapter 12 provides important information on humanism and religion and describes the development of a Portuguese maritime and commercial empire. Payne also discusses the problems Portugal encountered because of overexpansion and shows the continuity of Portuguese history during the sixty years of "nominal" Habsburg domination. Chapter 18 in volume two rapidly reviews the years under Habsburg rule and those following the Portuguese restoration under Joao IV in 1640. It also analyzes the economy of Portugal and Brazil in the seventeenth and early eighteenth centuries. In addition, there is a discussion of the reigns of Afonso VI (1656–1668), Pedro II (1668/1683–1706), João V (1706–1750), José I (1750–1777) and his minister Pombal, and Maria I, who, after becoming insane, was aided by her son, the future João VI, the latter monarch until his death in 1826. The author also provides a perceptive analysis of religion, the enlightenment and agriculture in Portugal. Chapter 22 discusses "Portugal under the Nineteenth-Century Constitutional Monarchy" and the events leading up to Brazilian independence. Throughout his narrative Payne makes frequent references to Brazil. There is an excellent bibliography. In addition, there are numerous maps, illustrations, and useful tables. Each volume has a convenient index to both volumes. This study is also available in paperback.

[28] William C. Atkinson. *A History of Spain and Portugal.* London: Penguin Books, 1960. 382 pp.

Succinct, well-written account that blends into one narrative the histories of Spain, Portugal, Spanish America, the Philippines, Portuguese Asia, Africa and Brazil. There are no subheadings or other divisions as Atkinson traces the history of the Iberian peoples. The period from the beginning of the fifteenth century to the independence movements is covered in six chapters and the early part of a seventh: "The End of the Middle Ages" (15th cent.); Part I of a two-chapter account of "Literature and the Arts"; "Involvement in Europe" (16th cent.); "The Age of Retribution" (17th cent.); Part II of "Literature and the Arts"; "No More Pyrenees" (18th cent.); and the beginning of "The Great Experiment." Though Atkinson's survey is difficult to use as a reference work, it does provide an excellent background for those who like history painted on a broad canvas. There is a two-page bibliographical note, plus a six-page chronological table, and a map of Spain and Portugal.

[29] António H. de Oliveira Marques. *History of Portugal.* 2 v. New York and London: Columbia University Press, 1972. viii, 507 pp.; 303 pp. [Volume I has the subtitle: *"From Lusitania to Empire"*]

To date, this two-volume work (also available in a more convenient one-volume paperbound edition) is the best general history of Portugal. It also has the advantage of presenting a Portuguese view of colonial Brazilian history. Providing a stronger emphasis on social and economic history than that available in the other accounts in English, Oliveira Marques also emphasizes a topical approach. Though the strongest parts of his study cover the Middle Ages and the First Portuguese Republic (1910–1926), the author has a number of useful chapters for those interested in colonial Brazil and its Portuguese background. Chapter III, for example, "The Beginnings of Expansion," describes the equipment and needs of the explorers, analyzes the voyages of discovery, and evaluates the initial results. The following chapter, "The Renaissance State," provides important insights into the Crown's growing power during the years of Portuguese expansion and how Portugal recovered from the severe agricultural and epidemic crises of the fourteenth and much of the fifteenth century. An overview of worldwide Portuguese expansion is found in chapter V, "Rise of Empire," where Oliveira Marques discusses Portuguese discovery and conquest in the years following the death of Henry "the Navigator" in 1460, the organization of the empire, and the problems encountered. "The Tridimensional Empire" (chapter VII) looks overseas with a topical discussion of the Portuguese in Asia and America from the mid-1500s through the seventeenth century along with the story of the Atlantic islands and Africa for much of the same time period. In chapter IX, Brazil—"the essence of the Portuguese empire"—from the late 1600s to 1822 is studied. Though most of chapter X, "Constitutional Monarchy," which begins the second volume, deals with the post-1822 years, there are several pages of useful information for better understanding Brazilian independence. The first volume contains 13 maps, 30 illustrations and three genealogical tables. There is an excellent bibliography (pp. 481–507). Unfortunately, in the hardcover edition, volume I has no index, it being contained only in volume II. The paperbound edition, which combines the two volumes in one, eliminates this serious inconvenience.

[30] Harold V. Livermore. *A History of Portugal.* Cambridge: The Cambridge University Press, 1947. xvi, 502 pp.

This is the best of Livermore's histories of Portugal, more complete and better organized than the other versions. It uses a combined chronological-topical approach with a strong emphasis on Portugal's political history. Social and economic factors are not neglected, however, though they do not receive the same attention as the political. There is a considerable amount of material on Brazil. Twenty-four of the book's twenty-six chapters deal with the period before 1834. Chapter XI discusses the rise of João I (1383–1433) and the Avis dynasty to power and the beginnings of Portuguese expansion with the conquest of Ceuta in North Africa (1415). The following chapter describes Portuguese discoveries along the coast of Africa and the Atlantic Islands and the colonization of the latter. The internal problems Portugal experienced following the death of João I which hampered overseas activity are recounted in Chapter XIII. The important events in the reigns of João II (1481–1495) and Manuel I (1495–1521) are detailed, as are the reassertion of the authority of the monarchy, the revival of the Portuguese commitment to overseas expansion, and the eventual harvesting of the wealth from the great discoveries. The sixteenth century, especially the years 1521–1580, beginning with successes at home and overseas during the early reign of João III and culminating in a series of disasters, the most notable being the destruction of much of the Portuguese nobility and the death of Sebastião I at Alcacer Quibir, is discussed in the chapter "From the Great Expansion to the Loss of Independence." The sixty years of Habsburg domination are covered in Chapter XVII, followed by a discussion of the restoration and the events leading up to and Portugal's role in the War of the Spanish Succession. "The Golden Age of Absolutism" analyzes the reign of João V (1706–1750) and is paralleled by "The Iron Age of Absolutism," which focuses on the reign of José I and his powerful minister Pombal (1750–1777). Chapters XXIII and XXIV carry the story through the reign of Maria I, the regency of the future D. João VI, and the crises caused by the Napoleonic invasion of Portugal in 1807, the transfer of the Court to Portuguese America, and the eventual independence of Brazil. There is a good bibliography (pp. 471–475) and an excellent "Reference Index," containing many useful facts about Portugal. There are 7 maps and 17 illustrations.

[31] H. V. Livermore. *A New History of Portugal.* Cambridge: At the University Press, 1966. xi, 365.

A New History of Portugal has about 30% less material on the 443 years that elapsed between the rise to power of João of Avis in 1383 and the death of João VI in 1826 than Livermore's earlier history **[30]**. However, the author continues to give attention to Portugal overseas—especially Portuguese America. About 25% of the pages dealing with the years 1500–1826 mention Brazil. His account of Portuguese history is done in chronological fashion and there are sections devoted to such topics as the capture of Ceuta in 1415, Prince Henry and his explorations, and the voyages of discovery, 1460–1495. A useful bibliographical note is found on pages 346–351. There are 7 maps and 17 illustrations, a number of the latter differing from those in **[30]**. A paperbound edition was published in 1969.

[32] H. V. Livermore. *A New History of Portugal.* 2nd edition. Cambridge: Cambridge University Press, 1976. ix, 408.

Identical to **[31]** for the years 1500–1822. There are some minor changes in the section on Salazar's New State (Chapter XII: "The Republic"). An additional fifty pages (Chapter XIII: "Dr. Caetano and the Revolution of 1974") bring the story of Portugal's history to early 1976. Unfortunately, the "Bibliographical Note" of the earlier edition **[31]** is omitted. There are 7 maps and 17 illustrations.

[33] H. V. Livermore. *Portugal. A Short History.* Edinburgh: Edinburgh University Press, 1973. 213 pp.

This newly written account attempts to give a greater emphasis to social and economic factors in Portugal's development as a nation than Livermore's earlier histories. Less than eighty pages deal with the years from the time of João I to the death of João VI in 1826. Brazil, however, is mentioned on almost half of these pages. The material for this period is covered primarily in chapters 4 through 6: "The Age of Discoveries";

"Peninsula Integration"; "The Restoration"; and "The Eighteenth Century." The first few pages of chapter 7 carry the account into the nineteenth century. There are 7 maps and 25 excellent illustrations, many of them different from those of Livermore's earlier histories of Portugal **[30]** and **[31]**. However, there is no bibliography and no notes.

[34] H. Morse Stephens. *Portugal.* London: T. Fisher Unwin, 1891. xxiv, 450 pp. [Also published in New York by G. P. Putnam's Sons, it was part of "The Story of the Nations" series.]

First published in 1891, this narrative history of Portugal is still of value. All but part of the last chapter deals with the period before 1822. The author uses a chronological approach and gives special attention to the personal and political lives of Portugal's monarchs and their consorts and children. Beginning on page 115, Stephens studies Portuguese expansion and the conquest of Morocco in 1415. Using the accounts of various chroniclers, he discusses the efforts of Henry, "the Navigator," and his successors to promote Portuguese overseas activities. There is a good discussion of some of the centralizing actions of João II (1481–1495) and his immediate successors, Manuel I (1495–1521) and João III (1521–1557). The author devotes one chapter (IX) to the Portuguese in Asia in the first half of the sixteenth century and another (X) to the Portuguese in Brazil during much the same time period. He follows this with an analysis of Sebastião's reign (1557–1578), that monarch's North African campaigns, culminating in the disaster of Alcacer-Quibir, and the fall of the House of Avis. Portuguese literature, the "Sixty Years' Captivity," the Revolution of 1640 and the English Alliance form the major topics of the next four chapters, with mentions of Brazil where appropriate. Eighteenth-century Portugal, with the long prosperous reign of João V (1706–1750), is discussed as are the career and administrative reforms of the Marquis of Pombal, who dominated Portuguese life from 1750–1777. The book's next-to-last chapter recounts the French invasion of Portugal and the resulting Peninsular Wars and gives a good insight into the chaos which that country was thrown—problems that would help give rise to Brazilian independence and absorb most of nineteenth-century Portugal's energies to remedy. The character of João VI and his queen, Carlota Joaquina, their reign and the independence of Brazil provide the finishing touches to Stephens's pre-1822 coverage. There is a list of the kings of Portugal, three useful genealogical tables (of the House of Avis, Manuel and his successors, and the Braganças), 44 plates and a map of Portugal. There is no bibliography.

[35] Charles E. Nowell. *A History of Portugal.* Princeton, New Jersey: D. Van Nostrand Company, 1952. xii, 259 pp.

This judicious, well-written survey covers the history of Portugal and her overseas empire to 1950. Devoting only two short chapters to the years prior to the battle of Aljubarrota in 1385, Nowell spends almost 20% of the book on the period to 1495 which he covers with two chapters: "The Early House of Avis" and "The Beginnings of National Greatness." Two additional chapters are devoted to the reign of Manuel I (1495–1521) and Portuguese overseas expansion. "The Portuguese Decline" discusses the reign of João III (1521–1557) and that of his grandson Sebastião I (1557–1578). Two chapters are devoted to literature and the arts during Portugal's "Golden Age." In "The Babylonian Captivity" Nowell argues that "Portugal began the sixty-year era of Spanish Hapsburg rule enjoying the nominal status of a junior partner kingdom. In the course of time it sank to the stature of a conquered province." The next century and a half is described in "Portugal Restored" and "Enlightenment and Revolution." The early pages of Chapter XIII, "The Constitutional Struggle," recount the chief events leading up to Brazilian independence. This brief survey contains a number of references to the history of colonial Brazil. There is a "Selected Bibliography" (pp. 243–249), a list of the rulers of Portugal, 6 maps (including several of Brazil) and 12 illustrations.

[36] Charles E. Nowell. *Portugal.* Englewood Cliffs, New Jersey: Prentice-Hall, Inc. 1973. xii, 178 pp.

This brief history of Portugal confines itself almost entirely to Europe, with only minor references to Brazil. However, its short, seven-to-ten-page chapters provide succinct and to-the-point background materials for anyone interested in the Portuguese antecedents to Brazilian history. Chapter Four surveys Portugal in the Middle Ages, while the following chapter discusses the accession of João I to power, with a few words on the efforts of the Avis dynasty to promote overseas expansion. "The House of Beja," the name sometimes applied to Manuel I, the Duke of Beja, and his successors, a branch of the Avis dynasty that presided over the golden years of Portuguese discovery and exploration, is the title given to chapter six. The next chapter, "Submergence and Reappearance," studies the Habsburg period, 1580–1640, the rise of Sebastianism, and the restoration of Brazilian independence under the Braganças. "A New Portugal" (chapter eight) discusses the second half of the seventeenth century, Bragança efforts to maintain Portugal's independence from Spain, and the problems leading to the overthrow of João IV's heir, Afonso VI, by his brother, the future Pedro II (1667–1706). The reign of João V (1706–1750), the reforms of Pombal (1750–1777) and their aftermath are covered in chapter nine, while chapters ten and eleven focus on the Napoleonic invasion, the transfer of the court to Brazil in 1807, the return of João VI to Portugal in 1821, and the proclamation of Brazilian independence by João's heir, Pedro I, in the following year. A bibliography is found on pages 169–173. There are two maps: one of Portugal, the other of central and southern Africa with inserts showing the Atlantic islands and Portuguese Guinea.

[37] J. B. Trend. *Portugal.* London: Ernest Benn Limited, 1957. xi, 218 pp.

This history of Portugal deals primarily with the period before 1600, having only a few scattered references to Brazil. It does, however, afford some useful background material. Chapter seven focuses on the revolution of 1383 that brought João of Avis to power. "Discovery and Pepper" indicate the topics of chapter eight. Much of the following chapter, "The Age of Camoens," discusses the effects of the maritime discoveries—especially those in Asia—on Portugal. In addition, there is a brief description of literature, art, and messianism in sixteenth-century Portugal. Part of chapter ten, "The Restoration, Methuen, Pombal," covers the commercial treaties between England and Portugal in the seventeenth century as well as the more famous but less important Methuen Treaty of 1703. There is also a discussion of the Marquis of Pombal (1750–1777) and his role in Portuguese history. Notes follow each chapter. There is a map of Portugal.

[38] Richard Pattee. *Portugal and the Portuguese World.* Milwaukee: The Bruce Publishing Company, 1957. vii, 350 pp.

Though this study was "intended primarily as a portrait of contemporary Portugal, the Portuguese people, and the world beyond the frontiers of Europe that were occupied by this enterprising nation and which still form a part of the empire," the author devotes the first half of the book to events in Portugal and its empire prior to 1826. "How Portugal Came to Be" takes the story from Portugal's origins to the late fifteenth century. The following chapter (III), "The Path of Empire: Portuguese Expansion Beyond the Seas," devotes more than twenty pages to Brazil with a special emphasis on early colonization, its African heritage, and the role of the *bandeirantes*. "Stress and Strain: The

Decline from Greatness" covers Portugal's history to Salazar's rise to power in the 1920s. It includes almost a dozen pages on Pombal and his policies, a number of which affected Brazil. A lengthy bibliography is found on pp. 330–345. There are 2 maps.

2. Special Aspects [Nos. 39–41]

An excellent study of Portugese society on the eve of expansion is found in António H. de Oliveira Marques, *Daily Life in Portugal in the Late Middle Ages* **[39]**. Magalhães Godinho **[40]** and **[41]** provides a good picture of Portugal and her empire from the mid-seventeenth to the early eighteenth century. He gives a special emphasis to socioeconomic conditions. Studies of English influence on Luso-Brazilian commerce are found in XVI, B, 4, a. [Nos. 616–620]

[39] António H. de Oliveira Marques. *Daily Life in Portugal in the Late Middle Ages.* Trans. L. S. Wyatt. Madison, Milwaukee, and London: The University Press, 1971. xvi, 355 pp.

Excellent social history of Portugal on the eve of expansion. The author treats in detail diet, dress, housing, hygiene, health, sexual mores, labor, faith, culture, amusements and death. A "Critical Bibliography" is found on pages 313–331. There are 99 illustrations, 3 maps and 2 genealogical charts. This is a translation of *A Sociedade Medieval Portuguesa: Aspectos de Vida Quotidiana.* Lisbon: Livraria Sá da Costa Editora, 1964.

[40] Vitorino Magalhães Godinho. "Portugal and her Empire," in F. L. Carsten, ed. *The Ascendancy of France, 1648–88* (Cambridge: At the University Press, 1961), pp. 384–397. [Volume V of the New Cambridge Modern History]

Good survey of the history of Portugal and her overseas empire in the mid-seventeenth century by one of Portugal's foremost historians. Magalhães Godinho studies Brazil's population centers and its sugar, tobacco, brazilwood, timber and hide production and points out that by the third quarter of the seventeenth century, the Portuguese "empire became essentially an Atlantic one, based on Africa and Brazil." The author argues that between 1654 and 1670, the annual total value of exports from Brazil to Portugal was nine to ten million *cruzados.* He also discusses the effects of the Restoration (1640) on Portugal and her empire, analyzes the Portuguese bureaucracy and the rise to power of the Portuguese nobility, and concludes that "after the Restoration, Portugal itself was in fact much more aristocratic in government than were the colonies." Magalhães Godinho claims that the overseas "*câmaras* had more influence than at home."

[41] Vitorino Magalhães Godinho. "Portugal and Her Empire, 1680–1720," in J. S. Bromley, ed. *The Rise of Great Britain and Russia, 1688–1715/25*. (Cambridge: At the University Press, 1970), pp. 509–539. [Volume VI of the New Cambridge Modern History]

Examines prices in Portugal and trade in Brazil and concludes that "Brazilian profits were being curtailed by a pincer movement constituted, on one hand, by the fall in market prices due to international competition, especially from the West Indies, and on the other by inelastic and even rising costs, due as much to international competition for slaves as to the presence of too many producers in a limited market." Magalhães Godinho also surveys commercial enterprise in Africa and Asia. He studies the factors leading to the Methuen Treaty of 1703, discusses the role of Portugal and Brazil in the War of the Spanish Succession, and analyzes frontier expansion and the discovery of gold in Portuguese America. He concludes with a description of nobility, clergy and commoner in late seventeenth and early eighteenth century Portugal. No notes.

B. Portuguese Overseas Expansion and its Antecedents [Nos. 42–51]

The best overview of Portuguese overseas expansion is Charles R. Boxer's *The Portuguese Seaborne Empire, 1415–1825* **[42]**. An earlier and shorter survey of Portugal overseas **[43]** was published by Boxer in 1961. An excellent survey of Portuguese maritime activity before the fifteenth century is found in Bailey W. Diffie's *Prelude to Empire. Portugal Overseas before Henry the Navigator* **[44]**, a brief synthesis of which is found in **[45]**. A more recent, lengthier and broader account by the same author **[46]** focuses on Portugal's overseas exploits from 1415 to 1500. Samuel Eliot Morison **[47]** discusses fifteenth-century voyages in the Atlantic and argues that there was no Portuguese voyage to Brazil before that of Pedro Álvares Cabral in 1500. The opposing view is held by Fidelino de Figueredo **[48]**, who also provides an overview of Portuguese overseas expansion. Thomaz Oscar Marcondes de Souza **[49]** discusses, then rejects, cartographic evidence for the discovery of Brazil in 1448. Charles Nowell **[50]** examines the controversy surrounding the encounters between João II of Portugal and Christopher Columbus. James Duffy **[51]** reviews contemporary narratives of shipwrecks that occurred during the period 1542–1649.

[42] Charles R. Boxer. *The Portuguese Seaborne Empire, 1415–1825.* New York: Alfred E. Knopf, 1969, xxvi, 415 pp.

Major overview of Portuguese overseas expansion. The prologue, "The Western Rim of Christendom," provides an excellent account of medieval Portugal. Chapter 1 discusses the conquest and exploration of Africa in the fifteenth century. "Slaves and Sugar in the South Atlantic (1500–1600)" (chapter 4) is probably the best short summary of Brazil's first century of settlement. The Dutch in Brazil, 1624–1654, are studied from a world perspective in chapter 5. "Revival and Expansion in the West (1663–1750)" shows the importance of Portugal's South Atlantic Empire and the effects of the Brazilian gold and diamond discoveries. "The Pombaline Dictatorship and its Aftermath (1775–1825)" is the subject of chapter 8. After using a chronological approach to the study of Portugal's overseas empire in Part I, Boxer switches to a topical approach in Part II. He investigates such topics as Brazil fleets, the controversies over "purity of blood" and "contaminated races," and the roles of town councillors and brothers of charity. The author also examines the lower strata of society (soldiers, settlers and vagabonds) as well as merchants, monopolists and smugglers. Culture and the enlightenment as well as messianism and nationalism are analyzed. There are a number of useful appendices for those interested in Brazil. A glossary is found on pages 388–393. The bibliography is on pages 394–415. There are sixteen illustrations and seven maps.

[43] Charles R. Boxer. *Four Centuries of Portuguese Expansion, 1415–1825: A Succinct Survey.* Johannesburg: Witwatersrand University Press, 1961. ix, 102 pp. [Reprinted. Berkeley: University of California Press, 1969.]

Parts I and II concentrate on Portuguese expansion in Africa and Asia, while III and IV focus mostly on Brazil. Part III, "The Struggle for Spices, Sugar, Slaves and Souls in the Seventeenth Century," begins with the death of Sebastião I in North Africa (1578) and the subsequent sixty years of Habsburg rule, discusses the Dutch in Brazil and other parts of the Portuguese empire, describes missionary activity, especially that of the Jesuits, analyzes the role of African and Amerindian slavery on Brazilian life, and recounts the effect of the scarcity of Portuguese women and widespread miscegenation on Portuguese American society. Part IV, "The Golden Age of Brazil in the Eighteenth Century," reviews early Portuguese coastal expansion in the sixteenth century, the advance of the frontier in the seventeenth, and the discovery of gold in Minas Gerais and its repercussions on the socioeconomic history of Brazil. Boxer then evaluates the role of the Marquis of Pombal (1750–1777), the suppression of the Jesuits, and the events leading to Brazilian independence. There is a tentative balance sheet and a "Bibliographical Note," pp. 94–96. Well annotated. Based chiefly on printed primary sources.

[44] Bailey W. Diffie. *Prelude to Empire. Portugal Overseas before Henry the Navigator.* Lincoln: University of Nebraska Press, 1960. xi, 127 pp.

Diffie argues that "without a Henry the Navigator there would have been no Atlantic discoveries, and without the preceding centuries of commerce and fishing, there would have been no Navigator." The author provides an excellent succinct survey of medieval Portuguese maritime history which he relates to the evolution of Portugal as a nation. He also discusses Portugal's Moslem heritage, the Christian crusades and reconquest, Portugal's role as "a wharf between two seas" (the Atlantic and the Mediterranean), the reign of D. Dinis (1279–1325), founder of the Order of Christ, promoter of commerce and agriculture, and the one who invited the Genoese Manuele Pessagno (Peçanha) and twenty Italian captains to help build up and sail the King's fleets. In addition, Diffie traces the development of commercial and maritime enterprises during the fourteenth century, analyzes the events leading up to the accession to the Portuguese throne by João of Avis, and concludes with a discussion of the Portuguese conquest of Ceuta in North Africa in 1415. Well documented. Bibliography. 3 useful maps.

[45] Bailey W. Diffie. "Portugal's Preparation for Exploration. A Functional-Cultural Interpretation," in Lindley Cintra, ed., *Actas* **[91]**, pp. 251–265.

Summary of **[44]**. Diffie challenges the view that Portuguese discoveries were accidental and discusses Portugal's maritime and commercial enterprises before the time of Henry the Navigator. Based on printed primary and secondary materials. 25 notes.

[46] Bailey W. Diffie and George D. Winius. *Foundations of the Portuguese Empire, 1415–1580.* Minneapolis: University of Minnesota Press, 1977. xxx, 533 pp.

In the first half of this major study (chapters 1–13), Bailey Diffie brings together a lifetime of research on the varied aspects of Portuguese overseas expansion and judiciously reviews the work of others. He tracks down and scrubs off a number of legends and myths that have become barnacles on the history of Portuguese expansion in the fifteenth century. For example, Diffie attacks the myth of the nautical school at Sagres. He points out that while it is clear that Henry "took more interest in African conquest and exploration than any other one person of importance in Portugal," the Portuguese prince "did not need to invent ships, train sailors, educate pilots, or give courage to his men. He found all of these at his command. What he needed to do, and what he did, was to give a focus to Portuguese energies—and he did it with only a small part of his energies, most of which went to govern his large estates and to further his economic interests. Exploration was a small part of his activities." In clear language, the author briefly surveys West-East relations from ancient times to the fourteenth century and Portuguese and European expansion prior to 1415. He then focuses on the capture of Ceuta, Portuguese activity in North Africa, and expansion into the Atlantic and down the African coast. Diffie also reviews the state of navigational science and maritime charts, analyzes Portugal's rivalry with Spain, and the treaty of Alcácovas (1479). He studies the overseas policy of João II, describing Christopher Columbus as "a Genoese who made a 'Portuguese' voyage for Spain." The author concludes his account with chapters on the voyages to India of Vasco da Gama and Pedro Álvares Cabral, the latter touching on Brazil in 1500. The second half of the book (chapters 14–22) is by George Winius and focuses on the first eight decades of Portuguese activity in India and the East. Though not of immediate interest to Brazilianists, Winius's account does help explain why the Portuguese concentrated on the East rather than Brazil for much of the sixteenth century. This well-documented study by Diffie and Winius includes 19 illustrations and 6 maps. The appendix includes both a list and discussion of confirmed and alleged discoveries made by European explorers in the fifteenth and sixteenth centuries. Included in this list is an excellent discussion of some of the controversies surrounding Amerigo Vespucci. The authors also provide a useful chronology of Portuguese expansion,

1415–1502 (pp. 465–471). There is a detailed and partly annotated bibliography on pp. 480–516.

[47] Samuel Eliot Morison. *Portuguese Voyages to America in the Fifteenth Century.* Cambridge: Harvard University Press, 1940. xv, 151 pp.

Morison describes the discovery of the Azores, discusses "the mythical islands of the Atlantic," and traces Portuguese efforts at discovery in the North Atlantic. He then analyzes the Portuguese "policy of secrecy." Finally, the author turns to the negotiations between Spain and Portugal during the 1490s and describes Vasco da Gama's instructions and sailing route to India and Pedro Álvares Cabral's voyage to Brazil. After examining evidence for an earlier discovery of Brazil, Morison concludes: "That there was no Portuguese voyage to Brazil before Cabral's seems certain. Caminha's description **[163]** and **[164]** of the week he spent in the Land of the True Cross, the late taking-possession and the council of ship-captains about sending the news home, indicate that Cabral was as much surprised as anyone at finding land in that part of the South Atlantic. . . . Every foreigner in Lisbon whose comment on Cabral's voyage has been preserved, believed that Brazil was discovered by Cabral, as did the Portuguese map-makers, the official Portuguese court chronicler, and the Portuguese historians of the sixteenth century." Well documented. Bibliographical footnotes. There is also a "Chronological List of Portuguese and Other Voyages to or toward America through 1500." 6 maps.

[48] Fidelino de Figueredo. "The Geographical Discoveries and Conquests of the Portuguese," *The Hispanic American Historical Review,* 6:1–3 (February–August, 1926), pp. 47–70.

After arguing that Portugal's "policy of silence" explains why pre-1500 geographical discoveries in Brazil are undocumented, the author analyzes the social conditions existing in fifteenth-century Portugal. He then discusses the contributions (and, at times, the historiography) of Portuguese naval construction and sailing ships, cartography and nautical astronomy. He concludes the article with a survey of the highlights of Portugal's overseas economic activities and a summary of that country's experiences in North Africa from 1415 to 1769. Though a half-century of recent scholarship has modified some of the author's conclusions, this article contains some useful information and insights. Undocumented. Based on two lectures delivered at the University of London in 1924.

[49] Thomaz Oscar Marcondes de Souza. "A Supposed Discovery of Brazil before 1448," *The Hispanic American Historical Review,* 26:4 (November, 1946), pp. 593–598.

Traces the history of the controversy concerning the correct interpretation of the legend "Ixola Otinticha" on the 1448 portolano of the Venetian navigator and cosmographer Andrea Bainco. The author argues convincingly that the legend refers to the Cape Verdean island of Santiago and not Brazil as some have claimed. Based on printed materials. 11 notes.

[50] Charles E. Nowell. "The Rejection of Columbus by John of Portugal," in *University of Michigan Historical Essays, 1937.* Ann Arbor, Michigan: University of Michigan Press, 1937. pp. 25–44.

Discusses Columbus's efforts to get backing from João II of Portugal in 1484, eight years before getting support from Ferdinand and Isabella. Nowell challenges the view that "the ideas and aims of Columbus underwent no material change in the years before 1492" and attempts to determine exactly why the Portuguese monarch refused to aid him. Las Casas's account is the only full one of Columbus's 1484 meeting with João II. The author argues that "Las Casas is suspiciously exact in writing of the Portuguese negotiations, of which he knew little." Nowell questions Las Casas's relation of the terms of Columbus's offer to King John as well as the awards claimed, showing that since Portugal also had the title of admiral, it would be strange for Columbus to ask the king "for an admiralty on the Castilian model." However, since Columbus was poor, "it is probable that the economic side of his proposal was roughly similar to what was finally agreed on in Spain." Columbus's later demands of Ferdinand and Isabella, if also made to João II, would have confused private initiative and national enterprise. Nowell argues that "for the Crown to outfit an adventurer, and then to step into the background in that adventurer's favor, was out of the question." The author also examines the scientific basis of Columbus's plans and argues that in 1484 Columbus "lacked the requisite intellectual background." In that year he "had not read a geographical work; nor had he made an independent observation that would be of any weight in convincing his listeners." Thus, Nowell concludes: "The Portuguese who rejected him had no choice. They did only what might have been expected of any well-ordered government dealing with an adventurer of vast pretensions but meager attainments." Based chiefly on printed primary materials. 62 notes.

[51] James Duffy. *Shipwreck & Empire. Being an Account of Portuguese Maritime Disasters in a Century of Decline.* Cambridge, Massachusetts: Harvard University Press, 1955. vii, 198 pp.

Analyzes eighteen contemporary narratives of Portuguese shipwrecks that occurred between 1552 and 1649. More than two-thirds of the authors were sailors, priests, pharmacists, or passengers who survived the shipwrecks. Duffy describes the ships, their crews and passengers, the voyage, the wreck, the march after reaching land, and the final outcome of the various tragedies. Of special interest to students of colonial Brazilian history is the account of the misadventures of the *Santo Antônio* **[185]**, which left Olinda for Lisbon in 1565 with Jorge de Albuquerque **[150]** aboard. Albuquerque, the son of Duarte Coelho **[149]**, first lord-proprietor of Pernambuco, managed to survive many harrowing experiences and later inherited his family's wealthy captaincy. Based chiefly on the accounts themselves.

C. The Papacy, The *Padroado* and the Demarcation Lines of 1493 and 1494 [Nos. 52–60]

Historians have focused a great deal of attention on the events of the early 1490s—an interest spurred on by the celebrations marking the 400th anniversary of Columbus's arrival in America. Edward Gaylord Bourne **[53]** wrote his doctoral dissertation on the Demarcation Line of Pope Alexander VI, a synthesis of which is found in **[52]**. Other authors of the late nineteenth century dealing with the diplomatic ramifications of Columbus's voyage include Henry Harrisse **[54]** and Samuel Edward Dawson **[55]**. These three accounts can still be read with profit, though they have been superseded in part by the brilliant detective work of H. Vander Linden **[56]**. Charles E. Nowell **[57]** also has clarified a number of points confused by earlier historians. William B. Greenlee **[58]** demonstrates how the papal and diplomatic events of the fifteenth century affected Brazilian history. The ecclesiastical aspects are reviewed by W. Eugene Shiels **[59]** and by James Muldoon **[60]**. Frances Gardiner Davenport **[104]** contributes a collection of well-translated and annotated documents which further help to illuminate many of the issues under discussion.

[52] Edward Gaylord Bourne. "The Demarcation Line of Pope Alexander VI," in *Essays in Historical Criticism* (New York: 1901), pp. 193–217. [Reprinted in 1967 by Books for Libraries Press, Inc., Freeport, New York.]

Argues that because Portugal had obtained papal bulls to confirm her discoveries in Africa, Spain was most anxious to obtain papal approval for Columbus's new discoveries. After a brief discussion of the three Alexandrine bulls, the author focuses on that dated 4 May 1493 and the boundary line drawn by the pope "from the North to the South pole, one hundred leagues west and south of any one of the islands known as the Azores and Cape Verde Islands. All lands discovered and to be discovered to the west and south of this line whether toward India or any other direction, not in the possession of any Christian prince at Christmas, 1492, should belong exclusively to Spain." João II of Portugal refused both to accept this line and to submit the matter to arbitration. The result was the 1494 Treaty of Tordesillas and a new dividing line, 370 leagues west of the Cape Verde Islands. Bourne discusses some of the scientific difficulties in measuring the 370 leagues and the controversy over which of the Cape Verde Islands should be the site for the measurement. The author then describes Magellan's voyage around the world and the problem of determining where the demarcation line should be in Asia. This, in turn, rekindled arguments over the demarcation line in America. Bourne concludes with a discussion of Spanish-Portuguese boundary disputes regarding Brazil, touching briefly on the founding of Colônia do Sacramento in 1680 and the abortive Treaty of Madrid (1750). Based on printed primary and secondary sources. Well documented.
Superseded in many respects by Vander Linden **[56]** and Nowell **[57]**.

[53] Edward Gaylord Bourne. "The Demarcation Line of Pope Alexander VI," (Ph.D. Dissertation: Yale University, 1892).

[54] Henry Harrisse. *The Diplomatic History of America. Its First Chapter: 1452–1493–1494.* London: B. F. Stevens, 1897. 230 pp. [Reissued by William C. Brown Reprint Library, Dubuque, Iowa.]

The author devotes short chapters to such topics as: papal grants to Portugal, 1452 to 1484; the response to Columbus by the Portuguese monarch João II after the former's return to Europe in 1493; Pope Alexander VI's four bulls of 1493; the Treaty of Tordesillas of 1494; the memorandum of the Catalan cosmographer Jaime Ferrer, the 1518 geographical compendium of Martín Fernández de Encisco, and efforts to determine the Treaty of Tordesillas' line of demarcation; and attempts to identify landmarks in northern Brazil. Map. 170 notes. Because of Vander Linden's research **[56]**, part of Harrisse's study has been superceded by more modern accounts.

[55] Samuel Edward Dawson. "The Line of Demarcation of Pope Alexander VI in A.D. 1493 and that of the Treaty of Tordesillas in A.D. 1494; with an inquiry concerning the Metrology of Ancient and Mediaeval Times," *Proceedings and Transactions of the Royal Society of Canada.* II Series, v. 5 (1899), pp. 467–546.

Challenges the view that Pope Alexander VI was "arrogant and presumptuous" and points out that "the popes were, in geographical questions, of necessity in advance of their age." The author describes the differences between a Papal Bull and a Papal Brief and discusses and compares various versions of the Alexandrine bulls of 1493. Despite its sometimes polemical tone, this article has valuable material for those interested in the topic. However, like Bourne **[52]** and Harrisse **[54]**, it, too, has been superceded in part by Vander Linden **[56]**. There are seven figures and maps. The appendix (pp. 529–546) contains the text and an English translation of several of Alexander VI's 1493 bulls and some of the correspondence between Ferdinand and Isabella and the Catalan cartographer, Jaime Ferrer. Though the article itself has no footnotes, the appendix is annotated.

[56] H. Vander Linden. "Alexander VI and the Demarcation of the Maritime and Colonial Domains of Spain and Portugal, 1493–1494," *The American Historical Review* 22:1 (October 1916), pp. 1–20.

Careful study, based on the examination of photographs of the transcripts of Alexander VI's papal bulls *Inter caetera* (May 3 and May 4) and *Eximiae devotionis* (May 3) of 1493, which shows that two of the documents were antedated—the first *Inter caetera* being expedited in April, the second in June and *Eximiae devotionis* in July. The bull of demarcation (a line probably suggested by Columbus one hundred leagues "to the west and to the south" of the Azores and the Cape Verde Islands) is the *Inter caetera* of May 4. The author challenges the view that the Pope acted as arbiter and argues that these documents "are acts of papal sovereignty in favor of a single power (Spain)." In fact, the different bulls of that year successively increased papal favors to Spain while cutting back on Portugal's prerogatives. Portugal, in turn, repudiated papal arbitration and entered into direct negotiations with Spain—diplomacy which resulted in the Treaty of Tordesillas of 1494. Based mainly on primary sources. 46 notes.

[57] Charles Edward Nowell. "The Treaty of Tordesillas and the Diplomatic Background of American History," in Adele Ogden and Engel Sluiter, eds., *Greater America. Essays in Honor of Herbert Eugene Bolton.* Berkeley and Los Angeles: University of California Press, 1945, pp. 1–18.

Points out that protection of the route to India took precedence over the one to Brazil in the concerns of João II. On 3 April 1493, a month after Columbus's return via Lisbon from his first voyage to America and before the famous pro-Spanish bulls of Pope Alexander VI were issued, the Portuguese monarch sent his diplomat, Rui de Sande, to Barcelona with a proposal that there should be a line of demarcation "extending across the Atlantic along the parallel of the Canaries. Portugal should own, or be entitled to claim, everything in the ocean south of the line, and Spain everything north, the Azores and Madeiras excepted." The Spanish monarchs, Ferdinand and Isabella, countered this proposal with a longitudinal rather than a latitudinal line which Alexander VI incorporated into his bull of 4 May 1493 (which was antedated, having been written in June of that year). The result was the threat of an armed clash between Spain and Portugal, finally resolved with the Treaty of Tordesillas of 7 June 1494. Nowell argues that João's agents in the Council of Castile kept him informed of every pending decision and that the Treaty of Tordesillas was a major victory for the king, whom he describes as "the finest statesman of the age." The author points out that João II "chose to ignore them [the Papal bulls] and thus to furnish no evidence, by word or deed, that he acknowledged their authority. At the same time, he avoided a rupture with the Church." Actually there were two treaties of Tordesillas. The first and better known one established a line from pole to pole, passing 370 leagues west of the Cape Verde Islands. But to keep the Spaniards from the African coast and to counter the papal bull *Dudum siquidem* of 26 September 1493, which "rescinded all earlier papal grants which had ratified Portuguese claims to Africa and the route to the Orient," a second treaty of Tordesillas was signed, reconfirming the Alcáçovas agreement of 1479. That earlier pact had acknowledged Spanish possession of the Canary Islands and Portugal's claims to Africa. Furthermore, as part of the Treaty of Tordesillas, both Spain and Portugal swore that "they would not seek, of the pope or any other prelate who could grant it, release from these treaties." Nowell also clears up two popular misconceptions regarding the 1494 treaty: 1) It was not an attempt to divide the earth between Spain and Portugal, since the wording indicates that it was concerned with dividing the Atlantic Ocean into spheres of influence. 2) It was not an amendment to Pope Alexander VI's pro-Spanish bulls. A useful bibliographical essay is appended (pp. 16–18).

[58] William B. Greenlee. "The Background of Brazilian History," *The Americas* 2:2 (October 1945), pp. 151–164.

Sketches fifteenth- and early sixteenth-century Portuguese explorations in Africa, Asia, and Brazil and discusses rivalries with Spain over spheres of influence in the newly "discovered" regions. The author analyzes the various papal bulls, especially the four of 1493, the Treaty of Tordesillas of 1494, and the Treaty of Saragossa in 1529–1530 regarding the division of the non-Christian world between Portugal and Spain. Based on printed primary and secondary sources. 18 notes.

[59] W. Eugene Shiels, S. J. *King and Church. The Rise and Fall of the Patronato Real.* Chicago: Loyola University Press, 1961. xiii, 399 pp.

Though chiefly concerned with Spain, Spanish America and the *patronato real,* the author discusses Portuguese precedents and translates two papal bulls directed to Portugal: *Romanus pontifex* of Nicholas V (1454) and *Inter caetera quae* of Calixtus III (1456). Shiels argues that the Portuguese foundation for its *padroado real* (royal patronage) "acted as an exemplar and proving ground for its Spanish counterpart." He also asserts that "the great bulls of patronage in the fifteenth century rest their grants squarely on the idea of crusade." The Portuguese vehicle for these privileges was the Order of Christ. The author devotes two chapters to the four Alexandrine bulls of 1493 with a special emphasis on the Spanish monarchs' duties regarding the conversion of the heathen and the establishment of the *patronato real.* Much of the book contains the original documents and their English translations. There is a bibliography on pp. 379–385.

[60] James Muldoon. "Papal Responsibility for the Infidel: Another Look at Alexander VI's *Inter Caetera*," *The Catholic Historical Review* 64:2 (April 1978), pp. 168–184.

Effectively argues that *Inter Caetera* was not "an assertion of long-dead papal claims to world domination but rather a carefully worded statement which balanced the rights of the infidels, the papal responsibility for preaching the Gospel, and the political realities of aggressive expansionism." Muldoon shows that *Inter Caetera* "reflected not simply Alexander's view of the papal role in the world, but, rather, a conception of papal responsibility for mankind rooted in the tradition of canon law that formed the intellectual framework within which the pope's curia operated." The author also analyzes the papal pronouncements of Alexander VI's predecessors and the writings of canon lawyers on relations between Christians and non-Christians and sees parallels between the statements of Eugenius IV (1431–1447) regarding Spanish and Portuguese activity in the Canary Islands and those of Alexander VI in reference to the problems raised by Columbus's voyage. Based on printed primary sources. 43 notes.

D. Brazil's Portuguese Heritage [Nos. 61–63]

Though Brazil's Portuguese background is referred to in many of the items included in this Guide, three articles, in particular, concentrate almost entirely on the relationship between Portugal and Brazil. Emílio Willems **[61]** and Stuart B. Schwartz **[62]** look at Brazil's debt to Portugal's cultural heritage. Donald Warren **[63]** concentrates on Portugal's spiritist traditions and how they affected Portuguese America. Other studies which devote attention to aspects of Portugal's political, economic, social or religious heritage when discussing Brazil include the accounts of Gilberto Freyre **[699]** and **[702]**. Harold B. Johnson **[155]** compares Portuguese grants and practices when examining the lord-proprietors of sixteenth century Brazil. Portuguese law and legal reforms are described by Stuart B. Schwartz **[284]**. The Portuguese military heritage of Brazil is explained by David Tengwall **[289]**. A. J. R. Russell-Wood **[300]** traces the history of the Misericordia and other Portuguese institutions offering social assistance before turning his attention to Brazil. The Portuguese background of the Order of Christ is analyzed by Francis A. Dutra **[297]**. Pombal's Portuguese reforms are analyzed by Dauril Alden **[274]** and Kenneth Maxwell **[719]**.

[61] Emílio Willems. "Portuguese Culture in Brazil," in Marchant, ed., *Proceedings* **[90]**, pp. 66–79.

After alerting the reader to the possibility that, in light of more research, parallel development rather than cultural borrowing might provide the explanation for similarities between some Portuguese and Brazilian behavior, the author discusses under the headings of family, rural community, religion and magic some common denominators in the Luso-Brazilian national character. Covers the late colonial as well as the postindependence period. Notes in the text refer to the appended bibliography. A short resume in Portuguese is also included.

[62] Stuart B. Schwartz. "The Uncourted *Menina:* Brazil's Portuguese Heritage," *Luso-Brazilian Review* 2:1 (Summer 1965), pp. 67–80.

Argues that the Portuguese contribution to Brazil's heritage, "obviously so crucial for an understanding of Brazil's past and present," is frequently neglected. The author discusses the characteristics of the Portuguese colonizer and the social and cultural traditions Portugal and Brazil share, pointing out parallels and cultural borrowings with a special emphasis on the virginity/virility complex, the family, attitudes towards work, folklore, and religion. Based entirely on secondary sources. 64 notes.

[63] Donald Warren, Jr. "Portuguese Roots of Brazilian Spiritism," *Luso-Brazilian Review* 5:2 (Winter 1968), pp. 3–33.

Using Inquisition records, folklore and literary sources, the author reviews the effects of witchcraft, sorcery, and Sebastianism in Portugal since 1400. He maintains that the Inquisition's concentration on "New Christians" or alleged crypto-Jews drove many "New Christians" out or down but left witches relatively unscathed: "Far from stamping out or even tampering with the superstition of witchcraft, as in hated Castile, Portugal let the mediums exist alongside or rather below the dominant national culture." Warren stresses that "folk spiritism continued to flourish in those very regions of Portugal from which so many future Brazilians were drawn" and argues that scholars must look "into Portuguese culture [as well as Brazil's Amerindian and African heritage] in search of spiritist tendencies." Based on printed sources. 98 notes.

III. The History of Brazil [Nos. 64–109]

A. General Accounts [Nos. 64–69]

There are four major surveys of Brazilian history in English, all of which may be read with profit. Burns **[64]** and Poppino **[66]** devote greater attention to the colonial period. Worcester's account **[65]**, though shorter on the preindependence years, provides useful information on Portugal. Calógeras **[67]** focuses mainly on the early nineteenth century. Two short general accounts that treat colonial Brazil briefly are those by Américo Jacobina Lacombe **[68]** and Andrew Marshall **[69]**.

[64] E. Bradford Burns. *A History of Brazil.* New York and London: Columbia University Press, 1970. xii, 449 pp.

Of all the general histories of Brazil in English, that by Burns devotes the greatest attention to colonial Brazil. After briefly surveying the physical geography of Portuguese America, the author describes the initial encounters and the subsequent confrontations between the Amerindian and the European. He then provides an account of Portugal's establishment of a colony in the new world. The main section on Portuguese America—"The Colonial Experience"—discusses the important role of the African and studies social amalgamation, territorial expansion, economic fluctuations, and political evolution. The early part of chapter III ("The Proclamation and Consolidation of Independence") describes the "spiritual formation of nationhood" and political independence. Appendix I (Chiefs of State of Brazil) lists the governors-general and the viceroys who administered Brazil during the colonial period. There is a glossary of Portuguese words used in the text (pp. 414–417), a chronology of significant dates in Brazilian history (pp. 418–422), and "Suggestions for Additional Reading" (pp. 423–431). There are 3 maps and "A Pictorial Study of Brazil," the latter with five photographs illustrating Brazil's colonial architecture.

[65] Donald C. Worcester. *Brazil. From Colony to World Power.* New York: Charles Scribner's Sons, 1973. x, 277.

Appropriately, the author introduces his history of Brazil with a survey of Portuguese history to 1500, focusing on some of the chief events and factors that aided overseas expansion. Chapter 2, "Early Colonial Brazil," covers the sixteenth and seventeenth centuries. "Sowing the Seeds of Independence" brings the story to 1821. Part of chapter 4, "The First Empire," discusses the events of the early 1820s leading to Brazil's break with Portugal. About one-fourth of Worcester's study covers the colonial period. There is a map and more than a half-dozen photographs illustrating aspects of Brazil's history before independence. The book contains a chronology (pp. 253–255), a glossary (pp. 257–260), and a list of suggested readings (pp. 261–264).

[66] Rollie E. Poppino. *Brazil. The Land and People.* 2nd ed. New York: Oxford University Press, 1973. viii, 385 pp.
[The first edition appeared in 1968.]

Poppino provides a good survey of the Portuguese background to the colonization of Brazil and studies the role of the lords-proprietor, governors, missionaries, settlers and *degredados* during the first hundred years of settlement in America. He also examines the social order that developed in sixteenth-century Brazil and which continued during much of the colonial period. Chapter III, "Trail Blazer, Cowboy, and Prospector," provides a panoramic view of the exploration and exploitation of Brazil's interior and is the best short treatment of the subject in English. "Boom and Bust" (Chapter 4) focuses on the cyclical pattern of Brazilian economic growth and traces the fluctuations of brazilwood, sugar, tobacco, gold, diamonds, leather, and cotton through more than four-and-a-half centuries. Part of chapter 5, "The Immigrant," deals with Portuguese colonists and the millions of African slaves who settled Brazil. There are 6 maps—especially good is that of colonial Brazil on page 70—and a political chronology (pp. 331–337). A comprehensive bibliography is found on pp. 338–369.

[67] João Pandía Calógeras. *A History of Brazil.* Trans. and ed. Percy Alvin Martin. Chapel Hill: University of North Carolina Press, 1939. xxiii, 374 pp. [Reprinted in New York: Russell & Russell, Inc. 1963]. Translated and adapted from *A Formação Histórica do Brasil.*

"Discovery and Exploration" quickly traces pre-Cabralian Portuguese expansion and then shows how Brazil expanded her boundaries during the three-and-a-quarter centuries after 1500. Chapter II, "The Economic Organization of the Colony," discusses Brazil's resources and population, with special attention paid to the role of the African slave. The third chapter, "Rio de Janeiro, Capital of Portugal," covers the period from 1808–1821. "The Independence of Brazil; Its Recognition by the 'Comitas Gentium' "(chapter IV) details the events of the 1820s. About 25 percent of the book deals with the colonial period, though almost half of that coverage focuses on the first quarter of the nineteenth century. There are some helpful notes by the translator. A bibliography is found on pp. 357–364.

[68] Américo Jacobina Lacombe. *Brazil. A Brief History.* Trans. W. A. R. Richardson. Rio de Janeiro: Ministry of Foreign Relations, 1954. 105 pp.

Based on a series of four lectures given in 1942 to the Anglo-Brazilian Cultural Society of Rio de Janeiro and geared to a British audience. The author, a distinguished Brazilian historian, reacts strongly against accounts that portray the history of Brazil "as having been a series of interesting coincidences, fortuitous circumstances and unconnected, fascinating adventures, culminating in a half-mad prince, who revolted against his father out of sheer obstinacy." This concise history consists of four chapters—"Colonization;" "The Era of Independence;" "The Brazilian Empire;" and "Republican Brazil"—the first two covering the period to 1822. In "Colonization" Lacombe provides an overview of Portuguese expansion, an analysis of the economic structure of colonial Brazil (with a special emphasis on brazilwood, sugar, gold and cattle), a discussion of sixteenth- and seventeenth-century foreign attacks on Portuguese America, a study of the role of the *bandeirantes* and the Jesuits, and a brief sketch of Brazil's administrative apparatus and culture. Part II contains a good survey of the European events leading to the transfer of the Portuguese court to Brazil, the elevation of Brazil to the status of a kingdom in 1815, the efforts of the Portuguese *Cortes* or Parliament to reduce Brazil to colonial status, and the proclamation of Brazilian independence by Pedro I. There is some documentation, but no index. A "Selected Bibliography in English" is found on pages 101–105.

[69] Andrew Marshall. *Brazil.* London: Thames and Hudson, 1966. 231 pp.

References to the colonial period are scattered throughout this short history of Brazil, but only chapter 3, "The Outline of the Past" (pp.

37–48), specifically focuses on Portuguese America before independence. The treatment, however, is uneven, with only one page devoted to the seventeenth century. Chapter 9, "The Faces of Culture" (pp. 145–156), discusses briefly the art, architecture and literature of colonial as well as modern Brazil. But most scholars would take issue with Marshall's remark that "the first taste of culture was given to Brazil not by a Portuguese but by a Dutchman in the seventeenth century." There is a "Select Bibliography" (pp. 211–212) and a "Who's Who" (pp. 213–223), the latter including 54 biographical sketches, 8 of which deal with the colonial period. About one-third of the 93 photographs help illustrate aspects of Brazilian history before independence. There are 4 maps.

B. Colonial Period [Nos. 70–80]

1. Books [Nos. 70–73]

The most complete account of colonial Brazil in English is Robert Southey's three-volume study **[70]**, first published in the early nineteenth century. Bailey W. Diffie's section on Brazil in his *Latin American Civilization: The Colonial Period* **[71]** remains one of the best brief statements on Portuguese America before independence. Felix Reichmann's series of essays **[72]** are interesting to read and helpful for beginners. Caio Prado, Jr. **[73]** looks at colonial Brazil on the eve of independence and provides a strong socio-economic analysis. His chief interest is the late eighteenth and the early nineteenth century. Though both Andrew Grant **[122]** and James Henderson **[123]** call their accounts *History of Brazil,* there is little history in them. The emphasis is more on Brazil's geography and economy.

[70] Robert Southey. *History of Brazil.* 3 v. London: Longman, Hurst, Rees and Orme, 1810–1819. xxxiv, 715 pp.; xvi, 718 pp.; xx, 950 pp. [The first volume was revised and enlarged in 1822. There have been several recent reprints. I have used the one by Lenox Hill (New York), 1970.]

"The history of Brazil is less beautiful that that of the mother country, and less splendid than that of the Portugueze in Asia; but it is not less important than either." With these words Robert Southey begins page one of his monumental three-volume history. His own evaluation, made in 1823, has withstood the test of time: "In many parts imperfect, it nevertheless is even now a great achievement. . . .Centuries hence, when Brazil shall have become the great and prosperous country which one day it must be, I shall be regarded there as the first person who ever attempted to give a consistent form to its crude, unconnected and neglected history." In the first volume, Southey prefaces Cabral's visit in 1500 with an account of the voyage of Vicente Yañez Pinzon to Brazil several months earlier. He describes the initial fifty years of Portuguese activity in America, but pays more attention to exploration in the Plata and the Amazon. He goes into great detail regarding Hans Staden's adventures, the practices of the Amerindians, the role of the governor-general, the missionary activity of the Jesuits, the settlement in Paraguay, the expulsion of the French from Rio de Janeiro and Maranhão, and the Dutch occupation of Brazil to 1640. He also analyzes further exploration of the Amazon region, paying considerable attention to Indian practices and customs. Volume two concludes the account of Dutch activity in northeastern Brazil with their ouster in 1654. Southey describes in great detail the Jesuit missions in Paraguay and recounts that region's history. He then outlines the major events in the coastal captaincies before focusing on Maranhão and its problems. The author concludes with a review of the state of Portuguese America in the seventeenth century. The third volume continues Southey's survey of seventeenth-century Brazil, discusses the gold discoveries in Minas Gerais, recounts the French attack on Rio de Janeiro, analyzes Indian-White relations in the Amazon and in Paraguay, evaluates the Pombaline era and various attempts at reform, weighs the effects of the expulsion of the Jesuits from Brazil, and reviews the various sections of Brazil at the end of the eighteenth and the beginning of the nineteenth centuries.

[71] Bailey W. Diffie. *Latin American Civilization: The Colonial Period.* Harrisburg, Pennsylvania: Stackpole Sons, 1945. xvi, 812 pp. maps, illus, charts.

Part III, Colonial Brazil, one of the best and most comprehensive short histories in English, is covered on pages 631–753. Diffie provides a useful survey of Brazil's discovery by Cabral in 1500, early settlement, the brazilwood trade, the captaincy or donatarial system which was inaugurated in the early 1530s, the institution of the governor-generalship in 1549, and the growing importance of sugar. He discusses French and English intervention, the union of crowns, 1580–1640, and the Dutch occupation of much of northern Brazil, the latter ending in 1654. Brazilian frontier expansion into the interior via the Rio São Francisco, colonization along the northeastern coast to the Amazon and northern Brazil, and thrusts by the *bandeirantes* south, west and north from São Paulo are analyzed. The discovery of large gold deposits in Minas Gerais, Mato Grosso and Goiás and their significance are detailed. The author describes colonial manufacturing and its chief characteristics and reviews the commerce of Portuguese America with a helpful discussion of Brazil's chief exports. Brazilian society and the role of Indians, Blacks and Portuguese and their interaction are delineated as is the class structure of the colony. Learning, literature, the eighteenth-century "academies" and the enlightenment along with art and architecture are sketched. There is a good section on the Church; and the activity of the regular clergy, especially the Jesuits, along with their work with the Indians, is evaluated. The author treats the Inquisition and its influence. The government of colonial Brazil and the changes that were effected in the eighteenth century are also studied. The section on Brazil contains several useful maps and graphs along with some excellent plates. Well documented.

[72] Felix Reichmann. *Sugar, Gold and Coffee. Essays on the History of Brazil Based on Francis Hull's Books.* Ithaca, New York: Cornell University Library, 1959. xxiii, 160 pp.

Easy-to-read and interesting series of essays on Portuguese expansion and Brazilian history to 1889. The author, making frequent references to rare books in the collection of Colonel Hull, outlines Brazil's sixteenth-century history with a special emphasis on the character of Amerindians, Africans and Portuguese and their intermingling. He analyzes Portuguese rivalries with the French, English and Dutch and discusses foreigners who visited or attacked Brazil during the sixteenth century. Shipping, sailors and piracy are examined as are Portugal's treaties with England in the seventeenth and early eighteenth centuries. After describing the gold discoveries, Reichmann discusses the Pombal (1750–1777)–Jesuit clash which resulted in that order's expulsion from Portugal and the Portuguese empire in 1759. The arrival of the Portuguese Court, Pedro I and the proclamation of Brazilian independence and his abdication in 1831, and Pedro II's life and reign to 1889 are also briefly described. The book concludes with an analysis of Brazil's wealth. Contains plates of almost two dozen title pages of rare books from the Hull collection, a discussion of the British-born engineer's career in Brazil, and a description of some of the most important works he gathered together. A bibliography is found on pp. 155–160.

[73] Caio Prado, Jr. *The Colonial Background of Modern Brazil.* Trans. Suzette Macedo. Berkeley and Los Angeles: University of California Press, 1967. 530 pp.

This important history of Brazil devotes most of its attention to the post-1750 years. Part One: "Population and Settlement" (which is subdivided into coastal settlement and that of the interior as well as currents of settlement and races) contains an excellent overview of Portuguese frontier expansion in Brazil. Unfortunately the book lacks a map, making these chapters doubly difficult to read, since often place name follows place name, separated every few paragraphs by a sentence or two that provides a theme or shows the region's economic importance. Part Two: "Material Life" provides an excellent overview of the economy of colonial Brazil, whether large-scale or subsistence agriculture, mining, stock raising, extractive products, crafts and industries, commerce, communications and transport. Part Three: "Social and Political Life" devotes chapters to social organization, administration, and social and political life. Though this pioneering work by a Marxist historian, because of its emphasis on social and economic history, is a milestone in Brazilian historiography, it is not without its flaws. The author seems to detest the Portuguese and their colonial system as well as Africans and Amerindians and denigrates their role in Brazil's pre-independence history. In addition, since he often fails to look at Brazil's history from a broader perspective, he falls into an overabundance of avoidable traps. Therefore, this book must be read with care. However, Caio Prado's contributions far outweigh his shortcomings. His chapter on administration is generally considered the best short statement on the subject. Well annotated.

2. Single Chapter Overviews [Nos. 74–80]

Manoel Cardozo **[74]** and **[75]** was one of the pioneers in the writing of these succinct overviews of colonial Brazilian history and few have matched his success. Other surveys written by Americans include those by Alexander Marchant **[76]** and Percy Alvin Martin **[77]**. Sérgio Buarque de Holanda **[78]** and **[79]** provides a brief Brazilian perspective, as does Eulália Maria Lahmeyer Lobo **[80]** in her chapter on the continuity of Brazilian history.

[74] Manoel Cardozo. "The Modernization of Brazil, 1500–1800: An Interpretive Essay," in Eric N. Baklanoff, ed., *The Shaping of Modern Brazil.* Baton Rouge: Lousiana State University Press, 1969. xviii, 164 pp.

This short introductory essay (pp. 3–18) traces economic development in Brazil from the sixteenth to the early nineteenth century and discusses the influence of religious, cultural and intellectual attitudes on Portugal and Portuguese America. In particular, Cardozo focuses on the chief economic activities that produced wealth and attracted immigrants to Portuguese America: Gathering brazilwood; raising sugar on the coast and cattle in the interior; growing tobacco; and panning for gold and diamonds. The author also discusses modernization efforts in the eighteenth and nineteenth centuries and concludes: "Providentially for Brazil, John VI arrived upon the scene [in 1808] and, with the good sense that always characterized him, decided that something radically new was needed. That is why he was determined to establish the 'Liberal System.' The modernization of the nineteenth century would essentially be carried out under this system." Based mainly on printed primary sources. 41 notes. This paper was originally presented at the Colloquium on the Modernization of Brazil held at Louisiana State University in Baton Rouge, February 23–25, 1967.

[75] Manoel Cardozo. "Dependency, 1500–1808," in Hill, ed., *Brazil* **[82]**, pp. 3–14.

Excellent overview of three centuries of Brazilian history by an outstanding authority on Portuguese America. Cardozo touches on the political, social, economic, religious and cultural life of colonial Brazil. Looking back at the colonial period, he concludes: "Much had been done since Cabral had landed in the New World. A continent had been conquered or carved out for future occupancy; a language, a culture, and a religion had been transplanted from Europe. . . .Brazil had reached a maturity that was to be one of the best guaranties of survival." There is a bibliography on page 371. No notes.

[76] Alexander Marchant. "Colonial Brazil," in H. V. Livermore, *Portugal and Brazil* **[81]**, pp. 283–301.

Marchant briefly discusses foreign and local challenges to Portuguese sovereignty in Brazil and shows how the mother country's strong social, cultural and economic influence kept Brazil Portuguese. He argues that although there were modifications, "some Portuguese characteristics or institutions, like the law, language, and religion, remained to a greater or less degree recognizably Portuguese and relatively unchanged by transplantation. Others, as, for instance, the latifundiary estate and the structure of the upper-class family, took on in Brazil variations that made them almost new things." The author points out how the same law codes applied to both Portugal and Brazil and shows how the Portuguese language and Catholicism—though remaining dominant—were modified by Brazil's African and Amerindian heritage. He also discusses Portuguese attempts at centralization, the development of Brazil's economy and the role of large landholding, sugar, and slave labor. The author traces the history of African and Amerindian slavery in Portuguese America. He discusses urban development, considering the Brazilian town as "the servant of the countryside." The role of the artisan is analyzed and some of the products made in Brazil are listed. Marchant gives the major characteristics of Brazil's population, its growth, distribution and racial composition. Leaning heavily on Gilberto Freyre's *The Masters and the Slaves* **[699]**, the author describes Portuguese America's social types and hierarchy. In his analysis of the colony's economy, he points out that "while the export economy of Brazil was organized capitalistically, the lives of most individuals (excluding some of those in the towns) within Brazil were but little affected by a money economy." There is a bibliographical note on pages 299–301. Undocumented.

[77] Percy Alvin Martin. "Portugal in America," *The Hispanic American Historical Review* 17:2 (May 1937), pp. 182–210.

Short survey of colonial Brazilian history, focusing on exploration, colonization, plantation life, race mixture, the role of the *bandeirantes,* and independence. Though it contains several factual errors, the speech does provide insights into historical research prior to the mid-1930s. Based chiefly on secondary sources. 39 notes. [Presidential Address, Pacific Coast Branch of the American Historical Association, December 1936].

[78] Sérgio Buarque de Holanda. "The History of a Demi-Continent," in Fulvio Roiter, ed. *Brazil.* New York: The Viking Press, 1971. pp. 74–88.

Sérgio Buarque de Holanda, one of twentieth-century Brazil's most important historians of the colonial period, contributed this survey of Brazil's past to accompany Roiter's photographic essay. About half of Buarque de Holanda's account covers the period before independence. The author describes the significance of brazilwood and sugar, two of Brazil's most important products during the first century and a half of settlement, and analyzes the role of the *bandeirantes* in territorial expansion west of the line of the Treaty of Tordesillas. The importance of gold discoveries in Minas Gerais in the mid-1690s and diamonds several decades later, the resultant influx of immigrants to Brazil, and the eventual transfer of political and economic power from the Northeast to Rio de Janeiro are explained. According to the author, "the colonial population increased tenfold within a century, from 300,000 inhabitants in 1700 to 3,000,000 in 1800." After briefly recounting some of the details of the Minas Conspiracy of 1789, Buarque de Holanda describes the impact on Brazilian life caused by the transfer of the Portuguese Court to America in 1808 and the events leading to independence. No notes.

[79] Sérgio Buarque de Holanda. "Outline of Brazilian History," *Travel in Brazil* 1:1 (1941). pp. 2–3.

This succinct survey by a distinguished Brazilian historian deals almost entirely with the colonial period. The author compares Portuguese attitudes to colonization in America with those of Spain and England. He also discusses the *bandeirantes* and their influence on the Brazilian frontier. The author concludes with an explanation of why European agricultural techniques were so slowly introduced into colonial Brazil. No notes.

[80] Eulália Maria Lahmeyer Lobo. "Conflict and Continuity in Brazilian History," in Keith and Edwards, eds., *Conflict and Continuity* **[84]**, pp. 268–296.

Provocative and informative overview that emphasizes continuity in Brazil's socio-economic history. Two points are stressed for the colonial period: 1) the importance of patterns of landownership, which, in turn, heavily influenced the economic and social structures in the colonial as well as the national period. The author lists such factors as scarcity of both Portuguese and Amerindian populations and the abundance of land in Brazil in promoting the development of latifundia. The Crown's need to attract private capital forced the Portuguese monarchs to make concessions to large landowners in Brazil. Also sugar and tobacco plantations and cattle-raising encouraged the formation of large estates; 2) economic growth based on the export of a few products. Shows that the seventeenth century was one of expansion for Portuguese Atlantic trade, while one of retrenchment for commerce between Spanish America and Spain. This pattern continued into the eighteenth century. However, the independence of Brazil coincided with the beginning of a long depression which Brazil shared with the United States and Britain, though the cycles in Brazil tended to last longer. The remainder of the article deals with Brazil since 1840. Based on some archival but mostly printed sources. 56 notes.

C. Collected Essays [Nos. 81-101]

This section includes all the collections containing at least two chapters on Colonial Brazil. The individual chapters are found under the topics with which they deal.

1. Luso-Brazilian History [Nos. 81-92]

a. GENERAL AND/OR REGIONAL [Nos. 81–86]

There are a number of excellent collections on Luso-Brazilian history. Harold V. Livermore and W. J. Entwistle's *Portugal* and Brazil **[81]** contains several fine surveys as does Lawrence Hill's Brazil **[82]** and T. Lynn Smith and Alexander Marchant's Brazil. Portrait of Half a Continent **[83]**—all of which rely on an interdisciplinary approach. Henry H. Keith and S. F. Edward's *Conflict and Continuity* **[84]** contains several scholarly essays and commentaries. E. Bradford Burns **[85]** has collected an excellent sample of writings on the historiography of Brazil. Charles Wagley **[86]** brings together some useful studies on the vast Amazon region.

[81] Harold V. Livermore and W. J. Entwistle, eds. *Portugal and Brazil: An Introduction.* Oxford: At the Clarendon Press, 1953. xi, 418 pp.

This collection was written to commemorate the memory of Edgar Prestage and Aubrey Fitz Gerald Bell. The sections of greatest interest to students of colonial Brazil include: **[76]** Alexander Marchant, "Colonial Brazil," pp. 283–301; **[760]** Robert C. Smith, "Baroque Architecture," pp. 349–384; **[800]** Joaquim de Sousa-Leão, "Decorative Art: The Azulejo," pp. 385–394; **[811]** Ann Livermore, "Music," pp. 394–403. There are more than two dozen plates and an index.

[82] Lawrence Hill, ed. *Brazil.* Berkeley and Los Angeles: University of California Press, 1947. xxi, 394 pp.

Contains the following chapters of interest for colonial Brazil: **[75]** Manoel Cardozo, "Dependency, 1500–1808," pp. 3–14; **[816]** Manoel Cardozo, "The Transition, 1808–1840," pp. 15–34; **[739]** Francisco Venâncio Filho, "Science," pp. 153–180; **[752]** Mario de Andrade, "Art," pp. 181–194. The book contains a bibliography for each chapter plus an index.

[83] T. Lynn Smith and Alexander Marchant, eds. *Brazil. Portrait of Half a Continent.* New York: The Dryden Press, 1951. viii. 466 pp.

This collection of essays had its origins in a special summer session held at Vanderbilt University in 1948. Professors from Vanderbilt's Institute for Brazilian Studies, those from other North American Universities and visiting professors from Brazil were invited to take part in these summer courses and contribute chapters to this collection. Chapters dealing with the colonial period include: **[114]** Alexander Marchant, "The Unity of Brazilian History," pp. 37–51; **[117]** Hilgard O'Reilly Sternberg, "The Physical Basis of Brazilian Society," pp. 52–85; **[118]** Preston E. James, "The Cultural Regions of Brazil," pp. 86–103; **[352]** Charles Wagley, "The Indian Heritage of Brazil," pp. 104–124; **[694]** José Arthur Rios, "The Cities of Brazil," pp. 188–208; **[705]** Antônio Cândido, "The Brazilian Family," pp. 291–312; **[302]** Roger Bastide, "Religion and the Church in Brazil," pp. 334–355; **[812]** Gerrit de Jong, Jr., "Brazilian Music and Art," pp. 423–448. There is also an excellent glossary (pp. 449–452). There are 48 illustrations and a map of Brazil. The book's 11 figures and 29 tables refer mainly to the period after independence.

[84] Henry H. Keith and S. F. Edwards, eds. *Conflict and Continuity in Brazilian Society*. Columbia, South Carolina: University of South Carolina Press, 1969. xiv, 312 pp. index.

Six of the papers along with their commentaries presented at the Seminar on Latin American History held at the University of South Carolina, October 19–21, 1967, and treating of Brazilian history prior to 1826 are contained in this collection: **[143]** Bailey W. Diffie, "The Legal 'Privileges' of the Foreigners in Portugal and Sixteenth-Century Brazil" (Commentary by Susan C. Schneider), pp. 1–24; **[322]** Dauril Alden, "Economic Aspects of the Expulsion of the Jesuits from Brazil:

A Preliminary Report" (Commentary by Fr. Mathias C. Kiemen, O. F. M.), pp. 25–71; **[735]** Manoel Cardozo, "Azeredo Coutinho and the Intellectual Ferment of His Times" (Commentary by E. Bradford Burns), pp. 72–112; **[822]** Alan K. Manchester, "The Transfer of the Portuguese Court to Rio de Janeiro" (Commentary by Richard Graham), pp. 148–190; **[893]** Harry Bernstein, "The Lisbon *Juiz do Povo* and the Independence of Brazil, 1750–1822: An Essay on Luso-Brazilian Populism" (Commentary by George E. Carl), pp. 191–230; and **[80]** Eulália Maria Lahmeyer Lobo, "Conflict and Continuity in Brazilian History," pp. 268–296.

[85] E. Bradford Burns, ed. *Perspectives on Brazilian History.* New York and London: Columbia University Press, 1967. xii, 235 pp.

This important collection of essays on the historiography of Brazil contains the following of importance to students of Portuguese America before independence: **[907]** E. Bradford Burns, "Introduction," pp. 1–20; **[922]** Karl Friedrich Philipp von Martius, "How the History of Brazil Should Be Written," pp. 21–41; **[930]** Pedro Moacyr Campos, "An Outline of Brazilian Historiography in the Nineteenth and Twentieth Centuries," pp. 42–89; **[923]** José Honório Rodrigues, "Problems in Brazilian History and Historiography," pp. 102–113; **[924]** José Honório Rodrigues, "The Periodization of Brazilian History," pp. 114–138; **[916]** João Capistrano de Abreu, "A Critique of Francisco Adolfo de Varnhagen," pp. 142–155; **[919]** José Honório Rodrigues, "Capistrano de Abreu and Brazilian Historiography," pp. 156–180; **[929]** Sérgio Buarque de Holanda, "Historical Thought in Twentieth-Century Brazil," pp. 181–196. Burns concludes with a useful "Bibliographical Essay on Brazilian Historiography," pp. 197–206. There are notes and a glossary.

[86] Charles Wagley, ed. *Man in the Amazon.* Gainesville: The University Presses of Florida, 1974. xvi. 330 pp.

Includes papers presented at the Twenty-third Annual Latin American Conference held at the University of Florida in Gainesville, February 18–21, 1973. Three chapters are of special interest to students of colonial Brazil: **[634]** Arthur Cesar Ferreira Reis, "Economic History of the Brazilian Amazon," pp. 33–44; **[633]** Lewis A. Tambs, "Geopolitics of the Amazon," pp. 45–87; and **[393]** Betty J. Meggers, "Environment and Culture in Amazonia," pp. 91–110. Unfortunately there is no index, though each chapter has a bibliography.

b. COLONIAL BRAZILIAN AND IMPERIAL PERSPECTIVES [Nos. 87–92]
Essays covering almost the entire span of the colonial period are found in Alden, ed., *Colonial Roots of Modern Brazil* **[87]**. Events leading up to independence are studied in a series of essays edited by A. J. R. Russell-Wood **[88]**. The imperial perpsective is covered briefly in Alden and Dean, eds., *Essays Concerning the Socioeconomic History of Brazil and Portuguese India* **[89]**. Livermore and Entwistle **[81]** also contains material on Portuguese Asia. The *Proceedings* or *Actas* of some of the Luso-Brazilian Colloquia **[90]**, **[91]**, and **[92]** include useful contributions in English on Portugal, colonial Brazil, and Portuguese Africa and Asia.

[87] Dauril Alden, ed. *Colonial Roots of Modern Brazil. Papers of the Newberry Library Conference.* Berkeley, Los Angeles, London: University of California Press, 1973. xiii, 294 pp.

The essays in this volume were originally presented in November, 1969, at the Newberry Library Conference on Colonial Brazil. Those published include: **[926]** Charles R. Boxer, "Some Reflections on the Historiography of Colonial Brazil, 1950–1970," pp. 3–15; **[152]** Francis A. Dutra, "Centralization vs. Donatarial Privilege: Pernambuco, 1602–1630," pp. 19–60; **[654]** David M. Davidson, "How the Brazilian West Was Won: Freelance and State on the Mato Grosso Frontier, 1737–1752," pp. 61–106; **[722]** Kenneth R. Maxwell, "The Generation of the 1790s and the Idea of Luso-Brazilian Empire," pp. 107–144; **[602]** Stuart B. Schwartz, "Free Labor in a Slave Economy: The *Lavradores de Cana* of Colonial Bahia," pp. 147–197; **[432]** Colin M. MacLachlan, "The Indian Labor Structure in the Portuguese Amazon, 1700–1800," pp. 199–230; **[567]** Harold B. Johnson, Jr., "A Preliminary Inquiry into Money, Prices, and Wages in Rio de Janeiro, 1763–1823," pp. 231–283. There is a useful glossary and an index.

[88] A. J. R. Russell-Wood, ed. *From Colony to Nation. Essays on the Independence of Brazil.* Baltimore and London: The Johns Hopkins University Press, 1975. xi, 267 pp.

Four of the papers included in this volume were initially presented at a symposium on Brazilian independence sponsored by the History Department at The Johns Hopkins University on 18 and 19 October 1972. The selections include: **[891]** A. J. R. Russell-Wood, "Preconditions and Precipitants of the Independence Movement in Portuguese America," pp. 3–40; **[892]** Emília Viotti da Costa, "The Political Emancipation of

Brazil," pp. 43–88; **[825]** Maria Odila Silva Dias, "The Establishment of the Royal Court in Brazil," pp. 89–108; **[879]** Stanley E. Hilton, "The United States and Brazilian Independence," pp. 109–129; **[709]** Stuart B. Schwartz, "Elite Politics and the Growth of a Peasantry in Late Colonial Brazil," pp. 133–154; **[692]** Richard M. Morse, "Brazil's Urban Development: Colony and Empire," pp. 155–181; **[733]** Manoel [da Silveira] Cardozo, "The Modernization of Portugal and the Independence of Brazil," pp. 185–210; **[731]** E. Bradford Burns, "The Intellectuals as Agents of Change and the Independence of Brazil, 1724–1822," pp. 211–246. There is a chronological table (pp. 247–250), a glossary (pp. 251–252), and an index.

[89] Dauril Alden and Warren Dean, eds. *Essays Concerning the Socioeconomic History of Brazil and Portuguese India.* Gainesville, Florida: The University Presses of Florida, 1977. xiv, 247 pp. index.

Contains two chapters dealing with aspects of Brazilian history prior to 1826: **[603]** Catherine Lugar, "The Portuguese Tobacco Trade and Tobacco Growers of Bahia in the Late Colonial Period," pp. 26–70; and **[292]** Michael C. McBeth, "The Brazilian Recruit during the First Empire: Slave or Soldier?" pp. 71–86.

[90] Alexander Marchant, ed. *Proceedings of the International Colloquium on Luso-Brazilian Studies.* Nashville, Tennessee: The Vanderbilt University Press, 1953. xii, 335pp.

The first Luso-Brazilian Colloquium was held in Washington, D. C., on 15–20 October 1950. Papers of interest to students of colonial Brazil include: **[61]** Emílio Willems, "Portuguese Culture in Brazil," pp. 66–79; **[757]** Robert C. Smith, "The Seventeenth- and Eighteenth-Century Architecture of Brazil," pp. 109–116; **[747]** John Bury, "Portuguese and Brazilian Architecture of the 17th and 18th Centuries: Relation of Exceptional Monuments to Their European Architectural Background," pp. 119–121; **[927]** Robert C. Smith, "Recommendations for Research and Research Aids in the History of the 17th- and 18th-Century Architecture of Portugal and Brazil," pp. 126–130; **[925]** Charles R. Boxer, "Some Considerations on Portuguese Colonial Historiography," pp. 169–180. This volume also contains a number of brief summaries in English. There are also some excellent photographs illustrating Luso-Brazilian art and architecture.

[91] Luis Filipe Lindley Cintra, ed. *Actas. III Colóquio Internacional de Estudos Luso-Brasileiros.* 2 v. Lisbon, 1959–1960. xxxix, 549 pp.; 470 pp.

The third Luso-Brazilian Colloquium was held in Lisbon, Portugal on 9–15 September 1957. Papers in English dealing with colonial Brazil are found in v. 2 and include: **[504]** John A. Hutchins, "Portugal's Interest in the Control of the Coast of Southern Brazil and the Mouth of the Rio de la Plata," pp. 173–187; **[429]** George C. A. Boehrer, "Some Brazilian Proposals to the Cortes Gerais, 1821–1823, on the Indian Problem," pp. 201–209; **[427]** Mathias C. Kiemen, O. F. M., "The *Conselho Ultramarino*'s First Legislative Attempts to Solve the Indian Question in America, 1643–1647," pp. 226–239; **[45]** Bailey W. Diffie, "Portugal's Preparation for Exploration. A Functional-Cultural Interpretation," pp. 251–265; and **[161]** Lewis Hanke, "The Portuguese and the Villa Imperial de Potosí," pp. 266–276.

[92] Padre Avelino de Jesus da Costa, ed. *Actas. V Colóquio Internacional de Estudos Luso-Brasileiros.* 5 v. Coimbra, 1965–1968. 545 pp.; 591 pp.; 567 pp.; 573 pp.; 420 pp.

The fifth Luso-Brazilian Colloquium was held at Coimbra, Portugal, on 2–8 September 1963. Papers published in English of interest to students of colonial Brazil include the following from v. II: **[510]** José Carlos Canales, "Rio Grande do Sul, Keystone of Platine Trade and Communications," pp. 171–191; and **[870]** Raul d'Eça, "A Little-Known Episode in the Early Negotiations Between the United States and Portugal for a Treaty of Commerce—Was Brazil the Cause for the Failure of the 1786 Treaty?" pp. 209–217.

2. Latin American History [Nos. 93–98]

Though the works cited below encompass all of Latin America, they each contain important sections on Brazil. Some chapters are reprints, while others are original. Julian H. Steward **[93]** edited the monumental *Handbook of South American Indians,* which is still useful for understanding the Indians of Brazil during the colonial period. Howard F. Cline **[94]**, in his two-volume collection on Latin American History, gathered together some of the earlier efforts to interpret the colonial Brazilian experience. Eight articles previously published in the *Publica-*

tions of the American Jewish Historical Society are reprinted in Martin A. Cohen, ed. **[95]**, *The Jewish Experience in Latin America.* Charles C. Griffin **[96]** edited two essays on Brazil in the collection, *Concerning Latin American Culture.* Robert B. Toplin **[97]** did the same in his *Slavery and Race Relations in Latin America*, as did Asunción Lavrin **[98]** in *Latin American Women: Historical Perspectives.*

[93] Julian H. Steward, ed. *Handbook of South American Indians.* 7 v. Washington, D. C.: Smithsonian Institution, Bureau of American Ethnology, 1946–1959.

The sections of Volume I of most interest for students of colonial Brazil include: **[368]** S. K. Lothrop, "Indians of the Paraná Delta and La Plata Littoral," pp. 177–190; **[369]** Antônio Serrano, "The Charrua," pp. 191–196; **[370]** Alfred Métraux, "Ethnography of the Chaco," pp. 197–370; **[378]** Robert H. Lowie, "Eastern Brazil: An Introduction," pp. 381–397; **[359]** Anibal Mattos, "Lagoa Santa Man," pp. 399–400; **[360]** Antônio Serrano, "The Sambaquís of the Brazilian Coast," pp. 401–407; **[373]** Alfred Métraux, "The Guato," pp. 409–418; **[408]** Robert H. Lowie, "The Bororo," pp. 419–434; **[371]** Alfred Métraux and Herbert Baldus, "The Guayakí," pp. 435–444; **[372]** Alfred Métraux, "The Caingang," pp. 445–475; **[394]** Robert H. Lowie, "The Northwestern and Central Gê," pp. 477–517; **[407]** Robert H. Lowie, "The Southern Cayapó, pp. 519–520; **[380]** Alfred Métraux, "The Guaitacá," pp. 521–522; **[379]** Alfred Métraux, "The Purí-Coroado Linguistic Family," pp. 523–530; **[381]** Alfred Métraux, "The Botocudo," pp. 531–540; **[383]** Alfred Métraux and Curt Nimuendajú, "The Mashacalí, Patashó, and Malalí Linguistic Families," pp. 541–545; **[384]** Alfred Métraux and Curt Ninuendajú, "The Camacan Linguistic Family," pp. 547–552; **[382]** Robert H. Lowie, "The 'Tapuya,'" pp. 553–556; **[385]** Robert H. Lowie, "The Cariri," pp. 557–559; **[388]** Robert H. Lowie, "The Tarairiu," pp. 563–566; **[386]** Robert H. Lowie, "The Jeico," pp. 567; **[387]** Alfred Métraux, "The Fulnio," p. 571; and **[389]** Alfred Métraux, "The Teremembé," pp. 573–574. An excellent bibliography to volume I is found on pp. 575–624.

Volume III, entitled *The Tropical Forest Tribes,* also contains much of value for those interested in colonial Brazil. It includes: **[374]** Robert H. Lowie, "The Tropical Forests," pp. 1–56; **[358]** Francisco de Aparicio, "The Archeology of the Paraná River," pp. 57–69; **[367]** Alfred Métraux, "The Guaraní," pp. 69–94; **[375]** Alfred Métraux, "The Tupinamba," pp. 95–133; **[398]** Curt Nimuendajú, "The Guaja," pp. 135–136; **[376]** Charles Wagley and Eduardo Galvão, "The

Tenetehara," pp. 137–148; **[364]** Betty J. Meggers, "The Archeology of the Amazon Basin," pp. 149–166; **[399]** William Lipkind, "The Carajá," pp. 179–191; **[390]** Curt Nimuendajú, "The Turiwara and Aruã," pp. 193–198; **[400]** Curt Nimuendajú and Alfred Métraux, "The Amanayé," pp. 199–202; **[401]** Curt Nimuendajú, "Little-Known Tribes of the Lower Tocantins River Region," pp. 203–208; **[403]** Curt Nimuendajú, "Little-Known Tribes of the Lower Amazon," pp. 209–211; **[402]** Curt Nimuendajú, "Tribes of the Lower and Middle Xingú River," pp. 213–243; **[404]** Curt Nimuendajú, "The Maue and Arapium," pp. 245–254; **[413]** Curt Nimuendajú, "The Mura and Piraha," pp. 255–269; **[414]** Donald Horton, "The Mundurucú," pp. 271–282; **[405]** Curt Nimuendajú, "The Cawahib, Parintintin, and their Neighbors," pp. 283–297; **[406]** Curt Nimuendajú, "The Cayabi, Tapanyuna, and Apiacá," pp. 307–320; **[421]** Alfred Métraux, "The Paressí," pp. 349–360; **[422]** Claude Levi-Strauss, "Tribes of the Right Bank of the Guaporé River," pp. 371–379; **[418]** Alfred Métraux, "The Chiquitoans and Other Tribes of the Province of Chiquitos," pp. 381–397; **[419]** Alfred Métraux, "The Chapacuran Tribes," pp. 397–406; **[420]** Alfred Métraux, "The Southeastern Panoan Tribes," pp. 449–452; **[416]** Alfred Métraux, "Tribes of the Juruá-Purús Basins," pp. 657–686; **[410]** Alfred Métraux, "Tribes of the Middle and Upper Amazon River," pp. 687–712; **[411]** Curt Nimuendajú, "The Tucuna," pp. 713–725; **[409]** Irving Goldman, "Tribes of the Uaupés-Caquetá Region," pp. 763–798; **[391]** John Gillin, "Tribes of the Guianas," pp. 799–860; **[392]** Alfred Métraux, "The Hunting and Gathering Tribes of the Rio Negro Basin," pp. 861–881; and **[351]** Julian H. Steward, "Culture Areas of the Tropical Forests," pp. 883–899. There is a glossary and a bibliography. Volume III contains 126 plates, 134 figures and 8 maps.

Volume V includes **[357]** Julian H. Steward, "The Native Population of South America," pp. 655–668.

[94] Howard F. Cline, ed. *Latin American History. Essays on Its Study and Teaching, 1898–1965.* 2 v. Austin and London: The University of Texas Press, 1967.

This important collection reprints almost a hundred essays, several of them dealing specifically with Brazilian history and many viewing Brazil within the context of Latin American history. The former include: **[110]** William R. Shepherd, "Brazil as a Field for Historical Study," I, 274–278; **[114]** Alexander Marchant, "The Unity of Brazilian History," II, 692–703; **[115]** Richard M. Morse, "Some Themes of Brazilian History," II, 703–716.

[95] Martin A. Cohen, ed. *The Jewish Experience in Latin America. Selected Studies from the Publications of the American Jewish Historical Society*. 2 vols. New York: KTAV Publishing House, 1971. lxxxiii, 497 pp. vi, 374 pp.

Volume II reprints eight articles on the Jews in colonial Brazil that originally appeared in the *Publications of the American Jewish Historical Society* **[337]** Herbert I. Bloom, "A Study of Brazilian Jewish History 1623–1654, Based Chiefly Upon the Findings of the Late Samuel Oppenheim," pp. 80–162; **[340]** Arnold Wiznitzer, "Jewish Soldiers in Dutch Brazil (1630–1654)," pp. 163–173; **[342]** Arnold Wiznitzer, "The Synagogue and Cemetery of the Jewish Community in Recife, Brazil (1630–1654)," pp. 174–177; **[345]** Cyrus Adler, "A Contemporary Memorial Relating to Damages to Spanish Interests in America Done by Jews of Holland (1634)," pp. 178–184; **[338]** Arnold Wiznitzer, "Isaac de Castro, Brazilian Jewish Martyr," pp. 205–217; **[347]** Arnold Wiznitzer, "The Members of the Brazilian Jewish Community 1648–1653," pp. 218–226; **[348]** Arnold Wiznitzer, "The Minute Book of Congregations Zur Israel of Recife and Magen Abraham of Mauricia, Brazil," pp. 227–312; **[343]** Arnold Wiznitzer, "The Exodus from Brazil and Arrival in New Amsterdam of the Jewish Pilgrim Fathers, 1654," pp. 313–330. In his introduction to volume I, Martin Cohen provides a fifty-six page survey of the role of the Jews in Latin America. The section on colonial Brazil is found on pp. lii–lx. The editor also provides notes on each of the articles. Those for volume II are found on pp. lxxiv–lxxviii. Pages lxxix–lxxxi provide a general bibliography of Latin American Jewish studies for the colonial period. At the end of volume II there are two indices: an "Index of Authors of Articles in the Anthology and Studies Mentioned Therein"; and an "Index of Names of Persons and Places Mentioned in the Anthology."

[96] Charles C. Griffin, ed. *Concerning Latin American Culture.* New York: Columbia University Press, 1940. xiv, 234 pp.

Includes papers read at Byrdcliffe, Woodstock, New York, in August of 1939. Those dealing with colonial Brazil were **[702]** Gilberto Freyre, "Some Aspects of the Social Development of Portuguese America," pp. 79–103; and **[753]** Robert C. Smith, "Brazilian Art," pp. 181–196.

[97] Robert Brent Toplin, ed. *Slavery and Race Relations in Latin America.* Westport, Connecticut: Greenwood Press, 1974. xiv, 450 pp.

This collection of essays edited with individual introductions by Robert Brent Toplin is Number 17 in Greenwood Press's Contributions in

Afro-American and African Studies. Though there are a number of essays on Brazil, only two deal with the period before independence: **[460]** Colin M. MacLachlan, "African Slave Trade and Economic Development in Amazonia, 1700–1800," pp. 112–145; and **[449]** Robert Conrad, "Nineteenth-Century Brazilian Slavery," pp. 146–175.

[98] Asunción Lavrin, ed. *Latin American Women: Historical Perspectives.* Westport, Connecticut: Greenwood Press, 1978. xiv, 345 pp.

Contains two chapters on Brazil: **[502]** A. J. R. Russell-Wood, "Female and Family in the Economy and Society of Colonial Brazil," pp. 60–100; and **[334]** Susan A. Soeiro, "The Feminine Orders in Colonial Bahia, Brazil: Economic, Social and Demographic Implications, 1677–1800," pp. 173–197.

3. Western Hemisphere History [Nos. 99–101]

Several important attempts have been made to place aspects of colonial Brazilian history in a hemispheric perspective. Each of the collections cited below contains two offerings on colonial Brazil: **[99]** David W. Cohen and Jack P. Greene, eds., *Neither Slave Nor Free;* **[100]** Richard Price, ed., *Maroon Societies;* and **[101]** A. Owen Aldridge, ed., *The Ibero-American Enlightenment.*

[99] David W. Cohen and Jack P. Greene, eds. *Neither Slave Nor Free. The Freedman of African Descent in the Slave Societies of the New World.* Baltimore and London: The Johns Hopkins University Press, 1972. xi, 344 pp.

This collection of essays grew out of a symposium on "The Role of the Free Black and Mulatto in Slave Societies of the New World" held at The Johns Hopkins University on 8 and 9 April 1970. Two of the participants, **[472]** A. J. R. Russell-Wood, "Colonial Brazil," pp. 84–133, and **[474]** Herbert S. Klein, "Nineteenth-Century Brazil," pp. 309–334, contributed chapters on the freedman in Brazil.

[100] Richard Price, ed. *Maroon Societies. Rebel Slave Communities in the Americas.* Garden City, New York: Anchor Press/Doubleday, 1973. vii, 429 pp.

Part Four deals with Brazil and includes: **[465]** R. K. Kent, "Palmares: An African State in Brazil," pp. 170–190; and **[469]** Stuart B. Schwartz,

"The *Mocambo*: Slave Resistance in Colonial Bahia," pp. 202–226. "Bibliographical Notes" are found on pp. 399–403 and the bibliography itself on pp. 404–416. There is an index.

[101] A. Owen Aldridge, ed. *The Ibero-American Enlightenment.* Urbana: University of Illinois Press, 1971. x, 335 pp.

A number of these essays were originally presented at a conference on the Ibero-American Enlightenment held at the University of Illinois, Urbana, in May of 1969. According to the editor, "the most pertinent of the papers presented at that time have been supplemented by others written subsequently." There are two important essays on the Luso-Brazilian enlightenment: **[732]** Manoel Cardozo, "The Internationalism of the Portuguese Enlightenment: The Role of the Estrangeirado, c. 1700–c. 1750," pp. 141–207; and **[730]** E. Bradford Burns, "Concerning the Transmission and Dissemination of the Enlightenment in Brazil," pp. 256–281. Unfortunately, the book has no index.

D. Collections of Documents [Nos. 102–109]

1. General [Nos. 102–103]

To date, only two general collections of documents on Brazilian history have been published in English. More complete by far is that of E. Bradford Burns **[102]**. There is a smaller collection by Russell H. Fitzgibbon **[103]**.

[102] E. Bradford Burns, ed. *A Documentary History of Brazil.* New York: Alfred A. Knopf, 1966. xii, 398 pp.

Excellent collection of more than 80 documents, about half of which deal with the colonial period. There is a useful introduction plus explanatory material prefacing each document. A number of these selections have been translated into English for the first time. Documents dealing with the history of Brazil to 1822 include: Excerpts from the Treaty of Tordesillas (1494) **[104]** and the letter of Pero Vaz de Caminha (1500) **[163]** and **[164]**; the royal letter of 1530 to Martim

Afonso de Sousa; a 1532 account by Pero Lopes de Sousa (Martim's brother) of an early settlement in Brazil; the royal letters granting Pernambuco to Duarte Coelho **[149]** and the charter itself (both 1534); an excerpt from the narrative of the English ship *Barbara* **[177]** in 1540; a selection from the French account of Jean de Lery **[184]**, first published in 1578; two Jesuit letters of 1558, one by Padre Antônio Pires, the other written anonymously, describing conversion efforts among the Amerindians; an excerpt from Father Cristóval de Acuña's account **[235]** of his explorations in the Amazon (1639); an account by Francisco Barreto of the first battle of Guararapes against the Dutch (1648); an excerpt from the English Richard Flecknoe's travel account **[261]** describing the sugar industry in Brazil (1654); an excerpt from Padre Antônio Vieira's **[315]** sermon condemning Indian slavery (1653); an excerpt from the Italian Jesuit Antonil's account of Brazil in the early eighteenth century describing the discovery of gold in Minas Gerais; an example of a colonial Brazilian land grant (1706); an excerpt from a letter describing a trip on the Tietê river in 1628; two accounts of a journey on the Tietê to Cuiabá in 1727; a 1734 account by José Peixoto da Silva of an overland trip from Saõ Paulo to Belém; excerpts from an eighteenth-century letter describing Portuguese activity in what is now southern Brazil; the Treaty of Madrid (1750); an excerpt from an English account by Thomas Turner **[226]** describing a slave revolt at the end of the sixteenth century; an excerpt from a memorandum to the King, dated 8 January 1720, warning of a slave rebellion; an excerpt from a letter of the Governor of Pernambuco in 1814 describing precautions being taken against a slave rebellion; Pombal's advice **[717]** of how to best govern Brazil; excerpts from the secret instructions of Viceroy Lavradio **[274]** to his successor (1779); excerpts from "Instruction for the Government of the Captaincy of Minas Gerais," written by José João Teixeira Coelho in 1780; two poems by Gregório de Matos **[714]** and **[715]**; an excerpt from José Basilio da Gama's epic poem *O Uruguay*; a selection from Sebastião José da Rocha Pita's *História da America Portuguesa* (1730), describing the captaincy of Bahia; a report by José Joaquim de Ataide, president of the literary society of Rio de Janeiro (1787); a description of the death sentence of Tiradentes for his role in the Minas Conspiracy; excerpts from Azeredo Coutinho's essay **[688]** on the commerce and products of Brazil (1794); excerpts from a letter of 1807 by João Rodrigues Brito describing some of Bahia's economic complaints; the decree of the Prince Regent João opening the ports of Brazil to foreign commerce (1808); the royal order of the Prince Regent revoking the prohibition of manufacturing (1808); the decree elevating Brazil to a kingdom (1815); instructions for the guidance of Pedro as regent of the kingdom of Brazil (1821); and the letter of Padre Belchior Pinheiro de Oliveira describing the *grito de Ypiranga*, considered the Brazilian proclamation of independence (1822). There are also two valuable appendices: "A Chronology of Significant Dates in Brazilian History" (pp. 387–390) and "Suggestions for Additional Reading in English" (pp. 391–398).

[103] Russell H. Fitzgibbon, ed. *Brazil. A Chronology and Fact Book, 1488–1973*. Dobbs Ferry, New York: Oceana Publications, 1974. vi, 150 pp.

Contains a 36-page chronology, each important date containing an explanatory paragraph. The colonial period is unevenly covered on pp. 1–13. The collection of documents (pp. 39–131)—more than half of which touch on Brazilian history before independence—includes excerpts from the Treaty of Tordesillas (1494) **[104]**, narratives describing early English trade (1540) **[177]** and the exploration on the Amazon (1639) **[235]**, an English account of Brazilian sugar production in 1654, the Treaty of Madrid (1750), the secret instructions of Viceroy Lavradio **[274]** to his successor (1779), the death sentence of Tiradentes (1792), excerpts from Azeredo Coutinho's essay **[688]** on the commerce and products of Brazil (1794), the decree opening the ports of Brazil in 1808, the edict elevating Brazil to the status of a kingdom (1815), and Pinheiro de Oliveira's contemporaneous account of the future Pedro I's proclamation of independence in 1822. Each document has a short introduction by the editor. Several of the document headings are misdated. A few of the excerpts were originally translated by Burns **[102]**. There is an appended list of eminent Brazilians, though only 2 of the 39 played a role in the history of colonial Brazil. A bibliography is found on pp. 143–145.

2. Special Aspects [Nos. 104–109]

There are three important collections of documents that focus on various aspects of the history of colonial Brazil and emphasize the years before 1600. Frances Gardiner Davenport **[104]** collects and translates the important papal bulls and international treaties that affected the history of colonial Brazil. Richard Hakluyt's *The Principal Navigations* **[105]**, first published in 1589 **[106]**, includes almost two dozen accounts in English on sixteenth-century experiences in Portuguese America. Hakluyt is updated and continued by Samuel Purchas **[107]**, *Hakluytus Posthumas or Purchas His Pilgrimes,* first published in 1625. Two useful eighteenth-century collections are that of Awnsham and John Churchill **[108]**, which emphasizes seventeenth-century travel accounts, and that of John Callander **[109]**, which reprints narratives dealing with voyages to the Southern Hemisphere.

[104] Frances Gardiner Davenport, ed. *European Treaties Bearing on the History of the United States and its Dependencies to 1648.* Washington, D. C.: Carnegie Institution, 1917, vi, 387 pp.

Very useful, carefully prepared collection which includes twenty papal bulls and treaties affecting Portugal and Portuguese expansion. Each document is prefaced by an informed introduction, a bibliography (which includes lists of manuscripts and printed texts, English translations, and contemporary and early writings and later publications on the bull or treaty being discussed), the text of the original (if possible) and an English translation. If a treaty is being translated, the date of ratification is also included. Davenport's collection contains: Doc. 1: Pope Nicholas V's bull *Romanus Pontifex,* 8 January 1455, which settled the conflict between Castile and Portugal over Africa and "granted Portugal exclusive rights in a vast southerly region." It also confirmed the same pontiff's *Dum Diversas* of 18 June 1452, which gave Afonso of Portugal "general and indefinite powers to search out and conquer all pagans, enslave them and appropriate their lands and goods." Doc. 2: *Inter Caetera,* 13 March 1456, the papal bull of Calixtus III, which "conferred upon the Portuguese military Order of Christ, of which Prince Henry ['the Navigator'] was governor, the spiritualities in all the lands acquired and to be acquired from Capes Bojador and Nao through the whole of Guinea and beyond its southern shore as far as to the Indians." Doc. 3: The ratification of the Treaty of Alcaçovas, 4 September 1479, between Spain and Portugal, and the additional articles by which "Ferdinand and Isabella bound themselves not to disturb Portugal in her possession of the trade and lands of Guinea, or of the Azores, Madeira, or Cape Verde Islands, or of any other islands in the region from the Canaries towards Guinea, and not to interfere in the conquest of Morocco." Portugal, in turn, ceded the Canary Islands to Castile. Doc. 4: Bull of Sixtus IV, *Aeterni Regis* of 21 June 1481, which confirms earlier papal bulls in favor of Portugal's "claim to exclusive rights in Guinea," and the provisions of the Treaty of Alcaçovas of 1479. Doc. 5: *Inter Caetera* of 3 May 1493, by which Pope Alexander VI "assigned to the present and future sovereigns of Castile the lands discovered and to be discovered by their envoys and not previously possessed by any Christian owner." Doc. 6: Pope Alexander VI's *Eximiae Devotionis,* antedated 3 or 4 May 1493 (but not expedited until July of that year), which reemphasized more emphatically concessions and privileges listed in the same pope's *Inter Caetera.* Doc. 7: The

Alexandrine bull, *Inter Caetera,* antedated 4 May 1493 (but not expedited until June of that year), restates the Borgia pope's earlier bulls on the subject, draws a line of demarcation, one hundred leagues west of the Cape Verde Islands, and grants Castile "the exclusive right to acquire territorial possessions and to trade in all the lands west of that line, which at Christmas, 1492, were not in the possession of any Christian prince." Doc. 8: Alexander VI's bull *Dudum Siquidem* of 26 September 1493 confirmed his earlier pro-Spanish bulls and "revoked all the earlier papal grants to Protugal which might seem to give her a claim to lands not already possessed by her." Doc. 9: According to the first of the two treaties of Tordesillas, 7 June 1494, between Spain and Portugal, "all lands lying east of a meridian located 370 leagues west of the Cape Verde Islands, and discovered by Portugal, were to pertain to that country and all lands west of the line, discovered by Spain, were to pertain to Spain." Doc. 10: Compact between Spain and Portugal, signed in Madrid on 7 May 1495, to provide for a meeting between Spanish and Portuguese commissioners to determine how to measure the line of demarcation agreed upon in the Treaty of Tordesillas. However, nothing further seems to have been carried out until 1512. Doc. 11: The papal bull *Ea Quae* by Julius II was one of three bulls dated 24 January 1506 which granted concessions to the Portuguese. It also confirmed the demarcation line of the Treaty of Tordesillas. Doc. 12: *Praecelsae Devotionis* of Pope Leo X and dated 3 November 1514 confirmed the bull of 7 June 1514, which gave to the king of Portugal "the patronage of ecclesiastical benefices in Africa and in all other places beyond the sea, acquired or to be acquired from the infidels, and subjected them to the spiritual jurisdiction of the Order of Christ." It also "granted to Portugal the lands and other property acquired from the infidels, not only from Capes Bojador and Nao to the Indies, but in any region whatsoever, even if then unknown." Doc. 13: Treaty between Spain and Portugal, concluded at Vitoria, 19 February 1524, regarding the possession of the Moluccas or Spice Islands. This provisional treaty provided that each country "should appoint three astrologers and three pilots" to determine a line of demarcation for Asia and name three lawyers to determine possession. Doc. 14: Draft of an unconcluded treaty between Spain and Portugal. The "junta of Badajoz" mentioned in the previous document was held from 11 April to the end of May 1524, when it was disbanded. "The Portuguese commissioners insisted that the 370 leagues should be measured from the eastern islands of the Cape Verde group, while the Spaniards were determined that the measurement should begin at the most westerly of these islands." The draft of the treaty is useful for detailing the various stages in these negotiations. Doc. 15: Treaty between Spain and Portugal concluded at Saragossa, 17 April 1529, but not ratified. However, most of its provisions were contained in another treaty of Saragossa signed five days later. One of the key provisions of both treaties was that Charles V gave up his right to the Moluccas for 350,000 ducats. Doc. 16: Treaty between Spain and Portugal concluded at Saragossa on 22 April 1529. Ratified by Spain on 23 April 1529 and by Portugal on 20 June 1530. The chief difference between this treaty and the earlier one was the omission of the requirement that "the Emperor [Charles V] should order his Royal Council to find out whether the treaty could be legally made without the approval of the *pueblos*." By the terms of the treaty of Saragossa, the Philippine islands fell within the Portuguese side of the Asian demarcation line. This provoked considerable controversy which was not resolved until the Treaty of Madrid, 1750, which "stipulated that the demarcation lines provided for in the bull of Alexander VI and in the treaties of Tordesillas and Saragossa should be annulled [and] that Spain should permanently retain the Philippines." Doc. 17: Articles concluded between France and Portugal at Lyons, 14 July 1536. This treaty "provided for the protection of the neutral commerce of Portugal" and certain Portuguese harbors "were opened to the French as places from which to pounce upon the enemy [Spain] or to which to bring the prizes they had made." In turn, at least for several years, French subjects were forbidden "to sail to Brazil, or Guinea, or the lands discovered by the Portuguese." Doc. 19: Articles concluded between Spain and Portugal in 1552 to protect "Spanish and Portuguese shipping against the French corsairs." Both countries agreed to provide coastguards and to share convoys and some defense expenses in the region of the Atlantic side of the Iberian peninsula and the Azores. Doc. 37: Treaty of alliance between Portugal and France concluded at Paris, 1 June 1641. Doc. 38: Treaty of truce and commerce between Portugal and the United Netherlands, concluded at the Hague, 12 June 1641. Ratified by the king of Portugal on 18 November 1641 and by the States General on 20 February 1642. Both these treaties were attempts to gain allies for Portugal in the aftermath of that country's overthrow of Spanish Habsburg rule in December of 1640.

[105] Richard Hakluyt. *The Principal Navigations Voyages Traffiques & Discoveries of the English Nation Made by Sea or Over-land to the Remote and Farthest Distant Quarters of the Earth at any time within the compasse of these 1600 Yeeres.* 3 vols. London: George Bishop, Ralph Newbery, and Robert Barker, 1598–1600. 619 pp.; 525 pp.; 868 pp.; [Reprinted. 12 volumes. Glasgow: James MacLehose and Sons, 1903–1905]

Volume XI [III of the 1600 edition] contains most of the accounts dealing with Brazil: **[170]** Martin Fernández de Enciso, "A short description of the river of Marannon or Amazones, and the Countries thereabout, as also of the sea of Freshwater, taken out of an ancient Discourse of all the Portes, Creekes, and Havens of the West Indies, Written by Martin Fernandez de Enciza, and dedicated to Charles the Emperour, Anno 1518," pp. 19–22; **[174]** William Hawkins, "A brief relation of two sundry voyages made by the worshipful M. William Haukins . . . knight, late Treasurer of her Majesties Navie, in the yeere 1530 and 1532," pp. 23–25; **[178]** Anthony Garrard, "An ancient voyage of M. Robert Reniger and M. Thomas Borey to Brasil in the Yeere of our Lord 1540," p. 25; **[179]** Edward Cotton, "A voyage of one Pudsey to Baya in Brasil anno 1542," p. 25; **[195]** John Whithall, "A letter written to M. Richard Stapers by John Whithall from Brasil, in Santos, the 26 of June 1578," and "A copie of the letters of the Adventurers for Brasil sent to John Whithall dwelling in Santos by the Minion of London. Anno 1580 the 24 of October in London," pp. 26–33; **[199]** Thomas Grigges, "Certaine notes of the voyage to Brasil with the Minion of London aforesaid **[195]**, in the yere 1580. written by Thomas Grigs Purser of the said ship," pp. 34–39; **[224]** Francisco Soares, "A letter of Francis Suares to his brother Diego Suares dwelling in Lisbon, written from the river of Jenero in Brasill in June 1596 concerning the exceeding rich trade newly begunne betweene that place and Peru, by the way of the river of Plate, with small barks of 30. and 40. tunnes," pp. 39–43; **[221]** James Lancaster, "The well governed and prosperous voyage of M. James Lancaster, begun with three ships and a galley-frigat from London in October 1594, and intended for Fernambuck, the port-towne of Olinda in Brasil. In which voyage (besides the taking of nine and twenty ships and frigats) he surprized the sayd port-towne, being strongly fortified and manned; and held possession thereof thirty dayes together (notwithstanding many bolde assaults of the enemy both by land and water) and also providently defeated their dangerous and almost inevitable fireworks. Heere he found the cargazon or freight of a rich East Indian carack; which together with great abundance of sugars, Brasil-wood, and cotton he brought from thence; lading therewith fifteene sailes of tall ships and barks," pp. 43–64; **[225]** Feliciano Coelho de Carvalho, "A speciall letter written from Feliciano Cieza de Carvalsho [sic] the Governour of Parajua [Paraiba] in the most Northerne part of Brasil, 1597, to Philip the second king of Spaine, answering his desire touching the conquest of Rio Grande, with the relation of the beseiging of the castle of Cabodelo by the Frenchmen, and of the discoverie of a rich silver mine and diverse other important matters," pp. 64–72; **[196]** Anonymous, "A ruttier or course to be kept for him that will sayle from Cabo Verde to the coast of Brasil, and all along the coast of Brasil unto the river of Plate," pp. 73–85; **[205]** Lopez Vaz, "An extract out of the discourse of one Lopez Vaz a Portugal, touching the fight of M. Fenton with the Spanish ships, with a report of the proceeding of M. John Drake after his departing from him to the river of Plate," pp. 92–95; **[198]** Anonymous, "A ruttier which declareth the situation of the coast of Brasil from the Isle of Santa Catelina unto the mouth of the river of Plata, and all along up within the sayd river, and what armes and mouthes it hath to enter into it, as farre as it is navigable with small barks," pp. 96–101; **[187]** Francis Drake, "The famous voyage of Sir Francis Drake into the South sea, and therehence about the whole Globe of the earth, begun in the yeere of our Lord, 1577," pp. 101–133; **[191]** Nuno da Silva, "The relation of a Voyage made by a Pilot called Nuno da Silva for the Vice-roy of new Spaine, the 20. of May, in the yere of our Lord 1579. in the citie of Mexico, from whence it was sent to the Vice-roy of the Portugall-Indies: wherein is set downe the course and actions passed in the Voyage of Sir Francis Drake that tooke the aforesayd Nuno da Silva at S. Iago one of the Islands of Cabo Verde, and caried him along with him through the Streights of Magellan, to the Haven of Guatulco in new Spaine, where he let him go againe," pp. 133–147; **[193]** Edward Cliffe, "The voyage of M. John Winter into the South sea by the Streight of Magellan, in consort with M. Francis Drake, begun in the yeere 1577. By which Streight also he returned safely into England the second of June 1579. contrary to the false reports of the Spaniards which gave out, that the said passage was not repasseable: Written by Edward Cliffe Mariner," pp. 148–162; **[200]** Luke Ward, "The Voyage intended towards China, wherein M. Edward Fenton was appointed Generall: Written by M. Luke Ward his Viceadmiral, and Captaine of the Edward Bonaventure, begun Anno Dom. 1582," pp. 172–202; **[211]** John Sarracoll, "The voyage set out by the right honourable the Earle of Cumberland, in the yere 1586. intended for The South Sea, but performed no farther than the latitude of 44. degrees to the South of the Equinoctial, Written by M. John Sarracoll marchant in the same voyage," pp. 202–227; **[210]** Lopez Vaz, "A discourse of the West Indies and South sea written by Lopez Vaz a Portugal, borne in the citie of Elvas, continued unto the yere 1587. Wherein among divers rare things not hitherto delivered by any other writer, certaine voyages of our Englishmen are truely reported: which was intercepted with the author thereof at the river of Plate, by Captaine Withrington and Captaine Christopher Lister, in the fleete set foorth by the right Honorable the Erle of Cumberland for the South sea in the yeere 1586," pp. 227–290; **[208]** Francis Pretty, "The admirable and prosperous voyage of the Worshipfull Master Thomas Candish [Cavendish] of Trimley in the Countie of Suffolke Esquire, into the South sea, and from thence round about the circumference of the whole earth, begun in the yeere of our Lord 1586 and finished 1588. Written by Master Francis Pretty lately of Ey in Suffolke, a Gentleman employed in the same action," pp. 290–347; **[209]** Thomas Fuller, "Certaine rare and special notes most properly belonging to the voyage of M. Thomas Candish [Cavendish] next before described; concerning the heights, soundings, lyings of lands, distances of places, the variation of the Compasse, the just length of time spent in sayling betweene divers places, and their abode in them, as also the places of their harbour and anckering, and the depths of the same, with the observation of the windes on severall coastes: Written by M. Thomas Fuller of Ipswich, who was Master in the desire of M. Thomas Candish in his foresaid prosperous voyage about the world," pp. 348–381; **[212]** William Magoths, "A briefe relation of a voyage of The Delight a ship of Bristoll one of the consorts of M. John Chidley esquire and M. Paul Wheele, made unto the Straight of Magellan: with divers accidents that happened unto the company, during their 6 weekes abode there: Begun in the yeere 1589. Written by W. Magoths," pp. 381–389; **[215]** John Jane, "The last voyage of the worshipfull M. Thomas Candish [Cavendish] esquire, intended for the South sea, the Philippinas, and the coast of China, with 3 tall ships, and two barks: Written by M. John Jane, a man of good observation, imployed in the same, and many other voyages," pp. 389–416.

In addition to the many accounts in volume XI, volume II contains **[173]** Robert Thorne, "A declaration of the Indies and lands discovered, and subdued unto the Emperour, and the king of Portingal: And also of other partes of the Indies and rich countries to be discovered, which the worshipful M. Robert Thorne merchant of London (who dwelt long in the citie of Sivil in Spaine) exhorted king Henrie the eight to take in hand" and "The book made by the right worshipful M. Robert Thorne in the yeere 1527. in Sivil, to Doctour Ley, Lord ambassadour for king Henry the eight, to Charles the Emperour, being an information of the parts of the world, discovered by him and the king of Portingal: and also of the way to the Moluccaes by the North," pp. 159–181.

Volume VI includes: **[206]** Edward Cotton, "Certaine remembrances of an intended voyage to Brasill, and the River of Plate, by the Edward Cotton, a ship of 260 Tunnes of Master Edward Cotton of Southhampton, which perished through extreme negligence neare Rio grande in Guinie, the 17 of July 1583," pp. 408–412.

[106] Richard Hakluyt. *The Principall Navigations Voiages and Discoveries of the English Nation.* London 1589.
[Reprinted in 2 v. with an introduction by David Beers Quinn and Raleigh Ashlin Skelton and with a new index by Alison Quinn. Cambridge: Published for the Hakluyt Society and the Peabody Museum of Salem, 1965.]

This was the first edition of Hakluyt's monumental work. The later three-volume edition was published 1598–1600.

[107] Samuel Purchas. *Hakluytus Posthumus or Purchas His Pilgrimes Contayning a History of the World in Sea Voyages and Lande Travells by Englishmen and Others.* 20v. Glasgow: James MacLehose and Sons, 1905–1907. [Originally published in 4 v. in 1625.] Issued by the Hakluyt Society. Extra Series, nos. 14–33.

In addition to syntheses of a number of accounts appearing in Hakluyt **[105]**, Purchas included a number of important new accounts. Most of the accounts dealing with Brazil appeared in volume 16: **[194]** Peter Carder, "The Relation of Peter Carder of Saint Verian in Cornwall, within seven miles of Falmouth, which went with Sir Francis [Drake] in his Voyage about the World, begun 1577. who with seven others in an open Pinnasse or Shallop of five tuns, with eight Oares, was separated from his Generall by foule weather in the South Sea, in October, Anno 1578. who returning by the Straites of Magellan toward Brazill, were all cast away, save this one only afore named, who came into England nine yeeres after miraculously, having escaped many strange dangers, aswell among divers Savages as Christians," pp. 136–146; **[216]** Thomas Cavendish, "Master Thomas Candish his discourse of his fatall and disastrous voyage towards the South Sea, with his many disadventures in the Magellan Straits and other places; written with his owne hand to Sir Tristam Gorges his Executor," pp. 151–177; **[218]** Anthony Knivet, "The admirable adventures and strange fortunes of Master Antonie Knivet, which went with Master Thomas Candish in his second voyage to the South Sea. 1591," pp. 177–289; **[226]** Thomas Turner, "Relations of Master Thomas Turner, who lived the best part of two yeeres in Brasill, &c. which I received of him in conference touching his Travels," pp. 290–291; **[229]** Robert Harcourt, "A Relation of a voyage to Guiana performed by Robert Harcourt of Stanton Harcourt in the Countie of Oxford Esquire. To Prince Charles," pp. 358–402; **[231]** William Davies, "A Description and Discovery of the River of the Amazons, by William Davies Barber Surgeon of London," pp. 413–416; **[207]** Fernão Cardim, "A Treatise of Brasil, written by a Portugall which had long lived there," pp. 418–517; **[184]** Jean de Lery, "Extracts out of the Historie of John Lerius a Frenchman, who lived in Brasill with Mons. Villagagnon, Ann. 1557. and 58," pp. 518–579.

[108] Awnsham and John Churchill. *A Collection of Voyages and Travels, Some Now First Printed from Original Manuscripts, Others Now First Published in English.* 6 v. 3rd ed. London: H. Lintot and J. Osborn, 1744–1746.

This is one of the best collections of travel accounts published in the eighteenth century, and a worthy successor to Hakluyt **[105]** and Purchas **[107]**. The third edition is probably the most accessible. Volume 2 contains **[259]** Johan Nieuhoff, "Voyage and Travels into Brazil, and the Best Parts of the East Indies," pp. 1–302; Volume 5 includes **[648]** James Barbot, "A Description of the Coasts of North and South Guinea, and of Ethiopia Inferior, Vulgarly Angola; Being a New and Accurate Account of the Western Maritime Countries of Africa.... And a New Relation of the Province of Guiana, and of the Great Rivers of Amazons and Oronoque in South-America," pp. 1–668; and **[265]** Anthony Sepp, S. J. and Anthony Behme, S. J., "An Account of a Voyage from Spain to Paraquaria," pp. 669–695; Volume 6 has **[234]** Nicholas del Techo, S. J., "The History of the Provinces of Paraguay, Tucuman, Rio de la Plata, Parana, Guaira, and Uruaica," pp. 3–116. In 1747 two more volumes (sometimes described as volumes 7 and 8, though they were published separately), "compiled from the curious and valuable Library of the late Earl of Oxford." added further accounts to the Churchill collection. Volume 7 reprints **[231]** William Davies, "A True Relation of the Travels and Most Miserable Captivity of William Davies, Barber-Surgeon of London, under the Duke of Florence," pp. 475–488. Volume 8 contains **[188]** Sir Francis Drake, "The World Encompassed," pp. 433–476. Pagination varies with edition. I have used the 1752 edition for volumes 7 and 8.

[109] John Callander. *Terra Australis Cognita: or, Voyages to the Terra Australis, or Southern Hemisphere, during the Sixteenth, Seventeenth, and Eighteenth Centuries.* 3 v. Edinburgh: A. Donaldson, 1766–1768. [Reprinted by N. Israel/Da Capo Press, 1967.]

The compiler reprints many descriptions of colonial Brazil. Volume I contains mostly accounts from Hakluyt **[105]** and Purchas **[107]**: **[167]** Amerigo Vespucci, "Voyages to Magellanica, 1501," pp. 53–61; **[167]** Amerigo Vespucci, "Americo's Fourth Voyage in 1503," pp. 61–63; **[184]** Jean de Lery, "Villegagnon to South America," pp. 212–277; **[187]** Sir Francis Drake, "Sir Francis Drake to Magellanica and Polynesia," pp. 283–321; **[191]** Nuno da Silva, "Nuno da Silva to Magellanica," pp. 321–336; **[193]** Edward Cliffe, "John Winter, to Magellanica," pp. 337–355; **[204]** Pedro Sarmiento de Gamboa, "Pedro Sarmiento to Magellanica," pp. 363–378; **[200]** Luke Ward, "Fenton's Voyage to Magellanica, Written by His Vice-Admiral Ward," pp. 378–412; **[208]** Francis Pretty, "Thomas Cavendish, to Magellanica," pp. 424–470; **[209]** Thomas Fuller, "Notes of the Heights, Soundings, Latitudes, and Distances, from the Journal of Thomas Fuller, Master on board Mr. Cavendish's Ship called the Desire," pp. 471–494; **[216]** Sir Thomas Cavendish, "Sir Thomas Cavendish to Magellanica, for the Second Time," pp. 494–516.

There is also a discussion of the voyage of Binot Paulmier de Gonneville **[138]**, pp. 63–73. Volume II includes extracts from **[219]** Sir Richard Hawkins, "Sir Richard Hawkins to Magellanica," pp. 3–142; and **[233]** Garcia de Nodal, "Garcia de Nodal, to Magellanica," pp. 269–273. There is also a discussion of the brief visit to Brazil of George Spilberg (pp. 191–217). Volume III reprints parts of **[267]** William Dampier, "William Dampier's last Voyage to Australasia," pp. 66–143; **[629]** William Funnell, "Funnell, to Magellanica," pp. 145–227; **[630]** Woodes Rogers, "Woodes Rogers, to Magellanica and Polynesia," pp. 231–379; and **[526]** Amédée François Frézier, "Monsieur Frézier to Magellanica," pp. 386–439. Callander also greatly abridges the accounts of such other visitors to Brazil as George Shelvocke **[527]**, Jacob Roggeveen **[632]**, George Anson **[530]**, and John Byron **[573]**.

IV. The Individuality of Brazil: The Land and the Environment [Nos. 110–123]

William R. Shepherd **[110]** presents a few ideas on the uniqueness of Portuguese America and why it should be studied. The national characteristics of Brazil are discussed by José Honório Rodrigues **[111]**. Joaquim Nabuco **[112]** and E. Bradford Burns **[113]** trace the growth of a national spirit in Brazil during the colonial period. Alexander Marchant **[114]** discusses the unity of Brazilian history and compares colonial Spanish and Portuguese American experiences. Richard M. Morse **[115]** focuses on factors that enabled Brazil to remain unified while Spanish America fragmented. In addition, he analyzes Brazil's regionalism. Diversity in Brazil is also discussed by Roy Nash **[116]**, Hilgard O'Reilly Sternberg **[117]**, and Preston E. James **[118]**. James **[119]** also provides an excellent review of Brazil's geography. Janet D. Henshall and R. P. Momsen, Jr. **[120]** describe Brazil's resources and their development. Warren R. Fish **[121]** traces the evolution of Brazilian dietary habits.

[110] William R. Shepherd. "Brazil as a Field for Historical Study," *The Hispanic American Historical Review* 13:4 (November 1933), pp. 427–436.

The author discusses Brazil's great wealth and then describes Portuguese America's similarities and differences with Spanish America and the United States. Shepherd then briefly surveys the history of Brazil and its natural resources. He also discusses some of the sources for the writing of Brazilian history. No notes.

[111] José Honório Rodrigues. *The Brazilians. Their Character and Aspirations.* Trans. Ralph Edward Dimmick. Austin and London: University of Texas Press, 1967. xxiv, 186 pp.
[Translation of *Aspirações Nacionais.* São Paulo, Editôra Fulgor, 1963].

Though most of this study by one of twentieth-century Brazil's foremost historians deals with the period after independence, there are many useful insights into the history of the colonial period. The author discusses many of the centrifugal tendencies in Brazil's colonial history. He then points out that "it was Dom João, the regent, later king, who during the thirteen years of his residence in Brazil, centralized the government, united the captaincies, dissipated prejudices, and, through the experience provided in common living, paved the way for the consolidation of the country." José Honório Rodrigues also argues that, despite the great deal of racial mixture in Portuguese America, "the Brazilian people are far more homogeneous in terms of culture, language, and stage of historical development than the peoples of other countries of comparable size or population." There are good sections on miscegenation, racial tolerance, and "psycho-social integration." The author also provides a useful discussion of national characteristics, as well as the problem of regionalism. Notes. There is a bibliography on pp. 159–172.

[112] Joaquim Nabuco. *The Spirit of Nationality in the History of Brazil.* New Haven, 1908. 14 pp.

This address, delivered in 1908 before the Spanish Club of Yale University, is one of the few historical writings in English by this famous Brazilian abolitionist, diplomat and historian. More than half of his survey deals with the colonial period. Nabuco traces the growth of a national spirit in Brazil. He argues that "distance and abandonment to its own resources, reliance on itself alone, engendered in every settlement a feeling of separate nationalism, which shows itself very early already in the Colonial times." The author discusses the important role of the Jesuits and claims that "without the religious fervour [of Catholicism] Brazil would have probably been cast into several moulds, acquiring different nationalities: Portuguese, French, Spanish, and most probably English." Nabuco indicates that the effort to oust the Dutch in the mid-seventeenth century "had the perseverance and the obstinacy of fully grown national spirit." He also stresses Brazil's good fortune, pointing to the Amazon basin and commenting that "if Portugal had not merged into the Spanish monarchy in 1580, Spain would most surely have disputed the Amazon river, whose mouth had been discovered by a Spaniard, Yañez Pinzon, in 1500, and which had first been navigated down from the Andes to its mouth by a Spaniard, Orellana, in 1542." Nabuco concludes his discussion of the colonial period by arguing that "it was also to the flight of the Royal Family to Rio de Janeiro that we owed the rare fortune that attended our Independence."

[113] E. Bradford Burns. *Nationalism in Brazil. A Historical Survey.* New York: Frederick A. Praeger, 1968. ix, 158 pp.

Chapter II, "The Formation of Brazil and the Cult of Nativism" (pp. 12–28) contains a useful survey of the writings of many of the sixteenth-, seventeenth-, eighteenth-, and early nineteenth-century observers who "praised the richness and potential of the American colony; all expressed optimism about its future." Burns argues that "by the end of the eighteenth century, the intellectual elite had created a spiritual foundation for Brazil, and the nativism they expounded accelerated the alienation of the Brazilians from the Portuguese." Documented. There is an excellent bibliographical essay on pp. 143–152.

[114] Alexander Marchant. "The Unity of Brazilian History," in Smith and Marchant, eds., *Brazil* **[83]**, pp. 37–51.

Lists the principal characteristics of Portuguese America and compares them with those of Spanish America. Marchant discusses native populations, administrative machineries, attitudes and policies, economies, local governments, expansion, and the role of the family in Ibero-America. He also discusses the unity of Brazilian history and describes some of the difficulties Brazilian historians have faced. 2 notes.

[115] Richard M. Morse. "Some Themes of Brazilian History," *The South Atlantic Quarterly* 61:2 (Spring 1962), pp. 159–182.

Morse lists and describes seven regions of Brazil and discusses Brazilian regionalism and its diversity. He then asks and tries to answer the question: "Why did Portuguese America—roughly a third of modern Latin America in size and population—remain single while Spanish America split into what are now eighteen republics?" Three factors are pointed out: 1) "Brazilian institutions developed more freely in response to their New World setting—and interacted more freely with each other"; 2) the character of the Portuguese American economy (by 1822, "Brazil's principal regions of settlement . . . were achieving complementariness in the exchange of the products of farm, ranch, and mine, an exchange made possible by a growing tissue of land and river routes"); 3) "the nature of the leadership under which Brazil made the transition to independence." In regard to the last point, Morse argues that four factors—"legitimacy, constitutionalism, nationalism, and personalism"—were needed for a country to survive independence with a modicum of peace and stability. These requirements were met in Brazil by such leaders as José Bonifácio de Andrada and Dom Pedro I. Based on printed sources. 25 notes.

[116] Roy Nash. *The Conquest of Brazil.* New York: Harcourt, Brace & World, 1926. xvi, 438 pp. [Reprinted. New York: Biblo and Tannen, 1968.]

"All the world knows of the brilliant folk who dwell on the shores of Guanabara Bay; knows Rio the gorgeous and São Paulo the industrious. He who reads herein will learn something, too, of the man who dwells in the mud hut: of the *gaucho* who rides herd over the cattle on the pampas of Rio Grande do Sul, the *matuto* who makes his clearing in the edge of the jungle, the *sertanejo* produced by the droughts and famines of the arid northeast, the *seringueiro* who gathers rubber in the wet, wet waste of Amazonas." With these words Roy Nash sets the scene for his exuberant, pioneering work on Brazil, its land, its people, and its tremendous potential for greatness. In this influential book, Nash studies "the seed"—the racial components of Amerindians, Africans and Portuguese—that will make up Brazil's population. He then looks at "the soil"—the topography, climate, forests, pastures and fauna—of Brazil. "The Sowing" gives the author the opportunity to trace four centuries of Brazilian history, most of it dealing with the period before independence. The remaining three parts of the book deal mainly with the years after 1822, though there are references to the colonial period, especially when the author discusses housing in rural Brazil, cattle raising and mining. There is a useful bibliography of books in English on Brazil (pages 399–401), listed chronologically by publication date. There are 8 useful maps and 77 illustrations, many of them of interest.

[117] Hilgard O'Reilly Sternberg. "The Physical Basis of Brazilian Society," in Smith and Marchant, eds., *Brazil* **[83]**, pp. 52–85.

Excellent introduction to Brazil's natural environment by one of that country's foremost geographers. The author provides an overview of the geography of Portuguese America, corrects a number of misconceptions, and then describes the following major geographical regions: Amazonia, Nordeste, Central-Western Plateau, Pantanal, Serra do Espinhaço, the São Francisco Valley, the Southern Plateau, and the Atlantic Seaboard. 48 notes.

[118] Preston E. James, "The Cultural Regions of Brazil," in Smith and Marchant, eds., *Brazil* **[83]**, pp. 86–103.

James studies "the relation of man to the land in the different parts of Brazil" from the beginning of the colonial period to 1950. The author lists and describes seven cultural regions of Brazil: Northeast, the Eastern Littoral, the Southeast, São Paulo, the South, the Sertões, and the North. These regions "are a product of the impact of history on the facts of the physical and biological habitat." 5 notes.

[119] Preston E. James. *Latin America.* 4th ed. New York: The Odyssey Press, 1969. xx, 947 pp.

"Portuguese South America" is covered on pp. 683–871. For those interested in colonial Brazil this study by Preston James is the most useful of the texts on Latin American geography. The general introduction discusses the land, with its surface features, climate, weather, natural vegetation, and mineral resources; the people, with a special discussion of Brazil's early racial ingredients; and the course of settlement. James then studies six major regions of Brazil: The Northeast, the East, São Paulo, the South, the Center-West, and the North. Though all four editions have useful maps, the fourth edition has some excellent additional ones. The third edition (1959) covers Brazil on pp. 381–568. The section on Brazil in the first edition (1942) was also published separately.

[120] Janet D. Henshall and R. P. Momsen, Jr. *A Geography of Brazilian Development.* London: G. Bell & Sons, 1974. x, 305 pp.

Though this book deals mostly with the twentieth century, the chapters on the land, the Indian, and the evolution of the economy deal in large part with the colonial period. There is also useful information in the sections on the economic regions of Brazil and mineral resources development. Notes. There are 17 maps.

[121] Warren R. Fish. "Changing Food Use Patterns in Brazil," *Luso-Brazilian Review* 15:1 (Summer 1978), pp. 69–89.

Traces the evolution of food habits from preconquest times when manioc ranked as the dominant crop supplemented by maize, sweet potato, beans and peanuts on the one hand and fish and animal protein on the other. The colonial period is covered on pp. 70–76. Because the humid tropical environment of the Northeast was unsuitable for many of the European crops to which the Portuguese settlers were accustomed, manioc, maize and fish dominated the diet of the newcomers. The seventeenth century brought several significant variations in the use of native foods. Maize became important in the region around São Paulo, while in Bahia, African influence began to dominate eating habits. In the Northeast beans became increasingly popular. By the eighteenth century, the preference for maize over manioc spread northward and at the end of the colonial period, rice became more and more important. Based on secondary sources. Notes.

A. Contemporary Narratives [Nos. 122–123]

Two early nineteenth-century accounts of Brazil's geography and resources are Andrew Grant's *History of Brazil* **[122]** and James Henderson's *A History of Brazil* **[123]**, both of which have much more information on geography than on history. Henderson's account is more valuable, because it includes large sections of Padre Manuel Aires de Casal's *Corografia Brazilica*—a detailed description of the state of Brazil on the eve of independence.

[122] Andrew Grant. *History of Brazil, Comprising a Geographical Account of that Country, Together with a Narrative of the Most Remarkable Events Which Have Occurred There since its Discovery*. London: Henry Colburn, 1809. 304 pp.

Andrew Grant, a physician, dedicated this book "to the merchants of Great Britain, trading to Brazil." Grant lists and discusses Brazil's flora and fauna and that colony's chief products. He devotes several chapters to the Amerindians, arguing that "the native Brazilians differ very little in stature or complexion from the Portuguese themselves; but some of the tribes greatly exceed them in strength and vigour." Indian women are "extremely prolific, and seldom miscarry. Child-birth among them is not attended with those consequences which result from it in civilized states." The author briefly outlines Brazil's discovery by Cabral, the grants to the lords-proprietor, and the arrival of the governor-general in 1549, then discusses at some length Villegagnon and the French in Rio de Janeiro and later French activity in northern Brazil. Grant devotes most of his history to the Dutch in Brazil, writing three chapters to the subject (pp. 47–90). He sketches briefly Portuguese activity in the Amazon and the Plata regions. The author is uncomplimentary about the role of Catholicism in Brazil: "The cupidity of the parish priests is, however, amply gratified by the contributions they contrive, under various pretexts, to levy on the superstitious, ignorant, and bigotted inhabitants." Much of the second half of his account contains descriptions of the major towns and captaincies in Brazil and their chief economic resources. There are lengthy sections on Rio de Janeiro and Salvador. Grant relies heavily on travellers' accounts, especially those of Lindley **[613]**, Staunton **[588]**, and Nieuhoff **[259]**. However, he frequently provides wrong baptismal names for many of the prominent figures in Brazil's colonial history. There are also a substantial number of factual errors—especially those dealing with chronology. An appendix (pp. 295–304) is entitled: "Medical Hints for Europeans Migrating to Brazil."

[123] James Henderson. *A History of the Brazil; Comprising its Geography, Commerce, Colonization, Aboriginal Inhabitants, &c.* London: Longman, Hurst, Rees, Orme, and Brown, 1821. xxiii, 522 pp.

Though the title is a misnomer (since there is relatively little history in Henderson's account), this book is useful to those interested in colonial Brazil. According to the author, "the object of this Work is to describe the state of the Brazil, from its first discovery down to the present time;—to trace distinctly the boundaries of the twenty-two provinces which it comprises, their sub-divisions into comarcas or districts, and their rivers; to enumerate the povoaçoes or establishments in each province, consisting of cities, towns, (and the dates they were so erected by his present Majesty, or previously,) *freguezias,* (parishes,) *arraials, aldeias,* (villages,) *presidios,* (garrisons,) hermitages &c. with the nature of their agricultural productions, the composition of their inhabitants, whether whites, mulattos, mamalucos, mesticos, Christianized Indians, or Africans." However, comparatively little of this work is Henderson's, much of it being a paraphrase or—at times—a direct translation of

Padre Manuel Aires de Casal's two-volume *Corografia Brazilica, ou Relação Historico-Geografica do Reino do Brazil,* which was first published in Rio de Janeiro in 1817. Since the *Corografia Brazilica* is a major source for the state of Brazil on the eve of independence, Henderson's heavy reliance on it brings much of Aires de Casal's compendium to the attention of English-speaking readers. Chapter I of *A History of the Brazil* describes Henderson's voyage from England to Rio de Janeiro. Chapter II, "From the First Discovery Down to the Arrival of the Royal Family There," includes the historical parts of Aires de Casal's lengthy introduction, but omits the Portuguese author's brief general description of Brazil's geography, flora and fauna. Though Henderson's two chapters (III and IV) on Rio de Janeiro are covered by Aires de Casal in one in volume II, the remainder of *A History of the Brazil* follows the *Corografia Brazilica* fairly closely. With the exceptions mentioned above, both works having matching chapters on each of the provinces of Portuguese America, beginning with the southernmost ("Province of Rio Grande do Sul") and ending with the northernmost ("Province of Guiana"). Henderson's account is enhanced by 28 interesting plates depicting life in various parts of Brazil.

V. Brazil in the Sixteenth and Early Seventeenth Century, 1500–1640 [Nos. 124–162]

A. Discovery, Exploration and Conquest [Nos. 124–137]

A recent general overview of discovery, exploration and conquest in South America is found in Samuel Eliot Morison's *The European Discovery of America. The Southern Voyages. A.D. 1492–1616* **[124]**. In his introduction to *The Voyage of Pedro Alvares Cabral,* William B. Greenlee **[163]** probably gives the best treatment to date in English on Brazil and the Cabral expedition. James Roxburgh McClymont **[125]** also provides a brief biography of Cabral. Bailey W. Diffie **[46]**, Samuel Eliot Morison **[47]**, Alexander Marchant **[126]**, and Charles Nowell **[127]** discuss whether the "discovery" of Brazil was accidental or intentional. The role of Amerigo Vespucci in the exploration of Brazil has been hotly debated. Diffie, in an appendix to his excellent *Foundations of the Portuguese Empire* **[46]**, provides a good evaluation of the controversy. Samuel Eliot Morison **[124]** argues the case against Vespucci. Germán Arciniegas **[128]** is sympathetic to the Florentine, as is William Greenlee **[129]**. Arthur Davies **[130]** attempts to explain some of the inconsistencies in Vespucci's account of his third voyage of 1501–1502. Edzer Roukema **[131]** studies "Brazil in the Cantino Map" of 1502 and a map of Guiana and North-East Brazil later in the same decade **[132]**. Some of the confusion surrounding Fernão Loronha and the rental of Brazil in 1502 is cleared up by John Vogt **[133]**. A useful overview of the first half-century of Brazilian history is provided by William Greenlee **[134]**. John Vogt **[135]** discusses brazilwood and the first economic cycle of Brazilian history, 1500–1530. Alexander Marchant **[136]** and John F. Weir **[137]** view the first eighty years of Portuguese exploration and development in America, as do the more general surveys by Diffie **[71]**, Sanceau **[146]**, and Southey **[70]**.

[124] Samuel Eliot Morison. *The European Discovery of America. The Southern Voyages. A.D. 1492–1616.* New York: Oxford University Press, 1974. xvii, 758 pp.

"The Discovery of Brazil, 1500–1508" is covered on pages 210–235. Morison also has interesting sections on "Vespucci and Solis, 1499–1516" (pp. 272–312); "The Conquest of the River Plate, 1534–1580" (pp. 562–584); "France and Portugal in Brazil, 1504–1568" (pp. 585–595); and "The Voyages of Thomas Cavendish, 1586–1593" (pp. 709–726).

[125] James Roxburgh McClymont. *Pedralvarez Cabral (Pedro Alluarez de Gouuea). His Progenitors, His Life and His Voyage to America and India.* London: Bernard Quaritch, 1914. 72 p. Text: pp. 1–36.

Provides useful genealogical and biographical information on the commander of Portugal's second expedition to India and chief "discoverer" of Brazil. 56 notes. Based on printed primary sources. Appendix has 6 additional notes and includes the translation of seven documents, six of them from the Arquivo Nacional da Torre do Tombo, Lisbon.

[126] Alexander Marchant. "The Discovery of Brazil: A Note on Interpretations," *The Geographical Review* 35:2 (April 1945), pp. 296–300.

Reviews Admiral Gago Coutinho's article "Descobrimento do Brasil" and challenges the thesis that Brazil was known to the Portuguese prior to 1500 and that Pedro Álvares Cabral's visit there en route to India was planned. The author argues against those who make Portugal's policy of secrecy the explanation for the lack of documentation on Portuguese America in the late fifteenth century. Based on primary and secondary sources. 16 notes.

[127] Charles E. Nowell. "The Discovery of Brazil—Accidental or Intentional?" *The Hispanic American Historical Review* 16:3 (August 1936), pp. 311–338.

Reviews the evidence for possible knowledge of Brazil by the Portuguese prior to 1500 and argues against those who explain Cabral's discovery of Brazil by storms, currents or loss of direction. Based on primary and secondary sources. 79 notes.

[128] Germán Arciniegas. *Amerigo and the New World. The Life & Times of Amerigo Vespucci.* Trans. by Harriet de Onís. New York: Alfred A. Knopf, 1955. xvi, 323 pp.

Arciniegas provides an interesting description and discussion of Vespucci's second voyage when he touched Brazil the first time. The author also gives a useful narrative of the background (Manuel I's invitation to Vespucci, the latter being in Seville) to Vespucci's third voyage, 1501–1502, when the Florentine in Portuguese service sailed along the coast of Brazil to Patagonia. The concluding chapter provides an account of the controversy over Vespucci's veracity, the author finding him to be a truthful observer of what he did and saw. There is a bibliography on pp. 315–323.

[129] William B. Greenlee. "The Captaincy of the Second Portuguese Voyage to Brazil, 1501–1502," *The Americas* 2:1 (July 1945), pp. 3–12.

After examining the claims made on behalf of Amerigo Vespucci, Gonçalo Coelho, André Gonçalves, Gaspar de Lemos, Nuno Manoel and Fernão de Loronha as leaders of the follow-up voyage to Pedro Álvares Cabral's 1500 expedition which touched Brazil, the author argues that Vespucci, who was called to Lisbon from Seville to aid the voyage, probably acted as chief pilot and that Loronha served as commander. Based on printed primary and secondary sources. 20 notes.

[130] Arthur Davies. "The 1501–02 Voyage of Amerigo Vespucci," *Actas do Congresso Internacional de História dos Descobrimentos.* 6 volumes. (Lisbon, 1961), III, 111–122.

The author examines letters, maps, and other documents that refer to Vespucci's voyage to Brazil in 1501–02. He then correlates this material in an attempt to reconstruct the route actually followed by Vespucci. 21 notes.

[131] Edzer Roukema. "Brazil in the Cantino Map," *Imago Mundi* 17 (1963), pp. 7–26.

The Cantino map, "the earliest map containing a recognizable picture of part of the Brazilian coast," was made in Lisbon in late 1502 by an unknown, but "generally well-informed," cartographer for Alberto

Cantino, agent of Ercole d'Este, Duke of Ferrara. Roukema examines Cabral's visit to Brazil in 1500 and attempts to discover Cabral's first anchorage. To better understand the places mentioned on the Cantino map, Roukema studies the additional discoveries of: 1) the returning provision caravel (1500); 2) João da Nova, captain of the third Portuguese India fleet to sail from Lisbon; and 3) André or Afonso Gonçalves in 1501–1502. The author argues that the Brazil section of the map developed in three stages based on the above-mentioned discoveries. Roukema concludes that "the Cantino map contains no traces of the 1501–1502 voyage in which Vespucci took part." Based chiefly on printed primary sources. Map. 69 notes.

[132] Edzer Roukema. "The Coasts of North-East Brazil and the Guianas in the Egerton Ms. 2803," *Imago Mundi* 15 (1960), pp. 27–31.

The author examines the Egerton map, thought to date from 1508, and concludes that although "from Cabo de S. Agostinho to just east of the Rio Mossoró mouth (c. de s. augustino to s. maria) the coast represented is basically correct," there is confusion over the remainder of the coast with some sections accurate but others very confusing. Almost a century later much of the confusion still had not been cleared up. Roukema quotes approvingly the comment of Captain Lawrence Keymis in 1596 "that no sea-card that I have seene at any time, doth in any sort neere a truth, describe the coast." Map. 10 notes.

[133] John L. Vogt. "Fernão de Loronha and the Rental of Brazil in 1502: A New Chronology," *The Americas* 24:2 (October 1967), pp. 153-159.

Studies two contradictory Italian sources—the Genoese Pietro Rondinelli, writing in 1502, and the Venetian Leonardo Masari, reporting four years later—regarding the exact terms and length of Loronha's brazilwood monopoly. The author concludes that Rondinelli's report was the more accurate. He believes that Loronha's three-year lease was not renewed and that the Bretoa expedition of 1511 (in which Loronha and his associates were involved) occurred when "trade with the New World seems to have been opened to all interested parties who petitioned the Crown for permission to send a ship there and agreed to pay the royal duties imposed on goods coming from that land." Based on archival (Arquivo Nacional da Torre do Tombo, Lisbon) and printed primary materials. 20 notes.

[134] William B. Greenlee. "The First Half Century of Brazilian History," *Mid-America* 25:2 (April 1943), pp. 91–120.

Valuable chronological account detailing the major happenings in Portuguese America from the time of Cabral's arrival there in 1500 to the departure from Lisbon in 1549 of Tomé de Sousa, Brazil's first governor-general. The author summarizes not only Portuguese activity but also that of the French, Spanish and English. He also places Brazilian exploration and settlement in the context of Portuguese overseas activity in Africa and Asia. Furthermore, he includes a discussion of the achievements and failures of the lord-proprietors and their settlers as well as the early clergy. Based on printed sources and secondary works. Map. 56 notes.

[135] John Leonard Vogt, Jr. "Portuguese Exploration in Brazil and the *Feitoria* System, 1500–1530: The First Economic Cycle of Brazilian History," (Ph.D. Dissertation: University of Virginia, 1967). 216 pp.

Analyzes the earliest period of Portuguese involvement in Brazil—the time of the *feitoria* system when trading posts dealing in dyewood were dotted along the Brazilian coast. Following several years of private monopoly (under Fernão de Loronha) the dyewood trade was opened to all interested Portuguese traders and it flourished between 1505 and 1516. The three main centers were at São Vicente, Itamaracá, and Cabo Frio. Following 1516, however, increasing French raids and a price slump in the dyewood market undermined the trade. In 1531, the Portuguese Crown intervened to defeat the French and to settle colonists in Brazil. The new colonists built on the foundations laid by the *feitoria* system, making use of the *feitoria* sites for towns and the established relations with Indians for recruiting a labor force. DAI 28/07-A (pp. 2635–2636).

[136] Alexander Marchant. *From Barter to Slavery. The Economic Relations of Portuguese and Indians in the Settlement of Brazil, 1500–1580.* The Johns Hopkins University Studies in Historical and Political Science. Series 60, no. 1. Baltimore: The Johns Hopkins University Press, 1942. 160 p. [Reprinted in 1966 by Peter Smith, Gloucester, Massachusetts.]

Divides the first eighty years of the history of Portuguese America into three periods: 1) 1500–1530 (dominated by brazilwood traders and coastguards); 2) 1533–1549 (characterized by the presence of *donatários* or lords-proprietor who were given great powers and large tracts of land in order to promote settlement); 3) 1549–1580 (a period of attempted centralization and royalization marked by the arrival of the governor-general and the Jesuits and their usual close cooperation). At the same time, the author traces the development of the Brazilian economy from barter to slavery with the initial brazilwood trade gradually being replaced or surpassed by the sugar plantation and its need for disciplined labor on a large scale and the effect these changes had on Portuguese-Indian race relations. Based almost entirely on printed primary sources. Map. Bibliographical note, pp. 144–151.

[137] John F. Weir. "The Colonization of Brazil to 1580," (Ph.D. Dissertation: University of Southern California, 1947).

Studies settlement in Brazil from Cabral's visit in 1500 to the beginning of the union of crowns in 1580. The period 1500–1530 is described as "Thirty Years of Neglect." During this era, Brazil was visited by the Portuguese chiefly for brazilwood. At the same time, the French seriously challenged the Portuguese, French ships in Brazilian waters almost equalling those of the Portuguese. The author feels that the succeeding epoch in Brazilian history, the "Period of Captaincies," was not a success since only two of the captaincies were really successful and the French presence was not eliminated. During the years of the royal governorship, 1549–1580, the Portuguese continued to develop the colony, finally driving out the French and making Brazil "Portuguese America." The author concludes that "by 1580 Brazil's future development was started in the direction it was to go."

B. Non-Portuguese Efforts at Exploration and Settlement in Sixteenth-Century Brazil and the Legal "Privileges" of Foreigners [Nos. 138–145]

Martine Emert's doctoral dissertation **[138]** surveys European voyages to Brazil before 1532 with a special emphasis on those of the French. Regina Tomlinson **[139]** studies the French in Portuguese America to 1550 from a French viewpoint, while Kenneth Umstead **[140]** approaches French activity in the New World from a hemispheric perspective. Charles Nowell **[141]** emphasizes French attempts at colonization—especially those of Nicolas Durand de Villegagnon. Manoel Cardozo **[911]** provides a good discussion on one of the French visitors in his article on the Franciscan Friar André Thevet. French-Indian relations are discussed in Hemming **[423]** as well as in some of the more general studies of the sixteenth century like those of Sanceau **[146]**, Weir **[137]**, and Marchant **[136]**. Robert Southey **[70]** and Bailey Diffie **[71]** also examine in some detail foreign rivalries in Portuguese America during the first century of colonization. The struggle over Rio de Janeiro—because of the role the Portuguese Jesuits and the third-governor general of Brazil, Mem de Sá, played—is also described in accounts by Dominian **[305]**, Jacobsen **[304]**, Espinosa **[306]**, and Butler **[271]**. Bailey Diffie **[142]** and **[143]** discusses the role of foreigners in Portugal and in Brazil during the sixteenth century. Good accounts of English mercantile activity in Brazil during the last quarter of the sixteenth century are found in Kenneth Andrews **[144]** and T. S. Willan **[145]**.

[138] Martine Emert. "European Voyages to Brazil before 1532: A Chapter in International Rivalry in America," (Ph.D. Dissertation: University of California, Berkeley, 1944). 281 pp.

Though Emert examines all the known voyages to Brazil before 1532, almost half of the dissertation focuses on the Portuguese-French rivalry for control of Brazil. After surveying early diplomatic and maritime efforts to gain possession of Brazil and to trade there, the author discusses its economic attractions—especially brazilwood, but also *cassia,* cotton, monkeys and parrots. Chapters three and five—"The French and Portuguese Gain a Toe Hold (1500–1513)" and "French Antagonism and French Achievement (to 1526)"—argue that "until 1532 the French dominated the Brazilian scene and were the only Europeans to make their cultural influence felt." Emert discusses in detail the 1504 visit of Binot Paulmier de Gonneville to Brazil and Portuguese expeditions such as that of the *Bretôa* to gather brazilwood. The author also describes Portuguese-Spanish rivalries—especially in the region of La Plata. The voyage to the Plata (1515–1516) of Juan Díaz de Solís, a Portuguese in the service of Spain, is recounted as is the later voyage of Sebastian Cabot (1526–1530). In the last chapter Emert gives an account of the capture of *La Pèlerine* and the destruction of the French trading post in Pernambuco by the Portuguese. She concludes: "The French had forced the defensive colonization of Brazil; but the carving of empire was slow, and the men from Brittany and Normandy continued trading up and down the long coast line for almost another century." There are eight useful maps. An "Essay on Authorities" is found on pp. 276–281. Based on printed primary and secondary materials.

[139] Regina Johnson Tomlinson. *The Struggle for Brazil. Portugal and "The French Interlopers" 1500–1550.* New York: Las Americas Publishing Co., 1970. 127 pp.

Tomlinson discusses the probable visit to Brazil of the 120-ton French vessel *L'Espoir* from Honfleur in 1504 and the efforts of subsequent entrepreneurs and corsairs to establish ties with Portuguese America. She also describes the diplomatic activity between the kings of France and Portugal surrounding the exploits of these "interlopers." During the long and largely inconclusive negotiations, French activity in Brazil continued as did Portuguese efforts to stop it. One French ship, *La Pèlerine,* landed in Pernambuco and traded with the Indians. Loaded with goods, it attempted to return to France only to be captured en route to Marseilles by the Portuguese. Later the same year, the Portuguese under Pero Lopes de Sousa captured the French trading post at Pernambuco and executed its leader and twenty other Frenchmen. Tomlinson points out that "some Frenchmen conformed to Indian customs in order to establish better trade relations, others because they preferred their manner of living." As for the trade itself, "the French sent guns and powder, knives, hatchets, mirrors, combs, scissors, beads and other trinkets. In exchange, they received Brazilwood, cotton, feathers, skins, monkeys, parrots, humming birds, gold, grain, and medicines." The author describes the role of such entrepreneurs and privateers as Jean Ango and Jean Fleury. She concludes with a discussion of Hans Staden's experiences in Brazil **[181]** and the role of the French in helping effect his escape from his Indian captors. The appendix includes a document in French regarding the 1504 visit of *L'Espoir:* "Voyage du Capitaine Paulmier de Gonneville au Bresil." There is a bibliography on pp. 121–127. Documented.

[140] Kenneth H. H. Umstead. "The French in the Americas during the Sixteenth Century," (Ph.D. Dissertation: University of California, Berkeley, 1940). 203 pp.

Umstead studies the French in America from a hemispheric perspective. Brazil is covered on pp. 118–165. The author points out that almost from the beginning of the sixteenth century, brazilwood "and other exotic products were sought after, from the Pernambuco to the Rio de Janeiro coasts." Profits from Brazil during these years approximated 100% for the French. Though "most of the shipping to the Americas was carried on by private individuals or associations of shippers," the French crown also aided and even, at times, sent out expeditions. The author discusses early French attempts to trade and settle in Brazil and Portuguese efforts to oust these "interlopers." Most of Umstead's study focuses on the first half of the sixteenth century. There is, however, an appendix which contains a "Chronology of the French in Brazil from the Time of Villegagnon to the End of the Century" (pp. 185–188). Based on printed primary and secondary materials.

[141] Charles E. Nowell. "The French in Sixteenth-Century Brazil," *The Americas* 5:4 (April 1949), pp. 381–393.

Provides convincing evidence that Nicolas Durand de Villegagnon, who set up a French settlement at Rio de Janeiro in 1555, "was a private adventurer undertaking a purely secular adventure" rather than the founder of a Huguenot colony. Though Villegagnon later welcomed Calvinist colonists as a "prop for his Brazilian colonial enterprise," the initial outpost contained Catholics. Perceptive analysis of the religious underpinnings of French settlement in Brazil and the conflicts caused by Catholic-Protestant rivalries during the decade following the establishment of "Antarctic France." Based on printed primary and secondary sources. 45 notes.

[142] Bailey W. Diffie. "Foreigners in Portugal and the 'Policy of Silence,'" *Terrae Incognitae. The Annals of the Society for the History of Discoveries.* 1(1969), pp. 23–34.

Balanced discussion of the theoretical "policy of silence," which alleges that for more than half of the fifteenth century, Portuguese monarchs followed a policy of secrecy with respect to Portuguese explorations and discoveries. The author also traces the role of foreigners in Portuguese commerce and exploration as well as in the dissemination of news of Portuguese discoveries. Based on printed primary and secondary materials. 35 notes.

[143] Bailey W. Diffie. "The Legal 'Privileges' of the Foreigners in Portugal and Sixteenth-Century Brazil," in Keith and Edwards, eds., *Conflict and Continuity* **[84]**, pp. 1–19.

After giving numerous examples of legal foreign participation in Portuguese commerce during the fourteenth and fifteenth centuries, when thousands of foreigners made Portugal their home, the author shows how the foreigners continued this activity during most of the first two centuries of Portuguese overseas expansion, playing significant roles in exploration and trade. Special attention is paid to the activities of Italians, Germans and Flemings. It was not until the end of the sixteenth century that Portuguese exclusivity began to be emphasized. Based on printed primary and secondary sources. 37 notes. Susan Schneider's commentary (pp. 20–24) provides supplemental and comparative information—especially regarding the policy of Spain towards foreigners—and brings Diffie's account to the end of the eighteenth century. 11 notes.

[144] Kenneth R. Andrews. *Elizabethan Privateering. English Privateering during the Spanish War, 1585–1603*. Cambridge: At the University Press, 1964. xv, 297 pp.

An excellent chapter entitled, "The Portuguese Trades," describes in detail English efforts at trade in Brazil, with Englishmen supplying manufactures for brazilwood and sugar. Andrews describes the voyages of the *Minion* in 1580 **[199]**, Captain Edward Fenton in 1582–1583 **[200]** and **[201]**, and the *Merchant Royal* in 1583. He also describes the effects on Brazilian shipping of the English alliance with Dom António (the Prior of Crato), pretender to the Portuguese throne held by Philip II of Spain. Andrews asserts that "the Portuguese Brazil trade suffered more heavily than any other from the depredations of English privateers. It required forty or fifty ships a year to carry away the sugar and brazilwood to Europe, and in the three years following the Armada English privateers captured no less than thirty-four such vessels." As a result, great amounts of sugar entered Europe. Andrews describes in some detail the Lancaster expedition against Pernambuco **[221]**, **[222]**, **[223]**. He concludes by arguing that "the English merchants thus turned from trade to plunder. Clearly this was not a change they themselves desired, but one forced upon them by the trend of political circumstances and the aggressiveness of certain of their compatriots. Once plunder replaced trade, the merchants made the best of it, and the profits they made on captured sugar and brazilwood contributed to the mounting stock of fluid resources available for commercial expansion. But from the fast-growing Brazil trade itself they found themselves almost completely excluded by the Dutch." Well annotated.

[145] T. S. Willan. *Studies in Elizabethan Foreign Trade.* Manchester: Manchester University Press, 1959. ix, 349.

In the chapter entitled, "The Factor or Agent in Foreign Trade," Willan describes problems the factors, merchants, and crew of the *Minion* faced in its trading voyage to Brazil in 1580. The author adds much new material to Grigge's brief account published in Hakluyt **[105]**. Willan also briefly describes the 1583 trading voyage to Olinda of the *Royal Merchant* as well as some of the repercussions from Edward Fenton's voyage of 1582 **[200]** and **[201]**. Willan shows "how trade could be affected by lawlessness at sea and by the Spanish conquest of Portugal, . . . [and] how difficult it was to trade profitably in regions where no permanent factors were established." The chapter, "Sugar and the Elizabethans," frequently mentions Brazil, but only in general terms.

C. The Donatarial Captaincies [Nos. 146–155]

Little has been done in English on the histories of the individual captaincies into which Brazil was divided in the 1530s. Diffie **[71]**, Marchant **[136]**, Sanceau **[146]** and Greenlee **[134]** give good descriptions of their foundings and initial vicissitudes as well as brief sketches of their early proprietors. Harrison **[148]** has the only general history of a captaincy—Paraiba do Sul from 1533 to 1753. Francis A. Dutra **[149]** contributes a revisionist study of the first lord-proprietor of Pernambuco, and Boxer **[150]** does the same for the third. In addition, Boxer **[185]** contributes a translation and a discussion of Jorge de Albuquerque's experiences while returning to Portugal in 1565. In his study of Matias de Albuquerque, Dutra **[272]** surveys the second half of the sixteenth century as well as the first quarter of Pernambuco's seventeenth-century history. The practice of the governors-general spending a great deal of time in Pernambuco rather than in Bahia, the capital, is discussed by Dutra **[151]** and **[152]**, both accounts giving a picture of the captaincy in the late sixteenth and early seventeenth century. Military and defense in Pernambuco in the 1620s are discussed at great length by Dutra **[153]**. For the Portuguese background of the extensive privileges given to the *donatários* or lords-proprietor, see Alexander Marchant **[154]** and Harold B. Johnson **[155]**. The early royal ordinances—including those affecting the lords-proprietor—have also been studied by Silva Rego **[147]**.

[146] Elaine Sanceau. *Captains of Brazil.* Porto: Livraria Civilização Editora, 1956(?). viii, 380 p. 2nd ed. 1965.

An easy-to-read account of the first seven decades of Portuguese activity in America. The author focuses on the customs and life-style of the Brazilian Indians and the first Portuguese discoverers and their interaction. She then gives a captaincy by captaincy account of the efforts of the first lords-proprietor (*donatários*) to colonize their land grants. The latter part of her narrative deals with the arrival of the first governors-general and the early bishops, Jesuit missionary activity, and the struggle against the French in what is now Rio de Janeiro. Relies almost exclusively on printed primary sources. The bibliography is on pp. 365–367.

[147] António da Silva Rego. *Portuguese Colonization in the Sixteenth Century: A Study of the Royal Ordinances (Regimentos).* Johannesburg: Witwatersrand University Press, 1959. Reprinted 1965. viii. 116 p. (Publications of the Ernest Oppenheimer Institute of Portuguese Studies of the University of the Witwatersrand, Johannesburg: 1).

After surveying the background of Portuguese overseas expansion, the author discusses the most important of the sixteenth-century standing orders or instructions (*regimentos*). Those analyzed for Brazil include the charters of the lords-proprietor and the instructions given to Tomé de Sousa, the first governor-general, and Antônio Cardoso de Barros, the chief treasury official. Silva Rego also describes the *regimentos* for Pedro Álvares Cabral, India and southeast Africa, and the charter granted to Paulo Dias de Novais (Angola). Based chiefly on printed primary sources.

[148] William Fredric Harrison. "A Struggle for Land in Colonial Brazil: The Private Captaincy of Paraiba do Sul, 1533–1753" (Ph.D. Dissertation: University of New Mexico, 1970). 301 pp.

Examines the rivalries of various interest groups in Paraiba do Sul from 1533–1753. The working out of these rivalries, such as that between cattlemen and sugar growers, cattlemen and religious orders, Brazilian-born rural landowners and the Portuguese-born lord-proprietor of the captaincy, gave Paraiba do Sul its peculiar history. Unique to this captaincy was the fact that "cattlemen were able to suppress the sugar industry for two hundred years on alluvial plains which were ideally suited for the cultivation of sugar cane." Based on Alberto Lamego's eight-volume document collection, *Terra Goitaca*, Brazilian archival materials, especially those in Campos, and printed sources. DAI 31/10-A (p. 5319).

[149] Francis A. Dutra. "Duarte Coelho Pereira, First Lord-Proprietor of Pernambuco: The Beginning of a Dynasty," *The Americas* 29:4 (April 1973), pp. 415–441.

Includes an analysis of the first two decades of Pernambuco's history as a donatarial captaincy (1534–1554) as well as a revisionist biography of Duarte Coelho. The author points out that although after the first lord-proprietor's death, the "absence of strong leadership caused the captaincy to drift, . . . Duarte Coelho's efforts had not been in vain. The momentum he had provided during those initial years of colonization increased with each passing decade. His dream of a stable agrarian colony became increasingly a reality." Based mainly on archival and printed primary sources. 105 notes.

[150] Charles R. Boxer. "Jorge de Albuquerque Coelho: A Luso-Brazilian Hero of the Sea, 1539–1602," *Luso-Brazilian Review* 6:1 (Summer 1969), pp. 3–17.

Brief biography of the third *donatário* of Pernambuco, younger son of Duarte Coelho **[149]**, the first of that captaincy's lords-proprietor. The author emphasizes Jorge's adventure-filled voyage in 1565 on the *Santo Antônio* **[185]** and his role in the North African battle of Alcacer-Quibir in 1578. Based on printed primary and secondary accounts. 25 notes.

[151] Francis A. Dutra. "A New Look into Diogo Botelho's Stay in Pernambuco, 1602–1603," *Luso-Brazilian Review* 4:1 (Summer 1967), pp. 27–34.

Focuses on Desembargador Belchior do Amaral's 1603 Lisbon investigation of Diogo Botelho, Brazil's eighth governor-general, which accused the governor of illicit activities and disobedience and recommended his removal. The author argues that this *devassa* probably gives a truer picture of Botelho's behavior than a similar inquiry made in Pernambuco the same year. Based on extensive use of documents from Spanish and Portuguese archives. 39 notes.

[152] Francis A. Dutra. "Centralization vs. Donatarial Privilege: Pernambuco, 1602–1630," in Alden, ed., *Colonial Roots* **[87]**, pp. 19–60.

Discusses the evolution of donatarial rights and privileges from the time Duarte Coelho was awarded the lord-proprietorship of Pernambuco in 1534. The author describes efforts during the first two decades of the seventeenth century by the four governors-general who established residence in Pernambuco for part of their administrations to interfere in the political and economic life of the captaincy. The arrival in 1620 of Matias de Albuquerque, brother of the fourth *donatário,* as governor and *capitão mor* of Pernambuco after almost fifty years of absentee rule by the lords-proprietor, however, produced a stop to this erosion of donatarial rights and privileges, though not before several bitter conflicts with the governors-general and their protégés and the *Relação* [High Court] in Bahia. Based mainly on archival (Spanish and Portuguese) and printed primary materials. 150 notes.

[153] Francis A. Dutra. "Matias de Albuquerque and the Defense of Northeastern Brazil, 1620–1626," *Studia* 36 (July 1973), pp. 117–166.

A detailed account of the state of Pernambuco's fortifications in 1620 and the efforts of Matias de Albuquerque, that captaincy's newly appointed governor and *capitão mor* to repair old defences and add new ones. When Bahia, the capital of Brazil, fell to the Dutch in 1624 and the Portuguese governor-general was captured, Matias was named governor-general of Brazil. Dutra discusses Albuquerque's efforts to free Bahia from Dutch control, put down Indian revolts in Paraiba and drive the Dutch fleet from the latter captaincy's Baia da Traição. Based chiefly on Spanish and Portuguese archival materials and printed primary sources. 164 notes. 2 maps.

[154] Alexander Marchant. "Feudal and Capitalistic Elements in the Portuguese Settlement of Brazil," *The Hispanic American Historical Review* 22:3 (August 1942), pp. 493–512.

After describing and analyzing the debate between those who interpret early Brazilian settlement in feudal terms and those who consider it capitalistic, with special attention to the views of Carlos Malheiro Dias, Roberto G. Simonsen, J. F. de Almeida Prado and Raul de Andrade de Silva, the author discusses the language of the *cartas de doação* and the *forais* granted to the lords-proprietor. He examines three fifteenth-century types of capitalistic enterprise (the overseas trading company, royal monopoly, and the donatary system combining commerce with colonization), and provides a useful survey of the early experiences of such *donatários* (lords-proprietor) as Pedro de Gois, Vasco Fernandes Coutinho, Martim Afonso de Sousa, and Duarte Coelho **[149]**. Marchant concludes that the *donatários* "were not members of a feudal society and they did not found feudal landholdings in Brazil. . . . On the other hand, the *donatários* were clearly capitalistic in the sense of investing money for profit. They were planter capitalists and not primarily traders, and their investment was in land and slaves." Based on printed primary and secondary materials. 61 notes.

[155] Harold B. Johnson. "The Donatary Captaincy in Perspective: Portuguese Backgrounds to the Settlement of Brazil," *The Hispanic American Historical Review* 52:2 (May 1972), pp. 203–214.

Compares a late fourteenth-century royal grant of *senhorio* (seignory) with a similar sixteenth-century grant in the Azores and shows what was old and new in the 1534 grant made to Duarte Coelho **[149]**, the first lord-proprietor of Pernambuco. The author argues the thesis that "Portugal's unique experience in repopulating empty spaces during the centuries of Reconquest" was "the prime factor which fitted it to undertake the colonization of Brazil." He also clears up much of the confusion surrounding the sterile controversy whether the donatarial captaincies were feudal or capitalistic. There is a useful discussion of the juridical and pragmatic reasoning behind such institutions as the *doação, foral,* and *sesmaria.* Based on printed primary and secondary sources. 27 notes.

D. Spanish Domination, 1580–1640 [Nos. 156–157]

This important topic still remains mostly neglected by historians. A good overview of what research has been accomplished and what remains to be done is found in Stuart B. Schwartz **[156]**. His doctoral dissertation on the *Relação* or High Court, 1609–1630, is the best and most extensive treatment of the period **[283]**. See also his broader study, *Sovereignty and Society in Colonial Brazil* **[284]**. Two other useful studies are Boxer's **[277]** biography of Salvador de Sá and Dutra's **[272]** study of Matias de Albuquerque. For administration during the union of crowns, see Joyce's **[268]** study of the Conselho da Fazenda. Engel Sluiter **[157]** provides a short introduction in English to *O Livro que da razão*—a detailed description of Brazil in the early seventeenth century.

[156] Stuart B. Schwartz. "Luso-Spanish Relations in Hapsburg Brazil, 1580–1640," *The Americas* 25:1 (July 1968), pp. 33–48.

Discusses and analyzes the historical literature on Brazil during the sixty-year union of crowns, when Portugal and Spain were jointly ruled by the Spanish Habsburgs, Philip II, Philip III, and Philip IV. Treats a wide variety of topics with a special emphasis on administrative, economic and racial themes. Relies heavily on archival and printed primary sources. 64 notes.

[157] Engel Sluiter, ed. "Report on the State of Brazil, 1612," *The Hispanic American Historical Review* 29:4 (November 1949), pp. 518–562.

The editor gives a useful four-page introduction in English to this important source for early seventeenth-century Brazil. The document itself is transcribed in Portuguese with footnotes in English. The introduction has 20 notes.

1. Portuguese Adventurers, Sailors and Merchants in Sixteenth- and Seventeenth-Century Spanish America [Nos. 158–162]

There has been an increasing interest in the Portuguese who were involved in the New World outside of Brazil. One of the most famous of the early adventurers was the shipwreck Aleixo Garcia, whose efforts to invade the Inca Empire are recounted by Nowell **[158]**. Henry Keith **[159]** studies those Portuguese who drifted to the Spanish Caribbean. The Portuguese in the La Plata region, Potosí and Peru are discussed in some detail by Hanke **[160]** and Harry E. Cross **[162]**. Boxer **[277]**, in his biography of Salvador de Sá, has an interesting discussion on these "Peruleiros."

[158] Charles E. Nowell. "Aleixo Garcia and the White King," *The Hispanic American Historical Review* 26:4 (November 1946), pp. 450–466.

Through a judicious comparison of extant source materials the author attempts to reconstruct the exploits of Aleixo Garcia, the Portuguese shipwreck from the 1515 Juan Dias de Solís expedition, who crossed the Chaco and invaded the Inca empire in the company of a large contingent of Indians several years before the arrival of Pizarro. Based on printed primary and secondary sources. 74 notes.

[159] Henry H. Keith. "New World Interlopers: The Portuguese in the Spanish West Indies, From the Discovery to 1640," *The Americas* 25:4 (April 1969), pp. 360–371.

Analyzes the role of the Portuguese in the Spanish Caribbean and the reasons for their presence. The author argues that the majority of Portuguese probably arrived illegally "on the pretext of bad weather and need for supplies" and as slave contractors, smugglers and sailors. After discussing the tendency of Spaniards to identify Portuguese merchants as "New Christians" and describing a 1606 report of 125 foreigners in Venezuela, 115 of whom were Portuguese, Keith concludes that most Portuguese "were rapidly assimilated . . . and became for all purposes Spanish American colonials." Based on archival and secondary materials. 37 notes.

[160] Lewis Hanke. "The Portuguese in Spanish America, With Special Reference to the Villa Imperial de Potosí," *Revista de Historia de America* 51 (June 1961), pp. 1–48.

Survey of individual Portuguese—many of whom were suspected of secretly being Jews—and their influence in Spanish America, especially in the Plata region, Potosí, Peru, and Venezuela. Special attention is paid to Antônio Leon Pinelo and his family, Enrique Garces, Lourenço de Mendoça, and António de Acosta, the latter reputed author of the *Historia de Potosí,* copies of which have not come to light.

Based on archival information and printed primary and secondary sources. 142 notes.

[161] Lewis Hanke. "The Portuguese and the Villa Imperial de Potosí," in Lindley Cintra, ed., *Actas* **[91]**, II, 266–276.

Preliminary version of **[160]**. 59 notes.

[162] Harry E. Cross. "Commerce and Orthodoxy: A Spanish Response to Portuguese Commercial Penetration in the Viceroyalty of Peru, 1580–1640," *The Americas* 35:2 (October 1978), pp. 151–167.

Cross opens the article by quoting the Inquisition in Lima regarding Portuguese mercantile activity in Peru: "They have made themselves masters of commerce. The Merchant's Street is almost theirs; the Merchant's Lane is all theirs, as are most of the retail booths. . . . As a result, they have gained control of merchandising. . . . The Spaniard who has not a Portuguese as a business partner has limited chances for success." He then examines the role of the Inquisition which had been established in Lima since the 1570s in challenging and eventually eliminating Portuguese competition. Cross argues that "nearly two-thirds of all convictions in the purge of 1635–1639 were Portuguese with commercial connections." He analyzes the economic repercussions of the Inquisition's activity and tries to determine the extent to which the Inquisition was "acting as an agent of the Spanish monopolists of Lima." He concludes that "by the time of the dissolution of the union of Spain and Portugal in 1640, most of the remaining Portuguese merchants in Lima were inescapably locked in the Inquisitional jail." Based on some archival, but mostly printed primary, sources. 61 notes.

VI. Contemporary Narratives: Brazil, 1500–1640

[Nos. 163–236]

A. Early Discoveries, 1500–1530 [Nos. 163–173]

The major study and documents for understanding the visit of Pedro Álvares Cabral to Brazil in 1500 is found in William Brooks Greenlee **[163]**. The letter of Pero Vaz de Caminha, the scribe who accompanied Cabral, translated by Greenlee, is also translated by Charles David Ley **[164]**. Donald Weinstein **[165]** translates and annotates Pietro Pasqualigo's 1501 oration to Manuel I of Portugal. The first printed reference to the discovery of Brazil is found in a *Copy of a Letter of the King of Portugal Sent to the King of Castile* **[166]**. Martin Waldseemüller's *Cosmographiae Introductio* gave the name "America" to the Western Hemisphere. It was accompanied by an account of the four voyages of Amerigo Vespucci **[167]**. Some of the Vespucci correspondence was translated by Sir Clements Markham **[168]**. Markham is clearly unsympathetic to his subject. John Parker **[169]** translates and comments on a four-page newsletter describing a voyage made by two Portuguese ships to the Rio de la Plata about 1514. Martin Fernández Enciso **[170]**, **[172]** described the Amazon and its inhabitants in 1519. He also described much of the rest of the coast of Brazil. Chapter VI of Antonio Pigafetta's journal of the voyage of Magellan **[171]** provides an interesting account of Brazil. Roger Barlow **[172]** describes his visit to Brazil in 1526 and includes much of Enciso's *Suma de Geographia* in his description of the coast. Robert Thorne **[173]** relates the diplomatic controversies between the Spaniards and the Portuguese over the newfound discoveries.

[163] William Brooks Greenlee, ed. *The Voyage of Pedro Álvares Cabral to Brazil and India from Contemporary Documents and Narratives.* London: Printed for the Hakluyt Society, 1938. lxix, 228 pp.

This important study by Greenlee gathers together and translates into English all the extant primary source materials on Pedro Álvares Cabral's visit to Brazil in 1500. The author's introduction (pp. xi–lxix) discusses the preparations for this follow-up voyage to India in the wake of Vasco da Gama's earlier expedition and the voyage itself. Greenlee examines the sources and recounts the little that is known of the life of Pedro Álvares Cabral. He studies in detail the various theories offered to explain why Cabral actually touched Brazil on his way to India and reduces them to four: 1) fortuitous; 2) intentional because of prior discovery; 3) intentional for discovery; and 4) intentional for reasons of navigation. Greenlee also studies the various claims for the prior discovery of Brazil and concludes that "it seems probable that Cabral's fleet was the first to reach the shores of Brazil under the Portuguese flag. The westward diversion of the fleet, during which Brazil was visited, seems to have been made not for one but for several reasons. The chief motive was to follow the most practicable and safest route to the Cape of Good Hope." There are a number of useful maps and illustrations, and an excellent appendix on the 13 ships, the captains, the factors, the writers, the pilots, the interpreters, the friars and priests, and other personnel that were part of the expedition. A detailed bibliography is found on pages 203–212. Documents translated into English that refer to Cabral's visit in Brazil include: The letter of Pero Vaz de Caminha to King Manuel, 1 May 1500; the letter of Master John (personal physician and surgeon of Dom Manuel I and astronomer of the fleet) to King Manuel, 1 May 1500; and the letter of King Manuel to Ferdinand and Isabella, 29 July 1501, where he tells the monarchs that Cabral "reached a land which he newly discovered, to which he gave the name of Santa Cruz. In it he found the people nude as in the first innocence, gentle, and peaceable. It seemed that Our Lord miraculously wished it to be found, because it is very convenient and necessary for the voyage to India, because he repaired his ships and took water there." In addition, there is an anonymous narrative by a member of the expedition and a letter sent to Venice by Giovanni Matteo Cretico, 27 June 1501. The two letters of 1 May 1500 were written in Brazil.

[164] Charles David Ley, ed. and trans. *Portuguese Voyages, 1498–1663.* New York: E. P. Dutton, 1947. xxii, 360 pp.

Contains "The Discovery of Brazil. Letter of Pero Vaz de Caminha, Written in Porto Seguro of Vera Cruz on the First Day of May in the

Year 1500" (pp. 39–59). Pero Vaz de Caminha was the scribe who accompanied Pedro Álvares Cabral on Portugal's follow-up voyage to India. This letter describes the discovery of Brazil, the Amerindians and their way of life, and the flora and fauna of the new land. It also gives a good insight into early Portuguese attitudes regarding Brazil and its population. Ley's translation is annotated, though the notes (53) are not continuous.

[165] Donald Weinstein, ed. *Ambassador from Venice. Pietro Pasqualigo in Lisbon, 1501.* Minneapolis: University of Minnesota Press, 1960. 112 pp.

In his Latin oration to Manuel I of Portugal on 20 August 1501, Pietro Pasqualigo exclaimed: "What kingdom is there on earth, what nation so remote and so far removed from commerce with all men, that has not been reached by your fame? In this brief time a world of other lands entirely unknown to Ptolemy and Strabo and to the rest of the world's writers has been discovered and made known to men through your diligence and under your direction." In his commentary Donald Weinstein spends several pages discussing whether Pasqualigo was referring to Brazil and concludes that he was not, since "these are undoubtedly references to Africa and India." The editor analyzes Cabral's visit to Brazil. Pasqualigo's account was first published in December of 1501. Weinstein includes a facsimile of the only known copy in the United States (from the James Ford Bell Collection of the University of Minnesota Library). Well documented. There is a useful index.

[166] Sergio J. Pacifici, trans. *Copy of a Letter of the King of Portugal Sent to the King of Castile Concerning the Voyage and Success of India.* Minneapolis: The University of Minnesota Press, 1955. 24 pp.

As John Parker pointed out in his introduction, "On October 28, 1505, there appeared in Rome a news tract printed by John of Besicken which purported to be a 'Copy of a letter of the King of Portugal sent to the King of Castile concerning the voyage and success of India.' Although certain textual evidence tends to indicate that this was merely a news publication with a spectacular title, it is nevertheless significant, for it not only gives a contemporary account of these first four commercial ventures to India by the Portuguese, but it also contains the first printed reference to the discovery of Brazil." After describing the composition of the 1500 armada that was to sail to India, the letter reports that "Pedro Álvares Cabral was the Captain General of the afore-mentioned armada. Sailing past Cape Verde, they sighted a land which had recently come to be known in our Europe, to which they gave the name of Santa Cruz, and this because they had a very high cross erected on its shore. Others call it New Land, that is, New World. This land, where they came ashore, is situated on the 14th meridian beyond the tropic of Cancer, as the sailors found its position by means of their quadrants and astrolabes, since they sail in those parts with astrological instruments. This land is situated 400 leagues west-southwest of the afore-mentioned Cape Verde. We have previously advised Your Lordship of its inhabitants, fertility, size, and condition and whether it is an island or a continent. The armada, upon its departure, left two Christians to chance. It was carrying 20 convicts, previously condemned to death, to be left wherever the Captain might deem fitting. Later on, one of these two Christians came back with another armada we had sent directly to that land. This man knew their language and gave information about everything." 6 notes. There are facsimile reproductions of the first and last pages of the original published version of the letter. Only 4 copies of the first edition are known. One of them belongs to the James Ford Bell Collection.

[167] Martin Waldseemüller. *The Cosmographiae Introductio of Martin Waldseemüller in Facsimile. Followed by the Four Voyages of Amerigo Vespucci, with their Translation into English; to Which Are Added Waldseemüller's Two World Maps of 1507*. Introduction by Prof. Joseph Fischer, S. J. and Prof. Franz von Wieser. Edited by Charles George Herbermann. New York: United States Catholic Historical Society, 1907. vii, 151 pp. CIII.

This is considered the best of the facsimile editions of Waldseemüller's *Cosmographiae Introductio,* which is important because it gives the name "America" to the part of the world where Brazil was located. After discussing Europe, Africa and Asia, Waldseemüller adds: "Now, these parts of the earth have been more extensively explored and a fourth part has been discovered by Amerigo Vespucci (as will be set forth in what follows). Inasmuch as both Europe and Asia received their names from women, I see no reason why any one should justly object to calling this part Amerige, i.e., the land of Amerigo, or America, after Amerigo, its discoverer, a man of great ability. Its position and the customs of its inhabitants may be clearly understood from the four voyages of Amerigo, which are subjoined." In the appended "The Four Voyages of Amerigo Vespucci," the third voyage mentions Vespucci's sighting of Brazil: "In the course of the voyage from Cape St. Augustine, we sailed 700 leagues—100 toward the west and 600 toward the southwest. Should any one desire to describe all that we saw in the course of that voyage, paper would not suffice him. We did not, however, discover anything of great importance with the exception of an infinite number of cassia trees and of very many others which put fourth a peculiar kind of leaf. We saw, in addition, very many other wonderful things which it would be tedious to enumerate." Scholarship has challenged the authenticity of Vespucci's authorship of "The Four Voyages," though it is clear that he visited Brazil on his 1501–1502 voyage. Good discussions of Waldseemüller and Vespucci are found in Borba de Moraes **[20]**, II, 364–368 and 345–357, respectively.

[168] Clements R. Markham, ed. *The Letters of Americo Vespucci and Other Documents Illustrative of His Career.* London: Printed for the Hakluyt Society, 1894. xliv, 114 pp.
[Issued by the Hakluyt Society. 1st series, no. 90. Reprinted. New York: Burt Franklin, 1964.]

Includes a translation of the letter concerning the four voyages **[167]** and the account of the third voyage (to Brazil) of 1501–1502.

[169] John Parker, ed. *Tidings Out of Brazil.* tr. Mark Graubard. Minneapolis: The University of Minnesota Press (James Ford Bell Collection), 1957. 48 pp.

Translation with notes and commentary of *Copia der newen Zeytung aus Presillg Landt,* a four-page newsletter describing a voyage made by two Portuguese ships to the Rio de La Plata about 1514. 29 notes. Bibliography.

[170] Martin Fernández de Enciso. "A short description of the river of Marannon or Amazones and the Countries thereabout, as also of the sea of Fresh-water, taken out of an ancient Discourse of all the Portes, Creekes, and Havens of the West Indies, Written by Martin Fernandez de Enciza, and dedicated to Charles the Emperour, Anno 1518," in Hakluyt, *The Principal Navigations* **[105]**, XI, 19–22.

Martin Fernández de Enciso was a conquistador who saw service in the West Indies during the early years of the sixteenth century. Despite its early publication date (the first edition was published in Seville in 1519), his survey is surprisingly accurate for Brazil. Borba de Moraes **[20]**, I, 244, considered it to be "the first work in Spanish to describe America." It was translated into English by John Frampton and published in London in 1578 with the title, *A Briefe Description of the . . . Bayes and Havens of the West India.* According to the account in Hakluyt, "all this coast from the Cape of S. Austine unto Marannon is a cleare coast & deep, but neer to the river are certaine sholds towardes the East part. And by the West part the river is deepe, and it hath a good entrie. From this river Marannon, unto the river which is called The sea of fresh water, are 25 leagues: this river hath 40 leagues of bredth at the mouth, and carieth such abundance of water that it entreth more then 20 leagues into the Sea, and mingleth not it selfe with the salt water. . . . The Indians of this countrey have their lips made full of small holes in 4 parts, & through those holes be put small rings, and likewise at their eares: & if any man aske of them where they had their gold, they answere, that going up by the river so many dayes journey, they found certaine mountains that had much of it, and from those mountains they brought it when they would have it, but they made no great account of it, for they neither buy nor sell, and amongst them is nothing but change. In this countery they eate bread of rootes, and Maiz, and they eate certaine rootes which they call Aies and Batatas, but the Batatas bee better then the other rootes, and being rawe they have a smell of Chestnuts: they are to be eaten rosted. These Indians doe make wine of the fruit of Date-trees."

[171] Antonio Pigafetta. *The Voyage of Magellan. The Journal of Antonio Pigafetta.* Trans. Paula Spurlin Paige. Englewood Cliffs, New Jersey: Prentice-Hall, 1969. xvii, 149 pp.
[This is a facsimile edition of *Le voyage et navigation faict par les Espaignols es Isles de Mollucques* published in Paris in 1525.]

According to Borba de Moraes **[20]**, "this edition is a resume, written by Jacques Antoine Fabre from the manuscript presented by Pigafetta to Louise de Savoie." It is the first printed account of Magellan's expedition. Chapter VI describes Brazil—a land "very vast and larger than Spain, Portugal, France and Italy combined, very vast indeed. The people have no religion and they live by the laws of nature and reach an age of 125 and 140 years. Both the men and the women go naked, and they live in long houses that they call *boii*, and they sleep in a cotton net that is tied to two large trunks in the middle of the house, and they build their fires inside on the ground. A hundred men with their women and children can sleep in each of these." Pigafetta observed that the Indians of Brazil "have boats made out of a single tree trunk that they call *canoes*, which they hollow out with stone axes, for they work with stone as we work with iron, which they do not possess. Thirty or forty men can ride in a canoe and they row it with oars that resemble a baker's shovel." The author described their custom of eating human flesh, their trading practices, and the collecting of Brazilwood. He concludes his discussion of Brazil with the comment that "it would be easy to convert these people to the faith of Jesus Christ." This translation and facsimile edition is from a rare copy of the 1525 edition in the William L. Clements Library, University of Michigan.

[172] Roger Barlow. *A Brief Summe of Geographie*. Ed. E. G. R. Taylor. London: For the Hakluyt Society, 1932. lvi, 210 pp.
[Issued by the Hakluyt Society. 2nd Series, no. 69.]

Although, as the editor points out, *A Briefe Summe* "embodies an almost word for word translation" of Martin Fernández de Enciso's *Suma de Geographia* (published in Seville in 1519), it also contains a good deal of additional material gathered by Barlow on his trip to America in 1526. Barlow spent about three months in Pernambuco that year: "from the cape sent augustine to parnambuc is 12 leges at northe northwest in 7 degrees 3/4, where the king of portugale hath a house of factorie for his brasyl, w[ch] brasill the indies do cutte downe and bryng to the portugales that reside there for bedestones, glasse and other trifles, and so thei pile it up by the waters side as thei do in kent pile there bilet, and everie ij or iij yere the king of portugale sendeth certin shippes and carveles for it." Barlow and Enciso stated that "the people of this cost bothe men and women go nakyd, paynte ther facys and bodies of dyvers facions and the menne when thei go to warre paynte ther facis after a grym fashion and hathe ther lippes full of holes and thorough them thei put long peces of cristall and tuskys of wylde bestes, and ther bodies be dressed w[t] popingaie fethers of diverse coloures." This is an important, yet often neglected, account for early sixteenth-century Brazil.

[173] Robert Thorne, "A declaration of the Indies and lands discovered, and subdued unto the Emperour, and the king of Portingal: And also of other partes of the Indies and rich countries to be discovered, which the worshipful M. Robert Thorne merchant of London (who dwelt long in the citie of Sivil in Spaine) exhorted king Henrie the eight to take in hand" and "The book made by the right worshipful M. Robert Thorne in the yeere 1527. in Sivil, to Doctour Ley, Lord ambassadour for king Henry the eight, to Charles the Emperour, being an information of the parts of the world, discovered by him and the king of Portingal: and also of the way to the Moluccaes by the North," in Hakluyt, *The Principal Navigations* **[105]**, II, 159–181.

Contains an interesting account by an English observer of the rivalries and diplomatic maneuverings between Spain and Portugal regarding the various demarcation lines and overseas expansion: "So that plainely it should appeare by reason, that the Portingals should leave these Islands of Cape Verde and land of Brasil, if they would have part of the Spicerie of the Emperours [Charles V]: or els holding these, they have no part there. To this the Portingals say, that they will beginne their 180 degrees from the selfe same Cape Verde: for that it may extende so much more toward the Orient, and touch these Islandes of the Emperours: and would winne these Islandes of Cape Verde and land of Brasil neverthelesse, as a thing that they possessed before the consent of this limitation was made. So none can verely tell which hath the best reason. They be not yet agreed, Quare sub Judice lis est. But without doubt (by all conjectures of reason) the sayd Islands fall all without the limitation of Portingal, and pertaine to Spain, as it appeareth by the most part of all the Cardes made by the Portingals, save those which they have falsified of late purposely." There is an interesting map of the world showing Spanish and Portuguese possessions.

B. Initial Settlement, 1530–1580 [Nos. 174–198]

William Hawkins **[174]** provides a brief account of his voyage to Brazil in 1530. The Veedor, Alonso **[175]**, describes a visit to Bahia in 1535. R. G. Marsden **[177]** has edited the transcripts of the testimony of eight survivors of the *Barbara* which spent time in Brazil in 1540. Anthony Garrard **[178]** informed Hakluyt of a trip to Brazil in 1540 by Robert Reniger and Thomas Borey. Edward Cotton **[179]** reported a visit to Bahia in 1542 by "one Pudsey of Southampton." Friar Gaspar de Carvajal's account of the Francisco de Orellana's voyage of discovery down the Amazon is found in **[180]**. Hans Staden **[181]** visited Portuguese America twice. The second time, in southern Brazil, he was captured by Indians. His account is one of the most famous narratives of sixteenth-century Brazil. Luis L. Dominguez **[182]** edited the accounts of Ulrich Schmidt and Alvar Nuñez Cabeza de Vaca regarding their experiences in the Plata region. Schmidt visited São Vicente and Cabeza de Vaca journeyed through southern Brazil. Two valuable French accounts are those of the Franciscan friar André Thevet **[183]**, who arrived near Rio de Janeiro in 1555, and the Calvinist Jean de Lery **[184]**, who followed Thevet to Brazil two years later. Afonso Luis **[185]** described the maritime adventures of Jorge de Albuquerque, the future lord-proprietor of Pernambuco, during his return to Portugal in 1565. Pero de Magalhães **[186]** provides a detailed account of Brazil in the 1570s. Francis Drake **[187]** and **[188]** sailed along the Brazilian coast in 1578 on his way around the world. In addition to Drake's account, there are those by Francis Fletcher **[189]**, John Cooke **[190]** and the Portuguese pilot, Nuno da Silva **[191]** and **[192]**. Several ships belonging to the Drake expedition became separated and returned to Brazil. Edward Cliffe **[193]** relates the story of John Winter and Peter Carder **[194]** describes his encounters with the Tupinamba and his stay of several years in Bahia with the Portuguese. Hakluyt printed a letter from John Whithall **[195]**. Whithall, known in Santos as João Leitão, invited English merchants to trade there. Several anonymous descriptions of the coast of Brazil **[196]**, **[197]**, and **[198]** also date from this period.

[174] William Hawkins. "A voyage to Brasill, made by the worshipfull M. William Haukins of Plimmouth, father to sir John Haukins knight now living, in the yeere 1530," in Hakluyt, *Principall Navigations* **[106]**, pp. 520–521.

William Hawkins was "one of the principall Sea Captaines in the West partes of England in his time, not contented with the short voyages commonly then made onely to the knowen coastes of Europe, armed out a tall and goodly ship of his owne of the burthen of 250 tunnes, called the Pole of Plimmouth, wherewith hee made three long and famous voyages unto the coast of Brazill, a thing in those dayes very rare, especially to our Nation." After trading on the African coast, Hawkins sailed to Brazil, where he used "such discretion, and behaved himselfe so wisely with those savage people, that he grew into great familiaritie and friendship with them. Insomuch that in his 2. voyage, one of the savage kings of the Countrey of Brasill, was contented to take shippe with him, and to bee transported hither into England." The Brazilian chieftain was presented to Henry VIII. In the Amerindian's cheeks "were holes made according to their savage maner and therein small bones were planted standing an inche out from the said holes, which in his own Countrey was reputed for a great braverie. He had also another hole in his nether lippe, wherein was set a precious stone about the beignesse of a pease: All his apparell, behaviour and gesture, were very strange to the beholders." The Brazilian Indian spent about a year in England. He died on the voyage back to Brazil. This account was reprinted in Hakluyt, *The Principal Navigations* **[105]**, XI, 23–25, under the title of "A brief relation of two sundry voyages made by the worshipful M. William Haukins of Plimouth, father to Sir John Haukins knight, late Treasurer of her Majesties Navie, in the yeere 1530 and 1532." See also Markham **[220]**.

[175] Alonso (Veedor). "Narrative of the Events Which Happened in the Fleet of Simon de Alcazaba Who Went Out as Governor of the Province of Leon in the Parts of the South Sea. Having to Pass the Strait of Magellan He Took Two Ships, the *Capitana* called *La Madre de Dios* and the Other Called *San Pedro* in Which were Embarked, Including Passengers and Sailors, 250 Persons," in Markham, ed., *Early Spanish Voyages to the Strait of Magellan* **[176]**, pp. 133–156.

This ill-fated voyage of 1534–1535 was plagued by misfortune almost from the time it embarked from San Lucar de Barrameda in September of 1534. Markham describes the story of the expedition as "one of mutiny, murder, and terrible suffering." It is of interest to Brazilianists because the *San Pedro,* on which Alonso was aboard, stopped at Bahia on 28 July 1535 enroute to Spain: "In this port there is a Christian named Diego [Diogo] Alvarez who had lived there for 26 years, married, with a wife and children. With him there were six or seven other Christians who had escaped from a caravel which was wrecked two or three months ago. Of these four came with us." When the Spaniards went ashore for provisions, they were attacked by Indians. But "after two days Diego Alvarez pacified the natives, and we went on shore again to obtain provisions. We remained until the 7th of August and purchased what we needed. Being at anchor, three or four days before we were to sail, the boat of the large ship, our consort, arrived with 20 men, the ship having been lost on the shoals of Tenereques. The natives attacked the shipwrecked crew, killing some, while others fled and hid themselves on shore. Out of a crew of 110 persons not more than these 20 escaped. Among them were the mate, the carpenter, the purser, and a nephew of the master. The ship was valued at 10,000 ducats. We made sail on that day, Sunday the 8th of August, being All Saints."

[176] Sir Clements Markham, ed. *Early Spanish Voyages to the Strait of Magellan.* London, 1911. xii, 288 pp. [Issued by the Hakluyt Society. 2nd Series, no. 28. Reprinted in Nendeln, Liechtenstein: Kraus Reprint, 1967.]

Contains two accounts of interest to Brazilianists: **[175]** Alonso (Veedor), "Narrative of the Events Which Happened in the Fleet of Simon de Alcazaba Who Went Out as Governor of the Province of Leon in the Parts of the South Sea. Having to Pass the Strait of Magellan He Took Two Ships, the *Capitana* called *La Madre de Dios* and the Other Called *San Pedro* in Which were Embarked, Including Passengers and Sailors, 250 Persons," pp. 133–156; and **[233]** Bartolomé Garcia de Nodal and Gonzalo de Nodal, "Narrative of the Voyage Which by Order of His

Majesty and Advice of the Royal Council of the Indies the Captains Bartolomé Garcia de Nodal and Gonzalo de Nodal Brothers and Natives of Pontevedra Undertook for the Discovery of the New Strait of San Vicente and Reconnaissance of that of Magellan," pp. 169–276.

[177] R. G. Marsden, ed. "Voyage of the *Barbara* to Brazil. Anno 1540," *The Navy Miscellany*. London: Navy Record Society Publications, 1912. II, 1–66.

Includes transcripts of the testimony in a piracy hearing of eight of the survivors of the *Barbara* of Dartmouth. Those involved gave a detailed description of their adventures in Brazil and the Spanish West Indies. Soon after leaving England, the crew of the *Barbara*—which included not only Englishmen but about twelve Frenchmen (one of whom was the pilot and several others "spechemen" or interpreters)—seized a Spanish bark from Biscaya as well as a smaller Portuguese vessel. The Englishmen kept the Biscayan bark, putting the Spanish sailors on board the Portuguese ship. Then both the *Barbara* and the Biscayan vessel sailed towards Pernambuco, touching at the island of Fernão de Noronha—"a goodly Ilande, whiche they named Phelippe and Jacobbes Ilande, because ther wer no people inhabityng therin; sayeng that the same Ilande was full of small trees and fowles, where they founde freisshe water. And there dyvers of ther company wente on lande and fette freisshe water for the shypp." George Moone, one of the deponents in the hearing, further reported "frome whiche Iland they sayled to the mayne lande of Brasile where they arryved the iiijth day of Maye nere a place called Potaiewe, and there came to an ancker within half a myle of the mayne lande, where they rod iij or iiij dayes. In whiche tyme they sente the boate withe the specheman and certen wares on lande sondrey tymes, where they spake withe the people of the countrey, and had frome them white hennys and cockes and a grene popyniay. And one tyme they brought a man of that countrey on borde, and an an other tyme ij men, and sent them on land agayne." However, as John Wardall, another witness in the proceedings, added, they were told that "here is no brasell [wood] to get, for we be fallen xl^ty^ leages to lye warde of that place wherethe brasell dothe growe, for the people sayde that they wolde not brynge it so farre unto us." So the voyagers "weyd ther ancker and turned to the estewarde purposying to fetche the countrey where the Brasell wood growethe." According to Wardall, "thethur we came and there ankoryd, and our pilotte with our specheman wente on shore, and dyd speake withe the people; and so doon they dyd come on borde us, and they sayde they wer glad of our comyng and promesed us to have of ther commodyties for our wares gladly, as our specheman tolde us. This doon our master commaunded us withe the captayne and pilotte to goe a shore and there to build an house; and at ther commaundment we so dyd, and caryed wares on lande, and dyd bye and sell with them for cotten; and there we were for the space of xijth dayes, and bought certen cottens in them for our wares. And there came to us a Portyngale and a Frencheman and certen of the same countrey with them by lande, and asked of us whence we were, and we sayd of Englande, and he demaunded us wherefore we dyd enterprise to come there. We answered we came for the trade of merchaundyse as they and other doe with us, etc. And then he commaunded us in his kynges name for to avoyde the countrey, and not to tary therin upon payne of a further dyspleasure to us hereafter ensueing. Then we made hym answer that we wolde not departe for hym for thuttermoste that he coulde do in any weys to us. And upon the sayd answer he departed in a greate fury, and sayd he wolde make us repente the tyme that ever we dyd enterprise do boldely and wolde not avoyde at his commaundemente, and so wente his wey. And we contynued in our trade with the people of the countrey still." Several days later, the crew of the *Barbara* caught the Frenchman mentioned above trying to cut the cables of their ship. Shortly thereafter, "oure specheman and xij[th] moe of the Frenchemen of our company which did use to lye on shore in oure house to make our markettes withe the people of that countrey dyd ron away in that sayd nyght, and caryed withe them all the wares whiche were on lande in our bowthe withe them clene, and had withe them an Englishe man, whiche was our cockswayne." Sixteen members of the *Barbara* followed in pursuit, but the French "besett our company withe people of the countrey, and so in conclusion set uppon them, and dyd slay them all save one man by the councell of the Frencheman and the Portyngale." The Amerindians pressed their attack further. "The same after none there came above a m[11] of the people and sette our bowthe on fyer, we beyng within; in so moche as then they burned all our cotten that we had bought that we saved not a dell of it. Then we fought with them iiij houres by the clocke, and in conclusion we beate them of, but dyvers of our men were hurte." The next day "the people of the countrey returned agaynste us agayne and a greate nomber of them, and dyd shote at us, and beate us of the lande, and wolde not suffer us to lande ther no more. And at that tyme we toke iij of them and brought them on borde with us, and there we dyd ride that daye, and coulde not be suffered to come on lande." The Englishmen then decided to return to England. They loaded everything into the *Barbara* and burnt the Biscayan bark. However, soon after leaving Brazil the *Barbara* sprung a leak and the English were diverted to the Spanish West Indies. Near Santo Domingo they captured a ship from Seville (the *San Barbara*), laden with sugar for its return voyage.

They transferred the cargo from the *Barbara* to the Spanish ship and continued their journey to England. The *Barbara* was abandoned to the Spaniards. Upon their return to Dartmouth, the thirteen able-bodied survivors ("for all the reste was dedde and sycke"), their new ship and cargo were seized by English officials.

[178] Anthony Garrard. "An ancient voyage of M. Robert Reniger and M. Thomas Borey to Brasil in the yeere of our Lord 1540," in Hakluyt, *The Principal Navigations* **[105]**, XI, 25.

According to Anthony Garrard, a merchant of London, "M. Robert Reniger, M. Thomas Borey, and divers other substantial and wealthie marchants of Southampton" often frequented Brazil in the 1540s. See also Hakluyt, *Principall Navigations* **[106]**, p. 521.

[179] Edward Cotton. "A voyage of one Pudsey to Baya in Brasil anno 1542," in Hakluyt, *The Principal Navigations* **[105]**, XI, 25.

Edward Cotton of Southampton reported that "one Pudsey of Southampton, a man of good skill and resolution in marine causes, made a voyage . . . 62 yeeres agoe to Baya de todos los Santos the principall towne of all Brasil, and the seate of the Portugal vice-roy [governor-general] and of the bishop, and that he built a fort not farre distant from that place, in the foresaid yeere 1542."

[180] José Toribio Medina. *The Discovery of the Amazon According to the Account of Friar Gaspar de Carvajal and Other Documents.* Trans. Bertram E. Lee. Ed. H. C. Heaton. New York: American Geographical Society, 1934. xiv, 467 pp.

An English translation of the important account by the Spanish Dominican Fray Gaspar de Carvajal of Francisco de Orellana's voyage of discovery down the Amazon in 1542. Orellana was part of Gonzalo Pizarro's expedition that left Ecuador in February of 1541 and reached the mouth of the Amazon at the end of August, 1542. As they neared the end of their voyage Carvajal reported that they continually passed "by settled country, where we secured a certain amount of food, although only a small amount, because the Indians had carried it off, but we found a few roots which they call "inanes [yams]," [and so we remained alive], for, if we had not found these, we should all have perished from hunger: thus we came out of there very short of supplies. In all these villages the Indians met us without weapons, because they are a very docile people, and they gave us to understand by signs that they had seen Christians [before]. These Indians are at the mouth of the river through which we came out, where we took on water, each one a jarful, and some half an *almud* of roasted maize and others less, and others [supplied themselves] with roots, and in this manner we got ready to navigate by sea wherever fortune might guide us and cast us, because we had no pilot, nor compass, nor navigator's chart of any sort, and we did not even know in what direction or toward what point we ought to head." Carvajal stated that "all the tribes that there are along this river down which we have passed . . . are people of great intelligence and [are] skillful men, according to what we saw and to what they appeared to be from all the tasks which they perform, not only in carving but also in drawing and in painting in all colors, very bright, such that it is a marvelous thing to see. We passed out of the mouth of this river from between two islands, the distance from the one to the other being four leagues measured across the stream, and the whole [width], as we saw farther back, from point to point must be over fifty leagues: it sends out into the sea fresh water for more than twenty-five leagues; it rises and falls six or seven fathoms. We passed out, as I have said on the twenty-sixth of the month of August, on Saint Louis' Day, and we [always] had such good weather that never in our course down the river or on the sea did we have squalls, and that was no small miracle which Our Lord God worked for us." Well-annotated with excellent introductions and explanatory chapters. The appendix contains "Selections from Oviedo's 'Historia de las Indias' Bearing on Orellana's Two Expeditions" (pp. 383–448).

[181] Hans Staden. *The True History of His Captivity. 1557.* Trans. and ed. Malcolm Letts. London: George Routledge & Sons, 1928. xx, 191 pp. There is an earlier English translation by Albert Tootal with annotations by Richard F. Burton. *The Captivity of Hans Stade of Hesse in A.D. 1547–1555 Among the Wild Tribes of Eastern Brazil.* London: Printed for the Hakluyt Society, 1874. xcvi, 169 pp. 1st Series, no. 51. The original German edition was published in 1557.

Hans Staden "of Homberg in Hesse" travelled from Germany to Portugal, where he "obtained employment as a gunner" on a boat "bound for Brazil on a trading voyage." Hans Staden made two voyages to Portuguese America. The first was to Pernambuco. "On the 28th day of January, we sighted a spit of land called Cape de Sanct Augustin. Eight miles farther on we reached the harbour of Prannenbucke (Pernambuco), having been eighty-four days at sea without sighting land. In this place the Portuguese had a settlement called Marin [Olinda]. The commander was named Artokoslio [Duarte Coelho, first lord-proprietor], to whom we delivered our prisoners and some of our cargo, intending to sail away and take in fresh cargo elsewhere." However, "it so happened that the savages who inhabit this place rebelled against the Portuguese who had enslaved them, and the commander besought us for the love of God to occupy a settlement called Garasu, five miles from the harbour of Marin where we lay, which had been attacked by the savages. The people at Marin were powerless to help the settlers, for they feared an attack from the savages. Accordingly we set off to Garasu with forty men from our ship travelling there in a small boat. The settlement lay in an arm of the sea which extended two miles inland. The defenders numbered some ninety Christians under arms. To them might be added thirty Moors and Brazilian slaves, the property of the settlers. The attackers were estimated to number about 8,000; we were closely invested and had only a palisade of rails to protect us." After successfully helping to lift the siege at Iguarrassu, Hans Staden eventually returned to Portugal, arriving at Lisbon about 8 October 1548. On his second voyage, he sailed from San Lucar for America, leaving Spain on 25 April 1549. After visiting the island of Santa Catarina, Hans Staden sailed northward, but was shipwrecked near São Vicente. He and some of his companions "travelled overland to Sancte Vicente where the Portuguese received us kindly and entertained us for a time, after which each one of us began to work to maintain himself." Hans Staden provides an interesting description of São Vicente: "Sancte Vincente is an island and lies close to the mainland. In it are two settlements: the one called in the Portuguese tongue Sancte Vincente, and in the savage tongue Orbioneme: the second settlement is situated some two miles away and is called Uwawa Supe. There are also certain houses in the island called Ingenio where sugar is made. The Portuguese live in the island and are friendly with a Brazilian tribe called Tuppin Ikin. The country of the Tuppin Ikins reaches for eighty miles inland and for about forty miles along the coast. This tribe is encompassed to the north and south by hostile tribes. Those to the south are called Carios **[367]**; those to the north are named Tuppin Imba [Tupinamba] **[375]**. They are also known by their foes as Tawaijar, which is to say enemy. The Portuguese have suffered much injury from these people, and even today they go in fear of them." One day, while hunting in the forest, Hans Staden was captured by some Tupinamba. He wrote that "they took me into the huts where I had to lie in a hammock while the women surrounded me and beat me and pulled at me on all sides, mocking me and offering to eat me. Meanwhile the men had assembled in a hut by themselves, drinking a drink which is known as Kawi, and having their gods, called Tammerka, about them, to whom they sang praises, since these gods, they said, had foretold my capture. I could hear this singing, but for half an hour none of the men came near me, and I was left with the women and children." Hans Staden then describes in great detail his experiences as a captive of the Tupinamba and the customs and cannibalism of those Indians. Finally, in October of 1554, Hans Staden managed to escape aboard a French ship and reached France about 20 February 1555. Part II contains "A True and Brief Account of all that I learnt concerning the trade and manners of the Tuppin Inbas, whose captive I was." It is composed of thirty-six chapters and along with the accounts of his two voyages to Brazil is rightly considered to be a major source for the history of the Tupinamba. Many of Hans Staden's observations were independently confirmed by the Frenchman Jean de Lery **[184]**, who spent two years near Rio de Janeiro, 1556–1558.

[182] Luis L. Dominguez, ed. *The Conquest of the River Plate (1535–1555). I. Voyage of Ulrich Schmidt to the Rivers La Plata and Paraguai. From the Original German Edition, 1567. II. The Commentaries of Alvar Nuñez Cabeza de Vaca. From the Original Spanish Edition, 1555.* London, 1891. xlvi. 282 pp.

Schmidt accompanied the expedition of the Spaniard Don Pedro de Mendoza to the Rio de la Plata. Dominguez argues that "it appears that Schmidt was not enlisted among the soldiers of Mendoza, but came as an employee of the house of Welzer and Niedhart, who owned the vessel which took him." In his account, Schmidt describes in detail the Indians, including the Cariós (Guarani) **[367]**, that he encountered, his visit to the island of Santa Catarina for provisions, and, at the end of his stay in the Plata region, his journey from Asunción to Brazil "with twenty Indians in two canoes." After much travelling, he arrived at the settlement of João Ramalho, a Portuguese exile who had gone native and fathered a large progeny of mestiço offspring. Schmidt observed that "fortunately for us he was not at home, for this place certainly appeared to me to be a robbers' haunt. The said chief was at this time gone to another Christian at Vicenda [São Vicente] in order to make an agreement. Both are (with eight hundred Christians living in the two villages) subjects of the King of Portugal, and the aforesaid Johann Reinmelle [Ramalho] has, according to his own account, lived, ruled, made war, and conquered in India [Brazil] for a period of four hundred (forty) years. Therefore, he may legitimately claim to rule the land for another. And because the Portuguese will not recognise his authority, they wage war. This said Reinmelle can, in one single day, gather around him five thousand Indians, whereas the king is not able to bring two thousand together, so much power and consideration has he got in the country. When we came to the village, the son of the said Reinmelle was there, and he received us very well, though we had to look closer after him than after the Indians." Schmidt eventually continued on "to a little town called S. Vicenda [São Vicente] at twenty-miles distance, where we arrived on July [June] 13th, 1553, St. Anthony's day, and found there a Portuguese ship laden with sugar, Brazil wood and wool, belonging to Erasmus Schetzen. His factor is at Lisbon, and is called Johann von Husen, and he has another factor in Vicenda whose name is Peter Rössel. Messrs. Schetzen and Johann von Hulsen own a good number of villages and sugar factories in that place, where sugar is made all the year round." Schmidt set sail from São Vicente for Lisbon on 24 June 1553. However the ship became disabled and "had to return to land, and came to a seaport named Spiritu Sanctu, situated in Brazil, in India, and belonging to the King of Portugal. There are Christians living in that town with their wives and children, and they make sugar. They also have cotton-wool and Brazilian wood, besides other kinds of wood that are found there. Between S. Vicenda and Spiritu Sanctu there are plenty of whales, which do great harm; for instance, when small ships sail from one port to another (these small ships are anyhow somewhat larger than the greatest ships at home), these whales come forward in troops and fight one another, then they drown the ship, taking it down along with the men."

The Commentaries of Alvar Nunez Cabeza de Vaca describe the adventures of the *adelantado* of the Plata region. Earlier Cabeza de Vaca had explored much of the southern part of what is now the United States. On this expedition, after arriving at the island of Santa Catarina, he travelled overland with part of his expedition to Asunción, leaving the others to go by sea to the Rio de la Plata. The *Commentaries* recount his journey through southern Brazil to Paraguay. The author describes how "in nineteen days they crossed great mountains, cutting roads through forests, to enable the men and the horses to pass, for all the land was uninhabited. And at the end of these nineteen days, having exhausted the provisions which they had carried when they began their march, and having nothing left to eat . . . they discovered the first inhabitants, who are called 'del campo', where they found certain villages of Indians." The author points out that "when the Indians knew of the arrival of the governor and his people, they went out to meet him laden with plenty of provisions, showing great joy at their arrival. The governor received them affably, and besides paying the value of the provisions into the hands of the chiefs, he graciously gave them many shirts and other things, with which they remained satisfied. This is a people and tribe called Guaranis **[317]**; they are cultivators, sowing maize twice in the year, and also cassava. They rear fowls as in our Spain, and geese; keep many parrots in their houses and occupy much land, and the whole are of one language. They eat human flesh, as well that of their Indian enemies as of Christians; they also eat one another. This people is very fond of war, and they seek it; they are very vindictive."

[183] André Thevet. *The New Found Worlde or Antarctike.* London: Thomas Hacket, 1568. 138 l.
[A facsimile edition was published by Theatrum Orbis Terrarum and Da Capo Press, 1971.]

English translation of the French Franciscan friar's *Les Singularitez de la France Antarctique*, published in Paris in 1557. André Thevet accompanied Villegagnon to the region around Rio de Janeiro in 1555. He spends the early part of his account describing the African coast and the Canary, Madeira and Cape Verde islands. There are few details on the French settlement in Brazil. Most of Thevet's attention is devoted to the Amerindians and the flora and fauna of eastern South America. More than a dozen-and-a-half chapters describe the Amerindian. Thevet points out that "these poor people live without Religion, and without Lawe." He enumerates their physical characteristics and discusses their eating and drinking habits. "It is easy to be knowne, that these wilde men of America have no more civilitie in their eating, than in other things, for as they have no lawes to take the good, & to eschue the evil, even so they eat of al kinds of meats at al times and houres, without any other discretion." The Amerindians "live all naked euen as they come out of their mothers wombe, as well men as women without any shame. If you woulde know whether they do it of indigencie, or for the extreme heate, I answere that they may make themselues clothing of cotton as well as to make them beds thereof to rest in. . . . They have this opiniõ, that being naked and without apparell, they are more nimbler and better disposed to all kynde of exercises." Thevet also provides one of the earliest descriptions of tobacco: "They gather this herbe very charely, and dry it within their little cabanes or houses. Their maner to use it, is this, they wrappe a quantitie of this herbe being dry in a leafe of a Palme tree which is very great, & so they make rolles of the length of a cãdle, & than they fire the one end, and receiue the smoke therof by their nose and by their mouthe. They say it is very holesome to clense & consume the superfluous humors of the brain. Moreouer being taken after this sort, it kepeth the parties from hũger & thirst for a time, therefore they use it ordinarily. Also whẽ they haue any secrete talke or coũsel among them selues, they draw this smoke, &

then they speake." The author describes "howe these Barbarous and wilde men put their enimies to death, that they have taken in the warre, and eate them." He discusses diseases, cures, and funeral and burial ceremonies. He describes the Plata and Amazon regions and their inhabitants and concludes with descriptions of Florida, Canada, and the Azores.

[184] Jean de Lery. "Extracts out of the Historie of John Lerius a Frenchman, who lived in Brasill with Mons. Villagagnon, Ann. 1557. and 58," Purchas, *Purchas His Pilgrimes* **[107]**, xvi, 518–579.

The French Calvinist, Jean de Lery, arrived in Brazil in the beginning of March of 1557 and departed on 4 January 1558. He was part of Villegagnon's settlement near Rio de Janeiro. His account, *Historie d'un voyage faict en la Terre du Bresil,* published in 1578, is an important source for the ethnography and natural history of sixteenth-century Brazil. Excerpts, translated into English, were published by Purchas. "Because the Brasil tree is the most famous of all that soile (from whence also that Countrie hath taken the name) especially for the colour which our Dyers make therewith, I will desribe it in this place. This Tree therefore is called by the Barbarians, Araboutan, and equalleth our Oake in height and plentie of Boughes. Some of these are found, the thicknesse whereof containeth full as much as three men can fathome." Lery then describes the brazilwood trade with the Portuguese and the French: "Except the Merchants were holpen by the Inhabitants, they could scarce lade a Ship with that Timber within a yeare, both for the hardnesse, and therefore the difficultie in cutting, and also chiefely, because that Countrie wanteth all labouring Beasts, and therefore it is to be carried upon the shoulders of men. The Barbarians being hired for Garments, Shirts, Cappes, Knives, and other Merchandizes, doe not onely cut, cleave, and make round that Timber, but also laying it upon their bare shoulders, carrie it into the Shippes, and sometime in most cumbersome places, lying three or foure miles distant from the wood to the shoare." As for the wood's quality as a dye, Lery recounted that "one of our men desired to wash our shirts, and unawares, put the ashes of the Brasil wood into the lye, whereby they were so surely died with a red coloure, that although they were washed, they never changed the same, and being so died with that colour, we were to put them on." Lery devotes much of his attention to the customs of the Indians: "They so hate adulterous women, that it lyeth in the Husbands power either to kill the adultresse, or at the least, to put her away with great ignominie and reproach. This surely is true, that they are not very carefull of preserving the chastitie of unmarried women: nay, they easily prostitute them to any man." Lery continues: "I have observed that the younger sort both men and women are not very much given to lust: and I would our Countrey people could moderate themselves aswell in this behalfe. But that I may attribute no more unto them then is meete, I remember, that often in their brawling they used to object this reproach Tyvire, that is, Buggerers, one unto another, whereby we may conjecture, that that hainous and abhominable wickednesse raigneth among them." The French observer also was impressed with the practices surrounding childbirth: "The women great with childe, abstained only from the greater burthens, and performe the other accustomed duties. And surely the women much exceed the men in labour, for the men (save that sometimes in the Morning, never at noone, they place certaine Trees to make Gardens) spend the time in warfare, hunting, fishing, making of woodden Clubs, Bowes, Arrowes, and other things of that kinde. As touching the travell of women; I and another Frenchman lodging in a certaine Village, about midnight heard a great out-cry of a woman, and supposing she had beene surprized by the cruell beast Jan-ouare, we arose, and ran unto her, and found the woman in travell, to whom the Husband performed the office of a Midwife: he receiving the Infant in his armes, cut the navell string asunder with his teethe, but pressed downe the Nose (for they esteeme the beautie of children to consist in the flatnesse of the Nose) the new borne Infant is presently washed, and painted by the Father with colours blacke and red: then, not being wrapped in swadling-clouts at all, it is put into a Cotton hanging beddle. But if it bee a Male childe, the Father will give him a little woodden Sword, a small Bow and little Arrowes, presently after his birth, and lay them in the bedde with the childe. . . . Their nourishment, beside the Mothers Milke, is chewed Meale, and every most tender kinde of meate. The woman lately delivered lieth downe two daies only, or three daies at the most. Afterward putting the little childe in a Cotton Scarffe, shee either goeth to the Garden, or to dispatch her other businesse."

[185] Charles R. Boxer, trans. and ed. *Further Selections from the Tragic History of the Sea, 1559–1565. Narratives of the Shipwrecks of the Portuguese East Indiamen Aquia and Garça (1559), São Paulo (1561) and the Misadventures of the Brazil-ship Santo Antônio (1565).* Cambridge: The Cambridge University Press, 1968. x, 170 pp.
[Published for the Hakluyt Society. 2nd Series. no. 132.]

Translates and discusses the narrative, *Navfragio que passov Iorge Dalbvqverqve Coelho, Capitao & Gouernador de Paranambuco* [*Shipwrech Suffered by Jorge de Albuquerque Coelho, Captain and Governor of Pernam-*

buco] by Alfonso Lusi (pp. 109–159). The first chapter of the *Naufrágio* describes the exploits of Jorge de Albuquerque **[150]** son of Duarte Coelho **[149]**, the first lord-proprietor of Pernambuco. Jorge had returned to Brazil from Portugal with his older brother Duarte Coelho de Albuquerque, the Captaincy's secondlord-proprietor, in "1560, when he was twenty years old" and spent five years fighting rebellious Amerindians and helping restore order in Pernambuco. The remaining chapters of the narrative deal with the maritime adventures Jorge experienced while trying to return to Portugal in 1565. On pages 12 –21 of the introduction, Boxer discusses other aspects of Albuquerque's life as well as problems regarding the authorship of the *Naufrágio*. Upon his brother's death in 1581, Jorge de Albuquerque became the third lord-proprietor of Pernambuco though he never returned again to Brazil, dying in Lisbon in 1601. Based on printed primary and secondary materials. Well documented. There is a bibliography on pp. 158 –164.

[186] Pero de Magalhães [de Gandavo]. *The Histories of Brazil.* 2 v. Trans. John B. Stetson, Jr. New York: The Cortes Society, 1922. 60 pp. plus facsims.; 266 pp.
[Reprinted in one volume by Kraus Reprint Co.]

Contains a facsimile edition of the exceedingly rare *História da Provincia Santa Cruz* (1576) and its translation into English as *The History of the Province of Santa Cruz* plus an English translation of the same author's later manuscript account, "Tratado da Terra do Brazil" ("Treatise on the Land of Brazil"). The *Historia* has been called "the first history of the Portuguese discovery of and settlement in Brazil." *The Histories of Brazil* include a discussion of the little that is known about Pero Magalhães de Gandavo's life, a brief bibliographical history including a description of the known copies of that work, and a literary appreciation. Magalhães de Gandavo himself justified writing an account of the first seven decades of Brazil's history as follows: "Since foreigners held it in higher esteem and know its peculiarities more thoroughly than we . . ., it seems a fitting and necessary thing that our own people should have the same information, especially so that all those who live in poverty in these kingdoms might have no hesitancy in choosing it for their own support; for the land itself is so favourable to all who seek it, that it will give shelter and relief to all, no matter how poor or destitute they may be." He describes the founding of Brazil, some of its chief characteristics, the captaincies and their settlement and colonization, their plants, fruits, animals, reptiles, birds and fish. Magalhães de Gandavo devotes three chapters to a description of the Amerindians of Brazil and discusses Jesuit attempts at converting the natives to Christianity. He concludes with a chapter, "About the Great Riches Which They Expect in the Regions of the *Sertão*." As for the "Treatise," the translator points out that although it "is more succinct than the printed account, it should not be considered lacking in interest, for in it the author refers to some particulars which he omitted in the other." A portrait of the important captaincy of Pernambuco as well as a sample of the author's approach and style is found in chapter II: "The Captaincy of Pernambuco is five leagues from Tamaracá toward the south, in the altitude of eight degrees, and the Captain and Governour is Duarte Coelho Dalbuquerque. There are two towns; the principal one is called Olinda and the other Garassû, which is four leagues inland. There are about a thousand inhabitants in this Captaincy. There are twenty-three sugar mills of which three or four are not yet completed. Some mills function with oxen, and these are called *tripiches* [sic: trapiches]; they make less sugar than the others, but the majority of them in Brazil function with water. Each one of these mills makes three thousand *arrobas* [of sugar] per year. In this Captaincy they make more sugar than in the others, for there are years when they exceed fifty thousand *arrobas*, although the yield is not certain but depends upon the crop and the weather. This is one of the rich districts of Brazil; there are many Indian slaves, which are the principal commodity of the region: here they buy them and take them to all the other Captaincies, because there are more of them and they are cheaper than anywhere else on the coast: there is much brazilwood and cotton, from which the inhabitants are getting rich. The haven where the ships enter is a league from the town of Olinda: they disembark on the beach, and also in a little river which flows right up to the city itself. More ships from Portugal come to this Captaincy each year than to any of the others. There is in the Captaincy a monastery of the Fathers of the Company of Jesus." Stetson has contributed a series of excellent notes—not only to the text, but to the introductory material as well. There are also some valuable illustrations.

[187] Francis Drake. "The famous voyage of Sir Francis Drake into the South sea, and therehence about the whole Globe of the earth, begun in the yeere of our Lord, 1577," in Hakluyt, *The Principal Navigations* **[105]**, XI, 101–133.

On 15 November 1577, Francis Drake and five ships sailed from Plymouth. After coasting along Northwest Africa and visiting the Cape Verde Islands, Drake sailed toward South America. "From the first day of our departure from the Islands of Cape Verde, wee sayled 54. dayes without sight of land, and the first land that we fell with was the coast of Brasil, which we saw the fift of April [1578] in ye height of 33. degrees towards the pole Antarctike, and being discovered at sea by the inhabitants of the countrey, they make upon the coast great fires for a sacrifice (as we learned) to the devils, about which they use conjurations, making heapes of sande and other ceremonies, that when any ship shall goe about to stay upon their coast, not onely sands may be be gathered together in shoalds in every place, but also that stormes and tempests may arise, to the casting away of ships and men, whereof (as it is reported) there have bene divers experiments." On "the seventh day in a mightie great storme both of lightning, rayne and thunder," the ships were dispersed. However, they were reunited at the Cape of Joy "where every ship tooke in some water. Heere we found a good temperature and sweete ayre, a very faire and pleasant countrey with an exceeding fruitfull soyle, where were great store of large and mightie Deere, but we came not to the sight of any people; but traveiling further into the countrey, we perceived the footing of people in the clay-ground, shewing that they were men of great stature. Being returned to our ships, we wayed anchor, and ranne somewhat further, and harboured our selves betweene a rocke and the maine, where by meanes of the rocke that brake the force of the sea, we rid very safe, and upon this rocke we killed for our provision certaine sea-wolves, commonly called with us Seales. From hence we went our course to 36. degrees, and entred the great river of Plate."

[188] Sir Francis Drake. *The World Encompassed.* London: Nicholas Bourne, 1628.
[The best reprint is edited by Sir Richard Carnac Temple. *The World Encompassed and Analogous Contemporary Documents Concerning Sir Francis Drake's Circumnavigation of the World.* London: The Argonaut Press, 1926. lxv, 235 pp.]

Drake's own account of his voyage was first published by his nephew in 1628. It varies slightly from the account found in Hakluyt **[187]**. "Passing thus, in beholding the most excellent works of the eternall God in the Seas, as if we had beene in a garden of pleassure, April 5, we fell with the coast of Brasill, in 31 deg. 30 min., towards the pole Antartick, where the land is lowe neere the sea, but much higher within the countrie, hauing in depth not aboue 12 fathome, 3 leagues off from the shoare, and being descried by the inhabitants, we sawe great and huge fires made by them in sundry places, which order of making fires, though it be vniversal, as well among Christians as heathens, yet it is not likely that many doe vse it to that end which the Brasilians doe: to wit, for a sacrifice to deuills, whereat they intermixe many and diuers ceremonies of coniurations, casting vp great heapes of sand, to this end, that if any ships shall goe about to stay vpon their coasts, their ministring spirits may make wrack of them, whereof the Portugalls by the losse of diuers of their ships, haue had often experience." Drake continued: "In the reports of Magellanes voyage **[171]**, it is said that this people pray to no maner of thing, but liue only according to the instinct of nature; which if it were true, there should seeme to be a wonderfull alteration in them, since that time, being fallen from a simple and naturalll creature to make Gods of Deuills. But I am of the minde, that it was with them then, as now it is, onely they lacked then the like occasion, to put it in practise, which now they haue; for then, they liued as a free people among themselues, but now, are in most miserable bondage and slavery, both in body, goods, wife, and children, and life itselfe to the Portugalls, whose hard and most cruell dealings agasint them forceth them to flie, into the more vnfruitful parts of their owne land, rather there to starue, or at least liue miserably with libertie, then to abide such intollerable bondage as they lay vpon them, using the aforesaid practises with deuills, both for a reuenge against their oppressors and also for a defence, that they haue no further entrance into the country. And supposing indeed that no other had vsed trauell by sea in ships, but their enemies onely, they therefore vsed the same at our comming: notwithstanding, our God made their deuilish intent of none effect; for albeit there lacked not (within the space of our falling with this coast) forcible stormes and tempests, yet did we sustaine no dammage, but onely the seperating of our ships out of sight for a few dayes. Here our Generall [Drake] would haue gone a shore, but we could finde no harbor in many leagues." Temple, in the 1926 edition, includes Nuno da Silva's relation **[191]** as well as that of Edward Cliffe **[193]**. Temple also transcribes an account from Francis Fletcher, Drake's chaplain **[189]** and another by John Cooke **[190]**, a mariner in the *Elizabeth*, one of the expedition's six ships. The editor also includes a report by Sarmiento de Gamboa, regarding Drake's "robberies on the coasts of Chile and Peru." Several years later, Sarmiento de Gamboa would play a role in Brazilian history **[204]**.

[189] Francis Fletcher. "The First Part of the Second Voiage about the World Attempted Continued and Happily Accomplished Within the Tyme of 3 Years by M[r] FFrancis Drake, at her Highness Commaund & His Company Written & Faithfully Layed Downe by FFrancis FFletcher Minister of Christ, & Preacher of the Gospell Adventurer & Traueler in the Same Voyage," in Temple, ed., *The World Encompassed* **[188]**, pp. 87–142.

Francis Fletcher, a gentleman-volunteer as well as chaplain to Sir Francis Drake, initially was impressed with the sight of Brazil: "After so longe but a sweet & pleasant trauaile before remembred by the prouidence of God we chanced & fell in the sight of Brasilia where at the first the land seemed to make vs a faire offer of opertunity to do that wch we had long desyred & now was most necessary for vs that is to trimt our shippes being verry fowle for the land seemed to be verry Pleasant a fare bay & a sandy ground fitt for our Purpose & to incourage the rather som of the poople being in sight did shew themselues verry joyfull to see vs in draweing to stand inward towards their land but the case was quickly altered sweet meates would haue sower sawce & long delights was likely to haue sower gaule & Bitternes. for we had not longer held our way inward but the sight of land was taken from vs & that sodainly wth such a hastynes as if it had been a most deadly fogg wth the palpabel darkenes of Egipt that neuer a shipp could see another in the neck wherof did follow such extreame stormes as heauen & earth had gon togeither & rootes of the Rocks & the bottom of the Sea should haue been discouered & that wch was a signe of a desperat state to vtter distruction wee were vpon a Leeshore & the shoalds increased vpon vs. so that if the Portugall Pilot had not ben apointed of God to do vs Good we had perished without remembrance for he being well acquainted wth the bloudy gouernment of this gouernm^{t} the Portugalls was not ignorant of the state of this part of the countrye & knowing the present danger he presently tryed to returne as we could or els no way but Iminent death wherin though we made all possible speed yet one of our shipps touched wth the shoalds: but by gods providence came cleere away & being cast about to the seas euen against the streames our fleet was so seperated that in many monthes after we came not together againe." Fletcher claimed that the Admiral's pilot, Nuno da Silva **[191]** and **[192]** explained the incident as follows: "When they [the Indians] see anny shipps vpon their coasts the shoare being sandy, they cast the Sand vp into the ayre wherof ariseth sodainly such a hazynes as a most gross & thick fogg that there followeth a Palpable darkenes that the Land cannot be seen no nor the heauens besides this they hurle the sands into heapes. wch as they increase so the shoalds increase in the way of the shipps in the seas to Ground them. & withall such horrible fearefull & intollerable winds, Raines, & stormes that there is no certainty of life one moment of tyme whereof we had present Experience, & had perished if God had not in his Mercy & power prevented the same, by this means did they continually ouerthrow the Portugalls when they cam wth their armies of Men, & theire Armathos that is their huge shipps of Warrs against them. whereof many had ben cast away & non that euer cam in the dance did euer Escape. & they supposing vs to be Portugalls & therefore their deadly enemies being not acquainted wth anny other Poople to frequent their Land but they, did practise against vs as against them."

[190] John Cooke. "John Cooke's Narrative," in Temple, ed. *The World Encompassed* **[188]**, pp. 142–168.

John Cooke, "a mariner in the *Elizabeth,*" one of the five English ships in Francis Drake's **[185]** expedition around the world also described Brazil: "Havynge thus in the begyninge of Februarye put of the Iland of Cape de Verde, we had not the syght agayne of any land vntill the vi of Aprill that we fell with coste of Brazylle. . . . The vij. day, in a myghty greate storme, bothe of lighteninge, rayne, and thundar, we lost the Canter, now named the Xpofere [i.e., Christopher]; but the xj. day aftar, by our Generals greate care and dyspersynge, his ships found hir agayne, by means especially that the mastar coasted always by the shoare and keping it in syght. Here where we found owr Canter, owr Generall named this Cape, Cape Joie: here every shipe toke in some water. Then we wayed ancker and rann somewhat fordar, and harbored ower selvs betwene a rokke and the mayne, where by means of the rokk that brake the foarce of the sea, we ryde very safe. Vpon this rocke we kyld some seyls for owr provysyon, but not very many, for that this place had not the multitude as aftarwards we found. Here were entered the great ryvar of freshe watar called the ryvar of Plat, and ran into 5. 4. and 3. fadome and halfe of freshe watar, where we fild in freshe watar by the ships syde; for that owr Generall could find here no harborowe as he expected, he bare owt agayne to sea."

[191] Nuno da Silva. "The relation of a Voyage made by a Pilot called Nuno da Silva for the Vice-roy of new Spaine, the 20. of May, in the yere of our Lord 1579. in the citie of Mexico, from whence it was sent to the Vice-roy of the Portugall-Indies: wherein is set downe the course and actions passed in the Voyage of Sir Francis Drake that tooke the aforesayd Nuno da Silva at S. Iago one of the Islands of Cabo Verde, and caried him along with him through the Streights of Magellan, to the Haven of Guatulco in new Spaine, where he let him goe againe," in Hakluyt, *The Principal Navigations* **[105]**, XI, 133–147.

Interesting account by the Portuguese pilot who was forced to accompany Francis Drake along the coast of Brazil and around the coast of South America. Drake freed him off the coast of Mexico, whereupon Nuno da Silva was taken into custody by Spanish authorities. Silva describes his early adventures as follows: "Nuno da Silva borne in Porto, a Citizen and inhabitant of Guaia [Gaia], saith, that hee departed out of his house in the beginning of November in the yeere of our Lord 1577, taking his course to Cabo Verde, or The greene Cape, where he anchored with his Shippe close by the Haven of the Island of Sant Iago, one of the Islandes of Cabo Verde aforesayde, beeing the nineteenth of January in the yeere of our Lord 1578. And lying there, there came sixe ships, which seemed to be Englishmen, whereof the Admirall boorded his ship, and by force with his men tooke him out of his ship, bringing him in the boate aboord the Admirals shippe, leaving some of his best men aboord his ship. . . . And Nuno da Silva saith, the cause why they kept him on boord was, because they knew him to bee a pilot for the coast of Brasilia, that hee might bring them to such places in those countryes as had fresh water." Nuno da Silva reported that "being put off from the Island of Brava, they helde their course to the land of Brasilia, which they descried upon the first of Aprill, under the height of thirtie degrees: and without landing or taking in fresh water, they helde on their course to Rio de la Plata, that is, The river of silver, lying under five and thirtie degrees, little more or lesse: where they went on land, and provided themselves of fresh water."

[192] Zelia Nuttall, ed. *New Light on Drake. A Collection of Documents Relating to His Voyage of Circum Navigation, 1577–1580.* London: Printed for the Hakluyt Society, 1914. lvi, 443 pp.

This volume contains many documents from Spanish archives on Drake's voyage around the world. Zelia Nuttall has translated them and provided excellent introductions and notes. Of chief interest to students of Luso-Brazilian history are the materials on Nuno da Silva, the Portuguese pilot seized by Drake. It was Silva who guided the English along the coast of Brazil. Included is the sworn deposition of Nuno da Silva before the Tribunal of the Inquisition of Mexico on 23 May 1579. "Nuno da Silva, Portuguese pilot, married, citizen of the town of Gaia, in the district of the city of Oporto, and a native of Lisbon, son of Alvaro Joanez, seaman, and of Joan da Silva, his wife, was brought up by the latter until he had reached the age of eight years, after which his uncle Adan Fernandez, a pilot, took him to Brazil. The deponent remained in his uncle's company and made voyages in vessels belonging to the Armada of the King of Portugal until he reached the age of twenty years, when his uncle died. The deponent continued to navigate between Portugal and Brazil, first as a sailor, then as a pilot, and finally as captain and pilot combined, of merchant vessels. In the month of November of the past year of 1577, he sailed from the said city of Oporto as pilot of a vessel bound for the Island of La Palma to fetch a cargo of wines destined for Brazil. Having loaded his ship he continued his voyage to Cape Verde Island; and, as he was about to enter the port to fetch water, an English Corsair [Drake] with six ships of his company and one which he had taken, and which he afterwards abandoned, sallied forth to meet him and seized his vessel [on the 20th of January, 1578]. Taking the deponent's ship and all her crew to the Island of Brava, twelve leagues distant from Cape Verde, the Corsair landed the men there but kept with him the vessel laden with wine and other merchandise, leaving the deponent on board with forty or fifty Englishmen." Nuno da Silva's description of Brazil differed substantially from those of Drake **[187]**, **[188]**, Fletcher **[189]** and Cooke **[190]**: "Navigating towards Brazil and reaching its coast in a latitude of 13 degs. the Corsair did not dare take water for fear of the galleys which are usually there, and therefore waited until reaching the river of La Plata which is in 35 degs." Nuno da Silva was accused of heresy and he confessed that he "had twice partaken of Communion according to the English mode of administering it." Nuttall also includes other documents relating to Nuno da Silva after he was released.

[193] Edward Cliffe. "The voyage of M. John Winter in the South sea by the Streight of Magellan, in consort with M. Francis Drake, begun in the yeere 1577. By which Streight also he returned safely into England the second of June 1579. contrary to the false reports of the Spaniards which gave out, that the said passage was not repasseable: Written by Edward Cliffe Mariner," in Hakluyt, *The Principal Navigations* **[105]**, XI, 148–162.

Edward Cliffe, a seaman aboard the *Elizabeth*, "of 80 tunnes in burthen" commanded by John Winter and one of the five ships in the Drake expedition, gives the latitude as 31° 30′ (Drake's account **[187]** gave it as 33°) when Brazil was sighted on 5 April 1578. The expedition passed through the Straits of Magellan "into the South sea the 6 of September." But in late September and early October the *Elizabeth* became separated from the remaining ships. John Winter and his crew then returned through the Straits of Magellan and on 11 November sailed northeast for the Plata river, in the vicinity of which they built a pinnace, took on water, "and afterward departed the first of Januarie 1579, and ran towards the North till the 20 of the said moneth, and then we arrived at an island which lieth on the coast of Brasil, neere to a towne called sant Vincent inhabited by the Portugals." The Englishmen got caught in a bad storm and lost their pinnace and eight men in it. The *Elizabeth* was also in danger, though it finally "ran into a place called Tanay, where we roade under an island and tooke in wood and water." Cliffe reported that while they "stayed there, there came 3 Portugals aboord us in a canoa, to knowe what wee would have, or of what countrey we were. To whom our Captaine made answere: that we were Englishmen, and had brought commodities for their countrey, if they would trafficke with us: whereat they greatly marveiled. For they saide that they never heard of any English ship to have bene in that countrey before; and so they went to land againe, having one of our men with them to speake with the Governour of the towne, and we kept one of them for a pledge. Shortly after there came another canoa aboord us with one Portugal and al the rest naked men of the countrey: of whom wee had two small Oxen, one yong Hogge, with certaine hennes: also Pome-cytrons, limons, oranges, and other fruites of the countrey. For the which our Captaine gave to them linnen cloth, combes, knives, and other trifles. In the meane time the Governour of the towne sent word that we should have nothing, unlesse we would bring our shippe into the haven. Whereunto our Captaine would in no case consent: for all their practise was to have gotten us within their danger, nevertheles we came somewhat neere the towne with our ship, as though wee would have gone in; but we never meant it. Here we tooke in our man; and set the Portugal pledge on land. After that we went to an iland called the isle of Sant Sebastian; where wee tooke fish. Here the Portugals betrayed us, if a Brazilian one of their slaves had not bene. For he store from them, & shewed unto us by signes, that the Portugals were comming with their canoas to take us, as it fell out in deed: for the next morning they shewed themselves with 12 or 16 canoas, some of them having 40 men in them. The same night two of our men ran away with our boat to the Portugals. And thus we came away from thence toward our owne countrey the 17 of March [of 1579]: and had sight of the Cape of sant Augustine, lying in 8 degrees to the Southward of the line. After that we had sight of an island lying within 3 degrees of the Equinoctial, called the isle of Fernando de Loronha."

[194] Peter Carder. "The Relation of Peter Carder of Saint Verian in Cornwall, within seven miles of Falmouth, which went with Sir Francis [Drake] in his Voyage about the World, begun 1577. who with seven others in an open Pinnasse or Shallop of five tuns, with eight Oares, was separated from his Generall by foule weather in the South Sea, in October, An[no] 1578. who returning by the Straites of Magellan toward Brazill, were all cast away, save this one only afore named, who came into England nine years after miraculously, having escaped many strange dangers, aswell among divers Savages as Christians," in Purchas, *Purchas His Pilgrimes* **[107]**, XVI, 136–146.

Carder gives the reader an interesting account of his lengthy encounters with the Tupinamba: "Here I staied among them (being well entertained) for certaine moneths, untill I had learned most part of their language, in which meane space I noted their manners, which were as followeth. They went out to the warres armed at my first comming, onely with Bowes and Arrowes, some three or foure hundred at a time, and when they had the victory of their enemies, they tied one of their Captives to one of their company with Cotten cords fast arme to arme, and bringing them home, within two or three daies after they would tie them to a poast, and with a massie club of red wood one of the strongest of the company (after they have drunke a certaine strong drinke with dancing round about him) at one blow slits his head a sunder." In one battle, two hundred of the enemy were killed and twenty taken prisoner. The Amerindian "King . . . caused many of thir carkases to be broyled upon the coals and eaten. . . . Those twenty prisoners which we brought home were afterward killed, rosted and eaten." Carder pointed out that "the chiefest riches which we found here was their drinke which they used to make themselves drunke withall; their Cotten Beddes and their Tobacco. As for Gold and Silver they neither seeke, nor make any accompt thereof." The Englishman eventually made his way to Bahia where he was befriended by "one Antonio de Pa[i]va in the towne which could speake good English, and was a lover of our Nation, and brought me directly unto his house." The author spent several years in Bahia, "in which meane space, first I spent part of my time in going into the fields as overseer of my friends Negros and Savages in their planting and dressing of their Sugar Canes, and in planting of Gingers, which grow there exceeding well, but is a forbidden trade to be transported out for hindering of other places, and in cutting downe of Brasil-wood, and in bringing it downe by Rivers upon rafts unto the Port where the Ships doe lade it, and in seeing them gather their Cotten wooll, and picking the seedes out of it, and packing the same, and in gathering of the long Pepper both white and red." Carder continued: "After I had spent, some yeare and an halfe in this businesse, my friend Antonio de Payve having a small Barke of his owne, which he employed in carrying of wares from Port to Port, and for bringing of Sugars to places where Ships should lade, used me, knowing I had bin brought up to the Sea, in these his businesses. Our first Voyage was to Ilheos, where we left some wares and staied there some monteh; then we went to Puerto Seguro, and there tooke in some Sugars for Linnen Cloth, Bayes, Wine and Oyle. Then returning home, shortly after we were set forth againe in the same Barke to Spirito Sancto and Saint Vincent, and the River Jenero, where discharging our wares to certaine Factors, and receiving Sugars and Cotten Wooll aboord, we returned safely home." Eventually Antonio da Paiva helped him escape to Pernambuco, where he eventually boarded a ship for England, arriving "in the haven of Chichister, in the end of November 1586. nine yeares and foureteene dayes after my departure out of England with Sir Francis Drake in his Voyage about the World."

[195] John Whithall. "A letter written to M. Richard Stapers by John Whithall from Brasil, in Santos, the 26 of June 1578," in Hakluyt, *Principall Navigations* **[106]**, pp. 638–641.

Interesting letter from John Whithall, known in Santos as João Leitão. Whithall agreed to marry the daughter of "Signior Iosso Dore," a Genoese living in Brazil. The author boasted that Dore "hath but onely this childe which is his daughter, which he hath thought better bestowed upon me then on any Portingall in all the country, and doth give with her in marriage to me part of an Ingenio which he hath, that doth make every yeere a thousand roues of suger. This my marriage will be woorth to me two thousand duckets, little more or lesse. Also Signior Iosso Dore my father in law doth intend to put into my handes the whole Ingenio with sixtie or seventie slaves, and thereof to make me factor for us both. I give my living Lord thanks for placing me in such honor and plentifulnesse of all things." John Whithall also reported that the provedor and the captain of São Vicente "have certified me few dayes past, that they have discovered certaine mines of silver and golde." They also welcomed "a shippe with goods to come from London hither." The author sent a lengthy list of products that should be sent to Santos and promised that "this voyage is as good as any Peru voyage." The letter is followed by "A copie of the letters of the Adventurers for Brasil sent to John Whithall dwelling in Santos, by the Minion of London. Anno 1580 the 24 of October in London" (pp. 640–641). In addition to the goods requested by Whithall, the merchants sent "as many other things as we thought might any wayes pleasure you, or profit the country." They also reported: "We have sent you copper cauldrons for your engenios with iron, and all other necessaries for your purpose, and artificers to set the same: and as we have at your request beene at great charges in sending these men, so we pray you let us have lawfull favor in like courtesie to favor all our causes. And if any of our mariners or passengers should in any respect of displeasure against their company, or in hope of preferment of mariage or otherwise, would procure to tary and dwell there, and leave his charge or office, that they you will be a meane to the justice that such fugitives should be sent aboord the shippe as prisoners: for as you know, without our men we can not bring home our shippe." See also Hakluyt, *The Principal Navigations* **[105]**, XI, 26–33.

[196] Anonymous. “A ruttier or course to be kept for him that will sayle from Cabo Verde to the coast of Brasil, and all along the coast of Brasil unto the river of Plate: and namely first from Cabo Verde to Fernambuck,” in Hakluyt, *The Principal Navigations* **[105]**, XI, pp. 73–85.

This interesting rutter is followed by another giving instructions for sailing from Pernambuco to Bahia (pp. 75–77). It, in turn, is followed by another rutter describing the coast from Bahia de Todos os Santos to the Bahia das Ilhas (pp. 77–79). Directions are also given for sailing from Bahia das Ilhas to Porto Seguro (pp. 79–80) and from there to the Bahia do Espirito Santo (pp. 80–82). These are followed by “The course from the bay de Spirito Santo to the bay of S. Vincent, and the markes thereof. Also the course from Saint Vincent to the river of Plate” (pp. 82–85).

[197] Anonymous. “A very exact and perfect description of the distances from place to place, from the river of Plate, till you come to Pette Guaras, northward, and beginning againe at the river of Plate, till you come to the ende of the Streights of Magellan, Southwards, with the degrees of latitude, wherein every place standeth,” in Hakluyt, *Principall Navigations* **[106]**, pp. 803–808.

Brazil from the Rio de la Plata to just north of Paraiba is covered on pp. 803–806. A sample of the descriptions include the island of Santa Catarina in what is now southern Brazil. It “is a great Island of 8 Or 9 leagues long, which Island lieth north, and South: and on the East side, it hath no roade, but one small Island, which lieth at the south ende, and another at the north ende, called the Island of Arburetso, which sheweth as a great Baye, going in between S. Katherins Island, and the maine: in which Baye you may come to an anker, and there are many small Islands: and the northern ende of S. Katherins Island stands in 28 degrees.” Further northward, São Vicente “stands in 23 degrees, 30 minuts, and hath a small Island in the mouth, bearing west, northwest off you, and is called the Hennes gissard.” Rio de Janeiro is described thusly: “The river of Genero stands in 23 degrees and riseth with high hils, and one of the hils sheweth like the toppe of a shippe, and hath in the mouth many small Islands, and a high pinnacle on the West side, and is called the suger loafe.” Much further along the coast is Porto Seguro which “hath great red cliffs which stand at the foote of the towne.” Bahia de Todos os Santos was distinguished by its white sand, while “the marke of Fernambucke is the Towne it selfe [Olinda], standing upon a high hil by the water side.”

[198] Anonymous. "A ruttier which declareth the situation of the coast of Brasil from the Isle of Santa Catelina unto the mouth of the river of Plata, and all along up within the sayd river, and what armes and mouthes it hath to enter into it, as farre as it is navigable with small barks," in Hakluyt, *The Principal Navigations* **[105]**, XI, 96–101.

Contains a good description of the coast of southern Brazil: "From the Isle of Santa Catelina (which is on 28 degrees of Southerly latitude) unto Rio Grande is fortie leagues. This river by another name is called Ygai. The Island of Santa Catelina is sixe leagues in length: It hath two small Ilands on the North side betweene the maine land and it: and on the South side it hath a shoald of rockes, which lyeth hidden very neere unto the poynt of the Isle. You are to passe betweene the firme land and the poynt of the Isle." Further south, "from Santa Catelina to the haven of Biaza, which by another name is called la Laguna, are twelve leagues: it is a good haven within: but you must stay the full sea to enter it, because it hath shoaldes in the mouth, and it may be knowen by a small Island which lyeth a league into the sea which is called La Isla de Raparo, that is The Island of succour or defence, and you must ride there to search the chanell." From Laguna to the Rio de la Plata "there is no haven for a ship to harbour it selfe. And Rio Grande hath many shoalds in the mouth thereof. It is a river that none but very small shippes can enter into. And this river divideth the countrey of the people called Carios **[367]** from other nations which are called Guaves. And from this river unto the entrance of the mouth of the river of Plate it is al a plaine land, and very low: you must saile all along two or three leagues into the sea from the shore, untill you come to certaine Islands which lye twelve leagues from the mouth of the river of Plate. From Rio Grande unto these Islands are 68 leagues."

C. Spanish Domination, 1580–1640 [Nos. 199–236]

The years 1580–1640 spanned the period during which the three Spanish Philips (II, III, and IV) were also kings of Portugal. Thomas Grigges **[199]** mentions the Spanish invasion of Portugal in his account of the *Minion*'s trading adventures in Santos. Luke Ward **[200]** provides a cautious account of the misadventures of Captain Edward Fenton in

Brazil. E. G. R. Taylor **[201]** fills in much that is omitted by Ward and includes 82 documents on the voyage. Elizabeth Story Donno **[202]** publishes the entire diary of Richard Madox, Fenton's chaplain. Portions of the diary had been published by Taylor. Clements Markham **[203]** includes part of the journal of William Hawkins, another participant on the voyage. Edward Fenton did not have a monopoly on misadventures. Pedro Sarmiento de Gamboa **[204]** encountered problem after problem—many in Brazil—on his expedition to the Straits of Magellan. The encounter of part of the Sarmiento expedition with that of Fenton is briefly discussed both by Markham **[204]** and by Lopez Vaz **[205]**. Not all English voyages to Brazil—for example, that of the Edward Cotton **[206]**—reached their destination. The Jesuit Fernão Cardim **[207]** gives a good account of the Indians in Brazil in the early 1580s. Francis Pretty **[208]** relates how Thomas Cavendish briefly visited Brazil on his trip around the world, 1586–1588. Thomas Fuller **[209]** who accompanied Cavendish, left a brief description of the Brazilian coast. Lopez Vaz **[210]** also provides a picture of Brazil in the 1580s. John Sarracoll **[211]** describes the Withrington and Lister attack on Bahia in 1587. William Magoths **[212]** gives an account of an English privateering voyage along the coast of Brazil. Magoths's relation is annotated and discussed by Kenneth R. Andrews **[213]**. E. G. Ravenstein **[214]** has edited the adventures of Andrew Battell, who was part of Abraham Cocke's expedition to the Plata region in 1589. John Jane **[215]** and Thomas Cavendish himself **[216]** describe Cavendish's last voyage and his experiences in Brazil. A definitive edition of the Cavendish narrative has been edited by David Beers Quinn **[217]**. Another member of the Cavendish expedition was Anthony Knivet, who was left for dead on the island of São Sebastião and captured by the Portuguese. An account of his adventures is found in **[218]**. Richard Hawkins **[219]** visited Espirito Santo toward the end of 1593. He also left a description of coastal Brazil. The two contemporary accounts of James Lancaster's capture and sack of Recife **[221]** and **[222]** have been reprinted and annotated by Sir William Foster **[223]**. Francisco Soares **[224]** describes Brazil's trade with Potosí in 1596. Feliciano Coelho de Carvalho **[225]**, governor of Paraiba, relates many of the problems the Portuguese were encountering in his captaincy and that of Rio Grande do Norte during the late 1590s. Thomas Turner **[226]**, who resided in Pernambuco during the latter part of the same decade, mentions Brazilian Indians and African slaves in his relation. The works and voyages of John Davis, a participant in Cavendish's last voyage to Brazil, are found in **[227]**. Later, he twice visited the island of Fernão de Noronha. Though he never visited Brazil, Jan Huygen van Linschoten **[228]** was well acquainted with many who did. Most of his description of Brazil focuses on the Amerindians. Robert Harcourt's relation of his voyage to Guiana is found in **[229]** and **[230]**. William Davies **[231]** describes the Amazon region, where he spent ten weeks in 1608. François Pyrard of Laval **[232]** visited Bahia for more than two months on his return to Europe from Asia. Bartolomé Garcia de Nodal and Gonzalo de Nodal **[233]** left a description of their visit to Rio de Janeiro in 1618. The following year after exploring the Straits of Magellan they stopped briefly in Pernambuco. The struggle of the Guarani Indians and the Jesuits against the marauding "Mameluco" *bandeirantes* from São Paulo is described by the Belgian Jesuit Nicholas del Techo **[234]**. The Jesuit Cristóval de Acuña **[235]** travelled down the Amazon from Quito with Pedro Teixeira **[636]** in 1639. His account of the Amazon was first published in 1641. There is a good translation and commentary on Acuña's journey in Markham's *Expeditions into the Valley of the Amazons, 1539, 1540, 1639* **[236]**.

[199] Thomas Grigges. "Certaine notes of the voyage to Brazil with the Minion of London aforesaid, in the yere 1580. written by Thomas Grigs Purser of the said ship," in Hakluyt, *The Principal Navigations* **[105]**, XI, 34–39.

In response to the letter of John Whithall **[195]**, a ship, the *Minion* of London, sailed to Brazill. "The first land that wee fell with upon the coast of Brasill was the yland of S. Sebastian, where we arrived on the 14. day of January in the yeere 1581. The 16. day Thomas Babington, and others in our pinnesse, went a shoare to Guaybea, where they met with John Whithall his father and mother in lawe, who having received letters from thence to be delivered at Santos came abord, and then we weyed and set saile, and the 28. day wee arrived at the yland of Santa Catelina [not to be confused with the island of Santa Catarina further south], near the entrance of Santos." On 18 February, "the captaine of Santos came abord our ship, by whom we had knowledge of foure great French ships of warre, that had bene at the river of Jenero [Rio de Janeiro], which there tooke three Canoas, but were driven from thence by their castles & forts, and were looked for here at Santos. Whereupon the Captaine requested us to lend them some armour and artillery, and we lent them twentie calivers, and two barrels of powder." On 23 February, "the Captaine and Justices of Santos wished us to tary in their road till the last of April, for they had sent a barke of Santos to Baya at the kings charges, to know whether we should have trade there or no, and this barke could not returne before that time. About this time there arrived at Fernambuck a shippe from Portugall, which brought newes that the Islands, Indies, and Portugall it selfe was molested and troubled by the Spaniards, and that the Portugales had both English and

Frenchmen to Lisbone to defend them against Spaine." Almost two months later, on 22 April, "our Master and Thomas Babington having some talke and conference with the Padres of Santos, they (our men being ready to go to the River of Jenero) tolde them, that they were sorry for our banishment from the Church, and that the Ministrador [*Administrador*] had written from Rio de Jenero, that forasmuch as these twentie yeres or more the English nation had denied the Church of Rome and her proceedings, therefore the Ministrador commanded that none of us should come to their Church: the Padres willed us herein to have patience, and to take it in good part, and promised to stand our friends in their word and writing, both to the Ministrador and to the Bishop of Baya, and further requested all our English company to have no ill opinion of them. The 28. of April we laded sugars into our ships. . . . The 10. day of June wee gratified one Iosto Thorno, dwelling in Santos, with some of our English victuals, and intertained him in good sort in our ship."

[200] Luke Ward. "The Voyage intended towards China, wherein M. Edward Fenton was appointed Generall: Written by M. Luke Ward his Viceadmiral, and Captaine of the Edward Bonaventure, begun Anno Dom. 1582," in Hakluyt, *The Principal Navigations* **[105]**, XI, pp. 172–202.

Originally destined for the East Indies, this expedition was aptly described by Luke Ward as "a troublesome voyage." After trading in Africa, Fenton set sail for Brazil and arrived near the island of Santa Catarina in December of 1582. The English planned to sail to Peru in search of Spanish treasure, but after taking a Spanish prize they learned "that the Spanish fleet was before the streights of Magellan." Fenton then decided to sail northward to São Vicente and trade there. He arrived off São Vicente on 19 January 1583. "The 20 day in the morning, being calme, the generals pinnesse came in to the shore, with intent to sound the entrance, but seeing three canoas, with ech at the least twenty men, whereof the greater part were naked Indians, which rowed, the rest Portugals, they returned aboord again. The canoas came with a flag of truce within, calling of our ship, and we shewed them the like, asking what we were, and of what nation: at length one Portugall went aboord the admirall by whom the generall sent a letter to the governour, craving a pilot to bring in our ship of courtesie, and to have traffique." Fenton anchored until the bar could be sounded. "The 21 day about three a clocke afternoone, came a canoa, with the old Genouois named Josephy Dory, a Fleming named Paul Badeves, and Steven Repose a Portugall, and brought a letter from the governor, and withall, answere of feare and doubts of us &c. After many speeches and requests a banket was made them, and the generall in his pinnesse with his musicke, & trumpets; and I in my skiffe with trumpets, drum and fife, and tabor and pipe, accompanied them a mile up the river: at going off, we saluted them with a volley of three great pieces out of ech ship." On the 22nd of January, Fenton and his advisers decided to give presents of cloth to the governor and the three Europeans mentioned above. But the governor was, at least for the moment, "unwilling to speake with them." After much deliberation, the English decided to sail on, Fenton giving "the three cloake-clothes, to Joseph Dory, to Paulo Baudevese, and to Steven Repose, to ech of them one, which were before cut out for them: and so friendly we and they departed about two a clocke after noone." Later that same afternoon Fenton encountered three Spanish ships of the Sarmiento de Gamboa expedition **[204]** and a battle ensued. According to Ward's account, Fenton then sailed along the Brazilian coast past the island of Fernão de Noronha northward to England where he arrived at the end of May of 1583. The original instructions (which were not followed) are reprinted on pp. 163–171.

[201] E. G. R. Taylor, ed. *The Troublesome Voyage of Captain Edward Fenton, 1582–1583*. Cambridge: At the University Press, 1959. lvii, 333 p.
[Issued by the Hakluyt Society. Second Series, no. 113.]

Fills in much that is missing from Luke Ward's account **[200]** and is essential for understanding the English expedition to Brazil in 1582–1583. There is an excellent introduction by Taylor, who provides a brief but useful sketch of what transpired in Santa Catarina, Santos and São Vicente. She also discusses the many letters of marque given Englishmen by Dom António, pretender to the Portuguese throne. There are 82 documents, many previously unpublished. Among the latter is the official narrative of Richard Madox, one of the two chaplains on the expedition and registrar, about one-fourth of his valuable private diary, the sea journal of Edward Fenton in the Galleon *Leicester*, and a translation of a Portuguese sea manual containing information on the coast of Brazil. Also included are excerpts from the official Portuguese inquiry held at São Vicente on 8–9 February 1583. Andrés de Aquino, leader of the three Spanish ships that attacked Fenton's expedition off São Vicente, described the ships as "two English corsair galleons of great strength who had occupied the [port] and terrorized the inhabitants with their threats." Witnesses included Braz Cubas, *alcaide-mor* of Santos, Simão Machado, governor of Santo Amaro, João Baptista Malio, overseer of a sugar plantation, and three other royal officials of the colony. Though their testimony is not included, the questions they were asked are reprinted. In addition, there is some interesting correspondence regarding the Fenton expedition from the Spanish ambassador to England, Bernardino de Mendoza.

[202] Elizabeth Story Donno, ed. *An Elizabethan in 1582. The Diary of Richard Madox, Fellow of All Souls.* London: The Hakluyt Society, 1976. xvi, 365 pp.
[Issued by the Hakluyt Society. Second Series, no. 147.]

Includes the entire diary and the register of Richard Madox, chaplain and registrar of the Galleon *Leicester*, and the diary of John Walker, chaplain and registrar of the *Edward Bonaventure*, both part of Edward Fenton's expedition of 1582–1583 **[200]** and **[201]**. Elizabeth Story Donno provides a useful introduction and includes an account of the activities of the Fenton expedition in Brazil and raises questions not discussed in Taylor's introduction **[201]**.

[203] William Hawkins. "Journal of the Voyage under Captain Fenton (1582) kept by William Hawkins," in Markham, ed., *The Hawkins Voyages* **[220]**, pp. 353–363.

This document (unfortunately much mutilated by fire) contains useful information on the Captain Edward Fenton expedition **[200]**, **[201]**, **[202]**, **[204]**, and **[205]**. Hawkins gives a good description of what happened at Espirito Santo on the return to England after the episode at São Vicente. The English arrived at Espirito Santo on 22 February and sailed on 5 March.

[204] Clements R. Markham, ed. *Narratives of the Voyages of Pedro Sarmiento de Gamboa to the Straits of Magellan.* London, 1895. xxx, 401 pp.
[Issued by the Hakluyt Society. 1st series, no. 91. Reprinted. New York: Lenox Hill (Burt Franklin), 1970.]

Markham translates five accounts, the most important for Brazilianists being the "Concise Narrative by Pedro Sarmiento de Gamboa, Governor and Captain-General of the Strait of the Mother of God, formerly called the Strait of Magellan, and of the settlements made and which may be made for his Majesty," written in December of 1589. Sarmiento de Gamboa, "one of the most eminent Spanish scientific navigators of the sixteenth century," was leader of the ill-starred expedition sent to build forts and set up a colony at the entrance of the straits of Magellan. This contingent spent March to November of 1582 in Rio de Janeiro. Though Sarmiento de Gamboa held the post of Governor and Captain General, Diego Flores de Valdes was "General of the Sea." Both men clashed continually during the expedition, each blaming the other for the many mishaps that occurred. Many of the Spaniards became ill during the voyage: "The Governor [of Rio de Janeiro], Salvador Correa, and the citizens of the town, being extremely poor, did what they could, but Diego Flores never gave any more, not even ordinary rations for healthy men, so that 150 died, and others, seeing this, deserted. Pedro Sarmiento, seeing the danger at hand, arranged that the settlers should be lodged in the houses of the inhabitants of the land, where they were cared for and cured, and not more than four died." While the expedition was wintering in Rio, a great deal of pilfering took place. "It was a cause for sorrow and regret to see the thousand ways in which the provisions, stores, and munitions, as well as fittings of the fleet were robbed and wasted, and the materials for construction of fortifications and houses, down to needles and thread." These goods were then sold "to the inhabitants of the city of Rio de Janeiro and of San Vicente, and afterwards at Bahia. . . . Many other things, such as wire, iron and steel, and clothing, were exchanged for Brazil wood to take to Spain and sell." Sarmiento de Gamboa further charged that Diego Flores and other officials divided among themselves "the money paid by the Portuguese." In fact, the expedition's "Treasurer set up a tent like a pedlar, with the cloth, canvas, wine, old and new stores, iron and steel tools. . . . Thus men who had not a real, got plenty at Rio de Janeiro, and were possessed of sugar and other merchandise to take to Spain." What corruption failed to dissipate, the climate did. "During this wintering at Rio de Janeiro all the ships were attacked by worms and bored, receiving notable harm and deterioration, except those of your Majesty, which had their bottoms covered with lead. For the great heat, with the mud and swampy ground, creates these worms, and boils the wood, cordage and nails of the ships. So that, at the time of departure, the greater part was reduced to cinder. Even the iron was rotten to such an extent that it could be ground with the hand, an unheard of thing. Thus what was worked with hoes, spades, or adzes came to pieces in the hands like paper, and at the least blow fell in bits on the ground." To make matters worse, "the ships being ready to start on the voyage for the Strait, many of the masters and captains secretly loaded their ships, during the night, with Brazil wood, which is as heavy as iron and very bad for the vessels, as it breaks them and pulls them to pieces. They put so much on board that the ships were very low, and in order to put the Brazil wood under hatches, a quantity of the stores for the Strait were left on the deck, and exposed to be lost, as happened, in the first heavy weather. I considered, as one acquainted with the sea and zealous for the service of God and the King, that these proceedings were most harmful, and that it might be concluded from them that, the first time the wind blew from the south, these captains would make sail for Spain without stopping in Brazil, to sell their dye wood." Sarmiento de Gamboa describes the experiences of the expedition at Santa Catarina, the failure of part of the expedition to enter the Straits of Magellan, and the return to Brazil. At São Vicente, several of the Spanish ships encountered Edward Fenton's expedition **[200]**, **[201]**, **[202]**, **[203]**, and **[205]**. Sarmiento de Gamboa also visited Pernambuco, Salvador, and Espírito Santo, before being captured by the English near the Azores on the return home.

[205] Lopez Vaz. "An extract out of the discourse of one Lopez Vaz a Portugal, touching the fight of M. Fenton **[201]** with the Spanish ships, with a report of the proceeding of M. John Drake after his departing from him to the river of Plate," in Hakluyt, *The Principal Navigations* **[105]**, XI, 92–95.

The author briefly describes the expedition of Pedro Sarmiento de Gamboa **[204]** to the Straits of Magellan and the encounter of part of the fleet with English ships captained by Edward Fenton. "This fleete because it was late, did winter on the coast of Brasil, in the river of Jenero." Later, after sailing southward and staying at the island of Santa Catarina, Diego Flores, who was in charge of naval operations, "founde a barke wherein were some fryers going for the river of Plate: which friers told him of two great English ships, and a pinnesse, which had taken them, but tooke nothing from them, nor did them any harme, but onely asked them for the king of Spaines ships. Hereupon Diego Flores knowing that these English ships would goe for the Streits, determined to go thither, although it was in the moneth of Februarie, and choosing 10 ships of the 15 that were left, hee left two ships which were not in case to goe to sea at the Island, and into the other three ships which were old, and shaken with the storme hee put all the women and sicke men in all the fleete, and sent them to the river of Jenero, and he with the other 10 returned again for the Streits. The three ships in which the sicke men and women were, went to Brasil, and there they found within the port of S. Vincent the ships before mentioned [of Captain Edward Fenton]. They would have had the English men to have gone out of the harbour, and thereupon they fell to fight, and because that these three ships were weake with the storme, and the men that they had were the worst in all the fleete, the Englishmen easily put them to the worst, and sunke one of them, and might have sunke another, if the Englishmen would. . . . So the Englishmen went from this port to Spirito Santo, where they had victuals for their merchandise, and so they went backe for England, without doing of any harme in the Countrey."

[206] Edward Cotton. "Certaine remembrances of an intended voyage to Brasill, and the River of Plate, by the Edward Cotton, a ship of 260 Tunnes of Master Edward Cotton of Southhampton, which perished through extreme negligence neare Rio grande in Guinie, the 17 of July 1583," in Hakluyt, *The Principal Navigations* **[105]**, VI, 408–412.

The *Edward Cotton*, "with 83 men of all sortes furnished, and fully appointed for the voyage, began to set saile from Hurst Castle upon Friday the 20 of May, Anno 1583." The account includes the agreement between Edward Cotton, owner of the ship and its cargo, and the captain, lieutenant, pilot and merchant aboard the vessel. The latter are instructed "to make their first port at Santos and Saint Vincent, and there to revictuall and traffike, and from thence to the River of Plate to make their voyage by the traine, and hide of the seales, with such other commodities as are there to be had." In a postscript, Cotton went into greater detail: "At your comming to the Isle of Saint Sebastian, upon the coast of Brasill, you shall according to your discretions, make sale of such commodities, as you may thinke will be thereabout well vented, and likewise to buy commodities without making longer stay there then your victuals be providing, but rather to bespeake commodities against your returne from the river of Plate, especially of Amber, Sugar, Greene ginger, Cotton wooll, and some quantitie of the peppers of the countrey there. Also for Parats and Munkies, and the beast called Serrabosa. Also you shall barrell up of the beefe called Petune, two or three barrels, and to lose no good oportunitie, to gather of the Indian figges, and the graines of them to preserve drie, in such quantitie as conveniently may be done: and touching the making of the traine, and the preserving of the hides, I leave it wholly to the order and the discretion of the chiefe of the companie." The *Edward Cotton* never reached Brazil, being shipwrecked off the Guinea coast in July of 1583.

[207] Fernão Cardim. "A Treatise of Brasil, written by a Portugal which had long lived there," Purchas, *Purchas His Pilgrimes* **[107]**, XVI, 417–517.

This is a translation of the Jesuit Padre Fernão Cardim's "Do clima e terra do Brasil" and "Do principio e origem dos indios do Brasil," stolen from him by the English when they seized his ship as he was returning to Brazil from Rome in 1601. Cardim first arrived in Brazil in 1583 and died there in 1625. The account translated into English and published by Samuel Purchas was probably written in 1584. "The Climate of Brasill generally is temperate, of good, delicate and healthfull aire, where the men live on even to 90. 100. and more yeeres, and the Countrie is full of old men. Generally it is neither cold nor hot, though from the River of Januarie, unto Saint Vincent, there be colds and heates, but not very great." As for the dietary habits of the Indians, Cardim writes: "The ordinary food of this Country that serveth for Bread, is called Mandioca, and they are certaine roots like Carrots, though they are greater and longer: these shoot out certaine stemmes or branches, and growed to the height of fiteene spannes. These branches are very tender, and have a white pith within, and at every spanne it hath certaine joynts, and of this bignesse they are broken, and set in the ground as much as is sufficient for to held them up and within sixe or nine moths have so big rootes that they serve for food. This Mandioca contayneth many kindes in it selfe, and all are eaten, and they are preserved under the earth three, foure, or unto eight yeeres, and needs no seasoning, for they doe no more but take them out and make fresh meate every day, and the longer they are under the earth the bigger they grow and yeeld the more. . . . Of these rootes crushed and grated they make a Meale that is eaten, it is also layd in steepe till it corrupt, and then cleansed and crushed, they make also a Flowere, and certaine Cakes like children very white and delicate. This roote after it is steeped in water, made in balls with the hands, they set it upon hurdles at the smoake, where it drieth in such manner that it is kept without corrupting as long as they list, and after scraped and stamped in certaine great trayes, and sifted, there remayneth a Flowre whiter then of Wheate, of the which being mingled in a certaine quantitie with the raw, they make a certaine Bisquet, which they call Of the warre, and it serveth the Indians and the Portugals by Sea, and when they goe to Warre, as Bisket. Another Bisket bread is made of very water of the greene Mandioca, if they let it congeale, and dry it at the Sunne, or at the fire: this is above all most white, and so pleasant and delicate, that it is not made for every one. Of this Mandioca dryed at the smoake they make many sorts of broaths, which they call Mingaos, so healthfull and delicate that they give them to them that are sicke of a Feaver, in stead of Caudles and Restoratives, and of the same they make Cakes, Simnels, Frutters, little Pyes, Cheef-cakes of Sugar &c. And mingled with the flowre of Milet, or of Rice, they make leavened bread, that it seemeth of Wheat. This same Mandioca dryed at the smoake, is a great remedie against poison, chiefly of Snakes." Fish were plentiful in Brazil. In addition, "because this coast is full of many Bayes, Nookes, and Creekes, there came great store of Whales to these Concaves chiefly from May to September, when they spawne and bring up their young, and also because they come to the great store of fish that at this time there is in these Creekes. They are sometime so many that ye may see fortie or fiftie together, men doe say that they doe cast the Amber that they find in the Sea, and whereof they also feed, and therefore is some of it found in this Coast. . . . It is very dangerous to saile in small Barkes along this Coast, for besides other dangers, the Whales overwhelme many."

[208] Francis Pretty. "The admirable and prosperous voyage of the Worshipfull Master Thomas Candish [Cavendish] of Trimley in the Countie of Suffolke Esquire, into the South sea, and from thence round about the circumference of the whole earth, begun in the yeere of our Lord 1586 and finished 1588. Written by Master Francis Pretty lately of Ey in Suffolke, a Gentleman employed in the same action," in Hakluyt, *The Principal Navigations* **[105]**, XI, 290–347.

Thomas Cavendish and three ships sailed from Plymouth on 21 July 1586. "The last of October running West Southwest about 24. leagues from Cape Frio in Brasile, we fell with a great mountaine which had an high round knoppe on the top of it standing from it like a towne with two little Ilands from it. The first of November wee went in betweene the Iland of Saint Sebastian and the mayne land, and had our things on shore, and set up a Forge, and had our caske on shore: our coopers made hoopes, and so we remayned there untill the 23. day of the same moneth: in which time we fitted our things, built our Pinnesse, and filled our fresh water. And while our Pinnesse was in building, there came a Canoa from the river of Jenero, meaning to goe to S. Vincent, wherein were sixe naked slaves of the Countrey people, which did rowe the Canoa, and one Portugal. And the Portugal knewe Christopher Hare Master of the Admirall, for that Master Hare had bene at Saint Vincent in the Minion of London in the yeere 1581. And thinking to have John Whithall **[195]** the Englishman which dwelleth at Saint Vincent come unto us, which is twentie leagues from this Harborough with some other, thereby to have had some fresh victuals, we suffered the Portugal to goe with a letter unto him, who promised to returne or send some answere within ten dayes, for that we told him we were Marchants, and would traffique with them: but we never received answere from him any more; and seeing that he came not according to appoyntment, our businesse being dispatched wee weyed anchor, and set sayle from S. Sebastian on the 23. of November."

[209] Thomas Fuller. "Certaine rare and special notes most properly belonging to the voyage of M. Thomas Candish [Cavendish] next before described **[206]**; concerning the heights, sounding, lyings of lands, distances of places, the variation of the Compasse, the just length of time spent in sayling betweene divers places, and their abode in them, as also the places of their harbour and anckering, and the depths of the same, with the observation of the windes on severall coastes: Written by M. Thomas Fuller of Ipswich, who was Master in the desire of M. Thomas Candish in his foresaid prosperous voyage about the world," in Hakluyt, *The Principal Navigations* **[105]**, XI, 348–381.

Includes "A note of the heights of certaine places from the coast of Brasill to the South sea" and "Soundings on the coast of Brasil." Fuller also describes the visit he made to Brazil with Cavendish: "Wee departed from the coast of Guinea for the coast of Brasil the 10 day of September, and wee had sight of the coast of Brasil the 26 day of October, being sixe leagues to the Northwards of Cape Frio: and from thence wee were sailing unto the iland of S. Sebastian untill the 31 and last day of October, where wee watered and set up our pinnesse: and we ankered on the Northwest part of the iland in tenne fadoms, and stayed there untill the 23 day of November." Fuller also provides "A note of our finding of the winds for the most part of our voyage 1586."

[210] Lopez Vaz. "A discourse of the West Indies and South sea written by Lopez Vaz a Portugal, borne in the citie of Elvas, continued unto the yere 1587. Wherein among divers rare things not hitherto delivered by any other writer, certaine voyages of our Englishmen are truely reported: which was intercepted with the author thereof at the river of Plate, by Captaine Withrington and Captaine Christopher Lister, in the fleete set foorth by the right Honrable the Erle of Cumberland for the South sea in the yeere 1586," in Hakluyt, *The Principal Navigations* **[105]**, XI, 227–290.

The first third of this account deals mostly with the Spanish Indies and includes an account of early efforts to explore the river of Marannon [Amazon]. The author then spends about five pages describing Brazil: "All the coast betweene the saide river and the river of Plate, is called The coast of Brasill, taking that name from a kinde of wood in the same countrey, called Brasill-wood, whereof there is great store in those partes. This coast of Brasill was first discovered by Pedro Alvarez Cabral **[163]** and **[164]**, in the second voyage which the king of Portugall caused to be made to the East Indies: and the foresayde Pedro Alvarez tooke possession of this land for the king of Portugall: whereupon the king Don Emanuel hearing newes thereof sent presently shippes to discover the whole countrey, and found it to be part of America otherwise called The West Indies: for which cause there grewe some controversie betweene him and the king of Spaine: but being kinsmen and great friends to one another, they agreed in the end, that the king of Portugall should holde all the countrey that he had discovered, the which was (as I have said) from the river of Marannon to the river of Plate; albeit the Spaniards affirme, that it stretcheth no further then the Iland of Santa Catelina; whereupon there have risen many controversies betweene the Portugales and Spaniardes, which have cost many men their lives." In 1587, the Englishman Christopher Lister and his men "found the king of Portugales armes graven on a rocke by the sea side [of the Rio de la Plata]; which are thought to have beene there engraven by one Martin Alonso de Souza, who was sent by the king Don Emanuel [sic] to discover this coast. Therefore I thinke the Portugales have reason for that which they alleage concerning the extension of the said coast of Brazil. Wherfore the king of Portugal gave this land to diverse of his gentlemen to inhabite. Most of the naturall inhabitants of this countrey are very rude, and goe starke naked both men and women, and are maneaters; for which cause they make warres one against another to get men to eate; they are stout and good bow-men. The first place inhabited on this coast beyonde the river of Marannon is called Fernambuck so named by the Indians, but in Portugall it is called Villa de Olinda. Before you come to this place there is a port called Parajua [Paraiba], unto which port not many yeeres past the Frenchmen hearing of the troubles which were then in Portugall resorted, and built there a fort; whereunto certaine French ships made yeerely voyages to lade Brasill-wood. But they of Fernambuc, with the helpe of the Spaniardes, went and burnt five French shippes within the port, and tooke the fort it selfe, and the Frenchmen that were there fled part into the mountaines, and part of them were slaine; so that since that time the Spaniardes have inhabited there till this present. Nowe to returne to Fernambuck inhabited by a Portugall Captaine called Duarte Coelio, it is the greatest towne in all that coast, and hath above three thousand houses in it, with seventie Ingenios for sugar, and great store of Brasill-wood and abundance of cotton, yet are they in great want of victuals: for all their victuals come either from Portugall or from some places upon the coast of Brasill. The harbour of this towne is a barred harbour, and fit onely for small barkes: this place belongeth as yet unto the sonne of Duarte Coelio. Beyond this towne lyeth the Cape of Sant Augustin, and next thereunto is the river of Sant Francisco, which is a great river. Betweene this river and Baya it is all a wildernesse inhabited with cruell salvages, for whomsoever they take they kill and eate him. The towne of Bayha belongeth to the king, and therefore the governour of all the coast keepeth his residence in the same, as also the bishop. It containeth 1000 houses, & 40 Ingenios for sugar, and hath much cotton, but no Brasill-wood at all . . .. The next towne upon the coast called As Ilhas [Ilheus], or The Iles, is but a small towne, containing not above 150 houses, and but three Ingenios for sugar. Most of the inhabitants are labouring men, which use to carry victuals in their small barkes unto Fernambuck: their Lord is called Lucas Giraldo. The next place unto this is called Puerto Seguro: it consisteth of 4 small townes, which containe not in all above 300 houses. The inhabitants of this towne also live by carrying of victuals along the coast; and the towne it selfe belongeth to the Duke de Avero . . .. The next habitation of Christains beyond these sholdes [de Abrolhos] is Espirito Santo which consisteth of two townes, both of them contayining about 300 houses: and they belong to a gentleman called Vasques Fernandes de Coutinho. From hence you passe along the coast to the river of Jenero, which hath about three hundred houses . . .. There are at this present onely two Ingenios, but great store of Brasill-wood, with plentie of victuals. From this river of Jenero they passe along the coast to Sant Vincente, which hath 4 townes, the greatest whereof is called Santos, and consisteth of foure hundred houses, there are also three Ingenios . . .. This countrey belongeth to a Gentleman called Martin Alonso de Souze: this is the last inhabited place upon all the coast of Brasill. This coast of Brasill is very full of mountaines and hath much raines falling upon it, for which cause they cannot goe from towne to towne by land; all the habitations of this countrey are by the sea side. From Sant Vincente the coast is all mountainous, till you come to the Ile of Santa Catelina, and from this Iland till you come even to the straights of Magellan, the coast is very plaine and without woods."

[211] John Sarracoll. "The voyage set out by the right honourable the Earle of Cumberland, in the yere 1586. intended for The South Sea, but performed no farther than the latitude of 44. degrees to the South of the Equinoctial, Written by M. John Sarracoll marchant in the same voyage," in Hakluyt, *The Principal Navigations* **[105]**, XI, 202–227.

This is the account of the voyage of Robert Withrington and his vice-admiral, Christopher Lister, and their attack on Bahia. Withrington and Lister left England in August of 1586. After visiting the African coast, they set sail for the Straits of Magellan. Short of the Rio de la Plata, they took a Portuguese ship "wherein there was for Master or Pilote an Englishman called Abraham Cocke **[214]** borne in Lee." The ship had "sugar, rice, Marmalade, and Sucket. . . . They had abord also 45. Negros, whereof every one in Peru yeeldeth 400 duckets a piece, and besides these, there were as passngers in her, two Portugal women and a childe." The next day they took the first ship's consort. In this ship, beside a "good store of sugar, Marmalade, and Succats," there were also "about 35. Negro women, and foure or five friers, of which one was an Irish man, of the age of three or foure and twentie yeeres, and two Portugal women also, which were borne in the river of Jenero. Both these ships were bought in Brasil, by a yong man which was Factor for the bishop of Tucaman, and the friers were sent for by that bishop to possesse a new Monasterie, which the bishop was then a building. The bookes, beads, and pictures in her, cost (as one of the Portugals confessed) above 1000. duckats." Several weeks later the leaders of the expedition decided that it would be "good for the wealth of our voyage, the health of our men, and safetie of our ships, to goe roome with the coast of Brasill, where by Gods grace wee shall well victuall our selves, both with wine which is our greatest want, and other necessaries. Beside, it is given us here to understand by the Portugals which we have taken, that there is no doubt but that by Gods helpe and our endevour, wee shall bee able to take the towne of Baya, at our pleasure." Sarracoll describes in detail the unsuccessful efforts of Withrington, Lister and their forces to capture Bahia. Though the English failed to seize the Brazilian capital, they were able to kill a number of Brazilians and destroy a sugar plantation. Sarracoll reported that on 16 May 1587 "we went to certaine Ingenios of Portugals, where we found the people fled and we entered their houses without resistance. We found in their purging house 1000 pots of sugar, some halfe purged, some a quarter, and some newly put into the pots: so that every man tooke his pot of sugar for their provision, and set all the rest on fire." Withrington and Lister finally sailed northward with plans to attack Pernambuco. But they overshot that captaincy and arrived in England at the end of September of 1587.

[212] William Magoths. "A briefe relation of a voyage of The Delight a ship of Bristoll one of the consorts of M. John Chidley esquire and M. Paul Wheele, made unto the Straight of Magellan: with divers accidents that happened unto the company, during their 6. weeks abode there: Begun in the yeere 1589. Written by W. Magoths," in Hakluyt, *The Principal Navigations* **[105]**, XI, 381–389.

On 5 August 1589 John Chidley and three ships sailed from Plymouth for Chile. Less than two weeks after departure, the *Delight*, captained by Andrew Merick, became separated from Chidley's ship but "constantly kept our course according to our directions along the coast of Brasil, and by the River of Plate, without touching any where on land untill we came to Port desire in the latitude of 48 degrees to the

Southward of the Equinoctial." The voyage was plagued with difficulties and after spending "6. weeks in the Streight striving against the furie of the elements, and having at sundry times partly by casualtie, and partly by sickness lost 38. of our best men, and 3. anckers, and nowe having but one ancker left us, and small store of victuals," the *Delight* left the Straits of Magellan. The Englishmen "returned backe [home] againe by The river of Plate; and sailing neere the coast of Brasill we met with a Portugal ship of 80. tunnes, which rode at an ancker upon the coast, who as soone as she descried us to chase her, incontinently weyed, & ran her selfe on ground betweene the yland of S. Sebastian and the maine land. But we for want of a good boat, and by reason of the foule weather, were neither able to bord her, nor to goe on shore. Thence in extreeme misery we shaped our course for the yles of Cape Verde, and so passing to the yles of The Azores, the Canaries being something out of our course." Finally, after landing at "Monville de Hage eight miles to the west of Cherbourg in Normandie," the author and three survivors made it to England. Two other survivors, including "Gabriel Valerosa a Portugal," remained in France. See also Andrews, ed., *English Privateering Voyages* **[213]**, pp. 65–71.

[213] Kenneth R. Andrews, ed. *English Privateering Voyages to the West Indies 1588–1595. Documents Relating to English Voyages to the West Indies from the Defeat of the Armada to the Last Voyage of Sir Francis Drake, Including Spanish Documents Contributed by Irene A. Wright.* Cambridge: At the University Press, 1959. xxvii, 421 pp.

As the title indicates, most of the material deals with the Caribbean. However, Andrews (pp. 65–71) includes and annotates William Magoths's account of John Chidley's voyage of 1589, first published in Hakluyt's *The Principal Navigations* **[105]**. In chapter III, Andrews also provides some background material for better understanding Magoths's narrative. In other parts of this annotated collection of documents there are scattered references to Englishmen involved in James Lancaster's Pernambucan expedition of 1594–1595 **[221]**, **[222]**, and **[223]**.

[214] Andrew Battell. *The Strange Adventures of Andrew Battell of Leigh, In Angola and the Adjoining Regions.* Ed. E. G. Ravenstein. London, 1901. xx, 210 pp.

Though Andrew Battell is more famous for his account of the two decades he spent in Angola and his description of life in West Africa, 1590–1610, he also provides some useful information about Brazil, 1589–1590. Battell was part of the 1589 expedition of Abraham Cocke of Limehouse to the Rio de la Plata. After some adversities in the vicinity of the mainland town of São Tome, located on the Gulf of Guinea, and the island of the same name, the author sailed to Brazil: "And running along the coast of Brasil till we came to Ilha Grande, which standeth in five [sic] degrees southward of the line, we put in betwixt the island and the main, and hauled our ships on shore, and washed them, and refreshed ourselves, and took in fresh water. In this island are no inhabitants, but it is very fruitful. And being here some twelve days there came in a little pinnace which was bound to the River of Plate, which came in to water and to get some refreshments: and presently we went aboard and took the Portugal merchant out of the pinnace, which told Abraham Cocke, that within two months there should two pinnaces come from the River of Plate, from the town of Buenos Aires. From this town there come every year four or five caravels to Bahia in Brasil, and to Angola in Africa, which bring great store of treasure which is transported overland out of Peru into the River of Plate. . . . This Portugal merchant carried us to a place in this island, where there was a banished man, which had planted great store of plantains, and told us that we might, with this fruit, go to the River of Plate: for our bread and our victuals were almost all spent." However, after arriving in the Plata region, they ran short of supplies. "Discomforted for lack of victuals," they sailed "northward again, to the isle of Sant Sebastian, lying just under the tropic of Capricorn. There we went on shore to catch fish, and some went up into the woods to gather fruit, for we were all in a manner famished. There was at that time a canoe fraught with Indians, that came from the town of Spiritu Sancto. These Indians landed on the west side of the island, and came through the woods and took five of us, and carried us to the River of Janeiro [Rio de Janeiro]. After this mischance our captain, Abraham Cocke, went to sea, and was never heard of more. When we that were taken and remained four months in the River of Janeiro, I and one Torner [Thomas Turner] were sent to Angola in Africa, to the city of Saint Paul."

[215] John Jane. "The last voyage of the worshipfull M. Thomas Candish [Cavendish] esquire, intended for the South sea, the Philippinas, and the coast of China, with 3 tall ships, and two barks: Written by M. John Jane, a man of good observation, imployed in the same, and many other voyages," in Hakluyt, *The Principal Navigations* **[105]**, XI, 389–416.

On 26 August 1591, Thomas Cavendish and five ships sailed from Plymouth: "The 29. of November wee fell with the bay of Salvador upon the coast of Brasil 12 leagues on this side Cabo Frio, where wee were becalmed untill the second of December: at which time wee tooke a small barke bound for the River of Plate with sugar, haberdash wares, and Negroes. The Master of this barke brought us unto an yle called Placencia [Ilha Grande] thirtie leagues West from Cabo Frio, where wee arrived the fift of December, and rifled sixe or seven houses inhabited by Portugales. The 11. wee departed from this place, and the fourteenth we arrived at the yle of S. Sebastian: from whence M. Cocke and Captaine Davis presently departed with The Desire and the blacke pinnesse, for the taking of the towne of Santos. The 15. at evening we anckered at the barre of Santos, from whence we departed with our boates to the towne; and the next morning about nine of the clocke wee came to Santos, where being discovered, wee were inforced to land with 24. gentlemen our long boat being farre a sterne, by which expedition wee tooke all the people of the towne at Masse both men and women, whom wee kept all that day in the Church as prisoners. The cause why master Candish desired to take this towne was to supply his great wants: For being in Santos, and having it in quiet possession, wee stood in assurance to supply all our needes in great abundance. But such was the negligence of our governour master Cocke, that the Indians were suffered to carry out of the towne whatsoever they would in open viewe, and no man did controll them: and the next day after wee had wonne the towne, our prisoners were all set at libertie, onely foure poore olde men were kept as pawnes to supply our wants. Thus in three days the towne that was able to furnish such another Fleete with all kinde of necessaries, was left unto us nakedly bare, without people and provision. Eight or tenne days after master Candish himselfe came thither, where hee remained until the 22. of January, seeking by intreatie to have that. whereof we were once possessed. But in conclusion wee departed out of the towne through extreeme want of victuall, not being able any longer to live there, and were glad to receive a fewe canisters or baskets of Cassavi meale; so that in every condition wee went worse furnished from the towne, then when wee came unto it. The 22. of January we departed from Santos, and burnt Sant Vincent to the ground. The 24. we set saile, shaping our course for the Streights of Magellan."

[216] Thomas Cavendish. "Master Thomas Candish his discourse of his fatall and disastrous voyage towards the South Sea, with his many disadventures in the Magellan Straits and other places; written with his owne hand to Sir Tristam Gorges his Executor," in Purchas, *Purchas His Pilgrimes* **[107]**, XVI, 151–177.

Recounts his last voyage to Brazil with an emphasis on the period after he had occupied and sacked Santos and burned São Vicente. Cavendish continued on toward the Straits of Magellan in order to embark on his Pacific voyage. However, he and his expedition were forced to spend "almost foure moneths betweene the coast of Brasile, and the Straights; being in distance not above sixe hundred leagues, which is commonly run in twentie or thirtie dayes: but such was the adversenesse of our fortunes, that in comming thither wee spent the Summer, and found in the Straits, the beginning of a most extreame Winter, not durable for Christians." Eventually they returned to Brazil for provisions. At first they "came to an anchor in the Bay of Saint Vincent, and being at an anchor there, the Gentlemen desired mee to give them leave to goe ashoare, to some of the Portugals Farme-houses, to get some fresh victuals, which I granted. . . . They went to a Sugar mill hard by mee where I rode (for that was my speciall charge, that they should never goe a mile from the ship) where they got some victuall, and came aboard againe very well." However, they were not as fortunate on their next foraging expedition. Cavendish reported that twenty-five men "were slaine with three hundred Indians, and eightie Portugals, which (in the evening) set upon them suddently." To avenge this he sailed northward to Espirito Santo, hoping to capture and plunder the town. However, he was unsuccessful.

[217] David Beers Quinn, ed. *The Last Voyage of Thomas Cavendish, 1591–1592*. Chicago and London: The University of Chicago Press, 1975. xi, 165 pp.

This is the definitive edition of the narrative **[216]** published in Purchas **[107]** and is based on the autograph manuscript of Cavendish's own account of the voyage. Thomas Cavendish was the third leader of a voyage to circumnavigate the world. This expedition was an attempt to do it a second time. As Quinn points out, the aim of the voyage was "plunder, trade, and discovery in that order but not necessarily with that emphasis." Thomas Cavendish arrived at Ilha Grande (or Placentia) on 5 December 1591 and attacked and occupied Santos from 16 December to 24 January 1592 when São Vicente was burned. He then left for the south Pacific but never was able to pass through the Straits of Magellan. He returned to Brazil and again attempted to raid São Vicente. Later he tried—unsuccessfully—to attack the town of Espirito Santo. He then sailed for St. Helena, but died "either in late October or more likely in November" of 1592. An excellent introduction (pp. 1–46), a reproduction of Cavendish's map of the South Atlantic (1588), and a chronological guide and track chart of Cavendish's last voyage accompany this facsimile edition. The introduction has 68 notes.

[218] Anthony Knivet. "The admirable adventures and strange fortunes of Master Antonie Knivet, which went with Master Thomas Candish in his second voyage to the South Sea. 1591," in Purchas, *Purchas His Pilgrimes* **[107]**, XVI, 177–289.

Anthony Knivet was a member of Thomas Cavendish's **[216]** and **[217]** expedition which sacked Santos in 1591. Knivet was left for dead on the Island of São Sebastião and captured by the Portuguese. He was brought into Rio de Janeiro and given to the man who had found him. Knivet spent eight years in Brazil and left a detailed account of his experiences. Though there are inconsistencies, exaggerations, and inaccuracies in his story, the narrative is generally considered to be reliable. He tried to escape from the Portuguese on several occasions, was recaptured and placed in servitude. Knivet lived among the Indians and provides detailed information regarding many of the tribes along the Brazilian coast. He accompanied Salvador Correia de Sá to Pernambuco and helped Feliciano Coelho **[225]** fight the Potiguar in Rio Grande do Norte. Earlier, he helped fight the warring Indians at Espirito Santo—"a kinde of Caniball, called Tomomynos; these are men of good stature, I have gone to warre against them, many times with the Portugals, at a place called Morogege; they had many Townes in the Ilands that stand in the River of Paraeva [Paraíba]; their Townes were all setled with great stones set together like pales, of a good height, & within that there are walls made of clay and stone, their houses are long all covered with the barks of trees, and the side of their houses are like hurdles made of Canes, in such sort that they may shoot out of them. We were at least five hundred Portugals, and three thousand Indians, in the siege against the City of Morogege, and many times the Tomomynos did set upon us with such violent force, that wee thought we should all have been slaine there, we were forced to settle our selves under a walk made with stone, clay, and logs, sending for succour to Spirito Santo. The Indians Tomomynos would stand upon the wall of their Citie, all decked with feathers, and their bodies all painted black and red, most ugly to be seene, with things in their hands like a wheele, all done with feathers, the which they would set on fire, and wave it about their heads, crying out to the Portugals, Lovas eyave pomombana, that is to say, Even as this you shall be consumed. After the fresh men came from Spirito Santo, they began to feare, and to steale out of the Towne. But when we saw that, we made things that the Portugal called Panesses (they are made of Canes, of seven or eight yars long, that no arrow can passe them) and those the Portugals and Indians that were on our side did carie before them like a wall, and so came to the wall of their Citie and brake it downe, with hurt and death of many on our side. Here our Captaine Martin de Sasa [Sá] was cast into the River by a Caniball, that tooke him in his armes, and in despight of us all carried him a stones cast, and threw him into the River, where he had beene drowned if it had not beene for a very famous Indian, called Patammycu, which was the same Martin de Sasa his slave. This Patammycu (that is to say, Long Tobacco, for the Indians take such names) killed the Caniball that would have drowned his Master and so saved him. That day wee had the victorie, and tooke 16000. of them, of the which wee put to the sword 1600. and all the rest we parted among the Portugals. After that, we tooke many small Townes, killing all the old men and old women, likewise we parted the rest that were serviceable, and so wee returned home."

[219] Richard Hawkins. *The Observations of Sir Richard Hawkins Knight, in His Voiage into the South Sea. Anno Domini 1593.* London: Iohn Iaggaard, 1622. [There are numerous reprints.]

Hawkins set sail from England in April of 1593. After visiting the coast of Africa and the Cape Verde Islands he arrived off Cape Santo Agostinho on 18 October of that year. By the end of the month he had reached the Bay of Espirito Santo and the port of Nossa Senhora de Victoria—a landmark that "is easie to be knowne, for it hath a great high hill over the port, which (howsoever a man commeth with the land) riseth like a bell." To refresh his sick sailors, Hawkins sought to trade with the Portuguese at Espirito Santo. The governor reported "that in consideration of the warre betwixt Spaine and England he had expresse order from his king not to suffer any English to trade within his jurisdiction, no, nor to land, or to take any refreshing upon the shore. And therefore craved pardon, and that wee should take this for a resolute answere: and further required us to depart the port within three days, which he said he gave us for our courteous manner of proceeding." Hawkins purchased "two or three hundreth oranges and lemmons, and some fewe hennes." He described Espirito Santo as follows: "Entering the port, within a quarter of a mile is a small village, and three leagues higher up is the chief towne; where they have two forts, one on eyther side of the harbour, and within them ride the ships which come thither to discharge, or loade. In the small village is ever a garrison of one hundreth souldiers, whereof part assist there continually, and in the white tower upon the top of the hill, which commaundeth it." Hawkins was impressed by the Brazilian Indians and their military prowess when allied to the Portuguese. He described Rio de Janeiro as having "a very good harbour, fortified with a garrison, and a place well peopled." He found Ilha Grande to be "some eight or ten leagues long, and causeth a goodly harbour for shipping. It is full of great sandie bayes, and in the most of them is store of good water; within this iland are many other smaller ilands, which cause divers sounds and creekes; and amongst these little ilands, one, for the pleasant scituation and fertilities thereof, called Placentia [Ilha Grande]. This is peopled, all the rest desert." Santa Catarina, the other important island off the southern coast of Brazil, "is a reasonable harbour, and hath good refreshing of wood, water, and fruit. It is desolate, and serveth for those who trade from Brasill to the river of Plate, or from the river to Brasill, as an inne, or bayting place." Hawkins concluded his description of Brazil by pointing out that "the commodities this country yeeldeth, are the wood called Brasill, whereof the best is that of Farnambuc (so also called, being used in most rich colours); good cotton-wooll, great store of sugar, balsamon, and liquid amber. They have want of all maner of cloth, lynnen, and woolen, of iron, and edge-tools, of copper, and principally in some places, of wax, of wine, of oyle, and meale (for the countrey beareth no corn), and of all maner of haberdashery-wares for the Indians."

[220] Clements R. Markham, ed. *The Hawkins Voyages during the Reigns of Henry VIII, Queen Elizabeth, and James I.* London: Printed for the Hakluyt Society, 1878. lii, 453 pp. [Issued by the Hakluyt Society. 1st Series, no. 57. Reprinted. New York: Burt Franklin, 1970.]

Useful collection that contains much of value for students of colonial Brazil. Of special interest are: **[174]** "The Voyage of Williams Hawkins in 1530," pp. 3–5; **[219]** "The Observations of Sir Richard Hawkins, Kt, in his voyage into the South Sea, A.D. 1593," pp. 83–329; and **[203]** "Journal of the Voyage under Captain Fenton (1582) kept by William Hawkins," pp. 353–363.

[221] James Lancaster. "The well governed and prosperous voyage of M. James Lancaster, begun with three ships and a galley-frigat from London in October 1594, and intended for Fernambuck, the port-towne of Olinda in Brasil. In which voyage (besides the taking of nine and twenty ships and frigats) he surprized the sayd port-towne, being strongly fortified and manned; and held possession thereof thirty dayes together (notwithstanding many bolde assaults of the enemy both by land and water) and also providently defeated their dangerous and almost inevitable fireworks. Heere he found the cargazon or freight of a rich East Indian carack; which together with great abundance of sugars, Brasil-wood, and cotton he brought from thence; landing therewith fifteene sailes of tall ships and barks," in Hakluyt, *The Principal Navigations* **[105]**, XI, 43–64.

In April of 1595 James Lancaster stormed the forts protecting Recife and captured the town "of above an hundred houses." According to the account of a chronicler aboard Lancaster's ship the *Consent,* the English "found in it great store of merchandizes of all sorts, as Brasil-wood, sugars, Calico-cloth, pepper, cynamon, cloves, mase, nutmegs, with divers other good things." Lancaster was later aided both by French privateers, to whom he gave much of Recife's store of Brazilwood, and Dutch merchants. The chronicler concluded: "We were at our comming foorth 15 sailes, that is, 3 sailes of Hollanders, (the one of 450 tunnes, the other of 350 tunnes, and the third of 300 tunnes), foure sailes of french, & one ship which the Admiral [Lancaster] gave the french Captain, 3 sailes of Captain Venners fleet of Plimmouth, and 4 sailes of our Admirals fleete, all these were laden with marchandizes, and that of good worth. We stayed in this harbour to passe all this business but onely 31 dayes, and in this time were were occupied with skirmishes and attempts of the enemie [the Portuguese] 11. times; in all which skirmishes we had the better, onely this last excepted. To God be the honour and praise of all, &c." See also Foster **[223]**, pp. 31–51.

[222] Henry Roberts. *Lancaster His Allarums. Honorable Assaultes, and Suprising of the Block-Houses and Store-Houses Belonging to Fernand Bucke in Brasill, With His Brave Attempt in Landing in the Mouth of the Ordinaunce There, Which were Cannons Culvering, Cannon Periall, and Sacres of Brasse; With Other Sundry His Most Resolute and Brave Attempts in that Country, from Whence He Laded of Their Spoyles and Rich Commodities He There Found Fifteene Good Ships; Which Was Sinemon, Sugar, Pepper, Cloves, Mace, Calloco-Cloth, and Brassel-Wood, With Other Commodities. With the Names of Such Men of Worth, Having Charge, Within This Most Honorable Attempt Lost Their Lives.* London: W. Barley, 1595.

The dedication, the short poem in the beginning about Lancaster's exploits in Pernambuco and the verse at the end eulogizing Captains Barker and Cotton who lost their lives in a last-minute attack on Portuguese artillery are the work of Henry Roberts, "a hanger-on at the courts of Elizabeth and James." However, the remainder of the account seems to have been written by a participant in the attack on Pernambuco in 1595. Some authors have suggested a common source for the version printed in Hakluyt **[221]** and the one printed through the efforts of Henry Roberts. The latter account is written less clearly but more flamboyantly. It also does not appear as accurate as the narrative published by Hakluyt. According to Roberts's account, the inhabitants of Recife and Olinda "which saw so much shipping, dreading what did follow, were gathered togither, by estimation to the number of 1000 men; and from their platforme, beeing oppisite with the harboughts mouth, well planted with cannon periall and sacars of brasse, plyed upon us with them, our shippes ryding within sacar-shot in the very face of them; yet did they not hurt any shippe." Then the English "by

Gods help and the gunners good industrie, beat their watchhouse about their eares." This, however, "made the faintharted swades to quaile, that their harts were in counsayle with ther heeles, which should be the best member. In the end, by generall consent, they agreed to see a littell more, intreating their heeles to be redy to make shifte for them." Though ousted from Recife, the Pernambucans did not give up. Roberts's narrative describes Portuguese resistance thusly: "Such was the pollicie of those base roges; who in the night at one time fyred iij carvills—a pollicie to their cost learned in England, but perfourmed like themselves; for the carvills with the fire taking, like harmelesse boates, a quite contrary way, ran ashore, consuming themselves without any annoyance to our ships, as they intended they should have done. This device sorting to no better effect, they made rafts with olde masts, and grapling them together, and planting them full of light wood, heath, and such, fired them and sent them amongst our shippes. For this devise our generall ordained from everie shippe two boates to be ready ahead each shippe, having in each one of them a graplet to throw on the rafts; which sunck them all, and never had any advantage to doe us harme." See also **[221]** and **[223]**.

[223] Sir William Foster, ed. *The Voyages of Sir James Lancaster to Brazil and the East Indies 1591–1603*. London, 1940. xl, 178 pp. [Reprinted 1967 by Kraus Reprint Limited. Nendeln/Liechtenstein.] [Issued by the Hakluyt Society. 2nd Series, no. 85.]

Pages 31–74 include two narratives of Lancaster's Pernambucan expedition of 1594–1595 which successfully attacked, captured and sacked Recife in mid-1595 and held it for about a month. The first account **[221]** (pp. 31–51) is from Hakluyt's *The Principal Navigations* **[105]** and contains 41 notes; the second is a reprint of the pamphlet, *Lancaster His Allarums* **[222]**, first published in 1595, and contains 48 notes. The editor's six-page introduction to these narratives is found on pp. xviii–xxiii.

[224] Francisco Soares. "A letter of Francis Suares to his brother Diego Suares dwelling in Lisbon, written from the river of Jenero in Brasill in June 1596. concerning the exceeding rich trade newly begunne betweene that place and Peru, by the way of the river of Plate, with small barks of 30. and 40. tunnes," in Hakluyt, *The Principal Voyages* **[105]**, XI, 39–43.

In this letter Francisco Soares gives a classic description of the Peru trade during the Habsburg period of Portuguese and Brazilian history. "Sir, we set saile from Lisbon the fourth of April 1596. and arrived her in this river of Jenero the twentie seventh of June next ensuing. . . . I hired a ware-house by my selfe, and landed my commodities. And now I am selling them as fast as I can; and sell them very well, and to great profit: for I have solde all our hats. I would I had brought forty or fifty dozen, by reason of the great utterance of them up into Peru, and into the new kingdome of Granada, by the way of the river of Plate. For here is passage every three or foure months with barks of thirty and forty tunnes a piece, which are laden with sugars, rice, taffataes, hats, and other kindes of commodities of this countrey, which are caried up the sayd river of Plate in the sayd barks, and thence are conveyed up into Peru. And these barkes are but tenne or twelve dayes going up the sayd river to Peru. And within foure and five moneths after, the sayd barkes come downe this river againe laden with reals of plate, and bring downe from those places no other commodities but treasure. It is a woonderfull thing to beholde the great gaine and profit which is gotten in this river and in this countrey. I am ashamed to write it, fearing that I shall not be beleeved. For the imployment of one hundred ducats in Spaine, being brought hither, will yeeld twelve hundred and fifteene hundred ducats profit. This trade hath beene used but within this yeere. For wee can goe up to the mines of Potosi, which are the best and the riches mines in all Peru. If the merchants of Spaine and Portugall did know this trade, they would not send nor venture so much merchandise to Cartagena as they doe. For up this river is a great deale the neerer way, and the easier to go to Peru. For the Peruleiros or merchants of Peru, which dwell there, come downe to this harbour and river of Jenero, and bring with them fifteene thousand and twentie thousand ducats in reals of plate and gold, and imploy it heere in this river in commodities: and when heere are no commodities to be had for money in this place, then these merchants of Peru are constrained to go to Baia and Fernambuc, and there to imploy their money. I would I had brought good store of silks, and not these kinds of commodities which I did bring. For heere is more profit to be had a great deale then in the voyage of Angola."

[225] Feliciano Coelho de Carvalho. "A speciall letter written from Feliciano Cieza de Carvalsho the Governour of Parajua [Paraiba] in the most Northerne part of Brasil, 1597, to Philip the second king of Spaine, answering his desire touching the conquest of Rio Grande, with the relation of the besieging of the castle of Cabodelo by the Frenchmen, and of the discoverie of a rich silver mine and diverse other important matters," in Hakluyt, *The Principal Navigations* **[105]**, XI, 64–72.

This interesting letter, intercepted by the English, describes many of the problems the Portuguese were encountering on the northeastern frontier of Paraiba and Rio Grande do Norte during the late 1590s. Feliciano Coelho de Carvalho describes the difficulties he had had getting help from Pernambuco: "I certified Manuel Mascarenhas [governor and *capitão-mor* of Pernambuco] of these informations by my letters, requesting him to send me with all expedition those souldiers which were in garison in Fernambuck to ayde me, and to defende this Captaineship from the enemie. But the Friers [Franciscan] of The Covent would not consent thereunto, nor suffer them to be sent unto me." The author had similar problems with D. Francisco de Sousa, governor-general of Brazil, who "doth spend your Majesties treasure in building his owne Ingenios or sugar-milles." Thus, "Your Majestie must give order, that the rest of the Governours shall ayde and assist me in these warres: otherwise of my selfe I am not able to doe more than I have alreadie done in defending of this countrey against our enemies which are many." Furthermore, Coelho de Carvalho complained that "here are neither shot, powder, nor any thing els to defend us from our enemies; nor any that wil put to their helping hands for the defence of this countrey, & the service of your Majestie." The governor of Paraiba describes several encounters he had with the French and their Indian allies. He then remarks that "if Don Francisco de Sousa had sent mee those two hundred and fiftie souldiers which I did send for, which were in garison in the castle of Arrecife, which doe nothing but spend your Majesties victuals and treasure, and had not sent them to Baiha, where there was no neede, these warres of Petiguar had bene ended long agone, and had saved your Majesty a great deale of charges which you had spent in folowing of this conquest of Rio Grande." Coelho de Carvalho also was at odds with the Franciscans in Paraiba. "Furthermore, it may please your Majestie to under stand, that the chiefest Friers of this Monasterie of S. Antonie have complained on me to the lord Governour generall, and have caused great strife and debate betweene him and me touching the government and rule of these Indian townes. For the Friers would command and governe both the Indians and their townes as well in Ecclesiasticall as Temporall causes, as touching the punishment of the bodies of such as are offenders. But I have resisted them in your Majesties name, and have alleagued, that none but your Majestie must rule and governe them and their countrey, and that the townes appertaine to your Majestie, and not unto the Friers. But the Governour hath written a letter unto me, signifying that he hath pronounced a sentence against me in the Friers behalfe." In addition, "the Indians have complayned against me, because I have burned their villages in this last rebellion. Wherefore, if your Majestie doe not send some order for this countrey and see into these cases, it will breed great dissention and rebellion among us, and we shall be readie to cut one anothers throat before it be long." However, claims that "a Frenchman called Daurmigas, which hath discovered and found great store of silver in a place called Copaoba . . . but 6 dayes journey from this Captaineship" proved to be false.

[226] Thomas Turner. "Relations of Master Thomas Turner, who lived the best part of two yeeres in Brasill, &c. which I received of him in conference touching his Travels," Purchas, *Purchas His Pilgrimes* **[107]**, XVI, 290–291.

According to Anthony Knivet **[218]**, Thomas Turner was an English gentleman who was residing in Pernambuco in the latter part of the 1590s. Knivet reported that "Master Turner by my advice, went to the River of Janero [Rio de Janeiro], and from thence to Angola, where he made great profit of his Merchandize, for which hee thanked me after we met in England." The two also crossed paths in Lisbon around the year 1600. Turner was an acquaintance of Samuel Purchas to whom he gave the following information: "Brasilian Indians are Canibals, and not for revenge only, but for food also devoure mans flesh. The Portugals make not slaves of them, nor can enjoyne them worke, by reason of a commission to the contrarie obtained by the Jesuites: neither do they winne of them ought but by faire meanes. They are most excellent Archers, go starke naked, the womens haire long and blacke, harsh as a Horsetaile." Turner was also impressed by the large numbers of African slaves that were imported. With exaggeration, he recounted that "out of Angola is said to bee yeerely shipped eight and twenty thousand slaves and there was a Rebellion of slaves against their Masters, tenne thousand making a head and barracadoing themselves, but by the Portugals and Indians chased, and one or two thousand reduced. One thousand belonged to one man, who is said to have tenne thousand slaves, Eighteene Ingenios, &c. his name is John de Paus [João Pais of Pernambuco], exiled out of Portugall, and heere prospering to this incredibilitie of wealth." Turner concluded his account by remarking that "Brasill is full of Mines, if the King would suffer the digging them."

[227] Albert Hastings Markham, ed. *The Voyages and Works of John Davis the Navigator*. London: Issued by the Hakluyt Society. 1st series, no. 59. [Reprinted: New York: Burt Franklin, 1970.]

The editor points out that "among the distinguished English seamen of the sixteenth century, John Davis of Sandridge stands out conspicuously as the one who, more than any other, united the qualities of a daring adventurer with those of a skilful pilot and a scientific navigator." He was part of the 1589 expedition of the Earl of Cumberland, which captured several ships from Brazil. One was from Pernambuco, "a ship of some 110 tuns burden, fraighted with 410 chestes of Sugar, and 50 Kintals [quintals] of Brasill-wood, every Kintall contayning one hundred pound weight. we tooke her in latitude nine and twentie degrees, about two hundred leagues from Lisbone westwards." Davis was also a participant in Thomas Cavendish's last voyage to Brazil **[216]** and **[217]**. Markham reprints John Jane's account of Cavendish's experiences **[215]**, pp. 93–128. In 1598 Davis was "chiefe Pilot to the Zelanders in their East-India Voyage." However, "unconstant weather and bad windes" brought him to "a small Ile named Fernando Loronha," where he anchored on the northside: "We found in this Iland twelve Negroes, eight men, foure women. It is a very fruitful Isle, and hath exceeding good water, it aboundeth with Goates, it hath also Beefes, Hogs, Hens, Mellons, and Ginnie Corne: with plentie of fish and Sea-birds. These Negroes were placed here by the Portugals to manure the Ile. Three yeeres past in which there hath no ships beene with them" In late December of 1604, on another voyage to the East Indies, this time with Sir Edward Michelborne, he again visited the island: On "the sixe and twentieth, our Generall went on shore to see the Iland, and marching up and downe in the same, wee found nothing but a wild Countrey, inhabited onely by sixe Negros, which live like slaves. In this Iland have beene great store of Goates and some wild Oxen; but by reason the Portugall Carakes sometimes use to water here when they go into the East-Indies, and that these poore slaves are left there as their servants, to kill and drie Goates against their comming thither, they have destroyed both Goats and Oxen, so that wee could find but few. In this Iland are great store of Turtle-Doves, Alcatrazes, and other Fowle, which we killed withour Pieces, and found them to be very daintie meate. Also heere is good store of Maiz or Guynie Wheat. Here are likewise plentie of rotten Trees, whereupon groweth the fine Bombast, and abundance of wild Goards, and Water-melons. When we were furnished with wood and water we came aboord."

[228] Jan Huygen van Linschoten. *Discours of Voyages into Ye East & West Indies.* London: John Wolf, 1598. 462 pp.
[There is a facsimile edition published in 1974 by Theatrum Orbis Terrarum, Amsterdam/Walter J. Johnson, Norwood, New Jersey. It is no. 675 in The English Experience Series.]

Born in Holland in 1563, Jan Huygen van Linschoten sailed to India in April of 1583 with the newly appointed archbishop of Goa, Frei Vicente da Fonseca, former chaplain of Sebastião I. Linschoten is best known for his personal accounts of Portuguese Asia. Though he never visited Brazil, he was acquainted with those who had and his pages on Portuguese America contain valuable material. Most of his description of Brazil is found in book two (pp. 242–264) and focuses on the Indians.

He is most interested in their customs and way of life and gives special emphasis to their food and drink, wars, arms, treatment of prisoners, religious practices, marriage practices, laws, and healing and burial techniques. He also describes Brazil's flora and fauna. Though the author includes a brief description of the seacoast of Portuguese America in book two of his discourse, chapters 55 to 62 of book three (pp. 423–429) provide detailed instructions on how to sail to Brazil and navigate along its coastline.

[229] Robert Harcourt. "A Relation of a voyage to Guiana performed by Robert Harcourt of Stanton Harcourt in the Countie of Oxford Esquire. To Prince Charles," in Purchas, *Purchas His Pilgrimes* **[107]**, XVI, 358–402.

Robert Harcourt set sail for Guiana from Dartmouth on 23 March 1608. Though most of his account deals with the Guianas, he does have an interesting description of the Amazon River: "The ninth day of May, we fell into the Current of the great and famous River of Amazones, which putteth out into the Sea such a violent and mightie streame of fresh water, that being thirtie leagues from land, we drunke thereof, and found it as fresh and good as in a Spring or Poole." Harcourt reported that "this River for the great and wonderfull breadth (contayning at the mouth neere sixtie leagues) is rightly termed by Josephus Acosta the Empresse and Queene of all Flouds, and by Hieronymous Girava Tarraconensis: it is said to bee the greatest not onely of all India, but also of the whole world; and for the greatnesse, is called of many the Sweet Sea. It riseth and floweth from the Mountaine of Peru, and draweth out her streames in many windings and turnings under the Equinoctiall, for the space of one thousand and five hundred leagues and more: although from her Fountaines and Springs unto the Sea it is but sixe hundred. When we entred into the aforesaid Current, we sounded, and had fortie foure fathome water, sandie sounding. The tenth day the colour of the water changed, and become muddie, whitish, and thicke."

[230] Sir C. Alexander Harris, ed. *A Relation of a Voyage to Guiana by Robert Harcourt 1613 with Purchas's Transcript of a Report Made at Harcourt's Instance on the Marrawini District.* London: Printed for the Hakluyt Society, 1928. xii, 191 pp.
[Issued by the Hakluyt Society. 2nd series, no. 60.]

Reprints and annotates the first edition (1613) of Robert Harcourt's *A Relation of a Voyage to Gviana. Describing the Climat, Scituation, Fertilitie, Prouisions and Commodities of that Country.* Harcourt **[229]** gives a good description of the mouth of Amazon. His account was published by Purchas **[107]**. The editor, in the appendix, includes new material from the second edition (1626) of Harcourt's *Relation.* Part of Harcourt's revised account describes a joint Spanish-Portuguese attempt to drive out the English from the Amazon region: "Whereupon 3 ships were sent from Spaine, that had their directions and commission to fall with Brasill, & to take in there a competent force to effect the same; which ships with 300. Portugals and Spaniards, accompanied with about 1500. of their Indians in their *Periagos* came into the riuer in the pursuite of this designe, but being constrained to stop many Tides, and to passe many narrow channels, before they could come to our Country-men, they were so closely watched by them and their Indians, that many of their said enemies were slaine by ambush in the way, euery bancke and bushy couert seruing our side for a sufficient retrenchment; which aduantage was still followed vpon the enemie after their landing: but by reason of the want of gouernment, and that the small number of ours were dispersed, and some would not, and others could not conueniently meete together, way (at last) was giuen vnto the enemie. by running vp farther into the Country and the inland parts, (where they might remaine secure against a farre greater force) so that the enemie not daring any farther attempt (through want of experience in the Country, & the enmitie of our Indians,) after they had done some spoile about the houses, were forced to withdraw themselves into their ships, and to depart the river, leauving some of their men thereabouts, then to beginne that actuall possession, which the Count of Gondomar had two yeares before bouldly affirmed to be in being."

[231] William Davies. *A True Relation of the Travailes and Most Miserable Captivitie of William Davies, Barber-Surgeon of London, under the Duke of Florence.* London: Nicholas Bourne, 1614. 20 pp.

William Davies was enslaved in the Mediterranean, and—while still a slave—served as physician aboard an Italian ship during an expedition to the Amazon. In chapter 5 of this short account, Davies describes the Amazon region where, in 1608, he spent ten weeks, "seeing the fashion of the people and countrie there." He reported that "this Countrie is altogether full of Woods, with all sorts of wilde Beasts. . . . Also these Woods are full of Wild-fowle of all sorts, and Parrats more plentifull then Pidgeons in England, and as good meate, for I have often eaten of them. Also this Countrey is very full of Rivers, having a King over everie River. In this place is continuall Tempests, as Lightning, Thunder, and Raine, and so extreame, that it continues most commonly sixteene or eighteene houres in foure and twentie. . . . This Countrie is full of Muskitas, which is a small Flie, which much offends a Stranger comming newly into the Countrie." Davis also described the Amerindians he encountered: "They are altogether naked, both men and women, having not so much as one threed about them to cover any part of their nakednesse, the man taketh a round Cane as bigge as a pennie Candle, and two inches in length, through the which hee puls the fore-skinne of his yard, tying the skinne with a piece of the rinde of a Tree about the bignesse of a small pack-threed, then making of it fast about his middle, hee continueth thus till hee have occasion to use him: In each Eare hee weareth a Reede or Cane, which hee bores through it, about the bigness of a Swannes Quill, and in length halfe an inch, and the like through the midst of the lower lippe: also at the bridge of the Nose hee hangs in a Reede a small glasse Beade or Button, which hanging directly afore his Mouth, flies too and fro still as he speakes, wherein hee takes great pride and pleasure. Hee weares his Haire long, being rounded below to the neather part of his Eare, and cut short, or rather as I judged pluckt bald on the crowne like a Frier. But their women use no fashion at all to set forth themselves, but starke naked as they were borne, with haire long of their Heads, also their Breasts hang verie low, by reason they are never laced or braced up: they doe use to annoint their Bodies, both Men and Women, with a kind of redde Earth, because the Muskitas, or Flies shall not offend them." The author also provides a description of their sleeping habits: "They have a kinde of Net make of the rinde of a Tree which they call Haemac, being three fathome in length, and two in breadth, and gathered at both ends at length, then fastning either end to a Tree, to the full length about a yard and halfe from the ground, when hee hath desire to sleepe, he creepes into it." This account is reprinted in A. & J. Churchill **[108]**. The part on the Amazon is also found in Purchas **[107]**.

[232] Albert Gray and H. C. P. Bell, trans. and ed. *The Voyage of Francois Pyrard of Laval to the East Indies, the Maldives, the Moluccas and Brazil.* 2 v. in 3. London, 1887–1890 [Reprinted by Lenox Hill (Burt Franklin), 1971.] Hakluyt Society. 1st series. vols. 76–77.

Translated from the French edition of 1619. Pyrard of Laval spent a little more than two months in Bahia before returning home in October of 1610. An account of his Brazilian experiences is found in Volume II:2, pp. 306–331.

Pyrard of Laval observed that "into this bay [of All Saints] fall many fine rivers which are navigable far inland for boats and barques and serve to supply the country with commodities." The Frenchman continued: "The city of St. Salvador is high-pitched on the summit of a mountain of difficult ascent, which on the seaside is sheer. Everything brought to the town or exported in gross has to be raised or lowered by a certain engine. No waggons are used, because it were too troublesom and expensive, whereas by this machine the cost is slight." In contrast to later visitors to Bahia, the author admired the lower city: "At the foot of this mountain, for more than a quarter of a league, are well-built houses on both hands, forming a long and handsome street, well crowded with all manner of merchants, craftsmen, and artisans. There also are the cellars and warehouses for the receipt and despatch of merchandise, whether of the king or of private persons." In addition, "the city is walled and well built; it is a bishopric, and contains one college of Jesuits (besides others in the country), a monastery of Franciscans, another of Benedictines, another of Carmelites: all these have handsomely built churches. Great numbers are continually converted to the Christian religion, albeit they are not so firm in the faith as are the East Indians after their baptism, but remain as fickle and hare-brained as before." Pyrard of Laval also observed that "there is a hospital in the town, ordered after the manner of Spain and France. Also a Misericordia, and a very fine cathedral church or Assee, with a dean and canons, but no Inquisition. . . . The King of Spain maintains in the town of St. Salvador three companies of infantry of 100 men each, whereof one is on guard every day at the residence of the viceroy, or Governor of Brazil."

[233] Bartolomé Garcia de Nodal and Gonzalo de Nodal. "Narrative of the Voyage Which by Order of His Majesty and Advice of the Royal Council of the Indies the Captains Bartolomé Garcia de Nodal and Gonzalo de Nodal Brothers and Natives of Pontevedra Undertook for the Discovery of the New Strait of San Vicente and Reconnaissance of that of Magellan," in Markham, ed., *Early Spanish Voyages to the Strait of Magellan* **[176]**, pp. 169–276.

This expedition left Lisbon on 27 September 1618. On 15 November of that year they "entered the harbour of Rio de Janeiro to repair the mast on board the Admiral, which was sprung. Presently we anchored before night, and the Governor Ruy Vaz Pinto sent an Alcalde, and other persons with him, to know what the ships were. A reply was returned that we were ships of the King our Lord, and that in the morning an account would be given of our arrival. The next day was Friday, the 16th of November. Captain Bartolomé Garcia de Nodal, commander of the caravels, went on shore to have an interview with the Governor. The Captain Gonzalo de Nodal remained on board, to take the ships further in with the tide, and to see that the crew did not desert. When the ships had taken up their berths, the Governor came on board, and put the crews in prison, to secure those who came by force [most of the crew had been impressed in Portugal]. After the address which the Governor made to them, they came quite willingly, and the Captain Gonzalo de Nodal went with them, encouraging them and telling them not to be downhearted, as he would soon let them out again. He charged the Alcalde of the prison to treat them well, and not to put them in the calaboose. With that they were content." The authors also provide a valuable portrait of Martin de Sá, one of the most important men in Rio de Janeiro: "On Saturday, the 24th of November, Martin de Sá arrived from his estate. He was a Knight of the Order of Christ, son of the Marquis of Las Minas. He came in a canoe with other gentlemen who brought with them two Benedictine friars. The canoe had more than forty Indians with paddles, who made her fly, and she was so large that, besides the 40 Indians with paddles, she carried 12 or 15 persons, and could have taken more. She had a bronze figurehead. Arriving at the ships and having paid his visit, he offered service to His Majesty. Besides all this Senhor de Sá delivered a very honorable address to the men, explaining to them that the enterprise on which they were engaged was one of great importance, and in conclusion expressing his confidence that deceit would not be found among Portuguese, but if one was caught on shore without leave from his captain, after the ships sailed, he would be hanged without confession, wherever he might be caught. . . . The Senhor is a man of much substance, is much feared, and all treat him with respect." The expedition left Rio de Janeiro on 1 December 1618. After exploring the straits of Magellan and part of the west coast of Patagonia, they sailed for Spain. On their return voyage they stopped at Pernambuco on 1 May 1619, "happy at having arrived there in safety. At Pernambuco they were astonished at the shortness of our passage . . . Here we refitted, and took in wood and water, and other things that were necessary. We found here 28 ships laden with sugar for the kingdom of Portugal. On the 12th and 13th of May, being Sunday and Monday, 13 more sugar ships arrived from Bahia, to join company with those in this port, and them a fine fleet was formed of 40 ships great and small. On Tuesday the 14th of May we left the port of Pernambuco on our return to Spain."

[234] Nicholas del Techo, S. J. "The History of the Provinces of Paraguay, Tucuman, Rio de la Plata, Parana, Guaira and Uruaica and Something of the Kingdom of Chili, in South America," in A. and J. Churchill, *A Collection of Voyages and Travels* **[108]**, VI, 3–116.

Nicholas del Techo (Du Toit) was a Belgian Jesuit missionary who worked in Paraguay from the time of his arrival in the 1640s until his death in 1685. His account, *Historia Provinciae Paraquariae Societatis Iesu* was published at Liege in 1673. Since he did not arrive in Paraguay until the 1640s, Father Nicolas del Techo relies heavily on Padre Antonio Ruiz de Montoya's important and rare account, *Conquista Espiritual Hecha por los Religiosos de la Compañia de Iesus, en las Provincias del Paraguay, Parana, Uruguay, y Tape,* published in Madrid in 1639, for the events of the 1620s and 1630s. In his preface to the English translation of Nicholas del Techo's narrative, Churchill points out that "the Author having design'd this for a History of his Order; has fill'd a considerable part of it with the Lives, particular Actions, Preaching and Teaching of his Brethren the Jesuits, and inserted abundance of Miracles, and other pious Matter, which is not the Subject of this present Work, nor likely to be at all acceptable to the Reader. . . . Therefore those religious Narrations are either quite left out, or if any thing be said of them, it is so concise as may no way be tedious, but rather afford something of variety." Of special interest to students of Brazilian history is the description of Guairá and the attacks of the *bandeirantes* on the Jesuit missions there. "Guaira is a large Country, part of the Province of Paraguay, Bordering on Brasil Eastward, and shut in by the River Parana on the West. Its breadth from the Plains of the Uruaicans in the South, to the Woods and inaccessible Marshes in the North, is not certainly known, but reaches a vast extent of Ground." Initially, Jesuit efforts were successful in that province. "Christianity now Dayly increas'd, and it was to be hop'd, that all the Province of Guaira would soon embrace the true Religion, when the Devil envying this Success, either by himself or by his Agents the Mamalucs, contriv'd the Destruction of the new Colonies built in Guaira by the Fathers of the Society. The Mamalucs being the prime Actors in this Tragedy, it seems but reasonable we should give an account of their Original, Country, Manners and Allies." The author briefly discusses early colonization in Brazil. "The European Planters for a long time preserv'd their native Honour, till the European Women failing, they began to mix with that barbarous Race, and corrupted the Noble Portugueze Blood. This mixture, in process of time, running through them all, and bad Sons succeeding good Fathers, and worse Grandson; the Sons that generous Portugueze breed, being so often mix'd, degenerated, so that there nothing remain'd among the Posterity of those first renowned Conquerors of Brazil, but their Names. The Portugueze disdaining to call this Generation by their Name (as Orlandinus in his History of the Society observes) gave them the barbarous Title of Mamalucs; that since they are like them in nothing else, they may not be alike in Name. This deprav'd Race was increased by the addition of worse Companions, who resorted to them in great numbers from other places, being invited by Liberty, and the good disposition of the place. For Piratininga [São Paulo], as to situation and fruitfulness of Soil, furnishes such as desire to live wickedly and daintily, with Necessaries and

Safety. It is fifteen Leagues from the Ocean, and a little South of the Tropick of Capricorn. Being therefore in a temperate Climate, it produces most things necessary for life, so that it not only furnished it self, but the rest of Brazil, which is so luxuriant by reason of the great Heat and Moisture, with plenty of Corn and Cattle. It produces Sugar, and is said not to want Gold Mines. There is but one way thither from the Ports upon the Ocean, which is over craggy Mountains, and very difficult to pass; and so narrow, that a very few may keep out any numbers. This fertility of the Soil, and inaccessibleness of the place, draws many, who are forced to fly for their Crimes, or desire to commit them to fly thither out of Europe and Brazil. Thus Men of several Nations, and guilty of all Crimes, having found out a place suitable to their Inclination, and joining in amity with the Mamalucs, began to treat the Indians after a far different manner from the first generous Portugals, who first planted Colonies in Brazil." Techo describes many of the attacks of the mamelucos or *bandeirantes* on Guaira. One of the earliest included "900 Mamalucs, and 2200 Tupims, (these are fierce Indians, in League with the Mamalucs)." The author reported that "a numerous Company of Mamalucs under the command of Simon Alvarez, assaults the Town [San Antonio], plunders it, spares none, cuts off such as oppose him, secures the prime Men, drives away the weak Multitude, robs F. Mola of all he had, tho he us'd all means to move those Robbers to commiseration; but finding no humanity among them, and despairing of defending the Bodies, apply'd himself to procure the health of the Souls of those poor People, baptizing, instructing, and otherwise helping them, as occasion would permit in that short time, and this not without danger of his Life, one of these Miscreants aiming to kill him, had not another of the Gang obstructed him. About 2500 Indians are said to have been taken at this Invasion by the Robbers; the Shepherd was left without his Flock, lamenting the loss of his dear Children in God, whom he saw drove away like Sheep before his Face, without hopes of Redress." Techo follows this account with numerous others describing the depredations of the Brazilian *bandeirantes* ["Mamalucs"] of the Jesuit Missions in Guairá.

[235] Cristoval de Acuña. *Voyages and Discoveries in South America the First Up the River of Amazons to Quito in Peru, and Back Again to Brazil.* London: C. Buckley, 1698. viii, 190 pp.

Acuña's account of his voyage with Pedro Teixeira **[636]** down the Amazon from Quito was entitled *Nuevo Descubrimento del Gran Rio de las Amazonas* and published in Madrid in 1641. According to Clements R. Markham **[236]**, "an English translation, from the French, was published in London, in 1698. It is full of omissions, mistakes, and long interpolations in the text." The French translation dates from 1682. Markham **[236]** retranslated the rare 1641 Spanish edition into English. He points out that "the narrative of Acuña is the earliest published account of the river of the Amazons in existence." Further, "Acuña, who was rector of the [Jesuit] college at Cuenca, accompanied Teixeira in his returning expedition from Quito, down the Napo and Amazons to Pará; with orders to observe everything on the way; to note down the names of all Indian tribes, their manners and customs; the names of the rivers flowing into the Amazons; the natural productions of the country; and to send in a full report to the council of the Indies, on his return to Spain. These instructions were ably carried into execution by the good father."

[236] Clements R. Markham, ed. *Expeditions into the Valley of the Amazons, 1539, 1540, 1639.* London: 1859. lxiiii, 190 pp. Issued by the Hakluyt Society. 1st series, no. 24.
[Reprinted. New York: Burt Franklin, 1964].

Contains accounts of the expeditions of Gonzalo Pizarro (1539–1542) **[180]**, Francisco de Orellana (1540–1541) **[180]**, and the Jesuit Father Cristoval de Acuña (1639) **[235]**. Markham also provides "A List of the Principal Tribes in the Valley of the Amazons." He includes a lengthy 64-page introduction which recounts the various efforts to explore the Amazon region in the sixteenth and seventeenth centuries. The first 21 pages review early Spanish exploration efforts; the remainder focus on Portuguese attempts, that of Acuña and Teixeira **[636]**, and those of Samuel Fritz **[325]** and **[319]**, La Condamine **[656]** and others. Father Cristoval de Acuña was lavish in his praise of the area's natural riches: "The regions bordering on the Amazons require no supplies from foreign lands; the river is full of fish, the forests of game, the air of birds, the trees are covered with fruit, the plains with corn, the earth is rich in mines, and the natives have much skill and ability." Acuña reported that his expedition encountered more than 150 tribes. He describes the arms and tools they use, their means of communication and their religious practices. The Jesuit explorer was optimistic regarding the conversion of the Amerindians: "These tribes of infidels have good dispositions, with fine features, and are of a colour not so dark as those of Brazil. They have clear understandings, and rare abilities for any manual dexterity. They are meek and gentle, as was found in those who once met us, conversed with us confidently, and eat and drank with us, without ever suspecting anything. They gave us their houses to live in, while they all lived together in one or two of the largest in the village;

and though they suffered much mischief from our friendly Indians, without the possibility of avoiding it, they never returned it by evil acts. All this, together with the slight inclination they display to worship their own gods, gives great hope that, if they received notice of the true Creator of heaven and earth, they would embrace His holy law with little hesitation." The Jesuit describes an alcoholic drink made from manioc roots much esteemed by the Amerindians. "It is sometimes so strong that it might be taken for grape wine, and intoxicates the natives, making them lose their judgment. With the help of this wine they celebrate their feasts, mourn their dead, receive their visitors, sow and reap their crops; indeed there is no occasion on which they meet that this liquor is not the mercury which attracts them, and the riband which detains them." After describing the manioc, fruit, fish and game that the Amerindians consume, Acuña lists the potential products for European use the Amazon region provides: medicinal drugs, timber and materials for ships, cocoa, tobacco, and cotton. However, he was most impressed by the possibilities for sugar production: "It is the most noble, most productive, most certain, and most valuable to the royal crown; and many farms ought to be established, which in a short time would restore the losses on the Brazilian coast [from the Dutch]." Appended to Acuña's account is a "Memorial Presented to the Royal Council of the Indies, on the Subject of the Above Discovery, after the Rebellion of the Portuguese. A. D. 1641." There is no index to this volume.

VII. The Dutch in Brazil, 1624–1654 [Nos. 237–253]

A good introduction to Dutch maritime activity against Spain, Portugal and their colonies is found in Sluiter **[237]**. The best and most exhaustive general treatment of the Dutch in Brazil is by Charles R. Boxer **[239]**, a summary of which is found in **[240]**. Boxer also has written an excellent overview of the Dutch overseas experience in his *Dutch Seaborne Empire, 1600–1800* **[238]**. For the attack on Bahia in 1624 and threats to other parts of northeastern Brazil in the 1620s, see Dutra **[153]**, Edmundson **[241]**, and Boxer **[277]** and **[239]**. Edmundson **[242]** and **[243]** also gives a detailed description of the early Dutch campaigns in Pernambuco in the 1630s. The recovery of Angola in 1648 is covered by Boxer **[244]** as are the events leading up to the fall of Pernambuco to the Portuguese **[245]**.

The administration of Count Maurits of Nassau is covered in detail by Boxer **[239]**, with a footnote by James Van der Veldt **[260]**. In the Dutch leader's entourage were the artists Frans Post and Albert Eckhout, both of whom left important paintings recording their experiences. Erik Larsen **[246]** discusses not only Post and Eckhout, but the brothers Peeters, all of whom painted scenes of seventeenth century Brazil of value to historians. Joaquim de Sousa-Leão has provided a book-length, richly illustrated study of Frans Post **[247]** plus an article and a postscript on some of his paintings **[248]** and **[249]**. Post's landscapes have also been studied by Robert C. Smith **[251]** and **[252]**. Lygia da Fonseca Fernandes da Cunha [250] reproduces several of Post's paintings on Pernambuco and gives a short introduction on the Dutch painter. Michael Benisovich **[253]** examines tapestries with Brazilian themes.

Gonsalves de Mello **[349]** discusses the Dutch Calvinists and religious toleration in northern Brazil. R. Herbert Minnich **[350]** deals with the question of whether there were Mennonites in Dutch Brazil. A number of Jews were also active in Dutch Brazil. Arnold Wiznitzer discusses their role in his general history of the *Jews in Colonial Brazil* **[335]** as well as in a number of articles, including a biographical sketch of Isaac de Castro **[338]** and estimates of the number of Jews **[339]**, Jewish soldiers **[340]** and Jewish sugar mill owners **[341]** in Dutch Brazil. Wiznitzer describes the Jewish synagogue and cemetery in Dutch-controlled Recife **[342]** and **[346]**. He also recounts the exodus of Jews from Brazil after the Dutch surrender **[343]**. Cyrus Adler **[345]**, Herbert I. Bloom **[337]** and Isaac S. Emmanuel **[336]** also discuss the role of Jews in Dutch Brazil.

[237] Engel Sluiter. "Dutch Maritime Power and the Colonial Status Quo, 1585–1641," *The Pacific Historical Review* 11:1 (March 1942), pp. 29–41.

The author focuses on the Dutch and shows how their success in combining trade and war won them a vast commercial and colonial empire in Africa, Asia and the Americas by 1641. Though at the close of the sixteenth century neither Spain nor Portugal had lost any overseas territory to the French, Dutch or English, this record would not remain unblemished. Sluiter outlines several periods of Dutch overseas expansion. The first phase, 1585–1597, was entirely commercial. Dutch ships and crews helped Portuguese merchants carry European cargoes to Brazil and bring back sugar and brazilwood. For Brazil, the second phase, 1598–1605, was characterized by tremendous growth in Dutch commerce. Though Spanish-Portuguese forces were engaged in hostilities with the Dutch in other parts of the world, the Twelve Year Truce, 1609–1621, saw Dutch-Brazilian trade increase even more: "In 1621 ten to fifteen ships were built annually in the United Netherlands exclusively for the Brazil trade, forty to fifty thousand chests of Brazilian sugar a year were imported, and twenty-nine sugar refineries in Holland were kept busy as a result of the traffic. It was then authoritatively stated that from one-half to two-thirds of the carrying trade between Brazil and Europe was in Dutch hands." In addition, the Dutch began to colonize the region of Guiana and the Amazon. The end of the Twelve Year Truce in 1621 and the inauguration of the Dutch West India Company the same year set the stage for Dutch military activity in northeastern Brazil, 1624–1654. Based chiefly on archival and printed primary sources. 71 notes.

[238] Charles R. Boxer. *The Dutch Seaborne Empire, 1600–1800*. London: Hutchinson, 1965. xxvi, 326 pp. maps. illus.

Excellent collection of essays on Dutch overseas expansion. Against the background of eighty years of war and the problems of nation building, Boxer, using a topical approach, describes Dutch society, the commercial attitudes of burghers and merchants, the role of Calvinism, techniques of trade and seafaring, racial attitudes, etc. There is a useful bibliography on pp. 307–314. Boxer also provides a helpful chronology, 1568–1795, on pp. 295–299.

[239] Charles R. Boxer. *The Dutch in Brazil, 1624–1654*. Oxford: Clarendon Press, 1957. xiii, 327 p.

Detailed account of the origins of the Dutch West Indian Company and its activities in Brazil. The 1624–1625 Bahia episode is sketched briefly with most of the focus on a careful analysis and description of the Portuguese-Dutch struggle in Pernambuco and other areas of the Brazilian Northeast from 1630–1654. Throughout the study, the author makes references to events, personalities and decisions in both the United Provinces of the Netherlands and Portugal and relates them to happenings in America. Boxer concludes with a short chapter on the diplomacy between 1655 and 1669 that finally settled matters, even though the Dutch had left Brazil in 1654 after signing the Capitulation of Taborda. Based on extensive use of Dutch as well as Portuguese primary archival and printed materials. "Bibliographical Note": pp. 291–301; Bibliography: pp. 302–309.

[240] Charles R. Boxer. "In the Time of the Flemings: The Dutch in Brazil, 1624–1654," *History Today* 4:3 (March 1954), pp. 159–168.

Excellent synopsis of his later *The Dutch in Brazil, 1624–1654* **[239]**. 2 notes. 7 illus.

[241] George Edmundson. "The Dutch Power in Brazil (1624–1654). Part I. The Struggle for Bahia (1624–1627)," *The English Historical Review* 11:42 (April 1896), pp. 231–259.

Good descriptive survey of the Dutch capture of Bahia in 1624, its restoration by the combined Spanish-Portuguese armada in 1625, and

Piet Heyn's 1627 attacks on shipping in Bahia's harbor. Based on some archival but mostly printed Dutch, Spanish and Portuguese primary sources. 112 notes.

[242] George Edmundson. "The Dutch Power in Brazil. Part II. The First Conquests," *The English Historical Review* 14:56 (October 1899), pp. 676–699.

After briefly describing Piet Heyn's successful capture of the Spanish silver fleet off Matanzas, Cuba, in 1628, the author narrates the Dutch preparations for the attack on Pernambuco and the Portuguese efforts under Matias de Albuquerque in late 1629 and early 1630 to defend that captaincy. The successful Dutch invasion of February 1630 is detailed as is Albuquerque's efforts to keep the Dutch hemmed in Olinda and Recife during the remainder of that year. Based almost entirely on printed primary sources. 79 notes.

[243] George Edmundson. "The Dutch Power in Brazil. Part II. The First Conquests (Continued)," *The English Historical Review* 15:57 (January 1900), pp. 38–57.

After describing the famous sea battle between the forces of António de Oquendo and Adriaan Janzoon Pater in August 1631, the author details efforts by the Dutch to reinforce their position in Pernambuco after capturing Recife and Olinda in 1630 and by the Portuguese under Matias de Albuquerque to recapture the political and economic center of the captaincy. Edmundson ends his account with the return of the Dutch commander, Colonel Diederick van Waerdenburgh, to Holland in March of 1633. Based on printed primary materials. 60 notes.

[244] Charles R. Boxer. "Salvador Correia de Sá e Benevides and the Reconquest of Angola in 1648," *The Hispanic American Historical Review* 28:4 (November 1948), pp. 483–513.

After discussing Dutch successes in the Portuguese South Atlantic from 1624 through much of the 1640s, the author describes in detail the successful efforts of Salvador Correia de Sá (1594–1688), overseas councillor, general of the Brazilian fleets, and governor-general of Angola, in organizing and leading the Lisbon-Rio de Janeiro-Luanda expedition that eventually recaptured the latter city and the rest of that colony from the Dutch in 1648. Based mostly on printed primary sources. 25 notes. 2 appendices.

[245] Charles R. Boxer. "The Recovery of Pernambuco, 1645–1654," *Atlante* 2:1 (January 1954), pp. 1–17.

Using both Dutch and Portuguese sources, the author challenges the view that the Dutch loss was a foregone conclusion and discusses the many factors that resulted in the ultimate expulsion of the Hollanders. Extensive use of unedited Portuguese Overseas Council records. 45 notes.

[246] Erik Larsen. "Some Seventeenth-Century Paintings of Brazil," *The Connoisseur* 175:704 (October 1970), pp. 123–131.

Focuses on the artists who accompanied Count Maurice of Nassau to Dutch Brazil, 1637–1644. Six were attached to his service, the most important and famous being Frans Post and Albert Eckhout. The author reproduces and describes two of Post's paintings: "Landscape in Brazil"—hitherto unpublished—which shows a sugar plantation complex, and "Cottages in the Interior." Larsen argues that Eckhout probably also painted Brazilian landscapes, although none have survived. The Brazilian paintings of Eckhout that are extant (in the Copenhagen Museum) deal with Indians, Africans, and Mulattoes and were part of Count Maurice's gift to the King of Denmark. The remainder of the article discusses the artistic work of the brothers Peeters, Bonaventura and Gillis, to whom Larsen attributes a series of paintings which he also reproduces and describes: "Recife and Its Harbor," "Battle Between Dutch Regulars and Indians," "Dutch Vessel Standing off the Brazilian Coast," "Redskins on the Shore," and "Dutch Man-of-War Arriving in the West Indies." The first two are by Gillis Peeters, the last three by Bonaventura. The author feels that these five paintings are historically accurate and that one or both of the brothers visited Brazil in the service of Maurice of Nassau. Based on primary source materials. 8 illus. 43 notes.

[247] Joaquim de Sousa-Leão. *Frans Post, 1612–1680.* Amsterdam: A. L. van Gendt, 1973. 176 pp.

The most impressive and important work to date in English on Frans Post, the Dutch artist who accompained Count Maurice of Nassau to Brazil, 1637–1644, and whose watercolors are of importance both to students of Brazilian history and those of Dutch art. About 140 paintings by Post on Brazil are known, nearly half of them dated. Sousa-Leão in a series of short chapters provides historical background regarding the Dutch in Brazil, discusses Post's importance for

Brazilianists, examines the Dutch artist's life and artistic output, describes the gift of a number of his paintings to Louis XIV of France by Nassau, and provides a *catalogue raisonné* of Post's paintings as well as his drawings. This well-documented work contains 5 color plates and 227 in black and white.

[248] J[oaquim] de Sousa-Leão. "Frans Post in Brazil," *The Burlington Magazine* 130 (March 1942), pp. 58–61, 63.

Frans Post (1612–1680) was one of six painters in the service of Prince Maurice of Nassau during the latter's stay as governor of Dutch Brazil. The author discusses the works of the "first landscape painter in the Americas" who portrayed life on sugar mills, urban and church architecture, and the flora and fauna of Northeastern Brazil both during his stay in the New World as well as after his return to Europe. The latter paintings, though based on Brazilian motifs, were often the product of his imagination. 2 plates (6 illustrations in black and white). 4 notes.

[249] J[oaquim] de Sousa-Leão. "Frans Post: A Postscript," *The Burlington Magazine* 83:486 (September 1943), pp. 216–217.

The postscript is to his earlier article in English on Frans Post **[248]**. To his list of paintings by the Dutch artist, Sousa-Leão adds two Brazilian landscapes owned by the Duke of Buccleuch. He also offers two conjectures on how they might have arrived in England: 1) The paintings may have been a gift from Louis XIV's collection to the Duke of Montagu, ambassador to the French Court at the end of the seventeenth century; 2) Post may have visited England after his sojourn in Brazil. 3 illus. No notes.

[250] Lygia da Fonseca Fernandes da Cunha. *Frans Post. Pintor do Brasil Holandês/Artist in Dutch Brazil.* (n.p.; n/d). Introduction and watercolor titles in both English and Portuguese.

Frans Post was commissioned by Count John Maurice of Nassau-Siegen "to depict representative scenes of tropical Brazilian civilization." After giving a brief account of Brazil's sixteenth- and seventeenth-century historical background, the names of several prominent historians of the period and important studies on the paintings of Frans Post, the author describes the influence of artistic trends in Holland on Post's work and quotes and cites a number of conclusions from Erik Larsen's *Frans Post, interprète du Brésil.* 7 illus.

[251] Robert C. Smith, Jr. "The Brazilian Landscapes of Frans Post." *The Art Quarterly* 1:4 (Autumn 1938), pp. 238–267.

After discussing the Pernambucan background, the Dutch invasion of 1630, and the changes made during the governorship of the Count of Nassau (1637–1644), the author focuses on the life and paintings on Brazilian themes of Frans Post (1612–1680), a member of the artistic and scientific mission that accompanied Count Johan Maurits to Brazil in 1637. The author describes ten landscapes of Post's Brazilian period, his working drawings for Barlaeus' *Rerum per octenium in Brasilia* and his subsequent paintings on Brazilian life after returning to Europe in 1644. Smith concludes that Post provides "excellent testimony of what Pernambuco was like in the time of the Dutch, an invaluable record of sixteenth and seventeenth century colonization in South America." 35 notes. 19 illus. An appendix includes a partial list (63) of Post's landscapes.

[252] Robert C. Smith, Jr. "Three Brazilian Landscapes by Frans Post," *Bulletin of the Pan American Union* 73:5 (May 1939), pp. 271–275.

Describes three landscapes by Frans Post, the Leyden-born painter, who accompained Maurice of Nassau to Brazil in 1637 and remained there with his patron until 1644. The first of these landscapes (from the Collection of Carl Freund, New York) is dated 1642 and titled "The Fortifications of Recife." It includes a Dutch planter, a black servant and a mulata laundress in the foreground. The second painting (from the Collection of Julius H. Weitzner, New York) is not dated. It is entitled "Ruins of the Basilica of Olinda," the church having been "one of the most imposing buildings erected by the Portuguese in Brazil prior to the coming of the Dutch." The third landscape (from the Collection of R. G. Ward, London) is also undated. It is titled "View of a Plantation in Pernambuco," and shows dancing slaves in the foreground. According to Smith, "these three landscapes represent the divergence in the master's work. If the first through the brilliance of its technique and the clarity of its mood offers delight to the connoisseur of painting, the other two afford invaluable information for the student of northeastern colonial Brazil." 3 illus. No notes.

[253] Michael Benisovich. "The History of the 'Tenture des Indes,'" *The Burlington Magazine* 83:486 (September 1943), pp. 216–225.

For students of Portuguese America, this article is a long footnote to the Brazilian saga of Albert Eckhout and Frans Post, two of the Dutch painters who accompained Prince Maurice of Nassau to Brazil in 1637. The author describes and discusses five tapestries with Brazilian themes made for Louis XIV by the Gobelins factory and now preserved in the Museé des Gobelins in Paris. Part of the design of these tapestries seems to have followed "as nearly as possible the paintings by Eckhout and by Post." 2 illus. 18 notes.

VIII. Frontier Expansion and the Bandeirantes

[Nos. 254–258]

The best and most useful introduction to the subject is found in Richard Morse's **[254]** collection of selections and source materials. Caio Prado, Jr., **[73]** and Rollie Poppino **[66]** also provide useful syntheses of the efforts of Brazilian explorers to open up new territory and discuss the various types of frontiers. Normano **[657]** has useful information on the economic and demographic effects of new frontiers in Brazilian history. Mary Lombardi **[937]** analyzes the literature on the frontier in Brazilian history. Manuel Cardozo **[255]** describes the efforts of Dom Rodrigo de Castel-Branco to discover mineral wealth in Brazil. The same author **[256]** and Paul Kigar **[257]** have contributed studies of Fernão Dias Pais and his search for emeralds in the seventeenth century. Virginia Freehafer **[258]** provides a biographical sketch of Domingos Jorge Velho, who explored much of the interior of northeastern Brazil.

[254] Richard M. Morse, ed. *The Bandeirantes. The Historical Role of the Brazilian Pathfinders.* New York: Alfred A. Knopf, 1965. 215 pp.

One of the best of the Borzoi Books on Latin America. Not only contains an excellent introduction (pp. 3–36), but includes translations into English of representative selections from some of the best Portuguese writings on the subject, such as those of Teodoro Sampaio, Myriam Ellis, José de Alcantara Machado, Jaime Cortesão, Sergio Buarque de Holanda, Afonso d'Escragnolle Taunay, and Cassiano

Ricardo. Morse also includes translations from documents and manuscripts of such seventeenth- and eighteenth-century figures as Justo Mansilla, Simon Maceta, Fernão de Sousa Coutinho, João da Cunha Souto Maior, Domingos Jorge Velho **[258]**, André João Antonil (Giovanni Antônio Andreoni) and Frei Gaspar da Madre de Deus. For comparative purposes, there are excerpts from Percy Alvin Martin's "Minas Geraes and California" **[903]** and Mario Góngora's *Los Grupos de Conquistadores en Tierra Firme (1509–1530)*. There are a map, glossary (p. 212), and a "Bibliographical Note" (pp. 213–215).

[255] Manoel da Silveira Soares Cardozo. "Dom Rodrigo de Castel-Blanco and the Brazilian El Dorado, 1673–1682," *The Americas* 7:2 (October 1944), pp. 131–159.

After quickly tracing sixteenth- and early seventeenth-century efforts by Portugal to discover mineral wealth in Brazil, the author focuses on the exploits of a Spaniard in Portuguese service, D. Rodrigo de Castel-Blanco, and what turned out to be one of the most ambitious—though unsuccessful—attempts ever made to discover valuable minerals in Portuguese America. Based on archival (especially the Arquivo Historico Ultramarino, Lisbon) and printed materials. 136 notes, map, facsimile of D. Rodrigo's signature.

[256] Manoel S. Cardozo. "The Last Adventure of Fernão Dias Pais (1674–1681)," *The Hispanic American Historical Review* 26:4 (November 1946), pp. 467–479.

Provides biographical data on the career of Fernão Dias Pais and gives details of this famous bandeirante's unsuccessful and fortune-consuming search for emeralds in what is now Minas Gerais—an expedition which cost him his life. Based mostly on printed primary sources. 64 notes.

[257] Paul Donovan Kigar. "The Emerald Hunter," *Américas* 26:6-7 (June–July 1974), pp. 8–14.

Popularized retelling of the quest for precious stones in the interior of Brazil by the *bandeirante* Fernão Dias Pais, "Governor of all the men of war and all others who go to discover the mines of Silver and of Emeralds." The sixty-six-year-old emerald hunter left São Paulo in 1674 with about 680 men, of which only about six percent were white.

After much suffering by Dias Pais and the handful of men who remained, green stones were discovered. Before they could be appraised, however, the famed *bandeirante* died in 1681 on the return journey home after spending seven long years in the sertão, exploring much of what are now the states of São Paulo and Minas Gerais, and exhausting his personal and family fortune. In line with his request, his remains were buried in front of the high altar of the Benedictine monastery in São Paulo that he helped to build. Unfortunately for the survivors of the expedition, the green stones were discovered to be tourmalines and not emeralds. 1 map; 12 illustrations. No notes.

[258] Virginia Freehafer. "Domingos Jorge Velho. Conqueror of Brazilian Backlands," *The Americas* 27:2 (October 1970), pp. 161–184.

Study of the famous *bandeirante* who in the last half of the seventeenth century explored much of the interior of northeastern Brazil and settled in what is now the state of Piaui. The author concentrates on Velho's exploits in fighting and "civilizing" hostile Indians and destroying Palmares, Portuguese America's most famous stronghold of escaped slaves, as well as his attempts to gain the promises made in his campaign contract to wipe out the Black rebels. Freehafer shows how Velho became a victim of the Portuguese Crown's efforts to tighten its Brazilian land legislation and bring more centralized authority to the interior of the Northeast and analyzes his dispute with D. Frei Francisco de Lima, bishop of Pernambuco. Based entirely on printed materials, especially the documents published by Ernesto Ennes in *As Guerras nos Palmares* (1938). 72 notes.

IX. Contemporary Narratives: Brazil, 1640–1700

[Nos. 259–267]

Johan Nieuhoff **[259]** describes Recife and Olinda in the 1640s as well as much of Dutch-occupied northeastern Brazil. James Van der Veldt **[260]** translates a letter of John Maurice of Nassau, Governor of the Dutch Colony in Brazil, 1636–1644. The Irish Jesuit and literary figure, Richard Flecknoe **[261]**, visited Rio de Janeiro in the late 1640s. Gabriel Dellon **[262]** and **[263]** describes his three-and-a-half-month-long stopover in Salvador in 1676. Two German Jesuits, Anthony Sepp and Anthony Behme **[265]**, describe their trans-Atlantic voyage, make references to Brazil and discuss the Paraguayan missions. At the end of the seventeenth century, the Sieur Froger **[266]** visited Rio de Janeiro on his voyage to the Straits of Magellan and stopped at Salvador on his return. William Dampier **[267]** anchored at Bahia in March of 1699.

[259] Johan Nieuhoff. "Voyage and Travels into Brazil, and the Best Parts of the East Indies," in A. and J. Churchill. *A Collection of Voyages and Travels* **[108]** II, 1–302.

Johan Nieuhoff spent more than eight-and-a-half years in America during the Dutch occupation of northeastern Brazil. He arrived in Recife on 15 December 1640 and sailed again for Holland on 23 July 1649. His account of Brazil and his experiences there are found on pp. 1–135. Nieuhoff provides interesting information about the island of Fernão de Noronha, which he passed by on his voyage to Brazil. The island, which had been occupied by the Dutch in 1630, was temporarily deserted by them because "of the vast number of rats, which consumed all the fruits of the earth." However, the author points out that it was "a very fruitful island, and abounding with fish, the inhabitants of Receif being used to send their fisherboats thither, which return commonly well freighted with fish." Nieuhoff then describes Dutch-occupied northeastern Brazil, beginning with the Rio São Francisco, "the largest and most considerable in those parts" and "the common boundary of the captainship of Parnambuco and Bahia dos todos los Santos, or the Bay of All Saints. In some places it is so broad that a six-pounder can scarce reach over it, and its depth is eight, twelve, and sometimes fifteen yards; but it admits of no ships of burthen, because its entrance is choak'd up with sands." Moving northward, the author describes Sergipe del Rei and the village of Porto Calvo, the latter "built upon a rising ground, about four leagues from the sea-shore." Located at the confluence of four small rivers, Porto Calvo "has two streets, the chief of which runs parallel with the river, from one fort to the other, and is call'd St. Joseph's street; it contain'd no more than three houses of one story high, and about thirty-six others cover'd with pantiles, being only built upon the ground." Nieuhoff provides a description of the *quilombos* of Palmares: "The lesser Palmairas, which is inhabited by six thousand negroes, lies about twenty leagues above the Alagoas. . . . The village consists of three streets, each near half a league in length. Their huts are made of straw twisted together, one near another, their plantations being behind. They retain something of the religious worship of the Portugueses, but have their peculiar priests and judges. Their business is to rob the Portugueses of their slaves, who remain in slavery among them, 'till they have redeemed themselves by stealing another: But such slaves as run over to them, are as free as the rest. Their food is dates, beans, meal, barley, sugar-canes, tame-fowl (of which they have great plenty) and fish." According to the author there was also a "greater Palmairas" located "betwixt twenty and thirty leagues distant behind the village of St. Amar, near the mountain of Bebe, being surrounded with a double inclosure. About eight thousand Negroes are said to inhabit the vallies near the mountains, besides many others, who dwell in lesser numbers of fifty or a hundred, in other places. Their houses lie straggling, they sow and reap among the woods, and have certain caves whither they retreat in case of necessity. . . . Under the government of count Maurice [of Nassau], the Negroes of this Palmairas did considerable mischief, especially to the country people about the Alagoas; to repress which, he sent three hundred firelocks, one hundred Mamelukes, and seven hundred Brasilians [Indians]." Nieuhoff gives a good description of the captaincy of Pernambuco, especially Recife, the island of Antonio Vaz, Mauritsstad, and the city of Olinda. "In the time of the Portugueses, all the ships coming out of the sea did unload on the village of Povoacano, or the Receif, and the goods were from thence in boats and lighter conveyed up the river Biberibi, to the suburbs of Olinda. Before the building of Maurice's town [by the Dutch] most of the traffick was in the Receif, where all the great merchants had their habitations, and from hence the sugar was transported into Holland. To prevent the frauds in the customs, it was surrounded with pallisadoes, and a goodly hospital was erected for the conveniency of the sick and wounded, and the education of orphans, under the tuition of four governors, and as many governesses. . . . To the south of the Receif, opposite to it, lies the isle of Anthony Vaez, so called by our people, from its ancient possessor. It is about half a league in circuit, being divided from the Receif by the Salt-River, or Biberibi. On the east side of this island, count Maurice laid the foundation of a city, which, after his own name, he called Maurice's town or city; the ruins of the churches or monasteries of the city of Olinda, furnished the materials for the building of it, which were from thence carried to the Receif, and so transported to this place." Nieuhoff also describes Recife: "At a small distance from the Receif, or Maurice's town, to the north, is the ruinated city of Olinda, once a famous place among the Portugueses; the whole product of Brasil, being from thence transported by sea into Europe. The best part of the city was built upon divers hills; towards the sea, on the south side, these hills were pretty plain, extending to the sea-shore, which has a very white sand all along that coast: Towards the land side, or the north, those hills are more steep and craggy, full of thorn-bushes, intermixed with a few orange-trees. These hills are an additional strength to the place, which besides this, was guarded by several bastions to the land side, though by reason of the great variety of hills contained in its circuit, it was a difficult task to bring the fortifications into a regular form. There is a very fair prospect from the higher part of the town, both to the south and north, or to the sea and land side, by reason of the great quantity of circumjacent trees, which continue green all the year round. You may also from thence see the isle of Anthony Vaez, and Maurice's town." Nieuhoff describes the rest of Dutch Brazil and its flora and fauna. He then makes some interesting observations on Brazil: "Brasil is a country exceedingly well qualified by nature for the producing of all things, which are generally found in the West-Indies, under or near the same climate; except, that hitherto no gold or silver mines have been discovered here worth taking notice of. But next to gold and silver, the sugar claims the precedency here before all other commodities. Among all the harbours and places of the West-Indies, there is not one that can compare with Brasil, either for the product, or conveniency of transportation of sugar; the whole coast of Brasil being full of small rivers, which flowing through the adjacent valleys, disembogues in the sea; from whence the sugar-mills built in the valleys reap the benefit of saving vast charges, which else must be bestowed upon labourers and carriages; whereas these rivers drive the mills, serve for the transportation of sugar to other places, and furnish them at an easy rate with what commodities they stand in need of." The author spends the last hundred pages of his account giving a detailed narrative of Dutch-Portuguese rivalry in Brazil, 1643–1647, as well as a description of Brazil's products and Amerindian and African population.

[260] James Van der Veldt. "An Autograph Letter of John Maurice of Nassau, Governor of the Dutch Colony in Brazil (1636–1644)," *The Americas* 3:3 (January 1947), pp. 311–318.

Prints and translates a letter from the Oliveira Lima Library Collection written in 1647 by John Maurice of Nassau to his panegyrist, Gaspar Barlaeus, regarding the latter's account of Nassau's eight years as governor of Dutch Brazil. The translator provides biographical details about both men and a short sketch of the Dutch West India Company and its role in Portugal's South Atlantic Empire. Van der Veldt concludes by discussing Dutch activity in West Africa under the Count's orders. 3 notes.

[261] Richard Flecknoe. *A Relation of Ten Years Travells in Europe, Asia, Affrique and America.* London, n.d. [1656]. 176 pp.

Richard Flecknoe, the Irish Jesuit priest and poet, was given 200 coroas by D. João IV to help defray the expenses of a voyage to Brazil. He sailed for Portuguese America in 1648 in the fleet of Salvador de Brito Pereira, the new governor of Rio de Janeiro. Flecknoe stayed six months in Rio. He described the town thusly: "The town of St. Sebastian is situate in a plain some mile in length, bounded at either end with rising hills, the inmost towards the lake inhabited and enclosed by the Benedictines, and the outmost towards the sea by the Fathers of the Company [Jesuits]; upon which hill was formerly situated the ancient town (as the ruins of houses, and the great Church, yet remaining, testify) till for the commodity of traffic, and portation of merchandise, it was by degrees reduced unto the plain, their buildings being but low, and streets not above three or four, the principal regarding the haven. Behind the town is a great plain some two mile over, part of it bushy, part woody, and part meadow ground, beyond which you find a country so wholly different from ours, as there is not a tree nor plant, bird, beast, nor anything you ever saw in Europe to be found." Flecknoe also describes the cultivation and processing of sugar in Rio de Janeiro in the mid-seventeenth century: "Their sugar-canes are pruned to the height of standing corn; nor need they other culture, but every second year to cut them close by the roots, as we do osiers, when against the next year they never fail to spring up again, the flags of which canes are of a pleasant green, and show afar off just like a field of corn; which being ripe about the month of June, they joint them in pieces some feet long, and carry them to the mill, turned by oxen, or water, consisting of two round cylinders, about the bigness of millposts, plated with iron, which turning inwards, and joining as close together as they can meet, so squeeze the canes in passing through them, as they come out on the other side all bruised, and dry as cakes, which were all liquid before; which liquor is conveyed by troughs to certain cauldrons, where it is boiled, still retaining its amber colour, till poured out at last into their forms or coolers, with a certain lee 'tis rendered white. And in these mills (during the season of making sugar) they work both day and night, the work of immediately applying the canes into the mill being so perilous as if through drowsiness or heedlessness a finger's end be but engaged between the posts, their whole body inevitably follows, to prevent which, the next Negro has always a hatchet ready to chop off his arm, if any such misfortune should arrive."

[262] Gabriel Dellon. *A Voyage to the East-Indies: Giving an Account of the Isles of Madagascar, and Mascareigne, of Suratte, the Coast of Malabar, of Goa, Gameron, Ormus, and the Coast of Brasil, with the Religion, Customs, Trade, &c. of the Inhabitants.* London: D. Browne, A. Roper, and T. Leigh, 1698. 248 pp.
[This is a translation of *Relation d'un voyage des Indes Orientales*, published in Paris in 1685.]

Dellon, a French "Doctor of Physick," is probably most famous for the account of his experiences with the Portuguese Inquisition at Goa **[263]**. On his return to Portugal as a prisoner, he visited Salvador from 20 May to 3 September 1676. During his stay he became "intimately acquainted with a certain Merchant, a Spaniard by Birth, but who having lived for a considerable time in those parts, gave me an exact account of the whole state of affairs of this Country." Chapter XXVI is devoted to the inhabitants of Brazil. Dellon claimed "that the Native Brazilians are to this day, Idolaters; That they are much addicted to Witchcraft, or at least are reputed so to be; they are very superstitious, have neither Temples nor Feasts, and adore the Devil. Their Hair they wear of a great length, their Complexion is swarthy, they go Naked, are naturally Brave and Nimble, and never forgive an Injury." On the other hand, "the Portugueses in Brasil, live here for the most part after the same manner as they do in other places, where they have settled their Colonies. . . . They compel the Neighbouring Brasilians to obey them, and are so well provided in their Garrisons as not to stand in fear either of the Brasilians or Europeans, in case they should come to Attack them." Finally, "the vast number of Slaves used by the Portugueses in Brasil, and the Hardship wherewith they are treated, not having a sufficient allowance for their sustenance, and being to be Punished in a most severe manner for the least faulte, proves the occasion of great disorders and outrages, which are committed by the Slaves, both in City and Country. They are for the most part Negroes, brought thither from Angola, and the Guinea Coast, their chief Employment being to work in making of Sugars, and Planting of Tobacco. They are brought to Market in whole Droves, where they are Bought and Sold no otherwise than we do our Cattle. Those who have great Plantations have several hundreds of them at a time, who are under the tuition of certain Commissaries, who are sometimes more cruel than their Masters. Those who have no Grounds of their own, give their Slaves leave to work where they can, provided they pay them a certain Tax Monthly or Weekly." Chapter XXVII, "Of the City and Port of the Bay of All Saints," describes whaling activities and briefly describes the Brazilian capital. Dellon observed that Bahia was "the residence of the Governour in chief of the Brasil Coast. 'Tis true the Governor of the City has no Authority over the rest, yet is he considered as the chief, because he takes place of all the rest. It was strongly discoursed whilst I was in Brasil, that there was to be sent thither a Vice-Roy, with the same Prerogative and Authority as the Vice-Roy of the Indies residing at Goa." In his chapter on "The Manners and Customs of the Inhabitants," Dellon claimed that "there is scarce any other place where Debauchery has got such an ascendant as here. The Women are generally great Admirers of all Strangers, but especially of the French." The author spends the remainder of the chapter by giving a description of the misadventures of "a Young French Man who Practised Physick in Brasil and married a Brazilian girl." After staying in Brazil almost three-and-a-half months, Dellon sailed with the Portuguese fleet of "thirty Sail, two and twenty of this Fleet being bound for Lisbon, the rest, being eight for Oporto." The author stayed six months in Lisbon before being permitted to return to France. Appended to his account is a chapter on Pernambuco (which Dellon did not visit)—based on Monsieur de Rennefort's *History of the East Indies*.

[263] Gabriel Dellon. *Account of the Inquisition at Goa.* Hull: I. Wilson, 1812.
[This is a translation of *Relation de l'Inquisition de Goa.* Paris, 1688.]

Of the first 39 chapters, 33 treat of his experiences with the Inquisition at Goa. Chapter 40 is of interest to students of colonial Brazil, since he adds material not found in **[262]**: "I was conveyed in irons on board a vessel on the boat bound for Portugal, and committed to the custody of the boatswain, who undertook to deliver me to the Inquisition at Lisbon; and the captain having received his final dispatches, we weighed anchor the 27th of January, 1676, and on the same day my chains were taken off. Our voyage to the Brazils was favourable. We arrived there in the month of May. On dropping anchor in the Bay of All Saints, my guard took me ashore to the Governor's palace, and thence to the public prison, where I was left in charge of the gaoler. I remained in the prison all the time the ship was in the port, but by the favour of some friends I had in the country, I was allowed to be at liberty in the day time, and shut up during the night only. The prison of the Bay is more commodious than any I had seen, except those of the Holy Office. Above the ground floor, which is tolerably clean and well lighted, there are several apartments appropriated for persons charged with slighter offences, or who are rich or well connected. There is also a chapel in which the Holy Mass is celebrated on Fridays and Festivals; and there are many charitable persons in the town, who contribute to the necessities of the prisoners."

[264] Anant Kakba Priolkar. *The Goa Inquisition.* Bombay, 1961. xii, 189 pp., 109 pp.

Part II contains excerpts from **[263]**.

[265] Anthony Sepp, S. J. and Anthony Behme, S. J. "An Account of a Voyage from Spain to Paraquaria," in A. and J. Churchill, *A Collection of Voyages and Travels* **[108]**, V, 669–695.

Interesting account of both the voyage from Cadiz to Buenos Aires and the missionary experiences among the Indians of Paraguay. Father Sepp and his companions sailed from Spain on 17 January 1691 and arrived at Buenos Aires on 30 March. He reported in detail the hardships of ocean travel. "The Captain allow'd me no other place to lie in than a narrow Cabin about 5 Foot long, and not above 2 and a half broad; and my beloved Companions Place, I mean Father Anthony Behme and another Austrian Father's were so short, that all that while they were not able to lie streight in it. . . . There was a little Window to let in the Air, but this being shut for the most part, to keep out the Sea Waves, we spent our time in Darkness; besides which the scent of the

Water in the Ship was so nauseous to us, that we were ready to be suffocated with it, and were on the other Hand no less pester'd with thousands of Mice and Rats, some whereof were not much less than Cats, and made a most terrible Noise. The smell of the Onions and Garlick, and of stinking Tobacco, of about 600 Pullets, 280 Sheep, and 150 Hogs, which were not far from our Quarters, were no small addition to the rest of our Troubles. To add to our Affliction we had for our Diet nothing but stinking Meat, and Biskets full of Maggots, the first having been Salted a Year, and the last Baked two Years before our departure." In an earlier letter Father Sepp had written that "the rest of the Missionaries were forced to take up their quarters in the Fore-castle of the Ship, exposed to the Injuries of the Weather and Air, and for an additional Plague were constantly incommoded with the stench of the Hen's Dung, which were kept thereabouts." On "the 2d of March we sailed along the Coast of Parnambuco in Brasil, where Father Anthony Vieraone [Vieira] of our Society, a Portuguese by Birth, and formerly Chaplain to Queen Christine of Sweden, lives in the Jesuits College." Near the mouth of the Rio de la Plata, "about Noon we came to the Isle Meldonato; and a Rumour being spread in Spain, that the Portugueses had taken the Post and Fortified themselves in that Island, the Governour of Buenos Ayres (pursuant to his Orders received from his Catholick Majesty) went a shoar in the said Island with some Gentlemen and Souldiers, to know the Truth thereof, they took a view of the whole Island, and found neither Men nor the Footsteeps of Men, much less any Houses or Fortifications; but prodigious numbers of fat Oxen, Cowes, Calves and Horses, the Grass being so high, that it almost covered the Cattle, notwithstanding they were very large." After resting at Buenos Aires, Father Sepp was assigned to the reduction of Japegu [Yapeyu] on the Uruguay river. "Three hundred Indian Christians were appointed with certain Vessels to carry us up the Stream; but before we embarqued, it will be requisite to give you a Description of these Vessels, which are call'd Canoes by the Spaniards. They take the Trunks of two large Trees, about 70 or 80 Foot long, and 3 or 4 Foot diameter; these two Trees they fasten together, like our Float-Woods, yet at the distance of a Pace from one another; this Interstice they fill up with Canes of about 12 Foot in length, and 2 Foot in depth; and upon it erect a certain Hut of small Canes and Straw, sufficient to contain conveniently enough 2 or 3 Persons; the Sides are commonly of Straw or Cane, covered with the same, over which they lay an Ox's Hide. On one side it has a little Window, and on the other the Door, made likewise of an Ox's Hide. In these Huts the Missionaries divert themselves during the Voyage, with as much satisfaction as if they were in a Palace, and perform the same Religious Exercises, as if they were in one of their Colleges, without the least Interruption; the Indians rowing very orderly without the least Noise, so that you shall scarce hear them speak a word all Day long." The German Jesuit was not overly impressed with the abilities of the Indians. "A Missionary in these Parts, must submit to all Functions, the Indians being so Stupid, that they are not capable of undertaking the most frivolous Thing, without a plain Direction. Whence it came that it was a Question among the first Missionaries sent hither, Whether these People were capable of receiving the Sacraments or not. But as Stupid as they are at Inventing, so happy they are in imitating, provided you give them a Model; thus if you shew one of these Indian Women a Piece of Bone-Lace, she will unrip some part of it with a Needle, and will make another after it, with so much exactness, that you shall not know one from the other." The reduction of Japegu [Yapeyu] is located near the town of Itaqui in Rio Grande do Sul.

[266] François Froger. *A Relation of a Voyage Made in the Years 1695, 1696, 1697 on the Coasts of Africa, Streights of Magellan, Brasil, Cayenna, and the Antilles, by a Squadron of French Men of War, under the Command of M. de Gennes.* London, 1698. 173 pp.

The Sieur Froger, "Voluntier-Engineer on board the English Falcon," was part of the abortive expedition headed by De Gennes to establish a French colony at the Straits of Magellan. Froger first visited Rio de Janeiro whose bay he described as the "safest and most convenient in America." As for the city itself: "'Tis large and well built, and the Streets are Streight, so that the magnificent Structures of the Jesuits and Benedictins that terminate them on both sides, each on a small Ascent, render the Prospect very delightful." The inhabitants of Rio he found to be "polite, and endow'd with a Gravity customary to their Nation: They are Rich, take much delight in Trading, and keep a great number of Negro-Slaves, besides divers entire Families of Indians, whom they maintain in their Sugar Plantations." The people had "a very great Respect for the clergy." But Froger was not impressed by the religious of the city: "Uncleanliness is not the only Vice peculiar to these lewd Monks: They live in gross Ignorance, so that very few of them understand the Latin tongue." Bested in trade by the governor of Ilha Grande, Froger declared: "We were oblig'd to afford our Commodities at a cheaper rate than they bear in Europe; which sufficiently shews the sinister Practices of that Nation, of whom three quarters are originally Jews." He was, however, favorably impressed with Salvador and its excellent Bay of All Saints which he visited on his return from the Straits of Magellan: "They take a great Number of Whales therein, build very fine Ships, and they had one then upon the Stocks that would carry sixty pieces of Cannon." Froger found the city itself to be "large, well built, and very populous. . . . It's high and low, and scarce one straight Street therein, it's the Capital City of Brazil, an Archiepiscopal See, and the Residence of the Viceroy. This place is honoured with a Sovereign Council, and the Privilege to coin Money." Froger's observations about the local ladies reveal insights into his own character as well: "They are never allowed to see any Body, and go not out of doors at any other time but on Sunday early in the Morning, to Go to Church. They are a very jealous People, and 'tis a kind of point of Honour for a Man to stab his Wife, when he can convict her of being unfaithful to his Bed; tho' for all that, this cannot hinder many of them from finding out a way to impart some of their Favours to us Frenchmen, whose winning and free Conversation they are mightily in love with."

[267] William Dampier. *A Voyage to New Holland, &c. In the Year 1699.* London: James Knapton, 1703, xii, 162 pp.
[In 1729, the same publisher issued a four-volume account of Dampier's voyages. The Argonaut Press published a reprint of the 1729 edition in 1939, edited by James A. Williamson.]

William Dampier (1652–1715), described by Borba de Moraes **[20]** as "a combination pirate, adventurer and explorer," originally planned to stop at Pernambuco, but fear of mutiny prompted him to sail on to Bahia, "the most considerable Town in Brazil whether in Respect of the Beauty of its Buildings, its Bulk, or its Trade and Revenue," where he arrived on 25 March 1699. Dampier describes the bay and its fortifications. He lists the city's thirteen churches, chapels and monasteries and its hospital and nunnery. The author also reports on the palaces of the Archbishop and the Governor (Dom João de Lencastre) as well as the planters' townhouses. There were four hundred soldiers in the garrison and a thousand available for militia duty. Thirty ships from Europe were at anchor, most of them arriving in February or March and returning the end of May or June. Dampier enumerates the items involved in Bahia's trade with Europe and mentions the shipping used in the Guinea as well as the coastal trade. Many of the smaller coastal crafts were manned by Black slaves. Whaling and shipbuilding were other maritime activities. In addition to merchants, there were also "other pretty wealthy Men, and several Artificers and Trades-men of most Sorts, who by Labour and Industry maintain themselves very well; especially such as can arrive at the Purchase of a Negro-Slave or two." All, "excepting People of the lowest Degree," owned household slaves, the wealthier also being accompanied or carried by slaves while making visits in town, "for they take a Piece of Pride in greeting one another from their Hammocks." Dampier listed smiths, hatters, shoemakers, tanners, sawyers, carpenters, coopers, tailors, and butchers as the chief artisans in the Brazilian capital. They, in turn, frequently bought slaves and trained them. Many slaves were used as stevedores and porters. African slaves made up the majority of the population. According to Dampier, many of the Portuguese who were bachelors kept black women as mistresses "tho' they know the Danger they are in of being poyson'd by them, if ever they give them any Occasion of Jealousy." After describing crime in the Brazilian capital, the author discusses in some detail the surrounding countryside and its flora and fauna. During Dampier's month-long stay in Bahia, the Viceroy of Goa arrived "in a great Ship, said to be richly laden with all Sorts of India Goods; but she did not break Bulk here, being bound Home for Lisbon" in company with the other Portuguese ships loading in Bahia. The author finally set sail on 23 April 1699 after having his ship scrubbed and taking on water, rum, oranges, sugar and ballast, omitting fowl, which he found to be "lean and dear." Includes a map of his voyage, and plates showing various landmarks of Bahia and a drawing of plants found in Brazil.

X. *Administration in Brazil* [Nos. 268–293]

A. Portuguese Councils [No. 268]

Another neglected topic in colonial Brazilian history has been administration. The only detailed study in English of a Portuguese Council has been that of Joyce **[268]**. Boxer **[277]** provides an excellent summary of the Portuguese overseas administrative apparatus during the sixteenth and seventeenth centuries in his study of Salvador de Sá. Alden **[274]** does the same for the eighteenth century in his biography of the Marquis of Lavradio. The activities and procedures of the Portuguese Overseas Council are discussed in Dutra **[294]** regarding the naming of bishops for Brazil, and Bardwell **[279]** and Tengwall **[289]** respectively, for the appointment of governors and *sargentos-mores* for Portuguese America. The role of the Overseas Council in drawing up Indian legislation is handled by Kiemen **[425]** and **[427]** and Fonseca **[428]**. During the sixteenth and early seventeenth century, the Mesa da Consciência e Ordens played an important role in drawing up Indian legislation. Kiemen **[425]** provides a short sketch of some of the Mesa's duties as does Boxer **[277]** in his biography of Salvador de Sá. Dutra **[297]** and **[475]** describes its role in administering the military orders of Christ, Santiago and Avis.

[268] Joseph Newcombe Joyce, Jr., "Spanish Influence on Portuguese Administration: A Study of the Conselho da Fazenda and Habsburg Brazil, 1580–1640," (Ph.D. Dissertation: University of Southern California, 1974). 455 pages.

A record of the Conselho da Fazenda (Council of Finance), the Habsburg institution charged with administering the finances of Portugal and its empire. It was at its most influential during the years 1610 to 1630. Brazil was an important area under its jurisdiction and the council was involved with Brazil's development, expansion and safety.

The interdependence of finances and defense meant that the council had to address itself to rescuing the empire, particularly Brazil, from the Dutch. Its failure to effectively meet that responsibility led to its decline in the 1630s. In spite of several instances of renewal it continued to decline and eventually lost most of its responsibilities to the Overseas Council, a new institution formed in 1643 after Portugal's revolt for independence from Spain. Based on a study of that body's correspondence in Spain and Portugal, especially in the Arquivo Histórico Ultramarino, Lisbon.
DAI 38/03-A (p. 1751).

B. Governors-General and Viceroys [Nos. 269–275]

The first three governors-general—Tomé de Sousa **[269]**, Duarte da Costa **[270]**, and Mem de Sá **[271]**—have been ably studied by Ruth Lapham Butler. Diogo Botelho's Pernambucan stay is analyzed by Francis A. Dutra **[151]** as are those of his immediate successors, Diogo de Meneses, D. Francisco de Sousa and D. Luis de Sousa, in the same author's "Centralization vs. Donatarial Privilege" **[152]**. Dutra also provides a biography of Matias de Albuquerque, governor-general of Brazil, 1624–1626 **[272]**. Stuart B. Schwartz **[273]** discusses the administration of Afonso Furtado de Castro, governor-general of Brazil, 1671–1675. For the eighteenth century there are two studies by Dauril Alden **[274]** and **[275]** on the Marquis of Lavradio, viceroy of Brazil in Rio de Janeiro, 1769–1779.

[269] Ruth Lapham Butler. "Tomé de Sousa, First Governor-General of Brazil, 1549–1553," *Mid-America* 24:4 (October 1942), pp. 229–251.

Though recent research has modified some of the author's introductory remarks on conditions in Brazil before 1549, the main section of the article provides a valuable and judicious assessment of Sousa's achievements during the slightly more than four years he served in Portuguese America. Of particular value is the item-by-item summary of the governor-general's *regimento* (standing orders) with a discussion of how well these instructions were implemented. Based on printed sources and secondary works. 55 notes.

[270] Ruth Lapham Butler. "Duarte da Costa, Second Governor-General of Brazil," *Mid-America* 25:3 (July 1943), pp. 163–179.

From the few extant documents for the stormy years of Duarte da Costa's administration (1553–1557), the author provides an evaluation of his efforts and their effects on Brazil and concludes that despite his good intentions, the governor was "unhappy, inept, and unimaginative." Based on printed sources. 56 notes.

[271] Ruth Lapham Butler. "Mem de Sá, Third Governor-General of Brazil, 1557–1572," *Mid-America* 26:2 (April 1944), pp. 111–137.

Focuses mostly on Mem de Sá's activities outside the Brazilian capital of Bahia with a special emphasis on his struggles against the French and the Indians during his slightly more than fourteen-year presence in Brazil as governor-general. Contains several errors regarding Sá's authority in Brazil and is the weakest of the author's studies on the governors-general. Based on printed materials. 70 notes.

[272] Francis Anthony Dutra. "Matias de Albuquerque: A Seventeenth-Century *Capitão-Mor* of Pernambuco and Governor General of Brazil," (Ph.D. Dissertation: New York University, 1968). 416 pp.

This study analyzes the early career of Matias de Albuquerque (1595–1647), a young military figure during the period of Habsburg domination, and clarifies the role of Pernambuco in Brazilian politics during the last days of that captaincy's "golden age" as a proprietary colony. The grandson of Duarte Coelho **[149]**, son of Jorge de Albuquerque **[150]** and brother of Duarte de Albuquerque Coelho, respectively the first, third and fourth *donatários* or lord-prorietors of Pernambuco, Matias served as *capitão-mor* of his family's captaincy (1620–1626) and governor-general of Brazil (1624–1626). As the first male member of his family to preside over the captaincy in almost half a century, Matias devoted his efforts to restoring donatarial authority. The capture of the governor-general of Brazil by the Dutch in 1624 and the naming of Matias as his successor provided a resolution to many of the "states rights" problems Pernambuco had faced. The abolition of the *Relação* or High Court in 1626—largely through the efforts of the Albuquerque Coelho family—made the triumph complete. In addition to successfully regaining many of his family's donatarial privileges in Pernambuco, Matias restored that captaincy's hegemony over much of

northern Portuguese America, thereby limiting Bahia's influence to the south. Military matters absorbed much of Matias de Albuquerque's energy. After the fall of Bahia to the Dutch in 1624, Matias was the leading Portuguese military figure residing in Brazil. By sending men and supplies to the Portuguese forces in Bahia, Albuquerque facilitated the Iberian victory of 1625. His alertness to the Dutch menace prevented the Hollanders from inflicting heavy damage on his captaincy and the area to the north. Based on extensive use of archival materials in Portugal, Spain and Brazil.
DAI 29/12A (p. 4421).

[273] Stuart B. Schwartz, ed. *A Governor and His Image in Baroque Brazil. The Funereal Eulogy of Afonso Furtado de Castro do Rio de Mendonça by Juan Lopes Sierra.* Trans. Ruth E. Jones. Minneapolis: University of Minnesota Press, 1979. xi, 216 pp.

Contains an English translation of the eulogy (completed in 1676) of the Viscount of Barbacena, Afonso Furtado de Castro do Rio de Mendonça, governor-general of Brazil, 1671–1675. Schwartz includes some excellent introductory material on Portuguese America in the seventeenth century including an analysis of economic causes of Brazilian expansion and a biography of the governor-general. Schwartz points out that the governor-general "demonstrated very little sympathy for the Indians who endangered the colony and hindered its expansion." It was during Afonso Furtado's administration that Dom Rodrigo de Castel-Blanco **[255]** arrived to undertake the discovery of mines—a project that failed. In his eulogy of the governor-general, Juan Lopes Sierra not only sketches the key events in Afonso Furtado's administration but describes his pious works. He concludes with a detailed description of the funeral ceremonies and the governor's tomb. Schwartz, in his introduction, provides information on the little-known author of the eulogy, who described himself as "a rustic in the sciences." There are several excellent appendices. Appendix A (Personalia) provides biographical sketches of some of the key figures in Brazil during the governor-general's term of office: Estevão Ribeiro Baião Parente, Francisco Fernandes do Sim, Rodrigo de Castel-Blanco **[255]**, Bernardo Vieira Ravasco, João Peixoto Viegas, João de Matos de Aguiar, Antônio Guedes de Brito, and Pedro Gomes. Appendix B contains "A Note on Portuguese and Brazilian Military Organization." Appendix C is a genealogy of Afonso Furtado. Appendix D includes a table of weights, measures and currency. There are 66 notes to the introduction and 83 notes to the text of the eulogy. There is also a useful map of the Bahian *sertão* in the seventeenth century.

[274] Dauril Alden. *Royal Government in Colonial Brazil With Special Reference to the Administration of the Marquis of Lavradio, Viceroy 1769–1779.* Berkeley and Los Angeles: University of California Press, 1968. xvii, 545 pp.

This is a well-researched and thorough study of the Marquis of Lavradio, viceroy of Brazil from 1769–1779, and his times. The author discusses Lavradio's apprenticeship as governor-general of Bahia, 1768–1769, his promotion to the viceroyship in Rio de Janeiro, and the ten years of his administration, especially the problems he faced in the new Brazilian capital (1763) and in the "debatable lands" to the south of Rio Grande do Sul and Santa Catarina in the aftermath of the abortive Treaty of Madrid (1750). There is also an excellent section on the economic problems southern Brazil encountered during the last half of the eighteenth century. Attempts at economic development are discussed as are the viceroy's struggles against smugglers and contrabandists. The author also evaluates Lavradio as an administrator and discusses his relationship with governors in the other captaincies in Brazil. There is a good discussion of Sebastião José de Carvalho e Melo, Marquis of Pombal **[717]** the dominant minister of Portugal, 1750–1777, one of whose proteges was Lavradio. Alden concludes with a useful critique of colonial Brazilian history. Based on archival research in Brazil as well as printed primary and secondary sources. There is an excellent annotated bibliography on pages 513–533.

[275] Dauril Alden. "The Marquis of Lavradio, Viceroy of Brazil (1769–1779), and the Climax of Luso-Spanish Platine Rivalry," (Ph.D. Dissertation: University of California, Berkeley, 1959). 554 pp.

Alden remarks in his preface that "this study forms a portion of a larger work in progress on the administration of Dom Luis de Almeida, second Marquis of Lavradio" **[274]**. Therefore the author limits his thesis to an analysis of the most critical problem confronting Lavradio—the struggle between Spain and Portugal for control of southern Brazil. The first two chapters of Part I deal with Lavradio's early career in Bahia, the position of viceroy of Brazil in general and Lavradio's administration in particular. Chapters three and four provide the background for Alden's lengthy discussion on the conflict over the "debatable lands." Part II and its six chapters contain a detailed examination of the decade 1769–1779—a decisive one in Luso-Spanish rivalry in the Plata region. There is an excellent bibliography on pp. 521–554. Based on archival materials in Brazil. The frontispiece is a portrait and signature of Lavradio. 11 maps and a chart.

C. Governors and *Capitães-Mores* [Nos. 276–281]

David P. Henige **[276]** provides a comprehnsive and accurate list of three centuries of governors in Portuguese America. Biographies of sixteenth-century governors in Brazil have been neglected by historians. For the first half of the seventeenth century, see Dutra **[272]** and his study of Matias de Albuquerque, governor and *capitão-mor* of Pernambuco, 1620–1626. Boxer **[277]** and Cardozo **[278]** provide biographies of Salvador Correia de Sá, governor of Rio de Janeiro from 1637–1643. Ross Bardwell **[279]** has done a collective biography of the more than three hundred candidates for the one hundred and ten job openings as governors in Portugal's South Atlantic Empire in the second half of the seventeenth century. Robert White **[280]** has provided a biography of Gomes Freire de Andrade, governor of Rio de Janeiro from 1733–1763, while Charles Dorenkott **[281]** has done the same for José da Silva Pais, governor of Santa Catarina, 1739–1749. Dauril Alden **[274]** draws a brief sketch of the Marquis of Lavradio's service in Bahia as captain-general (1768–1769) before being transferred to the post of viceroy of Rio de Janeiro. Robert C. Smith **[609]** performs a similar task for Marcos de Noronha e Brito, Conde dos Arcos, captain-general for Bahia, 1810–1818, who had moved north after being viceroy of Rio de Janeiro from 1806–1808.

[276] David P. Henige. *Colonial Governors from the Fifteenth Century to the Present. A Comprehensive List.* Madison: University of Wisconsin Press, 1970. xx, 461 pp.

In this very useful compilation, Portugal Overseas is covered on pages 227 to 273. Henige gives a general introduction along with short, one paragraph surveys for each captaincy or jurisdiction. Includes bibliographies.

[277] Charles R. Boxer. *Salvador de Sá and the Struggle for Brazil and Angola, 1602–1686.* (London: The Athlone Press, 1952). xvi, 444 pp.

Much more than a biography, this excellent study provides the reader with a fine insight into the history of Portugal and its South Atlantic Empire from 1580–1680 and is the best account of that period in English. Boxer discusses the career of Salvador Correia de Sá, his early visits to Brazil, mostly in search of mines, and his knighthoods in the Order of Santiago and later that of the Order of Christ. Sá's skirmishes with the Dutch and his appointment as *alcaide-mor* of Rio de Janeiro

"for all the days of his life" are recounted as well as his service in Paraguay and Tucumán and his return to the Iberian peninsula. Salvador de Sá was governor of the captaincy of Rio de Janeiro (1637–1643) during the Bragança Restoration and proclaimed for João IV. Returning to Europe, he was appointed general of the Brazil fleets. In 1648, Sá recaptured Luanda in Angola from the Dutch. He was named Captain General of Brazil's Southern Captaincies eleven years later. While there he extinguished a revolt in Rio de Janeiro against his family, the Sás having played a dominant role in that captaincy for almost a century. Sá returned to Portugal for the last time in 1663 to continue his service as overseas councillor, a position to which he was first appointed in 1643. He was disgraced in 1667 because of his support for Afonso VI in that monarch's struggle against his brother, the future Pedro II. But in 1669, Sá was restored to favor and continued to serve as an overseas councillor, signing his last *consulta* in January of 1681 and dying sometime during that decade. Based on research in Portuguese, Brazilian, English, Dutch and Angolan archives and on printed primary and secondary sources. There is an excellent bibliography on pages 408–423.
See also **[278]**.

[278] Manoel Cardozo. "Notes for a Biography of Salvador Correia de Sá e Benavides, 1594–1688," *The Americas* 7:2 (October 1950), pp. 135–170.

Gives a special emphasis to the Brazilian career of Salvador de Sá, "the last great representative of a family long prominent in Brazilian affairs." Most of the article deals with Sá's activities while governor of Rio de Janeiro (1637–1643), his relationship with the Jesuits, his proclamation in favor of D. João IV, and his continued interest in discovering mines. Cardozo also discusses Sá's role in the recapture of Luanda and as governor of Angola as well as his work on the Overseas Council in Lisbon. Based on archival (Arquivo Histórico Ultramarino, Lisbon) and primary printed materials. 134 notes.

[279] Ross Little Bardwell. "The Governors of Portugal's South Atlantic Empire in the Seventeenth Century: Social Background, Qualifications, Selection, and Reward," (Ph.D. Dissertation: University of California, Santa Barbara, 1974). 281 pp.

Explores the backgrounds of 110 successful and 220 unsuccessful candidates for posts as governors in Portugal's South Atlantic Empire in the seventeenth century. The Overseas Council and the King were in

agreement that military proficiency was the primary requirement for the post. Nobility was another criterion, and since the old titled nobility was largely uninterested in overseas duty, members of the new nobility (awarded patents during the inflation of honors) and soldiers of fortune (granted patents of nobility because of their military service) were chosen. The Overseas Council, according to the author, acted conscientiously in appointing colonial governors, not generally permitting offices to be obtained by wealth or family influence. Based on archival materials in the Arquivo Histórico Ultramarino and the Arquivo Nacional da Torre do Tombo, both in Lisbon.
DAI 35/11-A (p. 7205)

[280] Robert Allan White. "Gomes Freire de Andrada: Life and Times of a Brazilian Colonial Governor, 1688–1763," (Ph.D. Dissertation: The University of Texas at Austin, 1972). 286 pp.

Biography of the influential royal governor Gomes Freire de Andrada, first Count of Bobadela, who "ruled longer and with more influence than any other royal governor in the history of the Portuguese colonial empire." Administering southern Brazil from 1733 to 1763, Gomes Freire was directly involved with the principal issues of the day, such as gold mining, antismuggling regulations, diamond production, betterment of life in Rio de Janeiro, and the struggle with the Spaniards in the south. Based on Brazilian archival materials.
DAI 34/05-A (p. 2540)

[281] Charles Joseph Dorenkott, Jr. "José da Silva Pais: The Defense and Expansion of Southern Brazil, 1735–1749," (Ph.D. Dissertation: The University of New Mexico, 1972). 339 pp.

Examines the accomplishments of José da Silva Pais, military engineer and hero of the War of Spanish Succession, who was appointed governor of Rio de Janeiro in 1735. After strengthening the defenses of that port city, he became involved in moves to defeat the Spanish in the La Plata region. The first Portuguese settlement in Rio Grande do Sul was founded by him and he was the first governor of that territory. Later he was also the first governor of Santa Catarina (1739–1749). Based on Brazilian archival materials as well as printed primary and secondary sources.
DAI 33/07-A (p. 3533)

D. Financial Administration [No. 282]

One of the most neglected topics in colonial Brazilian history has been financial administration. Manoel Cardozo **[282]** discusses the collection of the royal fifth in Minas Gerais in the late seventeenth and early eighteenth century. He **[298]** also discusses the collection of the tithe in Minas Gerais. Caio Prado, Jr. **[73]** devotes a chapter to financial administration with an emphasis on the eighteenth century. Dauril Alden **[274]** provides a good discussion of some of the Pombaline economic and administrative reforms. Kenneth Maxwell **[719]** also contributes some useful information on the Pombaline reforms.

[282] Manoel S. Cardozo. "The Collection of the Fifths in Brazil, 1695–1709," *The Hispanic American Historical Review* 20:3 (August 1940), pp. 359–379.

Lists and discusses the various proposals made to the Crown and the Overseas Council for ways to collect more efficiently the royal fifths on Brazilian gold during the early years of the mining boom in Minas Gerais. Suggestions included more strategically located and better regulated smelting houses, inspection stations on the principal roads leading to Rio de Janeiro, São Paulo, Bahia and Pernambuco, the establishment of royal mints in Rio de Janeiro and Bahia, and farming out the royal fifth. Based almost entirely on archival materials in the Arquivo Histórico Ultramarino, Lisbon. 101 notes.

E. Magistrates and Justice [Nos. 283–286]

Stuart B. Schwartz has done much to fill the gap in our knowledge of colonial Brazil's judicial system. The early years of the *Relação* or High Court are carefully analyzed in his doctoral dissertation **[283]**, while his published work, *Sovereignty and Society* **[284]**, provides an overview of the High Court's activities and its relationship to the rest of Brazilian society for the period to 1751. The magistrates themselves are studied by Schwartz **[285]**, who uses a collective biography approach. Theresa Sherrer Davidson **[286]** describes the Brazilian inheritance of Roman law.

[283] Stuart Barry Schwartz. "The High Court of Bahia: A Study in Hapsburg Brazil 1580–1630," (Ph.D. Dissertation: Columbia University, 1968). 414 pp.

A study of justice in Habsburg Brazil, particularly of the High Court of Bahia (*Relação*), established in 1609. The judges, all lawyers trained at the University of Coimbra and most of them with experience as magistrates in Portugal, owed their position to the Crown. Generally they gave to the King their first loyalty even though many magistrates were drawn into alliances with the Bahian elites. Court decisions supporting legislation against Indian enslavement and favoring the tenant farmer against big plantation owners reflect the Court's independence from the sugar aristocracy. Before the Court was abolished in 1626 (until 1652) due to an alliance of sugar planters with the Pernambucan lord-proprietor and his family who desired its end, it had brought justice to a broader group of the colonial population than theretofore. DAI 29/02-A (p. 531)

[284] Stuart B. Schwartz. *Sovereignty and Society in Colonial Brazil. The High Court of Bahia and its Judges, 1609–1751.* Berkeley, Los Angeles, London: University of California Press, 1973. xxvii, 438 pp. illus.

Important discussion of justice and the judicial bureaucracy in Brazil with an emphasis on the years 1609–1626. The author discusses justice and its implementation in Portugal and the Portuguese overseas empire, paying special attention to the role of the *ouvidor-geral* and his subordinates in sixteenth-century Brazil. There is a fine analysis of Spanish reforms during the union of crowns (1580–1640) and a useful description of the institution of the first *Relação* or High Court for Brazil. The background of the various magistrates who served from 1609 to 1626 is discussed as is the social milieu of Bahia. There is a valuable chapter, "Judges, Jesuits, and Indians," and an analysis of the problems the High Court faced and why it was suppressed. The concluding part of his study is entitled, "The *Relação* Reborn, 1652–1751." In it Schwartz discusses problems concerning justice in Brazil and studies the backgrounds of the judges serving on the High Court of Bahia during the years 1652 to 1759 and their interaction with Portuguese American society. Based on extensive archival research in Portugal, Spain, Brazil and England. There is an excellent bibliography on pp. 401–429.

[285] Stuart B. Schwartz. "Magistracy and Society in Colonial Brazil," *The Hispanic American Historical Review* 50:4 (November 1970), pp. 715–730.

After outlining the rise of the magistrates, "the core of the Portuguese imperial bureaucracy," both at home and abroad, the author analyzes the socioeconomic backgrounds and careers of a hundred such magistrates who served on the Brazilian High Court *(Relação)* between 1609 and 1759. Schwartz concludes: "While the formal structure of administration placed Brazil in a classic colonial position, the informal structure allowed colonial interest groups to treat the magistrates as simply another source of power subject to alliance and cooptation." Based on archival and printed materials as well as secondary sources. 45 notes.

[286] Theresa Sherrer Davidson. "The Brazilian Inheritance of Roman Law," in James B. Watson *et al. Brazil: Papers Presented in the Institute for Brazilian Studies, Vanderbilt University*. (Nashville: Vanderbilt University Press, 1953), pp. 59–90.

After discussing the law of the Roman empire, the Visigothic codes, and the Ordenações Afonsinas (the latter published in 1446 by Afonso V of Portugal), the author focuses on the Ordenações Manuelinas (1521) and the Ordenações Filipinas (1603), both of which had an important influence on Brazil. Davidson points out that the "code, known as the Ordenações Manuelinas, was in effect throughout the remainder of the sixteenth century. During this time Portugal was engaged in colonizing Brazil, and, except as to matters for which specific provision had been made in grants and charters of captaincies, which, in general, did not affect the private law, the Ordenações Manuelinas, together with subsequent Portuguese legislation, constituted the law of Brazil. The next, and for Brazil the final, Portuguese code was the Ordenações Filipinas of 1603. This was a revision of the preceding code, accomplished mainly by the addition of subsequent legislation. As in the earlier codes the dependence upon Roman law in the formulation of a great part of its provisions is obvious." The author also discusses the effect of the "Law of Good Reason," of 18 August 1769 which "limited the use of the Roman law as a subsidiary source." Much of the latter part of the article deals with twentieth-century Brazilian jurisprudence. Based on printed primary and secondary materials. 107 notes. There is a bibliography on pp. 89–90.

F. Local Administration [Nos. 287–288]

Charles R. Boxer **[42]** provides an overview of local administration overseas in his *Portuguese Seaborne Empire.* He has a section on Bahia in *Portuguese Society in the Tropics* **[287]**. A. J. R. Russell-Wood **[288]** examines the town council in Minas Gerais.

[287] Charles R. Boxer. *Portuguese Society in the Tropics. The Municipal Councils of Goa, Macao, Bahia and Luanda, 1510–1800.* Madison and Milwaukee: The University of Wisconsin Press, 1965, xvi, 240 pp.

Bahia is covered on pp. 72–109 and there is a general introduction on pp. 3–11. The author presents a brief but useful overview of a much neglected topic and discusses the town council's composition, its sources of income, its efforts at promoting health and welfare, and its relationship with the Brazil Company, representatives of the Crown and the higher clergy. Based mainly on printed primary sources. There is a bibliography on pp. 219–231.

[288] A. J. R. Russell-Wood. "Local Government in Portuguese America: A Study in Cultural Divergence," *Comparative Studies in Society and History* 16:2 (March 1974), pp. 187–231.

Russell-Wood argues that the town council in Brazil "exemplified, as did the *Relação* (High Court), the *Fazenda Real* (Treasury), the judicial, military and ecclesiastical authorities, and the semi-bureaucratic *Santa Casa da Misericordia,* the conservative and non-innovative policy adopted by the Portuguese Crown towards an empire ranging from the Moluccas to Mato Grosso." To support this argument, the author studies the town council in eighteenth century Minas Gerais with a special focus on that of Vila Rica (Ouro Preto). He provides a good insight into the duties and the daily workings of the town council or *sendado da câmara* and its role in society as well as the responsibilities of the councillors and how they actually carried them out. Russell-Wood also describes the salaried officials the *câmara* employed and the social services they furnished. He also points out that "there was convergence of jurisdiction over a single area in the persons of several individuals on the one hand, and convergence of responsibilities for numerous branches of local government in a single individual on the other." A comparison of town councils in Brazil with those in Spanish and Anglo America concludes the study. For students interested in social science language and models, Russell-Wood provides a "theory of converging structures analysis" (pp. 188–192). The remainder of the article, however, is a straightforward overview of important aspects of local government in eighteenth-century Minas Gerais. Based on extensive use of town council records from Ouro Preto (Vila Rica). 173 notes.

G. Military [Nos. 289–293]

The most complete study to date of the military in colonial Brazil is David L. Tengwall's **[289]** analysis of the role of the *sargento-mor* in the seventeenth century. Robert A. Hayes **[290]** attempts a general survey of the colonial period and emphasizes the influence of the militia. Since all the governors of seventeenth-century Brazil had military experience, see Ross Bardwell's **[279]** study of the governors in Portugal's South Atlantic Empire. Stuart B. Schwartz **[273]** also offers a brief survey of the military in seventeenth-century Brazil. The earlier part of the seventeenth century is covered by Francis A. Dutra **[153]**, who studies the defense of Pernambuco and the Northeast during the 1620s, and Charles R. Boxer **[277]**, who analyzes defensive measures in southern Brazil in his biography of Salvador Correia de Sá. Military aspects of the struggle against the Dutch are best treated by Boxer **[239]** in his study of the Dutch in Brazil. George Edmundson **[241]**, **[242]**, and **[243]** furnished additional details on the early fighting. The role of the military in Bahia in the late colonial period is examined by John N. Kennedy **[606]** and F. W. O. Morton **[607]**. The military history of southern Brazil during the eighteenth century—especially the struggle against the Spaniards in the Plata region—is traced by Joseph Dorenkott **[281]** in his study of José da Silva Pais and Dauril Alden **[274]** and **[275]** in his biography of the Marquis do Lavradio. Robert A. Hayes **[291]** briefly studies the role of the military in the early nineteenth century, as does Michael C. McBeth **[292]** and **[293]** in his studies on the First Empire. The role of the military engineer is discussed by David Tengwall **[289]** and Robert C. Smith **[765]**. The efforts of the military in the seventeenth century to achieve status by obtaining memberships in the military orders of Christ, Santiago and Avis are studied by Francis A. Dutra **[297]** and **[475]**.

[289] David Lewis Tengwall. "The Portuguese Military in the Seventeenth Century: The *Sargento Mor* in the Portuguese South Atlantic Empire, 1640–1706," (Ph.D. Dissertation: University of California, Santa Barbara, 1978).

Traces the role of the *sargento-mor* in Portugal during the reigns of Sebastião I (1557–1578) and Philip I (1580–1598) and compares it to that of the *sargento-mor* of Brazil and the various captaincies during the late sixteenth and seventeenth centuries with a special emphasis on the period following the Portuguese Restoration of 1640. Using a collective biography approach, Tengwall studies the social and professional backgrounds as well as the military experience of the *sargentos-mores* serving in many of the captaincies as the chief military figures after the governor and *capitão-mor*. The *sargentos-mores*' opportunities for promotion, social advancement (patents of nobility and membership in the military orders of Christ, Santiago or Avis) and crown rewards are analyzed. The role of the Portuguese Overseas Council and its decisionmaking procedures are also examined. Based almost entirely on Portuguese archival and printed primary materials.

[290] Robert A. Hayes. "The Formation of the Brazilian Army and the Military Class Mystique, 1500–1853" in Henry H. Keith and Robert A. Hayes, eds., *Perspectives on Armed Politics in Brazil.* Tempe, Arizona: Arizona State University Press, 1976, pp. 1–26.

Traces the close relationship between the military and civilians that developed during the colonial period when all able-bodied males were expected to serve in the militia. At the same time, as the author shows, military men were assigned to a great variety of nonmilitary jobs. The arrival of the Portuguese Court to Brazil in 1807 brought a number of important changes for the military. New ministries for military affairs were established and steps were taken to create "a true national army." However, when Pedro I came to power, he chose Portuguese-born officers over those born in Brazil and clashed with native-born civilian leaders. This disillusioned many Brazilians, both soldiers and civilians, and eventually "brought about the unification of those leaders for the purpose of ending his rule." Thus, from a military point of view: "Because they were denied the role of true professionals and were called upon to serve society in many unique ways, Brazilian army officiers inevitably developed interests in virtually every aspect of their society, including politics. As one result, military men came to view the welfare of the army and the nation as one." Pages 1–3 contain a useful overview by the editors of Hayes's chapter; pages 4–19 cover the period to 1825. Unfortunately, the survey of the colonial period is marred by an inordinate number of factual errors. Based entirely on printed works, most of them secondary. 50 notes. This book itself has a glossary, but no index.

[291] Robert Ames Hayes. "The Formation of the Brazilian Army and Its Political Behavior (1807–1930)," (Ph.D. Dissertation: The University of New Mexico, 1969). 242 pp.

Attempts to study the development of the Brazilian army from 1807 to 1930. Part I deals with the period before 1889. The author argues that "prior to 1807, Brazilian military forces are seen as sharing a certain homogeneous quality with society itself which made the militia, the fundamental force of the period, an effective fighting unit despite its relatively unprofessional standards of training and equipment." But in 1807, according to Hayes, this homogeneous quality began to break down as a result of "a split between the planter class, the principal source for the national political elite until 1889, and the remainder of society, including the military class."
DAI 30/04-A (pp. 1613–1614).

[292] Michael C. McBeth. "The Brazilian Recruit during the First Empire: Slave or Soldier?" in Alden and Dean, eds., *Essays Concerning the Socioeconomic History of Brazil and Portuguese India* **[89]**, pp. 71–86.

Quotes a decree of 1764 calling for the enlistment into the army of "lazy and unemployed young men who are a burden on the rest of society" and shows that a similar philosophy influenced recruitment practices during the First Empire (1822–1831). The author describes recruitment methods and the swearing-in ceremony as well as the supplies, housing, rations, wages, duties, and punishments the new soldiers received. The sixteen-year term of duty was so severe that many compared it to slavery. Not surprisingly, desertion was common. One contemporary remarked that during the Cisplatine War (1825–1828), the system of sentinels "seemed designed more to impede desertion of our own men than to detect an enemy attack, because the sentries look inwards toward the encampment." Faced with growing military insubordination and rebellion in the late 1820s, many felt that a change in philosophy was needed. The imperial army was greatly reduced and a National Guard—"a militia designed to watch over the army"—was created in 1831 by the Regency. As one newspaper approvingly remarked, care should be taken "not to put arms in the hands of a mass of men who either hate our system or have no interest in public order." Based on archival and printed primary sources. 46 notes.

[293] Michael Charles McBeth. "The Politicians vs. the Generals. The Decline of the Brazilian Army During the First Empire, 1822–1831." (Ph.D. Dissertation: University of Washington, 1972). 291 pp.

Most of the dissertation focuses on the years 1822–1831. There is, however, a survey of the military during the period before independence.
DAI 33/08-A (p. 4312)

XI. Religion in Brazil [Nos. 294–350]

A. The Catholic Church [Nos. 294–334]

1. Hierarchy, Secular Clergy, Laity [Nos. 294–302]

With the exception of Francis A. Dutra's study on the Brazilian hierarchy in the seventeenth century **[294]**, little has been written on the Brazilian bishops. Burns **[734]** and Cardozo **[735]**, though writing about the eighteenth-century bishop of Pernambuco, Azeredo Coutinho, focus more on his social, economic and political writings and say little about his role as a churchman. Leslie Rout **[490]** challenges the assertion of Sir Harry Johnston **[447]** that there were black bishops in eighteenth-century Brazil. Bailey Diffie **[71]** and Robert Southey **[70]** have some useful information on church administration and the secular clergy, but these topics have been largely neglected by other historians. The Portuguese clerico-military Order of Christ and its role in Brazil is discussed by Dutra **[297]**. Manoel Cardozo **[298]** has a valuable article on another important topic—that of tithes—in his study detailing their collection in Minas Gerais in the eighteenth-century. Fernando de Azevedo **[743]** provides a good discussion of education and religion in his massive study on Brazilian culture, which can be supplemented by the brief sketch of Amoroso Lima **[296]** on education in Brazil, most of which was in Jesuit hands prior to their expulsion in 1759. René Ribeiro **[486]** and Roger Bastide **[483]** discuss the Christianization of the newly arrived Africans and their descendants. Important comparisons between Spanish and Portuguese missionary activity, with some interesting observations on why the Church developed differently in Spanish America and Brazil, are provided by Ricard **[295]**.

The lay brotherhoods (*irmandades*) have recently been the subject of a good deal of research. A pioneering study is that of Manoel Cardozo **[299]** for colonial Bahia. Russell-Wood **[300]** has focused on Bahia's Santa Casa da Misericordia, while both he **[488]** and Patricia

Mulvey **[487]** have analyzed the black and mulatto brotherhoods in Brazil as a whole. An attempted overview of the role of black brotherhoods in Portuguese America is found in Julita Scarano **[489]**. Other social aspects of the Church's role in Brazil are discussed by Roger Bastide **[302]**.

[294] Francis A. Dutra. "The Brazilian Hierarchy in the Seventeenth Century," *Records of the American Catholic Historical Society of Philadelphia* 83: 3–4 (September–December 1972), pp. 171–186.

Analyzes the role of the Overseas Council in recommending prelates for Brazil and evaluates the performances of the bishops and archbishops who served in Portuguese America during the seventeenth century. Based on archival and printed sources. 62 notes.

[295] Robert Ricard. "Comparison of Evangelization in Portuguese and Spanish America," *The Americas* 14:4 (April 1958), pp. 444–453.

Provocative essay on similarities and differences between the development and influence of the Church in Brazil and in Spanish America. The author discusses and compares demographic factors, the extent of the two empires, the rapidity of European occupation, the nature of colonization, the approaches and contributions of the mendicant orders and the Jesuits, the influence of the Council of Trent, the implementation of the *Patronato* and the *Padroado Real,* the strength of sociopolitical institutions and the Inquisition, and variations in mission techniques. Based on printed works. 6 notes.

[296] Alceu Amoroso Lima. "Religious Education in Brazil," *The Americas* (October 1958), pp. 159–170.

Divides Brazilian religious education into four periods, the first, 1553–1759 (pp. 159–161), and part of the second, 1759–1891 (pp. 161–164), coming before independence was achieved in Portuguese America. During the first phase, "education—profane as well as religious—of children and youth remained practically speaking for two centuries in the hands of the Jesuits." However, in the second period, when public authorities replaced the suppressed Jesuits as the chief educators in Brazil, the author argues that "religious instruction remained a family affair." Undocumented.

[297] Francis A. Dutra. "Membership in the Order of Christ in the Seventeenth Century: Its Rights, Privileges, and Obligations," *The Americas* 27:1 (July 1970), pp. 3–25.

Shows that despite constant efforts at reform the military and crusading aims of the Portuguese Order of Christ were anachronisms by the seventeenth century and that membership was becoming increasingly honorific. The author discusses in detail the requirements of the Order, its rule and regulations, the rewards it offered and the ease with which dispensation could be received. Problems faced by New Christians, as well as Blacks and Amerindians, are also analyzed. Many of the examples are drawn from the cases of those who served in Brazil or were born there. Based on Portuguese archival and printed primary materials. 1 table. 120 notes.

[298] Manoel S. Cardozo. "Tithes in Colonial Minas Gerais," *The Catholic Historical Review* 38:2 (July 1952), pp. 175–182.

After defining the tithe and tracing its history, collection, and role in financing not only religious but also secular projects, the author focuses on Minas Gerais, where tithes were customarily farmed out. After comparing tithe receipts and clerical salaries and expenses, Cardozo concludes that "the Crown's financial obligations to the Church in Minas Gerais were not adequately discharged during the eighteenth century." Based on some archival but mostly printed sources. 42 notes.

[299] Manoel S. Cardozo. "The Lay Brotherhoods of Colonial Bahia," *The Catholic Historical Review* 33:1 (April 1947), pp. 12–30.

After quoting liberally from the comments of both Portuguese and foreign visitors to Bahia on that city's many churches and chapels and its processions and other religious practices, the author discusses the role of the numerous *irmandades* (lay brotherhoods) located in the longtime capital of Brazil. He then describes the fourteen chapters of the original (1699) statutes of the Black brotherhood of St. Anthony of Categerona which flourished in the eighteenth century, concluding with a description of the revisions made in 1764. Relies heavily on colonial travellers' accounts and the copy of the brotherhood's statutes located in the Oliveira Lima Library at The Catholic University of America. 55 notes. See also **[487]**, **[488]**, and **[489]**.

[300] A. J. R. Russell-Wood. *Fidalgos and Philanthropists. The Santa Casa da Misericordia of Bahia, 1550–1755*. Berkeley and Los Angeles: University of California Press, 1968. xvii, 429 pp. illus.

Not only describes the history of the Misericordia of Bahia and its efforts to provide social assistance to the people of Bahia but also gives the reader a glimpse into the social, political, and economic structure of a multiracial slave society. The author discusses the history of the Brotherhood of Our Lady, Mother of God, Virgin Mary of Mercy (*Misericordia*) from its beginnings in Lisbon in the late fifteenth century and its rapid spread throughout Portugal and the Portuguese empire. After sketching the history of Bahia, capital of Brazil from 1549 to 1763, and its Misericordia, founded shortly after the city was established by Tomé de Sousa, the first governor-general, Russell-Wood describes the Misericordia's role in the administration of charity as well as the class, creed and color of the organization's administrators. The author then focuses on some of the Misericordia's chief works of mercy: supplying dowries, arranging burials, helping prisoners, taking care of foundlings, attempting to cure the sick in the Hospital of St. Christopher, and maintaining a retirement house for "young girls of middle class families who were of marriageable age and whose honour was endangered by the loss of one or both parents." Based on archival research in Brazil. A useful annotated bibliography is found on pp. 386–406.

[301] A. J. R. Russell-Wood. "The Santa Casa da Misericordia of Bahia: A Social Study, 1550–1750" (Ph.D. Dissertation: Oxford University, 1967).

Earlier version of Russell-Wood **[300]**.

[302] Roger Bastide. "Religion and the Church in Brazil," in Smith and Marchant, eds., *Brazil* **[83]** pp. 334–355.

About one-third of this article deals with the colonial period. Bastide discusses the influence of missionaries—especially the Jesuits—and analyzes the effects of Portuguese America's Amerindian and African heritages on Catholicism in Brazil. The role of the plantation chaplains is analyzed. The author discusses the efforts of the Church "to break down the institution of the private chaplains—a struggle that continued through independence and the Empire. Bastide argues that by the end of the seventeenth century, "the mulatto, who had lacked the right to enter the orders, could finally penetrate there. The Church became the channel of social ascension and was increasingly so in the eighteenth century and under the Empire." The author concludes his section on the colonial period by asserting: "Thus it was that owing to the action of these two factors, the divorce of the Church and patriarchalism and the rise of the little people and free mulattoes (who rose not only by the way of the Church but also through the army and the lower posts of the new imperial administration), the Church gradually became democratic." Based on printed sources. 24 notes.

2. Religious Clergy and Missionaries [Nos. 303–334]

For a variety of reasons—including the scattered number of Amerindians to be converted and Portuguese America's small diocesan ecclesiastical apparatus—the religious orders played a major role in colonial Brazil, not only numerically but also in art, architecture, literature and education. Their role in the Brazilian economy has yet to be carefully studied. There is a preliminary report of Jesuit wealth in Alden **[322]**. Susan Soeiro **[332]** and **[333]** has studied the socio-economic role of the Poor Clare Convent in Salvador.

a. JESUITS [Nos. 303–325]

Of all the religious orders in Brazil, the Jesuits have been the most studied. Jerome V. Jacobsen **[303]** gives a good insight into the Order's early activities in Portugal and Brazil. There are a number of biographical studies of sixteenth-century Jesuits who worked in Portuguese America. Nóbrega, the first provincial of the Jesuits in Brazil, is also studied by Jacobsen **[304]**. Two accounts of Anchieta's life and activities are found in an article by Manuel Espinosa **[306]** and a book-length study by Helen Dominian **[305]**. A seventeenth-century account **[324]** has been translated into English. Anchieta's literary achievements are ably discussed by Oscar Fernández **[307]** and Richard Preto-Rodas **[308]**. Manuel Espinosa has also provided excellent biographical sketches of other important Jesuits who lived in sixteenth-century Brazil: Luis da Grã **[309]**, Fernão Cardim **[310]** and Cristóvão de Gouveia **[311]**. Much of what is known about the Jesuits as well as the Portuguese experience in America during the first century of colonization in Brazil is found in the Jesuit letters. A good discussion of this correspondence is found in Burns **[312]** and **[313]**. The same author also translated four of these letters, dating from 1549 to 1558 **[323]**.

One of the most important figures in the Portuguese world of the seventeenth century was the Jesuit Antônio Vieira. Though no full-length study has yet appeared on this important preacher, prophet, missionary, diplomat and statesman, there is a good introduction by Charles R. Boxer **[315]**. Vieira's messianic ideas are discussed by Robert Ricard **[316]**, while his preaching techniques are analyzed by Mary C. Gotaas **[317]**. Another seventeenth-century Jesuit missionary and explorer was Father Samuel Fritz, who left an account of his experiences in the Amazon **[325]** which have been summarized by Derek Severn **[319]**. Magnus Mörner **[314]** discusses the role of the Jesuits in the Plata region and makes references to Brazil. Some of the anti-Jesuit writings of the eighteenth century are discussed by Sister Mary Agneta Reagan **[320]** and Ernesto Ennes **[321]**. Jesuit missionary activities among the Indians have been ably summarized by Dauril Alden **[426]**. He also examines the economic aspects of their expulsion **[322]**. Since the Jesuits played such an important role in colonial Brazilian history, they get frequent mention in a number of other accounts, the most useful being Schwartz's study of the High Court **[284]**, Boxer's biography of Salvador de Sá **[277]**, and his chapter on Jesuit activity in the Amazon region in *The Golden Age of Brazil* **[548]**.

[303] Jerome V. Jacobsen. "Jesuit Founders in Portugal and Brazil," *Mid-America* 24:1 (January 1942), pp. 3–26.

After reviewing how Portuguese- and English-speaking historians have described Jesuit activities in sixteenth-century Brazil, the author sketches the early successes and failures of the Jesuits in Portugal with an emphasis on their educational efforts and the role of their leader, Simon Rodrigues. Jacobsen concludes with a similar sketch for sixteenth-century Brazil, stressing the problems the Jesuits encountered and their achievements during the first decade after their arrival in Portuguese America in 1549. Based primarily on the printed works of Francisco Rodrigues, S. J., *História da Companhia de Jesus da Assistencia de Portugal*, and Serafim Leite, S. J., *História da Companhia de Jesus do Brasil.* 48 notes.

[304] Jerome V. Jacobsen. "Nóbrega of Brazil," *Mid-America* 24:3 (July 1942), pp. 151–187.

Following a brief review of the early career of Padre Manuel da Nóbrega (ca. 1517–1570) in Portugal is an examination of the problems this first Jesuit Provincial of Brazil and his colleagues encountered in

Portuguese America after arriving there in 1549 in the company of Tomé de Sousa, the first governor-general. Special emphasis is placed on the padre's activity amongst the Indians, his organizational efforts in Bahia and other parts of northern Brazil, the continuation of his missionary policy in São Vicente and São Paulo, his role in the conquest and settlement of Rio de Janeiro, and his rectorship of the Jesuit College there. Based on printed sources, especially the Jesuit letters. 88 notes. 1 map.

[305] Helen G. Dominian. *Apostle of Brazil: The Biography of Padre José de Anchieta, S. J. (1534–1597).* New York: Exposition Press, 1958. 346 p.

Based chiefly on the letters and reports of Anchieta and other Jesuits serving in sixteenth-century Brazil, this study is the most complete account in English of the famous native of the Canary Island. Anchieta became a Jesuit missionary and spent most of his life in Portuguese America working with the Indians in the region of São Paulo, helping oust the French from Rio de Janeiro, serving from 1567–1577 as rector of São Vicente, Superior of Santos and São Paulo, and leading his order in the following decade as the fifth provincial of Brazil. Since Anchieta's career was so intertwined with the history of Portugal's first century of colonization, this biography also provides a useful introduction to sixteenth-century Brazil. There is a bibliography.

[306] J. Manuel Espinosa. "José de Anchieta: 'Apostle of Brazil,'" *Mid-America* 25:4 (October 1943), pp. 250–274 and *Mid-America* 26:1 (January 1944), pp. 40–61.

After reviewing and analyzing the various attempts at writing a suitable biography of Padre José de Anchieta (1534–1597), the author concentrates on Anchieta's first fourteen years in Brazil, when, as a Jesuit scholastic and missionary, he played a major role in the founding of São Paulo de Piratininga, the conquest and colonization of the surrounding area, and the pacification efforts at Iperoig. Also summarized is Anchieta's career in the years following his ordination to the priesthood at Bahia in 1566, during which he served as superior of his order's residence at São Vicente, Jesuit Provincial for all of Brazil, and, finally, near the end of his life, superior of the residence at Espirito Santo. The article concludes with a survey of the Jesuit's literary career. Based mostly on printed primary sources, especially Anchieta's letters. 158 notes.

[307] Oscar Fernández. "José de Anchieta and Early Theatre Activity in Brazil," *Luso-Brazilian Review* 15:1 (Summer 1978), pp. 26–43.

Discusses several of the *autos* or morality plays of the Jesuit José de Anchieta, the most important figure in the sixteenth-century Brazilian theatre and compares them with similar dramatic pieces written and performed in Spain and Portugal. Anchieta frequently blended three languages—Tupí, Castilian and Portuguese—into his dramas. For example, one of the best and longest of these plays—"Na festa de São Lourenço" (On the feast of St. Lawrence), which deals with the Roman martyrdom of the early Christian saint—contains almost 1,500 lines of verse, more than half of which are in Tupí, 40 in Portuguese and the rest in Castilian. Heavily didactic—though not without their lighter moments—these dramatic pieces usually depicted a struggle between Good and Evil and were used to teach the tenets of Christianity to the Indians and to encourage both them and the European colonists to lead more moral lives. They often combined classical themes, events in the lives of the saints and the Scriptures, with references to sixteenth-century Brazilian life, and tell much about the customs, problems and way of life of both Indians and colonists. Based primarily on the printed works of Anchieta. 30 notes.

[308] Richard A. Preto-Rodas. "Anchieta and Vieira: Drama as Sermon, Sermon as Drama," *Luso-Brazilian Review* 7:2 (December 1970), pp. 96–103.

Analyzes the literary and ascetic values of Padres José de Anchieta (1534–1597) and Antônio Vieira (1608–1697), shows how both Jesuits were influenced by the Counter-Reformation, and discusses and compares their use of theatrical techniques. Based mostly on printed primary sources. 28 notes.

[309] J. Manuel Espinosa. "Luis da Grã, Mission Builder and Educator of Brazil," *Mid-America* 24:3 (July 1942), pp. 188–216.

Considered by the author to be one of the three most important Jesuits (along with Anchieta and Nóbrega) to serve in Brazil in the sixteenth century and described as "an eloquent and tireless preacher, a fine teacher, and a remarkably able missionary," Padre Luis da Grã (ca. 1523–1609) spent fifty-six years in Portuguese America as *colateral* or sort of vice-provincial (with Nóbrega), provincial, and seven times rector both of the college at Bahia as well as that of Pernambuco.

Espinosa, however, focuses on the years 1560–1566, a period of intensive development when Grã, the "Apostle of Northern Brazil," was reforming and extending the mission system in Bahia and the surrounding captaincies, consolidating smaller Indian villages into larger *aldeias*. The author concludes that "Grã's labors among the Indians around Bahia constitute one of the most glorious chapters in sixteenth-century Jesuit missionary history." Based chiefly on printed primary sources, especially Jesuit letters. 85 notes.

[310] J. Manuel Espinosa. "Fernão Cardim, Jesuit Humanist of Colonial Brazil," *Mid-America* 24:4 (October 1942), pp. 252–271.

The author provides a biographical sketch of Cardim as well as an analysis of the published writings of this famous Jesuit who spent almost forty years in Brazil. Cardim (1548?–1625) **[207]**, considered one of the most reliable informants regarding the last two decades of Brazil's sixteenth-century history, served as secretary to the Jesuit Visitor, Cristóvão de Gouveia, and later was rector of the Jesuit Colleges of Bahia and Rio de Janeiro, Procurator of the Brazilian Province at Rome, captive of English pirates, and Provincial and Vice-Provincial of the Jesuits in Portuguese America. Based on printed primary and secondary sources. 53 notes.

[311] J. Manuel Espinosa. "Gouveia: Jesuit Lawgiver in Brazil," *Mid-America* 24:1 (January 1942), pp. 27–60.

This is both a brief biography of Padre Cristóvão de Gouveia (1542–1622), who, in 1582, after twenty years of service to his order in Portugal, was named the second visitor of the Jesuit missions in Brazil, and a description of the day-to-day spiritual and material problems faced there by the Jesuits along with observations about the Indians and Blacks with whom they came into contact. Arriving in Brazil in 1583, accompanied by Padre Fernão Cardim, the historian of the visitation, Gouveia spent the next five years visiting every Jesuit residence in Portuguese America and is credited with reorganizing their activity in Brazil—his rules and instructions constituting the general usage of the order until its suppression in 1759. The author provides much useful information on the educational, social, cultural and economic life of Brazil in the latter part of the sixteenth century. Relies heavily on the first two volumes of Serafim Leite's ten volume *História da Companhia de Jesus no Brasil* as well as printed Jesuit letters and accounts. 65 notes.

[312] E. Bradford Burns. "The Brazilian Jesuit Letters. A Sixteenth Century View of Portuguese America," *Revista da Faculdade de Ciencias.* (Coimbra, Portugal), 39 (1967), pp. 5–15.

Stresses the historical value of approximately 120 extant letters written by more than twenty-five different Jesuits during the first decades after their arrival in Brazil in 1549. The author considers "these letters to be the most important source for a study of sixteenth-century Brazilian history." Based mostly on printed Jesuit letters. 34 notes.

[313] E. Bradford Burns. "The Sixteenth-Century Jesuit Letters of Brazil," *Historical Records and Studies* 49 (1962), pp. 57–76.

Samples 124 letters written by Jesuits from Brazil in the sixteenth century on such topics as religion, the Indians, Portuguese-Indian relations, French "interlopers," descriptions of Portuguese America, the efforts of various colonists to settle the new land, and the types of Portuguese who came to Brazil. The author concludes: "The Jesuit letters provide a rich source of information . . . about nearly every subject of importance for the study of mid-sixteenth-century Brazilian history." Based almost entirely on printed Jesuit letters.

[314] Magnus Mörner. *The Political and Economic Activities of the Jesuits in the La Plata Region. The Hapsburg Era.* Trans. Albert Read. Stockholm: Library and Institute of Ibero-American Studies, 1953. xv, 255 pp.

Contains a brief background chapter on the history of Brazil during the sixty years of Spanish domination. Mörner includes a discussion of Spanish and Portuguese boundaries in America, a sketch of Portuguese colonial administration, a survey of the role of the Church regarding the Indian question, and an account of the *bandeiras* emanating from São Paulo. In the main section of his study, Mörner succinctly discusses the interest of Portuguese Jesuits in establishing missions in the Plata region during the sixteenth century. He also touches on Luso-Brazilian trade with that area. Mörner then describes in some detail the penetration of *bandeiras* from São Paulo into Spanish territory beyond the Rio Paranapanema, where "the Jesuits had eleven reductions in Guairá in different stages of development around the year 1628." The author recounts the story of the eventual evacuation of the Jesuit-led Indians from Guairá. He further details Paulista threats—this time, to the mission Indian population on the Rio Uruguay and in the region of Tape—and Spanish Jesuit retreats. Mörner briefly describes Portuguese expansion into the Plata region and the founding of Colônia do Sacramento in 1680, the renewed attacks by the Paulistas, and Spanish reaction to the establishment of Colônia do Sacramento. In discussing the political and economic role played by the Jesuits in the Plata region, Mörner makes some comparisons with the activities of Portuguese Jesuits in Maranhão and Pará. The book also contains a collection of statistical data for La Plata and Paraguay, several useful appendices, a detailed bibliography, a glossary, and three maps.

[315] Charles R. Boxer. *A Great Luso-Brazilian Figure. Padre Antônio Vieira, S. J., 1608–1697*. The Fourth Canning House Annual Lecture. London, Hispanic and Luso-Brazilian Councils, 1957. 32 pages. (Reprinted in 1963.)

Excellent biographical sketch of the famous Lisbon-born Jesuit writer, preacher, prophet, missionary, diplomat and statesman—"the most remarkable man in the seventeenth-century Luso-Brazilian world." The author quotes liberally from Vieira's writings and sermons, stressing his three lengthy stays in Brazil, his attitudes towards Portuguese colonists and officials in America, the Amerindian, and African slavery. Boxer also discusses Vieira's role in the formation of the Brazil Company and the ouster of the Dutch from the Brazilian Northeast, his sympathies for the plight of New Christians, his struggle with the Inquisition and his messianic views. Based on printed primary sources. 52 notes. Appendix.

[316] Robert Ricard. "Prophecy and Messianism in the Works of Antônio Vieira," *The Americas* 17:4 (April 1961), pp. 357–368.

A review of Raymond Cantel's *Prophetisme et messianisme dans l'oeuvre d'Antonio Vieira* (Prophecy and Messianism in the Works of Antônio Vieira). Ricard discusses the major tenets of Vieira's messianic ideas, the Judaic and New Christian influences, and the atmosphere in Portugal preceding and during the famed Jesuit's lifetime. After comparing Vieira's writings with several similar ideas of the Peruvian Franciscan, Fr. Gonzalo Tenório, the author concludes that Vieira's theories "were only an aspect of the widespread eschatological movement which was provoked in the sixteenth century by the sudden discovery of a new and unknown humanity." 8 notes based on printed primary and secondary sources.

[317] Mary C. Gotaas. "Bossuet and Vieira. A Study in National Epochal and Individual Style," (Ph.D. Dissertation: The Catholic University of America, 1953).
See also **[318]**.

[318] Mary C. Gotaas. *Bossuet and Vieira. A Study in National, Epochal and Individual Style*. Washington, D. C.: The Catholic University of America Press, 1953. Reprinted by AMS Press in 1970.

Publishes the forward, chapters II and IV and the conclusion of the above-mentioned doctoral dissertation **[317]**. Using a small sample of the Baroque sermons of Antônio Vieira (1608–1697), the author points out and discusses the chief themes and techniques used by the famous Jesuit preacher and missionary and compares them with those of his French contemporary, Jacques-Benigne Bossuet (1627–1704). Because the excerpts from Vieira's sermons frequently are left untranslated, the value of this study is diminished for those who do not read Portuguese.

[319] Derek Severn. "A Missionary on the Amazon," *History Today* 25:4 (April 1975), pp. 279–286.

Biographical sketch of Father Samuel Fritz (1654–1724), the Bohemian-born Jesuit who spent thirty-seven years as a missionary in that part of the Amazon Basin which was claimed by Spain but contested by the Portuguese who from their base in Pará harassed and captured him and some of his Indian converts. Based mostly on George Edmundson, ed., *Journal of the Travels and Labours of Father Samuel Fritz* **[325]**. No notes.

[320] Sister Mary Agneta Reagan. "The Role Played by Gomes Freire de Andrade in the Exile of the Jesuits from the Portuguese Empire," (Ph.D. Dissertation: The Catholic University of America, 1978). 253 pp.

Examines the role Gomes Freire de Andrade **[280]** played in the expulsion of the Jesuits from the Portuguese empire in 1759 and the suppression of their order by Pope Clement XIV in 1773. Andrade was a skilled crown official who led the commission chosen to carry out the terms of the Treaty of Madrid. His report to Lisbon from Paraguay that the Indians resisted the occupation by the Spanish-Portuguese troops of the lands awarded Portugal in the treaty also mentions that a few

Jesuits had stirred up trouble. The author claims that Pombal seized on these remarks, putting all the blame for resistance on the Society of Jesus. The propaganda was picked up and used by other enemies of the Society. Three popes were exposed to Andrade's remarks. The importance of these writings in the campaign to suppress the Jesuits cannot be determined, but they do link Andrade, willingly or not, to Pombal's scheme to destroy the Society of Jesus. Research was based on Gomes Freire de Andrade's letters to the Portuguese Overseas Council, 1735–1760, and on archival research at both the Secret Vatican Archives and the Jesuit Archives in Rome.
DAI 39/04A (p. 2480)

[321] Ernesto Ennes. "Teresa Margarida da Silva e Orta, a Brazilian Collaborator in the Anti-Jesuit Propaganda of Pombal," *The Americas* 2:4 (April 1946), pp. 423–430.

Discusses anti-Jesuit sentiment during the administration of the Marquis of Pombal and analyzes a letter of Brazilian-born D. Teresa Margarida da Silva e Orta, a former owner of a sawmill in Maranhão, to Frei Manuel do Cenáculo, concerning accounts she was preparing regarding the alleged misdeeds of the Jesuits. Includes new biographical data on "the first Paulista authoress." Based on archival research and secondary sources. 13 notes.

[322] Duaril Alden. "Economic Aspects of the Expulsion of the Jesuits form Brazil: A Preliminary Report," in Keith and Edwards, eds., *Conflict and Continuity* **[84]**, pp. 25–65.

Important study that examines the sources of Jesuit wealth in Brazil and describes and analyzes the conflicts between the Jesuits and their rivals before 1722 as well as anti-Jesuit campaigns from that time to their suppression in 1759. Based mostly on printed primary materials. 133 notes. Followed by Mathias C. Kiemen's useful commentary (pp. 66–71) based on his experiences in Portuguese archives. 4 notes.

i. Contemporary Narratives, 1549–1759 [Nos. 323–325]

E. Bradford Burns **[323]** has translated four Jesuit letters describing their work in Brazil and dating from 1549–1558. In 1617, Sebastião Beretario **[324]** published a biography of Padre José de Anchieta, the famous Jesuit missionary who worked in Brazil during most of the second half of the sixteenth century. George Edmundson **[325]** has translated a contemporary account of the missionary activities of the

Jesuit Father Samuel Fritz **[319]**, who was based in Spanish America but who came into frequent contact with the Portuguese.

[323] E. Bradford Burns. "Introduction to the Brazilian Jesuit Letters," *Mid-America* 44:3 (July 1962), pp. 172–186.

Translates four letters written by the Jesuits about sixteenth-century Brazil and prefaces the first three by putting them into historical perspective. The first letter was written by Manuel de Nóbrega from Bahia in August of 1549; the second was penned by João Azpilcueta from Porto Seguro on 24 June 1555; the third is by Padre Antônio Pires from Bahia and dated 19 July 1558. The author of the fourth letter is not certain, though it, too, was sent from Bahia and dated 12 September 1558. Based on printed sources. 12 notes.

[324] Sebastiano Beretário. *The Lives of Father Joseph Anchieta, of the Society of Jesus; the Ven. Alvera von Virmundt, Religious of the Order of the Holy Sepulchre; and the Ven. John Berchmans, of the Society of Jesus.* London: T. Richardson and Son, 1849. xiv, 412 pp.

Number 17 of the collection *The Saints and Servants of God,* this biography of Anchieta is a translation of *Iosephi Anchietae Societatis Iesu Sacerdotis in Brasilia Defuncti Vita* first published in 1617. Beretário relied heavily on the manuscript account of Anchieta's life by Father Pero Rodrigues, the Jesuit Visitor to Angola and Provincial of Brazil (1594–1603), who completed the biography in January of 1607. The English version of Beretário's account contains nineteen short chapters plus an epilogue by the translator and is found on pp. 1–176. Beretário quickly traces Anchieta's birth, education, early life, and entrance into the Jesuits in chapter one. He then briefly describes the new Jesuit's voyage to Brazil and provides a description of Portuguese America. Beretário details Anchieta's early activities in Brazil, giving special prominence to his peacemaking efforts with the Amerindians and the Portuguese. After describing Anchieta's ordination to the priesthood and the success of his missionary activities, Beretário devotes several chapters to Anchieta's administrative abilities as Superior at Espirito Santo, Rector of the Jesuit College of St. Vincent in Bahia, and finally Provincial of his Order. The last chapter discusses "the high esteem in which he was held by all ranks of people after his death." There are constant references to supernatural events associated with Anchieta, though, as Pero Rodrigues himself pointed out, some of these "miracles" were the result of Beretário's faulty translation from Portuguese into Latin. Many of Anchieta's biographers, however, have relied heavily on Beretário's account. No notes.

[325] George Edmundson, ed. *Journal of the Travels and Labours of Father Samuel Fritz in the River of the Amazons Between 1686 and 1723.* London, 1922. viii, 164 pp.
[Issued by the Hakluyt Society. 2nd Series, no. 51. Reprinted. Nendeln/Liechtenstein: Kraus Reprint, 1967.]

Translation of "Mission de los Omaguas, Jurimaguas, Aysuares, Ibanomas, y otras Naciones desde Napo hasta el Rio Negro" [Mission to the Omaguas, Jurimaguas, Aysuares, Ybanomas and Other Nations From the Napo to the Rio Negro], which contains "a full narrative of the life and labours of Samuel Fritz." The Bohemian-born Fritz (1654–1724) became a Jesuit in 1673 and eventually was sent to the Spanish Jesuit College at Quito, Ecuador. In 1686, he took charge of Christianizing the Omaguas **[410]**. After seeking medical help from the Portuguese at Pará, the Jesuit missionary was detained there for two years (1689–1691). Freed, he returned to the Omaguas after a short stay at Lima. For many years he was superior of the Amazon missions. However, much of his work with the Indians was moving them up river out of the reach of the Portuguese. Though some efforts were initially made by the Spaniards to protect the Indians, Father Samuel Fritz was informed in 1711 that because of lack of funds, little more could be done to defend the Marañon missions. The following year many of the Omaguas dispersed. However, a few were gathered together and a new mission was established on the Ucayali River in 1712. Though no longer superior of the Marañon missions, Fritz worked among the Indians of the region until his death in 1724. There is a good introduction by Edmundson to the narrative, including a discussion of the act of possession by Pedro Teixeira **[636]** in 1639 and Portuguese claims to the region.

b. FRANCISCANS [Nos. 326–330]

The second most-written-about religious Order in Brazil during the colonial period is the Franciscans. Though it was a Franciscan who said the first mass in Brazil in 1500, their role in Portuguese America was somewhat sporadic until the end of the sixteenth century. Van der Vat **[326]** provides a useful sketch of Franciscan activity during the first century of colonization in Brazil. Venâncio Willeke **[327]** discusses the Order's work in Pernambuco and provides a good overview of Franciscan missionary enterprises in northern Brazil during the colonial era **[328]**. The greatest Franciscan missionary activity was probably in the Amazon region. Ferreira Reis **[329]** describes their early labor there, and Luiza da Fonseca **[330]** and **[428]** provides a biographical sketch of Frei Cristóvão de Lisboa, the first *custos* or administrator of his Order in that region. He was both a defender of the Indians and a naturalist. Mathias Kiemen **[425]** makes frequent mention of Franciscan missionary efforts in Maranhão and Pará in his study of Indian policy in that region. The study of Franciscan activity in other parts of Brazil, especially in the seventeenth and eighteenth centuries has been neglected, though Manoel Cardozo **[735]**, in his study on Azeredo Coutinho, makes some interesting comments regarding their attempts at educational reform in Rio de Janeiro.

[326] Odulfo Van der Vat, O. F. M. "The First Franciscans of Brazil," *The Americas* 5:1 (July 1948), pp. 18–30.

A critical analysis of Franciscan chronicles detailing activities of their Order in Brazil before the arrival in 1585 of Frei Melquior de Santa Catarina and his companions to establish a friary in Olinda and to found the custody of St. Anthony in Portuguese America. The author pays special attention to the list of sixteenth-century missionary undertakings and their chronology found in Frei Antônio de Santa Maria Jaboatão's *Novo Orbe Serafico Brasilico* (the first part of which was printed in 1761), pointing out and correcting its exaggerations and errors. The friars who accompanied Frei Melquior are also identified. Based mostly on printed chronicles. 9 notes.

[327] Venâncio Willeke, O. F. M. "The Mission of São Miguel de Una in Pernambuco, Brazil," *The Americas* 13:1 (July 1956), pp. 69–74.

Traces the history of the mission at Una (today, Barreiros), located in southern Pernambuco and founded sometime between 1589 and 1593 by Franciscan missionaries. Turned over to diocesan clergy in 1619, who were followed by the Jesuits five years later, the mission was devastated by the Dutch in 1636, restored, and eventually placed again in the hands of the Franciscans, this time from 1681 to 1742 or 1743, when Carmelite Observants took over. The mission was also destroyed during the War of the Mascates in 1710 and rebuilt. According to the author, "São Miguel de Una was the first Christian nucleus of the present-day diocese of Garanhuns." Based on some archival but mostly printed primary materials. 17 notes.

[328] Venâncio Willeke, O. F. M. "Three Centuries of Missionary Work in Northern Brazil: Franciscan Province of St. Anthony, 1657–1957," *The Americas* 15:2 (October 1958), pp. 129–138.

The author reviews Franciscan activity in sixteenth-century Brazil, with special mention of that Order's centers in Pernambuco and Paraiba. Willeke lists twenty-five Indian missions founded or administered by the friars after 1681. The author also provides a discussion of some of the problems the Franciscan missionaries faced in their work with the Indians. Almost the entire article deals with the colonial period. Based on manuscript as well as printed sources. 41 notes.

[329] Arthur Cesar Ferreira Reis. "The Franciscans and the Opening of the Amazon Region," *The Americas* 11:3 (January 1955), pp. 173–193.

Discusses the role of the Franciscans of the Province of Santo Antônio in the spiritual conquest of Maranhão and Pará during the seventeenth and eighteenth centuries. The author also briefly touches on English, French and Dutch interlopers, Jesuit-Franciscan conflicts, and the latter order's relations with the Portuguese colonists. Two-thirds of the article deals with the first two decades of the Franciscan presence in northern Brazil and a special emphasis is given to "the Defender of the Indians," Frei Cristóvão de Lisboa, who spent twelve years (1624–1636) in the Amazon region. Based on printed primary sources. 22 notes. A nine-page document in Portuguese, entitled "Relação Sumaria do que obrou a Provincia de Santo Antônio por seus filhos em serviço de ambas as Magestades," is appended.

[330] Luiza da Fonseca. "Frei Cristóvão de Lisboa, O. F. M., Missionary and Natural Historian of Brazil," *The Americas* 8:3 (January 1952), pp. 289–303.

After surveying some of the problems encountered in the exploration and colonization of Maranhão and Pará and the conversion and treatment of the Indians, the author sketches a few of the highlights in the life of the first Franciscan *custos* for that region, Frei Cristóvão de Lisboa, who left Lisbon for his post in 1624. There is also a special discussion of his contribution as a natural historian. After returning to Portugal, Frei Cristóvão was named Bishop-Elect of Angola, but was never installed in his diocese. The brother of the famed author, Manuel Severim de Faria, Frei Cristóvão died in 1652. Based almost entirely on archival materials (Arquivo Histórico Ultramarino and the Biblioteca Nacional, both in Lisbon). 32 notes. Appendix. Two documents are transcribed on pp. 357–359.
See also **[428]**.

c. BENEDICTINES AND CARMELITES [No. 331]

Other than the review article by Oliver Kapsner on the Benedictines in Brazil **[331]**, there are no studies in English focusing exclusively on either the Carmelites or the Benedictines. There are, however, scattered references in such studies of the Amazon region as those by

Mathias Kiemen **[425]** and Dauril Alden **[665]**. The artistic and architectural aspects of the important monasteries and churches of these two Orders are studied in a number of works listed in Section XX.

[331] Oliver Kapsner, O. S. B. "The Benedictines in Brazil," *The American Benedictine Review* 28:2 (June 1977), pp. 113–132.

Though a number of excellent books and articles have been published in Portuguese on the important role of the Benedictines in Brazil, no book or article on that Order has appeared in English. To remedy this neglect Oliver Kapsner has contributed a twenty-page review article occasioned by the 1976 publication in Salvador of Dom José Lohr Endres, O. S. B.'s important compilation, *Catalago dos Bispos, Gerais, Provinciais, Abades, e Mais Cargos da Ordem de S. Bento do Brasil, 1582–1975*. [Catalogue of Bishops, Generals, Provincials, Abbots and Others in the Order of St. Benedict in Brazil, 1582–1975]. Kapsner provides a useful sketch of the initial Benedictine foundations in Salvador, Rio de Janeiro, Olinda, and São Paulo during the last two decades of the sixteenth century. All four were quickly elevated to the status of abbeys—the first three before 1600—and are still in existence. From these four abbeys others were founded during the first half of the seventeenth century: "By 1650 the Brazilian Benedictine Province consisted of seven abbeys and four priories"—each with its own novitiate for the training of new members. The abbeys in Salvador and Olinda were looted and damaged during the Dutch invasions and occupations, 1624–1654. Later, two special Benedictine houses of study were established for aspiring members of that Order—one at Rio de Janeiro, the other at Salvador or Olinda. The author concludes his discussion of the colonial period (pp. 113–123) by pointing out some of the problems Benedictines faced during the Pombaline era. Pages 128–130 contain a list and brief historical description of the fourteen Benedictine foundations made in Brazil since 1582. (The author lists fifteen, but one of these was in Belgium). Though the article is useful for Benedictine history, there are a number of errors (mostly dates) on events in Brazil. Based on printed materials. 23 notes.

d. NUNS [Nos. 332–334]
Nuns—expecially the Franciscan Poor Clares of Bahia—have been studied by Susan Soeiro **[332]** and **[333]**. The same author also has provided a recent overview of the economic, social and demographic implications of convent life in Bahia **[334]**.

[332] Susan A. Soeiro, "A Baroque Nunnery: The Economic and Social Role of a Colonial Convent: Santa Clara do Desterro, Salvador, Bahia, 1677–1800," (Ph.D. Dissertation: New York University, 1974). 299 pp.

Illuminates socioeconomic factors in late seventeenth- and eighteenth-century Bahia, as well as recording the history of the convent Santa Clara do Desterro during that time period. The religious proved to be from wealthy merchant backgrounds as well as from the sugar elites. Upper-class women lacking necessary marital dowries found acceptance in the convent, thereby helping to preserve class lines in society. Nuns engaged in amorous as well as money-making activities. The convent was a money-lender, mainly for the planters, and an urban landlord. Reforms which took place in the eighteenth century are listed. Figures and tables in the appendix illustrate the main thesis. DAI 35/07A (pp. 4350–4351)

[333] Susan A. Soeiro. "The Social and Economic Role of the Convent: Women and Nuns in Colonial Bahia, 1677–1800." *The Hispanic American Historical Review* 54:2 (May 1974), pp. 209–232.

Informative analysis of the role of upper-class women in colonial Bahia, especially those connected with the Poor Clare convent of the Desterro, the first nunnery founded in Brazil (1677). The social background, motivation, and daily routine of the nuns are examined as well as the socioeconomic activities of the convent itself. Based largely on archival and printed primary sources. 1 table, 2 graphs, 74 notes.

[334] Susan A. Soeiro, "The Feminine Orders in Colonial Bahia, Brazil: Economic, Social, and Demographic Implications, 1677–1800," in Asunción Lavrin, ed., *Latin American Women* **[98]**, pp. 173–197.

The author points out that "conventual life answered both sacred and profane callings and served religious and secular needs. Convents could and did offer a foster family and an alternative life-style to women seeking refuge from temporal society. They provided education and taught domestic skills. As forerunners of contemporary welfare agencies, nunneries gave shelter and support to destitute and single women. Religious houses served as convenient and respectable repositories for daughters of families whose high social standing and low finances precluded them from sufficiently endowing their female children for marriage." Soeiro then compares convents in colonial Salvador with those of Spanish New Spain. She also discusses "the social composition and purpose of the nunnery," especially in Bahia. She concludes that "nunneries ultimately served as institutions buttressing an elitist system of values and stratification in Bahian society." Bahia's four convents were Santa Clara do Dêsterro **[332]**, founded in 1677, Nossa Senhora da Conceição da Lapa (1773), Nossa Senhora da Merçes

(1735), and Nossa Senhora da Soledade e Coração de Jesus (1741). Based largely on archival and printed primary materials. 105 notes.

B. Jews and "New Christians" [Nos. 335–348]

Thanks mainly to Arnold Wiznitzer, there has been a considerable amount of writing on Jews in Brazil. A good general introduction is found in Wiznitzer **[335]**. His survey includes a valuable section on the Inquisition in Bahia and Pernambuco, 1591–1595, and 1618 in the former captaincy. The main portion of Wiznitzer's study and the subject of his many articles deals with Jewish activity during the Dutch occupation of northeastern Brazil, 1630–1654. A useful critique of Wiznitzer's work is provided by Isaac Emmanuel **[336]**. The numerous articles by Wiznitzer include a study of Isaac de Castro **[338]**, who was captured in Bahia after journeying there from Amsterdam via Dutch Brazil and eventually burned at the stake in Lisbon; an estimate of the number of Jews **[339]** and the number of Jewish soldiers **[340]** in Dutch Brazil, 1630–1654; the number of Jews in the sugar industry **[341]** in Bahia and Pernambuco before the Dutch invasion, during the Dutch occupation, and in Rio de Janeiro at the end of the seventeenth century. In addition, Wiznitzer **[342]** describes the Jewish synagogue and cemetery in Recife during the Dutch period and recounts the exodus of Jews from Brazil **[343]** after the Dutch surrender in 1654. Herbert Bloom **[337]** provides a useful study of the Jewish presence in Dutch Brazil, 1623–1654. Sidney Raizman **[344]** gives a short biographical sketch of the famed Brazilian-born dramatist, António José da Silva, who was known as "The Jew."

Among non-Jewish writers, Charles R. Boxer provides a balanced and judicious analysis of Jewish and "New Christian" activities in sixteenth- and seventeenth-century Brazil and parts of Spanish America in his study of Salvador de Sá **[277]** and does the same for northeastern Brazil under Dutch domination **[239]**.

[335] Arnold Wiznitzer. *Jews in Colonial Brazil.* New York: Columbia University Press, 1960. x, 227 pp.

Useful description of the activities of the Portuguese Inquisition regarding Jews in Brazil with a special emphasis on the visitation of

Heitor Furtado de Mendoça to Bahia and Pernambuco, 1591–1595, and that of Marcos Teixeira to Bahia in 1618. However, the main portion of the book deals with the role of the Jews during the Dutch conquests, 1624–1654. The author concludes with a chapter on Brazilian New Christians during the remainder of the colonial period, 1654–1822. Based on some archival but mostly printed primary and secondary materials. There is a bibliography on pp. 199–205.

[336] Isaac S. Emmanuel. "Seventeenth-Century Brazilian Jewry: A Critical Review," *American Jewish Archives* 14:1 (April 1962), pp. 32–68.

A lengthy and detailed discussion of Arnold Wiznitzer's *Jews in Colonial Brazil* **[335]**, in which the author makes significant corrections, points out important omissions, and adds considerable data on Jews in seventeenth-century Brazil. Based on archival as well as printed sources. 67 notes. 2 tables.

[337] Herbert I. Bloom. "A Study of Brazilian Jewish History 1623–1654, Based Chiefly Upon the Findings of the Late Samuel Oppenheim," *Publications of the American Jewish Historical Society* 33 (1934), pp. 43–125. Reprinted in Cohen **[95]**, II, 80–162.

Pioneering effort in English to place in proper perspective Jewish conduct in Brazil and Amsterdam during the period when the Dutch West India Company was attempting to capture and colonize the northern half of Portuguese America. The author concludes that the Jewish population in Dutch Brazil was much more conspicuous than that of their fellow religionists in Amsterdam. Many of the Jews in Dutch Brazil were allied to the ruling Protestant Dutch minority and actively engaged in all branches of the sugar industry as well as other wholesale and retail enterprises. Because of such activities, hatred for them by many Catholic Portuguese both within and outside Dutch Brazil was especially intense and Jews, when captured by the Luso-Brazilian forces, were frequently singled out for special punishment. The Oppenheim papers "consist of many photostats of original documents, translations from the various documents, and typewritten translated copies of photostats, also personal notes and comments upon material, abstracts and translations of both contemporary and more recently printed books, corrections of printed works on the subject and comparisons of these." 196 notes; 3 appendices.

[338] Arnold Wiznitzer. "Isaac de Castro, Brazilian Jewish Martyr," *Publications of the American Jewish Historical Society* 47:2 (December 1957), pp. 63–75. Reprinted in Cohen **[95]**, pp. 205–217.

Biographical sketch of Isaac de Castro (alias José de Lis), a Jewish missionary, who in 1641 at sixteen years of age left Amsterdam for Dutch Brazil and three years later journeyed to Bahia to teach and provide spiritual direction to Judaizers there. Shortly after arriving in the Brazilian capital, he was denounced to the bishop (who was also a deputy of the Portuguese Inquisition), arrested, and sent to Portugal for trial. After resisting efforts to convert him to Catholicism, Isaac de Castro was burned alive at the stake in December of 1647. The article contains a good description of an auto-da-fé and the procedures of the Portuguese Inquisition. Based on archival (especially dossier 11550 of the Archive of the Inquisition at the Arquivo Nacional da Torre do Tombo, Lisbon) and printed primary materials. 23 notes. Appendix.

[339] Arnold Wiznitzer. "The Number of Jews in Dutch Brazil (1630–1654)," *Jewish Social Studies* 16:2 (1954), pp. 107–114.

Provides convincing evidence that D. Luis de Meneses's often-cited figure of 5,000 Jews in Dutch Brazil in 1654 is greatly exaggerated. Using a Dutch census list of 1645–1646, the record book of the Congregation Zur Israel of Recife for the years 1648–1653, and Saul Levi Mortera's account for 1654, the author argues that Jews in Dutch Brazil never surpassed 1,450 (about half the total white civilian population during the peak year of 1645) and that after the beginning of the Portuguese rebellion that same year, the Jewish population steadily decreased to about 720 in 1648 and 650 in 1654. Based on printed and manuscript primary sources and secondary works. 30 notes. 2 appendices.

[340] Arnold Wiznitzer. "Jewish Soldiers in Dutch Brazil (1630–1654)," *Publication of the American Jewish Historical Society* 46 (September 1956), pp. 40–50.
Reprinted in Cohen **[95]**, II, 163–173.

Brief discussion of Jews who fought against the Portuguese in Brazil. The author argues that Jews participated in the Dutch expedition to Pernambuco in 1630 and served in the militia of Dutch Brazil as well as in the Dutch navy, with many Jewish soldiers being killed in action. Based on archival (Dutch) and published primary sources and secondary materials. 42 notes.

[341] Arnold Wiznitzer. "The Jews in the Sugar Industry of Colonial Brazil," *Jewish Social Studies* 18:4 (July 1959), pp. 189–198.

Lists and describes some of the more important Jewish sugar mill owners and those active in sugar production, arguing that "Jews were not only technicians and administrators of *engenhos* (mills), but also proprietors in Brazil during the latter half of the sixteenth century." Estimates the number of Jewish mill owners in Bahia and Pernambuco in 1600, in northeastern Brazil during the Dutch occupation (1630–1654), and in Rio de Janeiro at the end of the century. Concludes that the "important role they had played in this industry for two centuries had been destroyed by the persecutions of the Inquisition in the first decades of the eighteenth century." Based mostly on printed materials and secondary sources. 39 notes.

[342] Arnold Wiznitzer. "The Synagogue and Cemetery of the Jewish Community in Recife, Brazil (1630–1654)," *Publication of the American Jewish Historical Society* 43:2 (December 1953), pp. 127–130. Reprinted in Cohen **[95]**, II, 174–177. See also **[346]**.

Short account of the seventeenth-century history of the Jewish synagogue and cemetery in Recife. After the Dutch were ousted from Brazil in 1654, the synagogue was given to João Fernandes Vieira and the cemetery to Henrique Dias, both of whom were important leaders in the struggle against the Dutch. The author attempts to locate the sites of these two Jewish centers in modern-day Recife. Based on some archival but mostly printed primary materials. 16 notes.

[343] Arnold Wiznitzer. "The Exodus from Brazil and Arrival in New Amsterdam of the Jewish Pilgrim Fathers, 1654," *Publication of the American Jewish Historical Society* 44:2 (December 1954), pp. 80–97. Reprinted in Cohen **[95]**, II, 313–330.

Discusses in some detail the 1654 Capitulation of Taborda—the agreement between the defeated Dutch and the victorious Portuguese and Brazilian forces—signed near Recife. Special attention is paid to provisions affecting Jews and the successful efforts of the Portuguese commander Francisco Barreto to insure that the Jews were protected. The author then focuses on the adventures of the twenty-three Jews who, after a number of misfortunes in the Caribbean, finally arrived in New Amsterdam, and corrects earlier accounts of their odyssey. Based on archival and printed sources. 55 notes. 2 appendices.

[344] Sidney I. Raizman. "António José da Silva 'The Jew,'" *Jewish Social Studies* 13:4 (October 1951), pp. 325–332.

Short biographical sketch of the Brazilian-born dramatist, António José da Silva (1705–1739), nicknamed "The Jew," who was beheaded and burned for being a Judaizer. The author argues that the Coimbra-trained writer who was arrested on several occasions (his mother was the daughter of a New Christian sugar plantation owner near Rio de Janeiro) "actually created the national theatre in Portugal, transmitting to posterity the customs, humor and folklore of the Portuguese." Based principally on secondary materials, especially those of António Baião and Mendes dos Remedios. 26 notes.

1. Contemporary Narratives, 1630–1654 [Nos. 345–348]

Cyrus Adler **[345]** translates and discusses Esteban de Aires Fonseca's charges against the Jews in Brazil. Arnold Wiznitzer **[346]** describes and translates the Minute Book of the Congregation Zur Israel of Recife and Magen Abraham of Mauricia **[348]** and transcribes and analyzes the signatures of 170 members of the two congregations **[347]**.

[345] Cyrus Adler, "A Contemporary Memorial Relating to Damages to Spanish Interests in America Done by Jews of Holland (1634)," *Publication of the American Jewish Historical Society* 17 (1909), pp. 45–51. Reprinted in Cohen **[95]**, II, 178–184.

The document referred to was authored by Esteban de Aires Fonseca. Henry C. Lea had summarized it in *A History of the Inquisition of Spain,* III, 279. Evidence to date shows that Fonseca's charges against the Jews were grossly overstated. Adler provides an English translation of this document from the Archivo General de Simancas, Spain.

[346] Arnold Wiznitzer. *The Records of the Earliest Jewish Community in the New World.* New York: American Jewish Historical Society, 1954. xiii, 108 pp.

Brings together three previously published articles and translations but with slight changes and additions. The footnote numbers are also somewhat different. Includes Wiznitzer **[348]** (though the description of the Minute Book and the translation are separated as Parts I and

IV); Wiznitzer **[347]**, which composes Part II; and Wiznitzer **[342]** which makes up Part III. There is an index.

[347] Arnold Wiznitzer, "The Members of the Brazilian Jewish Community 1648–1653," *Publication of the American Jewish Historical Society* 42:4 (June 1953), pp. 387–395.

Lists 170 signatures of members of the Congregation Zur Israel of Recife and Magen Abraham of Mauricia. These signatures were affixed to the Minute Book of these congregations. Wiznitzer points out that "the first names of the Brazilian Jews were all Hebrew names." In addition, the Jews in Brazil with Portuguese or Spanish family names were former Catholics or descendants of Catholics who had returned to Judaism either before they had come to Dutch Brazil or after the occupation of a part of Brazil by the Dutch in 1630." 2 plates. 20 notes. Reprinted in Cohen **[95]**, II, 218–226.

[348] Arnold Wiznitzer, "The Minute Book of Congregation Zur Israel of Recife and Magen Abraham of Mauricia, Brazil," *Publication of the American Jewish Historical Society* 42:3 (March 1953), pp. 217–302.

Wiznitzer points out that during the colonial period of Brazilian history, "Jews could openly profess Judaism in Brazil only for a period of twenty-six years (1624–1625 and 1630–1654) when first, Bahia, and later, the northern captaincies of Brazil were occupied and administered by Holland." In his lengthy introduction (pp. 217–257) to the Minute Book of the two Jewish congregations, Wiznitzer describes and synthesizes the material in the 28 page manuscript. He discusses the plenary meeting of 1648, central control by the Congregation Zur Israel, election of officers and functionaries and their duties, religious services and education, social welfare, finances, justice and the enforcement of law, and minutes of the meetings of the Mahamad or executive committee, 1649–1653. The translation of the Minute Book into English is found on pp. 260–293. The introduction has 28 notes. There is a glossary (pp. 294–302). 4 illus.
Reprinted in Cohen **[95]**, II, 227–312 (without the 4 illus.).

C. Protestants [Nos. 349–350]

Outside the years when the Dutch occupied Brazil, Protestantism played a very minor role in Brazil, its practice being confined to a few British merchants and a number of the travellers who used Brazil as a port of call. José Antônio Gonsalves de Mello **[349]** examines Dutch Calvinism and toleration in northern Brazil in the seventeenth century and R. Herbert Minnich **[350]** discusses whether there were Mennonites in Dutch Brazil.

[349] José Antônio Gonsalves de Mello. "The Dutch Calvinists and Religious Toleration in Portuguese America," *The Americas* 14:4 (April 1958), pp. 485–488.

Discusses the evolution of Dutch Calvinist attitudes regarding liberty of conscience and liberty of cult towards both Catholics and Jews in the Brazilian Northeast from 1630 to 1654. Based on Dutch archival and printed sources. 8 notes.

[350] R. Herbert Minnich. "Seventeenth Century Mennonites in Brazil," The *Mennonite Quarterly Review* 48:3 (July 1974), pp. 388–390.

An attempt to corroborate Friedrich W. Brepohl's assertion that three Mennonite agricultural experts arrived in Dutch Brazil with Count John Maurice of Nassau in 1637 and that one of them recommended that "other Mennonites be invited to settle in Dutch Brazil to establish family-size farms and till the soil." Based on printed materials as well as correspondence with Dutch archives and C. R. Boxer. 15 notes.

XII. The Amerindian [Nos. 351–436]

A. General Accounts and Special Aspects [Nos. 351–353]

There have been few general studies in English on the Indians of Brazil before the arrival of the Portuguese and during the colonial period. A good deal of information on the subject is found in John Hemming's *Red Gold* **[423]**. Julian H. Steward **[93]** has edited a number of tribal and linguistic studies about the Indians of Brazil in volumes I and III of the monumental *Handbook of South American Indians*. But with the possible exception of his own "Cultural Areas of the Tropical Forests," **[351]**, it includes no survey of the Brazilian Indians as a group. To a certain extent, this deficiency is remedied by Charles Wagley's **[352]** overview of the Brazilian Indian. Francis A. Dutra **[353]** describes the couvade, a practice common to many of the Indians of Brazil.

[351] Julian H. Steward. "Cultural Areas of the Tropical Forests," in Steward, ed., *Handbook* **[93]**, III, 883–889.

Steward discusses the chief similarities and differences between the basic and marginal Tropical Forest cultures. Since the Tropical Forest and its culture encompassed more than Brazil and did not include the Gê tribes of eastern Brazil and some of the tribes of the Plata region, the author's synthesis falls short of being an overview of the Amerindian population of Portuguese America. 1 map.

[352] Charles Wagley. "The Indian Heritage of Brazil," in Smith and Marchant, eds., *Brazil* **[83]**, pp. 104–124.

Excellent overview dealing mostly with colonial Brazil. Wagley estimates the pre-Cabralian Amerindian population at no more than 1,500,000 and emphasizes the diversity of culture and language among the Indians living in the eastern half of South America: "The lack of cultural, linguistic, and political unity among the Brazilian tribes was a major factor leading to their lack of resistance to the small groups of Europeans who came to Brazil in 1500 and to the rapid disintegration of organized Indian society along the coast." Admitting exceptions, Wagley classifies the Amerindian in Brazil into two main groups: "(1) Those who were primarily horticulturalists and fishers inhabiting rain-forest country—the Tropical Forest cultures, and (2) those who depended upon hunting, fishing, and gathering for their livelihood, or who combined these occupations with a weak and incipient horticulture and who inhabited open plains country or desert-like arid plateaus—the Marginal and semi-Marginal cultures." Of all the Indians heritages in Portuguese America, that of the coastal Tupí "had the most significant influence upon the formation of Brazilian national culture." Wagley challenges the view that the Indian male was merely "the hunter, fisherman, and warrior disdainful of agriculture, as some writers on Brazil **[699]** would have us believe." The author then devotes almost five pages to the extinct Tupinamba, a generic name for various coastal Indians sharing a Tupi heritage. He points out that "Tupinamba agricultural techniques were exceedingly inefficient, in comparison with those developed by the native peoples of Mexico and Peru." He also discusses the Tupinamba and the products they raised, their social and political organization, religion, the role of shamans, the practice of ritualistic cannibalism and its relationship to warfare, and the decimation of the Indians by disease. Wagley concludes his survey with a brief description of the Amerindian in the Amazon region and the Brazilian northeast. 2 maps. 22 notes.

[353] Francis A. Dutra. "The Couvade in Brazil: A Survey," *Proceedings of the Oklahoma Academy of Science* 47 (1968), pp. 307–314.

Describes and discusses the practice of "rites of passage" by the Brazilian Indians and its variations in different regions of Portuguese America from the colonial period to the present. Based on printed sources. Bibliography.

B. Population Studies [Nos. 354–357]

Careful population studies in English on pre-Cabralian Brazil have been somewhat neglected. Attempts to remedy this deficiency have been made byiJohn Hemming in a lengthy appendix to his *Red Gold* **[423]**. William B. Denevan **[354]** and **[355]** makes estimates for "Greater Amazonia." A valuable observation on the question of territoriality is found in Thomas P. Myers's brief note **[356]**. An earlier statement on the Amerindian population of Brazil in 1500—seen within the context of all of South America—is found in Julian H. Steward **[357]**.

[354] William M. Denevan. "The Aboriginal Population of Amazonia," in William M. Denevan, ed. *The Native Population of the Americas in 1492.* (Madison: The University of Wisconsin Press, 1976), pp. 205–234.

Using estimated habitat densities for the upper Amazon region of eastern Peru and northeastern Bolivia, Denevan attempts "to utilize the same method and habitat densities in order to derive a total potential aboriginal population for greater Amazonia"—a term that "includes roughly the area of South America east and south of the Andes and north of the Tropic of Capricorn, except for the Gran Chaco region. Greater Amazonia thus incorporates all the tropical lowlands and plateaus of interior South America, an area substantially larger than the Amazon Basin proper." The author examines subsistence patterns and resources of the following components of "Greater Amazonia": The lowland savanna habitat; Mojos population; the floodplain habitat; the coastal habitat, the upland forest habitat; the upland savanna habitat; and the lowland forest habitat. He then arrives at "a total estimated aboriginal, or initial contact, population for greater Amazonia" of 6,800,000, which he considers to be a conservative estimate and which "approximates [Henry F.] Dobyns' figure of 6,000,000 for all of tropical South America—a larger area." In an addendum, the author takes into account Thomas P. Myers's 1976 article **[356]**, "Defended Territories and No-man's-lands," which argued that "because of hostility many Amazon tribes were separated from one another by a no-man's land of unoccupied territory that in some instances was almost as large as the territory occupied." Denevan then reduces by 25% his figure of 6.8 million, arriving at a new one of 5.1 million, which he believes "is a reasonable buffer adjustment until the situation is better understood." 1 map; 3 tables; 12 footnotes and numerous bibliographic references.

[355] William M. Denevan. "The Aboriginal Population of Western Amazonia in Relation to Habitat and Subsistence," *Revista Geográfica* 72 (June 1970), pp. 61–86.

Earlier version of **[354]**. 3 tables. Bibliographical references are found on pp. 84–86.

[356] Thomas P. Myers. "Defended Territories and No-man's-lands," *American Anthropologist* 78:2 (June 1976), pp. 354–355.

Part of a continuing debate on the question "of territoriality among certain hunter-gatherer societies." For the colonial period, Myers cites Juan Salinas de Loyola's account of his voyage up the Ucayali River in the 1570s as evidence that Amazon tribes were "separated from their neighbors . . . by a no-man's land." The are five bibliographic references.

[357] Julian H. Steward. "The Native Population of South America," in Steward, ed., *Handbook* **[93]**, V, 655–668.

Steward discusses some of the methodological problems faced by writers in estimating the Amerindian population in South America before the arrival of the European. The author surveys the methods and population estimates of such authors as Paul Rivet, Carl Sapper, Angel Rosenblat, and Alfred L. Kroeber. He then makes his own estimates. Table 2 is especially useful for Brazil because Steward's population estimates correspond to each of the tribal and/or linguistic divisions studied in volumes I and III of the *Handbook of South American Indians*. Steward estimates that there were 1,100,000 Amerindians in Brazil in 1500. 3 tables.

C. Archaeology [Nos. 358–366]

There is a growing volume of writings in English on the archaeology of pre-Cabralian Brazil. Francisco de Aparicio **[358]** studies the Paraná River delta. Problems surrounding the "Lagoa Santa Man" are briefly described by Anibal Mattos **[359]**. Antônio Serrano **[360]** discusses the heaps of mollusk shells or *sambaquís* along sections of the Brazilian coast. The most rewarding finds have been made near the mouth of the Amazon. Betty J. Meggers and Clifford Evans **[361]** review the archaeology of the mouth of the Amazon and present revised versions of their dissertations. Meggers **[362]** focused on Marajó Island; Clifford Evans **[363]** examined the archaeology of the coast between the mouth of the Amazon and French Guiana. Betty J. Meggers **[364]** provides an overview of the archaeology of the Amazon basin. Helen Constance Palmatary **[365]** studies the archaeology of the Lower Tapajós valley. Artistic archaeological finds are described by Angyone Costa **[366]**.

[358] Francisco de Aparício. "The Archeology of the Paraná River," in Steward, ed., *Handbook* **[93]**, III, 57–69.

The author claims that "a brief analysis of the archeology of the Paraná demonstrates three distinct archeological complexes: two in the region of the Delta, and a third which is found along both shores of the river above the Delta." Sixteenth-century observers name the Querandí and the Guaraní as being in the Paraná region. However, excavations have revealed materials of still other Amerindian influences. Aparicio points out that "the sites along the shores of the Paraná are characterized by modeled pottery figures or plastic representations, with which are associated quantities of potsherds, plain, incised, and in a few cases, painted. By and large, however, the materials, which are almost exclusively ceramics, are of rather poor quality and of monotonous uniformity." Animals and birds, especially the great parrots, appear to be favorite subjects of the pottery. 2 plates; 2 figures. There is a bibliography on p. 66.

[359] Anibal Mattos. "Lagoa Santa Man," in Steward, ed., *Handbook* **[93]**, I, 399–400.

Brief discussion of the fossil remains discovered in the highland of Minas Gerais. The author reviews the different finds and concludes that "it has become evident that there were two or three types of Lagoa Santa man." Some of these may have lived along the coast. See Serrano **[360]**.

[360] Antônio Serrano. "The Sambaquís of the Brazilian Coast," in Steward, ed., *Handbook* **[93]**, I, 401–407.

The word "sambaquís" refers to the "heaps of mollusk shells which occur in the shape of cordons or mounds along a large section of the Brazilian coast." Some of these mounds are found along such fresh water rivers as the Amazon. "In both cases these shell deposits often conceal archeological remains and burials of peoples who, in ages past, dwelt along the coast of Brazil." The author examines the morphology of the *sambaquís* and their antiquity and concludes that the older view that there was a single *sambaquí* culture can no longer be held. Serrano claims that "the cultures which flourished along the coast on the *sambaquís* are mere littoral occurrences of other cultures of wide geographical distribution." The author defines four culture phases: southern, archaic, middle, and Amazonian. Bibliography. 4 plates.

[361] Betty J. Meggers and Clifford Evans. *Archeological Investigations at the Mouth of the Amazon.* Washington, D. C. Government Printing Office, 1957. xxviii, 664 pp.
[Also published by the Smithsonian Institution, Bureau of American Ethnology: Bulletin 167]

Though portions of this important study are chiefly of interest to archaeologists there are a number of useful sections for students of colonial Brazilian history. "Ethnographic Definition of Tropical Forest Culture" provides a succinct summary of material in volume III of Steward **[93]**. There are also geographical descriptions of the territory of Amapá (Brazilian Guiana) and the islands of Marajo, Mexiana and Caviana. Of special value to historians is the chapter entitled "The Historical Aftermath." The authors give a chronology of European contact and include a two-and-a-quarter page length table of European exploration and settlement with headings of year, event, and sources. There is also a most useful section on the ethnohistory of the territory of Amapá and the islands at the mouth of the Amazon, wherein the authors discuss tribes, population, culture, subsistence and settlement patterns, transportation, manufacturers, dress and ornament, social organization, recreation, life cycle, religion and warfare. Meggers and Evans conclude with an "ethnohistorical-archeological correlation" and a chapter on the "Implications of the Cultural Sequence at the Mouth of the Amazon." There is a bibliography of literature cited. 112 black and white photographs, 206 figures and maps, 21 tables within the text and 52 in the appendix.

[362] Betty Jane Meggers. "The Archeological Sequence of Marajó Island, Brazil, with Special Reference to the Marajoara Culture," (Ph.D. Dissertation: Columbia University, 1952). 397 pp.

Traces the evolution of Indian culture on the island of Marajó at the mouth of the Amazon and argues that "the Marajoara Phase, with artificial mounds, elaborate and diversified ceramics, pottery stools and tangas, and secondary urn burial provides a strong contrast with the earliest cultures." Mounds have been found on much of the eastern half of the island. From a study of the ceramics, Meggers points out that the "Marajoara culture possessed social stratification and occupational division of labor, and that its history on Marajó is one of decline." The author concludes that "the remnants of the declining Marajoara Phase were absorbed or expelled by the expansion from the mainland of the Aruã **[390]**, who possessed a typical Tropical Forest type culture with small scattered villages and simple utilitarian pottery." It was the Aruã Indians whom the Europeans first encountered on eastern Marajó in 1500. Based on archaeological field work on the island of Marajó in 1949–1950.
DAI 12/04 (p. 413).

[363] Clifford Evans. "The Archaeology of the Territory of Amapá, Brazil (Brazilian Guiana)," (Ph.D. Dissertation: Columbia University, 1950). 209 pp.

Examines the coast of Brazil between the mouth of the Amazon and French Guiana and claims that the territory of Amapá "was occupied by three distinct pottery-using phases"—Aruã, Mazagão and Ariste—the last two contemporaneous. The author concludes: "1) There is no evidence that any important migrations passed along the coast and up the Amazon; 2) Rather than being the nucleus of a developing Tropical Forest type of Culture, Brazilian Guiana was not occupied by ceramic-using peoples until relatively recently; 3) The relationship shown between the Mazagão Phase and the Middle Orinoco cultures of Venezuela points to the likelihood of an inland rather than a coastal migration route; 4) Except for the Aruã the cultures of the Territory of Amapá neither exerted nor received influence from any of those occupying the islands of Marajó, Mexiana and Caviana." Based on archaeological field work in 1949.
DAI 10/03 (pp. 4–5).

[364] Betty J. Meggers. "The Archeology of the Amazon Basin," in Julian H. Steward, ed., *Handbook* **[93]**, III, 149–166.

Meggers points out that "stone is scarce in most of the valley and was not a major item in the material culture. Few stone tools, mainly polished axes and celts, have been recovered. The perishable objects which took their place have not survived. Metal tools are rare and were acquired by trade from the Andes and later from the Europeans. As a result, pottery is almost all the archeologist can hope to find." In addition, "written sources leave much to be desired." The author divides the Amazon region into four areas: Marajó Island, Northeast Brazil, Santarem and its environs, and the Middle Amazon. Marajó Island "is characterized by the presence of mounds containing burial urns and domestic pottery . . . and by a distinctive style of decoration in which painted and incised designs are prominent." Santarem has neither mounds nor burial urns. However, burial urns are found in the Middle Amazon. In general, agriculture in the Amazon region "was supplemented by hunting, fishing, and gathering." Meggers argues that "the high development of the ceramic art, as well as the amount of labor which would have been required to build the stone walls along the coast and the mounds of Marajó, presupposes relatively large communities and indicates an economic and social organization advanced enough to permit the expenditure of large amounts of time and effort on projects unprofitable from the point of view of subsistence." 4 plates, 2 figures, 1 map. Documented.

[365] Helen Constance Palmatary. "The Archaeology of the Lower Tapajós Valley, Brazil," in *Transactions of the American Philosophical Society*. New Series. Volume 50, Part 3 (1960), pp. 1–243.

The author describes the geography of the Tapajós river area, sketches the history of the region's early contact with Europeans, and discusses Tapajó civilization. In the last-mentioned section, Palmatary describes Tapajó social organization, language, religion, disposal of the dead, food, handicrafts and weapons. She then discusses the chief archaeological sites. Most of the monograph deals with the pottery of the region, which is catalogued and described in detail. Palmatary also compares Marajó **[362]** and Tapajó ceramics and analyzes non-Tapajó wares. There is an interesting discussion of pipes and the use of tobacco. The author tries to determine "whether or not the Portuguese, who established themselves in the Amazon Valley rather late in Brazilian history and who were familiar with smoking customs before they arrived, were not, at least, the principal bearers of the bowl pipe into the Rio Tapajós and neighboring areas." There is also a section on the use of stone implements and jewelry. A bibliography is found on pp. 117–122. 6 maps. 121 plates.

[366] Angyone Costa. "Manifestations of Art in Brazilian Archaeology," *The Studio* 126:607 (October 1943), pp. 119–120.

The author points out that although a number of Brazilian tribes produced ceramics, "the producers of artistic ceramics were very few." Three groups—two from the Amazon region (that of Marajó and that of Santarém), and one from Guiana (the Cunani)—were the creators of native porcelain with pretensions to beauty." Angyone Costa describes some of their handiwork. The article also includes figures from Amazonian rock inscriptions.

D. Tribal and/or Linguistic Studies [Nos. 367–422]

1. The Indians of the Plata Region and Southern Brazil [Nos. 367–373]

Probably the most famous Indians of the Plata region were the Guaraní. Alfred Métraux **[367]** provides a brief account of their history and culture. S. K. Lothrop **[368]** describes the Indians of the Paraná delta and the Plata coast. The Charrua are discussed by Antônio Serrano **[369]**. Alfred Métraux **[370]** presents an excellent overview of the ethnography of the Chaco. The same author and Herbert Baldus **[371]** describe the Guayakí of eastern Paraguay. Métraux also studies such non-Guaraní Indians of southern Brazil as the Caingang **[372]** and the Guató **[373]**.

[367] Alfred Métraux. "The Guaraní," in Steward, ed., *Handbook* **[93]**, III, 69–94.

Métraux points out that "The Guaraní were first known as Carijó or Cario, but the name Guaraní finally prevailed in the 17th century. At this time, the Guaraní were the masters of the Atlantic Coast from Barra de Cananéa to Rio Grande do Sul, and from there their groups extended to the Paraná, Uruguay, and Paraguay Rivers." The author further adds that "since the 18th century, the Guaraní groups who had remained independent and had not been collected in missions have been distinguished from the Christianized Guaraní by the name Cainguá." Métraux examines the chief sources, the archaeology of the Guaraní area, and the conquest before examining in detail Guaraní culture. A good part of the author's discussion focuses on the topic of religion. "From the period of European Conquest to the present day, the Guaraní have been periodically stirred up by religious crises similar to messianic revivals in other parts of the world. Either a prophet would start a religious and political evolution by announcing the end of Spanish rule and the approach of a new golden age; or else some tribe would leave its territory in quest of the Land-Without-Evil." There is a bibliography on p. 94.

[368] S. K. Lothrop. "Indians of the Paraná Delta and La Plata Littoral," in Steward, ed., *Handbook* **[93]**, I, 177–190.

Lothrop relies heavily on the contemporary narratives of the sixteenth-century explorers, the accounts of eighteenth-century Jesuit missionaries, and early nineteenth century scientific accounts. He points out that a "study of historical sources indicates that the Indians dwelling on the shores of the Rio de la Plata and the lower Paraná River consisted primarily of plainsmen related to the Guaicuru." Into their midst had come an invading band of Guaraní, under whose influence the culture of some of their neighbors had been modified. The author attempts to reconstruct the history, language, subsistence activities, houses, dress and ornaments, weapons, warfare and social culture of the chief tribes of the region. Those mentioned by sixteenth-century explorers include the "Guarani de las islas," the Querandi, the Chana, the Mbegua, the Timbu, the Coronda, Quiloaza and Colastine. Those mentioned by seventeenth- and eighteenth-century writers include the Yaro and the Carcarana. There are two interesting early drawings of the Timbu. Bibliography.

[369] Antônio Serrano. "The Charrua," in Steward, ed., *Handbook* **[93]**, I, 191–196.

The Charrua inhabited parts of what are today Uruguay, Brazil and Argentina. Though originally the name was applied only to those who lived on the coast, it later was used to include a number of groups of the interior—some of which are treated in Lothrop **[368]**. There are 4 plates, one of which shows a group of Charrua in 1832. The other three provide examples of Charrua pottery, stonework and projectile points.

[370] Alfred Métraux. "Ethnography of the Chaco," in Steward, ed., *Handbook* **[93]**, I, 197–370.

Métraux points out that "the history of the Chaco in the sixteenth century cannot be separated from that of the conquest of the Rio de la Plata." In addition, "culturally as well as ecologically, the Chaco is a transitional zone between the tropical plains of the Amazon Basin and the barren pampas of the Argentine." The Portuguese shipwreck, Aleixo Garcia **[158]**, was "the first man to cross the Chaco and set foot in the empire of the Inca." Métraux provides a good description and evaluation of the sources useful for better understanding the ethnography of the Chaco. He then describes the chief tribes by linguistic group. One of the most important tribes speaking the Guaicuruan dialect was the Mbayá. "Changing from horsemen into boatmen and river pirates, they ambushed miners and colonists as they sailed from São Paulo to Matto Grosso on the Tacuary, Paraguay, and Cuyaba Rivers." Another tribe using the Guaicuruan dialect was the Abipon. In the early nineteenth century, members of this tribe served with José de Artigas, the hero of Uruguayan independence. Another important group was the Payaguá. "Since the beginning of the conquest of Paraguay, the Payagua are described as bold river pirates who, in their long and swift dugout canoes, sailed the Paraguay River from the Xarayes marshes to the Parana River." They "have a long record of hostility against the Spaniards and Portuguese.... They were a particular threat to the Portuguese of Matto Grosso travelling from São Paulo to Cuyabá." Also of importance were the Guaná, a name given to the eastern subtribes of the Paraguay basin. Métraux points out that in pre-Columbian times "the peaceful Guaná farmers had been subdued by the roving Mbaya and reduced to a condition of vassalage," which, as Ulrich Schmidel **[182]** observed in 1552, "was like that of German peasants to their feudal lords." The Mbayá also had Indian slaves. Both the Mbayá and the Guaná migrated from the Chaco to Mato Grosso during the latter part of the colonial period. The author then discusses the culture of the Indians inhabiting the Chaco region: subsistence activities, domesticated animals, houses and villages, furniture, dress and ornaments, transportation, manufactures, economic institutions, social and political organization, etiquette, warfare, life cycle, esthetic and recreational activities, religion, Shamanism and mythology. Métraux points out that "the adoption of the horse by the tribes living along the right bank of the Paraguay and Paraná Rivers broke the uniformity of culture which seems to have prevailed throughout the Chaco at the time of the Conquest." Furthermore, "the Chaco tribes which became equestrian rapidly developed along new lines and within a century formed a strongly stratified society differing sharply from that of the western and northwestern tribes, who carried on the democratic system formerly characteristic of all Chaco groups." The author emphasizes that "all Chaco Indians were extremely warlike; many still are. The most bellicose were the members of the Guaicuruan family, who were greatly feared not only by their neighbors but also by the Spaniards [and the Portuguese]." In warfare, "Indian tactics always aimed at avoiding casualties. Even the bellicose Abipon or Mbayá would flee if they suffered a few losses." For trophies, "the Indians took either heads . . . or scalps." Well illustrated. There is a lengthy bibliography on p. 370.

[371] Alfred Métraux and Herbert Baldus. "The Guayakí," in Steward, ed., *Handbook* **[93]**, I, 435–444.

The authors point out that "the Guayakí live in the dense forests of eastern Paraguay where hills and mountains separate the tributaries of the Paraguay River from those of the Paraná River." The Guayakí are one of the least-known tribes in the hemisphere. They were engaged in almost perpetual war against the Cainguá **[372]** and the Guaraní **[367]**. Métraux and Baldus attempt to reconstruct Guayakí subsistence activities, camps and houses, dress and ornaments, transportation, manufactures, social and political organization, life cycle, esthetic and recreational activities, religion, mythology, and medicine. There is a bibliography on p. 444.

[372] Alfred Métraux. "The Caingang," in Steward, ed., *Handbook* **[93]**, I, 445–475.

The term Caingang refers to "the non-Guaraní Indians of the States of São Paulo, Paraná, Santa Catarina, and Rio Grande do Sul, who previously were known as Guayaná, Coroado, Bugre, Shokleng, Tupí, Botocudo, etc. but who are all linguistically and culturally related to one another and form the southern branch of the Gê family." The Guayaná were first mentioned by Hans Staden **[181]**. Gabriel Soares de Sousa, in his account of Brazil in 1587, reported that "they were the masters of the entire coast of the present state of São Paulo, from Angra dos Reis to Cananéia." Métraux, however, states that "they shared the seashore with Guaraní-speaking Tupinikin." Tibiriçá, the Amerindian with whom the early missionaries and settlers of São Paulo frequently came in contact, was a Guayaná chief. Though the Caingang seem to have been sedentary agriculturalists, hunting played an important role in their economy. Métraux also points out that "river navigation never was so important to the Caingang as to their Tupí-Guaraní neighbors." In the nineteenth century, Jean-Baptiste Debret **[837]** depicted the Caingang in some of his watercolors. Though the author provides a good account of Caingang culture, most of the evidence dates from the postindependence period. 5 figs. There is a bibliography on p. 475.

[373] Alfred Métraux. "The Guató," in Steward, ed., *Handbook* **[93]**, I, 409–418.

Métraux points out that "the Guató inhabit the marshy and flooded plains of the upper Paraguay River Basin," south of the region of the Bororo **[408]**. There are a number of archaeological remains, including low mounds. "Pits, from which earth for the construction had been taken, remain near each mound. The accumulated earth contained animal bones, snail shells, stone fragments, and potsherds. The exceedingly crude pottery is very similar to that of the modern Guató." The Guató were mentioned in the *Commentaries* of Alvar Nuñez Cabeza de Vaca **[182]**. By the beginning of the nineteenth century, the Guató were much reduced in numbers and "wandered continually in dugout canoes," often cooking in their boats. There is a bibliography on p. 418. See also Métraux **[417]**, pp. 136–142.

2. The Coastal Indians and Their Immediate Neighbors [Nos. 374–390]

Robert H. Lowie **[374]** provides an overview of the Tropical Forest Tribes, among whom are the Coastal Tupí. Alfred Métraux **[375]** presents a synopsis of his several monographs on the Tupinamba. Charles Wagley and Eduardo Galvão **[376]** and **[377]** study the Tenetehara, a Tupí-Gaurani-speaking people of Maranhão and Pará. Robert H. Lowie **[378]** also surveys the non-Tropical Forest tribes of Eastern Brazil. Alfred Métraux examines the Coroado and Purí **[379]** as well as the Guaitacá **[380]** and the Botocudo or Aimoré **[381]**. Difficulties with the classification "Tapuya" are discussed by Lowie **[382]**. Métraux and Curt Nimuendajú examine the Mashacalí, Patashó, and Malalí **[383]** and the Camacan **[384]** linguistic families. Robert H. Lowie describes the Cariri **[385]** and the Jeico **[386]**. Alfred Métraux contributes a brief sketch on the Fulnio **[387]**. On or near the coast of northeastern and northern Brazil were the Tarairiu discussed by Lowie **[388]** and the Teremembe sketched by Métraux **[389]**. Also near the coast were some Indians belonging to the Northwestern and Central Gê. They are described by Lowie **[394]**. Nimuendajú **[390]** presents information on the Turiwara and, especially, the Aruã.

[374] Robert H. Lowie. "The Tropical Forests: An Introduction," in Steward, ed., *Handbook* **[93]**, III, 1–56.

The author provides a useful overview of the Tropical Forest environment. There are excellent descriptive lists both of cultivated plants and useful wild plants. Lowie discusses hunting, fishing, and food preparation. He describes in general terms the dwellings, clothing and body ornamentation of the Tropical Forest tribes as well as their modes of transportation and manufactures. Social and political organization, warfare, treatment of prisoners, and cannibalism are analyzed, as is the life cycle of birth, puberty, and death. The author also lists the art, games, dances, and music of the Tropical Forest Indians. There is a section on narcotics and intoxicating drinks. Lowie concludes with a consideration of religion, shamanism, medicine and etiquette. There is a bibliography on p. 56.

[375] Alfred Métraux. "The Tupinamba," in Steward, ed., *Handbook* **[93]**, III, 95–133.

Métraux uses the term Tupinamba to refer "to all the Indians speaking a Tupi-Guarani dialect, who in the sixteenth century were masters of the Brazilian shore from the mouth of the Amazon River to Canaéa in the south of the State of São Paulo. Though linguistically and culturally closely related, these Indians were divided into a great many tribes that waged merciless war against one another." The name Tupinamba also included such tribes as the Potiguara, Caeté, Tupinikin, Timimino, Tamoyo, Ararape, and Tupinakin, and such inland tribes as the Tabayara, Tupina, and Amoipira. Métraux points out that "several typical messianic outbursts took place in the second part of the 16th century when the various Tupinamba tribes were forced to yield ground to the Portuguese and were being either wholly outrooted or enslaved. Here, as elsewhere in the New World, these crises were prompted by shamans or prophets who announced the return of the mythical ages and the disappearance of the white scourge." Farming was of major importance, though the Tupinamba collected wild foods. Hunting "was a major masculine occupation." Fishing was also an essential part of the Tupinamba economy. These Amerindians also domesticated birds and wild pigs, agouti, monkeys and armadillos. Tupinamba villages "consisted of from 4 to 8 huge ceremonial houses built around a square plaza, where the social and religious life of the community centered." The Indians used stone axes for felling trees. Métraux describes Tupinamba dress and ornaments and examines their social and political organization, social control, justice, and etiquette. He discusses the Tupinamba life cycle of birth, puberty, and death, and the practice of war and cannibalism. Such esthetic and recreational activities as dancing, singing, playing musical instruments, smoking, and drinking are also analyzed. Métraux concludes his study of the Tupinamba with an analysis of their religious practices and mythology. There is a bibliography on p. 133.

[376] Charles Wagley and Eduardo Galvão. "The Tenetehara," in Steward, ed., *Handbook* **[93]**, III, 137–148.

The Tenetehara (also called Guajajara and Tembé) are a Tupí-Guaraní-speaking people who inhabited northern and northeastern Brazil, expecially Maranhão and Pará, during the colonial period. Both the French and the Portuguese encountered the Tenetehara during the second decade of the seventeenth century. According to the authors, "in the middle 17th century, the Jesuits made three separate expeditions up the Pindaré River for the purpose of bringing Tenetehara down the river and placing them in mission villages on the island of Maranhão." The Tenetehara, like the other coastal Tupí Indians, were agriculturalists. Wagley and Galvão point out that "formerly, only women planted and harvested cotton and peanuts, while the cultivation of manioc, maize, and other plants was the exclusive occupation of the men." Hunting and fishing were also important. The authors discuss the housing, clothing, manufactures, social and political organization, life cycle, esthetic and recreational activities, and religion of the Tenetehara. There is a bibliography on p. 148.

[377] Charles Wagley and Eduardo Galvão. *The Tenetehara Indians of Brazil. A Culture in Transition.* New York: Columbia University Press, 1949. xv, 200 pp.

Expanded version of **[376]**. Though most of this study deals with the twentieth century, there are some sections on the colonial period. The authors point out that "the original territory of the Tenetehara seems to have centered on the upper Pindaré River; all mention of them in the seventeenth and eighteenth centuries places them on this river, above the village of Monção." They trace the exploits of "the famous Indian hunter Bento Maciel Parente" who "with a force of 45 soldiers and 90 missionized Indians" warred against the Tenetehara "with fatal damage to that nation." The authors also discuss Jesuit efforts to protect the Tenetehara and establish them in missions. There is a useful map. 28 plates. A bibliography is found on pp. 189–190.

[378] Robert H. Lowie. "Eastern Brazil: An Introduction," in Steward, ed., *Handbook* **[93]**, I, 381–397.

As Lowie points out, many of the Tropical Forest tribes who inhabited geographical eastern Brazil are not included in this classification, which is reserved for such non-Tupí-Guaraní Indians as the Gê, Tapuyá, Bororo, and Botocudo. Though there is not a uniform culture among the tribes of eastern Brazil, they do have a number of common characteristics. They also share a number of traits with the Tropical Forest Indians, but "as a rule agriculture is less intensive than in the tropical forests." There is agriculture, but hunting and fishing seem more important. In addition, eastern Brazilian pottery "distinctly differs from either Tupí or Arawak ware." Lowie describes the culture of the Indians of eastern Brazil, giving special emphasis to subsistence activities, houses and villages, dress and ornaments, transportation, manufactures, social and political organization, warfare, life cycle, esthetic and recreation activities, supernaturalism, and mythology. The author points to the "extreme separatism" of the tribes in this classification.

[379] Alfred Métraux. "The Purí-Coroado Linguistic Family," in Steward, ed., *Handbook* **[93]**, I, 523–530.

The Coroado were located in the region of the Serra do Mar. Métraux points out that "during the 17th century, the Coroado were raided by the Paulistas and, as a result, they remained bitter enemies of the Whites until 1763, when they were induced to make peace. In 1767 they were placed under the authority of special government agents. Harshly treated by the colonists who exploited them, they were already in full decadence by 1813." The Purí inhabited the territory from the Paraiba river to the upper reaches of the Rio Doce. According to the author, "in the 18th century, several hundred Purí were lured to Villa Rica, where they were sold as slaves. About 500 in the region of Piranga and Santa Rita placed themselves under the protection of the Portuguese and were settled near Rio Pardo." Remnants of the tribe were seen by Prince Maximilian of Wied-Neuwied **[851]** and Spix and Martius **[546]**. Another related group were the Coropó, who "were acculturated and spoke Portuguese" by 1813. The Purí and the Coroado were poor farmers. The former "looted the fields of the colonists and of the civilized Indians, mainly for sugarcane, of which they were inordinately fond." Métraux discusses their culture in some detail. There is a bibliography on p. 530.

[380] Alfred Métraux. "The Guaitacá," in Steward, ed., *Handbook* **[93]**, I, 521–522.

Contemporary sources reveal that the Guaitacá "were the undisputed masters of the fertile Campos dos Goaitacazes that extended from the vicinity of Lagoa Feia to the mouth of the Parahyba River." In the sixteenth century, "the Guaitacá raided several times the Captaincy of Espirito Santo and, in one of their numerous battles against Portuguese troops, killed Fernão de Sá, the son of the Governor General of Brazil." In the early nineteenth century Prince Maximilian of Wied-Neuwied **[851]** encountered "in the village of São Lourenzo, near Rio de Janeiro, the remainder of the Guaitacá who had been settled in the Jesuit missions as well as others in the village of São Pedro dos Indios." There is a brief outline of the culture and a bibliography on p. 522.

[381] Alfred Métraux. "The Botocudo," in Steward, ed., *Handbook* **[93]**, I, 531–540.

The Botocudo or Aimoré, according to Pero de Magalhães **[186]**, in the sixteenth century were found "along the coast from the Capitania dos Ilheos to Porto Seguro." They had probably migrated from the interior of the *sertão* to pillage and kill in the coastal region. They are also mentioned by Cardim **[207]**. Métraux points out that "in the second half of the seventeenth century, perhaps in alliance with other tribes, they laid waste the towns of Porto Seguro, Santo Amaro, and Santa Cruz. For more than a hundred years they harassed the Mestizo and Portuguese settlements of the coast and remained the undisputed masters of the Serra dos Aimorés. Their raids led to bloody reprisals, and until the second half of the 19th century the colonists hunted them down." Métraux adds that "in the beginning of the 19th century there were already many families or bands settled near ranches, where they served as day laborers, or established in 'aldeas.' " The author provides a brief description of Botocudo subsistence activities, housing, dress and ornaments, transportation, manufactures, social organization, life cycle, medicine, esthetic and recreational activities, religion and mythology. Métraux argues that although "the Botocudo have repeatedly been branded as ferocious cannibals, . . . the evidence is dubious." A bibliography is found on p. 540.

[382] Robert H. Lowie. "The 'Tapuya,'" in Steward, ed., *Handbook* **[93]**, I, 553–556.

Lowie discusses the problems caused by the use of this term and points out that "earlier writers on eastern Brazil frequently applied it to any Indians obviously unrelated to the Tupí." In 1584, Padre Fernão Cardim **[207]** listed "76 'Tapuia' tribes, but indicates great diversity of speech and custom among them." Most of the Indians referred to as "Tapuya" seem to be located in northeastern Brazil. Lowie concludes that " 'Tapuya' is a blanket term like 'Digger Indian' or 'Siwash' in North America. No good purpose is served by considering them as a linguistic or ethnic unit. . . . There is no 'Tapuya' culture: except in quoting old writers on otherwise undefined groups so designated, the term should be eliminated from scientific usage." 1 fig. There is a bibliography on p. 556.

[383] Alfred Métraux and Curt Nimuendajú. "The Mashacalí, Patashó, and Malalí Linguistic Families," in Steward, ed., *Handbook* **[93]**, I, 541–545.

These Indians were originally located near the borders of the captaincies of Bahia, Porto Seguro and Minas Gerais. They were frequently in conflict with the Botocudo **[381]** and forced to migrate. They were described for the first time in the nineteenth century by Prince Maximilian of Wied-Neuwied **[851]** and Spix and Martius **[546]**. The authors briefly discuss their culture. There is a bibliography on p. 545.

[384] Alfred Métraux and Curt Nimuendajú. "The Camacan Linguistic Family," in Steward, ed., *Handbook* **[93]**, I, 547–552.

The authors point out that "the Camacan proper remained for many years hostile to the Portuguese and fought tenaciously against them until 1808. At the beginning of the last century, they lived in six or seven villages somewhat to the north of the Rio Pardo." In 1817, Camacan and Bahia were visited by Prince Maximilian of Wied-Neuwied **[851]**. Spix and Martius **[546]** observed another group of Camacan two years later. Métraux and Nimuendajú provide a brief account of their culture. There is a bibliography on p. 552.

[385] Robert H. Lowie. "The Cariri," in Steward, ed., *Handbook* **[93]**, I, 557–559.

Lowie points out that the Cariri formed "a distinct linguistic family" and inhabited the interior of northeastern Brazil. He lists 16 documented habitats for the colonial period. The author argues that "the Cariri were on a higher level of culture than most eastern Brazilians. They grew manioc, maize, beans, and cotton; slept in hammocks; made pottery molded at the base and coiled above, corresponding to the Shucurú ware of Cimbres, Pernambuco; and are even credited with having a simple loom." Much of what we know about them is provided by the Capuchin missionary Martin de Nantes, who published an account in French in 1706. The Cariri were "reduced in numbers through Portuguese and Dutch contacts" and later established in Jesuit *aldeias* west of Bahia. When Martius **[546]** visited them in 1818, there were about 600 survivors. Lowie provides a brief description of their culture. A bibliography is found on p. 559.

[386] Robert H. Lowie. "The Jeico," in Steward, ed., *Handbook* **[93]**, I, 567.

Little is known about this extinct Gê tribe. They were located near the Rio São Francisco in Piaui. The Jeico were mentioned by Padre Fernão Cardim **[207]** in the sixteenth century and Martius **[546]** in the beginning of the nineteenth century. There is a bibliography on p. 567.

[387] Alfred Métraux. "The Fulnio," in Steward, ed., *Handbook* **[93]**, I, 571.

Little is known about the Fulnio or Carnijó. They are first mentioned in 1758 and lived in the interior of Pernambuco. There is a brief bibliography on p. 571.

[388] Robert H. Lowie. "The Tarairiu," in Steward, ed., *Handbook* **[93]**, I, 563–566.

According to the author, "the Tarairiu were sublitoral, living not so far inland as the Cariri **[385]**, but back of the coast occupied by Europeans, possibly between Natal and Ceará, centering on what is now Rio Grande do Norte." During the Dutch occupation of 1630–1654, the Tarairiu usually sided with the Hollanders. Not surprisingly the best sources for the Tarairiu heritage are the Dutch. After the Dutch were ousted from Brazil the Tarairiu were almost annihilated by the Portuguese. Lowie provides a brief description of their culture. There is a bibliography on p. 566.

[389] Alfred Métraux. "The Teremembe," in Steward, ed., *Handbook* **[93]**, I, 573–574.

Métraux points out that the language of the Teremembe is unknown, but that it was not Tupi. In the seventeenth century, they lived along the shores of northern Brazil, "from the mouth of the Gurupy River or of the Tury River in the east to the mouth of the Paranahyba River." They are mentioned by such French visitors as Claude d'Abbeville and Yves d'Evreux. According to Métraux, "they were bitter enemies of the Tupinamba **[375]**, whom they attacked whenever they could ambush them. In 1674, because Teremembe had killed shipwrecked Portuguese sailors, the colonists led a bloody punitive expedition against them. At the end of the 17th century the remnants of the tribe were settled by the Jesuits in missions." The author provides a brief sketch of the Teremembe culture. There is a bibliography on p. 574.

[390] Curt Nimuendajú. "The Turiwara and Aruã," in Steward, ed., *Handbook* **[93]**, III, 193–198.

Little is known about the Turiwara during the colonial period. Francisco Xavier Ribeiro de Sampaio reported a tribe of that name on the lower Tocantins river during the late eighteenth century. There is more information regarding the Aruã. In the seventeenth century, this tribe inhabited the northeastern part of Marajo Island as well as other islands of the Amazon estuary. Nimuendajú points out that "the Aruã and the other tribes on Marajó Island were always hostile to the Portuguese of Belem, although they maintained friendly relations and commerce through the estuary of the Amazon with other nations, especially the Dutch." Padre Antônio Vieira **[315]** defended the Aruã, but expeditions were sent against them by local officials. Gradually, the Aruã and their neighbors migrated to Guiana. The year 1701 marked further conflict between the Aruã and the Portuguese. Later in the century, with French support, the Aruã attacked Portuguese settlements. Gradually more and more of the Aruã came under French influence. A bibliography is found on p. 198.

3. The Indians of the Guianas and the Rio Negro Basin [Nos. 391–392]

John Gillin **[391]** has the unenviable job of sorting out the myriad of tribes in the Guianas. Alfred Métraux **[392]** provides a survey of the hunting and gathering tribes of the Rio Negro Basin.

[391] John Gillin. "Tribes of the Guianas," in Steward, ed., *Handbook* **[93]**, III, 799–860.

The ehtnographic region of the Guianas includes much of northern South America. Brazilianists are mostly concerned with its southern boundary which "is the left bank of the Amazon River from its confluence with the Rio Negro to its northernmost mouth." Gillin divides the Guianas into three culture areas: coastal, inland mountain-savanna, and Amazonian, but it is a difficult region to analyze since migration and the mixing of cultures frequently have blurred distinctions. Furthermore, "the Guiana area as a whole is not strikingly distinctive, for it shares many traits and configurations in common with the other tropical regions of South America." Gillin points out that "from 1625 until the middle of the 19th century, Portuguese activity north of the Amazon River was confined largely to missionary explorations, desultory general exploring, and the establishment of a few towns." The author surveys the archaeology and the culture of the Guianas. He also gives a brief list of the many tribes of the region. There is a bibliography on pp. 858–860.

[392] Alfred Métraux. "The Hunting and Gathering Tribes of the Rio Negro Basin," in Steward, ed., *Handbook* **[93]**, III, 861–881.

Métraux points out that in this region "roam many groups of forest nomads. These little-known bands are surrounded with mystery and legends. . . . They represent a very ancient population which in some places has been destroyed or assimilated, but in other areas has succeeded in surviving." Almost all the information about tribes within Brazil dates from the postindependence period. There is a bibliography.

4. The Indians of the Eastern Amazon, Tocantins, Xingú, and Tapajós Rivers and Their Tributaries [Nos. 393–408]

A good introduction to the Amazon region is found in Betty J. Meggers's study, "Environment and Culture in Amazonia" **[393]**. Robert H. Lowie **[394]** surveys the Northwestern and Central Gê and Curt Nimuendajú devotes monographs to the Eastern Timbira **[395]**, the Apinayé **[396]**, and the Sĕrente **[397]**. He also **[398]** briefly discusses the Guajá. William Lipkind **[399]** describes the Carajá. The Amanayé are studied by Nimuendajú and Alfred Métraux **[400]**. Nimuendajú also mentions some of the little known tribes of the lower Tocantins river region **[401]** as well as those of the lower and middle Xingú river **[402]** and the lower Amazon **[403]**. In addition, he describes the Maué and Arapium **[404]**. Also on the Tapajós river were the Cawahib, Parintintin and their neighbors **[405]** along with the Cayabí, Tapanyuna, and Apiacá **[406]**—all studied by Nimuendajú. Robert H. Lowie concludes this section with studies on the Southern Cayapó **[407]** and the Bororo **[408]**.

[393] Betty J. Meggers. "Environment and Culture in Amazonia," in Wagley, ed., *Man in the Amazon* **[86]**, pp. 91–110.

The author briefly describes the environment of the Amazon basin and then focuses most of her attention on man's past in Amazonia. She points out that "in the absence of archeological information from the southeastern Amazon and in view of the ethnohistorical reports of the withdrawal of coastal groups into this region beginning during the latter half of the sixteenth century to escape Portuguese enslavement, it is possible that some or all of the Tupí-Guaraní groups in eastern Amazonia are post-European intrusions." Meggers also discusses aboriginal adaptation in various parts of the region as well as the ways Europeans utilized Amazonia. Map. Bibliographical references in the text.

[394] Robert H. Lowie. "The Northwestern and Central Gê," in Steward, ed., *Handbook* **[93]**, I, 477–517.

One of the most important of the Northwestern Gê tribes are the Timbira. They are "first mentioned in 1728 as extending east of the Parnahyba River [and] are recorded as hostile natives of Piauí as late as 1769." Their oldest chronicler was Francisco de Paula Ribeiro, who reported in 1815 and 1819 about the Indians living on the frontiers of Maranhão and Goiás. Spix and Martius **[546]** visited the Timbira in 1818 and 1819. Related to the Timbira are the Apinayé and the Northern Cayapó. The Central Gê are usually divided into the Akwẽ and the Acroá. The former include the Shacriabá, the Shavante, and the Sherente. Accounts describing the Akwẽ date from the early nineteenth century. According to the author, some of the Acroá "dwelt in the 18th century west of the São Francisco River, were settled in Piauí, and became extinct by 1850." Lowie points out that "contrary to widespread notions, the majority of the Gê have been farmers, especially the Apinayé **[396]**, with evidence for extensive manioc plantations going back to 1793." But "notwithstanding husbandry, wild species continued to loom large in aboriginal days." As for hunting, "except for the occasional digging up of armadillos from their burrows by women, the chase was a masculine occupation and an important one. The men hunted practically all mammals and birds except vultures." The author argues that "the preparation of food sharply distinguished the Northern and Central Gê from the Tupí. Lacking pottery, the Gê, including the Southern Cayapó **[407]**, steamed or baked food in earth ovens between the heated ground and the hot rocks or clay lumps. However, there was also broiling on a spit and roasting on a grate." The Gê had no intoxicating beverages. According to Lowie, water was their only drink. The author describes the culture of the Gê, their houses and villages, dress and ornaments, transportation, manufactures, political organization, social organization, warfare, life cycle, esthetic and recreational activities, and their religious practices. 8 plates. There is a bibliography on p. 517.

[395] Curt Nimuendajú. *The Eastern Timbira.* Trans. Robert H. Lowie. Berkeley and Los Angeles: University of California Press, 1946. x, 357 pp.

The author focuses on fourteen tribes which he groups under the heading, the Eastern Timbira. He classifies the Apinayé **[396]** as belonging to the Western Timbira. The territory of these northern Gê tribes "was simultaneously occupied by civilized newcomers along four distinct avenues of approach: (1) from São Luiz do Maranhão up the Mearim and Itapicuru; (2) from Pará up the Tocantins; (3) from Goyaz down the Tocantins; (4) from Bahia across the steppes to the northwest, across Piauhy." The last-mentioned invasion had the greatest effect on the Timbira. Nimuendajú traces the conquest and white settlement in Timbira territory and points out that "where force of arms failed the colonists often sought to gain their ends by false proposals of peace and mendacious promises, made through interpreters to the fortified Timbira; those who trustingly met the bandeira were then enslaved and massacred." Citing the statements of Francisco de Paula Ribeiro, an eyewitness to many of the events he recorded, Nimuendajú writes that "the Indians wars were due to the colonists' craving for slaves rather than to the need of opening up new territories." Nimuendajú studies their settlements and housing, dress and ornament, hygiene, and agricultural, fishing, and hunting techniques. He also examines their social life, ceremonies, religion, magic, and legends. 3 maps. 16 figures. 42 plates. There is a bibliography.

[396] Curt Nimuendajú. *The Apinayé.* Tr. Robert H. Lowie. Washington, D. C.: The Catholic University Press, 1939. vi, 189.
[Reprinted in the Netherlands by Anthropological Publications, 1967.]

The Apinayé are one of the Gê tribes. According to Nimuendajú, "the tribal domain embraced the triangle between the Rio Tocantins and the lower Araguaya, extending southward to about 6° 30′." Though Antônio Vieira **[315]** and other Jesuits frequented the Rio Tocantins during the years 1653–1658 in their search for Indians for the *aldeias* of Pará, they do not seem to have encountered the Apinayé. According to Nimuendajú, it was not until 1774 that "the first demonstrable contact of the Apinayé with civilization" occurred. "Towards the end of the eighteenth century the Apinayé first became known by that name when they undertook raids downstream in order to procure tools from the settlers." In 1793, Tomás de Sousa Vila Real wrote an account describing in some detail the Pinare or Apinayé. At that time they inhabited both banks of the Rio Araguaya, "had boats of their own and were able to navigate the river." Nimuendajú points out that "from 1797 on there was constant intercourse with civilization." The author provides a brief description of the land they inhabited and gives a detailed description of their social structure. Though most of the study deals with Nimuendajú's observations beginning with his first visit in 1928, there are continual references to the colonial period and, especially, Vila Real's account. The author claims that "agriculture seems to have been carried on to a considerable extent in ancient times and to have been more important economically than among the Eastern Timbira **[395]**. In 1793 Vila Real already noted extensive manioc plantations." There is a useful map. 30 figures. A bibliography is found on pp. 187–189.

[397] Curt Nimuendajú. *The Šerente.* Tr. Robert H. Lowie. Los Angeles: Southwest Museum, 1942. ix, 106 pp.

The Canella, other Eastern Timbira, and the Apinayé **[396]** are representative of the Northern Gê in the interior of Brazil. The Šerente belong to one of the two sub-branches that make up the Central Gê. The Šerente are closely related to the Savante. Nimuendajú argues that "essentially one in speech and custom, the two groups are distinct only in a local and political sense." The author points out that "the history of the two tribes opens with their resistance to gold prospectors from the south. At the margin of their territory were founded Crixás, Trahiras, São José do Tocantins, Agua Quente, and other settlements between 1732 and 1737; while Pontal, established in 1738, lies far within the Šerente country." He adds that "the Indians' opposition and their sanguinary attacks on goldseekers and settlers were the despair of the whites, but conditions in Goyaz were such that peaceable relations were practically impossible for the natives." The author then describes and analyzes their society. Most of the book deals with the post-1937 period, since only Johann Emanuel Pohl and Francis de Castelnau saw the Sĕrente before 1850. 3 plates. 4 figures. map. There is a bibliography on pp. 103–106.

[398] Curt Nimuendajú. "The Guajá," in Steward, ed., *Handbook* **[93]**, III, 135–136.

The author points out that "the tribe is rarely mentioned in literature. In 1774, Ribeiro de Sampaio mentions the Uaya among the tribes of the lower Tocantins." Most of what is known about their history and culture dates from the postindependence period. There is a bibliography on p. 136.

[399] William Lipkind. "The Carajá," in Steward, ed., *Handbook* **[93]**, III, 179–191.

According to Lipkind, "contact with the Carajá proper must have begun shortly after the founding of Santa Anna by Bartholomeu Bueno in 1682." The Carajá are "a river people who since pre-Columbian times have held as the central portion of their territory, the inland Island of Bananal, which is formed by the great fork of the Araguaya River." Lipkind discusses the archaeology as well as the culture of the Carajá. 7 figures. 3 plates. There is a very brief bibliography on p. 191.

[400] Curt Nimuendajú and Alfred Métraux. "The Amanayé," in Steward, ed., *Handbook* **[93]**, III, 199–202.

The Amanayé occupied parts of Maranhão, Piaui, and Pará. According to the authors, they "always occupied the upper Pindaré, the Gurupí, and the Capim Rivers, the middle Mojú River, and the central part of the right bank of the lower Tocantins below the mouth of the Araguaya, and were found only rarely away from this region." The year 1755 marks the date that they are first mentioned. The Amanayé are included in Francisco Xavier Ribeiro de Sampaio's account of Indians encountered on his expedition from Pará into the Brazilian interior along the Amazon and Negro rivers. Most of the information in the

Nimuendajú and Métraux coverage of this tribe dates from the postindependence period. There is a brief sketch of the Amanayé culture. A bibliography is found on p. 202.

[401] Curt Nimuendajú. "Little-Known Tribes of the Lower Tocantins River Region," in Steward, ed., *Handbook* **[93]**, III, 203–208.

Only two of the tribes listed—the Pacajá and the Jacundá—are of interest for the colonial period. According to the author, the former tribe "appears to have centered in the basin of the Pacajá de Portel River. It may also have lived in the lower Tocantins River and the lower Xingú River where a right tributary is named Pacajá (de Souzel) River." The French priest Yves d'Evreux, who was in northern Brazil in 1613 and 1614, mentions the Pacajá, as does Padre Acuña **[235]**, who encountered them in 1639. Shortly after mid-century, some of the Pacajá entered Jesuit missions. According to the author, a large number "escaped again to their own land. The others were sent to distant missions." By 1762–1763 they were almost extinct. Nimuendajú points out that "at the end of the 18th century and during the first half of the 19th century, the Jacundá lived on the Jacundá River, which empties into the Tocantins from right below Itaboca Falls." The Jacundá were first mentioned by Tomás de Sousa Vila Real in 1793. At that time "they lived at the headwaters of the Igarapé Guayapí (Jacundá River?) and occasionally appeared on the eastern bank of the Tocantins." There is a bibliography on p. 208.

[402] Curt Nimuendajú. "Tribes of the Lower and Middle Xingú River," in Steward, ed., *Handbook* **[93]**, III, 213–243.

The author divides the Amerindians of the region into three groups: "1) Canoeing tribes restricted to the Xingú, Iriri, and Curuá Rivers: Yuruna, Shipaya, Arupaí. 2) Tribes of the central virgin forest: Curuaya, Arara, Asuriní, and, formerly, Tacunyapé. 3) Savanna tribes that only temporarily invade the forest zone: North Cayapó **[394]**." Nimuendajú points out that manioc was the staple crop and "caimans, turtles, honey, and Brazil nuts were outstanding wild foods." He discusses efforts of both missionaries and secular authorities to "civilize" these various Indian tribes. After analyzing briefly the history, territory and number of each of the above-mentioned tribes, the author devotes pp. 225–243 to a discussion of their culture, with a special emphasis on subsistence activities, dwellings and villages, dress and adornment, transportation, manufactures, social and political organization, warfare and cannibalism, esthetic and recreational activities, and religion and shamanism. 7 figures. There is a bibliography on p. 243.

[403] Curt Nimuendajú. "Little-Known Tribes of the Lower Amazon," in Steward, ed., *Handbook* **[93]**, III, 209–211.

The author focuses on three tribes: The Aracajú, the Apotó, and the Pauxí. The first and third named Indians had contact with the Portuguese in the second half of the seventeenth century. Jesuit missionaries worked among the Aracajú and the Pauxi. Martius **[546]** visited the former in 1820. There is a bibliography.

[404] Curt Nimuendajú. "The Maué and Arapium," in Steward, ed., *Handbook* **[93]**, III, 245–254.

The Maué were located between the lower Tapajós and the Amazon Rivers. Portuguese Jesuits ministered to the Maué beginning in the second half of the seventeenth century. Nimuendajú discusses their culture, basing much of his discussion for the late colonial period on the writings of Martius, who visited the Maué in 1819. The Arapium, according to Father Samuel Fritz **[325]**, lived to the west of the lower Tapajóz. Some scholars have identified them with the Maué. Nimuendajú provides a brief sketch of the Arapium culture. A bibliography is found on p. 254.

[405] Curt Nimuendajú. "The Cawahib, Parintintin, and Their Neighbors," in Steward, ed., *Handbook* **[93]**, III, 283–297.

Nimuendajú points out that Cawahib "is the 18th- and early 19th-century name of a people who later split into some six groups or tribes, among them the Parintintin." The author adds that "in the 18th century, a tribe named Cabahiba lived on the upper Tapajóz River, between the confluence of the Arinos and Juruena Rivers and the mouth of the São Manoel River. Information about this tribe is scanty, partly because it never lived on the banks of the great river, unlike its neighbors, the Apiacá **[406]**." Nimuendajú shows that "as the name Cawahib gradually disappeared from the writings about Mato Grosso, Parintintin began to appear in Pará at the beginning of the 19th century. Parintintin is the name given the Cawahib by the Mundurucú **[414]**, its mortal enemies and neighbors to the north. The Mundurucú originally were concentrated in the region of the Rio das Tropas, but, since 1750, they have expanded mainly at the expense of the Cawahib." The author then focuses on the Parintintin. His discussion covers only the postindependence period. There is a bibliography on p. 297.

[406] Curt Nimuendajú. "The Cayabí, Tapanyuna, and Apiacá," in Steward, ed., *Handbook* **[93]**, III, 307–320.

Information on the Cayabí is derived from postindependence contact. The Tapanyuna (formerly the Arino) "lived on the right bank of the Arinos River and on the upper Tapajóz River." There are a number of early nineteenth-century references to the Tapanyuna. Nimuendajú points out that "the Apiacá are mentioned for the first time in itineraries of 1791 and 1805 published by Francis de Castelnau after his expedition to South America in 1843–1847. The Apiacá were considered to be "very numerous." Nimuendajú describes the Apiacá culture in some detail. The bibliography is the same as that in **[405]**.

[407] Robert H. Lowie. "The Southern Cayapó," in Steward, ed., *Handbook* **[93]**, I, 519–520.

Notice of the Southern Cayapó dates from the second half of the seventeenth century. They were located in Goiás, southeastern Mato Grosso, northwestern São Paulo, and western Minas Gerais. According to Lowie, "after endless fighting the Cayapó made peace in Goyaz in 1780." There is a brief sketch of their culture. A bibliography is found on p. 520.

[408] Robert H. Lowie. "The Bororo," in Steward, ed., *Handbook* **[93]**, I, 419–434.

The Bororo linguistic family was located in the Minas triangle, Mato Grosso, and western Goiás. The Bororo were predominantly hunters, gatherers, and fishermen. They were also good swimmers. As early as 1741, *aldeias* of Bororo were founded as protection against the southern Cayapó. Though Lowie discusses their culture in some detail, most of the evidence about the Bororo comes from late-nineteenth and twentieth century observers. 5 figs. 12 plates. There is a bibliography on p. 434.

5. The Indians of the Western Amazon Basin, the Madeira River, and Western Mato Grosso [Nos. 409–422]

Irving Goldman **[409]** discusses the Indians of northwestern Brazil in his analysis of the tribes of the Uaupés-Caquetá region. Alfred Métraux **[410]** describes the Omagua and other tribes of the middle and upper Amazon river, while Curt Nimuendajú **[411]** and **[412]** discusses the Tukuna. Moving southward, Nimuendajú **[413]** studies the Mura and Piraha, both of which were located near the Madeira River. Donald Horton **[414]** and Robert Murphy **[415]** examine the Mundurucú, enemies of the Mura. Alfred Métraux **[416]** surveys the tribes of the Juruá-Purús Basins. Turning toward the southeast, Métraux examines the tribes of eastern Bolivia and western Mato Grosso **[417]**, including the Chiquitoans and other tribes of the province of Chiquitos **[418]**, the Chapacuran tribes **[419]**, the Southwest Panoan Indians **[420]** and the Paressí **[421]**. Claude Levi-Strauss **[422]** concludes with a discussion of the tribes of the right bank of the Guaporé river.

[409] Irving Goldman. "Tribes of the Uaupés-Caquetá Region," in Steward, ed., *Handbook* **[93]**, III, 763–798.

According to Goldman, "the area designated here as the Uaupés-Caquetá region lies within a rough quadrilateral, bounded on the north by the Guaviare River separating the Columbian-Venezuelan llanos from the rain forest to the south; on the east by the Rio Negro, and its principal affluent, the Guainía River; on the south by the upper reaches of the Caquetá River; and on the west by the wall of the Andes. . . . The main streams of the area all drain into the Amazon." The author points out that "in 1784, the Portuguese, Manuel da Gama Lobo do Almada, ascended the Vaupés as far as Panoré and established mission stations as nuclei for Indian settlements. . . . None of these settlements took root. The Jesuits established contact with the Indians of the Rio Negro in the 17th century and, at the end of that century, the Carmelites founded missions on the upper Rio Negro and Rio Branco. Indian rebellions in the early and middle 18th centuries, led by chiefs of the Manao tribe near the present site of Manaos, virtually destroyed missionary influence in the area for almost a century." There is a lengthy description of the culture of the region. A bibliography is found on p. 798.

[410] Alfred Métraux. "Tribes of the Middle and Upper Amazon River," in Steward, ed., *Handbook* **[93]**, III, 687–712.

The author describes such Tupian tribes of the upper Amazon as the Cocama and the Omagua. Initially the Omagua came under Spanish influence. It was Spanish Jesuits who "started their missions among the Omagua at the request of these Indians, who sought protection against Portuguese slavers. During the 40 years following 1641, these slavers had reduced the Omagua from approximately 15,000 to 7,000 persons. After 1686, Father Samuel Fritz **[325]** spent many years among the Omagua, traveling, preaching, and founding . . . missions." Métraux points out that "during the war between Spain and Portugal at the beginning of the 18th century, the Portuguese attacked and destroyed the 33 Omagua settlements under the jurisdiction of the Jesuits. . . . In 1732, the Omagua, armed by the Jesuits, repelled a major Portuguese invasion. The Jesuits succeeded in warding off more Portuguese encroachments on their missions until their expulsion in 1767." Métraux discusses the culture of the Omagua in some detail. He also surveys the history and culture of some of the Arawakan tribes of the Middle Amazon, many of which were mentioned by Father Fritz. The author also describes some of the Arawakan tribes who lived between the Rio Negro and the lower Içá river. There is a bibliography on p. 712.

[411] Curt Nimuendajú. "The Tucuna," in Steward, ed., *Handbook* **[93]**, III, 713–725.

The Tukuna **[412]** "occupied the jungle tracts of the tributaries of the northern side of the Amazon-Solimões River. . . . They avoided the banks of the Amazon-Solimões, fearing the Omagua **[410]**, their traditional enemies of the islands." They were mentioned by Father Acuña **[235]** in the account of his expedition of 1639. Nimuendajú provides a survey of their culture. There is a bibliography on p. 725.

[412] Curt Nimuendajú, *The Tukuna.* Ed. Robert H. Lowie. Trans. William D. Hohenthal. Berkeley and Los Angeles: University of California Press, 1952. x, 207 pp.

Later and enlarged version of **[411]**. Nimuendajú describes the territory which the Tukuna inhabited and its climate. He points out that "the Tukuna tribe has not been prominent in the history of the Amazon region," being first mentioned by Cristobal de Acuña in 1641. Many of the writers who mention the Tukuna stress their rivalry with the Omaguas, "of the northern bank of the Solimões." Nimuendajú discusses the scientific observations of such visitors to the Tukuna as Padre

José Monteiro de Noronha (1768), Francisco Xavier Ribeiro de Sampaio (1774), and Johann Baptist von Spix (1820) **[546]**. Nimuendajú spends the remainder of the monograph analyzing the housing, subsistence patterns, clothing and ornament, art, social life, social organization, life cycle, magic, religion and legends of the Tukuna. The author makes frequent reference to colonial and nineteenth-century accounts of Tukuna life. Glossary. 18 plates. There is a bibliography on pp. 165–167.

[413] Curt Nimuendajú. "The Mura and Piraha," in Steward, ed., *Handbook* **[93]**, III, 255–269.

The Mura were located near the Madeira river. They were first mentioned by the Jesuit Bartolomeu Rodrigues in 1714. The Indians were hostile to the Jesuits and to the Portuguese. For over a century there were bloody encounters between the Portuguese and the Mura. According to Nimuendajú, "the Mura practiced farming before their pacification, but only on a small scale." The author adds that "the gathering of wild fruit was also important in their economy, but above all the Mura were fishermen." Nimuendajú describes the culture of the Mura. He points out that "when the Mura made peace in 1786, they were divided into many groups, each numbering 45 to 150 persons and having its own chief." The author discusses the warfare waged by the Mura and shows that "by the end of the 18th century, the Mura's most feared enemies were the Mundurucú **[414]**, who had come from the region of the Tapajóz River." The Piraha is a subtribe of the Mura. There is a bibliography on p. 269.

[414] Donald Horton. "The Mundurucú," in Steward, ed., *Handbook* **[93]**, III, 271–282.

Horton points out that "the Mundurucú are a Tupí-speaking people in the southwestern portion of the State of Pará and the southeastern corner of the State of Amazonas." Beginning in 1769, there are records of the Mundurucú moving northward along the Tapajós River and attacking a number of tribes. Eventually they encountered the Mura **[413]** who were located near the Madeira River. Horton states that later in the century, "except for minor conflicts with neighboring tribes, the Mundurucú abandoned warfare and gradually relinquished the great territory they had seized. Missions were established on the Tapajóz in 1799 and on the Madeira in 1811." The author relates that "the Mundurucú subsist partly on horticulture and partly on hunting, fishing, and gathering." He also discusses various aspects of their culture. There is a bibliography on p. 282.

[415] Robert F. Murphy. *Mundurucú Religion.* Berkeley and Los Angeles: University of California Press, 1958. iv, 146 pp. [University of California Publications in American Archaeology and Ethnology, v. 49.]

This study is based chiefly on field research by the author and his wife in Pará, Brazil in 1952 and 1953. Though it deals mostly with twentieth-century religious beliefs, there are some useful sections on the geography of the area (the region surrounding the Tapajós river) and the history of the Mundurucús. Murphy points out that the Mundurucú "arrived late on the Amazon historical scene, and were not noted in public reports until 1768." Though at that time they were reported to be near the Madeira river, "their center of strength remained roughly in their present habitat, and they fought a colonial military detachment in that region in 1795. Their defeat at the hands of government troops ended more than two decades of Mundurucú raids upon the Portuguese settlements of the Amazon and ushered in a period of peaceful relations and active alliance with the whites." There are two helpful maps. The bibliography is on pp. 145–146. 9 illus.

[416] Alfred Métraux. "Tribes of the Juruá-Purús Basins," in Steward, ed., *Handbook* **[93]** III, 657–686.

Métraux points out that "the basins of the Juruá and Purús Rivers which drain a large area of lowlands in the southwestern portion of the Brazilian Province of Amazonas, were the habitat of many tribes speaking dialects of Panoan, Arawakan, and Catukinan." The author lists the tribal divisions for the three dialects. According to Métraux, "tribes of this area are little known historically. Early explorers and missionaries largely by-passed them. The majority of the early accounts of travels and explorations of the Purús and Jurúa Basins date from the latter half of the 19th century and contain only fragmentary information on the Indians." There is a bibliography on p. 686.

[417] Alfred Métraux. *The Native Tribes of Eastern Bolivia and Western Matto Grosso.* Washington, D. C.: Government Printing Office, 1942. lx, 182 pp. [Smithsonian Institution. U. S. Bureau of American Ethnology. Bulletin 134.]

Earlier version of research by Métraux, much of which eventually appeared in volume III of the *Handbook of South American Indians* **[93]**. The author uses the same format. Of interest for the history of colonial

Brazil are Métraux's studies of the Southeastern Panoans **[420]**, pp. 45–50; Chapacuran tribes of the Guaporé river basin **[419]**, pp. 86–95; Chiquito and other tribes of the Province of Chiquitos **[418]**, pp. 114–134; Guato **[373]**, pp. 136–142; tribes of the Upper Guaporé river **[422]**, pp. 143–152 (authored in **[93]** by Claude Levi-Strauss); Chapacuran tribes of the Madeira River Basin **[419]**, pp. 158–160; and the Paressí **[421]**, pp. 160–170. 1 map. 5 plates. There is a bibliography on pp. 171–182.

[418] Alfred Métraux. "The Chiquitoans and Other Tribes of the Province of Chiquitos," in Steward, ed., *Handbook* **[93]**, III, 381–395.

The Chiquitoans inhabited an area "bordered on the south by the Chaco desert, on the east by the Paraguay River and the marshes of its upper course, [and] on the west by the Rio Grande." By the 1690s, "the Chiquito were constantly harassed by the Paulista slavers or mamelucos; entire tribes were exterminated or taken as slaves to the Brazilian coast. The Jesuits, aided by a small Spanish contingent, averted the total destruction of the Chiquito by defeating a party of slavers who had occupied the mission." Métraux points out that "during the three centuries after the Conquest, the Spanish and Portuguese slavers, as well as several epidemics, took a heavy toll of Chiquito." There is a brief survey of the Chiquito culture. A bibliography is found on p. 395. See also Métraux **[417]**, pp. 114–134.

[419] Alfred Métraux. "The Chapacuran Tribes," in Steward, ed., *Handbook* **[93]**, III, 397–406.

Métraux points out that the Chapacuran linguistic family includes a number of tribes, most of them living "on the lower and middle Guaporé River. One of these tribes was the Torá, who "originally lived on the Capanã River and later on the Maicy River, a little below the Machado River. About 1716, they sent war parties down the Madeira River to attack boats carrying cacao from Solimões to Pará. In 1719, a Portuguese expedition under João de Barros da Guerra destroyed a large number of Torá. Many Indians of this tribe were settled at Abacaxi and others were transported to Porto de Moz, at the mouth of the Xingu River, but many remained in or returned to the bush." The author describes the culture of the Chapacuran tribes. There is a bibliography on p. 406. See also Métraux **[417]**, pp. 86–95 and 158–160.

[420] Alfred Métraux. "The Southeastern Panoan Tribes," in Steward, ed., *Handbook* **[93]**, III, pp. 449–452.

Some of these tribes—e.g., the Caripuna—were among those encountered by Acuña **[235]** during his journey through the Amazon in 1639. "Their habitat was the Caldeirão and São Lourenzo Rivers, both small tributaries of the Madeira River." Métraux briefly discusses subsistence patterns, housing, clothing and adornment, transportation, manufactures, esthetic and recreational activities, and religion. There is a bibliography on p. 452. See also Métraux **[417]**, pp. 45–50.

[421] Alfred Métraux. "The Paressí," in Steward, ed., *Handbook* **[93]**, III, 349–360.

The Paressí (sometimes called the Pareti) were located in Mato Grosso in Central Brazil. Though Spaniards visited them in the seventeenth century, the first account of their culture dates from 1723. The Portuguese captain Antônio Pires de Campos discovered the Paressí in 1718 "on the highlands beyond the watershed of the Paraguay River" and described them in his "Breve Noticia." Métraux relates that "during the entire 18th century, the Paressí region was crossed by slavers and by adventurers in search of gold or diamond mines." The author provides a survey of their culture. 2 figs. 1 plate. There is a bibliography on p. 360. See also Métraux **[417]**, pp. 160–170.

[422] Claude Levi-Strauss. "Tribes of the Right Bank of the Guaporé River," in Steward, ed., *Handbook* **[93]**, III, 371–379.

The author points out that "since the 18th century, explorers, travellers, and missionaries have used the Guaporé River as a thoroughfare. . . . It is likely, therefore, that a thorough study of the tribes of the Guaporé River will show them to have suffered severely from the effects of that continuous traffic, perhaps almost to the point of extinction." Levi-Strauss also observes that "unlike most South American rivers, the Guaporé River is not the axis of a homogeneous culture area; it is a frontier rather than a link." José Gonçalves da Fonseca **[649]** visited the region in 1749 and left an account of his expedition. Levi-Strauss provides a brief discussion of tribal divisions and a survey of their culture. 3 figs. 1 plate. There is a bibliography on p. 379. See also Métraux **[417]**, pp. 143–153.

E. The Conquest of the Brazilian Indians [Nos. 423–433]

1. Overviews and Special Aspects [No. 423]

To date, only one study in English—John Hemming's *Red Gold* **[423]**—has focused on the Brazilian Indians and their encounters with the White Man in the colonial period. A number of other authors have touched briefly on the subject. There is a good discussion on Portuguese-Indian relations in Charles R. Boxer's *Race Relations in the Portuguese Colonial Empire* **[439]**. Especially good for the sixteenth century are sections of Stuart B. Schwartz, *Sovereignty and Society* **[284]** and **[431]**. See also Alexander Marchant, *From Barter to Slavery* **[136]**. Charles R. Boxer's two major works on the seventeenth century—*Salvador de Sá* **[277]** and *The Dutch in Brazil* **[239]**—have valuable chapters on European-Indian relations. The same is true for Boxer's *The Golden Age of Brazil* **[548]**, where he examines the first half of the eighteenth century. Robert Southey's three-volume *History of Brazil* **[70]** also makes frequent mention of the Brazilian Indian.

[423] John Hemming. *Red Gold. The Conquest of the Brazilian Indians.* Cambridge: Harvard University Press, 1978. xvii, 677 pp.

To date, the most detailed and comprehensive study in English of Indian-White relations in colonial Brazil. One-fifth of this lengthy account is devoted to the coastal Indian population and the initial reactions of the Portuguese and French to the natives of Brazil before the arrival of the Jesuits in 1549. A great deal of attention is paid to the Jesuits who "were never free to run their missionary world in the isolation they wanted. Throughout the two centuries of their administration, they fought long battles against two forces from across the Atlantic: the European colonists and their diseases." Special note is made of the plight of the Amerindians in the Amazon region and the role of the *bandeirantes* in raiding Jesuit missions and enslaving Indians in what is now southern Brazil. The book ends in 1760, shortly after the expulsion of the Jesuits. By this time, according to Hemming, "the balance of power between colonists and Indians had changed irretrievably." The book's title is derived from a remark by the Jesuit Antônio Vieira, who charged that expeditions into the interior of Brazil's Amazon region were really for the purpose of capturing Indians in order "to draw from their veins the red gold which has always been the mine of that province." In addition to 31 large illustrations, there are 21 smaller ones, the latter serving as part of the chapter headings. There are 4 excellent maps. There is also a glossary (pp. 502–504) and a bibliography (pp. 505–526). In the appendix, the author attempts to determine the Amerindian population of Brazil in 1500. Based largely on printed primary and secondary materials. Hemming has emphasized Brazilian sources rather than those in Portugal.

2. Portuguese Legislation Regarding the Brazilian Indian [Nos. 424–430]

Mathias C. Kiemen, O. F. M. **[424]** and **[425]** provides several useful surveys of Portuguese Indian policy for northern Brazil and the Amazon region. Dauril Alden **[426]** contributes a useful overview of Crown Indian legislation and the role of the Jesuits in its enforcement. Father Kiemen **[427]** also studies the efforts of the newly formed Conselho Ultramarino to solve the Indian question in the 1640s. Luiza da Fonseca **[428]** discusses the efforts of the Franciscan Frei Cristóvão de Lisboa on behalf of the Amerindian in the Amazon. George Boehrer **[429]** and **[430]** describes legislative attempts to come to grips with the Indian problem on the eve of independence.

[424]Mathias C. Kiemen, O. F. M. "The Indian Policy of Portugal in America with Special Reference to the Old State of Maranhão, 1500–1755," *The Americas* 5:2 (October 1948), pp. 131–171 and 5:4 (April 1949), pp. 439–461.

A useful survey of the laws promulgated by the Portuguese Crown for the protection and acculturation of the Brazilian Indian. The author gives a special emphasis to the seventeenth century. Based on printed primary and secondary materials. 120 notes. Bibliography.

[425] Mathias C. Kiemen, O. F. M. *The Indian Policy of Portugal in the Amazon Region, 1614–1693*. Washington, D. C.: The Catholic University of America Press, 1954. xii, 216 p.

Analyzes the evolution of Portuguese Indian legislation from 1570 to 1693 with a special emphasis on the Amazon region. The author gives a detailed explanation of the missionary activity and the approaches of both Franciscans and Jesuits to the Indians and the controversies that arose between the two religious orders over their different philosophies. Based on extensive archival research, especially in the Arquivo Histórico Ultramarino and the Arquivo Nacional da Torre do Tombo, both in Lisbon. There is a "Selected Bibliography," pp. 191–202.

[426] Dauril Alden. "Black Robes versus White Settlers: The Struggle for 'Freedom of the Indians' in Colonial Brazil" in Howard Peckham and Charles Gibson, eds. *Attitudes of Colonial Powers Toward the American Indian.* Salt Lake City: University of Utah Press, 1969, pp. 19–45.

Useful synthesis and overview of the Portuguese Crown's legislation regarding the Brazilian Indian and the latter's treatment by the Jesuits and the Colonists—especially those living in Maranhão-Pará and the region around São Paulo. Though the author covers the period from the arrival of the Jesuits in 1549 to their expulsion from Brazil two hundred and ten years later, the greatest emphasis is on the sixteenth and seventeenth centuries. Based on printed primary and secondary materials. 69 notes.

[427] Mathias C. Kiemen, O. F. M. "The *Conselho Ultramarino's* First Legislative Attempts to Solve the Indian Question in America, 1643–1647," *The Americas* 14:3 (January 1958), pp. 259–271.

Analyzes the way the Overseas Council during the first five years of its existence handled questions affecting the American Indian in the regions of Maranhão and Pará. After surveying the Council's approach to such matters as bad treatment by some of the Portuguese inhabitants, depopulation, temporal and spiritual administration of villages, rewards for loyalty, missionary activity and ransomed *indios de corda,* the author concludes that the Council's experiences and solutions "set a pattern for its future activities." Based largely on archival sources. 33 notes. Father Kiemen published an almost identical article with the same title in **[91]**, II, 226–239. In the latter publication, however, many of the quotations within the text are in Portuguese.

[428] Luiza da Fonseca. "In Defense of the Maranhão Indians of Colonial Brazil. A Report of Frei Christóvão de Lisboa, O. F. M., to the Conselho Ultramarino, Lisbon, October 29, 1647," *The Americas* 7:2 (October 1950), pp. 215–220.

Gives a biographical sketch of Frei Cristóvão de Lisboa, the Franciscan priest and missionary who was in charge of his Order's missions in Maranhão and who spent twelve years there. Upon his return to Portugal he gave information and advice to the Overseas Council—especially on questions affecting the welfare of the Brazilian Indians. In the appended document published in Portuguese, Frei Cristóvão argued that the Indians "have done us no injury, nor opposed the promulgation of the law of God." See also **[330]**.

[429] George C. A. Boehrer. "The Brazilian Proposals to the Cortes Gerais, 1821–1823, on the Indian Problem," in Lindley Cintra, ed. *Actas* **[91]**, II, 201–209.

Lists and discusses five proposals made to the Cortes but never acted upon. The most famous and best thought out of the proposals was that of José Bonifácio de Andrada e Silva. Other recommendations were made by José Caetano Ribeiro da Cunha and Francisco Ricardo Zany (both from Pará), the Bahian Domingos Borges de Barros (who recommended that the Protestant Moravian Brethren be invited to Brazil to work with the Indians), and the Pernambucan Francisco Moniz Tavares (who was impressed with William Penn's approach in North America). Based on archival and printed primary source materials. 29 notes.

[430] George C. A. Boehrer. "Variant Versions of José Bonifácio's 'Plan for the Civilization of the Brazilian Indians,'" *The Americas* 14:3 (January 1958), pp. 301–312.

Mainly an examination of the two different versions of José Bonifácio's program for civilizing the Brazilian Indian [*Apontamentos para a civilização dos indios bravos do Império do Brazil*]: one in manuscript form and written in 1821; the other published in Rio de Janeiro in 1823. Bonifácio made forty-four recommendations including intermarriage between Indians, Whites and Mulattoes, missionary activity by the Oratorians, peaceful expeditions into Indian territory, "caution against forcible Christianization and intensive agricultural labor, the careful supervision of contractual labor, and the establishment of a tribunal to supervise the work." Boehrer discusses the effect of Bonifácio's plan both on the Cortes Gerais in Portugal and the Constitutional Assembly in Brazil and concludes with a listing of the various attempts to reprint the program. Based on printed primary and secondary sources. 24 notes.

3. The Question of Indian Labor [Nos. 431–433]

Stuart B. Schwartz **[431]** has contributed a provocative and thorough article on the question of Indian labor in the sixteenth century. An earlier study of the problem is found in Alexander Marchant's *From Barter to Slavery* **[136]**. Colin M. MacLachlan has written two good studies on Indian Labor in the Amazon. The first **[432]** traces the evolution of Indian labor in the captaincies of Pará and Rio Negro in the eighteenth century. The second **[433]** focuses on the Indian Directorate and forced acculturation, 1757–1799.

[431] Stuart B. Schwartz. "Indian Labor and New World Plantations: European Demands and Indian Responses in Northeastern Brazil," *The American Historical Review* 83:1 (February 1978), pp. 43–79.

After analyzing some of the chief characteristics of the native populations the Portuguese encountered in Brazil in the sixteenth century, the author shows how the Europeans attempted to modify the Indians' traditional way of life and organize a variety of labor systems. But "faced with the increasing opposition of the crown to enslavement, the growing demands of the sugar economy, and the disastrous example of the 1560s [i.e., the demographic decline due to disease and famine], the colonists turned to the labor to be found in the Atlantic slave trade." The process, however, was a gradual one, taking about fifty years. "By the end of the sixteenth century, engenho labor forces were racially mixed and the proportion increasingly changed in favor of imported Africans and their offspring." The author gives a special emphasis to two sugar mills, Engenho Sergipe and Engenho Santana, both in Bahia, and attempts to determine the composition of the work force, the interaction of Amerindian, African, and Portuguese, the skills of Amerindians and Africans, both slave and free, and the prices of the former and the wages of the latter. Schwartz points out that "the colonists believed that, given the high mortality and low productivity of Indians, Africans were a better investment." He concludes: "Colonial slavery had emerged as the dominant mode of production, and the process of its emergence was not dictated by the market so much as by the organization of production." Based on archival and printed primary sources as well as secondary materials. 92 notes. 3 illus. and 6 tables.

[432] Colin M. MacLachlan. "The Indian Labor Structure in the Portuguese Amazon, 1700–1800," in Alden, ed., *Colonial Roots* **[87]**, pp. 199–230.

Useful and informative study that traces the evolution of Indian labor in the captaincies of Pará and Rio Negro in the eighteenth century. The author divides the period into three parts: 1) the mission system, 1700–1755; 2) the directory system, 1757–1798; 3) the postdirectory years and the reorganization of Indian labor. MacLachlan points out that "the Portuguese faced a scarcity of Indian labor and were forced to deal with Indian cultures not easily adaptable." Though by the eighteenth century in many areas of Brazil Indians were replaced by African slaves, in much of the Amazon they were not. The author reviews the chief characteristics of the mission system which carried over from the seventeenth century and which lasted to the mid-eighteenth century, studies its labor structure and its access to and its government and control of Indian labor. However, "under Pombal's influence [1750–1777] the old mission philosophy that emphasized conservation of the Indians gave way to a more dynamic attempt to introduce and eventually incorporate the Indians into Portuguese culture." This was the directory system, 1757–1798, which "transferred the temporary authority of the missionaries to secular administrators directly responsible to the governor." The author analyzes its labor structure as well as government labor requirements and shows how "the Crown hoped that ultimately they [the Indians] would not need direction and would be automatically absorbed into the economy as free and willing laborers." By the end of the eighteenth century, however, a severe labor crisis developed. As a result, a controlled labor market was organized to meet royal needs, while private employers were able to compete in the open market. The new system was basically a success. The Indians had adapted to the needs of the economy and "the evolution of a free labor system was almost complete." 123 notes. Based mostly on Brazilian archival and printed primary sources.

[433] Colin MacLachlan. "The Indian Directorate: Forced Acculturation in Portuguese America (1757–1799)," *The Americas* 28:4 (April, 1972), pp. 357–387.

Important study of Portuguese efforts to deal with the Amerindian after the abolition of the temporal authority of missionaries in 1755 and the expulsion of the Jesuits from Brazil in 1759. In 1755, Pombal, viewing "the mission system as an unnecessary, and perhaps dangerous barrier between the Crown and its Indian vassals" and "implementing long range plans for the economic and social integration of Amazonia," ordered that the Indians be placed under direct control of the Crown. His plan was to have both European and Amerindian live "under the same laws without distinctions based on origins." This task was entrusted to his brother, Francisco Xavier Mendonça Furtado, who had been appointed governor of the Amazon region in 1751. Called the Directorate, this new system of administering the former mission villages "forced the Indians to shoulder the responsibilities and assume the values of the European settlers or face extinction." Focusing on Pará and Rio Negro (Amazonas), MacLachlan examines the Directorate in theory, shows how it was modified by the Brazilian reality, and evaluates the apprenticeship program that lasted for forty-two years. The author concludes that "the previously controlled acculturation of the mission system, although, based more on a desire to isolate the Indian from European vice than an appreciation of the impact of cultural shock, undoubtedly would have permitted more Indians to survive by delaying the process so quickly and brutally achieved by the actual operation of the directorate." Based on extensive use of archival and printed primary souces. 108 notes.

F. The Indian in Art and Brazilian Literature

[Nos. 434–436]

David Miller Driver **[434]** discusses both French as well as Portuguese writers who described Brazil during the colonial period. Some of the engravings of Theodore de Bry, based on the woodcuts of Brazilian Indians printed in the accounts of Hans Staden **[181]**, André Thevet **[183]** and Jean de Lery **[184]**, are found in **[435]** and **[436]**.

[434] David Miller Driver. *The Indian in Brazilian Literature.* New York: Hispanic Institute, 1942. 182 pp.

The first two chapters contain valuable material on the colonial period. Driver points out that from the mid-sixteenth century the attitude of most of the missionaries to Brazil emphasized "the Indian's perfectability, not his perfection." The author argues that "it was not until the middle of the eighteenth century that we find, among the Portuguese friars, an example of idealization of the Indian along the lines followed by Las Casas and some of the early French writers." These French writers included Jean de Lery **[184]**, Yves d'Evreux, and Claude d'Abbeville. All visited Brazil in the sixteenth and early seventeenth centuries and "had considerable influence on Brazilians of the Romantic period."André Thevet **[183]**, on the other hand, "had little to do with establishing the noble savage ideal. He had a frank horror of the Indians." In his chapter, "First Manifestations of Indianism in Brazilian Literature," the author focuses on José Basilio da Gama (1740–1795) and his epic poem *O Uruguay*. Gama expresses " a strong sympathy for primitive races in revolt against their civilized masters." Driver also discusses Frei José de Santa Rita Durão (ca. 1717–1784) and his epic poem *Caramurú* and states that although Frei José "gives far more space to the description of Indians and their customs," his Indians have "none of that indomitable spirit and wild nobility to be found in the heroes of *O Uruguay*. His Indians are either humble allies or repugnant enemies." There is a bibliography on pp. 173–182.

[435] Michael Alexander, ed. *Discovering the New World. Based on the Works of Theodore de Bry.* New York, Hagerstown, San Francisco, London: Harper & Row, 1976. 224 pp.

The section, "Hans Staden **[181]** among the Cannibals of Brazil" (pp. 90–121) contains 29 plates from De Bry's *Americae Tertia Pars,* first published in 1592, along with excerpts in English from Hans Staden's account of his experiences in Brazil.

[436] Helmut Andrä and Edgard Cerqueira Falcão. *Americae Praeterita Eventa.* São Paulo, 1965. 289 pp.

Reprints 172 of the 173 copperplate engravings and a number of the maps and views from the *Historia Antipodum,* published in 1631 by Matthew Merian, son-in-law of one of Theodore de Bry's **[435]** sons. Of the plates, 12 depict Indians in sixteenth-century Brazil and there are 2 scenes from the early seventeenth century. In addition, there is a map of Pernambuco in 1630 with an inset of the Dutch storming the port of Recife. There are also two fine prospects of Olinda.

XIII. The African [Nos. 437–497]

A. South Atlantic Perspectives: Slavery and Its Justification [Nos. 437–444]

A good account of early attempts at African slavery and its justification is found in A. J. R. Russell-Wood's useful study **[437]**. Charles R. Boxer **[438]** and **[439]** discusses the "colour question" and race relations in the Portuguese overseas empire.

[437] A. J. R. Russell-Wood. "Iberian Expansion and the Issue of Black Slavery: Changing Portuguese Attitudes, 1440–1770," *The American Historical Review* 83:1 (February 1978), pp. 16–42.

Quoting extensively from the chronicles of Gomes Eanes de Zurara and João de Barros, the author attempts to show how the medieval concepts of "honor" and "just war" were modified to justify Portuguese expansion, beginning with the War against Morocco in 1415. Russell-Wood discusses the ideology of expansion, papal attitudes, justifications used by theologians and jurists, and the role of the Oder of Christ and its governor, the Infante D. Henrique ["the Navigator"]. The author samples the writings of such Iberian writers as Bishop Azeredo Coutinho, the Spanish Dominican Tomás de Mercado, Bartolomé Frias de Albornoz, the Jesuits Luis de Molina and Alonso de Sandoval, the Carmelite Amador Arrais, and Fernão de Oliveira as well as comments from Jesuits in sixteenth- and seventeenth-century Brazil. He concludes that "the debate in Portugal over black slavery and the slave trade never equalled that in Spain over the enslavement of Amerindians." Based chiefly on printed primary and secondary souces. 59 notes.

[438] Charles R. Boxer. "The Colour Question in the Portuguese Empire, 1415–1825," *Proceedings of the British Academy,* XLVII (1961), pp. 113–138.

Although the section on Brazil (pp. 132–138) composed only one-third of the author's 1961 Raleigh Lecture on History before the British Academy, there are other references to Portuguese America interspersed throughout the remainder of the article. After surveying race relations in Brazil Boxer concludes that "if the course of true love never did run smooth, neither did that of interracial integration." The author argues that "the existence of an effective colour-bar in colonial Brazil, at any rate at certain times in certain places, is evident from a survey of the conditions obtaining in the Church, in the army, and in the municipal councils." However, Boxer points out that the presence of such restrictions "does not . . . alter the fact that by and large the Portuguese did mix more with coloured races than did other Europeans, and they had, as a rule, less colour prejudice." Well documented. Based chiefly on printed primary sources. 61 (noncontinuous) notes.

[439] Charles R. Boxer. *Race Relations in the Portuguese Colonial Empire, 1415–1825.* Oxford: Clarendon Press, 1963. vii, 136 pp.

In the chapter entitled "Brazil and Maranhão" (pp. 86–130), Boxer discusses Jesuit approaches to Christianizing and Europeanizing the Amerindian and that Order's rivalries with Portuguese settlers over Indian labor. The author also analyzes Portuguese attitudes towards African slaves in Brazil [an earlier chapter is entitled "Morocco and West Africa"], quoting extensively from Antônio Vieira, the famed Jesuit preacher, and even more so from a 1764 pamphlet **[562]** in the form of a dialogue between a Lisbon lawyer and a slave-owning gold miner from Brazil. Those of mixed blood—expecially mulattoes—are also studied. Boxer concludes with an overview of the pros and cons of Portuguese treatment of people of color in their overseas "conquests." Based largely on printed primary sources. 40 bibliographical footnotes. These lectures were originally delivered at the University of Virginia in November of 1962.

1. Brazil and West Africa [Nos. 440–444]

Because of the large number of Africans who were transported to Brazil and the important commercial ties between the two regions, there is a growing interest in treating Brazil and Africa as a unit. The best overall survey is by José Honório Rodrigues **[440]**. A related article, "The Influence of Africa on Brazil and of Brazil on Africa," also by Rodrigues **[441]**, contains an excellent synthesis of the role of the African in Brazilian history. E. Bradford Burns **[442]** shows that "the conquest, settlement, and development of Brazil were a joint Afro-European enterprise." Pierre Verger **[443]** examines Bahia and the West African trade, 1549–1851. Anne Wadsworth Pardo **[444]** studies the interdependence of Angola and Brazil, 1648–1825.

[440] José Honório Rodrigues. *Brazil and Africa.* Trans. Richard A. Mazzara and Sam Hileman. Berkeley and Los Angeles: University of California Press, 1965. xxii, 382 pp.

Though the book covers the entire span of Brazilian history to 1960, there is much useful material for students of Portuguese America. Quoting approvingly the famed Jesuit Antônio Vieira's remark that "Brazil has its body in America and its soul in Africa," Rodrigues discusses the Brazilian image of Africa and colonial relations between the two regions, 1500–1800. During that time, several million slaves were sent from Africa to Brazil, often, as José da Silva Lisboa observed in 1781, in trade for "tobacco, either waste or second-grade leaf, and strong spirits." By the end of the colonial period, "Brazil's dependence upon the traffic in slaves, which was increasing in order to satisfy the demands of the coffee industry, led to expansion of commerce with Africa, gave business to traders, and because of the constant importation of slaves, increased the Africanization of the country." Rodrigues also studies the African contribution to Brazil, and later in the book, Brazil's contribution to Africa **[see also 441]**. A particularly provocative chapter (four), "Miscegenation and Relations Between Brazil's Whites and Africans," challenges a number of Gilberto Freyre's views **[699]** on the subject and argues that "the failure of miscegenation in Portugal's African colonies and its small success in her territories in Asia . . . indicates that the Portuguese colonist per se was not the decisive factor in the process." The author also discusses the question of racial prejudice in Brazil. Part of chapter six, "Modern Relations: 1800–1960," describes the effects of the antislave trade provisions in the treaties between Britain and Portugal, 1810–1817. He concludes his study of pre-Brazilian independence relations with Africa with an analysis of Brazilian attempts to dominate Portuguese territories there, 1818–1826. Based on printed primary and secondary materials. Well documented. There is no bibliography. This an abridged translation of the second edition of *Brasil e África: outro horizonte.* Rio de Janeiro: Editôra Civilização Brasileira, 1964. The first Brazilian edition dates from 1961.

[441] José Honório Rodrigues. "The Influence of Africa on Brazil and of Brazil on Africa," *The Journal of African History* 3:1 (1962), pp. 49–67.

Excellent synthesis on the role of the African in Brazilian history. The author traces the development of historical, anthropological and sociological research on the African in Brazil, distinguishes between Negro and slave, describes the African origins of many of the Brazilian slaves, and analyzes their influence on Brazil (especially on diet, dress, language, music, folklore, and religion), and their demographic contribution to Brazilian history. After comparing geographical similarities between Brazil and Africa, Rodrigues discusses Portuguese America's agricultural contributions to Africa: tobacco, mandioca, maize and nuts. He also briefly mentions Brazilians who were sent to Africa—most of them as exiles. Though there are references to post-independence Brazil, most of this article deals with the colonial period. Based on printed materials. 72 notes.

[442] E. Bradford Burns. "The Black in Brazilian History: An Exploratory Essay," *West Georgia College Studies in the Social Sciences* 8:1 (June 1969), pp. 52–61.

Points out that historians have neglected the history of Blacks in Portuguese America, even though at the time of independence two-thirds of Brazil's population were Blacks or Mulattoes. Burns argues and gives examples to show that "the conquest, settlement, and development of Brazil were a joint Afro-European enterprise. Neither race could have accomplished those tasks alone." Though the article deals with all of Brazil's history, more than half of the material is on the colonial period. Based mostly on secondary sources. 13 notes.

[443] Pierre Verger. *Bahia and the West African Trade, 1549–1851.* Ibadan: Ibadan University Press, 1964. 39 pp.

Good brief account of the commercial and cultural ties between Bahia and the west coast of Africa. Verger divides African immigration to Bahia into four periods: "1) the Guinea cycle during the second half of the sixteenth century. 2) The Angola cycle in the seventeenth century. 3) The Mina Coast cycle during the first three quarters of the eighteenth century. 4) The Bight of Benin cycle between 1770 and 1851." Most of the author's attention is focused on the Mina trade in the eighteenth century. He describes the importance of Brazilian tobacco in the slave trade. He also discusses the fort at Whydah and the rivalry between Bahian and Portuguese businessmen for supremacy in the Mina slave trade. Map and three plates. Well annotated.

[444] Anne Wadsworth Pardo. "A Comparative Study of the Portuguese Colonies of Angola and Brazil and their interdependence from 1648–1825," (Ph.D. Dissertation: Boston University Graduate School, 1977). 232 pp.

The slave-exporting colony of Angola was always closely tied to the colony of Brazil which needed Angola's slaves to produce its tropical goods for market. Brazil, involved in the reconquest of Angola from the Dutch in 1648, became increasingly dominant over the African colony. The author argues, for example, that "a pattern of administrative communication developed from Angola through Brazil to Portugal." Also, Brazil contributed military forces to Angola to keep order and open trade routes there. After 1676, the archbishop of Bahia included Angola in his jurisdiction. Portugal allowed Brazil control of her trade with Angola. These patterns of relationship continued until Brazil gained her independence. Angola, still a colony, then returned to the mother country's sphere.
DAI 38/04-A (p. 2286).

B. The African in Brazil [Nos. 445–460]

1. Overviews and General Studies [Nos. 445–449]

Thanks in large measure to Gilberto Freyre's pioneering study, *The Masters and the Slaves* **[699]**, the African in Brazil has been one of the most widely and best studied topics in colonial Brazilian history. A useful survey of the role of the African in Brazil is found in Arthur Ramos **[445]**. An older account, providing some general information on the subject, is that of J. K. Eads **[446]**. Another older view is that of Sir Harry H. Johnston **[447]**, who has a chapter, "Slavery under the Portuguese: Brazil," in his study, *The Negro in the New World.* J. V. D. Saunders **[448]**, in his article on Blacks in Brazil, relies heavily on the writings of Gilberto Freyre. Robert Conrad **[449]** reexamines slavery in nineteenth-century Brazil and discusses some of the earlier interpretations of the treatment of Brazilian slaves.

[445] Arthur Ramos. *The Negro in Brazil.* Trans. by Richard Pattee. Washington, D. C.: The Associated Publishers, Inc., 1939. v, 210 pp.

The author discusses the slave trade and the slave population in Brazil with an emphasis on the eighteenth and nineteenth centuries. Ramos describes various slave occupations, slave insurrections and runaway slaves with a special chapter devoted to the Negro Republic of Palmares. Abolitionism and the role of the Blacks themselves and brotherhoods for people of color in freeing slaves are analyzed, as well as the African's religious heritage and popular festivals and feasts. The Black Man's contributions to Brazilian music, painting, literature, and the sciences are also detailed. The participation of Blacks in the military, especially during the colonial period is discussed. The translator provides a brief survey of Brazilian history. There is a bibliography on pp. 193–196, followed by a good index.

[446] J. K. Eads. "The Negro in Brazil," *The Journal of Negro History* 21:4 (October 1936), pp. 365–375.

The first four pages have very general information on Blacks during the colonial period of Brazilian history. Based on some nineteenth- and twentieth-century travel accounts as well as printed secondary sources. Superseded by recent studies. 30 notes. Bibliography.

[447] Sir Harry H. Johnston. *The Negro in the New World.* New York: The Macmillan Company, 1910. xxix, 499 pp.

The author treats Brazil in chapter five, "Slavery under the Portuguese: Brazil," pages 77–109. Johnston argues that the Portuguese "rival the Spaniards for the first place in the list of humane, slave-holding nations, and even in Africa their treatment of their slaves (or slave-like apprentices of more recent date) was far less cruel than that of the Dutch, the British, or the French. Slavery under the flag of Portugal (or Brazil) or of Spain was not a condition without hope, a life in hell, as it was for the most part in the British West Indies and, above all, Dutch Guiana and the Southern United States." About half of the chapter deals with the period after independence. There are lengthy quotations from R. Walsh's *Notices of Brazil in 1828 and 1829* on the horrors of life aboard a slave ship and the indignities of the slave market for the captive African. The author also discusses manumission, the treatment of runaways, slave revolts—especially those in Bahia—and the religious and cultural life of Africans in Brazil.

Johnston argues that most of the cruelty to the slaves occurred during the Atlantic crossing and gives a sympathetic view of the Portuguese slave trade in Africa: "So far as the sum of human misery in Africa was concerned, it is probable that the trade in slaves between that continent and America scarcely added to it." This study is marred by a number of chronological as well as factual errors. The author also makes a number of statements that have been challenged by authorities on the subject. Based largely on printed travel accounts. There are a map and twenty-two interesting photographs.

[448] J. V. D. Saunders. "The Brazilian Negro," *The Americas* 15:3 (January 1959), pp. 271–290.

Studies Blacks in Brazil from a demographic, historical and social perspective. The author concentrates heavily on the colonial period in the first and third of these categories. Under the heading "The Demographic Aspect," Saunders reviews slave import records and argues that "by 1700 not more than 200,000 Negroes were to be found in Brazil." It was not until the eighteenth and nineteenth centuries that enormous numbers of Africans were brought to Portuguese America. As the author points out, "from 1798 to 1807, 75,150 slaves entered the port of Bahia alone." Slaves came from almost every part of Africa with Rio de Janeiro, Bahia and Pernambuco being the chief ports of entry. Under "The Historical Aspect," Saunders discusses the futile efforts of José Bonifacio in 1823 to abolish the slave trade and ameliorate the treatment of slaves. The later abolition movements of the nineteenth century are also mentioned. Finally, under "The Social Aspects," there is a lengthy discussion of general treatment and manumission based heavily on early nineteenth-century travel accounts, especially those of Henry Koster **[626]**, Karl Martius **[546]**, and Johann Rugendas. When discussing widespread miscegenation in Brazil, the author relies heavily on the writings of Gilberto Freyre **[699]**. Saunders concludes his overview with a discussion of sociolegal aspects of the definition of "whites" in Brazil. Based on printed primary and secondary sources. 39 notes.

[449] Robert Conrad. "Nineteenth-Century Brazilian Slavery," in Toplin, ed., *Slavery and Race Relations* **[97]**, pp. 146–175.

The author challenges those that hold "that the Latin American slave in general, and the Brazilian slave in particular, were introduced into a relatively humane slave system, that they were well protected by legal, ecclesiastical, and patriarchal traditions and institutions, and that freedom was a goal that they might reasonably have been expected to achieve." Conrad reexamines slavery in nineteenth-century Brazil and focuses on "aims and attitudes of the master class, slave mortality and population decline, manumission and illicit enslavement, the legal status of bondsmen, their punishments, marriage, and the integrity of the slave family." He concludes that "there exists . . . abundant and persuasive evidence that the reputation for mildness of Brazilian slavery, which was propagated even during the nineteenth century, is undeserved." Though there are scattered references to the period before 1822, most of Conrad's study emphasizes the years after independence. Based mostly on printed primary and secondary materials. 99 notes.

2. Regional Studies [Nos. 450–460]

a. LA PLATA AND SOUTHERN BRAZIL [Nos. 450–452]

Two doctoral dissertations—one by Russell E. Chace, Jr. **[450]**, the other by Evelyn Peterson Meiners **[451]**—examine African influences in the Plata region. Spencer Leitman **[452]** analyzes the role of slave cowboys in southern Brazil in the first half of the nineteenth century.

[450] Russell Edward Chace, Jr. "The African Impact on Colonial Argentina," (Ph.D. Dissertation: University of California, Santa Barbara, 1969). 235 pp.

Though many of the slaves entering the Plata through Buenos Aires continued on to Chile, Potosi or Peru, enough stayed in La Plata to compose one-third of that region's population by the end of the colonial period. The author argues that contraband trade may have supplied just as many Blacks as the legal traffic. Chace also shows how Portuguese merchants dominated most of the seventeenth-century slave trade to the Plata region. Africans in colonial Argentina were involved in pastoral as well as plantation activities and worked as skilled artisans. They were also used in domestic service and as status symbols. The author discusses treatment, manumission practices and the role of freedmen, some of the latter serving as soldiers.
DAI 32/01-A (p. 336)

[451] Evelyn Peterson Meiners. "The Negro in the Rio de la Plata," (Ph.D. Dissertation: Northwestern University, 1948).

[452] Spencer Leitman. "Slave Cowboys in the Cattle Lands of Southern Brazil, 1800–1850," *Revista de História* (São Paulo), 51:101 (January–March 1975), pp. 167–177.

Argues that "the most striking feature of Rio Grande do Sul, Brazil, in the first part of the nineteenth century was the presence of slave cowboys." Though the majority of slaves worked in that province's salt beef industries, domestic service, and manioc, maize and wheat fields, the slave cowboys played a role far out of proportion to their numbers. The author discusses various aspects of African slavery in southern Brazil and suggests reasons for the popularity of slave cowboys, a significant one being "that the riograndense rancher inside Uruguay felt more secure with a loyal force of slave cowboys at his back, rather than hired Uruguayan stockmen." Based on archival as well as printed primary and secondary sources. 38 notes.

b. RIO DE JANEIRO AND ITS ENVIRONS [Nos. 453–455]
Richard Graham **[453]** studies a 1791 inventory for a rural estate located outside Rio de Janeiro. Mary Karasch **[454]** examines slave life and **[455]** analyzes African occupations in Rio de Janeiro during the first half of the nineteenth century. Herbert S. Klein **[463]** examines the African slave trade to Rio de Janeiro, 1795–1811. James Patrick Kiernan **[477]** discusses the manumission of slaves in Paraty, 1789–1822. The role of African slaves in Rio de Janeiro in the seventeenth century is described by Charles R. Boxer **[277]** in his biography of Salvador de Sá.

[453] Richard Graham. "Slave Families on a Rural Estate in Colonial Brazil," *Journal of Social History* 9:3 (Spring 1976), pp. 382–402.

Examines a 1791 inventory of 1347 slaves listed by name, age, sex and family group, living on the Fazenda Santa Cruz, about 35 miles west of the city of Rio de Janeiro. A former Jesuit estate under royal control since 1759, the *fazenda's* major economic focus was cattle raising and the production of staples for the urban market. It contained 363 men, 448 women, and 536 children fourteen years of age or younger. The author makes some comparisons with an earlier inventory of 1768 and shows that "many of the accepted generalizations about slave life in Brazil and elsewhere do not hold true" and that "family life was both varied and more complex than was once thought." For example, almost 55% of the households were built around man and wife and over ¾ of the children were growing up with both a father and a mother; men tended to marry in their late twenties; and the proportion of skilled men to total population was high. Based largely on archival and printed primary source materials. 2 figures; 9 tables; 2 appendices. 40 notes.

[454] Mary Catherine Karasch. "Slave Life in Rio de Janeiro, 1808–1850," Ph.D. Dissertation: The University of Wisconsin, 1972. 613 pp.

The author discusses the African heritage, economic activity, and cultural accomodation of urban slaves in Rio de Janeiro during the first half of the nineteenth century. Increasing numbers were African-born (by 1849, 60% were Africans). Many of the slaves were male children and teenagers, both groups being in heavy demand by slaveowners. The author shows that Africans had a higher mortality rate than freedmen. Though masters had considerable success in training their slaves and promoting their adjustment to Portuguese life, many aspects of African culture remained. Karasch argues that "African religious leaders continued to minister to the religious needs of their people." She describes the attitudes of the Catholic Church and the military towards Blacks and Mulattoes. Though there were no slave revolts in Rio, a number of slaves did try to run away and organize *quilombos.* The majority of slaves were unskilled. However, a number of slaves were able to earn money and buy their freedom. Despite the fact that urban life in Rio de Janeiro provided slaves with a number of cultural and economic opportunities, Karasch concludes that "slaves did not have easy mobility or enjoy frequent emancipation and benevolent treatment." Research was based on travel accounts, newspapers, notarial and police records as well as other archival materials.
DAI 33/05-A (p. 2288)

[455] Mary Karasch. "From Porterage to Proprietorship: African Occupations in Rio de Janeiro, 1808–1850," in Stanley L. Engerman and Eugene D. Genovese, eds., *Race and Slavery in the Western Hemisphere: Quantitative Studies.* Princeton, New Jersey: Princeton University Press, 1975, pp. 369–393.

Mary Karasch describes the population of Rio de Janeiro and its composition during the first half of the nineteenth century and points out that during this time period "Rio was a city of slaves, but especially of African slaves." She states that "the majority of slaves were used for manual labor, but what is unique to Rio in the first half of the century is the variety of semiskilled and skilled manual occupations that were open to slaves." Karasch points out that "unless selected for special training, the average imported slave found himself assigned to an unskilled job. Whether he then improved his position or occupation frequently depended on the will of his master or on his own initiative.... The master obtained his share of the wage, but the slave could often keep and save or spend what he earned over and above what his master required.... Because they had access to money, *negros de ganho* were the ones among the unskilled slave workers who were most likely to accumulate enough funds to buy their freedom." There was a set hierarchy for the unskilled manual occupations as well as the semi-skilled and skilled ones. Karasch describes these occupations and the status and working conditions associated with them. She concludes that "because of the growing demand for workers to fill manual occupations between 1808 and 1850, slaves and freedmen had significant opportunities open to them, as long as the work involved labor that whites disdained." Based on archival and printed primary source materials. 4 tables. 55 notes.

c. MINAS GERAIS [No. 456]

It is almost impossible to discuss Minas Gerais in the eighteenth and nineteenth centuries without mentioning the African. A. J. R. Russell-Wood **[456]** is the only writer to date to focus entirely on the topic. However, almost all the studies mentioned in Section XV, C describe the role of the African in the economy and society of Minas Gerais. In addition, Herbert S. Klein **[473]** relies heavily on late colonial census data from Minas Gerais for his study on the colored Freedmen.

[456] A. J. R. Russell-Wood. "Technology and Society: The Impact of Gold Mining on the Institution of Slavery in Portuguese America," *Journal of Economic History* 37:1 (March 1977), pp. 59–83.

Describes how mining technology from simple panning for gold to the elaborate "washings" *(lavras)*, royal fiscal and administrative policies, labor needs, and demographic patterns affected the gold-bearing regions of Brazil, especially the captaincy of Minas Gerais. The author examines such topics as the ethnic origins of the African slaves, the importance of their skills in mining technology, the physical demands of gold mining, the problem of runaway slaves, the male-female ratios of the slaves and the Portuguese, the low incidence of marriage among both slaves as well as the general population, and the rapid development of a substantial population of free Blacks and Mulattoes. Russell-Wood shows how the above-mentioned factors affected both the miners and the slaves, compares the composition of the gold region's slave population with that of Brazil's coastal area, and argues that "the degree of freedom enjoyed by slaves in Minas Gerais was determined by different mining practices." Based largely on Brazilian archival materials. 68 notes.

There is a commentary by Joseph Love (pp. 84–86) calling for comparative research with mining areas like Potosí and Mexico to better determine how the type and state of mining technology affected the labor system in question. 7 notes.

d. BAHIA AND ITS NEIGHBORING CAPTAINCIES [Nos. 457–458]
The African heritage of Bahia is surveyed by Donald Pierson **[457]**. Because the African demographic and cultural influence was such a pervasive one in Bahia, almost all the works mentioned in Section XV, E devote considerable attention to Blacks. In addition, Stuart B. Schwartz **[468]**, **[469]**, and **[470]** examines slave resistance in Bahia and Ilheus. Howard M. Prince **[471]** studies slave rebellions in Bahia in the early nineteenth century. Schwartz **[476]** has written a model article on manumission in Bahia, 1684–1745. Jerry M. Turner **[458]** surveys Bahian slave society in the early nineteenth century before studying former Afro-Brazilian slaves who settled along the West African coast in the nineteenth and twentieth centuries.

[457] Donald Pierson. "The Negro in Bahia, Brazil," *American Sociological Review*, 4:4 (August 1939), pp. 524–533.

A survey of the African heritage of Bahia, much of it dealing with the colonial period. The author discusses manumission, the preservation of African cultural forms, miscegenation, and racial ideology. He argues that the African-born slaves' "acquaintance with the simple agriculture of a primitive village economy, and particularly their adjustment to the settled existence which it imposed, probably facilitated their accommodation to the plantation life of the Recôncavo." Furthermore, "slavery was principally characterized by the gradual and continuous growth of intimate personal relations between master and slave which tended to humanize the institution and to undermine its formal character." Based on printed sources. 21 notes.

[458] Jerry Michael Turner. "Les Bresiliens—The Impact of Former Brazilian Slaves upon Dahomey," (Ph.D. Dissertation: Boston University Graduate School, 1975). 417 pp.

The author examines Bahian slave society in the early nineteenth century before turning his attention to Africa. He then traces the

history of Afro-Brazilians, former slaves who managed to leave Brazil during the nineteenth and twentieth centuries and settle along the West African coast. There they were successful as artisans, merchants and interpreters. Being neither African nor European, they formed a culture for themselves known as Bresilien.
DAI 35/09-A (p. 6041).

e. PERNAMBUCO AND THE NORTHEAST [No. 459]
Though Pernambuco and the Brazilian Northeast were heavily dependent on African slavery, there has been little research in English on Blacks in that region during the colonial period. Many of the seventeenth-century Black and Mulatto freedmen military officers discussed by Francis A. Dutra **[475]** were Pernambucans. Billy Jaynes Chandler **[459]** points out that nearly half of the population of Ceará on the eve of independence was of African heritage.

[459] Billy Jaynes Chandler. "The Role of Negroes in the Ethnic Formation of Ceará: The Need for a Reappraisal," *Revista de Ciências Socias* 4:1 (1° Semestre de 1973), pp. 31–43.

Using the census reports for Ceará for the years 1804, 1808, 1813 and 1872, Chandler argues that "persons considered to be of recognizable Negroid stock (either whole or partial) consistently comprised near one half of the total population of Ceará." Furthermore, "the Indian contribution to both the culture and physical stock of the Cearense may have been exaggerated. The Indians of this area, never very numerous, were of a relatively low cultural level and quite fierce, qualities which limit peaceful contacts." The author urges that the role of Negro—previously ignored by historians of Ceará—be reappraised. He concludes that "the history of Negroes in this area is not chiefly that of a numerically insignificant enslaved group existing in a state of sexual lethargy but rather of a general element which was playing a vital and active role in the formation of the general population and its culture." There is an appendix with four tables breaking down the results of the abovementioned censi. 10 notes.

f. AMAZONIA [No. 460]
Comparatively little in English has been written on Blacks in the Amazon region. An excellent overview is found in Colin M. MacLachlan **[460]**. The role of Blacks in the Amazonian economy is briefly discussed by Sue Ann Gross **[638]** and Dauril Alden **[665]**.

[460] Colin M. MacLachlan. "African Slave Trade and Economic Development in Amazonia, 1700–1800," in Toplin, ed., *Slavery and Race Relations* **[97]**, pp. 112–145.

Important study of the efforts of the Portuguese to use African slavery as a remedy for improving less prosperous areas of colonial Brazil. MacLachlan points out that the "successful establishment of a plantation economy in the sugar-producing regions of colonial Brazil created a pattern for colonial development." As a result, "faith in the economic benefits of African slavery blinded the Portuguese to the limited agricultural potential of the Amazon." These attitudes were reinforced by pressures to replace Amerindian labor with that of enslaved Africans. The author studies the formation in 1690 of the Companhia de Cacheu e Cabo Verde and its efforts to import African slaves into the Amazon region. He also describes such problems that surrounded the importation of Blacks into the Maranhão-Pará region as complaints about the limited numbers and high prices of the slaves, the rivalry between São Luis do Maranhão and Belém do Pará over their apportionment, the limited capital of the Amazon region for investment in slave labor, the poor quality of the area's sugar, and the demand of the Pernambucan and Bahian slave markets for Africans. Given these difficulties, it is not surprising that up to 1750 only several thousand slaves had been imported into the Amazon region. When the future Marquis of Pombal came to power in 1750, he "viewed Belém do Pará as the northern anchor of imperial defenses, and he considered Mato Grosso, on the western frontier, as the keystone linking Pará with Rio de Janeiro in the south. A viable Paraense economy appeared vital to the grand design of empire that would be elaborated after 1750." The importation of large numbers of African slaves was considered to be a major aspect of the economic development of Amazonia. By the mid-1770s, the plantation crops of rice and cotton were Maranhão's principal export crops, while cacao, gathered by Indians in the Amazon forests, was the chief product exported by Pará—a clear indication of the diversity of Amazonia's economy. The Portuguese government, however, continued to promote the importation of black labor into both Maranhão and Pará. But, as MacLachlan points out, in the case of Pará "the crown once again failed to consider the ability of the region's products to support the cost of the African slaves." The author concludes with a comparison of the populations of Maranhão (46% black or mulatto slaves) and Pará (23% black or mulatto slaves). There are two appendices, one giving the number of African slaves landed at Belém do Pará, 1757–1800, the other giving figures for São Luis do Maranhão during the same period. Based chiefly on Portuguese and Brazilian archival materials. 101 notes.

C. The Slave Trade [Nos. 461–463]

The most extensive treatment of the slave trade—especially for the late eighteenth and early nineteenth centuries is Herbert S. Klein's *The Middle Passage* **[461]** which includes and updates some of his earlier studies on the subject like that on the Angolan slave trade **[462]** and on mortality and patterns of trade for Rio de Janeiro **[463]**. For the seventeenth century, Charles R. Boxer **[277]** provides a useful description in his biography of Salvador de Sá.

[461] Herbert S. Klein. *The Middle Passage. Comparative Studies in the Atlantic Slave Trade* (Princeton, New Jersey: Princeton University Press, 1978), xxiii, 282 pp.

After surveying the history of the slave trade in the Atlantic world to 1850, the author spends the next four chapters studying the Portuguese slave trade, especially that from Angola and its ports of Luanda and Benguela in the eighteenth century and that from other parts of Africa for the nineteenth. Using a variety of archival materials, the author attempts to determine the total volume of trade from Luanda and Benguela in the eighteenth century, the Brazilian ports of entry, the carrying capacity of the vessels employed in the trade, seasonal effects on slave imports and exports, ages and sex ratios of the slaves, and mortality rates. Commercial organization, both for the Portuguese Atlantic and for Brazil itself, is also studied. The remainder of the book covers the slave trade to Virginia, Jamaica, Cuba and French America. Based on multiarchival research in Portugal and Brazil. There are 34 graphs and tables for the Brazilian part of the study, plus an appendix of three tables. Well-documented and provocative study.

[462] Herbert S. Klein. "The Portuguese Slave Trade from Angola in the Eighteenth Century," *The Journal of Economic History* 32:4 (December 1972), pp. 894–918.

Discusses the organization, volume, rhythm, and direction of the Angola-Brazil slave trade as well as vessel types, capacities, actual and average loads, and male-female, adult-children ratios. The author also examines the papers of several merchants (especially those of Captain João Xavier de Proença e Sylva from Luanda) and discusses the effects of the Pombaline monopoly companies on trade patterns in the Portuguese South Atlantic. Based chiefly on archival (mostly Arquivo Histórico Ultramarino, Lisbon) and printed primary sources. 46 notes. 9 tables. Appendix (with 2 additional tables).

[463] Herbert S. Klein. "The Trade in African Slaves to Rio de Janeiro, 1795–1811: Estimates of Mortality and Patterns of Voyages," *Journal of African History* 10:4 (1969), pp. 533–549.

Careful study of 375 slave ships landing in Rio de Janeiro from 24 July 1795 to 18 March 1811. The author attempts to determine the number of African slaves imported and their mortality rate by year, month and season as well as by port of origin. Klein concludes by comparing "death rates of stable farming populations, epidemic disease outbreaks in these same populations, and mortality of soldiers and sailors in peacetime African activity." Based on archival (códice 242 in the Arquivo Nacional do Rio de Janeiro) and printed primary sources as well as secondary materials. 32 notes. 11 tables.

D. Slave Resistance and Revolts [Nos. 464–471]

Another topic that has gained increasing attention by students and scholars has been that of African resistance to Brazilian slavery. Flight was a common response to forced subjection. The most famous of the slave refuges or hideaways (*quilombos* or *mocambos*) was Palmares, in what is now the state of Alagoas in the Brazilian northeast, which has been studied by Charles E. Chapman **[464]**, R. K. Kent **[465]**, Ernesto Ennes **[466]** and Irene Diggs **[467]**. Stuart Schwartz **[468]** and **[469]** has examined several *quilombos* in Bahia. Runaways are also discussed in such broader studies as those of Karasch **[454]** and Russell-Wood **[456]**. On the topic of resistance and accommodation, Schwartz **[470]** provides an interesting note. Howard Prince **[471]** has studied Bahia, 1807–1835, the area with the highest frequency of slave revolts for a set period of time.

[464] Charles E. Chapman. "Palmares: The Negro Numantia," *The Journal of Negro History* 3:1 (January 1918), pp. 29–32.

Pioneering work in English on the most famous of the Brazilian *quilombos* or runaway slave havens. The author compares the final days of Palmares and its defenders with those of the beleaguered Iberian city of Numantia in Roman times. To be used with caution. Undocumented.

[465] R. K. Kent. "Palmares: An African State in Brazil," *Journal of African History* 6:2 (1965), pp. 161–175.

Describes and analyzes the evolution of Palmares from its foundation in the beginning of the seventeenth century until its destruction in 1694. The author emphasizes that this refuge of escaped slaves in northeastern Brazil "did not spring from a single social structure. It was rather an African political system which came to govern a plural society and thus give continuity to what could have been at best a group of scattered hideouts." After discussing Portuguese attitudes towards Palmares, Kent concludes that "Palmares was a centralized kingdom with an elected ruler" and argues that the political system derived from several Central African models and was "no small tribute to the vitality of traditional African art in governing men." Based entirely on printed primary and secondary sources. 2 illus. 90 notes. There are several erroneous dates in the first five pages.
Reprinted in Price **[100]**, pp. 170–190.

[466] Ernesto Ennes. "The Palmares 'Republic' of Pernambuco, Its Final Destruction, 1697," *The Americas* 5:2 (October 1948), pp. 200–216.

Translates and discusses a number of letters and legal documents from the Portuguese Overseas Archive in Lisbon regarding Palmares, the largest and most famous African slave-refuge in Brazil, and the preparation and activity of the expeditions which finally destroyed it. 4 notes.

[467] Irene Diggs. "Zumbí and the Republic of Os Palmares," *Phylon* 14:1 (March 1953), pp. 62–70.

Uses Edison Carneiro's study on the wars of Palmares and Ernesto Ennes' **[466]** article on the republic of Palmares and describes some of the Portuguese attacks on the famed *quilombo*. Diggs pays special attention to the 1694 siege led by the *bandeirante* Domingos Jorge Velho **[258]** and the commander-in-chief of the Pernambucan troops Bernardo Vieira de Melo which provided the deathblow to Palmares. However,

Zumbí, the leader of the *quilombo*, escaped. Two years later he was tracked down, betrayed and shot, "trapped in a trench 'but fighting back.'" The author, following Carneiro, points out that Zumbí did not hurl himself "theatrically over a precipice," as legend has it. Zumbí's head was cut off and publicly exhibited in Recife. Based on secondary materials. 15 notes. The author used a Spanish translation of Carneiro's study and has kept many of the terms in the article in Spanish rather than Portuguese.

[468] Stuart B. Schwartz. "Buraco de Tatú. The Destruction of a Bahian Quilombo," *Verhandlungen des XXXVIII. Internationalen Amerikanisten-kongresses. Stuttgart-Munchen, August, 1968.* v. 3 (1971), pp. 429–438.

After quickly surveying the formation of communities of runaway slaves (*quilombos*) in colonial Brazil and the Portuguese response to them, the author discusses the expedition of 1763 which destroyed a slave refuge housing approximately sixty-five inhabitants and located north of Salvador. He then attempts to reconstruct from the judicial records of the High Court (*Relação*) at Bahia the organization of the *quilombo* and the way of life of its members and reviews the sentences of the sixty-one fugitives who were captured as well as those handed down to their accomplices. Based heavily on archival materials. 28 notes. Appendix.
See also **[469]**.

[469] Stuart B. Schwartz. "The *Mocambo*: Slave Resistance in Colonial Bahia," *Journal of Social History* 3:4 (Summer 1970), pp. 313–333.

Includes substantial portions of Schwartz **[468]** but goes into more detail on factors promoting and hindering slave resistance and flight. Argues that the economy of *mocambos* in Bahia was based on theft, raids and extortion "rather than a return to African pastoral or agricultural pursuits." Based on multiarchival research and printed materials. 76 notes.
Reprinted in Price **[100]**, pp. 202–226.

[470] Stuart B. Schwartz. "Resistance and Accommodation in Eighteenth-Century Brazil: The Slaves' View of Slavery," *The Hispanic American Historical Review* 57:1 (February 1977), pp. 69–81.

Discusses a late eighteenth-century slave revolt and its aftermath in the captaincy of Ilheus. A group of about fifty slaves from the former Jesuit

Engenho Santana, one of the oldest and largest (about 300 slaves) in that region, killed the overseer, fled into the forest and established a *mocambo* or escaped slave community. The author describes attempts to recover the runaways and destroy their refuge and analyzes the treaty of peace the escaped slaves proposed. 10 notes. The appendix contains two documents in Portuguese, both of which are translated into English.

[471] Howard Melvin Prince. "Slave Rebellion in Bahia, 1807–1835," (Ph.D. Dissertation: Columbia University, 1972). 274 pp.

Analyzes several types of slave uprisings and upheavals which occurred in early nineteenth-century Bahia. The background to these insurrections is examined, particularly the characteristics of urban slavery, the geographical conisderations for *quilombos*, and the numbers and ethnic homogeneity of the African-born slaves. Each important incident of three types of upheavals (quilombo communities established, spontaneous outbreaks, planned insurrections) which occurred in Bahia between 1807 and 1835 is carefully explained with special attention paid to the largest insurgency, that of 1835, also called the "Revolt of the *Males*," which proved to be the last major slave insurrection in Bahia. All of the Bahian slave revolts were led by African-born rather than Brazilian-born Blacks, with the earlier rebellions led by Blacks of Hausa descent and the latter uprisings by those of Yoruba origin. DAI 35/12-A (p. 7847)

E. Freedmen [Nos. 472–482]

In recent years this neglected topic has been finally receiving the attention it has deserved. Two useful overviews are those of Russell-Wood **[472]** and Herbert Klein **[473]**. Francis A. Dutra **[475]** discusses problems that Black freedmen faced during the seventeenth century. There is an excellent article by Schwartz **[476]** on manumission in Bahia in the late seventeenth and early eighteenth century which should be compared with James Patrick Kiernan's study of Paraty **[477]** for the late eighteenth and early nineteenth century.

[472] A. J. R. Russell-Wood. "Colonial Brazil" in Cohen and Greene, eds., *Neither Slave Nor Free* **[99]**, pp. 84–133.

The most extensive study to date on the subject, this chapter provides a judicious overview of the role of freedmen in colonial Brazil. The author discusses their numbers, origins, methods of manumission, social and economic activities, and the problems they encountered. Crown legislation and a change in racial attitudes in the second half of the colonial period are also examined. The author concludes: "At no time did a mulatto, no matter how light-skinned, entirely cast off his ethnic origins and gain total integration into the white ruling class. All but a very few blacks and free mulattoes in colonial Brazil were born, lived and died in a social, economic and ethnic penumbra." Based on archival (Brazilian) and secondary sources. 120 notes. A bibliographical note is appended.

[473] Herbert S. Klein. "The Colored Freedmen in Brazilian Slave Society," *Journal of Social History* 3:1 (Fall 1969), pp. 30–52.

This survey of the role of freedmen in Brazil during the colonial period and the empire complements Russell-Wood's study **[472]**. The author points out that natural reproduction coupled with a constant process of emancipation enabled freedmen to be the fastest growing class in nineteenth-century Brazilian society. Klein argues that "the excessively high birth rate among the free colored would seem to indicate that this category was increasing through accessions from another class, most specifically from the slave group, a fact which could also account for the very low birth rate of slaves." Using data from Minas Gerais in 1814, the author states that a disproportionate male-female ratio among the slave (more male than female) and free-colored (more female than male) population suggests that large numbers of female infant slaves were being freed at birth. In addition, "a large proportion of the free-colored class originated from native-born children of white fathers and slave mothers." The author also discusses the role of freedmen in militia units, in the arts, and as artisans during the colonial period and concludes that "free men of color advanced rapidly in the arts, letters and liberal professions under the empire," though "the middle rank of Brazilian society were relatively more open to accepting mulattoes and blacks than was the upper elite." Based on archival as well as printed materials. 11 tables. 34 notes.

[474] Herbert S. Klein. "Nineteenth Century Brazil" in Cohen and Greene, eds., *Neither Slave Nor Free* **[99]**, pp. 309–334.

This is a slightly expanded version of his article, "The Colored Freedmen in Brazilian Slave Society" **[473]**. Contrary to the title, there is a good deal of information on the colonial period. Based on archival as well as printed materials. 11 tables. 45 notes.

[475] Francis A. Dutra. "Blacks and the Search for Rewards and Status in Seventeenth-Century Brazil," *Proceedings of the Pacific Coast Council on Latin American Studies* v. 6, pp. 25–35.

Points out that many who were awarded *habitos* or memberships in the Portuguese military orders of Christ, Santiago and Avis never received them, since they failed to pass the background examination—race, religion and class being the major obstacles. Though none of the military orders explicitly excluded people of color, Blacks, Amerindians, and those of mixed blood had considerable difficulties to overcome in gaining admittance because they or their parents or grandparents had been slaves or heathens, or both. The author examines all the seventeenth-century cases involving Brazilian Blacks and Mulattoes and concludes that no Brazilian Black was ever awarded a membership in the Portuguese military orders in that time period. According to a *consulta* of the Mesa da Consciência, Henrique Dias, the Black hero who helped drive out the Dutch from Brazil, though he was awarded a *habito*, never was allowed admittance into a Portuguese military order, receiving only a gold medal with the king's effigy so as not to lower the esteem with which *habitos* were held. Other Brazilian Blacks of slave heritage, such as Antônio Gonçalves Caldeira, Mestre de Campo of the Blacks and Pardos in Pernambuco, and Domingos Rodrigues Carneiro, a *sargento mor* in the same unit, also failed to gain admittance into the orders of Santiago and Avis, respectively. However, as the author points out, there were cases where Blacks who were not Brazilians actually received membership in the prestigious Order of Christ during the seventeenth century, the most famous case involving Dom Domingos, Prince of Warri, who became a member of that order in Lisbon in 1609. Based almost entirely on Portuguese archival materials. 46 notes.

[476] Stuart B. Schwartz. "The Manumission of Slaves in Colonial Brazil: Bahia, 1684–1745," *The Hispanic American Historical Review* 54:4 (November 1974), pp. 603–635.

Important analysis of more than a thousand letters of manumission from Bahia and its environs that challenges many of the earlier views on freedmen in Brazil. Schwartz's sample of 1,160 newly freed slaves reveals that half of them obtained freedom by purchase and almost 20% received conditional freedom. Furthermore, there was a 2:1 ratio of freed females to freed male slaves. Of those whose age could be determined 9.2% were five years old or younger; 35:6% were between the ages of 6 and 13; 52.3% between 14 and 45 and only 2.9% over 45 years old. Based primarily on archival materials (notarial records). 49 notes. 9 tables. 3 figures.

[477] James Patrick Kiernan. "The Manumission of Slaves in Colonial Brazil: Paraty, 1789–1822," (Ph.D. Dissertation: New York University, 1976). 353 pp.

A quantitative study of manumission in Paraty at the end of the colonial period. Compared to some other parts of Brazil, the frequency of manumission was not exceptional. The slave population increased by births and purchases five times faster than slaves were freed. Of those freed, two-thirds were females and a large percentage were children, mulattoes, and Brazilian-born Blacks. Reasons for manumission varied. Generally, it was not the sick and the elderly that were freed. Nor did many slaves purchase their freedom compared to those in large cities like Rio de Janeiro and Bahia. Though many were freed without any further obligations, freedom was usually granted conditionally and often occurred when an owner died and there were problems with dividing the estate. Women freed almost half of all the slaves manumitted in Paraty, though they owned only a small percentage of the slaves. Marriage and baptismal records indicate that it was miscegenation more than manumission that was the source of the growing free non-white population in this part of Brazil in the late eighteenth and early nineteenth century.
DAI-38/02-A (p. 966)

1. The Abolition of the Slave Trade [Nos. 478–482]

Several recent studies have appeared on the abolition of the Brazilian slave trade. The early part of both Leslie Bethell's book on the subject **[478]** and an article **[479]** contain useful information for the colonial period. Robert E. Conrad **[480]** has also examined the abolition of the slave trade and discusses the period before 1822. Two earlier studies on abolition—one by Jane Elizabeth Adams **[481]**, the other by Lawrence Hill **[482]**—examine early English efforts to abolish the slave trade to Brazil before 1822.

[478] Leslie Bethell. *The Abolition of the Brazilian Slave Trade. Britain, Brazil, and the Slave Trade Question, 1807–1869.* Cambridge: At the University Press, 1970. xvi. 425 pp.

The initial chapter, "First Steps towards Abolition, 1807–1822," and part of the second, "Independence and Abolition, 1822–1826," contain useful information for the colonial period. The author reviews the extent of slavery in Brazil, pointing out that "with the entire economic life of Portugal's overseas empire in Africa and America organised around the slave trade, abolitionist feeling was notably weak throughout the Luso-Brazilian world." When people, like the two Jesuits Antônio Vieira (1608–1697) and André João Antonil (1649–1716), had criticized slavery, "amelioration, not abolition, . . . had been their aim." Bethell discusses English efforts in April of 1807 (before the Portuguese Court was transferred to Brazil) to make Portugal follow England's lead in abolishing slavery. He then analyzes the abolitionist clauses in the Anglo-Portuguese Treaty of 1810 and the ways they were put in practice, pointing out that Portugal balked at English demands for immediate and total abolition. The Convention of 21 January and the Treaty of 22 January 1815, according to which Portugal, in exchange for a large financial indemnity, agreed to end the slave trade north of the equator, are also studied, as is the 1817 Additional Convention to the Treaty of 1815. Bethell shows how England continued her efforts to obtain stronger search treaties and enforce them more completely. He also discusses how the various European congresses, Vienna (1815), Aix-la-Chapelle (1818) and Verona (1822), handled the issue of slavery and the slave trade. Based primarily on Brazilian and British archival and printed materials.

[479] Leslie Bethell. "The Independence of Brazil and the Abolition of the Brazilian Slave Trade: Anglo-Brazilian Relations, 1822–1826," *Journal of Latin American Studies* 1:2 (November 1969), pp. 115–147.

An earlier but shorter version of the first two chapters of **[478]**. The paper on which this article was based won the First Rio Branco Prize of the Casa do Brasil, London, 1968. 80 notes.

[480] Robert Edgar Conrad. "The Struggle for the Abolition of the Brazilian Slave Trade, 1808–1853," (Ph.D. Dissertation: Columbia University, 1967). 392 pp.

The first part of this fine doctoral dissertation contains a valuable description of slavery in Brazil, the slave trade itself, and the effects of

slavery on the life of the slave. Conrad concludes that "Brazilian slavery, at least that associated with the coffee economy of the hinterland of Rio de Janeiro in the first half of the nineteenth century, was not the mild institution which it is sometimes purported to have been." The second part deals with efforts of Great Britain to abolish the slave trade to Brazil. There is valuable material on the period prior to Brazilian independence.
DAI 28/01-A (p. 1757).

[481] Jane Elizabeth Adams. "The Abolition of the Brazilian Slave Trade," *The Journal of Negro History* 10:4 (October 1925), pp. 607–637.

Approximately one-third of this article deals with slavery in Portuguese America and British efforts to abolish the slave trade and slavery during the period before Brazilian independence in 1822. After the act of 25 March 1807 which abolished the British slave trade, England tried to persuade other countries to do the same. This was done in congresses and through treaties. The author discusses English efforts to make Portugal abolish slavery in 1810 and points out that at the Congress of Vienna (1815) Great Britain "secured from Portugal the signing of a treaty for the abolition of the slave trade north of the Equator and an agreement to negotiate further at some future time upon the matter of total abolition." However, English efforts, and those of France, Austria, Prussia and Russia, to effect total abolition in the Portuguese empire failed. In 1822, the Duke of Wellington reported that "Portugal is the only Country in the World, which now, by Law, permits a trade in Slaves." Adams discusses the types of treaties in which England entered to stop the international slave trade and describes the events that led up to Brazil's promise to abolish the external slave trade as a condition of England's recognition of her independence. Based almost entirely on British printed primary sources. 138 notes.

[482] Lawrence Hill. "The Abolition of the African Slave Trade to Brazil," *The Hispanic American Historical Review* 11:2 (May 1931), pp. 169–197.

Most of the article deals with the period after Brazilian independence in 1822, though the first three pages provide a good synthesis of English pressures on Portugal and Brazil from 1807 to 1822 to abolish the international slave trade. Based on printed British and United States primary sources. 53 notes.

F. The African and Religion [Nos. 483–490]

A new and much-needed interest in the influence of religion—both African and its combination with Portuguese Catholicism—is becoming evident in the historiography of colonial Brazil. In addition to Freyre's pioneering study **[699]**, there is a translation of Roger Bastide's important analysis of African religions of Brazil **[483]**. There are also two provocative articles, one by Donald Warren **[484]**, the other by Mary Karasch **[485]**, the latter arguing that "the major influence of Africans in Brazil has been religious." René Ribeiro **[486]** has studied the influence of Christianity on Blacks in Brazil. Some of the most visible evidences of the role of Christianity in the lives of those of African heritage have been the Black and Mulatto Brotherhoods (*irmandades*), which have been studied by Manoel Cardozo **[299]** for Bahia and by Patricia Mulvey **[487]** and A. J. R. Russell-Wood **[488]** for all of Brazil. Russell-Wood's study of the Misericordia **[300]** also sheds light on the subject for Bahia. Julita Scarano **[489]** attempts an overall assessment of Brazil's Black Brotherhoods. Leslie Rout **[490]** questions the existence of Black Bishops in colonial Brazil.

[483] Roger Bastide. *The African Religions of Brazil. Toward a Sociology of the Interpenetration of Civilizations.* Trans. Helen Sebba. Baltimore and London: The Johns Hopkins University Press, 1978. xxviii, 494 pp. [Translation of *Les Religions Afro-Brésiliennes: Contribution à une Sociologie des Interpénétrations de Civilisations.* Paris, 1960]

This is an important book for those interested in Brazil's African heritage. In Part I, "The Dual Heritage," Bastide traces the importation of African slaves into Brazil and their interaction with the Portuguese. He points out that "despite the unfavorable conditions of slavery, which mixed ethnic groups, broke down African social structures, and imposed a new work rhythm and life style, the religions the blacks brought with them from beyond the Atlantic did not die." The author discusses the social framework in which these religions evolved. There is a section on slave protest and religion, with a discussion of Palmares and other *quilombos*. The religious element in some of the slave revolts—especially those in Bahia in the early nineteenth century—is also analyzed. Bastide studies in some detail the syncretism of African religions with Catholicism and the survivals of African religion. Part II, "A Sociological Study of the Afro-Brazilian Religions," discusses geographical influences, religious syncretism and messianism. He also describes how the African sects function. There is a useful glossary on pp. 469–481. Well annotated.

[484] Donald Warren, Jr. "The Negro and Religion in Brazil," *Race* 6:1 (January 1965), pp. 199–216.

The author argues that "religion, largely ignored in race-class studies, has been and continues to be an important if not critical factor which served the educated as a yardstick for telling who the Negro was in Brazil." According to Warren, the Brazilians have not only divided society into rich and poor and black and white, they have also distinguished between European and non-European Catholicism. To support his argument, the author analyzes three manifestations of non-European Catholicism, in this case Afrobrazilian religion: 1) fetishism; 2) religious brotherhoods of laymen (the *irmandades*); 3) cult groups and their growth. Though the article covers the subject from the sixteenth century to the present, a large part deals with the colonial period. This is a useful and interesting contribution on a relatively neglected topic. Based on printed sources. 52 notes.

[485] Mary Karasch. "Black Worlds in the Tropics. Gilberto Freyre and the Women of Color in Brazil," *Proceedings of the Pacific Coast Council on Latin American Studies* vol. 3 (1974), pp. 19–29.

Challenges Freyre's view in *The Masters and the Slaves* **[699]** that it was the Luso-Brazilian masters and their color blindness that promoted racial tolerance in Brazil and argues that in early nineteenth-century Rio de Janeiro "it was the poor whites and the people of color who reacted against the racism and class prejudice of the masters and who created their own way of life." As an example, the author points to the *irmandades* or brotherhoods of Rio. Though upper-class ones specifically excluded blacks and mulattoes, "many of the black and mulatto brotherhoods admitted people of all colors and civil status"—even whites. Attacking Freyre's image of the "passive, depraved slave woman," Karasch sees many women as actually passing on their African heritage, overcoming or resisting enslavement through manumission or flight (two-thirds of a sample of manumissions for Rio, 1808–1831, were for women), becoming businesswomen and property owners, and serving as religious leaders. The author concludes that "the major influence of Africans in Brazil has been religious," with women tending to preserve many of the rituals and beliefs brought from Africa. This African heritage was reinforced by new slaves coming from Africa, for as Karasch shows, the majority of slaves in Rio de Janeiro in the early nineteenth century came from West-Central Africa and less than ten percent were Brazilian-born. Based on archival research as well as printed primary and secondary sources. 28 notes.

[486] René Ribeiro. "Relations of the Negro With Christianity in Portuguese America," *The Americas* 14:4 (April 1958), pp. 454–484.

Important and provocative interpretation of the Africans' reaction to Christianity in Brazil. Ribeiro examines the African slave and the new social structure he or she encountered and concludes that for many Africans "agriculture became disconnected from its significance as a means of supporting humanity to that of an impersonal exploitation for lucrative purposes." In addition, the African became "separated from his tribal and family groups to become part of the anonymity of the slave quarters." The African, who was used to "a flexible religion in which there was close and even physical participation, such as the easy consulting of supernatural entities," soon became part of a society where "the rule was the rigourous observance of the precepts and rituals of Catholicism." This, the author feels, encouraged "the retention of pagan beliefs." Ribeiro discusses at length the protective systems and the reactions of the African to Christianity. Such reactions were as follows: When the Africans "were forced into the violent despoiling of all their values—rebellion, magic, clandestine continuation of their *ritos fetichistas* [fetishistic rituals]; when they were elevated in the social structure and were accepted in social organizations of prestige—the almost integral acceptance of Christianity or its reinterpretation; when relegated to the margins of society—an easy prey to the contra-acculturative action of individuals proselytized by more aggressive religions than Christianity, or seduced by the only religious structures which would open to them a worthy position and would, through an integral religious experience, assuage some of their most intense desires." Based on printed primary and secondary materials. 56 notes.

[487] Patricia Ann Mulvey. "The Black Lay Brotherhoods of Colonial Brazil: A History," (Ph.D. Dissertation: City University of New York, 1976). 349 pp.

Investigates the membership and functions of the black lay brotherhoods in colonial Brazil and offers a comparative study of 165 lay brotherhoods of slaves, free blacks, and mulattoes founded in the seventeenth and eighteenth centuries. In general, blacks could not rise above the middle levels of society in colonial Brazil. Through the lay brotherhoods Afro-Brazilians could exercise leadership in the black community and also find legal ways to achieve some justice for blacks in the church and society. The brothers built churches, organized festivals, loaned manumission money to slaves, and provided legal counsel for them as well as achieving some measure of parity in the use of local

churches. They also buried the dead, visited prisoners and the sick, provided dowries and gave sustenance to families of members who died or were destitute. Members and officers had great social prestige in the black community. The majority of members of the black lay brotherhoods were slaves, while freedmen were prominent as officers and financial backers. Men serving in black and pardo militias were also active in the confraternities. Most of the black lay brotherhoods were in eighteenth-century Minas Gerais. Bahia, Rio de Janeiro and Pernambuco were also centers of brotherhood activity.
DAI 37/03-A (p. 1743).

[488] A. J. R. Russell-Wood. "Black and Mulatto Brotherhoods in Colonial Brazil: A Study in Collective Behavior," *The Hispanic American Historical Review* 54:4 (November 1974), pp. 567–602.

Important discussion of the foundation, statutes, membership, wealth, functions and social philanthropy of the Black and Mulatto *irmandades* (lay brotherhoods) in Bahia, Minas Gerais and Rio de Janeiro. Based largely on Brazilian archival materials and printed sources. 67 notes.

[489] Julita Scarano, "Black Brotherhoods: Integration or Contradiction?" *Luso-Brazilian Review* 16:1 (Summer 1979), pp. 1–17.

Though the author discusses the Portuguese background of Brazil's *irmandades* or brotherhoods and compares them with the *cofradias* in Venezuela and Columbia during the colonial period, most of the article focuses on brotherhoods in eighteenth century Brazil. She points out that brotherhoods "acquired distinctive regional characteristics" and "became more social than religious" as the eighteenth century progressed. This was especially true in Minas Gerais "because of a royal decree which restricted the establishment of new regular religious orders." Black brotherhoods were "a typically urban phenomenon" and "acted as defenders of black interests." In addition, the brotherhood "gave the black a means of equalizing himself with the rest of the community." The author concludes that "without threatening the principle of slavery or its general acceptance the brotherhoods bettered the lives of some slaves and contributed to the growth of a special mentality." Based on archival as well as secondary materials. 61 notes.

[490] Leslie Rout, Jr. "The 'Black Bishops' Mystery," *Luso-Brazilian Review* 9:1 (Summer 1972), pp. 86–92.

Argues that no evidence can be found to substantiate the claims of Sir Harry Johnston **[447]**, repeated by Roy Nash in *The Conquest of Brazil* **[116]** and Frank Tannenbaum in *Slave and Citizen*, that before the end of the eighteenth century there were "black" bishops in Brazil. After criticizing the above-mentioned writers for failing to differentiate between blacks and mulattoes, the author emphasizes that even after independence, during the period of the monarchy, neither blacks nor mulattoes were permitted to enter seminaries unless they received special episcopal dispensation. Based on printed studies, most of them secondary. 26 notes.

G. Slavery and Race Relations Compared: Brazil and the United States [Nos. 491–495]

There are a growing number of studies on race relations from a comparative point of view, many of them discussing Brazil. Those specifically dealing with Brazil include the book and the article by Carl Degler **[491]** and **[492]**. Degler focuses mostly on post-1822 Brazil, though there is useful material on the colonial period. Two interesting earlier comparative studies are by Herbert B. Alexander **[493]** and E. Franklin Frazier **[494]**. Those interested in the comparative history of the treatment of slaves in the Americas are indebted to the excellent article by Eugene D. Genovese **[495]** which discusses three basic meanings of "treatment."

[491] Carl N. Degler. "Slavery in Brazil and the United States: An Essay in Comparative History," *The American Historical Review* 75:4 (April 1970), pp. 1004–1028.

Degler discusses the Tannenbaum and Elkins thesis and points out that Brazil and the United States were "the two most important slave societies in the New World." He also shows that "in both societies slavery occupied an important, if not actually a central, place in the economy." The author argues that although slavery was different in Brazil and the United States, the explanation for these differences lies "neither in the laws of the Crown nor in the attitudes and practices of the Roman Catholic Church in Brazil." Though there were dissimilarities based on demographic, economic and geographic factors reinforced by the fact that the slave trade lasted almost a half century longer in Brazil, Degler claims that these factors do not explain why "in Brazil the slave was feared, but the black man was not, while in the United States the black man as well as the slave was feared." In Brazil, "the slave trade came to an end principally because of pressure from outside the society." In the United States, "the widespread fear of Negroes also explains why all but one of the states prohibited the importation of slaves before the federal prohibition in 1808." Brazil never restricted manumission the way Anglo-America and, later, the United States did. The author concludes by suggesting that the differences between slavery in Portuguese America and Anglo America should be sought "among the inherited cultural patterns and social structures and values of the two countries." Based entirely on printed sources. 85 notes.

[492] Carl N. Degler. *Neither Black Nor White. Slavery and Race Relations in Brazil and the United States.* New York: The Macmillan Company, 1971. xvi, 302 pp.

Pointing out that "today Brazil and the United States contain more people of African descent than any other countries outside of Africa," the author discusses and compares slavery and race relations in the two nations. Though most of the book deals with the second half of the nineteenth and the twentieth century, there are brief discussions of runaways, slave revolts, the arming of slaves, laws based on race and class, and the role of mulattoes in Colonial Brazil.

[493] Herbert B. Alexander. "Brazilian and United States Slavery Compared: A General View," *The Journal of Negro History* 7:4 (October 1922), pp. 349–364.

Discusses and compares slave populations, family life, types of occupations, the role of religion, slave rights and privileges, slave resistance, and the role of freedmen. Relying heavily on such early nineteenth-century visitors to Brazil as Henderson [**123**], Koster [**626**], and Luccock [**844**], the author concludes that "it seems that the Brazilian institution of slavery was less brutal than the United States system." Though recent studies have modified some of Alexander's conclusions, his article is one of the best informed of the older attempts to compare slavery in Brazil and the United States. Based entirely on printed materials. 52 notes.

[494] E. Franklin Frazier. "A Comparison of Negro-White Relations in Brazil and in the United States," *Transactions of the New York Academy of Sciences*, II Series, vol. 6:7 (May 1944), pp. 251–269.

More than half of this article focuses on the colonial period. The author describes the early history of both Portuguese and Anglo America and interracial contact. He argues that "because of Puritanic mores and the higher status of women, there was a sense of sin and greater protest against concubinage in the South." Although, "the intense racial feeling in the South has sometimes been attributed to fear of insurrection," the same kind of emotions did not develop in Brazil where there also was fear of slave revolts. Frazier argues that in Brazil the African slaves "did not suffer the destruction of their social life nor experience the disintegration of their cultural heritage to the same extent as the slaves imported into the United States." Despite the discovery of African survivals in some isolated parts of the southern United States, "there is practically no evidence that African survivals have influenced the social development of the Negroes in the United States." In contrast, there was significant African influence on "the language, the diet and music of the Brazilians." In fact, such influences were "an integral part of the culture of Brazilian society." 38 notes.

[495] Eugene D. Genovese. "The Treatment of Slaves in Different Countries: Problems in the Applications of the Comparative Method," in Laura Foner and Eugene D. Genovese, eds. *Slavery in the New World. A Reader in Comparative History.* (Englewood Cliffs, New Jersey: Prentice-Hall, Inc., 1969), pp. 202–210.

This excellent article clears up a number of difficulties encountered by earlier writers on the comparative history of treatment of slaves in the Americas. Genovese distinguishes three types of treatment: 1) "day-to-day living conditions"; 2) "conditions of life"; and 3) "access to freedom and citizenship." He points out that distinctions must be made between the type of treatment that is being discussed and compared. The author concludes that "care in definition of terms and precision in comparison of the strictly comparable should take us a long way toward the solution of many problems, the ramifications of which far transcend the study of slavery." 19 notes.

H. The African in Brazilian Art and Literature and in the Accounts of Travellers [Nos. 496–497]

One-third of Raymond S. Sayers's fine study, *The Negro in Brazilian Literature* **[496]**, covers the colonial period. Margaret V. Nelson **[497]** reviews the chronicles of a number of the English-speaking travellers and visitors who were in Brazil during the first half of the nineteenth century and examines their comments on slavery and race relations.

[496] Raymond S. Sayers. *The Negro in Brazilian Literature.* New York: Hispanic Institute, 1956. 240 pp.

This excellent survey is much broader than the title indicates and one-third of the book is devoted to the period before 1822. Sayers prefaces his study with a survey of the Negro in the literature of the Iberian peninsula. He then examines references to those of African heritage made by the sixteenth-century chroniclers who lived in or visited Brazil. The seventeenth-century sermons of the Jesuit Antônio Vieira **[315]** are also studied as are the satires of Gregório de Matos **[714]** and **[715]**, the latter frequently castigating mulattoes and urban Blacks. The important eighteenth-century accounts of the Jesuit Antonil and Nuno Marques Pereira are also examined, especially regarding their references to the role of rural Blacks. There is a good discussion of a number of eighteenth-century defenders of mulattoes and Blacks. The attitudes of the poets of Minas Gerais—several of whom were involved in the Inconfidência Mineira—are also discussed. Special attention is paid to the mulatto poets Manuel Inácio da Silva Alvarenga (1749–1814) and Domingos Caldas Barbosa (1738–1800). Sayers argues that their careers "demonstrate that mulattoes were able to make a place for themselves in the literary world of the late eighteenth century." There is also a brief treatment of antislavery literature in Brazil before 1825. Unfortunately, for English-speaking readers, the lengthier selections from the pre-independence writings are left in Portuguese. However, there are sufficient examples in English to make this study profitable reading for those who do not read Portuguese. There is a detailed bibliography on pp. 225–234. 7 plates. Well documented.

[497] Margaret V. Nelson. "The Negro in Brazil as Seen through the Chronicles of Travellers, 1800–1868," *The Journal of Negro History* 30:2 (April 1945), pp. 203–218.

More than half the references are to travellers who were in Brazil before independence was proclaimed in 1822: Henry Koster **[626]**, Gilbert F. Mathison **[862]**, John Mawe **[563]**, and Thomas Lindley **[613]**. Other travellers cited were Thomas Ewbank, Louis and Mrs. Agassiz, William H. Edwards, and Prince Adalbert of Prussia. From a study of the above-mentioned travel accounts, Nelson concluded that the relationship between master and slave "was personal in each case, that there were good and bad masters in Brazil as elsewhere, and that government regulations were both inadequate and ineffective." Furthermore, "the living conditions of the slave varied from section to section and from occupation to occupation," and "slaves in the cities generally fared better than those in the country where hours of work were longer and where opportunities for earning extra wages were fewer." The author also concluded that "in general slaves in Brazil were less well cared for by the masters than those in other slave-holding countries, but that they had a better opportunity for providing for themselves." Nelson discusses such topics as the role of religion in the daily lives of the slaves, manumission, and the great variety of jobs performed by slaves. She also makes comparisons with the United States. Based entirely on the above-mentioned travellers' accounts. 75 notes.

XIV. Women in Colonial Brazil [Nos. 498–502]

Both Ann M. Pescatello **[498]** and Charles R. Boxer **[499]** have attempted overviews on the role of women in the Iberian world. In addition to the studies of Susan Soeiro **[332]**, **[333]**, and **[334]** on the Poor Clares and their nunnery in Bahia in the late seventeenth and eighteenth century, Russell-Wood **[501]** and **[502]** has contributed several overviews on the role of women in colonial Bahia. There is also a pioneering study by Ann Pescatello **[500]**, "Ladies and Whores." Ernesto Ennes **[321]** discusses the anti-Jesuit sentiments of a woman sawmill owner from Maranhão and Schwartz **[602]** shows how important widows were in the administration of sugar mills in the Brazilian Northeast.

Gilberto Freyre's provocative and controversial study, *The Masters and the Slaves* **[699]**, provides a good starting point for those interested in women in colonial Brazil, though a number of his interpretations have recently been under attack. For example, Mary Karasch **[485]** takes issue with Freyre in her discussion of the role of women in Rio de Janeiro in the early nineteenth century.

[498] Ann M. Pescatello. *Power and Pawn. The Female in Iberian Families, Societies, and Cultures.* Westport, Connecticut: Greenwood Press, 1976. xix, 281 pp.

In this pioneering and far-ranging survey, the author has some useful sections in chapter 2 ("Iberia: Frontiers, Fidalgos, Families, and Females") on the Portuguese background to female-male relationships and responsibilities. She also examines the role of prostitution and analyzes the role of women in the labor force. Chapter 6 ("America in the Reconquest: Empire, Miscegenation, and New Societies") contains a section entitled "Portuguese America: Brazil and the Maranhão." (pp. 144–150). Pescatello stresses the importance of the patriarchal, extended family on the attitudes and behavior of women in colonial Brazil. She argues that "marriage, more specifically the pawning of a woman, created a web of familial and social ties and obligation." The author also analyzes the "traditional double standard of morality." Notes. There is an extensive bibliography on pp. 235–273.

[499] Charles R. Boxer. *Women in Iberian Expansion Overseas, 1415–1815. Some Facts, Fancies and Personalities.* New York: Oxford University Press, 1975. 141 pp.

Chapter II, which covers Spanish and Portuguese America, contains most of the material on women in colonial Brazil. Boxer argues that "it is fairly safe to assert that Spanish-American women in the colonial period had, on the whole, a more enviable position that that of their Luso-Brazilian contemporaries." He points to "the rigorous seclusion in which the better class women were kept," and quotes approvingly Capistrano de Abreu's characterization of the Brazilian family: "Taciturn father, obedient wife, cowed children." After analyzing the influence of such factors as race and class on the treatment of Brazilian women, Boxer concludes that "small wonder if, under these circumstances, many aristocratic young ladies of Bahia preferred becoming Poor Clares in the well-endowed and relatively uninhibited Convent of the Desterro to either marriage or spinsterhood in a home of their own." Well annotated. Bibliographical notes.

[500] Ann M. Pescatello. "Ladies and Whores in Colonial Brazil," *Caribbean Review* 5:2 (April–June 1973), pp. 26–30.

Pioneering survey of the political, economic and social roles of women in Brazil during the first three centuries of Portuguese colonization. The author argues that "class, race, and religion, were underlying factors in almost any legislation restrictive of or beneficial to women." No notes.

[501] A. J. R. Russell-Wood. "Women and Society in Colonial Brazil," *Journal of Latin American Studies* 9:1 (May 1977), pp. 1–34.

Argues that women in Portuguese America "played a significantly more important role in the social, economic, and ideological development of the colony than has been appreciated." After quoting extensively from Nuno Marques Pereira's 1728 *Compendium* on what was to be expected of white women in Brazil, the author attempts to analyze the social role of single and married women and the socioeconomic role of widows as heads of households. Throughout the article, the author analyzes such themes as women's attitudes towards manual labor, treatment of slaves, religiosity, marriage and vanity. Based extensively on archival materials, especially those in Bahia and Minas Gerais. 69 notes. See also **[502]**.

[502] A. J. R. Russell-Wood. "Female and Family in the Economy and Society of Colonial Brazil," in Asunción Lavrin, ed., *Latin American Women* **[98]**, pp. 60–100.

An expanded version of **[501]**. The author has added a different introduction and a section on crown policy and colonial demography. One of the themes of Russell-Wood's study is that "in colonial Brazil the role of the female and her contribution to the economy and society were determined by a code of ethics, by theological doctrine, by canon and civil precepts, and by social and religious attitudes that had comprised the ethos of Catholic countries of Western Europe. This had been transferred to the New World, there to be preserved, strengthened, or modified to meet the needs of colonizing societies. The female, no less than the male, had been affected by social mores and economic change in Brazil." Based heavily on archival and printed primary materials. 80 notes.

XV. Colonization in Brazil: A Regional Approach

[Nos. 503–656]

A. La Plata, Southern Brazil, and the Conflict with Spain

[Nos. 503–542]

Almost from the very beginning of the Spanish and Portuguese presence in the region of La Plata there was conflict. Lewis A. Tambs **[650]** views the hostility within the context of seven centuries of Iberian rivalry, whether in Europe, Africa, the Atlantic islands or America. John A. Hutchins provides a useful overview of more than three centuries of controversy in both his doctoral thesis **[503]** and in a succinct summary of his research **[504]**. Martin Lowry **[505]** focuses on the years 1580–1630, during the union of crowns, while José Carlos Canales **[506]** continues the story to 1737. Magnus Mörner **[314]** discusses the role of the Jesuits in the Plata region, 1549–1700. Mario Rodríguez **[507]**, **[508]**, and **[509]** describes the events following the Bragança Restoration in 1640 and those leading up to the founding of Colônia do Sacramento on the northern bank of the Plata estuary by the Portuguese in 1680. Canales **[510]** discusses the early development of Rio Grande do Sul, as does Joseph Dorenkott **[281]** in his biography of José da Silva Pais. In *The Golden Age of Brazil, 1695–1750*, Charles Boxer **[548]** devotes an excellent chapter to Colônia do Sacramento and southern Portuguese America. He also handles the events leading up to the Treaty of Madrid in 1750, which Hildebrando Accioli **[511]** also discusses in his "Title to Empire." Dauril Alden **[274]**, in the more than two hundred pages of Part II ("The Debatable Lands") of his biography of the Marquis of Lavradio, sums up and reviews much of the above-mentioned research and brings the story to 1779. See also **[514]**. From a Spanish viewpoint, George Archuleta **[512]** in his doctoral dissertation looks at the region in the aftermath of the abortive treaty of Madrid and focuses on Pedro de Cevallos and Spanish efforts at retaliation against Colônia do Sacramento, Rio Grande do Sul, and Santa Catarina **[513]**. Moysés Vellinho **[515]**, in a series of essays, provides an interpretation of the region's rivalries from the point of view of an ardent Rio Grandense. John Hoyt Williams **[516]** adds an interesting sidelight as he analyzes requests of Paraguayan royalists for Portuguese aid against the revolutionaries from Buenos Aires in 1811.

Renewed Portuguese-Spanish hostilities during the first three decades of the nineteenth century are analyzed from a pro-Portuguese point of view by John Hann **[518]**, while Timothy Anna **[519]** and Enoch Resnick **[520]** and **[521]** discuss the repercussions of the 1816 Portuguese invasion of the Banda Oriental. John Street **[517]** examines the role of Lord Strangford in the Plata region, 1808–1815.

Gregory Brown **[522]** studies the evolution of small property agriculture in southern Brazil, 1747–1824. James Slade **[523]** discusses the rivalry between cattle barons and yeoman farmers in the same region, 1777–1889. Evelyn Peterson Meiners **[451]** and Russell Chace **[450]** analyze the role of the Black Man in the Plata. Clifton B. Kroeber **[524]** and **[525]** studies the growth of the shipping industry in the Plata region during the last years of the eighteenth and the first half of the nineteenth centuries.

[503] John A. Hutchins. "Portugal and the Plata: The Conflict of Luso-Hispanic Interests in Southern Brazil and the North Bank of the Rio de la Plata, 1493–1807," (Ph.D. Dissertation: American University, 1953).

[504] John A. Hutchins. "Portugal's Interest in the Control of the Coast of Southern Brazil and the Mouth of the Rio de la Plata," in Lindley Cintra, ed., *Actas* **[91]**, II, pp. 173–187.

Useful overview of more than three centuries of diplomatic and military disputes over Spanish-Portuguese boundaries in the region of the Plata. Although the 1494 Treaty of Tordesillas had established a demarcation line running from pole to pole 370 leagues west of the Cape Verde islands, there was neither agreement over the length of a league nor the Cape Verdean starting point. Furthermore, it was not until the middle of the eighteenth century that longitude could be determined accurately. Not surprisingly, each side tried to operate to its best advantage in the disputed area. The author traces this struggle to gain the upper hand, especially after 1680 when Portugal founded Colônia do Sacramento. No documentation.

[505] Martin J. Lowery. "A Back Door to the Empire: A Study of the Character of the Commerce of the Rio de la Plata, 1580–1630," (Ph.D. Dissertation: Loyola University, 1951).

[506] José Carlos Canales. "Rio Grande do Sul in Luso-Spanish Platine Rivalry, 1626–1737," (Ph.D. Dissertation: University of California, Berkeley, 1959). vii, 379 pp.

Canales describes the geography of Rio Grande do Sul and discusses the region's Amerindian inhabitants. He analyzes the first missionary frontier and the confrontation between Jesuits and *bandeirantes* over the control of the Indian. The author examines Portuguese Platine policy, the establishment of Colônia do Sacramento, the development of Santa Catarina, and the settlement of Rio Grande de São Pedro. He also studies Spanish responses, especially the founding of the Seven Missions and Montevideo.

[507] Mario Rodríguez. "The Genesis of Economic Attitudes in the Rio de la Plata," *The Hispanic American Historical Review* 36:2 (May 1956), pp. 171–189.

Analyzes and gives numerous seventeenth-century examples of the anticontraband attitudes of Spanish cattlemen in the Plata region towards Spaniards from Tucuman and Potosí, Portuguese entrepreneurs (during the union of crowns, 1580–1640) and Portuguese colonists from across the estuary at the newly founded outpost of Colônia do Sacramento (after 1680) as well as Dutch and other northern European traders (especially around mid-century). Argues that such antipathies accounted "for Spain's strengths in that area and the fierce resistance of her colonials to Portuguese aspirations in the Rio de la Plata." Based chiefly on Spanish and, to a lesser extent, Portuguese printed primary sources. 65 notes.

[508] Mario Rodríguez. "Colônia do Sacramento: Focus of Spanish-Portuguese Rivalry in the Plata, 1640–1683," (Ph.D. Dissertation: University of California, Berkeley, 1952). 334 pp.

The first three chapters of this well-researched thesis discuss the history of the Plata region from 1516 to 1672 with an emphasis on such themes as early Spanish-Portuguese rivalry, the "pull of Peru" and

Portuguese commercial infiltration during the union of crowns, and the Luso-Brazilian need for a port in that region. Rodríguez then turns his attention to Portuguese independence in 1640 and its influence on Brazil. He also recounts the role of the Portuguese Prince Regent (the future Pedro II) in the evolution of plans for establishing a colony on the banks of the Rio de la Plata and the part Manuel Lobo played in the founding of Colônia do Sacramento early in 1680. The author points out: "It was neither to the interest of Spain nor to that of her Platine colonials to have the Portuguese re-enter the trade of the Plata. Spain opposed this, for inevitably it would again drain away silver; the Plata colonials resisted because it threatened their hide industry. The Spanish Jesuits and their mission Indians fearing further Portuguese aggression likewise stood in opposition." The result was quick reaction by the Spaniards who captured Colônia in late 1680. However, Spanish possession was short-lived. A diplomatic victory returned it to Portugal in 1683. There are useful maps and an annotated bibliography (pp. 306–334). Based on archival and printed materials, especially the Bancroft Library's microfilm collection of documents from Lisbon's Arquivo Histórico Ultramarino.

[509] Mario Rodríguez. "Dom Pedro of Braganza and Colônia do Sacramento, 1680–1705." *The Hispanic American Historical Review* 38:2 (May 1958), pp. 179–208.

Views Portuguese interest in establishing a base at Colônia do Sacramento as part of the Brazilian reform plan of Dom Pedro II (Regent, 1667–1683, and King, 1683–1706) in which the monarch tried to make the administration of Portuguese America more efficient, develop and diversify the colony's economy and bring relief and prosperity to the royal treasury. Within this framework the author argues that the particular motives for setting up the Colônia outpost were (in order of importance): contraband trade with Potosí, access to the huge cattle herds of the Plata, defensive colonization (to protect mines the Portuguese hoped to discover and to buttress their claims to lands on Portugal's side of the Tordesillas line), and the Indian and possible mineral resources in that area. However, Portuguese efforts were frustrated by the strong opposition of Porteño cattlemen and the Spanish Jesuits and their Indians. Based extensively on Portuguese and Spanish primary sources. 96 notes.

[510] José Carlos Canales. "Rio Grande do Sul, Keystone of Platine Trade and Communications," in Costa, ed., *Actas* **[92]**, II, pp. 171–191.

After describing efforts of the *capitão mor* of Laguna, Francisco de Brito Peixoto, and other Portuguese frontiersmen to settle the Canal do Rio Grande do Sul, the key to land communication between Colônia do Sacramento and southern Santa Catarina, the author discusses the attempt of the "most ambitious expedition to the Rio de la Plata" to come to the aid of besieged Colônia, to attack Montevideo, and occupy Rio Grande do Sul. Though the 1735 Spanish siege was eventually lifted, other Portuguese objectives in the La Plata failed because of incompetence, indecisiveness and bad luck. However, on his return to Rio de Janeiro in 1737, General Silva Pais erected a fort on what is today Rio Grande, officially sanctioning earlier Portuguese movements into that area. Based on some archival and many printed primary sources. 122 notes.

[511] Hildebrando Accioli. "Title to Empire," *Américas* 2:5 (May 1950), pp. 20–23.

Studies the Treaty of Madrid, signed on 13 January 1750, "the first attempt to define a precise dividing line between Brazil and Spain's possessions in South America." Discusses the role of the *bandeirantes* and the union of crowns, 1580–1640, in blurring still further the already vague boundaries established by the Treaty of Tordesillas in 1494. The Treaty of Madrid was based on the principle of *uti possidetis* (lit. as you possess) and attempts were made to provide precise geographic definition to the boundaries. The treaty was also founded on mutual concessions: Portugal gave up Colônia do Sacramento founded in 1680 on the southern bank of the Rio de la Plata; Spain ceded the seven towns of Missões on the eastern bank of the Uruguay river. The Rio de la Plata river basin was to be in the hands of Spain, while the Amazon river basin was to go to the Portuguese. Portugal gave up its claim to part of the Philippines and the adjacent islands in exchange for recognition of its rights to land occupied in Mato Grosso and the Amazon river basin. The author pays a special tribute to the Brazilian-born Alexandre de Gusmão, one of the chief architects of the new treaty. It was Gusmão who drafted the instructions, proposals and counterproposals that were forwarded to Madrid. 7 illus. No notes.

[512] George Louis Archuleta. "Pedro de Cevallos and the Luso-Spanish Struggle in the Rio de La Plata (1750–1778)," (Ph.D. Dissertation: The University of New Mexico, 1973). 394 pp.

Analyzes the extent to which the Spanish and Portuguese clashed seeking territorial gain in the Plata region and southern Brazil between

1750 and 1778. Focuses on General Pedro de Cevallos, leader of the Spanish forces, who believed that force of arms not diplomacy would be decisive in this struggle. Jesuit-trained Cevallos disliked the terms of the Treaty of Madrid and protected the Guaranis and Jesuits in the mission areas ceded to Portugal. A year after the revocation of the treaty (1761) he led the forces that captured Colônia do Sacramento from the Portuguese and drove into Portuguese Rio Grande do Sul. Spain, forced by England to return Colônia in 1763, remained in Rio Grande do Sul. In 1776, the Luso-Brazilians finally managed to evict the Spanish from that province. Next Cevallos commanded a large armada sent to recover Rio Grande do Sul, a mission that failed. He did, however, recapture Colônia. Plans to retake Rio Grande were interrupted by the Treaty of San Ildefonso in 1777 which granted Colônia to Spain and Rio Grande to Portugal.
DAI 35/03-A (p. 1578).

[513] George Louis Archuleta. "Spanish Retaliation Against Portuguese America in 1776–1777," *Rocky Mountain Social Science Journal* 7:1 (April 1970), pp. 99–107.

Account of the 19,000 man Spanish expedition under Pedro de Cevallos which early in 1777 took Santa Catarina, captured and destroyed Colônia do Sacramento but because of storms failed to seize Rio Grande do Sul before an armistice stopped hostilities. The Treaty of San Ildefonso signed in October of the year restored Santa Catarina to Portugal. Viewed from a Spanish perspective and based almost entirely on printed sources, most of them secondary. 21 notes.

[514] Dauril Alden. "The Undeclared War of 1773–1777: Climax of Luso-Spanish Platine Rivalry," *The Hispanic American Historical Review* 41:1 (February 1961), pp. 55–74.

Detailed analysis of the military and diplomatic struggle between Spain and Portugal over Colônia do Sacramento and Rio Grande do Sul which was finally resolved by the Treaty of San Ildefonso (1777). Based on archival (Brazilian) and printed primary sources. 76 notes.

[515] Moysés Vellinho. *Brazil South: Its Conquest and Settlement.* Trans. by Linton Lomas Barrett and Marie McDavid Barrett. New York: Alfred A. Knopf, 1968. xv, 282 pp.
[This is a translation of *Capitania d'El Rei* Porto Alegre: Editora Globo, 1964.]

A series of essays on the colonial background of Brazil's southernmost state by an ardent Rio-Grandense. The author discusses early Spanish-Portuguese rivalries in the Plata region, the founding in 1680 of Colônia do Sacramento, which for the next century would be "choked off by enemy-held territory, besieged five times, thrice conquered and razed," and the effort of Silva Pais to settle sixty leagues to the north in what was to become Rio Grande do Sul. The diplomatic efforts by Spain and Portugal to resolve their territorial problems in that region are also recounted. The author describes the *bandeirantes'* long and bitter rivalry with the Jesuits and argues that the Jesuits "tenaciously held to the purpose of constructing an empire of their own in the heart of the new world." Vellinho praises the *bandeirantes* for destroying Jesuit Indian missions in what is now southern Brazil, thus opening up new areas to Portuguese settlement, and argues that the "*bandeirantes* have been vituperated unthinkingly and immoderately." After delineating the struggle over the Missiones Orientales and the role of Cristovão Pereira in the history of Rio Grande do Sul during the first half of the eighteenth century, the author concludes with a comparison between the Spanish part of the Plata region and Rio Grande do Sul and a discussion of the role of the frontier on the type of Portuguese spoken by the inhabitants of that region. Based entirely on printed primary and secondary sources. Documented. There is an extensive bibliography on pp. 247–258.

[516] John Hoyt Williams. "Governor Velasco, the Portuguese and the Paraguayan Revolution of 1811: A New Look," *The Americas* 28:4 (April 1972), pp. 441–449.

Discusses Paraguayan reaction to the efforts of the revolutionary junta in Buenos Aires to bring Paraguay under control after the successful overthrow of Spanish rule in the viceregal capital of the Rio de la Plata on 26 May 1810. Though the Argentine forces under Belgrano were defeated by creole troops, the Paraguayan governor, Bernardo de Velasco y Huidbro, disgraced himself by fleeing from the battle with his European advisers. Since Paraguayan opposition to Buenos Aires stemmed more from localism and distrust of the viceregal capital than a deep affection for the royalist cause, Velasco's cowardice was a mortal blow to the Spanish cause in Paraguay. To bolster his rapidly eroding position and at the urging of the ultraroyalist *cabildo* or town council of Asuncion, Velasco called upon Portuguese military aid to protect Paraguay from further incursions from Buenos Aires. Letters were written to Colonel Francisco das Chagas Santos, Portuguese commander in the Banda Oriental, asking for 200 troops of the line for Misiones, and to Diogo de Sousa, captain general of Rio Grande do Sul.

Sousa replied that he "had authority to aid the legitimate Spanish governors against the rebels, in order to protect . . . Carlota Joaquina" and offered 800 to 1,000 troops rather than the 200 for which Velasco had asked. Soon the number of regular Portuguese troops proffered to the Spanish governor of Paraguay reached 1,500, plus additional militia. Promises of Portuguese aid continued to escalate while threats from Belgrano and the Argentine rebels decreased. The Portuguese price was high. The Paraguayan royalists "must recognize the legitimate claim of Carlota Joaquina as heir to the Spanish Crown and its dominions." Though the *cabildo* and Velasco seem to have agreed to pay the price, there is a letter, dated 13 May 1811, seemingly in the Spanish governor's handwriting, which declined Portuguese troops but asked for 25,000 pesos in their place. Despite this letter (which may have been antedated), a note of 15 May 1811, informing Velasco that he was being deposed, claims that this action was being taken to prevent Paraguay from "being turned over to a 'Foreign Power,' Portugal." Velasco, pointing to his letter of 13 May 1811, claimed the charge was false. Whatever the truth of the matter, Velasco was deposed and arrested. Based on Paraguayan archival and printed secondary sources. 33 notes.

[517] J. Street. "Lord Strangford and Rio de la Plata, 1808–1815," *The Hispanic American Historical Review* 33:4 (November 1953), pp. 477–510.

An account of the efforts of Viscount Strangford, British Minister to the Portuguese Court at Rio de Janeiro from 1808–1815, to maintain peace among England's allies in the region of the Rio de la Plata, oppose French intervention and keep them out of South America, and promote British trade there. Though the greater part of the article deals with Strangford's relationship to Spanish America, there is important information on Brazil. Street claims that "stopping Portuguese aggrandizement in the South was . . . one of Strangford's major activities" during the period from 1808–1812. Initially—i.e., in 1807, when Spain and France were allies—the British War Secretary Castlereagh was willing to allow Portugal to take over the Spanish colonies bordering on Brazil in recompense for her losses in Europe and to prevent the French from seizing them. However, Spain's break with France and alliance with her former enemy, England, changed British policy. Though Street claims that Strangford's "ascendancy over the Portuguese Court was almost complete" and that he "had little trouble over purely Portuguese American affairs," his study reveals that the British minister had to constantly restrain the Portuguese from becoming involved in the Plata region. Initially Strangford was successful, though he had to send an agent to warn the Revolutionary Junta in Buenos Aires "not to provoke Rio de Janeiro by actions or declarations which could be interpreted as hostile." In April of 1811, Strangford managed to discourage Portuguese attempts at invading Paraguay. But later that year, "Portuguese troops entered the Banda Oriental at the invitation of Elio and Casa Iruja, ostensibly to help Montevideo to subdue the revolutionaries, though Strangford remained convinced that the Portuguese really intended to occupy the province for themselves." The Portuguese, on the other hand, argued that "the operation was intended to keep Brazil safe from revolutionary infection and to protect the interests of their Spanish ally." It was not until an armistice was arranged in 1812 that the Portuguese withdrew their troops. Strangford was also kept busy dealing with Carlota Joaquina, the Queen of Portugal and sister of Ferdinand VII, and her efforts to be recognized as ruler of Spanish America since her brother was a captive of Napoleon. Based largely on archival materials in the British Foreign Office and Archivo General de la Nacion, Buenos Aires. 54 notes.

[518] John Henry Hann. "Brazil and the Rio de la Plata, 1808–1828," (Ph.D. Dissertation: The University of Texas, 1967). 490 pp.

New look at the Platine policy of the Portuguese and Brazilian governments from 1808 to 1828, arguing that it was not simply a plan of imperialist expansion towards the Plata estuary. Analyzes the many complex factors that determined Luso-Brazilian moves in the area, culminating with João VI's policy in 1821 to allow Uruguayans their own choice of government. Dom Pedro was unable to effectively change this policy and, by 1828, most Brazilians accepted Uruguay's independence and opposed Argentine efforts to undo the settlement. DAI 28/10-A (p. 4091).

[519] Timothy E. Anna. "The Buenos Aires Expedition and Spain's Secret Plan to Capture Portugal, 1814–1820," *The Americas* 34:3 (January 1978), pp. 356–380.

Discusses Spain's response to Portugal's seizure of Montevideo in 1816 and its occupation of the Banda Oriental. The "Secret Plan" was for the Buenos Aires expedition to take Montevideo and use it as a land base to attack and subject the rebels in Argentina. But more importantly, it was hoped that such action would elicit a declaration of war from João VI at Rio de Janeiro which, in turn, would give Spain the excuse to attack

Portugal (Spanish land forces were gathered along the border in Extremadura) and unite the Iberian peninsula under the Spanish monarchy. "While Brazil was taking advantage of Spain's weakness to grab contiguous territory in South America, Spain would take advantage of Portugal's weakness to do the same in the peninsula." João VI's offer in 1820 to surrender Montevideo in exchange for "the guarantee of monarchy in Argentina to defend against the spread of South American republicanism" was refused. But the troops gathered at Cadiz and scheduled to sail on the expedition revolted and the plan came to naught. Based on Spanish archival and printed primary source materials. 69 notes.

[520] Enoch F. Resnick. "A Family Imbroglio: Brazil's invasion of the Banda Oriental in 1816 and Repercussions on the Iberian Peninsula, 1816–1820," *Revista de História* (São Paulo), 51:101 (January-March 1975), pp. 179–205.

Using a wide variety of primary sources—e.g., minutes of the Spanish Council of State, memoirs by Ferdinand VII's ministers, British newspaper accounts, and Spanish, Russian, British and American diplomatic correspondence—the author tries to explain the reaction of Ferdinand VII, his court and the Spanish people to the invasion of the Banda Oriental by João VI's Portuguese troops in 1816. He discusses the role of Maria Isabel de Bragança, Ferdinand's queen and João's daughter, and Carlota Joaquina, João's queen and Ferdinand's sister, the reaction of the Paris Conference, England's position and that of Russia, and the Spanish mobilization of troops on the Portuguese border. Resnick concludes by raising the question whether Spain's failure to act was because of a tacit agreement between João VI and Ferdinand VII regarding the Portuguese invasion of the Banda Oriental or because of an "inability to adopt resolute measures." 95 notes.

[521] Enoch F. Resnick. "Spain's Reaction to Portugal's Invasion of the Banda Oriental in 1816," *Revista de Historia de America* nos. 73–74 (January–December 1972), pp. 131–143.

Earlier version of **[520]**, but with a slightly different format and perspective. Discusses the reaction in Spain by government officials, the nation-at-large, the Court and the Royal Family to the Portuguese army's invasion of the Banda Oriental. Based on archival research. 48 notes.

[522] Gregory Girard Brown. "The Evolution of Small Property Agriculture in Southern Brazil: 1747–1824," (Ph.D. Dissertation: Northern Illinois University, 1978). 391 pp.

Between 1735 and 1748 an increasing number of immigrant families from the Atlantic islands of the Azores and the Madeiras were settled as homesteaders in southern Brazil to better establish Portuguese control in that area. Small farms were encouraged and diversification of products flourished during the Pombaline years. By 1800, small property owners were on the way of gaining social and economic significance in that part of Brazil, supplying the larger cities with considerable quantities of wheat and manioc. After 1815, however, when North America sought new outlets for their foodstuffs in Brazil, the small farmers of southern Brazil were forced out of their primary markets. This factor, plus others like lack of a suitable commercial infrastructure and natural problems like wheat rust, destroyed the prosperity and expansion of small property agriculture in southern Brazil. A switch to cattle raising and subsistence agriculture followed and a domestic elite based on large latifundia became the dominant force in Rio Grande do Sul and Santa Catarina.
DAI 39/06-A (pp. 3764–3765).

[523] James Jeremiah Slade III. "Cattle Barons and Yeoman Farmers: Land Tenure, Division, and Use in a County in Southern Brazil, 1777–1889," (Ph.D. Dissertation: Indiana University, 1972). 271 pp.

Analyzes land tenure patterns—their causes and effects—in São Lourenço do Sul, a county in Rio Grande do Sul. The first group to settle the land after it was definitively won from the Spaniards in 1776 was made up of a few military men who took over the prairies for cattle raising. They were displaced by a small number of more powerful men who amassed huge cattle holdings when the market in salted beef was flourishing. These men had little interest in the serra which was the other distinctive land formation in the region. That area was colonized by subsistence farmers who held small cattle and planting endeavors. After the mid-nineteenth century, colonists were brought over from Germany to the serra where they further developed the small-scale mixed agricultural pattern. The serra prospered as its agricultural products reached the cities. New trade, commercial activities and crafts developed. The Germans, however, were kept out of local politics by their own exclusiveness and by the political structure of the empire. During this time the ranch economy of the prairies remained substan-

tially unaltered. The pattern of large ranches on the prairie and family farms in the serra has lasted until the present.
DIA 30/01-A (p. 261).

[524] Clifton Brown Kroeber. *The Growth of the Shipping Industry in the Rio de la Plata Region, 1794–1860.* Madison: The University of Wisconsin Press, 1957. ix, 194 pp.

The Rio de la Plata and its tributaries drain an area of almost 1,200,000 square miles, including part of southern Brazil. Though this study is written from a Spanish perspective, there are a number of references to Portuguese America. Chapter one describes the Plata region and its rivers and includes a useful map. "Trade and Navigation in Colonial Times" (chapter two) provides a good picture of the significance of Portuguese infiltration into the region. In the remaining chapters Kroeber uses a topical approach and studies ports, ships, ownership and control of shipping, the commodities of trade, the coming of foreigners, the expansion of shipping, the development of shipping routes, and the struggle for free navigation. There are a substantial number of references to Brazil prior to 1822 interwoven into the narrative of such chapters. Table II shows Portuguese shipping in Buenos Aires, 1810–1817. Table IV is entitled "Nationality of Vessels in Coastal Trade to Buenos Aires from Brazil, 1818–1822." Based on Argentine and Paraguayan archival materials and printed sources. There is a detailed bibliography (pp. 167–175) and a helpful index.

[525] Clifton Brown Kroeber. "River Trade and Navigation in the Plata Region, 1800–1852," (Ph.D. Dissertation: University of California, Berkeley, 1951). vi, 376 pp.

An earlier version of **[524]**.

1. Contemporary Narratives, 1700–1822 [Nos. 526–542]

Most of the eighteenth and early nineteenth century accounts in English dealing with southern Brazil focus on the island of Santa Catarina. The famous French engineer in Spanish service, Amédée François Frézier **[526]**, visited Santa Catarina in 1712 and provided a detailed description of the island. Seven years later, Captain George Shelvocke **[527]** stopped for a month-and-a-half at Santa Catarina. William Betagh **[529]**, who was also on the expedition, gives a slightly different version of the Shelvocke visit. George Anson **[530]** and his expedition spent a little less than a month at Santa Catarina in 1740–1741. Other descriptions of that visit are contained in the diary of Captain Philip Saumarez **[531]**, eventually to be Anson's second-in-command, and the journal of Bulkeley and Cummins **[532]**. Santa Catarina was also visited by Antoine Joseph Pernety **[533]** and Bougainville in 1763, and by La Pérouse **[534]** in November of 1785. James George Semple Lisle **[535]** and some of his companions were set adrift near Rio Grande do Sul in August of 1797. His account of Rio Grande do Sul is one of the few in English for the time period. He also spent three weeks on the island of Santa Catarina before travelling on to Rio de Janeiro and Salvador. John Black **[536]**, who was set ashore with Semple Lisle, also left an account of his Brazilian experiences. Adam J. von Krusenstern **[537]**, Urey Lisiansky **[538]** and Georg Heinrich von Langsdorff **[539]** were part of the Russian expedition that circumnavigated the world, 1803–1806. All three left descriptions of Santa Catarina. John Mawe **[563]** stopped briefly at Santa Catarina in 1807. An American, Captain David Porter **[540]**, visited Santa Catarina during the War of 1812. Otto von Kotzebue and Adelbert von Chamisso **[541]** were part of another Russian scientific expedition to stop in Brazil. They spent most of December 1815 at Santa Catarina. The occupation of Montevideo by the Portuguese in 1816 is described in **[542]**.

[526] Amédée François Frézier. *A Voyage to the South-Sea and along the Coasts of Chili and Peru, in the Years 1712, 1713, and 1714.* London: Jonah Bowyer, 1717. 335 pp.

Frézier visited Santa Catarina in 1712 on his voyage to the Pacific and Salvador two years later on the return voyage. His description of Santa Catarina is detailed. He found the island to be "a continu'd Grove of Trees, which are all the Year green. There are no Places in it passable, besides what have been clear'd about the Dwellings; that is, 12 Or 15 Spots scatter'd about here and there along the Shore, in the little Creeks facing the Continent. The Inhabitants settled on them are Portugueze, some European Fugitives, and a few Blacks: There are also some Indians, who come voluntarily to serve them, or taken in War. Tho' they pay no Tribute to the King of Portugal, they are his Subjects, and obey the Governor or Captain he appoints to command them, if there be Occasion, against European Enemies, and the Indians of Brazil; with which last they are almost continually at War, so that they dare not go under 30 or 40 Men Together, well arm'd, when they penetrate up the Continent, which is no less embarass'd with Forests than the Island. That Captain commonly commands but three Years, and is subordinate to the Governor of Lagoa, a small Town 12 Leagues distant from the Island to the S. S. W. He had at that Time 147 Whites within his District, some Indians and Free Blacks, Part whereof are dispers'd along the Shore of the Continent. Their usual Weapons are Hunting-hangers, Bows and Arrows, and Axes: They have but few Firelocks, and seldom any Powder; but they are sufficiently fortify'd by the Woods, which an infinite Quantity of Brambles of several Sorts render almost impenetrable; so that having always a sure retreat, and but little Houshold-stuff to remove, they live easy, without any Fear of being robb'd of their Wealth. . . . Those People, at first Sight, appear wretched; but they are in Reality, happier than the Europeans; being unacquainted with the Curiosities and superfluous Conveniences so much sought after in Europe, they are satisfy'd without thinking of them. . . . The only Thing they are to be pity'd for, is, their living in Ignorance: They are Christians it is true, but how are they instructed in their Religion, having only a Chaplain of Lagoa, who comes to say Mass to them on principal Festivals of the Year? However, they pay Tythe to the Church, which is the only Thing exacted from them. In other respects, they enjoy a good Climate, and a very wholesome Air: They seldom have any other Distemper besides that they call Mal de Biche. . . . They also have many Medicines of the Simples of the Country, to cure other Distempers that may seize them." Frézier also described Salvador in detail. "The Access to it is so difficult, by reason of its great Steepness, that they have been forced to have recourse to Machines for carrying up, and letting down of Goods from the Town to the Port. . . . Tho' the Streets there are Straight, and of a good Breadth, most of them have so steep a Descent, that they would be impracticable for our Coaches, and even for our Chairs. The rich People, notwithstanding that Inconveniency, do not go a Foot; being always industrious, as well in America, as in Europe, to find Means to distinguish themselves from the rest of Mankind, they would be ashamed to make use of the Legs which Nature has given us to walk. They lazily cause themselves to be carry'd in Beds of fine Cotton, hanging by the Ends to a Pole, which two Blacks carry on their Heads or Shoulders; and to be there conceal'd." Frézier was impressed by the "six Companies of Regular Forces" maintained by the Crown "to secure these forts and the Town." The soldiers "are well disciplin'd and pay'd; those I saw were in a very good Condition, well arm'd, and full of fine Men; they want nothing but the Reputation of being good Soldiers." As for the inhabitants, Frézier reported that they "have an Out-side good enough as to Politeness, Neatness, and the manner of giving themselves a good Air, much like the French. I mean the Men only, for there are so few Women to be seen, that but a very imperfect Account can be given of them. The Portugueze are so jealous, that they scarce allow them to go to Mass on

Sundays and Holidays; nevertheless, in Spight of all their Precautions, they are almost all of them Libertines, and find Means to impose upon the Watchfulness of their Fathers and Husbands, exposing themselves to the Cruelty of the latter, who kill them without Fear of Punishment, when they discover their Intrigues. Instances hereof are so frequent, that they reck'ned above 30 Women murder'd by their Husbands within a Year."

[527] Captain George Shelvocke. *A Voyage Round the World by the Way of the Great South Sea, Perform'd in the Years 1719, 20, 21, 22 in the Speedwell of London.* London: J. Sennex, W & J. Innys, J. Osborn and T. Longman, 1726.
[There is a second edition, dated 1757, cited by Borba de Moraes **[20]**, II, 252–253.]

Captain George Shelvocke (1690–1728) was named to command the "Speedwell," the smaller of two ships commissioned to war against the Spanish in the Pacific. Shortly after the voyage began, the two ships were separated by a storm. From 23 June to 8/9 August 1719, Shelvocke and his often mutinous crew spent time at Santa Catarina, which is described in detail on pages 52–57. The island "is all over cover'd with inaccessible woods, so that excepting the plantations, there is not a clear spot upon it . . . and the main continent of Brazil it self may in this part be justly term'd a vast continu'd wilderness." The Captain describes the great quantity and variety of available fruit. In addition, the inhabitants "have the sugar cane very large and good, but make little or no use of it for want of utensils, so that the little molassus and rum they have, they sell very dear." Though there is not much game, "the woods are full of parrots, which are good eating." There was also an abundance of tasty fish and shellfish. "On the Savannas of Arezitiba on the Continent over against the southernmost part of St. Catharines, they have great numbers of black cattle." As for the Portuguese inhabitants: "It is certain that they are a parcel of Banditti, which come for refuge here from the neighboring and more strictly govern'd Colonies of Brazil; Emanuel Mansa, who was what they call'd the Captain of the Island, was still their Chief as much as in Frézier's time **[526]**. However, for my part, I can but do them the justice to say, that they traded with me very honestly, and were very civil to everyone but those who gave them . . . gross affronts." According to Shelvocke, one of the chief English troublemakers was Simon Hatley, the second captain: "I had daily complaints of his abusing their women in the grossest manner; and further, that he, and a gang that used to go about with him to buy fresh provisions, had threatened to ravish old and young, and set their houses on fire; nay and actually burnt one, which the inhabitants had permitted us to use as long as we had occasion for it." Shortly before Shelvocke and his crew sailed for Cape Horn, the Portuguese got their revenge by ambushing an English contingent looking for deserters. The author concludes: "As to their fine dwelling-houses mentioned by Monsieur Frézier, none of us cou'd see any such thing, nor have they any place worthy the name of a Town, nor any Fortification of any kind except the woods, which to them is a sure retreat and security against any enemy that may attack them. As to the Indians of this part, I can't say much of them, having never seen above 2 or 3 of them." Shortly before departing from Santa Catarina, Shelvocke encountered on 3 August 1719, the São Francisco Xavier, a "Portuguese man of war, of 40 guns and 300 men from Lisbon, bound to Macau in China, commanded by Captain La Riviere, a Frenchman," to whom he apologized for the unruly behavior of his men.

[528] Captain George Shelvocke. *A Privateer's Voyage Round the World.* London: Jonathan Cape, 1930.

One of the volumes in The Traveller's Library Series, this modern edition of Shelvocke's account **[527]** also includes remarks by William Betagh **[529]**, a detractor of Shelvocke, interspersed between chapters. Shelvocke was arrested on his return to England for conspiring to defraud the owners of their percentage of the profits from his privateering voyage. He wrote this account in defense of his conduct. Of particular interest to Brazilianists is the episode with the Portuguese merchantman near Cabo Frio and the events that took place on the island of Santa Catarina.

[529] William Betagh. *A Voyage Round the World. Being an Account of a Remarkable Enterprize, Begun in the Year 1719, Chiefly to Cruise on the Spaniards in the Great South Ocean.* London: T. Combes, J. Lacy, and J. Clake, 1728. 342 pp. and 3 unnum.

William Betagh was Captain of Marines on the Clipperton-Shelvocke expedition **[527]** and assigned to Shelvocke's "Speedwell." Betagh's book is a scathing attack on Shelvocke's leadership and challenges the veracity of his captain's account published two years earlier. On 5 June 1719, the "Speedwell" had met a Portuguese merchantman near Cabo Frio going from Rio de Janeiro to Pernambuco. The ship was loaded not only with "plantins, bananas, lemons, oranges, pomegranates, etc." but "above a dozen pieces of silk, several of which were flower'd with gold and silver, worth, at least, three pound a yard, by retale; several dozen of China plates and basins, a small Japan cabinet" and "a purse of 300 moydors." Shelvocke claimed that he sent a boarding party and some money to purchase supplies from the Portuguese. Later he discovered that his men had plundered the ship and kept the money—information Shelvocke had given to the captain of the Portuguese man-of-war which had stopped at Santa Catarina on 3 August 1719 on its way to Macau. Betagh claimed that the incident was one of piracy and the Shelvocke himself was involved. Both Selvocke and Betagh criticized the behavior of a Simon Hatley, which, Betagh wrote, "was so odious to the Portuguese inhabitants." The burning down of a settler's house was criticized by Betagh as "a brutish return to the people, who out of fear or complaisance had quitted their house, for our coopers and sail-makers to work in, and likewise served us for a guard house." Betagh also charged that Shelvocke had exaggerated his purchases at Santa Catarina and pocketed the money for himself. Shelvocke, he said, bought only four, not twenty-one, head of black cattle and five or six, not one hundred and fifty, bushels of cassava.

[530] George Anson. *A Voyage Round the World in the Years MDCCXL, I, II, III, IV.* London: John and Paul Knapton, 1748. 417 pp.
[There have been many other editions, one of the most recent being that edited by Glyndwr Williams and published by Oxford University Press in 1974.]

Since England was at war with Spain, Anson's voyage combined raids on Spanish possessions as well as exploration. His squadron of six ships, needing a port for the recovery of his sick and fresh supplies, anchored on 20 December 1740 at Santa Catarina, "celebrated by former Navigators for its healthiness and its provisions, and for the freedom, indulgence, and friendly assistance there given to the ships of all European Nations, in amity with the Crown of Portugal." But unknown to Anson, there had been a change in Portuguese policy in southern Brazil. In the days when Santa Catarina was visited by Frézier and Shelvocke, it had been "a retreat to vagabonds and outlaws, who fled thither from all parts of Brazil" and who "were extremely hospitable and friendly to such foreign ships as came amongst them." But "their former ragged bare legged captain" had been replaced by Dom José da Silva Pais who brought new laws and government and who placed "centinels at all the avenues, to prevent the people from selling us any refreshments, except at such exorbitant rates as we could not afford to give." The author charged Silva Pais with being involved in smuggling in the La Plata region and having "treacherously" given the Spaniards "an account of our arrival, and of the strength of our squadron." The author describes the harbor and its defenses, a battery and three other forts being under construction. "Fruits and vegetables of all climates thrive here, almost without culture, and are to be procured in great plenty; so that here is no want of pine-apples, peaches, grapes, oranges, lemons, citrons, melons, apricots, nor plantains." There was also an abundance of onions, potatoes, fresh water and good fish. On the other hand, the leader of the expedition found Santa Catarina "close and humid," bothered by mosquitoes by day and sandflies by night. The author gives a short sketch of the history of Brazil, with an interesting second-hand account of the recent gold and diamond discoveries with comments about slaves and the Portuguese Crown's efforts to control the Paulistas. Despite Anson's complaints, the expedition was supplied with fresh meat and allowed to get the water, wood, and naval supplies it needed. After a little less than a month at Santa Catarina, the squadron weighed anchor on 18 January 1741.

See also **[531]** and **[532]**.

[531] Leo Heaps. *Log of the Centurion. Based on the Original Papers of Captain Philip Saumarez on Board HMS Centurion, Lord Anson's Flagship during His Circumnavigation, 1740–44.* London: Hart-Davis, Mac Gibbon, 1973. 264 pp.

Philip Saumarez (1710–1747) was stationed on Anson's flagship and kept the Centurion's logs for the voyage. Third lieutenant when the voyage began, Saumarez was promoted to Captain and was Anson's second-in-command. The editor claims that Saumarez's log served as the basis for the popular account of the expedition published in 1748 **[530]**. The English anchored off the island of Santa Catarina in December of 1740. "There is a regular fortification laying on the north and likewise on the south side, but none of them seem calculated for resisting ships of war and probably are more designed to prevent privateers from annoying them and to preserve an appearance among the native Indians with whom they are generally at war." Formerly Santa Catarina had "been the rendezvous of fugitives and outlaws who just acknowledge the subjection to the Crown of Portugal, but in all other respects are quite licentious and have only an obscure person residing amongst them as their captain, commonly sent by the governor of Logons [Lagoa], a small place to the southward of this island. At present they are modelling it after the same plan that the rest of the principal ports on the coasts are governed by, having for their governors when we were there, a general officer who is likewise an engineer

and kept them under severe injunctions." Saumarez found the water to be "excellent and preserved beyond what I ever observed." He recorded the fact that "the woods abound with several medicinal and aromatic plants. One might imagine oneself in a druggist's shop." The island was beginning to develop. "At the southern entrance of the straits is a small town on the island side called La Villa de St. Katherina consisting of nearly 40 houses which is as yet in its infancy being lately begun." The region has much in its favor. Cattle, the officer reported, "are very plentiful thereabouts." He further observed that "the soil on this island is truly luxuriant and every way flatters the indolence of the inhabitants. There are fruits of most sorts with many vegetables growing spontaneously." On 18 January 1741, the expedition departed from Santa Catarina and continued southward toward Cape Horn.
See also **[532]**.

[532] John Bulkeley and John Cummins. *A Voyage to the South Seas, In the Years 1740–1741. Containing a Faithful Narrative of the Loss of His Majesty's Ship the Wager.* London: Jacob Robinson, 1743.
[A second edition with additions was published in London and Philadelphia: James Chattin, 1757. xxxii, 306 pp. There is also a good edition with an introduction by Arthur D. Howden Smith entitled *A Voyage to the South Seas in His Majesty's Ship the Wager in the Years 1740–1741.* New York: Robert M. McBride, 1927. xxxi, 212 pp.]

John Bulkeley and John Cummins were respectively gunner and carpenter on the supply ship *Wager,* which was part of Anson's expedition **[530]** of 1740–1741. They left England on 18 September 1740. On 19 December they reached the Island of Santa Catarina, where "the People were generally imploy'd in over-hauling the rigging, and getting aboard Water." On 17 January 1741, they set sail again. But on 14 May after passing around the tip of South America, the *Wager* "struck abaft on a sunken Rock" and "a short time after, she struck, bilged, and grounded between two small Islands." After nine months of suffering and more than a thousand leagues of travel they reached the northern banks of the Rio de la Plata, two days journey from Montevideo. They travelled on to Rio Grande do Sul. There "the Commandant, the Officers, and People of the Place, receiv'd us in a most tender and friendly Manner. They instantly sent on Board to the People four Quarters of Beef, and two Bags of Farine Bread. We were conducted to the Surgeon's House, the handsomest Habitation in the Place; where we were most hospitably entertain'd." The authors wrote of the "wonderful Change in our Diet; we live on the best the Country can produce, and have Plenty of every Thing." The same was not true for the soldiers in the Portuguese garrison who had "twenty Months Arrears due to them." On 2 February 1741, there were "Great Murmurings among the Soldiers; they detain'd the Brigadier from going back as he intended this Morning, till he promis'd to dispatch the Money, Cloaths, and Provisions, and to see their Grievances adjusted." Bulkeley and Cummins give a lengthy description of the soldiers' grievances and the crown officials' reactions. On 12 April the authors arrived in Rio de Janeiro where the governor provided them with "a convenient House, with Firing, and eight Vintins a Man per Day Subsistence-Money." Less than a month later, on 7 May, they "anchor'd before the city of Bahia." However, the Viceroy [the Count of Galveias] refused them provisions saying that "if he gave us any, it must be out of his own Pocket, therefore he would not supply us." This elicited the response that there never "was a worse representative of royalty upon the Face of the Earth, than this Vice-roy." They told the viceroy that "we had better been Prisoners to the King of Spain, who would allow us Bread and Water, than in a Friend's Country to be starv'd." During their stay in the Brazilian capital, Bulkeley and Cummins were mostly impressed with Bahia's whales: "Provisions here of all kinds are excessive dear, especially Fish, this we impute to the great Number of Whales that come into this Bay, even where the Ships lie at Anchor; the Whale Boats go off and kill sometimes seven or eight Whales in a Day. The Flesh of which is cut up in small Pieces, then brought to the Market Place, and sold at the rate of a Vintin per Pound; it looks very much like coarse Beef, but inferior to it in Taste. The Whales here are not at all equal in Size to the Whales in Greenland, being not larger than the Grampus." After spending four months in Salvador, "without any relief from the Governor or the Inhabitants, who behaved to us as if they were under a Combination to starve us," Bulkeley and Cummins set sail for Lisbon, 11 September 1741, "in Company with one of the King of Portugal's Ships of War, and two East-India Ships." After experiencing several bad storms and being separated from the rest of the fleet, the authors arrived in Lisbon on 28 November.

[533] Antoine Joseph Pernety. *The History of a Voyage to the Malouine (or Falkland) Islands, Made in 1763 and 1764, Under the Command of M. de Bougainville.* London: T. Jeffreys, 1771. xvii, 294 pp.
[This is a translation of *Histoire d'un voyage aux Isles Malouines, fait en 1763 & 1764.* Paris, 1770.]

Pernety and Bougainville visited the island of Santa Catarina in 1763 and devoted a chapter to their impressions. There is also a general chapter on Brazil. Included is a map of the island of Santa Catarina.

[534] John Francis Galaup de la Pérouse. *The Voyage of La Pérouse Round the World, in the Years 1785, 1786, 1787, and 1788.* Arranged by M. L. A. Milet Mureau. 2 vols. London: John Stockdale, 1798. clxxx, 290 pp.; viii, 442 pp. Translation of *Voyage de La Pérouse autour du monde, publié conformément au décret du 22 avril 1791 et rédigé par M. L. A. Milet-Mureau.* Paris: Imprimerie de la République an V [1797].

In 1785, La Pérouse, commanding two frigates, left France to begin a voyage of discovery and exploration in the Pacific Ocean. However, in 1788, after accomplishing much of his mission, La Pérouse and his expedition were lost. Fortunately, shortly before his death, La Pérouse sent many of his records by land to France. The result is this account. The French explorer visited the island of Santa Catarina, casting anchor on 6 November 1785. Chapter II (pp. 27–33) describes the island including "Nossa Senhora del Desterro, the capital of this commandery, where the governor resides. It contains, at most, 3000 inhabitants, and about 400 houses; and wears a very agreeable appearance." It was part of the government of Rio Grande which "extends from north to south 60 leagues, from the river St. Francis to Rio-Grande. Its population amounts to 20,000; but I have seen so great a number of children in some families, that I think it will soon be more considerable. The soil is extremely fertile, and produces, almost spontaneously, all sorts of fruits, vegetables and grain." But, La Pérouse observed, "not withstanding these advantages, the country is very poor, and absolutely destitute of manufactures; insomuch, that the peasants are almost naked, or covered with rags." The expedition was given help by the governor of the island, Dom Francisco de Barros. This "brigadier general of the infantry," according to La Pérouse, "spoke French with perfect ease, and his comprehensive knowledge inspired us with the fullest confidence." The French explorer felt that the populace of the island "were good, obliging, and of gentle manners; but they are very superstitious, and jealous of their wives, who never appear in public." Volume I includes a map of the world showing the route of La Pérouse. Opposite page 27 is an interesting view of the island of St. Catarina with a number of the inhabitants in the foreground.

[535] James George Semple Lisle. *The Life of Major J. G. Semple Lisle: Containing a Faithful Narrative of His Alternate Vicissitudes of Splendor and Misfortune.* London: W. Stewart, 1799. xxii, 382 pp.
[Borba de Moraes **[20]**, I, 422–423 cites a second edition of 1800.]

After being convicted of swindling, Major Semple Lisle spent two years as a prisoner at Newgate, after which he was sent to Australia aboard the *Lady Shore*. On the voyage to Rio de Janeiro, the crew mutinied and changed course for the Rio de la Plata. Semple Lisle, John Black **[536]**, one of the ship's officers, and others were allowed a boat and set adrift near Rio Grande do Sul. They arrived at São Pedro in the latter part of August of 1797. The description of Rio Grande do Sul at the end of the eighteenth century is one of the few in English: "The soil is fertile, producing all things in the greatest abundance, with which the inhabitants are well supplied; in fact, the luxury of the first class of the people is excessive, and such as one would scarcely expect in a place almost shut out from the rest of the world. The town of Port St. Pedro is situated about four leagues from the mouth of the river, from which the province takes its name; it is mostly of wood, ill-built, and straggling, with very few good houses; nor did I see above two or three that consisted of more than one floor. The Governor's house is small, but convenient and laid out entirely on a military plan. It consists of a suite of apartments, all on the ground floor. There is a handsome cathedral, with very suitable establishments about it; and I should suppose that here, as well as everywhere, the clergy are well taken care of." The author was impressed by the inhabitants of Rio Grande do Sul: "The poeple, unlike those of the mother country, are remarkably clean, and dress in a splendid manner; their linen, which seems with them a favourite article of dress, is exceedingly fine, and is always so clean that it really prepossesses a stranger in their favour; not withstanding I have ever carried cleanliness to a sinical nicety, I made but a second-rate figure at Port St. Pedro; for such is the effect of the sun, and the pure water, that their linen is white beyond all imagination." Furthermore, "the hospitality of the Rio-grandians far exceeds all I ever saw in any other part of the world." The major was also favorably impressed by the uniforms of the militia. "Besides the regular forces, the whole males are enrolled in the militia, and form, if not perhaps the best disciplined, by far the best dressed corps in the world; their waistcoats and breeches are generally silk, as are the linings of their coats; these, with the excessive whiteness and cleanness of their linen, render their appearance truly elegant." After about six weeks in Rio Grande do Sul, the author received permission to proceed to Rio de Janeiro. He began his journey by land. However, after arriving at the island of Santa Catarina (where he spent three weeks and "was treated with the most polite attention by the Governor and principal inhabitants of the island") he decided to complete his trip to Rio de Janeiro by sea. Semple Lisle was also well received at the viceregal capital. In general, he was favorably impressed with that part of Brazil: "The town is well built, busy, considerably large, and surrounded by gentelmen's seats and gardens. The palace [of the viceroy] is large, commodious, and magnificently furnished; the streets are remarkable well paved, but never lighted; the houses are generally good, but have, for the most part, lattice windows; and there are a prodigious number of rich churches. The vast influx of trade renders some of the inhabitants extremely opulent; and an air of plenty appears throughout the whole. The amusements are chiefly confined to the opera, for which they have a small theatre; but private societies are very engaging. The people are not, however, so hospitable as in some other places, particularly Rio Grande [do Sul]; but they are not morose, and treat their negroes remarkably well, many of whom at an early age are enabled to purchase their freedom." He felt that "the women here are by no means patterns of chastity; and those of the class of courtezans are remarkably extravagant in the prices they demand for their favors." The author spoke highly of Rio de Janeiro's soldiers: "The military establishment of the town of Rio de Janeiro consists of two squadrons of very fine dragoons, which serve as a guard to the Viceroy, two regiments of regulars, and a battalion of artillery, who, though far better in appearance than those in Portugal, are not to be compared to the militia. These consist, besides whites, of a black and a mulatto regiment; and the last, in appearance, exceeds any thing I have seen. At present, however, they are holiday soldiers, and almost without discipline, but a hard campaign or two would, in all probability, make them good troops. It must be remarked, that the mulatto militia are all men of some property, and dress at their own expence; they wear light blue, with red facings, and gay spangle silver lace, which gives them a remarkable showy look." Semple Lisle pointed out that "the reason why the regiments of colour are so much more splendid than the whites is owing to this circumstance: the whites are a promiscuous assemblage of *all* the males, poor and rich, whereas the others consist only of such as are rich enough to have been able to purchase their own freedom; besides, when once free, they, through superior industry, acquire independence much quicker than the others." From Rio de Janeiro, Semple Lisle sailed to Salvador to obtain passage to Lisbon. The major was impressed by Bahia's slaves: "Everywhere as I walked through the streets the strong and lusty appearance of the negroes forcibly struck me. I learnt that they came from a part of Africa different from those usually imported; and that their treatment far exceeded what they received at Rio de Janeiro." As for the remainder of that region's inhabitants, the major observed: "The inhabitants of Bahia are exceedingly hospitable, remarkably gay, and passionately addicted to gambling; they dress with more taste and richness than in any town I had seen; their linen is, as I have observed of Rio Grande, peculiarly fine and white. They live in a most sociable and pleasant manner, but whenever they meet, cards are introduced as a matter indispensable. Some very sumptuous dinners are given, and at every table the greatest variety of sweetmeats are served; this is the more easily done, as there sugar is equally cheap and good, and their fruits not less abundant than delicious."

[536] John Black. *An Authentic Narrative of the Mutiny on Board the Ship Lady Shore with Particulars of a Journey through Part of Brazil.* Ipswich: G. G. and J. Robinsons, 1798. viii, 64 pp.
[There is also a London edition of 1798.]

The *Lady Shore* was one of the ships taking English convicts to Australia. Black visited Rio de Janeiro and provides a short description of the Brazilian capital. See also Semple Lisle **[535]**.

[537] Adam J. von Krusenstern. *Voyage Round the World, in the Years 1803, 1804, 1805, & 1806, by Order of His Imperial Majesty Alexander the First, on Board the Ships Nadeshda and Neva.* 2 v. London: John Murray, 1813. xxxii, 314 pp.; 404 pp.

Krusenstern, captain of the *Nadesha*, was the leader of the Russian naval expedition organized to explore the northern Pacific. The Russians stopped at the island of Santa Catarina on 21 December 1803. Because of a broken mast on the *Neva*, the expedition did not leave Brazil until early February of 1804. Krusenstern was impressed by the hospitality provided the visitors by the Portuguese governor, Joaquim Xavier Curado. The author describes the town of Nuestra Senhora del Desterro "which is very pleasantly situated, consists of about 100 ill-constructed houses, and is inhabited by 2000–3000 poor Portuguese and negro slaves. The Governor's house and the barracks are the only buildings distinguished, by their appearance, above the rest." Krusenstern adds that at this time, the townspeople were "building a church, which in many catholic countries is thought much more of than either hospitals or any other useful building. I was not a little surprised at seeing one evening about ten o'clock, as I was going on board, several negro slaves of both sexes carrying stones for this purpose; but my astonishment diminished in some degree, when I considered that the reward of this religious zeal belonged less to them than to their masters." Krusenstern felt that Santa Catarina's defenses were in poor condition. Furthermore, "the garrison consists of about 500 men, who, notwithstanding the quantity of valuable diamonds and the 20 million of crusades [*cruzados*] which are annually sent from the Brazils to Lisbon, have for several years received no pay, a striking proof of the imbecility of the government. In order, however, to secure the garrison against starvation, every soldier receives for his daily maintenance twenty reis. . . . They are, however, very well clothed, owing probably to the care of the Governor and the commander of the regiment; the government, to judge from the manner in which it remits their pay, not

having the least share in it." Krusenstern pointed out that "the coast only is inhabited, and the people are exposed to the attacks of the natives, as happened even during our stay there. These attacks are not however attended with any bloody consequences; the natives are content to plunder, and carry off particularly the cattle belonging to the Portuguese." The author concludes, "Ships going round Cape Horn, or destined for the whale fishery upon this coast, cannot desire a better harbour than St. Catherine's to run into. It is infinitely preferable to Rio de Janeiro, where strangers, particularly if they arrive in merchant ships, are treated with the same insulting jealousy as in Japan."
See also **[538]** and **[539]**.

[538] Urey Lisiansky. *A Voyage Round the World in the Years 1803, 4, 5 & 6; Performed, by Order of His Imperial Majesty Alexander the First, Emperor of Russia, in the Ship Neva.* London: John Booth and Longman, Hurst, Rees, Orme, & Brown, 1814. xxi, 388 pp. maps, plates.
[A facsimile edition was published in 1968 by N. Israel/Amsterdam and Da Capo Press/New York.]

Part of the expedition that circumnavigated the world with Krusenstern **[537]**, Lisiansky and his ship *Neva* arrived in Santa Catarina at the end of December 1803 and departed in early February of 1804. Though initially suspicious of the Brazilians—he felt "that the Brazilians were very apt to make the common men drunk, and then buy of them clothes and other useful articles"—by the end of his stay he concluded that "the inhabitants of St. Catherine are civil and hospitable. La Pérouse **[534]** was right in saying that they are in general honest and disinterested, though there are individuals amongst them not quite deserving of that character." Lisiansky was particularly impressed with the help he received from the island's governor, Don Francisco Shever de Courado [Joaquim Xavier Curado]. Fresh provisions of every kind were available at moderate prices. The military force included 1,000 regulars and 3,000 militia. By the governor's account, Santa Catarina's population was 10,142 of which 4000 were Blacks—the condition of the latter being "less wretched than that of their brethren in the West Indies, or in any European colony I have yet visited." The Russian visitor was particularly taken with the African dances performed during Christmas holiday. The description of Santa Catarina is found on pages 30–41. There is a nice map in color of the harbor, 1804, facing page 40. This account was originally published in Russia in 1812 (2 v.).
See also **[539]**.

[539] Georg Heinrich von Langsdorff. *Voyages and Travels in Various Parts of the World During the Years 1803, 1804, 1805, 1806, and 1807.* Carlisle, Pennsylvania: George Philips, 1817. xvi, 617 pp.

Langsdorff, later to be Russia's consul to Brazil and eventually to lead a scientific expedition of his own **[741]**, had previously served as physician to Prince Christian de Waldeck. He joined the Russian scientific expedition under the leadership of Krusenstern **[537]**, which was planning to sail around the world. Late in 1803 it reached Brazil. Though many on the expedition wanted to visit Rio de Janeiro, fear of bureaucratic delays prompted Krusenstern to stop instead at the island of Santa Catarina "which had many superior recommendations as a place of refreshment." Langsdorff devoted chapter II (pages 42–77) to a description of his stay at Santa Catarina. "The principal place of the island, and the seat of the government, is the town of Nossa Senora do Desterro. It stands on the south-west side of the island, about ten sea-miles from the anchoring place . . . at the foot of a considerable hill, and contains between four and five hundred houses. The number of inhabitants in the island of Santa Catarina is reckoned at ten thousand, that of the whole government dependent upon the island at thirty-thousand. There are a great number of people among the inhabitants in easy circumstances, but few very rich. The houses are all built of stone, cemented with a kind of clayey earth: the streets are for the most part regular. Here are merchants, or rather traders, and mechanics, of every description; and great abundance of provisions of all kinds are daily brought to market for the country around. In the numerous shops are to be found almost all sorts of European merchandize that contribute to the support and convenience of life." Langsdorff found the inhabitants to be "pleasing, friendly, and prepossessing; great hospitality reigns among them, and they are very sociable with each other. They assemble together in the evening in little family parties, in which the Portuguese manners prevail entirely." He was impressed with the women of the island: "The females are not ugly. Among those of the higher classes we saw some who, even in Europe, might with justice have been pronounced handsome. They are in general of a middle stature, well made, with dark complexions, coarse dark hair and dark eyes full of fire; we saw, however, a few who were very fair. They received their guests with great courtesy, and are not restrained like the lovely sex in the mother-country, who are shut up the whole year through, and can only catch a sight of a stranger by looking through the key-hole or a crack in the door."

[540] David Porter. *Journal of a Cruise Made to the Pacific Ocean by Captain David Porter, in the United States Frigate Essex, in the Years 1812, 1813 and 1814.* 2nd edition. 2 vols. New York: Wiley & Halstead, 1822. vol. I: lxxvi, 246 pp. plates, map, table; vol. II. 256 pp. plates.
[The first edition, which is not as complete as the second, was published in Philadelphia in 1815 and entitled: *Journal of a Cruise Made to the Pacific Ocean by Captain David Porter in the United States Frigate 'Essex' in the years 1812, 1813, 1814. Containing Descriptions of the Cape de Verd Islands, Coasts of Brazil, Patagonia, Chili and Peru, and of the Gallapagos Islands; Also a Full Account of the Washington Groupe of Islands, the Manners, Customs, and Dress of the Inhabitants etc. etc.*]

Captain Porter's journal relates his wartime activities (War of 1812) against English shipping in the South Atlantic and South Pacific. The first two chapters of the first volume describe his encounters with Portuguese and English shipping to and from Brazil. There is also some interesting and useful information on his encounters with Portuguese coastal shipping in Brazil. He visited the island of Fernando de Noronha, "well fortified in every part, and its population consists of a few miserable, naked, exiled Portuguese, and as miserable a guard." He also anchored at Santa Catarina, the stopping off point for North Americans involved in the south Atlantic whaling industry, for reprovisioning. Porter speaks favorably of his visit to Brazil's southernmost captaincy: "The peasantry are well clad, and comfortable and cheerful in their appearance; the women are handsome and graceful in their manners; the men have the character of being extremely jealous of them, and I believe they have some reason to be so." The North American captain felt that the inhabitants of Santa Catarina "appear to be the most happy of those who live under the Portuguese government, probably because the more they are distant from it, the less they are subject to its impositions and oppressions."

[541] Otto von Kotzebue [and Adelbert von Chamisso]. *A Voyage of Discovery into the South Sea and Beering's Straits, for the purpose of Exploring a North-East Passage, Undertaken in the Years 1815–1818.* Trans. H. E. Lloyd. 3 vols. London: Longman, Hurst, Rees, Orme, and Brown, 1821.
[A facsimile edition was published in 1968 by N. Israel/Amsterdam and Da Capo Press/New York.]

This is an English translation of the three-volume Russian account published in St. Petersburg. The first two volumes were written by Kotzebue, commander of the expedition and captain of the *Rurick*. The third volume contains the account of Adelbert von Chamisso, the naturalist of the voyage. The expedition, financed by the Russian chancellor, Count Romanov, visited the island of Santa Catarina in December of 1815. Chamisso gave the more extensive account: "The government of the island of St. Catharine, contains, as we were informed, about 30,000 inhabitants; among whom, two blacks may be reckoned to one white. We found the slave-trade still carried on here; and this government alone requires, yearly, from five to seven ships full of negroes, reckoning each at a hundred, to supply the place of those who die on the plantations." Chamisso also observed that "the number of slaves is, in proportion, smaller on the more populous islands than the continent. Their food is meat and cassava. Those living in the houses of their masters, and such as are kept in poorer families, grow up more like human beings, than those who are compelled to work like mere machines. We were, however, never witnesses of any cruel treatment of them." The author reported that the town of Nossa Senhor de Destero "contains a convent for men; and of the monks not one dedicates his idle hours to any science. Dealers in butterflies are here called naturalists." Chamisso further noted that "the commerce of this colony is inconsiderable. Its harbour is only visited by American ships, to take in provisions when on their way to double Cape Horn, or go on the southern whale-fishery. Its productions are sugar, rum, rice, and coffee. Tobacco, mace, cassava (Jatropha manihot) fruite, &c. only for home consumption: they also grow corn, but with little success." The author found that "cheerfulness, cleanliness, and hospitality prevail among a people, whose means are but scanty. We were invited into the poorest huts, where the people entertained us with fruits, and offered us meat and cassava, but refused to accept any payment in return." Kotzebue, initially miffed by the reception he received from the governor Luis Maurício da Silveira—"He received me coolly, and did not seem disposed to comply with the orders from Rio de Janeiro, to afford every possible assistance to the *Rurick*"—had mixed impressions of the island: "The country about the shore was inhabited by the soldiers of the militia, who only render their services in times of danger; at other seasons they employ themselves on their rice and sugar plantations. Their houses are at some distance from each other, and their principal riches consist in the number of their negro slaves, who, like members of the family, work with their masters, and enjoy with him all that his house affords. The negroes in the town, on the contrary, are very unhappy; they are used for the most laborious works, like beasts of burthen; and are particularly employed to beat the rice out of the husks, for which such heavy clubs are given them, that it is with the greatest difficulty that they are able to wield them: they are driven to their work with a whip when their strength fails them; and, besides this, they have very miserable food. By this inhuman treatment, these unfortunate people are degraded to the level of brutes: they seem incapable of reflection or feeling; the sight is dreadful, and inspires commiseration. The most opprobrious term of abuse, among the Portuguese, is negro! The slaves of the soldiers are quite different men; they enjoy their existence as such, and we had every reason to be satisfied with our neighbors; they behaved very friendly to us, and practised towards us all the virtues of hospitality. The soldiers consider themselves very poor, because it is several years since they have received their pay; it is true they have no money, but they are never in want of the necessaries of life which the island produces; and, therefore, I consider them as very rich and fortunate people."

[542] *An Account, Historical, Political, and Statistical, of the United Provinces of Rio de la Plata: with an Appendix, Concerning the Usurpation of Monte Video by the Portuguese and Brasilian Governments.* Translated from the Spanish. London: R. Ackermann, 1825. x, 345 pp.

As the title indicates, it is the appendix (pp. 303–345) which is chiefly of interest to the Brazilianist. It contains a "Letter concerning the occupation of Monte Video, by the Portuguese and Brazilian Governments." An asterisk indicates that the "letter was addressed to a respectable person in London by another residing in the same capital." The correspondence traces some of the events that occurred after 1816 and accuses the Luso-Brazilians of having "violently pillaged the country, and, under the authority of the General, of more than four million head of vicunnas, which have been sent to the Brazilian territory, as is proved by the estimates made at the collecting houses in the passes of the frontiers." The appendix also charges "that, following the plan of peopling the country with Brazilians, whose numbers now exceed 1500, the General took away the lands from the natives, and assigned them to others, without giving the smallest compensation." In addition, "the province is not only not indebted for any public work to the invaders, but that, on the contrary, these very persons have ruined almost all the public works which it possessed prior to their entrance." In short, "in every point of view, is Monte Video a decaying colony, oppressed with poverty." There is a good map of the "Rios de la Plata, Parana, Uruguay, y Grande y los terrenos adjacentes," dated 1820. The first part of the *Account* contains a letter by Ignácio Benito Nuñez, dated 15 June 1824, entitled "A Political Review of the Causes of the Revolution in the United Provinces of Rio de la Plata, of its character and progress, and of the social organization with which it has terminated" (pp. 2–63). It is followed by "Documents referred to in the foregoing letter" (pp. 67–135).

B. São Paulo [Nos. 543–546]

Though a number of articles have been written in English on the Paulistas and the *bandeirantes* (many of the latter also natives of São Paulo), little has been written on São Paulo itself during the colonial period. Charles Boxer **[277]** has some short descriptions of sixteenth and seventeenth century as well as eighteenth-century **[548]** São Paulo. The most detailed account is Elizabeth Kuznesof's important doctoral dissertation on São Paulo's household composition and economy during the years 1765 to 1836 **[543]**. Richard Morse **[544]** briefly describes São Paulo's early urban history. Emílio Willems **[545]** studies society in some of the agricultural and cattle-raising regions of the captaincy. Antônio Cândido's research on the family in colonial Brazil **[705]** is based heavily on the São Paulo experience. For the *bandeirantes* themselves, see Section VIII [Nos. 254–258].

[543] Elizabeth Anne Kuznesof. "Household Composition and Economy in an Urbanizing Community: São Paulo 1765 to 1836," (Ph.D. Dissertation: University of California, Berkeley, 1976). 466 pp.

Explores the demographic responses to the changes São Paulo underwent from "domestic production for subsistence to production for market exchange" between 1765 and 1836. Whereas the nuclear family was the typical group in 1765, larger, more complex households accompanied the development of a mercantile economy. A trend arose to more and earlier marriages, more children per head of household and larger size households. Composite households, particularly female-headed households, increased markedly during this period.
DAI 38/03-A (p. 1592)

[544] Richard McGee Morse. "São Paulo City under the Empire (1822–1889)," (Ph.D. Dissertation: Columbia University, 1952). 367 pp.

Part of the first chapter—"Colonialism and New Stimulants (1820–1830)"—deals with the late colonial period. Colonial São Paulo is described. The author emphasizes "its isolation from the sea by the coastal range; its command of travel routes to the hinterland; the modest, subsistence economy of the environs; patriarchal class structure and customs; the socially integrating function of church ceremony; folkways of agrarian provincialism." Morse then analyzes São Paulo's role in Brazilian independence.
DAI 12/05 (pp. 738–739)

[545] Emílio Willems. "Social Differentiation in Colonial Brazil," *Comparative Studies in Society and History* 12:1 (January 1970), pp. 31–49.

A study, based on 1822–1824 census reports of ten localities specializing in agriculture and cattle raising within the captaincy of São Paulo, which challenges the stereotyped picture of a two-class society—one wealthy and powerful, the other, poor and powerless. An analysis of the population of all ten localities revealed a highly differentiated society and a rural middle class with some degree of social mobility. The author concludes that "the colonial society of southern Brazil was definitely not a caste society." Based on archival and printed materials. 6 tables; 3 footnotes plus numerous other references within the text to the appended bibliography.

1. Contemporary Narratives, 1700–1822 [No. 546]

Relatively few travellers visited São Paulo during the colonial period. There are, however, two important early nineteenth-century descriptions in English: One by John Mawe **[563]**, who visited São Paulo in 1808; the other by Spix and Martius **[546]**, who devoted a chapter to São Paulo, which they visited in the early part of their expedition of 1817–1820.

[546] Johann Baptist von Spix and Karl Friedrich Philipp von Martius. *Travels in Brazil in the Years 1817–1820 Undertaken by Command of His Majesty the King of Bavaria.* Trans. H. E. Lloyd. 2 v. London: Longman, Hurst, Rees, Orme, Brown, and Green, 1824. xix, 327 pp.; viii, 298 pp.

Unfortunately, this is only a partial translation of the three-volume account of their scientific expedition through Brazil, 1817–1820, *Reise in Brasilien*. The German version is more than twice as long as this translation. These two volumes discuss the voyage of Spix and Martius to America, their stay in Rio de Janeiro and excursions into the capital's environs, their journey from Rio de Janeiro to the city of São Paulo, treks to the Iron foundry at Ipanema and the town of Vila Rica and its environs, and encounters with the Coroado Indians. "The population of the city of S. Paulo, according to the latest accounts, including the dependent parishes, amounts to above 30,000 souls, of which the half are whites, or such as are called so, and the other blacks, or people of colour." Spix and Martius found that "the women of S. Paulo have the same simplicity as the men. The tone of society is jovial and unaffected, animated by ready and cheerful pleasantry. They have been unjustly accused of giddiness. If the spirit of conversation is strongly contrasted with the refined manners of their European relatives, among whom a jealous etiquette prohibits the unrestrained expression of feeling; their artless liveliness does not excite surprise, in a province where a free and simple mode of thinking has been retained, more than in any other part of Brazil." According to the authors, the women of São Paulo were "reckoned to be the handsomest women of Brazil." Spix and Martius observed that "convenience and cleaniness are more attended to than elegance and splendour in their household arrangements; and instead of the light North American furniture and French looking-glasses, which are seen in the other provinces, we found in the parlours (sala) only a row of heavy chairs, venerable for their antiquity, and a small glass, which, from its Nürenberg frame, the German recognizes for a countryman." In Minas Gerais, the two scientists encountered Coroado Indians **[379]**: "When we reached the huts, no female was to be seen, except a few old women; the men lay silent, motionless, and with their backs turned to us, in their hammocks. Our military guide went first into their habitations, saluted the savages, and gave them to understand, as well as his knowledge of their language would permit, that we had come from a very distant country to visit them, and to employ ourselves in collecting birds, butterflies and plants. This declaration seemed to make but little impression upon them, they swung, as before, silent in their hammocks, and looked at us only by stealth. Even good words and presents had no effect upon them."

C. Minas Gerais, Goiás and Mato Grosso [Nos. 547–563]

Manoel Cardozo's excellent study on mining in colonial Brazil **[547]** has much material on Minas Gerais. Also useful is Charles R. Boxer's *The Golden Age of Brazil* **[548]** which contains much information on Minas Gerais, Goiás and Mato Grosso for the years 1695–1750. Hans Mann **[549]** provides a photographic essay on Minas Gerais, many of the photographs and much of the text focusing on the colonial period. Sylvio de Vasconcellos **[550]** contributes a survey of that captaincy's cultural past. An excellent description of the excitement and chaos in Minas Gerais after the discovery of gold was announced is found in Cardozo **[551]**. W. P. Morrell **[552]** and Carlos Prieto **[553]** also contain useful material. Manoel Cardozo **[282]** discusses problems regarding the collection of the royal fifth. The same author **[554]** provides a good description of the civil war that broke out in the mining area between the Paulistas and the new arrivals. Robert Allan White **[555]** gives a detailed account of the inauguration of the capitation tax in Minas Gerais in 1735. Donald Ramos **[556]** sums up the first three decades of Ouro Preto's history, using a social history approach. Lawrence Nielson **[557]** discusses Sabará's society at the end of the eighteenth century. Ramos **[558]** also studies marriage and the family in Ouro Preto—this time in the late eighteenth and early nineteenth centuries. He **[559]** also studies the town's demographic character. Basílio de Magalhães **[560]** discusses the role of mule trains in the economic life of Minas Gerais. A brief description of diamond mining is found in Aires da Matta Machado Filho **[561]**. The art and architecture of Minas Gerais are reviewed in Section XXI, B, 2, d [Nos. 773–784].

[547] Manoel [da Silveira Soares] Cardozo. "A History of Mining in Colonial Brazil, 1500–1750," (Ph.D. Dissertation: Stanford University, 1939).

This is the best study on mining in colonial Brazil. Based on Portuguese archival materials, especially those in the Arquivo Histórico Ultramarino, Lisbon. The author describes the many sixteenth-century searches for "Eldorado," with a special emphasis on the efforts of Dom Francisco and Luis de Sousa, 1591–1613. Cardozo examines activity emanating from São Paulo and Bahia, 1613–1623, and Rio de Janeiro under Salvador Correia de Sá, 1637–1648. Other seventeenth-century quests for gold, silver and emeralds, especially those of Fernão Dias Pais and Dom Rodrigo de Castel-Blanco during the third-quarter of the century are also studied. The remaining half of Cardozo's dissertation focuses on the discovery of gold in Minas Gerais and its consequences. He provides an excellent social, economic, administrative history of that captaincy and concludes with a chapter on "The Age of Gold."

[548] Charles R. Boxer. *The Golden Age of Brazil, 1695–1750. Growing Pains of a Colonial Society*. Berkeley and Los Angeles: University of California Press, 1962. xiii, 443 pp.

This important study provides both a region-by-region analysis as well as an excellent overview of Portuguese America during its famous gold and diamond boom and assesses Brazil's role in Portugal's South Atlantic Empire. The author discusses the tensions caused by the various gold and diamond rushes, the expansion of slavery and the slave trade, the disputes between Jesuits and colonists and between merchants and planters, and international rivalries. Boxer concludes with a description of "Portuguese America in Mid-Century," based extensively on archival and, especially, printed primary sources. There are excellent maps and illustrations. The bibliographical references are included in the notes (pp. 375–418). There is a useful annotated bibliography (pp. 419–433).

[549] Hans Mann. *Minas Gerais.* Text in Portuguese and English by Silvio Castro. Rio de Janeiro: Livraria Kosmos Editora, 1961. 142 pp.

Photographic essay on Minas Gerais, whose area of 224,650 square miles makes it "larger than any European country except Russia." The future captaincy was largely neglected during the sixteenth and part of the seventeenth century until gold was discovered in the 1690s. The ensuing gold rush changed the region's landscape: "The conquest went forward particularly rapidly from 1699 to 1711. Temporary encampments struck root; towns were built, life developed." Though the gold and, later, diamond cycles lasted through much of the eighteenth century, other products—like cattle, sugar, maize, rice, beans, coffee and iron—grew in importance. In the nineteenth century stock and crop raising replaced to a great extent gold and diamonds. In the twentieth century, the iron and steel industry became important. More than half of the 159 photographs—all of which are captioned in both Portuguese and English—deal with the colonial period. There is an excellent series of photos on Ouro Preto, "the city of the gold cycle," including shots of such churches as those of Carmo, São Francisco de Paula, São José, and São Francisco de Assis, the former residence of the governors, the old *camara* or municipal council building, and the Casa dos Contos. Diamantina (formerly Tijuco), "the largest producer of diamonds in Brazil," and some of its artistic treasurers are also studied, as is Congonhas do Campo with its twelve prophets carved by Aleijadinho.

[550] Sylvio de Vasconcellos. "The Cultural Miracle of Minas Gerais," *Américas* 26:2 (February 1974), pp. 2–9.

An overview of the colonial past of Minas Gerais with a strong emphasis on its architecture, sculpture, painting, literature and music. The author devotes much attention to the work of Antônio Francisco Lisboa (Aleijadinho) and discusses the artistic style of the painter Manuel da Costa Ataíde. The interpretation of Minas Gerais' colonial heritage, however, is marred by many unsubstantiated and, at times, misleading generalizations, particularly when Minas Gerais is compared with coastal Brazil, the isolation of the mining region is described, and the Portuguese national character and that of Minas Gerais are discussed. 7 plates; 1 map. No notes.

[551] Manoel Cardozo. "The Brazilian Gold Rush," *The Americas* 3:2 (October 1946), pp. 137–160.

Excellent description of the excitement and chaos which resulted in Brazil and Portugal from the discovery of Gold in Minas Gerais. The author skillfully lets both the Brazilian participants and the Portuguese bureaucrats discuss in their own words their reactions to such varied problems as inflation, depopulation, conspicuous consumption, the presence of foreigners, lawlessness and immorality, and shortages of labor and food. Based almost entirely on unpublished archival materials. 136 notes.

[552] W. P. Morrell. *The Gold Rushes.* 2nd ed. (1st ed., 1940). London: Adam & Charles Black, 1968. xi, 427 pp. plates, 8 maps.

Brazil is covered in chapter II (pp. 17–42). A useful summary, the value of which is sometimes lessened by careless generalizations and misplaced footnotes. Based almost entirely on printed secondary sources. 9 notes. map; bibliography. Superseded by Cardozo **[551]**.

[553] Carlos Prieto. *Mining in the New World.* New York: McGraw-Hill Book Company, 1973. xvii, 239 pp.
[This is a translation and adaptation of *La Mineria en el Nuevo Mundo* with additions by Marvin D. Bernstein and Carleton Sprague Smith.]

Chapter V, "The Special Case of Brazil" (pp. 39–57), provides a good synthesis of the history of colonial Brazil with an emphasis on the search for precious minerals and the mining for gold, diamonds and iron. Scattered throughout this survey of mining in Latin America are useful sections on Brazilian mining legislation, slavery, the economic effects of mining, art, architecture and music in Minas Gerais and the independence movements and mining in Portuguese America. Chapter V has 23 helpful notes. The book has a good index and bibliography, the latter on pp. 167–219. There is also a valuable "Chronological Table of Discovery and the Development of Mining in the New World," pp. 152–166.

[554] Manoel Cardozo. "The *Guerra dos Emboabas*, Civil War in Minas Gerais, 1708–1709," *The Hispanic American Historical Review* 22:3 (August 1942), pp. 470–492.

After describing the boom conditions resulting from the discovery of gold in Minas Gerais, the author presents a detailed description of the events and personalities involved in the several-months-long civil war between Paulistas and newcomers to the mining area. Based largely on archival (Arquivo Histórico Ultramarino, Lisbon) materials. 103 notes.

[555] Robert Allan White. "Fiscal Policy and Royal Sovereignty in Minas Gerais: The Capitation Tax of 1735," *The Americas*, 34:2 (October 1977), pp. 207–229.

In this detailed account of the inauguration of the capitation tax in Minas Gerais in 1735, White shows "how royal officials sought to manipulate public opinion and persuade the people to obey the king's will." The author points out that the collection of the *quinto* or royal fifth was one of the most difficult tasks which officials faced in the Brazilian mining regions in the eighteenth century. Smuggling and evasion of the tax were so widespread that the Crown's share did not keep up with increased gold production. In 1720 Crown efforts to collect the full *quinto* had resulted in a bloody rebellion. Though Dom Lourenço de Almeida, governor of Minas Gerais (1721–1732), and the principal citizens agreed on a minimum 52 arrobas a year tax and the establishment of local smelting houses, by 1733 the royal fifth was a misnomer, since collections were below one-fifteenth of total annual production. This was the setting for a concerted effort by Crown officials to find a better solution. Brazilian-born Alexandre de Gusmão (1695–1753), private secretary to João V, assembled a group of administrators and charged them "with increasing the revenues from the mines, strengthening royal authority, and seeking ways to provide a legal basis for Portugal's territorial claims." Three of the most important of these officials were André de Melo e Castro, fourth Count of Galveias (1668–1753), who served seventeen years in Brazil, first in Minas Gerais as governor (1732–1735) and later as viceroy (1735–1750); Gomes Freire de Andrada (1688–1761), the most important of these administrators, initially governor of Rio de Janeiro in 1733 and of Minas Gerais as well beginning in 1735; and Martinho de Mendonça de Pina e de Proença, who left for Brazil in 1733 "to advise the governors on matters of taxation as a special consultant," and who served as interim governor of Minas Gerais from May of 1736 to the end of December of 1737, when the Spanish attack on Colônia do Sacramento forced Gomes Freire to return to Rio de Janeiro. White gives a detailed description of how each of the three men—Melo e Castro unsuccessfully—attempted to put a halt to some of the most flagrant abuses of royal authority in the mining region and implement the capitation tax. He also attempts to explain why Melo e Castro failed and Gomes Freire succeeded. Based largely on archival and printed primary materials. 98 notes.

[556] Donald Ramos. "A Social History of Ouro Preto: Stresses of Dynamic Urbanization in Colonial Brazil, 1695–1726," (Ph.D. Dissertation: The University of Florida, 1972). 464 pp.

Examines the social history of Ouro Preto (formerly Vila Rica) during the first quarter-century after the big discovery of gold in Minas Gerais. Well situated for trade, Ouro Preto was a center of commerce as well as gold mining. Merchants, though rich, could usually only enter the elite class when they entered mining or farming. Middle sectors were of varied components, although many members were white and born in Portugal. The town council created the guilds for artisans who were important in the community. Ownership of shops was an avenue into the middle classes for women and nonwhites. Freedmen and slaves were at the bottom of the social ladder. *Quilombos* were frequently established by runaway slaves in the area around Ouro Preto. The militia, kinship relations and lay brotherhoods are investigated as well as the physical organization of the town. The story of the successful campaign by the Royal government to gain control of this urban community is also recounted. Based heavily on Brazilian archival materials, especially those from Minas Gerais.
DAI 34/06-A (pp. 3319–3320)

[557] Lawrence James Nielsen. "Of Gentry, Peasants, and Slaves: Rural Society in Sabará and its Hinterland, 1780–1930," (Ph.D. Dissertation: University of California, Davis, 1975). 320 pages.

Studies the landowners, peasants and slaves who made up the rural society of Sabará, a region in Minas Gerais, from 1780–1930. The landed gentry, which dominated society, was a fairly open class in which wealth, ownership of land, and control of labor determined membership. High status within the group was attained by those who could successfully mediate between local society and the broader Brazilian government. Until the 1870s the landed elite relied on slave labor. Most slaves were of local or national origin and their life was harsh. The

peasant class, spared a hard exploitive relationship with the landowners, began to be tied to the land by sharecropping and similar schemes when abolition gained momentum. The peasants, a mixed racial group, using magic, homeopathic medicine and fictive kinship ties to cope with the world, farmed family plots by "paleotechnic agricultural methods."
DAI 36/07-A (pp. 4703–4704)

[558] Donald Ramos. "Marriage and the Family in Colonial Vila Rica," *The Hispanic American Historical Review* 55:2 (May 1975), pp. 200–225.

Uses the censuses of 1804 and 1815 to determine the structure and size of housefuls and households in Minas Gerais, the age, occupation and sexual, racial and marital status of household heads, and the age of the mother at the birth of the eldest residing child, etc. The author concludes that the role of women was significant in numerical and social terms and that nuclear and matrifocal families were much more common than the "traditional patriarchal, extended family based on coresidential patterns." Based largely on archival materials and printed sources. 73 notes. 13 tables.

[559] Donald Ramos. "Vila Rica: Profile of a Colonial Urban Center," *The Americas* 35:4 (April 1979), pp. 495–526.

Ramos examines Vila Rica in the early nineteenth century, during a period "of stable depression." Earlier, in 1720, its "central location, its burgeoning business community, its resources of precious gold, and the unruliness of the miners led to its selection as capital of the mining district of Minas Gerais." But gold production dropped drastically in the last three or four decades of the eighteenth century. Vila Rica's population declined from 20,000 to 9,000 and "was supported by commerce, the political bureaucracy which had evolved to govern the mining district, and residual gold deposits." After analyzing family life and organization Ramos concludes that "far from only the patriarchal, extended family, Vila Rica portrays the entire range of family relationships from solitaries to nuclear families to multiple families. Surprising is the substantial number of nuclear families and especially those headed by women. Equally surprising is the relatively small number of multiple and extended family units. This suggests that if the pattern of a patriarchal extended family had ever prevailed during the eighteenth century, shifts in economic organization had led to its ceasing to function as a residential group. The society of Vila Rica in 1804 emerges from this study as one which, in terms of size and composition, is closer to that of present-day Brazil than that of the commonly held image of colonial society." Based almost entirely on archival and printed primary source materials. 29 tables. 32 notes.

[560] Basílio de Magalhães. "The Packtrains of Minas-Gerais," *Travel in Brazil* 2:4 (1942), pp. 1–7, 33.

Points out that until the middle of the nineteenth century, the packtrain provided the chief method of transporting goods between the urban centers on the coast and the settlements of the interior. Muleteers or *tropeiros* (the Portuguese term was probably derived "from the military organization of the first convoys") played an important role in carrying gold from Minas Gerais to Rio de Janeiro, especially in the first half of the eighteenth century. When gold and diamonds began to peter out, coffee became an important product. The packtrains brought sugar, sugar scrapings, rolls of tobacco, and, later, manufactured goods, especially those from England, to the interior and cheese, coffee and cotton to the coast. One popular route was the Caminho Novo and part of the Caminho Velho which connected the interior to the coastal town of Angra dos Reis. Packtrains from Rio de Janeiro to Diamantina took more than a month to reach their destination. The author quotes from accounts of such early nineteenth-century visitors to Brazil as Mawe **[563]**, Saint-Hilaire, Spix and Martius **[546]** and describes the packtrains, their owners and the personnel who worked them, the latter's diet, the mules, the large rawhide trunks placed on each side of the animal, and the *ranchos,* which served as shelters and rest places. A number of these *ranchos* evolved into towns. 7 photographs. No notes.

[561] Aires da Matta Machado Filho. "Diamond Mining," *Travel in Brazil* 1:1 (1941), pp. 10–12.

The author attempts to discover the identity of the first discoverer of diamonds in eighteenth-century Brazil. After discussing a number of candidates for the honor, Matta Machado Filho gives the credit to Bernardo da Fonseca Lobo. The author briefly describes the early history of Diamantina (Tijuco), quotes a description of Brazilian diamonds by Spix and Martius **[546]** in 1818 and discusses the principal methods of mining the gems. Matta Machado Filho points out that "the greater part of the diamonds found for a long time came from the region of the Rivers 'Jequitinhanha' and 'Pardo,' the two main water courses of the Diamantina District." No notes. 3 illus.

1. Contemporary Narratives, 1700–1822 [Nos. 562–563]

Charles R. Boxer **[562]** translates an anonymous pamphlet of 1764 containing a dialogue between a miner and a Portuguese lawyer regarding the role and treatment of the African in the mining region. John Mawe **[563]** devotes seven chapters to Minas Gerais, which he visited shortly after the transference of the Portuguese Court to Brazil. Almost a decade later, Spix and Martius **[546]** travelled to Vila Rica and its environs and left an account of their observations.

[562] Charles R. Boxer. "Negro Slavery in Brazil. A Portuguese Pamphlet (1764)," *Race* 5:3 (January 1964), pp. 38–47.

Translation of the rare and anonymous pamphlet, *Nova e Curiosa Relação*, published in Lisbon in 1764, containing a dialogue between a miner who had been in Brazil and a Portuguese lawyer, the former defending poor and cruel treatment of the Black Man, the latter attacking such evils. 10 unnumbered notes.

[563] John Mawe. *Travels in the Interior of Brazil, Particularly in the Gold and Diamond District of that Fine Country.* London: Longman, Hurst, Rees, Orme, and Brown, 1812. vii, 366 pp.

Mawe, after some misadventures in the Spanish La Plata region, which he had visited in 1804, arrived at the island of Santa Catarina at the end of September, 1807, en route to Rio de Janeiro. He found that the houses of the island's chief town "are well built, have two or three stories, with boarded floors, and are provided with neat gardens, well stocked with excellent vegetables and flowers." Mawe also observed that "the lands capable of cultivation are under considerable improvement; a great extent of them was formerly covered with large trees, but as great quantities have of late years been cut down and used for ship-building, good timber may now be considered scarce. They grow flax here of a very fair quality, of which the fishermen make their lines, nets, and cordage." After leaving Santa Catarina, the author sailed northward to Santos, whose harbor "has a safe entrance and is very secure; it is a strait, having the island of St. Vincent to the left, for the extent of half a mile, when it takes a different direction. Here is situated the port, which has good anchorage, with regular soundings towards the shore, which shoals gradually." From Santos, Mawe travelled to São Paulo. The author's description of São Paulo is one of the few in English during the colonial period: "The population of this place amounts to full fifteen thousand souls: perhaps nearer twenty thousand; the clergy, including all ranks of religious orders, may be reckoned at five hundred. They are in general good members of society, free from that excessive bigotry and illiberality which is the reproach of the neighboring colonies, and their example has so beneficial an effect on the rest of the inhabitants, that I may presume to say, no stranger will be molested while he acts as a gentleman, and does not insult the established religion. His Excellency the Bishop is a most worthy prelate." Mawe observed that São Paulo had "few manufactures of any consequence; a little coarse cotton is spun by the hand, and woven into cloth, which serves for a kind of wearing apparel, sheets, &c. They make a beautiful kind of net-work for hammocks, which are fringed with lace, and form an elegant piece of furniture, being slung low, so as to answer the purpose of sofas. The ladies are particularly fond of using them, especially when the heat of the weather disposes them to ease and indolence. The making of lace is a general employment for females, some of whom excel in it. The shop-keepers here are a numerous class, who, as in most colonial towns, deal in almost every thing, and sometimes make great fortunes. Here are few doctors of medicine, but many apothecaries; some silver-smiths, whose articles are indifferent both in metal and workmanship; tailors and shoemakers in great numbers; and joiners, who manufacture very beautiful wood, but are not so moderate in their charges as the former classes of tradesmen. In the outskirts of the city live a number of Creolian Indians, who make earthen-ware for culinary purposes, large water-jars, and a variety of other utensils ornamented with some taste. The greatest proportion of the inhabitants consists in farmers and inferior husbandmen, who cultivate small portions of land, on which they breed large stocks of pigs and poultry for sale." From São Paulo, Mawe travelled to Rio de Janeiro. At the Brazilian capital he was able to present a letter of introduction from the Portuguese ambassador at London to the minister's brother, the Count of Linhares, who had just arrived with the Portuguese Court. This enabled Mawe to visit the gold and diamond mining regions of Minas Gerais, a description of which fills seven chapters in the author's account. He felt that "Villa Rica at the present day scarcely retains a shadow of its former spendour. Its inhabitants, with the exception of the shopkeepers, are void of employment; they totally neglect the fine country around them, which, by proper cultivation, would amply compensate for the loss of wealth which their ancestors drew from its bosom." Mawe describes the various washings and how gold and diamonds were extracted. He recounts how the African slaves were rewarded: "When a negro is so fortunate as to find a diamond of the weight of an octavo (17½ carats), much ceremony takes place; he is crowned with a wreath of flowers and carried in procession to the administrator, who gives him his freedom, by paying his owner for it. He also receives a present of new clothes, and is permitted to work on his own account. When a stone of eight or ten carats is found, the negro receives two new shirts, a complete new suit, with a hat and a handsome knife. For smaller stones of trivial amount proportionate premiums are given." Tejuco, the chief town of the diamond mining district, "owing to its situation by the side of a hill, is very irregularly built; its streets are uneven, but the houses in general are well constructed and in good condition, compared with those of other towns in the interior." Mawe provides a brief, secondhand sketch of the Brazilian Northeast and a more detailed one of Mato Grosso. Regarding the latter captaincy, the author received much of his information from a Colonel Martinez, "an engineer of extraordinary merit, who had made four journeys to Matto Grosso, and had resided there some years." Rio Grande do Sul is also described in some detail. The author concludes with some "General Observations on the Trade from England to Brazil."

D. Rio de Janeiro and Its Environs to 1808 [564–597]

In addition to accounts of the struggle against the forces of Antarctique France and the founding of Rio de Janeiro by the Portuguese found in Sanceau **[146]**, Butler **[271]** and Dominian **[305]**, Charles R. Boxer **[277]** in his biography of Salvador Correia de Sá provides the major study in English on the history of Rio de Janeiro during its first century of existence as a captaincy. Cardozo **[278]** also contributes some useful information in his notes on the life of Salvador de Sá. Overland routes from Rio de Janeiro and the difficulties in crossing the Serra do Mar are discussed by Richard Momsen **[564]**. Francis A. Dutra **[294]** describes the foundation of the diocese of Rio de Janeiro in 1676 and analyzes the behavior of its early bishops. Boxer **[548]**, in his survey of Brazil, 1695–1750, discusses the French attacks of Duclerc and Duguay-Trouin on Rio and provides a useful survey of that captaincy's history during the first half of the eighteenth century—a period of great growth because of the gold and diamond discoveries in Minas Gerais. Southey **[70]** also provides a colorful narrative of Rio de Janeiro's history. A French visit in 1748 is described by Manoel Cardozo **[566]**. Harold B. Johnson **[567]** analyzes money, prices and wages in the new capital of Brazil (after 1763) and Dauril Alden **[274]** provides a vast amount of information on Rio de Janeiro and its environs in the second half of the eighteenth century in his study of the Marquis of Lavradio. Alden **[569]** also traces the efforts of Manuel Luis Vieira to develop a rice mill in Rio de Janeiro. Rudolph Bauss **[568]** discusses the rise of Rio de Janeiro as Brazil's chief emporium in the late eighteenth and early nineteenth century. An impressionistic view of the city's social history during the same time period is found in Luiz Edmundo da Costa's *Rio in the Time of the Viceroys* **[570]**.

[564] Richard P. Momsen, Jr. *Routes Over the Serra do Mar. The Evolution of Transportation in the Highlands of Rio de Janeiro and São Paulo.* Rio de Janeiro, 1964. 173 pp.

In the early part of this study in historical geography (pp. 11–45), the author provides a useful synthesis of the problems the Portuguese experienced in crossing the Serra do Mar from the captaincies of São Vicente and Rio de Janeiro. Momsen describes the various routes built over this coastal escarpment. The earliest was from São Vicente to São Paulo and was primitive. The Jesuit missionary Simão Vasconcellos described it thusly: "The whole road was so difficult that at times we went along hanging by our hands." The author describes the "Caminho do Padre José" named after the Jesuit, José de Anchieta, and its development during the colonial period. The settlement of the captaincies of São Vicente and Rio de Janeiro are studied along with expansion into the interior and the need for additional routes over the Serra do Mar. Up to the end of the seventeenth century settlers from São Vicente were much more successful in overcoming obstacles traversing the escarpment than those from Rio de Janeiro. With the discovery of gold in Minas Gerais in the 1690s, there was a rush to open up more routes over the Serra do Mar to Rio de Janeiro. The author discusses the history of such routes as the Caminho Novo, the Caminho do Secretário, the Caminho do Tingua, the Caminho do Gago, and the Rio-São Paulo road. Momsen concludes his discussion of the colonial period with an analysis of the Serra do Mar routes, travel conditions, and the role of muleteers in the late eighteenth and early nineteenth century. He also describes the improvements made during João VI's stay in Brazil. The survey of the colonial period is based on secondary sources. There are several useful maps.

[565] Richard Paul Momsen, Jr. "Routes Over the Serra do Mar: An Historical Geography of Transportation in the Rio de Janeiro-São Paulo Area," (Ph.D. Dissertation: University of Minnesota, 1960). 425 pp.
DAI 22/01 (p. 226)

An earlier version of Momsen **[564]**.

[566] Manoel [da Silveira Soares] Cardozo. "A French Document on Rio de Janeiro, 1748," *The Hispanic American Historical Review* 21:3 (August 1941), pp. 425–435.

Anonymous account in French of a three-week visit of the fifty-gun man-of-war "Arc-en-ciel" to Rio de Janeiro. Gives a description not only of Rio's fortifications but of the city's social and economic life as well. Introduction and 9 notes in English. Document from the Biblioteca da Ajuda, Lisbon.

[567] Harold B. Johnson, Jr. "A Preliminary Inquiry into Money, Prices, and Wages in Rio de Janeiro, 1763–1823," in Alden, ed., *Colonial Roots* **[87]**, pp. 231–283.

Uses the records of four institutions of colonial Rio de Janeiro—the leper Hospital dos Lazaros, the Santa Casa da Misericordia, and the two brotherhoods of Sao Francisco de Penitencia and Sao Francisco de Paula—to determine prices for foodstuffs, building materials, slaves and salaries for the late eighteenth and the early nineteenth century. There is also a useful discussion of weights and measures, coinage, and the problems of inflation and deflation. The author concludes by comparing his findings for the economy of Rio de Janeiro with those of Ruggiero Romano [*Cuestiones de historia economica latino-americana*] for Santiago de Chile and Buenos Aires for the years 1765 to 1810. Johnson argues that "in contrast to the situation in Argentina or Chile, what prevailed in Rio was essentially a dual economy comprising a quasi-subsistence sector, largely outside the market, side by side with a sector of highly capitalized agriculture oriented to export markets whose profitability was largely determined by conditions exterior to the economy." Based on archival and printed primary materials. 57 notes. 3 tables. 20 figures. An appendix gives price series for nineteen commodities.

[568] Rudolph William Bauss. "Rio de Janeiro: The Rise of Late Colonial Brazil's Dominant Emporium, 1777–1808," (Ph.D. Dissertation: Tulane University, 1977). 406 pp.

Due to changes in the economy of southern Brazil after 1763, such as the expansion of agriculture and the development of Rio Grande do Sul, Rio de Janeiro became a prosperous commercial center with important trading ties rather than simply a transshipment locale. Merchants developed strong ties to agriculturists in southern Brazil as Rio flourished, enjoying a virtual monopoly over foreign trade in the south. Rio de Janeiro was also the center for the growing Brazilian

Atlantic seaboard trade. Likewise her smugglers grew wealthy from their illegal trade with Spanish America by using Rio Grande do Sul as a transfer point. In short, Rio became the center of an increasingly integrated national trade as well as a growing nationalism. This study examines Brazilian exports in the commercial relations of Portugal with a particular focus on Rio de Janeiro, the most important city after Lisbon in the Portuguese empire. Imports are also analyzed, especially the high prices they demanded, which impeded Brazilian economic development.
DAI 38/04-A (pp. 2294–2295).

[569] Dauril Alden. "Manoel Luis Vieira: An Entrepreneur in Rio de Janeiro during Brazil's Eighteenth Century Agricultural Renaissance," *The Hispanic American Historical Review* 39:4 (November 1959), pp. 521–537.

After reviewing some of the major fiscal and commercial problems facing Brazil and Portugal during the second half of the eighteenth century and the efforts of the Crown and various viceroys to stimulate production of new crops in Portuguese America, the author traces the efforts of Manoel Luis Vieira to develop a rice mill in Rio de Janeiro to provide the processed product for local consumption and export to Portugal. The many vicissitudes Vieira encountered are discussed. Based heavily on archival (Brazilian) and printed primary sources. 61 notes.

[570] Luiz Edmundo da Costa. *Rio in the Time of the Viceroys.* Trans. by Dorothea H. Momsen. Rio de Janeiro: J. R. de Oliveira & Cia., 1936. 353 pp.
[This is a translation of *O Rio de Janeiro do Tempo dos Vice-Reis,* published in Rio de Janeiro in 1932. The translator has added an epilogue (pp. 341–345).]

Opinionated, impressionistic and uneven account of life in Rio de Janeiro during the last half of the eighteenth and the early nineteenth centuries. Topics covered include housing, the slave market, taverns, churches, beggars, *festas,* dress, wigs, family life, books, the theatre, medicine and justice. Some of the material on slavery and family life has been superseded by newer studies. The best parts of the book deal with sedan chairs, coaches, headdresses, kitchens and cooking and some of the *festas* or celebrations. There is also useful information on eighteenth-century sumptuary laws. For those interested in architectural history, there are some valuable descriptions as well as photographs of some of the Brazilian capital's old buildings. There are also a number of pen and ink sketches of aspects of daily life accompanying the text. Despite the book's obvious defects, it is worth reading since it covers some topics on which nothing else appears in English. 34 photographs. There is a partial bibliography on pages 349–353.

1. Contemporary Narratives, 1700–1807 [Nos. 571–597]

Because of its location and importance, Rio de Janeiro was the most visited port in colonial Brazil during the eighteenth and early nineteenth centuries. Numerous accounts are available in English. Bartholomaeus Ziegenbalgh **[571]** published a letter of Jonas Finck describing Rio de Janeiro in 1711 and the siege of Duguay-Trouin. Neville Frowde's supposed visit to Rio de Janeiro in 1735 is described in **[572]**. John Byron **[573]** visited Rio in 1764. The following year, James Forbes **[574]** spent four months in the new Brazilian capital. Louis de Bougainville **[575]** stopped at Rio de Janeiro in 1767 for provisions during visits to the Plata region and Santa Catarina the same year. A member of Captain Cook's expedition **[576]** described Rio in late 1768. James Cook's account is found in **[577]**. The botanist Joseph Banks **[578]** also left a description of Rio de Janeiro. The North American whaler, Thomas Lothrop **[579]**, described his experiences in a letter from prison dated 1774. Arthur Phillip **[580]**, governor-elect of New South Wales, and his expedition spent from early August to early September of 1787 in Rio and spoke highly of the city and its viceroy. Several others who accompanied Governor Phillip—John White **[581]**, Watkin Tench **[582]**, David Collins **[583]**, John Hunter **[584]**, Philip G. King **[585]**, and John Easty **[586]**—also left accounts of their stay. John Barrow **[587]** and Sir George Staunton **[588]**, both of whom accompanied the Earl of Macartney's embassy to the Emperor of China, left descriptions of their visit to Rio de Janeiro in November and the first half of December of 1792. James Colnett **[590]** of the British Navy spent a little less than a month—from the latter part of February to mid-March of 1793—in the Brazilian capital. In November of 1796, the Protestant missionary James Wilson **[591]** visited Rio de Janeiro briefly. A deportee to New South Wales, the Irish-born George Barrington **[594]** stopped in Rio de Janeiro in the late eighteenth century. James Kingston Tuckey **[595]**, who visited Rio de Janeiro twice in the early 1800s, gives a detailed description of the city. The American Richard Jeffry Cleveland **[596]** visited Rio several times: 1802, 1806, and 1820. Another convict, James Hardy Vaux **[597]**, arrived in Rio in May of 1807 and left an interesting account of his stay.

[571] Bartholomaeus Ziegenbalgh, ed. *Propagation of the Gospel in the East: Being a Collection of Letters From the Protestant Missionaries, and other Worthy Persons in the East Indies.* Part III. London: J. Downing, 1718. xxiv, 233 pp.

In a letter dated 20 October 1711, Jonas Finck, a printer on his way to India as part of a Protestant mission to Malabar, describes his experiences in Rio de Janeiro since his arrival in August of that year. As a strict Protestant, he found Rio to be "a Place over-run with gross Idolatry and Superstition." Finck felt constrained to pose as a domestic, because "the Inquisition is (as in all the other Portuguese Territories,) so very Flagrant in Brazil, that one can't take sufficient Precaution amongst a People so much enslaved by the Authority of Rome. At our Arrival here near a Hundred Persons were just embarking for Portugal, in order to be tried there at the Holy Office. They were suspected of favouring Judaism." The author felt that "the Clergy are so Ignorant, that in Ten you hardly find one who has got so much Latin as to read Mass." In addition, "the common People are swallowed up in Sensuality and their Care centers in heaping up Gold and Silver." He described the Jesuit college as "a very stately Building." Finck had several conversations with the Jesuits and was surprised that they had no knowledge of Thomas-à-Kempis' *Christian Pattern* [*The Imitation of Christ*]. In Rio he "found very few Portuguese Books worth my purchasing." Jonas Finck devoted a paragraph to slavery: "The Negro-Slaves making up in Number near eight Thousand Souls, are in a pitiful Condition. All the Evidence they have of their Reception into the Christian Church, amounts to no more than the Knowledge they have of their being sprinkled with Water, together with the Pater-Noster, which they are taught to rehearse. Besides this, they have Images of some of their Saints, as for Instance, that of St. Francis, or St. Anthony, &c. hanging about their Neck, as a Badge of the Christian Religion." While the author was in Rio, the French "Admiral Trouin landed Three Thousand Five Hundred Men." Finck describes the siege of Rio de Janeiro. Finally, "the Eleventh of September, the French took Possession of the Town, and plundered it the Day following. They threatened to reduce the whole Town to a Heap of Rubbish, but the Portuguese prevented that by paying a Sum of 15000 l."

[572] [Edward Kimber]. *The Life, Extraordinary Adventures, Voyages, and Surprizing Escapes of Capt. Neville Frowde of Cork. In Four Parts. Written by Himself, and Now First Published from His Own Manuscript.* London: J. Brown, 1767. vii, 220 pp.

The author writes that in 1734 his ship was driven past Rio Grande do Sul to the Rio de la Plata. There he claims to have fought with a Spanish coastguard and barely weathered a terrible storm during which "our Mainsail was split, our Fore-mast brought to the Board, our Maintop-gallant-mast sprung in two Places, and to add to our Distress, in the Height of the Gale, our Guns to Windward broke loose, and with every yaw we thought would have beat out the Ship's Side." After many adventures—including capture by Indians—Frowde reached Rio de Janeiro. "As we were now, without Employment, we lived very sociably amongst the Portuguese, and had daily Invitations to their houses in Town and Country, where we diverted ourselves as much as Men could possibly do, whose Hearts, were set on Objects at so awful a Distance, as our Friends and native Country." Eventually Frowde sailed for Lisbon on 18 May 1735, anchoring in the Tagus on 12 September of that year. Though this book is included in Borba de Moraes **[20]**, I, 285, who cites a later edition (1792), all evidence suggests it is a novel. The first edition seems to have been published in 1758. There was another edition in 1773. Edward Kimber, the author, wrote a half-dozen similar accounts, one being *The Life and Adventures of Joe Thompson a Narrative Founded on Fact, Written by Himself*. Though Kimber was in Georgia in the early 1740s, there is no reason to believe that he was ever in Brazil. Some useful information on Edward Kimber is found in Sidney A. Kimber, "The 'Relation of a Late Expedition to St. Augustine,' with Biographical and Bibliographical Notes on Isaac and Edward Kimber," *The Papers of the Bibliographical Society of America* 28:2 (1934), pp. 81–96.

[573] John Byron. *Byron's Journal of his Circumnavigation 1764–1766.* Ed. by Robert E. Gallagher (Cambridge: At the University Press, 1964). lxxxii, 230.
[Issued by the Hakluyt Society. Second Series. No. 122.]

John Byron, who had been a midshipman on the ill-fated *Wager* **[532]** (which went on the rocks about 90 leagues off the Straits of Magellan), part of Anson's expedition of 1740, commanded the *Dolphin* on a voyage around the world in 1764–1766. He arrived in Rio de Janeiro in mid-September of 1764: "The City of Janeiro makes a very handsome appearance, is very large & governed by the Vice Roy of all the Brazils, who is as absolute as any Prince in the Universe; Several Instances of which he shewed whilst we were here.—When I visited him he received me with great form, above 60 Officers were drawn up before the Palace as well as a Captain's Guard, all extremely well clothed & very well looking Men. The Vice King with a number of Persons of the first distinction belonging to the Place received me at the head of the Stairs, upon which 15 Guns were fired from the nearest Fort, we then enterd into his Room of State & after conversing about a quarter of an hour in French, I took my leave & went out with the same forms I had come in with." After having Portguese caulkers repair his ship, he set sail on

October 21st, "glad to leave Rio de Janeiro where the heat was intollerable."

[574] James Forbes. *Oriental Memoirs: Selected and Abridged from a Series of Familial Letters Written during Seventeen Years Residence in India: Including Observations of Parts of Africa and South America, and a Narrative of Occurence in Four India Voyages.* 4 vols. London: T. Bentley, 1813. xxiii, 481 pp.; xv, 542 pp.; xii, 485 pp.; xi, 425 pp.
[There is also a second edition entitled: *Oriental Memoirs: A Narrative of Seventeen Years Residence in India.* Revised by his Daughter, the Countess de Montalembert. 2 vols. London: Richard Bentley, 1834. xix, 550 pp.; viii, 552 pp.]

In March of 1765, James Forbes sailed from England to work with the East India Company at Bombay. After stopping for a week on the island of Santiago in the Cape Verdes, he continued on toward the Cape of Good Hope. However, his ship sprung a leak and was forced to dock at Rio de Janeiro, where it remained from the end of June to the middle of October, undergoing repairs. Forbes was impressed by the scenery of Rio de Janeiro: "If I was pleased with St. Jago, I had much greater reason to be delighted with the Brazils: the grandeur of the mountains, the fertility of the valleys, the mildness of the climate, and the general beauty of animal and vegetable nature, render this part of South America very interesting; while the variety of trees and plants, the profusion of fruits and flowers, and the brilliancy of the birds and insects, afforded an ample scope for my earliest attempts in natural history." But he had a disdain for the people who lived in Brazil: "The manners and customs of the inhabitants are neither pleasing nor interesting: pride, poverty, indolence, and superstition, are the prevailing characteristics of these degenerate Portugueze; and seem to have entirely extinguished the noble virtues of their ancestors: their cruelty to the plantation negroes, and slaves of every description, is excessive: humanity shudders at the constant smack of the whip, and the loud cries for mercy, vainly implored by these poor wretches, from their tyrannic masters, who seem to have lost every sense of that divine attribute." On the other hand, he found Rio de Janeiro to be "a large city, with numerous churches, convents, and nunneries. . . . The splendour of the churches, the pompous ceremonies of the Romish worship, the various dresses of the monks and nuns, and the beauty of the gardens at their convents, were all attractive." Forbes remarked that "the native Brazilians are seldom to be seen at Rio de Janeiro; the few who yet remain live at a distance from the Portuguese settlements; and their manners and customs are little known." The author was impressed by Rio's jewellers' shops, which "make a grand display of diamonds, topazes, amethysts, and other precious stones, brought from the mines." Forbes's visit to Brazil is described in volume I of both editions.

[575] Louis de Bougainville. *A Voyage Round the World. Performed by Order of His Most Christian Majesty, In the Years 1766, 1767, 1768 and 1769.* Translated from the French by John Reinhold Forster, F. A. S. Dublin, 1772. xxxii, 480 pp.
[Translation of *Voyage autour du monde par la frégate du Roy 'La Boudeuse' et la flûte 'L'Etoile' en 1766, 1767, 1768 & 1769.* Paris, 1771.]

During this voyage Bougainville visited the Plata twice, interspersed with an excursion to Rio de Janeiro for provisions and a rendezvous with the *L'Etoile,* the French King's ship bound for India which would accompany the author on his trip around the world. Though Bougainville wrote that Rio de Janeiro was "the emporium and principal staple of the rich produce of the Brasils" and that he was assured by Monsieur de Commerçon, a naturalist aboard the L'Etoile, that Portuguese America "was the richest country in plants he had ever met with," the author was disappointed in finding in the Brazilian capital "neither biscuit, nor wheat , nor flour." Initially the Portuguese viceroy had been friendly to the French: "He even told us his intention of giving us a *petit souper,* or a collation, by the water-side, in bowers of jasmine and orange-trees; and he ordered a box to be prepared for us at the opera. We saw, in a tolerable handsome hall, the best works of Metastasio represented by a band of mulattoes; and heard the divine composition of the great Italian masters, executed by an orchestra, which was under the direction of a hump-backed priest, in his canonicals." Because "the Brasils, and the capital in it," had "been described by so many authors", Bougainville said little more about Rio de Janeiro, except that "the mint at Rio de Janeiro is one of the finest buildings existing. It is furnished with all the conveniences necessary towards working with the greatest expedition." The Frenchman was also impressed with the arrival of the fleets, "especially that from Lisbon [which] renders the commerce of Rio de Janeiro very flourishing. The fleet from Porto is laden only with wines, brandy, vinegar, victuals, and some coarse cloths, manufactured in and about that town. As soon as the fleets arrive, all the goods they bring are conveyed to the custom-house, where they pay a duty of ten per cent. to the king." Bougainville observed that "the greater part of the most precious merchandizes which arrive from Europe were sent from Rio de Janeiro to that colony [do Sacramento], from whence they were smuggled through Buenos Ayres to Peru and Chili; and this contraband trade was worth a million and a half piastres or dollars annually to the Portuguese. In short, the mines of the Brazils produce no silver, and all that which the Portuguese got, came from this smuggling trade. The negro trade was another immense object. The loss which the almost entire suppression of this branch of contraband trade occasion [because of the outbreak of hostilities between Spain and Portugal] cannot be calculated. This branch alone employed at least thirty coasting vessels between the Brasils and Rio de la Plata." When visiting the Plata region, however, the author observed that Colônia do Sacramento was "now so much surrounded by the new works, erected by the Spaniards, that it is impossible to carry on any illicit trade with it [i.e., Buenos Aires] unless by connivance; even the Portuguese, who inhabit the place, are obliged to get their subsistence by the sea from the Brasils." The author was much impressed by the collection and smuggling of diamonds: "Of all the contraband trades, that of diamonds is most severely punished. If the smuggler is poor, he loses his life; if his riches are sufficient to satisfy what the law exacts, besides the confiscation of the diamonds, he is condemned to pay double their value, to be imprisoned for one year, and then exiled for life to the coast of Africa. Notwithstanding this severity, the smuggling trade with diamonds, even of the most beautiful kind, is very extensive, so great is the hope and facility of hiding them, on account of the little room they take up." Bougainville's first visit to the Plata was from the end of January to the end of February 1767, his second covered the end of July and most of August the same year. He arrived in Rio de Janeiro on 21 June and left 14/15 July of 1767. Chapter V (pp. 72–86) covers his stay in the Brazilian capital.

[576] Anonymous. *A Journal of a Voyage Round the World in His Majesty's Ship Endeavour, In the Years 1768, 1769, 1770, and 1771.* London: T. Becket and P. A. De Hondt, 1771. 133 pp.
[A facsimile edition was published in 1967 by N. Israel/Amsterdam and Da Capo Press/New York.]

The earliest, though anonymous, account by a member of the Cook expedition which arrived in Rio de Janeiro on 13 November 1768 and departed on 8 December. The author describes the bay, its batteries and forts with comments on how it might be entered by a British fleet. He recounts how they were carefully inspected by both military and customhouse officials. Initially, the Portuguese Viceroy, Antônio Rolim de Moura, Conde de Azambuja, "a little old man" who "has enjoyed his present office about three years [sic], having formerly been governor of Bahia for a long time," though granting the *Endeavor* necessary supplies, prohibited anyone from coming on shore. The author suggests that some of the difficulties the British encountered might have been due to the evasive answers given to the viceroy, "Captain Cooke judging that such questions concerning a ship of war would be impertinent." This, along with the fact that while entering the harbor the English had "publicly taken surveys of the country" plus "some commercial disagreements, which at that time were supposed to subsist between Great Britain and Portugal doubtless excited unfavorable suspicions in the government of Rio [de] Janeiro, and occasioned the prohibitions" mentioned. The harbor had room for sixty or seventy ships and it actually contained several of four hundred tons. "The principal street is near an hundred feet in width, and extends from St. Benedict to the foot of Castle-hill; the inferior are commonly twenty or thirty feet wide. The houses adjoining to the principal street have three stories, but in other places they are very irregular, though built after the same manner as in Lisbon." Rio's four monastaries—those of the Benedictines, Carmelites, Franciscans and the Jesuits (the latter being used as a military hospital in 1768)—are described as is the viceroy's palace, where "the palace, mint, stables, gaol, &c. compose but one large building, which has two stories, and is ninety feet from the water." Blacks crowded around the water fountain waiting to fill their jars. "Negroes are almost the only people employed in selling the different commodities exposed in the market, and they employ their leisure time in spinning of cotton." The gentry used chaises drawn by mules, sedan chairs, and hammocks. Rio's apothecary shops served as coffee houses. "Beggars, who infest the streets of most European cities, are not to be found in this." The author also describes the climate and major products of Brazil's capital.

There is a good discussion of this account and its possible authorship in Beaglehole **[577]**, pp. cclvi–cclxiv.

[577] James Cook. *The Journals of Captain James Cook on His Voyages of Discovery. The Voyage of the Endeavour 1768–1771.* Ed. by J. C. Beaglehole (Cambridge: At the University Press, 1955).
Published for the Hakluyt Society. Extra Series No. 34.

Captain Cook arrived in Rio de Janeiro on 13 November 1768 for "Water and other refreshments." Though the Portuguese viceroy granted his request, restrictions were placed on Cook and his crew. The British explorer complained that the viceroy "obliged me to employ a person to buy them [provisions] for me under a pretence that it was the custom of the place." Cook finally "obtained leave for one of my people to attend the market to buy necessarys for my table and to assist the Agent to buy the things for the Ship." The viceroy, however, continued to keep a close watch, doubting that the Endeavour "is the Kings" and accusing the English of smuggling. Cook was especially upset that "a Spanish Packet (a small Brigg) from Buenos Ayres . . . met with very diferent treatment from us, no Guard was put over her and her officers and crew went where ever they pleased. " As the editor notes, however, "notwithstanding the Viceroy's restrictions, Monkhouse the surgeon landed every day to buy provisions, while both Solander and Banks managed to get ashore, and otherwise add to their collections." Cook gives a five-page account on the Brazilian capital, most of it information on entering the bay and a lengthy description "of the different forts that are erected for the defense of this Bay." He added that "for the defense of these Forts and the town the King of Portugal Maintains Seven Regments of Regular Troops, those I saw were well cloathed and in a good condition but this as I was told was not the case with the whole; besides these troops are three Regments of Militia two of Horse and one of foot, these consist of the principal inhabitants of the place who serve without pay." According to Cook, the Governor of Rio was "no friend to the English" and the Viceroy "as absolute as any Monarch on Earth and the people to all appearence as much slaves. This City and adjacent parts about the Bay are said to contain one hundred thousand Souls, but not much above a twentieth part are Whites the rest are blacks many of whom are free and seem to live in tolerable circumstances." The captain concludes his account of Rio de Janeiro by discussing the quality and prices of food and other provisions. The notes by the editor are excellent.

[578] J. C. Beaglehole, ed. *The Endeavour Journal of Joseph Banks, 1768–1771.* 2 v. Sydney: Angus & Robertson, 1962. xxvii, 476 pp.

Volume I covers the visit of the botanist Joseph Banks to Rio de Janeiro in November and December of 1768. Banks was a member of James Cook's expedition. The botanist described Rio de Janeiro as "regular and well built after the fashion of Portugal, every house having before its windows a Lattice of wood behind which is a little balcony. For size it is much larger than I could have thought, probably little inferior to any of our Countrey towns in England Bristol or Liverpool not excepted; the streets are all straight intersecting each other at Right angles and have this peculiar Convenience, that much the greater number lay in one direction and are commanded by the Gunns of their citadel calld St Sebastian which is situate on the top of a hill over looking the town." Banks noted that the city "is supplyd with water by an aqueduct which brings it from the neighbouring hills upon two stories of arches, said in some places to be very high; the water that this brings is conveyd into a fountain in the great square immediately opposite the Governors palace, which is guarded by a sentry who has sufficient work to keep regularity and order among so many as are always in waiting at this place; there is also water laid into some other part of the town but how it is brought there I could not hear, only that it was better than the fountain which is exceedingly indifferent." As for the churches, those in Rio "are very fine dressd out with more ornaments even than those in Europe, and all parts of their religion is carried on with more shew;

their processions in particular are very extrordinary, every day one or other of the parishes go in solemn order with all the insignia of their church, altar, host &c through their parish, begging for what they can get and praying in all form at every Corner of a street." Banks, though he spent a limited time ashore, claimed that "the Government of this place Seems to me to be much more despotick even that that of Portugal tho many precautions have been taken to render it otherwise." He also asserted that "this town as well as all others in South America belonging either to Spanyards or Portuguese has long been infamous for the unchastity of its women," though "I had not even the least opportunity to go among them." In addition, "assassinations are I fancy more frequent here than in Lisbon as the churches still take upon them to give protection to criminals." According to Banks, the Portuguese officials "have a very extrordinary method of keeping people from traveling—to hinder them I suppose from going into any districk where gold or diamonds may be found, as there are more of such than they can possibly guard, which is this: there are certain bounds beyond which no man must go, these vary every month at the discretion of the Vic[e]roy, sometimes they are a few sometimes many Leagues Round the City: Every man must in consequence of this come to town to know where the Bounds are, for if he is taken by the guards who constantly patrole on their edges he is infallibly put in prison, even if he is within them, unless he can tell where they are."

[579] Stanley F. Chyet, ed., "From a Prison in Brazil—1774," *The Americas* 35:4 (April 1979), pp. 573–580.

In July, 1773, the North American Thomas Lothrop, Captain of the brig *Leviathan*, and an employee of the wealthy merchant-shipper, Aaron Lopez, a Portuguese Jewish immigrant based in Newport, Rhode Island, arrived in Brazil. In September he was taken into custody as a smuggler and his boat confiscated. The Marquis of Lavradio, viceroy of Brazil, offered to write to the king of Portugal on Lothrop's behalf and have "your vessel's being given you again and a large gratification for your service with all other damages" in exchange for the captain's cooperation in aiding in the development of the Brazilian whaling industry. Lothrop made some efforts in that direction before deciding not to cooperate further with the Portuguese authorities. He wrote to Lopez: "I may say for your sake and my honor, I have refused making a fortune as I have had great offers to stay two or three years in this country." In a letter dated 11 December 1774, he also informed Aaron Lopez that "in some parts of this ocean there is great plenty of spermacetis, to my knowledge, but the Portuguese are as yet strangers and know but little how to carry on the business to profit or anything, making immense charge for nothing. The contractor hath a very profitable fishery of our right whale kind and in the year 1773 got one thousand and five; one with another produced fifteen pipes of oil manufactured in a scandalous manner and carried on with no ingenuity." According to the editor, Lothrop seems to have died in prison sometime in 1775. 6 notes.

[580] Arthur Phillip. *The Voyage of Governor Phillip to Botany Bay; With an Account of the Establishment of the Colonies of Port Jackson and Norfolk Island.* London: Printed for John Stockdale, 1789. 296 pp, 74 pp, 55 plates (8 maps and charts).

Arthur Phillip (1738–1814), governor-elect of New South Wales, spent a month (5 August to 4 September 1787) in Rio de Janeiro, reprovisioning his fleet before continuing on to Australia. Phillip had earlier seen service with Portugal and was known by the Viceroy of Brazil, Luis de Vasconcelos. The Governor spoke favorably about the Brazilian capital, calling the port "one of the finest in the world." Though Captain Cook **[577]** had complained about the poor treatment he and members of his expedition had received during his stay in Rio nine years earlier, "the reception given by the present Viceroy to Governor Phillip and his officers was very different: it was polite and flattering to a great degree, and free from every tincture of jealous caution." The only disappointment the visitors seemed to have had was they "did not find the ladies so indulgent as some voyagers have represented them." Philllip found provisions cheap and an abundance of meat, rice, fresh vegetables and rum—"wine was not at this season to be had, except from the retail dealers, less was therefore purchased than would otherwise have been taken"—were loaded aboard, along with a hundred sacks of cassava, the latter as a substitute for bread. The Governor was also impressed by "the great abundance of images dispersed throughout the city, and the devotion paid to them. They are placed at the corner of almost every street, and are never passed without a respectful salutation." He added, however, that "the strictness of manners in the inhabitants is not said to be at all equivalent to the warmth of this devotion." (pp. 20–35).
See also **[581]**, **[582]**, **[583]**, **[584]**, **[585]**, and **[586]**.

[581] John White. *Journal of a Voyage to New South Wales.* London: J. Debrett, 1790. 299 pp.
[There is a recent edition, edited by Alec H. Chisholm, with a biographical introduction by Rex Rienits. Published in Sydney, Australia: Angus and Robertson, 1962.]

John White, "Surgeon-General to the First Fleet and the Settlement at Port Jackson," arrived in Rio de Janeiro in early August of 1787 in the company of Arthur Phillip **[580]**, the governor-elect of New South Wales. White was one of the expedition's officers received by the Viceroy, the Count of Figueiro, Luis de Vasconcelos e Sousa, who "appeared to be of a middle age, somewhere between forty and fifty, stout and corpulent, with a strong cast or defect in both his eyes. He seemed to be a person of few words, but at the same time civil and attentive." The author was impressed by the celebration of the Prince of Brazil's birthday. The Englishman claimed that "the court [of the Viceroy] was brilliant, if a place where a female does not appear can be said to be brilliant; but this, I was informed, is always the case here. Those gentlemen who appeared in the circle were richly and elegantly dressed. The officers of the army and of the militia were particularly so, and that in a stile and fashion which did no small credit to their taste. The viceroy wore a scarlet coat trimmed with very broad rich gold lace, and his hair, according to his usual mode of wearing it, in a remarkably long queue, with very little powder; an article of dress to which I observed the Portugueze were not very partial, while, on the contrary, they were profuse in the use of pomatum." In general, White spoke highly of Rio de Janeiro: "The plan on which it is built has some claim to merit. The principal street, called Strait Street, runs from the viceroy's palace, which is near the south-east end of town, to the north-west extremity, where it is terminated by a large convent belonging to the Benedictine friars, situated on an eminence. The street is broad, well built, and has in it a great number of handsome shops. All the others are much inferior to this, being in general only wide enough to admit two carriages to pass each other in the centre." He found the houses to be "commonly two, and sometimes three, stories high, of which, even though inhabited by the most wealthy and respectable families, the lower part is always appropriated to shops, and to the use of the servants and slaves (who are here extremely numerous), the family rather chusing to reside in the upper part, that they might live in a less confined air. To every house there is a balcony, with lattice-work before it, and the same before all the windows. The churches are very numerous, elegant, and richly decorated; some of them are built and ornamented in a modern stile, and that in a manner which proclaims the genius, taste, and judgement of the architects and artists." White also provides a good description of Rio de Janeiro's military establishment: "The military force of Brazil consists of a troop of horse, which serve as guards for the viceroy, twelve regiments of regulars from Europe, and six raised in the country: these last enlist men of a mixed colour, which the former are by no means suffered to do. Besides the foregoing, there are twelve regiments of militia always embodied. This whole force, regulars and militia, except those on outposts and other needful duties, appear early in the morning, on every first day of the month, before the palace, where they undergo a general muster and review of arms and necessaries. The private men, although they are considered

as persons of great consequence by the populace, are, on the other hand, equally submissive and obedient to their officers. This strict discipline and regularity, as the city is in a great measure under military orders, renders the inhabitants extremely civil and polite to the officers, who, in return, study to be on the most agreeable and happy terms with them." The author found "the inhabitants in general" to be "a pleasant, cheerful people, inclining more to corpulency than those of Portugal; and, as far as we could judge, very favourably inclined to the English. The men are strait and well-proportioned. They do not accustom themselves to high living, nor indulge much in the juice of the grape. The women, when young, are remarkably thin, pale, and delicately shaped; but after marriage they generally incline to be lusty, without losing that constitutional pale, or rather sallow, appearance. They have regular and better teeth than are usually observable in warm climates, where sweet productions are plentiful. They have likewise the most lovely, piercing, dark eyes, in the captivating use of which they are by no means unskilled. Upon the whole, the women of this country are very engaging; and rendered more so by their free, easy, and unrestrained manner."
See also **[582]**, **[583]**, **[584]**, **[585]**, and **[586]**.

[582] Watkin Tench. *A Narrative of the Expedition to Botany Bay.* London: J. Debrett, 1789. 146 pp.
[There is a useful reprint of this account, annotated and edited by L. F. Fitzhardinge. *Sydney's First Four Years.* Sydney: Angus and Robertson, 1961.]

Watkin Tench was the captain of the marines on one of the English ships carrying convicts to Australia in 1787. En route, he, like the expedition's commander, Arthur Phillip **[580]**, the surgeon, John White **[581]**, and the marine John Easty **[586]** visited Rio de Janeiro. Tench devoted chapter V to his stay: "The height to which religious zeal is carried in this place, cannot fail of creating astonishment in a stranger. The greatest part of the inhabitants seem to have no other occupation, than that of paying visits and going to church, at which times you see them sally forth richly dressed, en chapeau bras, with the appendages of a bag for the hair, and a small sword: even boys of six years old are seen parading about, furnished with these indispensable requisites. Except when at their devotions, it is not easy to get a sight of the women, and when obtained, the comparisons drawn by a traveller, lately arrived from England, are little flattering to Portugueze beauty. In justice, however, to the ladies of St. Sebastian, I must observe, that the custom of throwing nosegays at strangers, for the purpose of bringing on an assignation, which Doctor Solander, and another gentleman of Mr. Cook's ship, met with when here, was never seen by any

of us in a single instance. We were so deplorably unfortunate as to walk every evening before their windows and balconies, without being honoured with a single bouquet, though nymphs and flowers were in equal and great abundance." Tench also observed that "the police of the city is very good. Soldiers patrole the streets frequently, and riots are seldom heard of. The dreadful custom of stabbing, from motives of private resentment, is nearly at an end, since the church has ceased to afford an asylum to murderers. In other respects, the progress of improvement appears slow, and fettered by obstacles almost insurmountable, whose baneful influence will continue, until a more enlightened system of policy shall be adopted. From morning to night the ears of a stranger are greeted by the tinkling of the convent bells, and his eyes saluted by processions of devotees, whose adoration and levity seem to keep equal pace, and succeed each other in turns. 'Do you want to make your son sick of soldiering? Shew him the Trainbands of London on a field-day. Let him who would wish to give his son a distate to Popery, point out to him the sloth, the ignorance, and the bigotry of this place.'" On 4 September 1787, Tench and the other members of the expedition set sail for Australia.
See also **[582]**, **[583]**, **[584]**, and **[585]**.

[583] David Collins. *An Account of the English Colony in New South Wales: With Remarks on the Dispositions, Customs, Manners &c. of the Native Inhabitants of That Country.* London: T. Cadell Jun. and W. Davies, 1798, xxxviii, 617 pp.
[A facsimile edition was published in Adelaide: Libraries Board of South Australia, 1971.]

David Collins was judge advocate and secretary of the colony. He sailed on the *Sirius* with Captain Phillip. His account adds information not contained in those of Arthur Phillip **[580]**, John White **[581]**, Watkin Tench **[582]**, John Hunter **[584]**, Philip G. King **[585]**, and John Easty **[586]**. In general, Collins was favorably impressed with Rio de Janeiro. "The palace of the viceroy stood in the Royal Square, of which, together with the public prison, the mint, and the opera-house, it formed the right wing. Of these buildings the opera-house alone was shut up; and we were informed. that the gloom which was thrown over the court and kingdom of Portugal by the death of the late king [Pedro III, consort of Maria I], had extended in full force to the colonies also; All private and public amusements being since that time discouraged as much as possible, the viceroy himself setting the example. Once a-week, indeed, his excellency had a music-meeting at the palace for the entertainment of himself and a few select friends; but nothing more." Collins pointed out that among the Brazilians "epidemic distempers were rare. . . . In their streets, however, were frequently seen objects of wretchedness and misery crawling about with most painful and disgusting swellings in their legs and privities. The hospital, which had formerly been a Jesuit's convent, stood near the summit of the hill, in an open situation, at the back of the town. From the great estimation in which English surgeons were held here, it would seem that the town is not too well provided in that respect. Senor Ildefonse, the principal in the place, had studied in England, where he went under the course of surgical education called walking the hospitals, and might by his practice in this place, which was considerable, and quite as much as he could attend to, have soon realized a handsome fortune; but we understood, that to the poor or necessitous sick he always administered gratis." The author had some interesting comments on the women of the Brazilian capital and their dress: "The women of the town of Rio de Janeiro, being born within the tropics, could not be expected to possess the best complexions; but their features were in general expressive—the eye dark and lively, with a striking eye-brow. The hair was dark, and nature had favoured them with that ornament in uncommon profession: this they mostly wore with powder, strained to a high point before, and tied in several folds behind. By their parents they were early bred up to much useful knowledge, and were generally mistresses of the polite accomplishments of music, singing, and dancing. Their conversation appeared to be lively, at times breaking out in sallies of mirth and wit, and at others displaying judgment and good sense. In their dress for making or receiving visits, they chiefly affected silks and gay colours; but in the mornings, when employed in the necessary duties of the house, a thin but elegant robe or mantle thrown over the shoulders was the only upper garment worn. Both males and females were early taught to dress as men and women; and we had many opportunities of seeing a hoop on a little Donna of three years of age, and a bag and a sword on a Senor of six. This appearance was as difficult to reconcile as that of the saints and virgins in their churches being decorated with powdered perruques, swords, laced clothes, and full-dressed suits."

[584] John Hunter. *An Historical Journal of the Transactions at Port Jackson and Norfolk Island with the Discoveries Which Have Been Made in New South Wales and in the Southern Ocean, Since the Publication of Phillip's Voyage.* London: John Stockdale, 1793. xviii, 583 pp.
[A facsimile edition was published in Adelaide: Libraries Board of South Australia, 1968.]

A member of Governor Phillip's expedition, John Hunter was "Second Captain of his Majesty's ship Sirius, with the rank of Post Captain, and with power to command her in the absence of her principal captain." Like Arthur Phillip **[580]**, John White **[581]**, Watkin Tench **[582]**, David Collins **[583]**, Philip G. King **[585]** and John Easty **[586]**, Captain

Hunter also kept record of his impressions. Compared to those of his colleagues, his account is brief. He was especially impressed with the reception he received from Luis de Vasconcelos, the viceroy of Brazil. On the 21st of August 1787, the anniversary of the Prince of Brazil's birthday, "half an hour after ten, the Vice-King received compliments upon that occasion; all the officers of our fleet which could be spared from duty on board, landed, and in a body went to the palace to make their compliments upon this public day; the viceroy upon this, as well as upon every other occasion, shewed us particular attention. We were the first company admitted into the levee-room, then the clergy and military, after which, the civilians and some of the military promiscuously." He also admired the city's churches, which "are very good buildings, and their decorations exceedingly rich, and they seem to have excellent organs in them."

[585] Philip G. King. "Remarks & Journal Kept on the Expedition to Form a Colony in His Majestys Territory of New South Wales under the Command of His Excellency Arthur Phillip Esq[r] His Majesty's Governor and Captain General of Ye Said Territory & Its Dependencies," in *Historical Records of New South Wales,* II, 513–660.

Lieutenant (later, Governor) Philip King was also a member of Arthur Phillip's **[580]** expedition who visited Rio de Janeiro and left an account of his observations. His narrative supplements those of **[581]**, **[582]**, **[583]**, **[584]**, and **[586]**. King was very much interested in the military aspects of Rio: "The harbour is spacious and safe, and ye largest I ever saw except Trincomalay [Trincomalee]. It is very well defended, yet I think ten sail of the line and 5,000 troops would give a good account of the gold crosses with which their churches are well furnished in a short time, if well conducted." Regarding the Viceroy and the military stationed in Rio, King wrote: "The title of ye Vice-King is Vice-King and Captain-General of ye Brazils by sea and land; his fixed salary is but £2,000 p. annum; however, if he wishes to treble that sum he has it much in his power. An officer of the rank of Lieut't-Colonel, who is stiled Adjutant des Ordres, is in constant attendance at the pallace to give out orders and transact all the military business. There are besides this officer, a great number of others who are likewise on constant duty at the same place. The troops are well disciplined and appointed, and ye subordination is kept very high. There are now about 5,000 troops, viz.:—ye regiments of Braganza, Estra Modo [Estremadura] and Moira [Moura]. These three regiments came from Lisbon in 1768, and were to remain only three years: however, they are not yet gone, or any likelihood of it. There are, besides, two companies of calvary and four companies of artillery with three provincial corps. The town can arm 6,000 trained men."

[586] John Easty. *Memorandum of the Transactions of a Voyage from England to Botany Bay 1787–1793. A First Fleet Journal.* Sydney, Australia: The Trustees of the Public Library of New South Wales in Association with Angus and Robertson, 1965. ix, 186 pp.

Interesting document because it gives a rare insight into the common man's view of Rio de Janeiro. John Easty, a private marine, part of a detachment to guard convicts, sailed from England on the *Scarborough* for Botany Bay. He arrived in Rio de Janeiro for the first time at the end of August 1787, departing on 4 September. Easty was impressed with the well-fortified and well-defended—six to seven thousand disciplined troops—"fine Large harbour" of Rio along with that region's many kinds of fruit and birds. The "natives of this place are of a Dark Clompecton much Like the Gipsies of England." Though the white women dressed like those in France, Spain and other foreign countries, male black slaves wore nothing "Ecept a Clout Jest round ther Privits." Black women wore "A Short kind of bed gowned wich jest Cover thier Brists and Shoulders and a Short Peticoat wich Come About half way down thier thies." Furthermore, "thay ware no kind of Shirts or Shifts So that thare Bellies is naked." On his return to England, Easty again visited Rio de Janeiro, this time from 7 February to 4 March 1793. He witnessed the Ash Wednesday Procession, of which he gives a detailed description, although Catholic religious practices in Brazil were "Enough to make a prodstant Shuder." He also chafed at the travel restrictions placed on foreigners in Rio.
See also **[580]**, **[581]**, **[582]**, **[583]**, **[584]**, and **[585]**.

[587] John Barrow. *A Voyage to Cochinchina in the Years 1792 and 1793.* London: T. Cadell and W. Davies, 1806. xviii. 447 pp.

Barrow visited Rio de Janeiro in 1792 in the company of the Earl of Macartney and Sir George Staunton **[588]** and devoted a lengthy chapter to its description. In many ways his observations parallel those of Staunton. For example, Staunton observed that "there were but two booksellers in Rio. Their shops contained only books of medicine and divinity." Barrow wrote: "One of the first objects of inquiry to an inquisitive traveller, on his entering a city or large town, is a bookseller's shop. . . . After a long search, and many inquiries, we at last discovered that there were two booksellers' shops in St. Sebastian; but it required less time time to find out that they contained nothing that was likely to be useful or interesting to us. Many old volumes on medicine and alchemy, still more on church history and theological disputations, and some few on the exploits of the house of Bragança, swelled their catalogues; nothing that related to the country was to be found." Barrow estimated that the population of the city of Rio was "at least sixty thousand souls, including slaves." However, he was disappointed that "there is neither inn, nor hotel, nor any kind of lodging or accommodation for the reception of strangers." Barrow was not overly impressed with the embassy's lodgings: "The house provided for the Ambassador was sufficiently large, but not very clean; and although it was represented as being completely furnished, there was, in reality, little in it beside some clumsy old fashioned chairs of heavy wood, a few tables, and wooden frames with cane bottoms, intended for bedsteads, but without either posts or curtains. Fortunately we took on shore our own bedding, by doing which we soon discovered that we had lost nothing in point of comfort, the Portugueze not being over nice in this respect." Barrow also challenged some of Cook's **[577]** comments about the wives and daughters of the Portuguese inhabitants: "I never could perceive in their conduct any thing that could warrant the opinion of their being more licentious, or more immorally inclined, than females are in other countries." He added: "That the ladies of Rio have a great deal of vivacity and little reserve I am free to admit, which indeed is not greatly to be wondered at. The whole day is spent at home in gloomy confinement; and they rarely see a human creature beside their own family, except in the evenings, when they appear in their balconies or go to vespers. At these moments they may be compared to birds that have escaped from the confinement of the cage."

[588] Sir George Staunton. *An Authentic Account of an Embassy from the King of Great Britain to the Emperor of China.* 2 v. London: W. Bulmer. 1797. xxxiv, 518 pp.; xx, 626 pp.

Authorship is sometimes attributed to the Earl of Macartney, who headed the Embassy. Both accounts are identical. Sir George Staunton was secretary to the Embassy and actually related the voyage. Only the first volume describes Brazil.

[589] Sir George Staunton, *An Historical Account of the Embassy to the Emperor of China.* London: John Stockdale, 1797. xv, 475 pp.

This is an abridged version of **[588]**. Staunton arrived in Rio de Janeiro on the *Lion* on 1 November 1792. He describes the city's buildings and adds that "there are three convents for men, and two for women; none of them remarkable for religious austerity. The ceremonies of religion, however, were strictly observed; and an addition had been made to them, by the ringing of bells, and launching of skyrockets, whenever any solemnities were performing in the churches. All classes of society have an insuperable attachment to gaiety and pleasure. The lower order appeared abroad in cloaks; those of the middling and higher ranks always in swords. The ladies had their hair hanging down in tresses, tied with ribands, and adorned with flowers; their heads were uncovered. They had, in general, fine dark eyes, and animated countenances; were fond of music, and their favourite instruments the harpsichord and guitar. A few of them shewed instances of extreme levity; and some of the men were accused of unnatural practices." As for recreation, Staunton wrote that "plays, operas, and masquerades were the innocent amusements of both sexes. A public garden, at one extremity of the town, by the sea side, was the favourite attraction; where, after their evening promenade, they frequently partook of banquets, rendered more zestful by the accompaniment of music and the display of artificial fireworks. This garden was laid out, with much taste, in grass plots, shrubberies and parterres; interspersed with shady trees, and arched alcoves decorated with flowers, Jessamines, and fragrant plants. Towards the middle, was a fountain of artificial rock work, ornamented with sculptural figures of two alligators, spouting water into a marble reservoir, in which aquatic birds, done in bronze, were sportively represented." In contrast to this opulence, "at Val Longo, in another part of the harbour, are warehouses for the reception and sale of slaves from Angola and Benguela, on the coast of Africa. Out of twenty thousand, purchased annually for the Brazils, Rio took five thousand, of which the average price was twenty pounds sterling each. The Queen of Portugal receives sixty thousand pounds per annum, into her privy purse, by a duty of ten thousand rees [*reis*], on each slave, paid before they are shipped from Africa." He described the Amerindians as "low in stature, muscular, stout and active; of a light-brown complection; straight black hair; little beard; long dark eyes, but with tokens of intellect. They entertained an implacable antipathy to the invaders of their country; they shun the settlements of the Portugueze, but massacre individuals, without remorse, whereever they are found scattered or unprotected." Staunton briefly describes Brazil and its resources. He also lists Rio de Janeiro's chief fortresses. On 17 December, after a month and a half in Rio, the Earl of Macartney's expedition left Brazil and continued on to China.

[590] James Colnett. *A Voyage to the South Atlantic and Round Cape Horn into the Pacific Ocean, for the Purpose of Extending the Spermaceti Whale Fisheries, and Other Objects of Commerce.* London: W. Bennett, 1798. xviii, 179 pp.

Captain Colnett of the Royal Navy arrived in Rio de Janeiro on 24 February 1793 in the ship *Rattler.* In Rio he "found Governor Phillips **[580]** on his homeward bound passage from Botany Bay, in the Atlantic transport" and presented him with a five-hundred pound turtle the *Rattler's* crew had caught. Though Colnett's account has little on Rio de

Janeiro itself, other than the observation that "the land-breeze, at this place, commences in the evening, and generally continues until the morning," he does provide a detailed description of the procedures foreign ships had to follow before entering port: "On the arrival of a ship off Santa-Cruz at the mouth of Rio Janeiro, the Patrimor [*Patrão-mor*] or harbour master comes on board, takes charge of the vessel, carries her into the harbour and moors her in good birth. Sometimes the mate is first taken out, as was the ceremony with me, to undergo examination; but the captain is not suffered to leave the ship without orders; neither will any supplies be admitted until a visit has been made by the officers of police, to enquire into the health of the crew, from whence you came, whither you are bound, what is the particular object of youi voyage, and the time you wish to stay. The mates are then taken on shore to be examined, when their declaration with that of the commanding officer, is laid before the Viceroy whose official permission must be given before any commercial intercourse can take place between the ship and the shore: the captain and officers must also sign a declaration, acknowledging that they and their crew consider themselves as amenable to the laws of the country, while they remain in it." In addition, "the commanders of merchant vessels are required to give one day's notice previous to their sailing from this port." Colnett left Rio de Janeiro in mid-March of 1793.

[591] James Wilson. *A Missionary Voyage to the Southern Pacific Ocean, Performed in the Years 1796, 1797, 1798, in the Ship Duff, Commanded by Captain James Wilson. Compiled from Journals of the Officers and the Missionaries; and illustrated with Maps, Charts, and Views, Drawn by Mr. William Wilson.* London: T. Chapman, 1799. c, 420 pp.
[There was also another edition with an identical title but different pagination published the same year by T. Chapman. It only contained 395 pages and was printed by T. Gillet. The edition cited in the main entry was printed by S. Gosnell.]

Though the captain, James Wilson, is frequently given credit for this account, the advertisement states that "the body of the journal is the composition of Mr. William Wilson [the chief officer], from the Captain's papers, his own, and the Missionaries' reports." On 24 September 1796, the *Duff,* carrying a contingent of English missionaries sponsored by the London Missionary Society, sailed from Portsmouth. The Protestants planned to establish a mission in Tahiti. On 12 November they arrived in Rio de Janeiro. "As soon as we had anchored, a guard-boat, with the proper officers, came alongside, in order to prevent smuggling, and watch that no person went from the ship unaccompanied by a soldier. It is remarked, that the government in this colony acts towards strangers with the most jealous caution." Wilson described the Brazilian capital thusly: "The inhabitants are a mixture of Portuguese, Mulattoes, and negroes, and their number in the city and suburbs cannot exceed two hundred thousand. The churches, monasteries, convents, the viceroy's palace, the hospital, and a few private houses, have a good appearance. The streets are narrow, but straight and regular. Their windows and the upper part of their doors being latticed with rods laid across each other, and close shut all day, a stranger walking along, and seeing women and children peep through these gratings, might suppose their dwellings are so many prisons." The author was scandalized by the Brazilians' religious practices: "This capital appears to exceed all popish places in the parade of religion. At the corner of every street is a figure of our Saviour and the Virgin Mary placed in a niche, or kind of cupboard, with a curtain and glass window before it; in the night, candles are lighted; and here the people stop to address their devotions, and the whole night long the voice of their chanting to these images may be heard. Even the common beggar makes a trade of religion, by carrying a little crucifix at his breast, which I suppose he may buy for a penny; at this the poorer sort cross themselves, and the beggar blessing them, must be paid for his benediction as well as the pope." The missionaries expressed similar sentiments after going ashore to visit the city. At the viceregal palace, "the colonel commandant and his lady shewed us the greatest politeness, and his lady was peculiarly attentive to our wives; and sorry we were that we could make no acknowledgements in return; especially when we saw their rooted superstitions, beads and crucifixes hung about their necks; and the cross and their saints were at the corner of every street, and before their houses: to these they bow and cross themselves as they pass. Indeed they seem sunk in idolatry. The number of their priests is immense. The town seemed not bigger than Bristol." The missionaries were also "shocked with the sight of a poor slave worn out with disease and labour, advancing with feeble crawl to the water's edge; and shortly after beheld a scene disgusting to humanity, a cargo of human beings exposed for sale, naked in the market-place; whilst others, in companies of six or seven chained together, were traversing the streets with burdens: we have seen their masters flog them like horses or dogs, so that our eyes have been filled with tears at the sight. When shall this barbarous traffic come to an end?" After spending a little more than a week in Rio de Janeiro "refitting our rigging, watering our ship, and procuring live stock, wine, &c. for sea store," the missionaries departed from Brazil on 20 November 1796. One of the plates depicts the harbor of Rio de Janeiro.

[592] James Wilson and William Gregory. *The Life and Dreadful Sufferings, of Captain James Wilson, in Various Ports of the Globe, including a Faithful Narrative of Every Circumstance during the Voyage to the South Sea Islands, in the Missionary Ship Duff, for the Propagation of the Gospel; with an Authentic and Interesting Account of the Sufferings and Calamities of the Missionaries, from the Year 1797, to the Present Time.* Portsea: G. A. Stephens, 1810.

Includes the earlier description of Rio de Janeiro found in Wilson **[591]**.

[593] John Griffin. *Memoirs of Captain James Wilson, Containing an Account of His Enterprises and Sufferings in India, His Conversion to Christianity, His Missionary Voyage to the South Seas, and His Peaceful and Triumphant Death.*

Includes the earlier description of Rio de Janeiro found in Wilson **[591]**.

[594] George Barrington. *A Voyage to New South Wales.* New York: John Swain, 1801. 184 pp.
[Borba de Moraes **[20]** describes a later, enlarged edition: *An Account of a Voyage to New South Wales.* London: M. Jones, 1810. 472 pp.]

The Irish-born Barrington visited Rio de Janeiro in the late eighteenth century while being deported to New South Wales as a pickpocket. Because he helped put down an attempt by some of the prisoners to take over the ship, he was given special treatment and allowed to go ashore. Barrington spent about three weeks in the Brazilian capital city, while the sick recovered and the ships were being "replenished with water, and loaded with vegetables and fruit of all kinds." The 1801 edition devotes only a page and a half to his visit. Barrington observed that "the city of St. Sebastian is tolerably large, and regularly built; but from its being situated on low swampy ground, surrounded by high hills, it is entirely excluded from the refreshing sea and land breezes, so that in the summer months, it is insupportably hot, and of course very unhealthy." He found the interior of the churches to be "decorated with the utmost profusion, and most of them furnished with an excellent organ, and tolerable good pictures over the different alters [sic]."

[595] James Kingston Tuckey. *An Account of a Voyage to Establish a Colony at Port Philip in Bass's Strait, on the South Coast of New South Wales, in His Majesty's Ship Calcutta, in the Years 1802-3-4.* London: Longman, Hurst, Rees, Orme, and Brown, 1805. xv, 239 pp.

Tuckey was first lieutenant of the *Calcutta*. He visited Rio de Janeiro twice, in 1802 on the voyage to Australia and again in 1804 on his return home. He gives a detailed description of Rio as well as an overview of Portuguese rule in Brazil, with information on Brazilian society, administration, and the economy.

[596] Richard J[effry] Cleveland. *A Narrative of Voyages and Commercial Enterprises.* 2 vols. Cambridge, Massachusetts: John Owen, 1842. xvi, 249 pp; viii, 240 pp.

Volume I contains a description of Rio de Janeiro which Cleveland visited in January of 1802: "The Viceroy permitted us to remain eight days. This was ample time to fill up our water-casks, to procure a supply of stock, vegetables, and fruit, and to ascertain if it were possible to dispose of our cargo to some one of the traders, who were here from the River Plate." Cleveland passed an interesting evening at the Theatre which he describes. His most useful description is that of "the Convent of Benedictines, which is beautifully situated on an eminence facing the harbour." Cleveland was given a tour of the interior of the monastery: "The profusion of ornaments and gold about the altar, which strikes the eye on first entering, is very grand and imposing, and probably produces the reverential effect intended on the majority of those who worship there." After visiting the church, "we passed up a flight of stairs to the cells and the dining room. The former are about twelve feet square, with one window, and are furnished each with a bed, a chair, and a table of ordinary manufacture. The latter is about sixty feet by thirty, with small windows near the ceiling. On one side, about midway of the room, is a pulpit, from which one of the brothers reads a sermon or homily, while the others are engaged at their meal." Cleveland then visited the library. "On the same floor, and in a delightful room, the large windows of which open upon the harbour, is the library, containing from ten to twelve thousand volumes, mostly in the French, Italian, and Latin languages." At the time of his tour the Benedictines there numbered "about forty good healthy-looking men, who may be supposed to be leading innocent lives, but certainly to appearance, very useless ones." The author also describes Rio de Janeiro's public gardens, the city itself and some of its buildings. Volume II describes several additional visits to Brazil by Cleveland. In October of 1806, he was forced to seek refuge and repairs in Rio de Janeiro because of a broken foremast. That same year he visited the island of Santa Catarina. "The houses are of very ordinary construction, generally of one story; and their furniture is of the rudest manufacture, and limited to articles of indispensable necessity." He concluded that "in consequence of the limited native commerce of St. Catharine's, and the small number of foreign ships which visit it, there are no inducements to the inhabitants to prepare such supplies of live stock, vegetables, and fruits, as are desirable for vessels touching there." Cleveland briefly describes some of his experiences along the coast of Pernambuco after the 1817 Revolt. He also narrates an unpleasant encounter he had with a customs-house officer during his stay in Rio de Janeiro in August of 1820.

[597] James Hardy Vaux. *Memoirs of James Hardy Vaux.* 2 vols. London: W. Clowes, 1819. xx, 247 pp.; vii, 227 pp.
[There is a reprint edited by Noel McLachland, *The Memoirs of James Hardy Vaux.* London: Heinemann, 1964. lxxv. 315 pp. It contains a useful introduction and notes.]

A gambler, con-man, and embezzler, James Hardy Vaux was convicted and deported to Botany Bay. After a number of adventures in Australia, Vaux received a free pardon and on 10 February 1807 set sail for England. Leaking, and short of water and provisions, his ship arrived in Rio de Janeiro on 22 May after fifteen weeks at sea. Vaux was impressed with the "long table of rules and ceremonies to be observed by our ship's company. . . . They related to the times and places of landing from boats; the behavior of the English when on shore; respect to be paid to the Catholic religion and its ministers, etc. . . . Among other injunctions it was expected that every Englishman on passing a church should move his hat, and pay the same compliment to the Image of the Virgin Mary, which you encounter at the corner of every principal street. . . . It was also required that every person on meeting the Host (which is a grand procession of priests, friars, &c., followed by an immense rabble) should bend on one knee, and so remain till the procession was past. The priests, on this occasion, carry gold or silver images of our Saviour and the saints, accompanied with musical instruments, flags, numerous lighted flambeaus, and every other device to render the scene at once grand, solemn, and impressive." The author further remarked: "It being the first Catholic country I was ever in, I was struck with admiration at the grandeur of the churches, the nightly exhibitions of fire-works, illuminations, ringing of bells, and other demonstrations of religious aspects, or what we should call superstition. But I am of opinion there is much policy in carrying these rites to such an extravagant pitch, for the population of this city being composed of negroes, in the proportion, I take it, of at least nineteen to one white, and the majority of the former being slaves, the splendour and enchanting effects of music, paintings, fire-works, processions, and other devices, together with the implicit devotion in which they are brought up to the Catholic religion, keep their minds in a continual state of resigned subjection, amuse their senses, and leave neither time, nor inducement to attempt, by acts of rebellion, a release from their habitual bondage." Vaux observed that "the Portuguese excel in music, particularly the violin and bass-viol; and there were frequently large parties of amateurs at our house, who formed a most delightful evening concert. This is, in fact, the custom of all people of fashion there, who, instead of meeting for the purpose of gaming as in London, adopt this much more laudable and rational mode of amusement." Vaux also provided a good description of certain aspects of slavery: "Another object of my attention was the slave-market, which is held on the arrival of a Guinea ship, in the suburbs of the city. These unfortunate beings are chained together, and driven to the scene of this disgraceful traffic, where they are sold like cattle or sheep in Smithfield. A healthy youth of about fifteen will produce from about thirty to fifty pounds, this being considered the most advantageous age at which a slave can be purchased. The condition of this unhappy class of persons is, however, much more tolerable in this city than a stranger would suppose. Most of the inhabitants possess a male or female, (some several,) exclusive of those employed in household affairs. These superfluous slaves are sent out in a morning to ply for hire on their owner's account, and obtain as much as they can by their labour; the majority of the women confine themselves to carrying water from the fountains, which they cry as the venders of milk do in London; and on being hailed, they stop and empty their vessel, for which they receive a vintain (about three halfpence;) they then return to the nearest fountain to replenish. I could not help being surprised at the large size of the vessels in which they carry this water on their heads; they are a kind of wooden casks, some of them holding at least ten gallons. . . . As the trade of water-carrying furnishes employment for many hundreds of negro women, and their continual resort to the fountains would occasion much confusion and quarrelling, a soldier is placed in attendance to preserve order, and the women seat themselves in a row on a long bench fixed on purpose, where they are obliged to wait for their turn to fill. It is a curious and interesting sight to observe these harmless and industrious creatures conversing with each other, and smoking their pipes, while they patiently await the sentinel's intimation to approach." The author concluded his section on slavery in Brazil with a discussion of the clothing of slaves and freedmen: "The men wear coarse jackets and trowsers, the women a sort of gown of blue cloth; but their linen is always remarkably white, of a fine texture, and beautifully wrought with ornamental work about the sleeves and bosom. They have also bracelets both on the wrists and ancles, and ear-rings, all of the purest gold. Both sexes are very cleanly in their persons, and of a most docile and gentle disposition." Vaux also described the opera in Rio, which he visited frequently during his stay. On 12 August 1807 he set sail for England.

E. Bahia and Its Subordinate Captaincies [Nos. 598–615]

Ruth Lapham Butler's studies of the first three governors-general—Tomé de Sousa **[269]**, Duarte da Costa **[270]**, and Mem de Sá **[271]**—provide useful information on the early history of Bahia. Alexander Marchant **[136]** and Elaine Sanceau **[146]** and their surveys of Brazil in the sixteenth century are also helpful. Stuart B. Schwartz **[898]** compares the first few decades of Bahia's history with that of Mexico. In his studies of the *Relação* **[283]** and **[284]** Schwartz also provides a good overview of the city and the royal captaincy. Russell-Wood **[300]** does the same in his study of Bahia's Misericordia. There is an excellent survey of Bahia's history, 1695–1750, in Charles Boxer's *Golden Age of Brazil* **[548]**. Boxer also examines the role of Salvador's town council during the colonial period **[287]**.

David Grant Smith **[598]** studies the mercantile class in Bahia and Lisbon during the seventeenth century. Boxer **[599]** discusses the correspondence of a Bahian merchant, João Serrão de Oliveira, in the mid-seventeenth century. Serrão de Oliveira soon moved to Lisbon, but kept his ties with Bahia. Rae Flory **[600]** analyzes Bahian society in the mid-colonial period. She and David Smith **[601]** pay special attention to Bahian merchants and planters in the seventeenth and early eighteenth century. Stuart B. Schwartz **[602]** studies the *lavradores de Cana*. Catherine Lugar **[603]** describes tobacco growers in the Brazilian *Recôncavo*. A. J. R. Russell-Wood **[604]** analyzes class, creed and color in colonial Bahia. Robert C. Smith **[605]** describes and analyzes four eighteenth-century views of Bahia. John N. Kennedy **[606]** examines the Bahian elites, 1750–1822, a number of them having ties with the military, on which F. W. O. Morton **[607]** concentrates. Morton **[608]** also has a provocative study on royal timber in late colonial Bahia. Robert C. Smith **[609]** discusses the career of the Conde dos Arcos, the early nineteenth-century governor-general of the captaincy of Bahia, who was responsible for a number of important public works as well as the Merchant's Exchange. The Jesuits, who played an important role in Bahia's colonial history are studied in section XI, A, 2, a. Bahia's art is discussed in detail in section XXI, B, 2, c [Nos. 765, 767–770].

[598] David Grant Smith. "The Mercantile Class of Portugal and Brazil in the Seventeenth Century: A Socio-Economic Study of the Merchants of Lisbon and Bahia, 1620–1690," (Ph.D. Dissertation: The University of Texas at Austin, 1975), 452 pp.

The author uses a collective biography approach to analyze the mercantile communities of seventeenth-century Lisbon and Bahia. These merchant groups are examined as to ethnic, geographical and social origin. Although in both cities most merchants were new immigrants, in Lisbon New Christians predominated, and in Bahia Old Christians were more numerous. Smith shows how careers were advanced through marriage alliances, personal ties and commercial partnerships. He highlights the surprising social mobility of successful merchants, where a rise from artisan to minor nobility was not uncommon in one generation. The upper strata of the mercantile class in Lisbon were merchant bankers with financial and other ties to the Crown. In Brazil the most successful merchants bought sugar and cattle land and worked themselves into the planter aristocracy. These merchants and planters "blended into a continuous social grouping with no clear-cut distinction." Politically the mercantile classes in Portugal and Brazil achieved no power due to several factors: religious persecutions of New Christians; contempt for the merchant trade; and the ability of the aristocracy to co-opt leading members of the mercantile community. Based on archival research in Brazil and Portugal.
DAI 37/01-A (p. 525).

[599] C. R. Boxer. "The Commercial Letter-Book and Testament of a Luso-Brazilian Merchant, 1646–1656," *Boletin de Estudios Latinoamericana y del Caribe* 18 (June 1975), pp. 49–56.

Discusses some of the correspondence found in the copybook of the merchant João Serrão de Oliveira. This valuable and rare manuscript contains copies of 349 letters written by the Bahian- and later Lisbon-based merchant during a ten-year period. Boxer lists the names of some of Serrão de Oliveira's correspondents as well as those of some of his relatives and friends, and gives details from a few of the letters. The author shows that the merchant had connections in Holland—even though northeastern Brazil was occupied during much of this time by the Dutch—in addition to those in Hamburg, Rouen, Venice and other parts of Europe as well as in Angola, Brazil and Portugal's Atlantic Islands. Boxer speculates whether Serrão de Oliveira "despite the conventionally devout phrasing of his will and despite the fact that he never seems to have got into trouble with the Inquisition" was secretly a Jew and concludes that "his letter-book of 1646–1656, taken in conjunction with his will, strongly supports David Grant Smith's contention

[598] that in terms of business associations, there was no division of Old and New Christians into separate groups." Based primarily on the *libro copiador* in the Lilly Library of Indiana University. 24 notes. The appendix contains a copy in Portuguese of the merchant's last will and testament.

[600] Rae Jean Dell Flory. "Bahian Society in the Mid-Colonial Period: The Sugar Planters, Tobacco Growers, Merchants, and Artisans of Salvador and the Reconcavo, 1680–1725," (Ph.D. Dissertation: The University of Texas at Austin, 1978). 394 pp.

Using a collective biography approach, the author analyzes various groups (sugar planters, tobacco growers, merchants, artisans) in Bahian society in order to define social differentiation, social mobility, social stereotypes, and social change in the early eighteenth century. The intermediate level of society included prosperous artisans, entrepreneurs, and tobacco farmers of diverse backgrounds, demonstrating the complexity of society as a whole. The Bahian elite, well-established land and sugar mill owners and their families, was not closed to wealthy businessmen who could buy land and mills, marry advantageously, and hold office. In the early eighteenth century merchants achieved a greater role in local institutions because of new commercial opportunities. This, however, did not lessen planter influence or mark a fundamental change in the makeup of the elite. The old sugar families dominated the militia as well as local government through new Reconcavo town councils. Most office holders of mercantile origins achieved their positions after marrying into Bahian high society or becoming planters and landowners. Based on archival research (notarial registers) in Bahia.
DAI 39/04-A (pp. 2477–2478)

[601] Rae Flory and David Grant Smith. "Bahian Merchants and Planters in the Seventeenth and Early Eighteenth Centuries," *The Hispanic American Historical Review* 58:4 (November 1978), pp. 571–594.

Challenges the contention of Russell-Wood and others that "the aristocracy [of colonial Bahia] always kept itself hermetically closed to any aspiration on the part of the *haute bourgeoisie*." After studying the "origins, marriage patterns, and economic activities of merchants, as well as their roles in key social and political institutions," the authors conclude that far from there being "a rigid division between merchants and planters" in Bahian society, there was "a continuum in which the local elite was set off from the rest of the population by an ill-defined and permeable barrier constructed from requirements of wealth, land ownership, family connections, and other intangible criteria." A substantial number of the more prosperous merchants were part of this elite. Flory and Smith show that the greater part of Bahia's merchant community was made up of Portuguese immigrants, most of them from northern Portugal. Of those who had wives, most were married to Bahian-born women whose fathers were often merchants or planters. In addition, merchants were active on municipal councils and in the Santa Casa da Misericordia in the seventeenth as well as the eighteenth century. They also held positions of leadership in the local militias. Based mainly on archival and printed primary sources. 3 tables. 60 notes.

[602] Stuart B. Schwartz. "Free Labor in a Slave Economy: The *Lavradores de Cana* of Colonial Bahia," in Alden, ed., *Colonial Roots* **[87]**, pp. 147–197.

Schwartz focuses on a neglected sector of Brazil's free population—the *lavradores de cana* or cane growers of Bahia. For his study he relies heavily on the papers of the plantation of Sergipe do Conde, "one of the largest and certainly the most famous of the sugar plantations in colonial Brazil," located in the midst of the Bahian Recôncavo. The author discusses land tenure, the size and distribution of land holdings, and patterns of settlement and land use in the Recôncavo. He then examines the needs and problems of the sugar industry. Schwartz attempts a social profile of the *lavrador de cana* and finds "a wide gulf existed between a cane grower who produced one *tarefa* a year and a man whose fields yielded forty or fifty *tarefas*." Though some *lavradores de cana* were wealthy and powerful, many others had fewer than six slaves. Schwartz concludes that "in Brazil the economic spectrum of the *lavradores de cana* was broad, but socially they must as a group be considered an adjunct to the wealthy planter class, men of more or less the same social origins, but lacking the economic foundations capable of fully supporting their desires." He also found a surprisingly large number of clerics and women listed among the *lavradores de cana* in Sergipe do Conde. Seventeen percent of the *lavradores de cana* in Pernambuco and Alagoas in 1639 (then under Dutch control) were women. The author concludes with a discussion of the conflicts, mobility and change the *lavradores de cana* experienced in the latter part of the seventeenth and the early years of the eighteenth century. Based largely on archival and printed primary materials. 4 maps. 2 graphs. 6 tables. 141 notes.

[603] Catherine Lugar. "The Portuguese Tobacco Trade and Tobacco Growers of Bahia in the Late Colonial Period," in Alden and Dean, eds., *Essays Concerning the Socioeconomic History of Brazil and Portuguese India* **[89]**, pp. 26–70.

In this well-organized chapter, the author focuses on tobacco growers in the district of the Bahian *Recôncavo*. She sees four stages in the development of commercial cultivation during the colonial period: 1) "ca. 1620–98: the establishment of the most characteristic features of tobacco cultivation and trade, including regional concentration of cultivation for export by growers in Bahia; the practice of labor-intensive techniques of cultivation with apparently few slaves; the development of markets in Europe and West Africa; the specialization in twist, or roll, tobacco"; 2) "1698–1750, growth: the expansion of the African market as a result of the strong demand for slaves in the Brazilian gold fields in the interior; increased production restrained only by the higher costs of slaves; the initiation of restrictions on the amount of tobacco to be employed in the slave trade"; 3) "1751–1815, diversification: efforts to promote the culture of Virginian and Cuban leaf varieties of tobacco with the expansion of trade to Europe in quality tobacco; a steady growth in both European and African exports, indicating increased levels of productivity and an increasing number of growers; some large, others quite marginal"; 4) "1815–35, transition: a temporary decline in productivity, owing to the shift of many large-scale growers from tobacco to cotton in response to the loss of African markets, lower prices for Brazilian tobacco in Europe, and disruption of agriculture during the independence struggle." Based on archival and printed primary sources. 1 map. 18 tables. 3 illus. 111 notes.

[604] A. J. R. Russell-Wood. "Class, Creed and Colour in Colonial Bahia: A Study in Prejudice," *Race* 9:2 (October 1967), pp. 133–157.

Though it is noted that the article "forms part of the author's forthcoming book, entitled *Fidalgos and Philanthropists*" **[300]**, this piece is not the usual modified chapter or earlier draft but a succinct perceptive overview of the three major factors—class, creed, and color—that determined socioeconomic relationships in colonial Bahia. The author discusses the reactions of travellers to these factors and analyzes the social structure of Bahia. He also studies the role of religion and the position of Jews in Bahian life. Russell-Wood concludes by examining the position of "coloureds, Negroes and Amerindians" in Bahian society and argues that "prejudices of class, creed and colour existed in colonial Bahia." Furthermore, "these prejudices were related to a substantial degree." Based heavily on Bahian archival materials and printed primary sources. 66 notes.

[605] Robert C. Smith. "Some Views of Colonial Bahia," *Belas Artes* (Lisbon), 2ª Serie, no. 1 (1948), pp. 31–47.

Describes and analyzes four eighteenth-century panoramic views of Bahia and its environs: 1) a watercolor of "the entrance to the harbor of Salvador with its forts, its hills and houses," the author of which is identified as João de Abreu e Carvalho, son of one of the most important Portuguese military engineers in seventeenth-century Brazil; 2) The Morgado de Santa Barbara, created in 1641 by Francisco Pereira and his wife, Andresa de Araujo, located at the foot of Salvador's Ladeira da Misericordia—a sketch probably required by the town council before major reconstruction could be undertaken. Its realism (buildings are shown in disrepair) and detail offer the historian much information on seventeenth-century construction techniques and architecture (structures no longer standing at the end of the following century are carefully represented); 3) A second drawing of the Morgado de Santa Barbara done at a later time and less carefully; 4) Part of the Reconcavo (on the far side of the Bahia de Todos os Santos) focusing on the towns of Cachoeira and São Felix. This sketch is part of a manuscript prepared by Dr. Joaquim do Amorim Castro and dated 1792 which describes the culture of tobacco. Based almost entirely on archival materials, most of them Brazilian. 61 notes.

[606] John N. Kennedy. "Bahian Elites, 1750–1822," *The Hispanic American Historical Review* 53:3 (August 1973), pp. 415–439.

Seriously challenges the view that native-born Brazilians were excluded from positions of power and argues that a study of Bahia's elite (i.e., "the wealthiest rural landowners, the wealthiest merchants, those who occupied the highest posts in the fiscal-administrative bureaucracy and those who held the highest ranks in the regular or reserve military forces") reveals that "Brazilian-born colonists held positions at all levels in the fiscal-administrative bureaucracy and in the military officer corps." The author claims that "the four sectors of the Bahian elite coalesced and formed one cohesive socioeconomic entity during the last half of the eighteenth century." Based on archival (especially the Arquivo Histórico Ultramarino, Lisbon) as well as printed primary sources and secondary materials. 89 notes.

[607] F. W. O. Morton. "The Military and Society in Bahia, 1800–1821," *Journal of Latin American Studies* 7:2 (November 1975), pp. 249–269.

Examines the backgrounds, functions and relationships to Bahian society of officers as well as enlisted men in both the professional military and the part-time or militia units. Morton shows that "all the rank and file and the bulk of the officers were recruited in Bahia itself." He also makes it clear that service as an officer was popular since, among other things, it bestowed or reinforced social status and carried privileges (one of the most important being the *foro militar*). The rank and file, on the other hand, were "predominantly poor, coloured and Bahian." The author analyzes recruiting practices, promotion procedures, conditions of service, and the rivalries between Portuguese- and Brazilian-born officers and concludes by describing the numerous conflicts that arose between various factions in the military in the decade following independence. Based largely on archival (both Portuguese and Brazilian) materials. 51 notes. 1 table.

[608] F. W. O. Morton. "The Royal Timber in Late Colonial Bahia," *The Hispanic American Historical Review* 58:1 (February 1978), pp. 41–61.

Interesting study of timber belonging exclusively to the crown *(madeiras da lei)* in southern Bahia, especially in the former proprietary colonies of Ilheus and Porto Seguro, and its relationship to the Portuguese shipbuilding industry both in Europe and in Bahia. The author discusses the *Reais Cortes* (royal logging operations) and the fifty or sixty individuals who formed the local elite of timber administrators, *fabricantes* (producers of timber) and owners of oxteams and ships. Morton views this system as "a variant of the familiar pattern of colonial Brazilian government in which the crown, in return for revenue and recruits, legitimized the control and exploitation of the countryside by local elites." However, as the volume of shipbuilding greatly increased, the timber supplies dwindled. At the same time, virgin forests were being destroyed by increased manioc cultivation. These changes, combined with what was seen as waste and inefficiency in the timber industry, caught the attention of Rodrigo de Sousa Coutinho, a strong advocate of active government and rational reform, who became Colonial Secretary in 1796. Soon there was a struggle between direct royal control represented by Baltasar da Silva Lisboa, *ouvidor* of Ilheus and the first judge-conservator of the *Reais Cortes,* and free enterprise, bolstered by the laissez-faire doctrines of Adam Smith, represented by José de Sá Bittencourt e Accioli, whose family held large estates in the same *comarca.* At issue was the *plano* of 1799 that "reserved all timber on crown land in Ilheus and Alagoas to the Royal Navy and which declared that certain *madeiras da lei* could be sold only to the Royal Arsenal at a set price. Private individuals had to purchase planks from the Royal Arsenal. Resistance came from the sawmill owners and from merchants and shipowners of Salvador. The sawmill owners withheld wood. Soon the government, faced with a number of difficulties, yielded to local interests. Based heavily on archival materials in Bahia and at the Biblioteca Nacional in Rio de Janeiro. 1 table. 55 notes.

[609] Robert C. Smith. "A Brazilian Merchants' Exchange," *Gazette des Beaux-Arts* 36 (July–September 1949), pp. 75–96.

Summarizes the career of Dom Marcos de Noronha e Brito, eighth Count of Arcos, Governor-General of the Captaincy of Bahia, who during his administration (1810–1818) was responsible for Salvador's first public park, paved city streets, built roads to outlying communities, helped set up the city's first printing press, opened in one of the rooms of his palace the town's first public library, and promoted the creation of a Merchants' Exchange. In the Count of Arcos' words, "a Merchants' Exchange is the most powerful means known to man to facilitate and multiply mercantile transactions, including at the same time useful establishment of principles of polish, exactitude and other commercial virtues." The author discusses the plans and building of this "edifice of elegant though inexpensive construction" and argues that the author of its design seems to have been Cosme Damião da Cunha Fidie, lieutenant colonel attached to the second infantry regiment of Bahia. Smith describes in detail the Exchange's measurements and architectural characteristics and discusses various English—and even possible North American—influences in its design. Because of its Merchants' Exchange, Salvador has "the honor of having inaugurated the neo-classic reaction in Brazil." Based on archival as well as printed primary and secondary sources. 14 illus. 54 notes.

1. Contemporary Narratives, 1700–1822 [Nos. 610–615]

Most of the travellers whose accounts are in English and who visited Bahia in the post-1700 period arrived there in the late eighteenth and early nineteenth centuries. Mrs. Nathaniel Kindersley **[610]** visited Bahia in 1764 and voiced disapproval of her stay there. John Brown **[611]** was one of three shipwrecks who eventually reached Salvador. James George Semple Lisle **[535]** was favorably impressed with Salvador in 1798. John Turnbull **[612]** who arrived in Salvador three years later, provides a sympathetic portrait of the former capital of Brazil. He was especially impressed with Bahia's shipbuilding. Thomas Lindley **[613]** gives a lengthy account of his experiences in Bahia from 1802–1803, during which time he was under arrest for dealing in contraband. Appended to his diary is a description of the captaincy of Porto Seguro. G. M. Keith **[614]** was unimpressed with his stay in Bahia in November of 1805. John White **[615]** visited Bahia briefly in September of 1819. In 1821–1822, Maria Graham **[628]** made two visits to Bahia. The first, in late 1821, lasted a little more than a month and a half. The second—of less than a month's duration—was made early the following year.

[610] Mrs. Nathaniel Kindersley [Mary Molesworth]. *Letters from the Island of Teneriffe, Brazil, the Cape of Good Hope, and the East Indies.* London: J. Nourse, 1777. 301 pp.

According to Borba de Moraes **[20]**, I, 368, "Mrs. Kindersley was the first woman to have left a narration of a voyage to Brazil." She visited Bahia in August of 1764 on her way to India. In a series of letters she voiced her disapproval of much of what she saw in the former capital of Brazil. She claimed that since the Bahian women were "brought up in indolence, and their minds uncultivated, their natural quickness shows itself in cunning. As their male relations do not place any confidence in their virtue, they in return use their utmost art to elude the vigilance with which they are observed; and to speak the most favorably, a spirit of intrigue reigns among them. Were I to tell you what the darkness of evening conceals, amongst such as are not to be seen in the day but in a church, it would look like a libel on the sex." Mrs. Kindersley wrote that "many of them, when they are quite young, have delicate features and persons, but there is a certain yellow tint in their complexions which is disagreeable, and beside they look old very early in life." The author pointed out that "the dress is calculated for a hot climate; the best-dressed woman I have seen, had on a chintz petticoat, a flowered muslin shift, with deep ruffles, and a tucker of the same sewed upon it, without any stays or gown, but a large sash of crimson velvet, thrown round and round her waist. Her hair was braided behind and fastened up with a great many combs; she had drops in her ears, and her hair was ornamented with a sort of egret, or rather a large lump of massive gold, embossed and set with diamonds; on her neck were several rows of small gold chain; and on her arms she had bracelets of gold of great thickness, and each of them wide enough for two. A pair of slippers like the sash, completed the dress."

[611] John Brown. *Narrative of the Dreadful Sufferings of Six Men, Who Left the Island of St. Helena in a Whale Boat.* Stirling: C. Randall, 1806, 8 pp.

According to Borba de Moraes **[20]**, I, 114–115, three survivors reached Bahia at Belmonte. Eventually they were taken to Salvador. Two of the three survivors went to Rio de Janeiro, where John Brown was hospitalized.

[612] John Turnbull. *A Voyage Round the World in the Years 1800, 1801, 1802, 1803, and 1804: in which the Author Visited Madeira, the Brazils, Cape of Good Hope, the English Settlements of Botany Bay and Norfolk Island; and the Principal Islands in the Pacific Ocean.* 2nd ed. London: A Maxwell, 1813. xv, 516 pp.

On the evening of 2 July 1801, John Turnbull left England. After stopping at the Madeira Islands, the author arrived at Salvador at the end of August. Chapter III (pp. 19–38) describes the city and its economy. "The houses have latice windows and balconies, but the streets in many parts of the town, are so narrow, that two neighbours in opposite balconies might almost shake hands. The population is estimated at from 90 to 100,000. The inhabitants may be classed into three divisions, whites, mulattoes, and blacks, of which the latter is by somewhat the largest." He visited the cathedral where he heard the Archbishop preach a sermon. He found the churches "corresponding in every respect both with the genius of their religion and the wealth of their settlement; they were magnificently adorned, and the ornaments of the images appeared to us to be very valuable." The churches were "crowded with all ranks of people, from the meanest slave to his excellency the governor himself." Turnbull describes a procession to the Virgin, almsgiving, and his encounter with a group of black musicians. He was particularly impressed with the large number of religious festivals. Of special interest to Turnbull was Bahia's ship-building industry. "Like all other new and unbroken countries, there is a greater want of workmen, than of materials. If carpenters or shipwrights were in greater numbers, vessels might be very cheaply built, from the great abundance and quality of the timber. The forests of the Brazils are not excelled, perhaps not equalled, by those of Europe. . . . The dockyear, from its commodiousness, and still more from its capabilities of further improvement and enlargement, attracted much of my attention, indeed much more than any other object whatever. It is a large square area of ground, immediately fronting the water, enclosed on all sides." The author was invited to inspect a sixty-four gun ship that was nearing completion—"a most complete, and well finished piece of workmanship; and, together with its neatness, to have a strength and substance, not to be excelled, and not commonly equalled in the European docks." He praised the Portuguese caulkers as "perhaps, the first in the world; for oakum, they make use of a fibrous bark, which they say is less subject to decay than that article. The common labourers in the dock I observed to be chiefly convicts, and others condemned to the works, as punishments for their civil crimes." In light of the troubled European situation because of the Napoleonic Wars, he suggested that England have her ships built in Brazil. In addition to the topics mentioned in the title of chapter IV (pp. 39–58), "Trade, Revenue, Price of Provisions,"

Turnbull makes some interesting comments on justice in Brazil: "The Portuguese laws, in many respects, are not severe. Executions are rare; punishment by torture is forbidden. The principal fault is in the insecurity of personal liberty, and the difficulty of procuring what, in England, is termed a fair trial. . . . Smuggling, however, is considered almost as bad as forgery in England, and punished with a rigour accordingly. The laws of debtor and creditor resemble those of Scotland: an insolvent debtor makes a cession of his goods to his creditor, and thenceforth is personally free." This chapter (four) is not found in the first edition.

[613] Thomas Lindley. *Narrative of a Voyage to Brasil: Terminating in the Seizure of a British Vessel, and the Imprisonment of the Author and the Ship's Crew, by the Portuguese.* London: J. Johnson, 1805. xxxi, 298 pp. [According to Borba de Moraes **[20]**, I, 415, Lindley's later *Authentic Narrative of a Voyage from the Cape of Good Hope to Brasil,* London, 1808, is not a new edition, but merely the first edition with a new title page.]

Thomas Lindley, his wife, and crew—along with a number of Portuguese officials from Porto Seguro—were arrested in 1802 for dealing in contraband. The Englishman was imprisoned for a little more than a year. The diary account of his imprisonment covers the period from 13 July 1802 (he was arrested the following day) to 5 August 1803, the date he escaped aboard a ship sailing to Portugal. From there, he managed to return to England. Lindley's diary (pp. 1–210) provides a good glimpse into legal proceedings and prison conditions in Brazil. Though the contrabandist's initial imprisonment was harsh, he eventually was given considerable freedom—an apartment in the fort commander's quarters and, later, liberty to walk around Salvador and its environs during the day. In his diary, he describes Salvador's Forte do Mar and Forte Barbalho (in both of which he was imprisoned), many of the city's churches and their ceremonies, and a number of officials with whom he came in contact. Lindley was surprised "to see how little subordination of rank is known in this country [Brazil]: France, in its completest state of revolution and citizenship, never excelled it in that respect. You see here the white servant converse with his master on the most equal and friendly terms, dispute his commands, and wrangle about them if contrary to *his better opinion*—which the superior receives in good part, and frequently acquiesces in. The system does not rest here; but extends to the mulattoes, and even to the negroes. One sees no humiliation except in the patient hard-working drudge, the native Indian. The same licentious freedom is found in their marine and troops." Appended to the diary are a "Description of the Province of Porto Seguro" (pp. 213–232) and a "Description of the Province of Saint Salvadore" (pp. 233–282). "In entering the port [of Porto Seguro], the view of the country is delightful. Near the water's edge is a range of fisherman's cottages; shaded with the waving cocoa in front, and each having its adjoining orange-ground. . . . The streets here are sufficiently broad, straight, but irregularly disposed; the houses are generally of one story, low, and ill built, —of soft clay bricks, cemented with the same, and plastered over: but they all appear dirty and wretched. About half a dozen are of two stories: the largest of which is a quadrangular town-house and prison of some extent, the house of the civil governor (formerly a college of jesuits), and one or two of the others are the residences of individuals. The church is plain and has glass windows; and is by far the best-erected building in the place." As for Salvador, Lindley found the buildings to be "chiefly of the seventeenth century, ill constructed, and from the slightness of the materials rapidly decaying, which diminishes the effect of many of them that once were sumptuous. As in all Catholic cities, the churches are the most distinguished edifices, and those on which the greatest attention and expence were originally lavished. The cathedral is large, but falling into ruin; while the college and archiepiscopal palace (or rather house) adjoining are kept in thorough repair: they were all, at the period of their erection, spacious buildings, and have a proud station on the summit of the hill, commanding the bay and surrounding country. The grand church of the ex-jesuits is by far the most elegant structure of the city. It is composed entirely of European marble, imported for the purpose at an immense cost, while the internal ornaments are superfluously rich." In the appendix itself, there are latitude and longitude tables, exchange rates, and a "copy of an order from the governor-general of Bahia, for the imprisonment of myself [Lindley] and wife."

[614] G. M. Keith. *A Voyage to South America, and the Cape of Good Hope; in His Majesty's Gun Brig the Protector.* London: Richard Phillips, 1810. 43 pp.

The *Protector*, commanded by Lieutenant G. M. Keith, was part of a contingent of English ships that sailed from Spithead for the Cape of Good Hope on 25 August 1805. Keith arrived in Bahia on 10 November 1805 after a visit to the Madeira Islands: "The appearance of the Bay of All Saints and the City of Salvador from the anchorage is very beautiful, and though certainly inferior to the Bay of Naples, is perhaps not far short of the view of Constantinople from the harbour, and in several respects resembles it on a smaller scale. The moment a person lands, however, the deception vanishes, for there never was a place of equal extent and importance, so dirty, miserable, and disgusting, in every sense of the word. The house inhabited by the governor (and dignified with the name of a palace) forms one side of a small square; the other being occupied by the common jail, which, with the wretches immured in it, must of course meet his eye fifty times in a day: so much for prospect and situation. In the streets you meet none except soldiers and slaves, with here and there a solitary friar, or a Portuguese gentleman borne in his palanquin, for as to the ladies without the walls of their houses, they are absolutely invisible. The Portuguese with their accustomed avarice, on the arrival of the fleet trebled the price of every article in their markets, from an orange to a pipe of wine; and not satisfied with this extortion, they unanimously refused to received any government bills whatever, unless at the enormous discount of 20 per cent. though payable ten days after sight; and at this rate, including the repairs, stores, and provisions, for the men of war and troops, with private purchases, they must have received at the lowest estimate 150,000 £ sterling." On 25 November Keith sailed for Rio de Janeiro, arriving in the harbor of the Brazilian capital on 3 December. The author only spent overnight in Rio. "The commander immediately waited on the viceroy, and having completed our water, we sailed again on the following day." Chapter VII (pp. 21–27) gives an account of Rio de Janeiro, with frequent quotations from Captain Cook's description. Keith states that "the churches are very fine; and there is more religious parade in this place, than in any of the popish countries in Europe; there is a procession of some parish every day, with various insignia, all splendid and costly in the highest degree. They beg money, and say prayers in great form at the corner of every street. . . . The military establishment here consists of twelve regiments of regular troops, six of which are Portuguese, and six creoles, and twelve other regiments of provincial militia. It is generally allowed, that the women both of the Spanish and Portuguese settlements in South America, make less scruple of granting personal favours, than those of any other civilized country in the world. Murders are frequently committed here; but the churches afford an asylum to the criminal."

[615] John White. *A Voyage to Cohin China.* London: Longman, Hurst, Rees, and Orme, 1824. xi, 372 pp.

John White, according to Borba de Moraes **[20]**, II, 376–377, visited Bahia briefly in September of 1819 when his ship was forced into port for repairs. He left a short account of his impressions.

F. Pernambuco and the Brazilian Northeast [Nos. 616–628]

In addition to the general accounts of Pernambuco's early history by Bailey Diffie **[71]**, Alexander Marchant **[136]**, and Elaine Sanceau **[146]**, there is a good discussion of the brazilwood trade at Itamarcá by John Vogt **[135]**. The lords-proprietor of Pernambuco in the sixteenth and early seventeenth century are covered by Francis A. Dutra in his biography of Matias de Albuquerque **[272]**. The same author provides a biography of Duarte Coelho, Pernambuco's first *donatário* or lord-proprietor **[149]** and a discussion of centralization vs. donatarial privilege **[152]**. Dutra also studies Diogo Botelho, the first of four governors-general to spend considerable time in Pernambuco in the seventeenth century **[151]**. The duties of a governor and *capitão-mor* are found in the same author's lengthy account of Matias de Albuquerque and the defense of northeastern Brazil in the 1620s **[153]**. Charles R. Boxer discusses the career of Jorge de Albuquerque, Pernambuco's third lord-proprietor in **[150]** and **[185]**. The Dutch invasion of 1630 is described by Edmundson **[242]** and **[243]** as well as Boxer **[239]** and **[245]**. The latter author gives an important overview of the Dutch occupation of northeastern Brazil. For other writings on the Dutch period, see section VII. Jews played an important role in Pernambuco and the neighboring captaincies, though most of the studies focus on the Dutch period. See section XI, B. Kempton E. Webb **[616]** provides some useful geographical information on colonial Pernambuco. For the eighteenth century there is George Starling's account of the War of the Mascates, 1710–1714, **[617]**. Charles Boxer devotes a chapter to the conflict in his *Golden Age of Brazil* **[548]**. Robert C. Smith **[619]** and **[620]** discusses brazilwood and the logging industry as well as the architecture of Recife **[618]** in the late eighteenth century. Bainbridge Cowell **[621]** studies the population of Recife and cityward migration during the eighteenth and nineteenth centuries. John Galloway **[622]** provides a historical geography of Pernambuco for much the same time period. Billy Jaynes Chandler **[623]** and **[624]** studies the Feitosa family and the backlands of Ceará.

[616] Kempton E. Webb. *The Changing Face of Northeast Brazil.* New York and London: Columbia University Press, 1974. xi, 205 pp.

Though most of this study focuses on the twentieth century, there are a number of useful sections on the colonial period. One of these is the first half of chapter 4 ("The Spread of Settlement and Land Use") where the author traces Portuguese expansion from the nuclei of such towns as Olinda and Igaraçú. Webb discusses westward expansion into the interior of northeastern Brazil and the role of cattle raising. He describes the granting of *sesmarias* and translates a grant made in 1665 by the Count of Óbidos, governor-general of Brazil. Chapter 5 ("The Zona da Mata") also has a section on the colonial period, as do chapters 6 ("The Sertão) and 8 ("The Brejos and Serras"). There is a glossary and a bibliography. 12 maps. 24 figures.

[617] George Westley Starling, Jr. "The War of the Mascates in Brazil, 1710–1714," (Ph.D. Dissertation: University of California, Berkeley, 1957).

Argues that the War of the Mascates should be compared with three other serious rebellions that took place between 1684 and 1714: The Beckman Revolt in Maranhão (1684); the War of the Emboabas in Minas Gerais (1710); and the Maneta Riots in Bahia (1711). Starling describes how "the political antagonisms, economic and social tensions, petty jealousies and hatreds which had developed in Pernambuco over the years reached a climax during the governorship of Sebastião de Castro e Caldas [1707–1710]." The rivalry between Recife and Olinda came to a head in 1709 with "the elevation of Recife to the status of a town independent of Olinda." Many saw this change of relationship between the two towns as "a victory for Governor Sebastião de Castro and the Portuguese merchants over the creoles, led by the planter aristocracy of Olinda." The author sees three phases in the ensuing civil war: 1) the seizure of Recife by the planters and the deprivation of the inhabitants of that town of their civil rights; 2) the recovery of the port city by the merchants seven months later, the resignation of the bishop as governor, the turning over of power to a creole junta, and civil war; 3) the repressive measures of the new governor, Felix José Machado de Mendonça, whose arrival ended the war, "but did not bring lasting peace." Starling argues that the War of the Mascates was not a separatist movement. It did, however, leave "a residue of colonial bitterness which lingered until Brazil's independence." Based on printed primary and secondary materials. 2 maps.

[618] Robert C. Smith. "The Caetano Prospect: An Eighteenth-Century View of Recife in Brazil," *The Americas* 10:4 (April 1954), pp. 391–408.

Fascinating description of a watercolor bound into the second volume of Luis dos Santos Vilhena's (ca. 1744–1814) manuscript study of Brazil at the end of the eighteenth century, where it illustrates a chapter on Pernambuco. The drawing, a copy of a panorama of 1759 by the Jesuit

Father José Caetano, shows the buildings of the town of Recife from the side facing the city of Olinda with such detail that it is important for the architectural as well as the urban history of Recife. It is accompanied by a map of Recife which Santos Vilhena copied from a plan of 1773—one of the few pre-1800 maps of a Brazilian town which indicates clearly the name of every street. The article also translates a number of excerpts from Vilhena's account of Pernambuco and gives a useful picture of the town's history. Based on printed primary and secondary sources. illus.; map; 71 notes.

[619] Robert C. Smith. "The Wood-Beach at Recife. A Contribution to the Economic History of Brazil," *The Americas* 6:2 (October 1949), pp. 215–233.

Description and discussion of a recently discovered late eighteenth-century painting (1788) which shows how brazilwood was stored and shipped at Recife. The work is very detailed and not only portrays and labels many aspects of the brazilwood and logging industry but also depicts a part of Recife that has been destroyed in the last century and a half. The article includes useful information on the brazilwood economy and life and architecture in Recife during the second half of the eighteenth century. Based mostly on archival (both Brazilian and Portuguese) materials. 80 notes.

[620] Robert C. Smith. "More About the Wood-Beach at Recife," *The Americas* 10:1 (July 1953), pp. 75–78.

Provides a biographical sketch of José de Oliveira Barbosa (1753–1844), the author of a watercolor describing the handling of brazilwood in late eighteenth-century Pernambuco. Oliveira Barbosa later served as governor of Angola (1810–1816) and after Brazilian independence was created Barão do Passeio Publico and Visconde do Rio Comprido. Based on printed sources, especially almanacs of the city of Rio de Janeiro. 11 notes.

[621] Bainbridge Cowell, Jr. "Cityward Migration in the Nineteenth Century. The Case of Recife, Brazil," *Journal of Interamerican Studies and World Affairs* 17:1 (February 1975), pp. 43–63.

Studies the population of Recife—the second largest of the Brazilian port cities to 1700, eventually falling to third behind Salvador and Rio de Janeiro, the latter moving into first place just before independence. The author gives five sets of population figures for the colonial period:

1710 (12,000); 1749 (16,000); 1782 (18,000); 1810 (26,000); 1822 (34,000)—and seven for the period after independence to 1920. Cowell argues that "neither natural increase nor the slave trade, then, explains the rapid growth of nineteenth-century Recife. The most important cause was voluntary migration to the city—from the interior of Brazil and from overseas. Samples of the urban population drawn from marriage registers show that in the last decades of colonial rule and the first turbulent years of independence (1790–1840), 29 percent to 35 percent of the population had been born outside the city." About half the article deals with the period prior to 1826. Based on Recife Parish records and printed primary and secondary sources. 5 tables; 2 maps. 14 notes. There is an appendix (Bibliographical References) for the many notes within the text.

[622] John Herbert Galloway. "Pernambuco, 1770–1920: An Historical Geography," (Ph.D. Dissertation: University of London, 1965).

[623] Billy Jaynes Chandler. *The Feitosas and the Sertão dos Inhamuns. The History of a Family and a Community in Northeast Brazil, 1700–1930.* Gainesville: University of Florida Press, 1972. xi, 178 pp.

Chapter II, "The First Century. The Formative Years" (pp. 6–45), is important for students of colonial Brazilian history since it is one of the most detailed accounts of eighteenth-century Ceará in English. The Inhamuns region borders eastern Piaui and is located "just north of the soutwestern corner of Ceará." After discussing the land's physical characteristics, Chandler describes some of the early *sesmarias* or land grants and recounts how Francisco Alves Feitosa, the founder of the branch of the family that was to play such an important role in that part of Ceará, consolidated his holdings and power. The author discusses the family's difficulties with the Indians of the Inhamuns. He details the role of the chief officials of eighteenth-century Ceará—the *capitão-mor,* the town councillors, and the *ouvidor* or crown judge—and reports on the region's ecclesiastical apparatus. Much of the chapter is devoted to the rivalry that broke out into armed conflict between the Feitosa and the Montes families in the mid-1720s and continued to simmer throughout most of the colonial period. There is also a good deal of material on the history of the captaincy of Ceará during the administration of the *capitão-mor* José Alves Feitosa, who held that post for thirty-two years, 1791–1823. This chapter is based on private archival materials as well as printed sources. There is a bibliography (pp. 171–175) and a glossary (pp. 177–178) but no index.

[624] Billy Jaynes Chandler. "The Inhamuns: A Community in the *Sertão* of Northeast Brazil, 1707–1930," (Ph.D. Dissertation: The University of Florida, 1967). 273 pp.

Records the history of the Inhamuns, an area in the *sertão* or backlands of southwest Ceará, from the first white settlement in 1707 until 1930. One or two prominent families dominated each period of its history. The Feitosas and the Montes family war of the 1720s resulted in the dominance of the Feitosas, lasting until the 1820s when the Fernandes Vieira family arose to become their rivals throughout the Empire years. Meanwhile, the socioeconomic basis of the community, a small group of *fazendeiros* on top of a pyramid of largely landless *moradores,* remained mostly unchanged. Based on archival research in Brazil, especially Rio de Janeiro and Ceará, and published documents.
DAI 29/01-A (p. 207)
See also **[623]**

1. Contemporary Narratives, 1700–1822 [Nos. 625–628]

John Atkins **[625]** anchored off Pernambuco in 1722 and left a brief description. In addition, three travel accounts which mention Pernambuco—all in the early nineteenth century—are worthy of note. The most detailed is Henry Koster's *Travels in Brazil* **[626]**. Koster arrived in Recife late in 1809 and spent almost a decade there. He also visited Paraiba, Rio Grande do Norte and Ceará as well as Maranhão. Charles Waterton **[627]** stopped of at Pernambuco in 1816 and devoted a chapter of his *Wanderings in South America* to a description of his stay. Maria Graham **[628]** arrived in Pernambuco in September of 1821 and spent several weeks there.

[625] John Atkins. *A Voyage to Guinea, Brasil and the West Indies; in His Majesty's Ships the Swallow and Weymouth.* London: Caesar Ward and Richard Chandler, 1735. xxv, 265 pp.

John Atkins was a surgeon in the British Royal Navy. Most of the book deals with his experiences in Africa. However, on 1 July 1722, he "made Cape Augustine in Brasil, a Portuguese colony, and anchored the 4th in Pernambuca Road, the next great Port of Trade in this Province to Bahia." On 12 July he left Brazil and continued on his voyage to the West Indies, which he describes in some detail. According to Borba de Moraes **[20]**, I, 45, the first edition is dated 1723.

[626] Henry Koster. *Travels in Brazil.* London: Longman, Hurst, Rees, Orme, and Brown, 1816. ix, 501 pp.
[There are several later editions. A second, in two volumes, was published in London in 1817. A similar two-volume edition was published in the same year in Philadelphia. A greatly abridged edition, edited by C. Harvey Gardiner, was published by Southern Illinois University Press in 1966.]

Born in Portugal, the son of a sugar dealer in Liverpool, Henry Koster originally visited Brazil for health reasons. He arrived in Recife in mid-December of 1809. The account of his lengthy stay is the most detailed description in English of Pernambuco and much of northeastern Brazil before independence. The island of Santo Antônio, which formed the center of the important town of Recife, "is composed chiefly of large houses and broad streets; and if these buildings had about them any beauty, there would exist here a certain degree of grandeur: but they are too lofty for their breadth, and the ground floors are appropriated to shops, warehouses, stables, and other purposes of a like nature. The shops are without windows, and the only light they have is admitted from the door. There exists as yet very little distinction of trades; thus all descriptions of manufactured goods are sold by the same person. Some of the minor streets consist of low and shabby houses." He was impressed by some of the province's educational facilities: "The public institutions are not many, but, of those that exist, some are excellent. The seminary at Olinda for the education of young persons is well conducted, and many of its professors are persons of knowledge and of liberality. Free schools are also established in most of the small towns in the country, in some of which the Latin language is taught, but the major part are adapted only to give instruction in reading, writing, and arithmetic. Neither in these nor in the seminary is any expense incurred by the pupils." Koster was not particularly sympathetic to Pernambuco's religious practices. He observed that "the number of churches, chapels, and niches in the streets for saints, is quite preposterous." Koster was disturbed that criminals performed "the menial offices of the palace, the barracks, the prisons, and other public buildings. They are chained in couples, and each couple is followed by a soldier, armed with a bayonet. The prisons are in a very bad state, little attention being paid to the situation of their inhabitants. Executions are rare at Pernambuco; the more usual punishment inflicted, even for crimes of the first magnitude, is transportation to the coast of Africa. White persons must be removed for trial to Baia, for crimes of which the punishment is death. Even to pass sentence of death upon a man of color, or a Negro, several judicial officers must be present." Koster includes several chapters (18–20) on the status and treatment of people of color in Pernambuco. "The militia regiments, commanded by mulatto and black officers, and formed entirely of men of these castes, are very superior in appearance." As for the slaves themselves, the author felt that "the lives of the slaves of Brazil have been rendered less hard and intolerable than those of the degraded beings who drag on their cheerless existence under the dominion of other nations." In his chapter on the "Impolicy of the Slave Trade," Koster argued that many Brazilians "suspect the motives of Great Britain in urging their government to abolish the trade." The author describes in detail his trips through the Northeast. He visited Paraiba, Rio Grande do Norte, and Ceará on one journey. In February of 1811, only eight days after completing this trip, urgent business forced him to leave Pernambuco for England via Maranhão. He spent six weeks in that part of Brazil, before sailing on his transatlantic journey. São Luis, "the metropolis of the *estado* or state of Maranhão, is the residence of a captain general and the see of a bishop. . . . The population may be computed at about 12,000 persons or more, including negroes, of which the proportion is great, being much more considerable than at Pernambuco. The streets are mostly paved, but are out of repair. The houses are many of them neat and pretty, and of one story in height; the lower part of them is appropriated to the servants, to shops without windows, to warehouses, and other purposes, as at Pernambuco. The family lives upon the upper story, and the windows of this reach down to the floor, and are ornamented with iron balconies. The churches are numerous." After a short visit in England, Koster returned to Pernambuco in late December of 1811. He again journeyed to England in 1815, thus ending his account. However, in late 1816, he returned to Pernambuco still another time, dying there in 1820. There are two good maps and eight plates in the first edition of Koster's travel account. The last chapter includes a copy of the 1810 treaty between Great Britain and Portugal. Excerpts from Dr. Manuel Arruda da Camara's two pamphlets—"A Dissertation upon the Plants of Brazil from which fibrous substances may be obtained . . ." and "An Essay on the utility of establishing gardens in the principal provinces of Brazil"—are found in the appendix (pp. 475–501).

[627] Charles Waterton. *Wanderings in South America, the North-West of the United States, and the Antilles, in the Years 1812, 1816, 1820 and 1824.* London: J. Mawman, 1825. vii, 326 pp.

Charles Waterton (1781–1865) first visited Guiana in 1805, managing his family's estates there until 1812 and nurturing his interest in natural history. Before making one of his many visits to England, Waterton made the first of his four journeys in 1812. Though he visited the Brazilian frontier, his second journey, which included a visit to Pernambuco in 1816, is probably of most interest to historians of colonial Brazil—though many of his descriptions of Indians, birds and animals from neighboring Guiana are also helpful. In general, Waterton was impressed with his stay in Pernambuco: "As you approach the shore, the view is charming. The hills are clothed with wood, gradually rising toward the interior, none of them of any considerable height. A singular reef of rocks runs parallel to the coast, and forms the harbor of Pernambuco. The vessels are moored betwixt it and the town, safe from every storm. You enter the harbour through a very narrow passage, close by a fort built on the reef. The hill of Olinda, studded with houses and convents, is on your right hand, and an island thickly planted with cocoa-nut trees, adds considerably to the scene on your left. There are two strong forts on the isthumus, betwixt Olinda and Pernambuco, and a pillar midway to aid the pilot. Pernambuco probably contains upwards of fifty thousand souls. It stands on a flat, and is divided into three parts—a peninsula, an island, and the continent." However, he felt that "the appearance of the houses" in Recife "is not much in their favour." In addition, "there is a lamentable want of cleanliness in the streets. The impurities from the houses and the accumulation of litter from the beasts of burden, are unpleasant sights to the passing stranger." But "in a week or two the stranger himself begins to feel less the things which annoyed him so much upon his first arrival, and after a few months residence, he thinks no more about them, while he is partaking of the hospitality, and enjoying the elegance and splendour within doors in this great city." Though he pointed out that the inhabitants pay little attention "to the common comforts which one always expects to find in a large and opulent city," he gave no indication of the revolt that would take place the following year. Instead, he pointed out that "the Captain-General of Pernambuco walks through the streets with as apparent content and composure as an English statesman would proceed down Charing-cross." A Catholic, Waterton digresses when describing the palace of the Captain-General—"once the Jesuits' college and originally built by those charitable fathers"—and spends several pages discussing Pombal's expulsion of the Jesuits from Brazil. Waterton observed that "the environs of Pernambuco are very pretty. You see country houses in all directions, and the appearance of here and there a sugar plantation enriches the scenery. Palm-trees, Cocoa-nut-trees, Orange and Lemon groves, and all the different fruits peculiar to Brazil, are here in the greatest abundance. At Olinda there is a national botanical garden; it wants space, produce, and improvement, The forests, which are several leagues off, abound with birds, beasts, insects, and serpents." The author describes in some detail the "pretty little village called Monteiro," located about six or seven miles from Recife. "The river runs close by it, and its rural beauties seem to surpass all others in the neighbourhood; there the Captain-General of Pernambuco resides during his time of merriment and joy." The author points out that "for three months in the year the environs of Pernambuco are animated beyond description. From November to March the weather is particularly fine; then it is that rich and poor, young and old, foreigners and natives, all issue from the city to enjoy the country, till Lent approaches, when back they hie them. Villages and hamlets, where nothing before but rags were seen, now shine in all the elegance of dress. . . . Some join in the merry dance, others saunter up and down the orange-groves; and towards evening the roads becoming a moving scene of silk and jewels. The gaming-tables have constant visitors." Fourteen days after leaving Pernambuco aboard a Portuguese brig, Waterton arrived at Cayenne, at that time under Portuguese control. Waterton provides several valuable pages of description of that French colony which had recently been captured by the forces of João VI.

[628] Maria Graham. *Journal of a Voyage to Brazil, and Residence There, During Part of the Years 1821, 1822, 1823*. London: Longman, Hurst, Rees, Orme, Brown, and Green, 1824. vi, 335 pp.

Maria Graham, the future Lady Calcott, visited Brazil on three different occasions: the first time before independence (late 1821 and early 1822); the second (1823) in the company of Lord Cochrane; and the third time, at the request of Dom Pedro I in 1824, to be the governess of his daughter, Maria da Gloria, the future queen of Portugal. On her initial voyage to Brazil, she visited Pernambuco, Bahia and Rio de Janeiro before continuing on to Chile. When Graham arrived in Pernambuco on 21 September 1821, she found the captaincy in a state of siege. A month earlier, "about 600 men of the militia and other native forces had taken possession of the Villa of Goyanna . . . where they had declared the government of Luiz do Rego [the pro-royalist governor of Pernambuco] to be at an end." The author is sympathetic to the rebel or patriot cause and visited the dissidents in early October to complain about their refusal to allow the ship's linen to be returned to Recife. She describes Recife, including its slave market, in some detail. She was horrified at the lack of proper burial for slaves left on the beaches. She found the slave market to be "thinly stocked, owing to the circumstances of the town; which cause most of the owners of new slaves to keep them closely shut up in the depots. Yet about fifty young creatures, boys and girls, with all the appearance of disease and famine consequent upon scanty food and long confinement in unwholesome places, were sitting and lying about among the filthiest animals in the streets." Calcott was greatly impressed by "the great preponderance of the black population. By the last census, the population of Pernambuco, including Olinda was seventy thousand, of which not above one third are white: the rest are mulatto or negro." She was disturbed that in Pernambuco "the very names of literature and science are almost unknown. The college and library of Olinda are in decay. There is not one book-seller in Pernambuco." The author concluded her visit to Pernambuco "with a firm persuasion that this part of Brazil at least will never again tamely submit to Portugal." Arriving at Salvador late in the evening of the 16th of October, she landed the next day "at the arsenal, or rather dock yard, where there is nothing of the neatness observable in such establishments at home." The lower town of Bahia she described as "without any exception, the filthiest place I ever was in. It is extremely narrow, yet all the working artificers bring their benches and tools into the street: in the interstices between them, along the walls, are fruit-sellers, venders of sausages, black-puddings, fried fish, oil and sugar cakes, negroes plaiting hats or mats, caderas, (a kind of sedan chair,) with their bearers, dogs, pigs, and poultry, without partition or distinction; and as the gutter runs in the middle of the street, everything is thrown there from the different stalls, as well as from the windows; and there the animals live and feed! In this street are the warehouses and counting-houses of the merchants, both native and foreign. The buildings are high, but neither so handsome nor so airy as those of Pernambuco." On 9 December, Maria Calcott sailed from Bahia. Six days later she arrived in Rio de Janeiro, which she described as "more like an European city than either Bahia or Pernambuco; the houses are three or four stories high, with projecting roofs, and tolerably handsome." After describing the agitation in that city after the departure of João VI, she points out that "there are a good many English shops, such as saddlers, and stores, not unlike what we call in England an Italian warehouse, for eatables and drinkables; but the English here generally sell their goods wholesale to native or French retailers. The latter have a great many ships of mercery, haberdashery, and millinery. For tailors, I think, there are more English than French, and but few of either. There are baker's shops of both nations, and plenty of English pot-houses, whose Union Jacks, Red Lions, Jolly Tars, with their English inscriptions, vie with those of Greewich or Deptford. The goldsmiths all live in one street, called by their name Rua dos Ourives, and their goods are exposed in hanging frames at each side of the shop-door or window, in the fashion of two centuries back. The workmanship of their chains, crosses, buttons, and other ornaments, is exquisite, and the price of the labour, charged over the weight of the metal, moderate. Most of the streets are lined with English goods." On 24 January 1822, Maria Graham set sail for another brief visit to Bahia, "where the election of the new provisional government" had just taken place. At Salvador she observed that "the language of the writers of gazettes here is much bolder than at Rio; and I think that there is here a truly republican spirit among a very considerable number of persons." She returned to Rio de Janeiro on 24 February 1822 and discovered that "the Prince Don Pedro has been very active, and has dismissed all the Portuguese troops." The author was impressed with the talent displayed by negroes and mulattoes, whom she claimed "are the best artificers and artists. The orchestra of the opera-house is composed of at least one-third of mulattoes. All decorative painting, carving, and inlaying is done by them; in short, they excel in all ingenious mechanical arts." On 6 March 1822, she sailed for Chile.

G. Islands Off the Brazilian Coast, 1700–1822
[Nos. 629–632]

Though there are no studies in English on the four most important islands off the Brazilian coast—Fernão de Noronha, Ilha Grande, Ilha de São Sebastião, and the island of Santa Catarina—there are many references to them in contemporary narratives.

1. Contemporary Narratives, 1700–1822 [Nos. 629–632]

Descriptions of the island of Santa Catarina are found in Section XV, A. William Funnell **[629]** visited Ilha Grande in late November and early December of 1703 and left an account of his impressions. The same island and the mainland town of Angra dos Reis was visited five years later by Woodes Rogers **[630]**. Edward Cooke **[631]**, who was part of the Rogers expedition, also related his experiences at Ilha Grande and Angra dos Reis. In 1721, Jacob Roggeveen **[632]** visited the island of São Sebastião near Santos.

[629] William Funnell. *A Voyage Round the World. Containing an Account of Captain Dampier's Expedition into the South-Seas in the Ship St. George, in the Years 1703 and 1704.* London: James Knapton, 1707. 300 pp.
[A facsimile edition was published in 1969 by N. Israel/Amsterdam and Da Capo Press/New York.]

On 24 November 1703, Funnell anchored off Ilha Grande, which he called Island Le Grand: "This is a very woody Island, and hath several very good springs of fresh Water upon it. The soil is black, and the Island is about nine Leagues round, and distant from the Main [Brazil] about three Miles. It is not inhabited by any other than Jaccals, Lyons, Tygers, &c. Which in the Night make a most hideous Noise, enough to terrifie any Man. About three Miles from this place is the main Land, all very mountainous and woody, where is a small Town of the Portugueze (called by the name of Le Grand Town), who come out of the Country for forty or fifty Miles round on Saint Andrews day, to pay their Devotions to that Saint, here being a small Church consecrated to his use. They abide here about fourteen Days, and then return to their own Dwellings. Here is Rum, Sugar, and several sorts of Indian Fruits to be had, but very dear by reason of their supplying the Town of St. Pauls with these Necessaries; near which Town is said to be a Gold-mine, accounted one of the richest yet known. It is distant from the Town of Le Grand about three hundred Miles; and is reckoned, by reason of the difficulty of the way and the vast high Mountains that intercept the passage, to be sixty days journey. At this place we wooded, watered, and refitted our Ship. Here our first Lieutenant (with eight of our Men,) our Captain and they falling out, went ashoar with their Goods, and left us." On 8 December 1703, Funnell left Ilha Grande for the island of Juan Fernandez. Opposite page 10, there is an interesting map of "The Great and Small Bay of Le Grande. Part of Brazile &c."

[630] Woodes Rogers. *A Cruising Voyage Round the World: First to the South-Sea, Thence of the East Indies, and Homewards by the Cape of Good Hope. Begun in 1708 and Finish'd in 1711.* London, 1712. xxii, 428 pp. maps.
[There is a paperbound edition, edited by Percy G. Adams and published in New York: Dover Publications, Inc., 1970.]

On his way around the world, Woodes Rogers touched Brazil in mid-November of 1708 and left in early December of the same year. He visited Angra dos Reis and Ilha Grande. At Angra, Rogers and some of his men, along with two trumpets and an oboe, were invited to take part in the celebration of the feast of the conception of the Virgin Mary: "The Ceremony held about two hours, after which we were splendidly entertain'd by the Fathers of the Convent, and then by the Governour at the Guard-House, His Habitation being three Leagues off. It's to be noted, they kneel'd at every Crossway, and turning, walk'd round the [Franciscan] Convent, and came in another Door, kneeling and paying their Devotion to the Image of the Virgin and her Wax-Candles. . . . The Town consists of about sixty low Houses built of mud, cover'd with Palmetto Leaves, and meanly furnish'd. They told us they had been plunder'd by the French, or perhaps they hid their Plate and other best Movables, because they were in doubt whether we were Friends or Enemies. They have two Churches and a Franciscan Monastery tolerably decent, but not rich in Ornaments: They have also a Guard-house, where there are about 20 Men commanded by the Governour, a

Lieutenant, and Ensign. The Monastery had some black Cattel belonging to it, but the Fathers would sell us none." In December, he visited Ilha Grande: "The Island abounds with Monkeys and other wild Beasts, has plenty of good Timber, Fire-wood, and excellent Water, with Oranges and Lemons, and Guavas growing wild in the Woods. The Necessaries we got from the Town were Rum, Sugar, and Tobacco, which they sell very dear, tho not good to smoke, 'tis so very strong. We had also Fowls and Hogs, but the latter are scarce; Beef and Mutton are cheap, but no great quantity to be had; Indian Corn, Bonanoes, Plantanes, Guavas, Lemons, Oranges, and Pine-Apples they abound with; but have no Bread except Cassado." He gives a short account of the Dutch episode in Brazil (1630–1654) and discusses the Amerindians and their customs, both based on the "Voyages and Travels into Brazil" by the Dutch traveller Johan Nieuhof **[259]**. He concludes his description of Brazil with a report on the Amazon based on his reading of Nicolas and Guillaume Sanson, Hakluyt's "Voyages" **[105]** and Purchas's "Pilgrimes" **[107]**.

[631] Edward Cooke. *A Voyage to the South Sea, and Round the World, Perform'd in the Years 1708,1709, 1710, and 1711, by the Ships Duke and Duchess of Bristol.* 2 vols. London: B. Lintot and R. Gosling, 1712. 432 pp.; xxiv, 328 pp.

Edward Cooke was the captain of the *Duchess* and was part of the expedition of Woodes Rogers **[630]**. He describes his visit to Angra dos Reis and Ilha Grande in November of 1708. On his arrival, Cooke "went to the Town in a Pinnace, with a Present for the Governor, and to acquaint him we were Friends. At our first Landing, the Portuguese fir'd several Shot, taking us for French; but were afterwards sorry for it, and receiv'd us very handily." On Sunday, the 28th of November, "the Governor, with several of the [Franciscan] Fathers, and others, came Aboard, and the Weather proving Rainy, stay'd all Night, I, with some others, being ashore to barter Rum, Sugar, Hogs &c." The author also provides "A short Description of the Island Grande, the Bay it forms, and the Town of Angra dos Reys on the Continent": ". . . This island lies near the Continent, and is plentifully stor'd with Wood and Water, but not inhabited. The Town of Angra dos Reys is on the Main, about three Leagues distant from the Island, very small, consisting of 50 or 60 Houses, low built, very indifferent, with Mud Walls, and cover'd with Palmito Leaves. However, it has a Franciscan Monastery, and two churches, decent, but not so richly adorn'd as in other places." The town had earlier been plundered by the French. This, according to Cooke, "might be the Reason why their Houses were no better furnished; as also their not being satisfy'd, whether we were Friends or

Enemies, might probably make them remove and hide the best of their Housholdstuff." On 30 November the Duchess weighed anchor and continued its voyage.

[632] Andrew Sharp, ed. *The Journal of Jacob Roggeveen.* Oxford: At the Clarendon Press, 1970. 193 pp., plates, maps, facsims.

In 1721–1722, Jacob Roggeveen led an expedition from the Netherlands down the coast of South America, round Cape Horn and across the Pacific Ocean to New Ireland. He reached the Brazilian coast on 9 November 1721 and stopped at the island of São Sebastião near Santos on the 16th. The Dutch commander sent a present of "Hollands butter, dried fish, cheese and a ham" and petitioned the Portuguese official in charge of the island for "cattle, sheep, pigs, fruits and all other vegetables, as well as water and firewood, paying for them as much as your Honour according to equity shall judge to be proper." The Portuguese were hesitant to fully grant Roggeveen's request both because of royal orders and the fear that the Dutch were pirates, the latter since "the inhabitants still had fresh and active in memory pillaging of this type inflicted in the previous war by the French." Because of this "fear of being plundered," the inhabitants had carried inland "all the livestock and other commodities of importance, even the bricked-in copper cauldrons of sugar mills." The Portuguese finally relented on condition "that the payment be made in current money" and let the Dutch land for a little more than a week. Roggeveen finally raised anchor on 1 December 1721 and continued southward. The editor has added helpful and informative notes.

H. Maranhão and Pará and the Conflict with the French, English and Dutch [Nos. 633–649]

Two general introductions to the Amazon region are found in Lewis A. Tambs, "Geopolitics of the Amazon" **[633]**, and Arthur Cesar Ferreira Reis, "Economic History of the Brazilian Amazon" **[634]**. Walter Breymann **[635]** discusses the attention both Portugal and Spain gave the Amazon region from 1540 to 1640, as well as foreign threats from the French, English and Dutch. George Edmundson **[636]** describes the exploration efforts of Pedro Teixeira on the Amazon. Mathias Kiemen **[425]** in his study of missionary activity in the Amazon region provides valuable information on that area's history. Robert Southey **[70]** also devotes considerable attention to the State of Maranhão and Pará in his three-volume history of colonial Brazil. Derek Severn **[319]** discusses the exploits of the Jesuit Samuel Fritz. Sue Ellen Gross **[637]** studies the economic life of Maranhão and Pará for the years 1686 to 1751. She **[639]** also analyzes Portuguese efforts to promote the exploitation of raw materials in the Amazon region, 1700–1750, and describes problems caused by the shortage of labor during the first half of the eighteenth century **[638]**. Colin MacLachlan **[432]** and **[433]** does the same for the captaincies of Pará and Rio Negro during the entire nineteenth century with his important studies on Indian labor. He also analyzes African labor in Pará during the eighteenth century **[460]**. Charles R. Boxer **[439]** contributes a study on race relations in Maranhão and Pará and provides **[548]** an overview of that region's history, 1695–1750, in his *Golden Age of Brazil*. Robin Anderson **[640]** discusses Pará in the period after 1758 and efforts at migration and settlement. Dauril Alden **[665]** compares cacao production in that region with other parts of the Americas. Though his chief emphasis is the late nineteenth century, Raul d'Eça **[641]** provides background material for disputes between Brazil and British, Dutch, and French Guiana. Donn Alan Williams **[642]** provides a four-century overview of the rivalry between Brazil and the French over Amapá in the Amazon basin. Andrew S. Szarka **[643]** describes French activity in Maranhão, 1697–1700. There is useful information on the Portuguese in the Amazon region in the first half of the seventeenth century in James A. Williamson, *English Colonies in Guiana and on the Amazon, 1604–1668* **[644]**. Father Aubrey Gwynn **[645]** studies Irish efforts to settle the Amazon. George Edmundson **[646]** and **[647]** does the same for the Dutch.

[633] Lewis A. Tambs. "Geopolitics of the Amazon," in Wagley, ed., *Man in the Amazon* **[86]**, pp. 45–87.

Tambs points out that "geopolitically, Amazonia is a linking or connecting subregion between two great strategic areas of Latin America, the Andean nexus of Charcas and the closed sea of the Caribbean." He then describes the five natural routes leading from the Pacific to the Atlantic—one of which "follows the equator from the freshlets of the Andes down the Amazon to the Atlantic." After discussing the geographical factors involved, the author discusses the historical background of the contest between Portugal and Spain for dominance in the Amazon region. Much of the chapter deals with the colonial period and Tambs gives a useful and succinct account of the struggle between the two Iberian powers. There are extensive bibliographic references. Based chiefly on printed sources. There are several helpful maps.

[634] Arthur Cesar Ferreira Reis. "Economic History of the Brazilian Amazon," in Wagley, ed., *Man in the Amazon* **[86]**, pp. 33–44.

The greater part of this chapter focuses on the colonial period. Ferreira Reis points out that "from their first contact with the region, the Europeans learned of a wealth of exotic plant species which might arouse the interest of world markets." However, the cooperation of "the local Indians who could identify the various species included in this natural wealth" was almost a *sine qua non* for "the commerical exploitation of these natural products." He then traces this relationship through the colonial period. The author also discusses efforts at agriculture, the role of African slaves, and the activities of missionaries. Though the Europeanized population of the Amazon region numbered only 23,510 in 1799, it grew to about a 100,000 by independence. Based on printed sources. 2 editorial notes plus bibliographic references in the text.

[635] Walter Norman Breymann. "The Opening of the Amazon, 1540–1640," (Ph.D. Dissertation: University of Illinois, 1950). 248 pp.

Records how the Amazon basin was gradually incorporated into the Iberian world in the century following Orellana's discovery of the river in 1540. Conquistadores from Peru who searched through the basin for wealth were the first to gain knowledge of the region. Missionaries followed from both sides of the Andes, recording more information about the basin. Northern Europeans challenged Iberian possession of the Amazon in the early seventeenth century, but were driven out by the Portuguese by 1640. Then, with new interest in the area, the Portuguese began a deliberate drive inland. Their effective occupation of the area was decisive in fixing the boundary between Spanish and Portuguese America in the mid-eighteenth century, despite Spanish claims based on the Treaty of Tordesillas and early exploration.
DAI 10/04-A (pp. 188–190).

[636] George Edmundson. "The Voyage of Pedro Teixeira on the Amazon from Pará to Quito and Back, 1637–39," *Transactions of the Royal Historical Society,* Fourth Series. London, 1920. III, 52–71.

After quickly discussing the background of early Spanish, Dutch and English attempts to explore and settle the Amazon region and the efforts of the Portuguese from 1615 onwards to claim the area and disperse foreign interlopers, the author focuses on the instructions of Philip IV to the Portuguese governor of Maranhão and to Spanish authorities at Quito and Cuzco to explore the Amazon. The former sent Pedro Teixeira and the latter Spanish soldiers and Franciscan missionaries, both reaching their destinations, Teixeira, Quito and several of the Franciscans, São Luis. On the return journey, Teixeira was accompanied by the Spanish Jesuit Cristoval de Acuña who published an account of his journey in 1641. Edmundson concludes by examining the conflicting accounts regarding Spanish-Portuguese boundaries in the Amazon region. Based mostly on archival materials and printed primary sources. 21 notes.

[637] Sue Ellen Anderson Gross. "The Economic Life of the Estado do Maranhão and Grão Pará, 1686–1751," (Ph.D. Dissertation: Tulane University, 1969). 219 pp.

Studies the economic life of Maranhão and Grão Pará between 1686 and 1751, a period of relative quiet and stability for that colony. Agriculture, trade, labor, and administration are among the topics examined. By 1751, the Portuguese settlers had established a fairly stable basis for continued prosperity and had raised the colony to a state of self-sufficiency within the empire. The author believes that growth would have continued after 1751 if the colony had been allowed to proceed along the patterns established between 1686 and 1751. Based on materials from the Arquivo Histórico Ultramarino, Lisbon.
DAI 30/06-A (p. 2441)

[638] Sue Ellen Anderson Gross. "Labor in Amazonia in the First Half of the Eighteenth Century," *The Americas* 32:2 (October 1975), pp. 211–221.

Discusses the perennial problem of labor shortages in northern Brazil and the legal and illegal methods used to obtain Indians, the mainstay of the Amazonian labor force. The author concludes with a discussion of efforts (largely unsuccessful) to attract shipments of black slaves from Africa and white immigrants from the Madeiras and the Azores in the years preceding the Pombaline era. Based almost entirely on archival (Arquivo Histórico Ultramarino, Lisbon) and printed primary sources. 64 notes.

[639] Sue Ellen Anderson Gross. "Agricultural Promotion in the Amazon Basin, 1700–1750," *Agricultural History* 43:2 (April 1969), pp. 269–276.

Discusses attempts by the Portuguese Crown to promote the exploitation of raw materials in Maranhão and Grão Pará by such incentives as tax exemptions and grants of Indians and by efforts to improve quality control. Special attention is paid to sugar, coffee, cinnamon, pepper, cacao and indigo. The author concludes: "Where Crown and colonial self-interest coincided, Crown plans met with success. But usually the colonists did not believe that their personal welfare would be served by behaving in accord with the Crown's conception of what was in Portugal's best interest." Based mainly on archival (Arquivo Histórico Ultramarino, Lisbon) and printed primary sources. 34 notes.

[640] Robin Leslie Anderson. "Following Curupira: Colonization and Migration in Pará, 1758 to 1930 as a Study in Settlement of the Humid Tropics," (Ph.D. Dissertation: University of California, Davis, 1976). 371 pp.

Records the efforts made to colonize and settle the humid tropical state of Pará. The first serious coordinated attempt at establishing a system of towns and villages in the lower Amazon basin was made by the Portuguese government between 1758 and 1798. This Directorate system had some success, maintaining sixty-one villages, in spite of numerous problems. Following a half-century lull, interest in settling the area revived in the 1850s. Between 1850 and 1930 forty-six colonies were established. However, setbacks were common and government interest waned after the collapse of the rubber boom in 1911. Although the social, ecological cost of settlement was great with a variety of glaring failures, the record shows that occupation of great humid tropics is possible and that people are willing to face the obstacles involved in settling there.
DAI 37/06-A (p. 3841)

[641] Raul D'Eça. "A History of the Conflict and Settlement of Boundaries between Brazil and the British, Dutch, and French Guianas," (Ph.D. Dissertation: George Washington University, 1936).

Contains useful material on the Colonial period.

[642] Donn Alan Williams. "Brazil and French Guiana: The Four-Hundred Year Struggle for Amapá," (Ph.D. Dissertation: Texas Christian University, 1975). 235 pp.

Analyzes European disputes over Amapá, 100,000 square miles of land in the Amazon basin. In the sixteenth and seventeenth centuries, the British, French and Dutch tried to establish themselves in the area. Although each founded a colony on the north coast of South America, only the French pursued further ambitions for Amapá. As they moved east from Guiana, they met the Portuguese moving west from Belem. In 1688 military units of the two European powers clashed. But Amapá remained mostly a no-man's-land for the next couple of centuries while the two contenders argued the issue in Europe. In 1807, the Portuguese Court moved to Brazil and effected the occupation of Amapá and French Guiana as well. Although Guiana was returned to the French after Napoleon's defeat, the issue remained alive because the boundaries were not clearly established. In 1841 Amapá was neutralized while diplomatic maneuvering continued. Finally in 1900, after binding arbitration, Amapá was awarded to Brazil.
DAI 36/05-A (pp. 3065–3066)

[643] Andrew S. Szarka. "Louis XIV and Brazil: The French Probe into Maranhão, 1697–1700," *Proceedings of the French Colonial History Society* 2 (1977), pp. 133–148.
See also **[648]**

[644] James A. Williamson. *English Colonies in Guiana and on the Amazon, 1604–1668*. Oxford: At the Clarendon Press, 1923. 191 pp.

The author has some useful material on the Portuguese in the Amazon during the first half of the seventeenth century. Williamson argues that the Dutch seem to have been the earliest pioneers in the Amazon as *settlers*, followed by the French in 1612 and the English. He discusses Portuguese efforts to oust the French in 1614–1615 and then focuses on their attempts to drive out the English. The Portuguese captured Purcell's plantation in 1629 and destroyed both North's Fort and Fry's plantation in 1631. In the following year the colonists of Cumau were forced to surrender to the Portuguese. In 1623 and 1625 the Portuguese also attacked Dutch and Irish settlements. There is a useful chronological table for the years 1594–1668 (pp. 185–187). Based mostly on archival and printed primary sources.

[645] Aubrey Gwynn, S. J. "An Irish Settlement on the Amazon (1612–1629)," *Proceedings of the Royal Irish Academy* 41C:1 (July 1932), pp. 1–54.

Detailed, judicious examination of Irish efforts to settle in the Amazon region. Father Gwynn describes in detail how the Irish settlement was "first established in 1612, found in a prosperous condition in 1620 and again in 1623, destroyed by [Pedro] Teixeira after the surrender of 1625, refounded by James Purcell and his companions in 1628, and finally destroyed by Teixeira for a second time in 1629." The article includes useful material on Portuguese operations in northern Brazil during the 1620s. The author also discusses two (unsuccessful) proposals—one by Gaspar Chillan to the Spanish Crown (1632), the other by Peter Sweetman to the Portuguese Crown (1644)—to settle Irish immigrants in the Amazon region under Iberian authority. The Chillan (in Spanish) and Sweetman (in Portuguese) proposals and the Iberian responses were earlier published by Gwynn in "Documents Relating to the Irish in the West Indies," *Analecta Hibernica* 4 (October 1932), pp. 139–286. The Chillan documents are found on pp. 172–182. Those dealing with Sweetman's plan are on pp. 196–203. Gwynn's article on Irish settlement is based largely on primary source materials. It contains 105 notes. 3 illus.

[646] George Edmundson. "The Dutch on the Amazon and Negro in the Seventeenth Century. Part I. Dutch Trade on the Amazon," *The English Historical Review* 18:72 (October 1903), pp. 642–663.

Though focusing on Dutch Settlement and trade in the Amazon during the second and third decades of the seventeenth century, this article contains much information on the efforts of Bento Maciel Parente, Luis Aranha Vasconcelos, and Pedro Teixeira in expelling the Dutch. In October of 1629 the garrison of the Dutch fort surrendered to a force of 120 Portuguese and 1600 Indians. "The Portuguese were from this time onwards masters of the Lower Amazon. After 1625 ingress to the main stream was barred at Corupá, and after 1629 such desultory trading on the part of the Dutch as still continued was confined to the immediate neighbourhood of the Cabo do Norte, and owed its existence to the passing visits of vessels laden with stores for one or more of the colonies on the Guiana coast." Based largely on primary sources. 79 notes.

[647] George Edmundson. "The Dutch on the Amazon and Negro in the Seventeenth Century. Part II. Dutch Trade in the Basin of the Rio Negro," *The English Historical Review* 19:73 (January 1904), pp. 1–25.

Analyzes trade between Dutch settlers on the Essequibo River with the Amerindians of the interior. Edmundson points out that Padre Cristoval de Acuña **[235]** found Dutch goods in the possession of Indians living in the Amazon-Rio Negro delta. Caribs "were for the greater part of two centuries not only the close allies but the commercial emissaries of the Dutch in their dealings with the tribes of the interior." The author shows that towards the end of the seventeenth century, "besides the presence of the Dutch two other causes contributed to arouse the Portuguese to a sense of the insecurity of their hold upon the river Amazon. Their possession of the northern mouth of the Cabo do Norte was threatened by the French from Cayenne, and that of the Solimões by the astonishing success of the Spanish Jesuit missions among the Omaguas **[410]** and Jurimaguas, under the direction of Padre Samuel Fritz **[325]**." Based on archival and printed materials. 79 notes.

1. Contemporary Narratives, 1700–1822 [Nos. 648–649]

John Barbot **[648]** discusses the rivalry between France and Portugal over Cayenne and "French Guiana." Charles Marie de la Condamine **[656]** describes Belém do Pará in the early 1740s. José Gonsalves da Fonseca **[649]** describes the river town of Camutá in 1749. The artists who acompanied Alexandre Rodrigues Ferreira **[742]** in the 1780s left excellent drawings of Belém's waterfront as well as many of the important religious and civic buildings of the city.

[648] John Barbot. "A Description of the Province of Guiana," An Appendix to "A Description of the Coasts of North and South Guinea, and of Ethiopia Inferior, Vulgarly Angola," in A. and J. Churchill, *A Collection of Voyages and Travels* **[108]** V, 1–668.

The section on the province of Guiana and a description of the island of Cayenne is found on pp. 548–571. John Barbot was "Agent General of the Royal Company of Africa, and Islands of America at Paris." His account is of interest to students of Brazilian history because of his description of the clash between the French and the Portuguese over the Amazon region. "The governor of Cayenne claims a jurisdiction over the countries of Guiana, from the great river of the Amazons on the east to the river Maroni at west north-west; and accordingly the late governor M. De Ferolles, who was major of the fort and garrison in my time, begun a road by land to the river of the Amazons, pretending to drive the Portugueses from the rivers Paron and Macaba, on which they have built three forts for their security. The French alledge, that those countries belong to the crown of France, and that it behoves them to defend them not only on account of the trade, but because there are silver mines; so that the country they pretend to, extends about an hundred leagues along the ocean, which is its boundary on the east and north; and this they call Equinoctial France. . . . The pretension of the French and Portugueseses to the sovereignty of this port of Guiana, have occasion'd many controversies and blows between them, and several negotiations have been set on foot, and regulations made, to adjust theose differences amicably." But, Barbot continued, "the Portugueses of Para, one of the captainships of Brazil, which reaches to the great river of the Amazons, envying the trade of the colony of Cayenne in this river, resolv'd several years ago, to secure it to themselves, by setting up a pretension, that their sovereignty in those parts of South-America had extended for a long time as far westward beyond the river of the Amazons, as the river Wiapoco, near cape Cassepourri; which, they said, was their boundary, and the separation from the French jurisdiction at Cayenne. The French, on the other hand, affirm'd, that the Portuguese limits could reach no farther westward then another river or channel, called Wiapoco, lying in the midst of the Archipelago of islands, at the mouth of the river of the Amazons, and almost a hundred leagues in breadth. The Portugueses persisted in their claim, aiming to secure to themselves the trade of the river of the Amazons, consisting in slaves, Manati, hammocks, green stones, fine feathers, and tygers skins; as also to possess soley the benefit of the Cacao trade in that part of Guiana, on the west side of the river of the Amazons, so very advantageous; the large country round about Macaba naturally abounding in plants of Cacao, growing of themselves, without any culture, in the woods. They made no scruple to fall out with the French on that account; so that at last force of arms was used by the contending parties reciprocally, as opportunity offer'd: but the Portugueses having been quick at erecting a small fort at Arowary, near Cape North, at the mouth of the river of the Amazons, and a very large one at Macaba, about sixty leagues up it, mounted with fourteen guns, and a little one at some distance from it, with the arms of Portugal on the gate, maintain'd their ground for a time, and very much molested the French trading that way either by sea or land: and many have been slain or injur'd on both sides, for the French struggled against their antagonists from Cayenne and Wiapoco, as much as they could." The aftermath of the War of Spanish Succession saw peace return to that region. The Portuguese "with great diligence rebuilt the fort at Arowary and Macada, and thus again peaceably possess the beneficial trade of cacao. However, it is to be observ'd that those nuts are nothing to the right Spanish, commonly known by the name of Caracas nuts, which are large and sweet; whereas these Portuguese nuts are small and bitter. These nuts the Portugueses convey in large canoos and barks to Para, whence great quantities are sent yearly to Lisbon. The canoos the Portugueses of Para make to carry on their trade in the river of the

Amazons, are extraordinary fine and large, all of one single tree, and some of them eight feet broad, and above sixty in length, with cabbins, wherein they can hang three hammocks in a row, and their Indians are very dextrous at navigating them." Barbot added that "the government of Para has above three thousand Indians, living in villages, about the town of that name, and maintained as a constant, regular militia, to serve upon all occasions. Those Indians are all baptiz'd and instructed in the Christian religion, with their whole families, by the labour of the jesuits, who have erected fine churches in the Indian villages, and employ those people in husbandry when the government has no occasion for their service in war." Barbot also has some interesting observations about the Indians of the Guianas: "Before the Europeans had furnish'd the Indians of Guiana with instruments of iron and steel for fishing, hunting, hewing of wood, and cultivating the ground, they made them of hard stones; and besides the endless labour of making, were at no less pains in using them; and perceiving they could do more work in a day with hatchets, bills, knives and hooks, than they could before in a month with their stone tools, they give any thing for such necessaries, and have quite left off the use of their own. . . . The Cassabi is the common bread of the country, especially among the poorer sort and slaves, and of all the Indians, not only of Guiana, but of a great part of South-America. It is made of the Mandioca root, which they scrape, and then press to get out the poisonous juice; being so rank a poison that half a glass of it swallow'd, will kill either man or beast, and yet it may be put into sauces and pottages, giving them a good relish, provided it be boil'd but ever so little, for then it loses that pernicious quality. They bake the Cassavi on large, thin, flat iron plates, over the embers, making it into cakes; which when new, are tolerable good food; but when stale and dry, very insipid and poor."

[649] José Gonsalves da Fonseca. "Voyage Made from the City of the Gram Para to the Mouth of the River Madeira by the Expedition which Ascended This River to the Mines of Mato Grosso, by Special Order of His Faithful Majesty in the Year 1749," in George Earl Church, ed. *Explorations Made in the Valley of the River Madeira, from 1749–1868.* London: Published for the National Bolivian Navigation Company, 1875, pp. 203–355.
[Translation of "Navegação feita da cidade do Gram Pará até a bocca do Rio de Madeira pela escolta que por este rio subio as minas do Mato Grosso."]

"The canoes of his Majesty started on the 14th of July from the port of the City of Gram Para, with the intention of making a voyage on the River Amazon, and from this to enter its affluent, the Madeira, along the south bank, and to make for the military stations of Mato Grosso, in accordance with the orders of our Lord the King." Thus begins Gonsalves da Fonseca's account. He describes the river town of Camutá, located on the banks of the Tocantins, "on a site but slightly elevated to the westward, where there is a plain of sufficient extent to build a better town than the present one, which consists of a small street of unpretending houses, and only two of them covered with tiles. There is a church, but it is a plain and poorly-built edifice. There is also a hospital of Mercenarios, which is not a better specimen of architecture than the church, but it affords greater facility for divine worship." The author reports that "the inhabitants live on their cleared plantations, on which they grow the mandioca-plant, cacao and tobacco. They likewise manufacture a large quantity of oil, which they usually extract from a species of chestnut which they gather on the islands. This oil is used in their lamps, and is called *andiroba.* It is manufactured throughout the state. The air of the river Tocantins is salubrious; the views are delightful. . . . The river abounds with fish, and the banks and islands with every kind of game, while the natives enjoy that fertility which nature spontaneously offers to them; and they might increase the utility of the products obtainable, if they cultivated the land with care. The soil on either margin is admirably adapted for any phase of agricultural industry." At Gurupá, eleven days and 91 leagues from Belém, was a military outpost of Santo Antônio. "This place is the reporting-station for canoes, whether on the up or down journey to or from the interior. At this outpost there is a chief captain as commandant, provided by his Majesty. The garrison consists of eighteen men and a captain, and other subordinate officers. . . . About a cannon-shot from the said station there is a village of indians who are used for garrison work. This place is missioned by the Capuchin Friars of the Province de Piedade. There was a tolerable number of indians located there, but repeated attacks of small-pox and measles have swept down many persons of both sexes and all ages." Eight days and 75 leagues later, Gonsalves da Fonseca arrived at the Tapajós, "rather a large river, and . . . a league wide at the mouth. . . . At the entrance of the Tapajos, towards the left, upon a rocky height, stands a fortress, regularly contructed, and quadrangular in form. It has a garrison of soldiers, commanded by a captain and a lieutenant. This fortification could never be useful to command the passage of the Amazon, since between the river and there work there are several islands, among which canoes might navigate without any danger, and evade the vigilance (if it were exercised) of the abovementioned garrison. The only purpose for which it could be convenient would be for the missionaries in the villages on the Tapajos. These are five in number, visited by the Fathers of the Companhia de Jesus [Jesuits]." The expedition arrived at the Madeira River on 25 September 1749. At the village of Dos Abacaxis or Topinatubas there had been "a considerable amount of sickness and mortality among the inhabitants. . . . In consequence of the mortality arising not only from the malignity of the climate, but also from the two epidemics of small-pox and measles, which ravaged the country from 1743 up to present year, 1749, less than a third part of the population remains. During the administration of Father João de S. Paio, of the order Da Compania [Jesuits], there were among the indians more than a thousand warriors and able-bodied men before the two plagues alluded to." The author describes 19 *cachoeiras* or waterfalls on the Madeira. He concludes his interesting narrative with an account of "navigation of the river Apore until arriving at the mines of Mato Grosso."

I. The Middle Amazon and the Far West [Nos. 650–656]

Lewis Tambs **[650]** and **[651]** provides two overviews of the Luso-Brazilian march to the West. A detailed description of the Portuguese occupation of the Middle Amazon and its effects on that region is given by David Sweet **[652]**. In his doctoral dissertation, "Rivers and Empire," David Davidson **[653]** carefully details the process by which the Brazilian West was won. Much of the earlier part of this material is synthesized in his study of free lance and state on the Mato Grosso frontier, 1737–1752 **[654]**. Robert C. Smith **[655]** describes some of the maps and watercolors of Colonel Francisco Requena, a Spanish boundary commissioner, who spent more than fifteen years attempting to mark the limits of the Amazon and some of its tributaries as required by the Treaty of San Ildefonso in 1777.

[650] Lewis A. Tambs. "March to the West: Seven Centuries of Luso-Brazilian Expansion, Origins to 1808," (Ph.D. Dissertation: University of California, Santa Barbara, 1967). xi, 326 pp.

Against the background of centuries of feuding between Spain and Portugal in the Iberian Peninsula, Africa and the Atlantic islands, the author discusses Spanish and Portuguese rivalries in the New World "despite delineation in 1494 of their respective domains in South America by the Treaty of Tordesillas." During the first American phase of this struggle, 1494–1580, Spain was the victor—especially in the

Plata river basin. However, during the next period, 1580–1640, the union of Crowns enabled the Portuguese to encroach steadily westward, especially from staging points like São Paulo in the south and Belém do Pará in the Amazon region. At times it was done peacefully, though violence was not unknown, as for example, when the Paulistas destroyed the Spanish Jesuit mission system in Guairá, and "thus broke the Paraná-Tocantins water barrier which approximated the location of the line of Tordesillas dividing the two Crowns." During the years 1640–1680 the Portuguese continued their encroachments onto the Spanish side of the 1494 line as *bandeirantes* searched for gold and slaves. In 1680, the Portuguese established Colônia do Sacramento on the northern banks of La Plata. Though Colônia was recovered temporaily by the Spaniards during the War of Spanish Succession, the Treaty of Utrecht restored it to Portugal. Meanwhile, gold had been discovered in Minas Gerais. Between 1715 and 1750 *bandeirantes* continued their movement westward, spurred on by the gold discoveries in Minas Gerais, Goias and Mato Grosso. Other Portuguese explorers followed the Amazon and its tributaries. Nor did the Treaty of Madrid in 1750 or that of San Ildefonso in 1777 check Brazil's westward march. As José de Carvajal y Lancáster remarked in the mid-eighteenth century: "Spain's greatest territorial losses have been to Portugal." Based mostly on printed primary and secondary materials. There are a number of excellent maps.

[651] Lewis A. Tambs. "Brazil's Expanding Frontiers," *The Americas* 23:2 (October 1966), pp. 165–179.

Overview of Portuguese expansion in South America from the seventeenth century to 1825, with a special emphasis on the eighteenth century. Tambs describes how the Bragança monarchs attempted to control South America's two main river systems—the Rio de la Plata and the Amazon—and points out that "by 1750, the Luso-Brazilians, employing their 'indirect methods of conquest' had tripled the extension of Portuguese America beyond that allowed by the Treaty of Tordesillas." The author discusses the efforts of D. Luis da Cunha, one of João V's chief advisers, to obtain a natural Platine frontier in the south, strengthen the borders in the Amazon region of northern Brazil and open up the west to Portugal. An example of D. Luis's interest in the Brazilian West was his recommendation that the Algarve in southern Portugal be exchanged for Chile in Spanish America. Tambs recounts the feeble and futile efforts of Spain to seize the Middle Amazon from the Portuguese during the War of the Spanish Succession. He also points out that with the gold strikes at Cuiabá in Mato Grosso further efforts at westward expansion were promoted by the Crown, especially through their governors at Pará. The Portuguese pushed southwest, "following the natural curve of the rivers flowing into the Amazon." In 1748, the captaincy of Mato Grosso was created. The author also discusses boundary disputes with Spain and concludes with a discussion of the Treaty of Madrid (1750) and its aftermath. Based entirely on printed primary and secondary sources. 51 notes.

[652] David Graham Sweet. "A Rich Realm of Nature Destroyed: The Middle Amazon Valley, 1640–1750," (Ph.D. Dissertation: The University of Wisconsin, Madison, 1974). 869 pp.

Records the process of social change that occurred in the Solimões and Rio Negro Valleys in northwestern Brazil during the first hundred years after penetration of the region by Portuguese adventurers and Dutch trade goods. European disease, trade goods, and individuals demanding goods and services had an overwhelming impact on local Indians and their cultures, resulting in social upheavals that were undirected by any effective government agency. Decimation of Indian populations, the destruction of self-sufficiency and the ecological balance were some of the consequences. Slave trading in Indians, both official and unofficial, was extensive and longlasting. The missionaries' connections with this trade are analyzed. Based on archival research in Portugal and Brazil.
DAI 38/01-A (pp. 498–499).

[653] David Michael Davidson. "Rivers and Empire: The Madeira Route and the Incorporation of the Brazilian Far West, 1737–1808," (Ph.D. Dissertation: Yale University, 1970). 535 pp.

Explains how some of Brazil's far-flung frontier lands were knitted together and integrated into a conscious Brazilian nationality. Focuses on the "Madeira Route" (the Guaporé-Mamoré-Madeira River Route) which, crossing 2700 miles between western Mato Grosso and Belém do Pará, became Brazil's western border according to the terms of the Treaty of Madrid (1750). In 1752, navigation and commerce were officially opened on the rivers. The author points out that the route served as a defense line as well as "a principal bureaucratic, logistic and commercial artery to the west." Though, commercially, the Madeira route was only partially a success, it did tie the Brazilian west to Pará and Lisbon.
DAI 31/06-A (p. 2838).

[654] David M. Davidson. "How the Brazilian West Was Won: Freelance and State on the Mato Grosso Frontier, 1737–1752," in Alden, ed., *Colonial Roots* **[87]**, pp. 61–106.

Traces the history of the line of Tordesillas and the efforts of the Portuguese to expand further west in America in their search for mines and natural boundaries, especially rivers. Davidson discusses the frontier lands that eventually became the Brazilian West and the rivalry over their possession between Spain, with her Spanish Jesuits, and Portugal, acting with a combination of *bandeirantes*, miners and merchants. The author argues that "the critical stage in the winning of the Brazilian West spanned approximately the years from 1737 to 1752, after the initial gold strikes and settlement, and during a time of increased state participation. Within this brief span the Portuguese occupied Mato Grosso, sketched a western border along the Guaporé, Mamoré, and Madeira rivers and, in opening up navigation between Mato Grosso and Pará along these same rivers in 1752, created a bureaucratic, commercial and logistic artery that, like its southern counterpart along the monsoon route, integrated the Far West into the Empire." He describes the role of two of João V's principal advisers—the Brazilian-born Alexandre de Gusmão and the elder statesman Luis da Cunha—in encouraging Portuguese expansion. They "considered the pasture lands of the South, the forest and agricultural products of the Amazon, and the mines of the Center and West more valuable to the metropolis than the scanty contraband trade conducted through Colônia [do Sacramento]." By 1745, in the face of Spanish hostility to their westward encroachments, the Portuguese sent missionaries into Mato Grosso to Christianize the Indians and to counteract the Spanish Jesuits. In addition, bishoprics were created in São Paulo and Mariana in Minas Gerais and prelacies were established in Gioás and Cuiabá to bolster Portugal's claims to the West. The role of frontiersmen and their interests and conflicts with Portuguese royal policy is analyzed along with the effects of the Treaty of Madrid (1750). Based on archival research in Brazil, Spain and Portugal as well as printed primary and secondary materials. Map. 104 notes.

[655] Robert C. Smith. "Requena and the Japura: Some Eighteenth-Century Water Colors of the Amazon and Other Rivers," *The Americas* 3:1 (July 1946), pp. 31–65.

Both the treaty of Madrid (1750) and the treaty of San Ildefonso (1777) provided for joint-commissions to determine the boundaries between

Spanish and Portuguese America. One of these groups devoted its attention to charting the "middle section of the Amazon and the courses of some of its tributaries." The Spanish commissioner was the military engineer and mapmaker, Colonel Francisco Requena y Herrera. Governor of the province of Maynas (which now forms part of Brazil, Colombia, Ecuador and Peru), Requena led a contingent of Spanish officials, soldiers and slaves for more than a decade and a half before leaving Belém for Europe in January of 1795. The Portuguese, on the other hand, had three commissioners during this period. Initially, its contingent was headed by Lieutenant Colonel Teodósio Constantino de Chermont. He was replaced by H. J. Wilkens who held the post until 1788, when he, in turn, was succeeded by the new governor of Rio Negro, Colonel Manoel da Gama Lobo de Almada. The author gives a detailed account of the problems these officials faced during their difficult task of establishing a line of demarcation. The Spanish commission was poorly equipped and fed. Both groups fell victim to sickness and waterfalls, desertion by their Indian contingents, and constant disputes over the boundaries themselves. A number of maps and watercolors by Requena have survived, and eight of the former and ten of the latter are in Washington, D. C. The maps are dated 1788–1789, but the watercolors are undated. The ten watercolors are probably part of a larger collection. They depict "two scenes of preparations for the journey, showing the use of rafts and the making of a canoe; two views of Maynas missions visited by the Spanish commission en route down the Amazon; six episodes from the expedition up the Japura and its tributaries." Professor Smith gives a careful and detailed description of each watercolor, quoting whenever possible from the comments of other visitors to that or nearby regions. Based on printed primary and secondary materials. 1 map. 15 illus. 160 notes.

1. Contemporary Narratives, 1700–1822 [No. 656]

There are few travel accounts for this part of Brazil. Charles Marie de la Condamine **[656]** describes his travels eastward from Quito to Belém do Pará in 1743. José Gonsalves da Fonseca **[649]** gives a detailed report of his voyage from Pará to the Madeira river and from there to the mines of Mato Grosso in 1749. There are some excellent plates showing towns and forts in the Brazilian West in Alexandre Rodrigues Ferreira **[742]**, who led a scientific expedition through much of that region in the late 1780s.

[656] Charles Marie de la Condamine. *A Succinct Abridgement of a Voyage Made within the Inland Part of South America; From the Coasts of the South-Sea, to the Coasts of Brazil and Guiana, down the River of Amazons.* London: E. Withers, 1747. xii, 108 pp.
[Translation of *Relation abrégée D'un voyage Fait Dans l'Interieur De l'Amerique Meridionale depuis la Côte de la Mer du Sud, jusqu'aux Côtes du Brésil & de la Guyane, en descendant La Rivière Des Amazones.* Paris, 1745.]

The only account in English of the expedition of Charles Marie de la Condamine (1701–1774) focuses on the French explorer's travels in Brazil's Amazon region. Travelling eastward from Quito in 1743, La Condamine left "Pevas, the last Spanish mission, [to go] to St. Paulo, the first of those of Portugal; which is under the care of some fathers of the order of Mount Carmel." In his account, the author provides a short history of earlier explorers in the Amazon and discusses the accounts of Padre Cristoval de Acuña **[235]** and Father Samuel Fritz **[325]**. He travelled along the Rio Negro, the banks of which were "peopled by Portugueze missions, of the same Carmelite monks, whom we had met on coming down the Amazon, since our having pass'd the Spanish missions." He recounts his visit to the town and "the Portugueze fortress of Curupá, which was built by the Dutch, when masters of Brazil. The king's lieutenant there received us with extraordinary honours, the three days we stay'd being one continual feast." La Condamine lists the many animals he saw. He also gives an interesting description of Belém do Pará and its commerce with Lisbon: "In effect, on coming to this place immediately after our leaving the woods of the Amazon, we could almost have fancied ourselves transplanted to Europe: We found ourselves in a large city, adorned with streets finely laid out, and handsome houses; most of them rebuilt within these thirty years, of stone and shards, as also magnificent churches." Appended to his account is a large detailed map entitled: "A Map of the Course of the Maragnon, or Great River of the Amazons."

XVI. The Economy [Nos. 657–690]

A. General Accounts [Nos. 657–658]

The economic history of Brazil has been sadly neglected by historians. Two attempts to survey the economy of Brazil with substantial sections on colonial Brazil are those of João F. Normano **[657]** and Celso Furtado **[658]**.

[657] João F. Normano. *Brazil. A Study of Economic Types.* Chapel Hill: University of North Carolina Press, 1935. xii, 254 pp.
[Reprinted: New York: Biblo and Tannen, 1968.]

Normano uses a "cyclical" approach in analyzing the economy of Brazil, whose history he views as "a sensational record with amazing fluctuations. It is a history of the appearance and disappearance of entire industries. Its leitmotif is the perpetual change of the 'kings,' Sugar, cacao, gold, tobacco, cotton, rubber, coffee—each of these products has its place in the history of the country and was at one time the axis of the national (or state) economy, lending to Brazil a temporary world supremacy." Furthermore, "the change of the leading commodities moved the economic frontier of the country. The sugar cycle formed agricultural nuclei; the gold cycle disturbed part of them and originated new pastoral and agricultural centers. Cacao and tobacco are more similar to sugar in their influence." Normano describes the chief economic types: the "conservative and stable" *fazendeiro*; the nomadic *bandeirante*; the *tropeiro*, the *sertanejo*, the urban *paulista*, and the foreigner. The author also examines the influence of Adam Smith's *Wealth of Nations* (1776) on Brazilian economic thought during the late colonial and early independence periods. In particular, Normano focuses on the writings of José da Silva Lisboa, the future Viscount of Cayrú. The author concludes his analysis of the economic history of Brazil before independence with a review of colonial currency and the first Bank of Brazil. Notes. A "Selected Bibliography" is found on pp. 231–254.

[658] Celso Furtado. *The Economic Growth of Brazil. A Survey from Colonial to Modern Times.* Trans. Ricardo W. de Aguiar and Eric Charles Drysdale. Berkeley and Los Angeles: University of California Press, 1963. x, 285 pp.
[Translated from *Formação Economica do Brasil* (Rio de Janeiro, Editora Fundo de Cultura, 1959)]

Pioneering effort at synthesizing the economic history of Brazil. The author has attempted "to present an introductory text, accessible to the reader without a technical background in economics." To a great extent he has succeeded. Three of the book's five parts deal with the colonial period (pp. 1–94): I. Economic Bases of Territorial Occupation; II. The Slavery Economy of Tropical Agriculture (Sixteenth and Seventeenth Centuries); III. The Slave Economy of Mining (Eighteenth Century). Portions of Part IV, "The Economy of Transition to Paid Labor (Nineteenth Century)," bring Furtado's account up to the independence period with chapters on "Maranhão and the False Euphoria at the End of the Colonial Epoch"; "Colonial Liabilities"; "Comparison with the Development of the United States"; and "The Long-Term Decline in Income Level in the First Half of the Nineteenth Century." In his treatment of the colonial economy, there are important sections on sugar, cattle-raising, cotton, gold and diamonds. There are also some good insights into the role of Britain in the Luso-Brazilian economy. Although the author tends to overgeneralize, this is a useful essay. However, a growing amount of new research is beginning to challenge some of Furtado's conclusions and raise new questions about the economic history of colonial Brazil. Annotated. Based on printed sources.

B. Special Aspects [Nos. 659–687]

1. Agriculture and Cattle Raising [Nos. 659–667]

Alexander Marchant **[136]** and John Vogt **[135]** describe the brazilwood industry in the sixteenth century. For the eighteenth century, there is a study by Robert C. Smith **[619]** and **[620]** on the Wood Beach at Recife. F. W. O. Morton **[608]** discusses the royal timber industry in eighteenth-century Bahia. The most detailed book in English on sugar is Noel Deerr's two-volume work, which devotes a chapter to Brazil **[659]**. Kit Sims Taylor **[660]** and **[661]** attempts to construct a model of the northeastern sugar economy from 1540 to 1810. Matthew Edel

[662] discusses Brazilian sugar in the seventeenth century and the competition it received from the West Indies. Stuart B. Schwartz **[602]** studies the role of free labor and the production of sugar. J. H. Galloway **[663]** reexamines the agricultural crisis in northeastern Brazil 1700–1750. Dauril Alden contributes two important studies—one on indigo production **[664]**; the other on cacao **[665]**. He also has useful comments on Brazil's agricultural "renaissance" of the eighteenth century in **[274]** and **[569]**. Rollie Poppino **[666]** provides a good overview of the cattle industry in colonial Brazil, with a special emphasis on the São Francisco River Valley. Sue A. Gross **[667]** studies the production of honey and beeswax. There is much useful information on agriculture and cattle raising in Caio Prado, Jr. **[73]**.

[659] Noel Deerr. *The History of Sugar.* 2 vols. London: Chapman and Hall, 1949–1950. xiv, 636 pp.

Volume I provides a history of honey and cane sugar from the beginning of time to the present. The history of beet sugar is discussed in volume II. The Portuguese colonies are covered on pages 100–114. Deerr traces the development of cane sugar production in the Atlantic islands of the Madeiras and São Tomé and its transfer to Brazil. Unfortunately, much of the information is garbled as the result of factual and/or typographical errors and mistranslations from the Portuguese. When using Portuguese sources, Deerr relies heavily on *Annuario Azucareiro* (1936) and Simonsen's *História Econômica do Brasil, 1500–1800.* Almost a third of the chapter concentrates on the years during which the Dutch dominated northeastern Brazil, 1630–1654. The early part of the second volume contains a brief history of slavery, its relationship to sugar production and the role of the Portuguese. The section on slave revolts and sugar plantations has a few references to Brazil. There is an interesting chapter (XXI) entitled "The Plantation and the Planter," but the references to Brazil diminish after 1822. Though the author brings together a vast amount of material on the history of sugar, much of the information is of uneven value. The parts on colonial Brazil should be used with caution. Documented. There are numerous illustrations.

[660] Kit Sims Taylor. "The Economics of Sugar and Slavery in Northeastern Brazil," *Agricultural History* 44:3 (July 1970), pp. 267–280.

Attempts to construct "a model of the northeastern sugar economy from 1540 to 1810 and to examine the process of growth and stagnation by which sugar cane established its stranglehold on the region." Based entirely on printed sources with heavy reliance on the writings of Roberto C. Simonsen, Caio Prado Jr., and Manuel Correa de Andrade. 62 notes. 1 table.

[661] Kit Sims Taylor. *Sugar and the Underdevelopment of Northeastern Brazil, 1500–1970.* Gainesville: The University Presses of Florida, 1978. viii, 167 pp.
[University of Florida Social Sciences Monograph Number 63.]

Three chapters deal with colonial Brazil: "The Historical Development of Sugar and Slavery in Brazil," pp. 13–25; "The Economics of Sugar and Slavery," pp. 26–41; and "Sugar, Slavery, and the Formation of Brazilian Institutions," pp. 42–57. Based mostly on printed secondary sources. "The Economics of Sugar and Slavery" was originally published in *Agricultural History* **[660]**.

[662] Matthew Edel. "The Brazilian Sugar Cycle of the Seventeenth Century and the Rise of West Indian Competition," *Caribbean Studies* 9:1 (April 1969), pp. 24–44.

Discusses the reasons for Brazil's loss of its dominant position in the world sugar market in the second half of the seventeenth century. The author analyzes the economics of Dutch investment in Brazilian sugar and argues that even if the Dutch had not been driven out of Brazil in 1654 (after occupying much of the northeast for more than two decades) they still would have helped develop the sugar industry in the Caribbean. In short, it was not incompatible for the Dutch to invest simultaneously in both areas. Based entirely on printed materials, most of them secondary. 7 tables; 2 figures; 7 notes, plus other references within the text to the appended bibliography.

[663] J. H. Galloway. "Northeast Brazil 1700–50: The Agricultural Crisis Re-examined," *Journal of Historical Geography* 1:1 (January 1975), pp. 21–38.

Challenges the view that the gold rush in Minas Gerais which began in the 1690s led to loss of population and the depression of the agricultural economy of the Northeast. The author examines sugar exports, tithe contracts, and slave imports and pinpoints the beginnings of the depression in the 1730s for Bahia and Pernambuco and more than a decade earlier for Paraiba and Itamaracá. Galloway concludes that the traditional dating of the start of the depression in the Northeast was two to three decades too early and that previously held statistics on the region's loss of population were exaggerated. In short, the economic difficulties of the four captaincies studied were caused more by severe droughts and the drop of sugar prices on the world market than by repercussions from the discovery of gold in Minas Gerais. Based mostly on archival materials in the Arquivo Histórico Ultramarino, Lisbon. 2 maps; 2 graphs; 2 tables. 53 notes.

[664] Dauril Alden. "The Growth and Decline of Indigo Production in Colonial Brazil: A Study in Comparative Economic History," *The Journal of Economic History* 25:1 (March 1965), pp. 35–60.

After discussing the world's sources of indigo and its importance as a dye in the European textile industry, the author analyzes the factors that promoted the cultivation of indigo in Brazil during the last three decades of the eighteenth century and led to its decline in the early years of the nineteenth. Argues that despite the presence of internal factors that might have curtailed the industry, it was external factors—especially the disturbed international situation in Europe caused by the French Revolution and the Napoleonic Wars—over which neither Brazilians nor Portuguese had control that led to its downfall. As a result, American indigo was replaced in European markets by indigo from India, with Britain assuming the dominant position in the trade. Based on archival and printed sources as well as secondary works. 101 notes.

[665] Dauril Alden. "The Significance of Cacao Production in the Amazon Region during the Late Colonial Period: An Essay in Comparative Economic History," *Proceedings of the American Philosophical Society* 120:2 (April 1976), pp. 103–135.

This important article covers more ground than its title indicates. Alden spends a little less than a third of his study recounting the story of cacao production in Spanish America and the Caribbean, before turning to Brazil. He traces the Portuguese presence in the Amazon region, problems related to the use of Indian labor, and Portugal's early reliance on wild rather than cultivated cacao. Alden describes the large numbers of canoes being sent up river to gather wild cacao and points out that "by the early 1730s cacao had become the Amazon's dominant export staple, a position it would continue to occupy for longer than a century." The author then tries to determine annual production of cacao and its value in Belém and in Lisbon. He investigates charges that the Jesuits were exporting excessive amounts of corn without paying the tithe—charges that Alden discovers to be clearly exaggerated, at least during the years 1743–1745 when "the missionaries' share of the cacao trade amounted to a modest 6.6%." The author also challenges the thesis of Manuel Nunes Dias regarding the Companhia do Grão Pará and Maranhão founded during the Pombaline era. Nunes Dias argues that prior to this company's formation, "the economy of the Amazon was entirely one of subsistence and that it was the company that first linked the Amazon's production centers to European markets." Alden compares data for the years 1730–1755 and 1756–1777 and shows that such claims are inflated. He concludes his study by examining Guy C. Callender's so called staple thesis—that "the prosperity of a colony or of a colonial region depended upon the development of a major export staple for which there was a metropolitan demand"—and its relationship to cacao and the Amazon. Based extensively on archival (especially in Lisbon) and primary printed sources. There are 7 figures and 10 tables. 188 notes. The appendix includes a table listing yearly cacao exports from Belém to Pará, 1730–1822, and a description of his statistical sources.

[666] Rollie E. Poppino. "Cattle Industry in Colonial Brazil," *Mid-America* 31:4 (October 1949), pp. 219–247.

The author traces the effect of cattle raising on Brazilian social and economic development with a special emphasis on the São Francisco River Valley. Since cattle were not indigenous to America, they had to be imported to Brazil from Portugal's Atlantic Islands. Quickly multiplying in their new environment, these cattle played an important role in the history of Portuguese America. Since Brazil was mostly an agricultural colony, cattle were needed for food, leather and transportation and to power sugar mills. The development of mining in the eighteenth century and the European need for hides in the "age of leather" promoted further expansion of the cattle industry, as did the custom of wrapping tobacco and cotton with leather. Based on printed primary and secondary sources. 97 notes.

[667] Sue A. Gross. "colonial Brazil, Land of Honey and Butter," *American Bee Journal*. October, November, December, 1972, pp. 380–381; 411, 452; 455.

Valuable survey of sixteenth-, seventeenth-, and eighteenth-century Portuguese, French, Dutch and German writings on the importance of bees and wasps and their honey (as food and medicine) and wax in colonial Brazil. Based mostly on printed primary sources. 77 notes.

2. Mining [Nos. 668–670]

The best overview of mining in Brazil is found in the 1939 dissertation of Manoel Cardozo **[547]**. An early study that needs to be updated and corrected is Theophilus Henry Lee, "A Historical Sketch of the Development of Mining in Brazil" **[668]**. A useful account of mining in both Spanish and Portuguese America is that of Carlos Prieto **[553]**. Gold and diamond mining and their repercussion on the society and economy of Brazil are also discussed in Section XV, C. Edward J. Rogers **[669]** and **[670]** briefly discusses the iron and steel industry in colonial Brazil.

[668] Theophilus Henry Lee. "A Historical Sketch of the Development of Mining in Brazil," *Archivos do Museu Nacional do Rio de Janeiro* 22 (1919), pp. 195–220.

More than two-thirds of this survey of mining in Brazil deals with the colonial period. The author spends considerable time on a description of the origins of Portuguese expansion and early settlement in Brazil before turning to the search for mineral wealth. He describes a number of the pre-1690 attempts to find precious metals and emeralds. He then discusses the gold strikes of the 1690s in Minas Gerais and those of the early eighteenth century in Goiás and Mato Grosso. The diamond finds in the Tijuco district of Minas Gerais are also recounted. The author concludes with a description of semiprecious stones and manganese and iron ore in Brazil. No notes. Unfortunately, this study is marred by a number of factual errors concerning Portuguese and Brazilian history.

[669] Edward Jonathan Rogers. "A Study of the Brazilian Iron and Steel Industry and its Associated Resources," (Ph.D. Dissertation: Stanford University, 1957). 460 pp.

Though most of this thesis deals with the twentieth century, there is some useful information on iron-working activities during the colonial period. The author describes the role of the Jesuits in working Brazilian iron, problems incurred with the use of the primitive Catalan forge, and the founding of a number of blast furnaces in the early nineteenth century, the latter after the arrival of the Portuguese Court in Brazil. DAI 17/07 (p. 1538).

[670] Edward J. Rogers. "The Iron and Steel Industry in Colonial and Imperial Brazil," *The Americas* 19:2 (October 1962), pp. 172–184.

After briefly describing Portuguese smelting techniques and efforts to set up forges and furnaces in Brazil during the first three centuries of the Portuguese presence, the author focuses on the attempts of three foreigners—Baron Guilherme de Eschwege, Frederico Guilherme de Varnhagen, and Jean Antoine de Monlevade—to set up iron works in Minas Gerais and São Paulo after the Court's arrival in Rio de Janeiro in 1808. Though Eschwege and Varnhagen remained in Brazil to 1821, competition from British-made iron and steel products and the difficulty in recruiting workers led to the decline of Brazilian technology for the remainder of the Empire. Most of the article deals with pre-1822 history. Based entirely on secondary sources. 53 notes.

3. Fishing and Whaling [No. 671]

Surprisingly, little has been published in English on this important subject. A useful introduction to Brazilian whaling is found in Dauril Alden's study of the sperm whale **[671]**.

[671] Dauril Alden. "Yankee Sperm Whalers in Brazilian Waters, and the Decline of the Portuguese Whale Fishery (1773–1801)," *The Americas* 20:3 (January 1964), pp. 267–288.

After surveying sixteenth-century accounts of whales in Portuguese American waters and the beginning of the Brazilian whaling industry in the following century, the author analyzes its expansion and consolidation under Pombal and his successors. Particular attention is paid to the role of New England whalers—especially those captured aboard the *Leviathan,* a brig owned by Aaron Lopez, the merchant prince of Newport, Rhode Island—in Brazilian waters and the problems encountered by the syndicate organized by Inácio Pedro Quintela, "one of the most illustrious businessmen of the Pombal era," which had the colony's whaling contract. Based mostly on archival and printed primary sources. 75 notes.
See also **[579]**.

4. Shipping, Trade and Commerce [Nos. 672–687]

Alexander Marchant **[672]** studies Brazil as a way station for the Portuguese India fleets and Charles R. Boxer **[673]** focuses on Bahia as a port of call on the round trip between Lisbon and Goa. There are a growing number of studies on shipping and commerce. Charles R. Boxer **[674]** discusses the role of Padre Antônio Vieira in the founding of the Brazil Company in 1649. David Grant Smith **[675]** analyzes the role of Old Christian merchants in the institution of the same company. Boxer **[676]** and **[677]** also contributes articles on England and the Brazil trade during the troubled years following the Portuguese Restoration of 1640. The same author **[678]** studies the interaction of Brazilian gold and British traders during the first half of the eighteenth century. Dauril Alden **[679]** reviews the "vicissitudes of trade" in the Portuguese Atlantic Empire during the same time period. Allan Christelow **[680]** examines Great Britain and the trades from Cadiz and Lisbon to Spanish America and Brazil, 1759–1783. Kenneth Maxwell **[718]** and **[719]** provides some useful information on shipping and commerce during the Pombaline era. A list of United States vessels in Brazil, 1792–1805, has been compiled by Charles Lyon Chandler **[681]**. Herbert Heaton **[682]** describes the experiences of John Luccock, a merchant adventurer in Brazil, 1808–1818.

[672] Alexander Marchant. "Colonial Brazil as a Way Station for the Portuguese India Fleets," *The Geographical Review* 31:3 (July 1941), pp. 454–465.

Argues that despite earlier expectations that Portuguese America would become a way station for the India fleets, only about twenty ships—all having broken off from the fleet because of extraordinary circumstances—stopped in Brazil in 230 years (between 1500–1730). Using Portuguese America as a stopping off point would have prevented fleets from following the navigational timetable that would have ensured the most successful voyages to India. Based largely on printed primary sources. 45 notes.

[673] Charles R. Boxer. "The Principal Ports of Call in the *Carreira da India*," *Luso-Brazilian Review* 8:1 (Summer 1971), pp. 3–29.

Describes the two principal ports of call on the round trip between Lisbon and Goa: Mocambique island on the outward voyage and Bahia on the return, the latter especially after 1663. Bahia was popular because of its geographical location and the many opportunities it offered for both legitimate and contraband trade in Indian textile, Chinese silk fabrics, teas and porcelain for Brazilian gold (after 1695), sugar, tobacco and hides. Based mainly on printed primary sources. 73 notes. Appendix.

[674] Charles R. Boxer. "Padre Antônio Vieira, S. J. and the Institution of the Brazil Company in 1649," *The Hispanic American Historical Review* 29:4 (November 1949), pp. 474–497.

After briefly surveying the serious diplomatic and military problems facing Portugal and her overseas empire during the critical years 1640–1654, the author describes the successful attempt of the Jesuit Antônio Vieira in getting financial support from his new Christian friends to put together Antônio Teles's armada which raised the Dutch blockade of Bahia and Salvador Correia de Sá's squadron that recaptured Angola. Boxer then details Vieira's efforts to organize a chartered company and convoy system (much of the capital being furnished by New Christian financiers) to protect Portuguese South Atlantic shipping against the enormous losses it was suffering from the Dutch. After discussing its regulations and privileges, the opposition of the Inquisition, and the successes of the first four years of its operation, the author concudes that despite its political and economic shortcomings, it was of tremendous strategic value and turned the tide for the Portuguese. Based largely on archival (British Museum) and printed Portuguese and Dutch primary sources. 16 notes. Appendix.

[675] David Grant Smith. "Old Christain Merchants and the Foundation of the Brazil Company, 1649," *The Hispanic American Historical Review* 54:2 (May 1974), pp. 233–259.

Discusses the social backgrounds and economic connections of those Old Christian merchants who were the major investors and directors of the Companhia Geral do Comércio do Brasil and offers convincing arguments that the Brazil Company was not founded with the "extorted" funds of New Christian merchants but "was simply one more in a long series of contracts authorized by the Crown for reasons of state and underwritten by businessmen for motives of profit." The author estimates that one-fourth to one-third of Lisbon's merchant bankers were Old Christians and views the denunciation of the Brazil Company by the Inquisition as part of its feud with the Jesuits and the backers of the Revolution of 1640. Based largely on archival materials. 77 notes.

[676] Charles R. Boxer. "English Shipping in the Brazil Trade, 1640–1665," *The Mariner's Mirror* 37 (1951), pp. 197–230.

Valuable and detailed discussion of both the contraband trade as well as that carried on via Portugal during the first quarter of a century following Portugal's successful revolt against Spain. The author traces the Brazil trade's fluctuations and shows how it was affected by European politics and diplomacy. Based mainly on archival and printed primary sources. 53 notes (not consecutive).

[677] Charles R. Boxer. "Blake and the Brazil Fleets in 1650," *The Mariner's Mirror* 36 (July 1950), pp. 202–228.

Clearly shows that although the English blockade of the Tagus by Admiral Blake in 1650 (because of D. João IV's sympathies towards Prince Rupert and the royalist [Stuart] cause) resulted in the capture of nine outward-bound ships of the newly formed Companhia Geral's second armada, a good part of Antão Temudo's fleet returning directly from Rio de Janeiro, and several other Portuguese ships, it failed to seize the main body of the "singularly rich" Brazil fleet of approximately seventy vessels convoyed by the Conde de Vila Pouca and the Portuguese Brazil Company. The safe arrival of these sugar-laden ships from Bahia was of tremendous importance both for Portugal's efforts to remain independent from Spain and Luso-Brazilian attempts to drive out the Dutch from Portuguese America. In reprisal for Blake's actions, English ships and property were sequestered both in Brazil and Portugal. Largely based on archival (especially Brazilian and Portuguese) and printed primary sources. 24 notes. Appendix.

[678] Charles R. Boxer. "Brazilian Gold and British Traders in the First Half of the Eighteenth Century," *The Hispanic American Historical Review* 49:3 (August 1969), pp. 454–472.

Surveys the economic situation in Brazil in the post-1668 period and the effects of the discovery of Brazilian gold in Minas Gerais in the 1690s on the Brazilian and Portuguese economy. Boxer then discusses the problems caused by smuggling, the Anglo-Portuguese trade and commercial treaties, the role of the English merchant community in Portugal and Brazil, and English shipments of Brazilian gold to England. Heavily based on archival (British Public Records Office) materials. 35 notes.

[679] Dauril Alden. "Vicissitudes of Trade in the Portuguese Atlantic Empire during the First Half of the Eighteenth-Century: A Review Article," *The Americas* 32:2 (October 1975), pp. 282–291.

An examination of five volumes of the correspondence (ed. by Luis Lisanti and entitled *Negócios Coloniais*) of the Lisbon merchant Francisco Pinheiro with a special emphasis on Brazil. Describes the commercial system in which Pinheiro operated and the problems which he and his agents and partners faced. 25 notes.

[680] Allan Christelow. "Great Britain and the Trades from Cadiz and Lisbon to Spanish America and Brazil, 1759–1783," *The Hispanic American Historical Review* 27:1 (February 1947), pp. 2–29.

Describes the changes in attitude of Spain and Portugal as well as Great Britain and many of the latter's merchants regarding commercial treaties, the fleet system, and mercantile activity in Latin America and Asia during the years Charles II and Pombal were in power. The author argues that the Iberian attacks on the commercial treaties with Great Britian "were mistaken to the extent that they were based upon faulty diagnoses of the sources of British commercial predominance, which rested upon superior technical and financial resources far more than it did upon treaty privileges." Based largely on archival (British and French) and printed primary sources. 116 notes.

[681] Charles Lyon Chandler. "List of United States Vessels in Brazil, 1792–1805, Inclusive," *The Hispanic American Historical Review* 26:4 (November 1946), pp. 599–617.

Lists the names and, where possible, the owner(s), captain, and port of debarkation of 83 ships from the United States and the reasons for their presence in Rio de Janeiro (a few arrived at the port of Desterro [now Florianopolis] in the captaincy of Santa Catarina)—mostly to be refitted or repaired or to obtain provisions, food and water. The author was unable to find records of American ships in Brazil in 1806 and 1807 but lists five vessels that visited Portuguese America in 1808 after that colony's ports were open to foreign trade. Based on eleven volumes of documents regarding the arrival and departure of foreign shipping at Rio de Janeiro from 1790–1806. The documents are in the Biblioteca Nacional do Rio de Janeiro. 4 notes.

[682] Herbert Heaton. "A Merchant Adventurer in Brazil," *Journal of Economic History* 6:1 (May 1946), pp. 1–23.

Well-written sketch of the personal and mercantile experiences of John Luccock, a Yorkshire merchant, who arrived in Rio de Janeiro in June of 1808 and returned to England in 1818. Because of the French occupation of Portugal in 1807 and the Non-Importation and Embargo Acts passed the same year by the U. S., British manufactured goods were shut out of some of their most valuable markets. Luccock, related by marriage to the Luptons, an important mercantile family, was given the assignment of opening new markets in Brazil for his father-in-law's cloths as well as other English manufactures accepted for sale on a commission basis. In 1820, Luccock published his own account entitled *Notes on Rio de Janeiro and the Southern Parts of Brazil* **[844]**. Based on primary materials. 12 notes.

a. ENGLAND AND PORTUGAL [Nos. 683–687]

The close economic and political ties between England and Portugal played an important role in the histories of both countries and that of colonial Brazil. V.M. Shillington and A. B. Wallis Chapman **[683]** provide a good survey of the commercial relationships between England and Portugal. A.B. Wallis Chapman **[684]** reviews the fluctuations in Anglo-Portuguese trade during much of Brazil's colonial history. Sandro Sideri **[685]** argues that the Anglo-Portuguese commercial treaties of 1642, 1654, 1661, and 1703 resulted in "strong dependence by Portugal on England." A. D. Francis **[686]** gives a detailed account of Anglo-Portuguese diplomatic and commercial negotiations leading to the Methuen treaty of 1703. H.E.S. Fisher **[687]** studies the expansion of English trade with the Portuguese world from 1700–1760 and its contraction in the decade of the 1760s. There is a useful discussion of Pombal's role in Anglo-Portuguese commercial affairs, 1750–1777, in Kenneth Maxwell **[718]** and **[719]**.

[683] V. M. Shillington and A. B. Wallis Chapman. *The Commercial Relations of England and Portugal.* London, 1907. xxxii, 342 pp. [Reprinted. New York: Burt Franklin, 1970.]

Part I focuses on the Middle Ages and traces the early political alliances and commercial relations between England and Portugal. Part II deals with the late fifteenth to the early nineteenth centuries and is important for Brazilianists. Chapter I discusses colonial rivalries between Portugal and England, 1487–1580, especially English attempts at trade with the Indies and Africa, Anglo piratical activities and Portuguese retaliation. Chapter II covers the sixty years of Habsburg dominion over Portugal, 1580–1640, and traces the activities of the Company of English Merchants trading with Spain and Portugal and difficulties in Anglo-Portuguese relations because of Spanish rule. The Anglo-Portuguese treaties of 1642 and 1654, especially the latter, are treated in Chapter III. Special emphasis is given to the role of the English merchants and their Lisbon factory on the provisions of the 1654 treaty.

The marriage of Charles II of England with Catarina of Bragança, along with the Anglo-Portuguese treaty of 1661, trade between England and Portugal, the competition of Brazilian sugar with that from the British Caribbean, and the factors leading to the Methuen treaty of 1703 are the subjects of chapter IV. Chapter V discusses the English factories in Portugal and the Brazil trade and provides some insights into the growing animosity in Portugal against English mercantile interests. Chapter VI focuses on the Company of the Wines of the Alto Douro during much of the Pombaline regime, 1756–1787. Also discussed is Portuguese sentiment against the gold drain to England; the establishment of the Junto do Comércio is also studied. The initial effects of the Pombaline trading companies on Anglo-Portuguese commerce, the eventual demise of these companies, and the growing importance of the Brazil trade for England, 1786–1807, are the chief topics covered in chapter VII. Based mostly on archival as well as printed primary sources.

[684] A. B. Wallis Chapman. "The Commercial Relations of England and Portugal, 1487–1807," *Transactions of the Royal Historical Society.* 3rd Series, I (1908), pp. 157–179.

Reviews the fluctuations in Anglo-Portuguese trade during the period of Portuguese overseas expansion and discusses the various treaties between the two countries and their effects. Chapman points out that by the end of the eighteenth century a change was taking place in the trade relationship and "Portugal seemed for once to be on a commercial equality with England." She shows that "Brazil, instead of making gold its staple, began to produce raw cotton in increasing quantities, and this at a time when the English cotton manufactures were developing with unparalleled speed. . . . In 1791 England was sending gold to Lisbon, and Lisbon gold to Brazil." But these developments, the author asserts, were halted by the outbreak of the French Revolution. Based heavily on English archival sources. 72 notes.

[685] Sandro Sideri. *Trade and Power. Informal Colonialism in Anglo-Portuguese Relations.* Rotterdam: Rotterdam University Press, 1970. xi, 256 pp.

Sideri argues that "the Anglo-Portuguese commercial treaties of 1642, 1654, 1661 and finally 1703 (Methuen Treaty) established and codified an internal division of labour between the two countries." As a result, Portugal, which "at the end of the 17th century really produced both wine and cloth," was forced into an unfavorable economic position.

Sideri sees Portugal's "political and military weakness plus her colonial ambitions" as the reason for the four abovementioned treaties. "The Anglo-Portuguese relationship which emerged from this economic arrangement was one of strong dependence by Portugal on England, although it reinforced the Braganza House and the landed interests, thus the aristocracy and the Church." Sideri concludes that "the large and chronic deficit created by this type of international division of labour in the Portuguese balance of payments caused Brazilian gold (about 1700–1760) to outflow entirely from Portugal and to be directed mostly to England." The author discusses Pombal's policies and his efforts to resist this dependence. However, "the serious attempts to develop and industrialize Portugal in the 1770s and to make the colonies (mainly Brazil) more instrumental to such a goal were defeated by external events"—especially the Napoleonic invasions and "the reaction of the landed aristocracy." Based largely on printed sources. There is a bibliography on pp. 243–256.

[686] A. D. Francis. *The Methuens and Portugal, 1691–1708*. Cambridge: At the University Press, 1966. xv, 397 pp.

Detailed account of Anglo-Portuguese diplomatic and commercial relations, 1691–1708, from an English point of view. Francis discusses at great length the careers of John Methuen and his eldest son, Paul, both of whom served as British ministers to Lisbon. He also examines their success in arranging a commercial and defensive treaty with Portugal that was to have important repercussions on both England and Portugal for much of the eighteenth century. There are numerous references to Brazil as well as an interesting description of Pedro II of Portugal and his kingdom in the 1690s and early 1700s. Based heavily on British archival materials and travellers' accounts.

[687] H. E. S. Fisher. *The Portugal Trade. A Study of Anglo-Portuguese Commerce, 1700–1770*. London: Methuen & Co. Ltd., 1971. xvi, 171 pp.

Fisher discusses the expansion of English trade with Portugal and its empire to 1760 and its contraction in the decade of the 1760s. He shows how "the growth of population and output greatly enlarged effective demand in Brazil for manufactured goods, especially textiles." In addition, "the market for foreign manufactures in Portugal also benefited from the impact the growth of Brazilian wealth made on metropolitan Portugal." However, wartime conditions (Portugal entered the Seven Years War in 1762) and the decline in Brazil's gold and diamond output were responsible for the contraction of Anglo-Portuguese commerce, for, as the author points out, "the decline in Brazil's prosperity also seriously depressed the incomes of the Portuguese Crown and the mercantile communities in Lisbon and Oporto." Fisher describes the commercial organization of Anglo-Portuguese trade: textiles to Portugal and Brazil, foodstuffs to Portugal, the wine trade, the employment of merchant shipping, and the amount of bullion transferred to England. The author also studies the seasonal and yearly fluctuations in the trade, pointing out that "such fluctuations were quite marked. They stemmed essentially from variations in agricultural activity whether in England, Portugal or Brazil—that is, from agriculture as both a source of output and and as a source of incomes—and from variations in the output of the Brazilian mines. But there were other causes, notably the timing of the Portuguese trading fleets to and from Brazil and the effects of war." Fisher concludes with a chapter on the role of the Portugal trade and English economic development. There are numerous references to eighteenth-century Brazil. Based largely on English archival materials and printed primary sources. The printed sources are listed on pp. 155–162. There are 15 appendices dealing with the Portuguese trade. 2 maps; 11 plates.

C. Contemporary Narratives [Nos. 688–690]

There are three interesting contemporary accounts in English on the economy of colonial Brazil. José Joaquim da Cunha de Azeredo Coutinho **[688]** contributed a thoughtful essay on the commerce and products of Brazil. His analysis can be supplemented by the 1809 marginalia by an American or Englishman familiar with Brazil **[689]**. Thomas Ashe **[690]** wrote a guide to consumer wants and needs of Brazilians and described how England could fill them, given the disruption caused by the Napoleonic Wars.

[688] José Joaquim da Cunha de Azeredo Coutinho. *An Essay on the Commerce and Products of the Portuguese Colonies in South America, Especially the Brazils.* London, 1807. v, 198 pp.
[The first edition, entitled *A Political Essay on the Commerce of Portugal and Her Colonies, Particularly of Brazil in South America,* was published in 1801.]

The comments of the translator, though exaggerated, are worth noting: "The work before us contains more useful information, respecting the natives, the climate, the soil, the productions, the commerce, the navigation, and the capabilities, of the Portuguese colonies, but especially Brazil, than has ever yet been communicated to the public." The author, a native of Brazil and bishop of Pernambuco, 1795–1802, is accurately described by the translator as "a man at once distinguished by rank, talents, literature, and local knowledge." Though Azeredo Coutinho **[734]**, **[735]** provides a general survey of Brazil's resources, almost half of the essay focuses on the need for developing Brazil's maritime industry. He argues that "it is necessary to establish good dockyards, separated from the men of war docks, in the principal harbours of Brazil, where the materials for shipbuilding are the best and cheapest; so that the merchants may have full liberty to get ships built, and sent off when they please; and also that all the provinces should take care to raise a sufficient number of able masters and ship-wrights. In the royal dock-yards in Portugal, the number of workmen is often greater than is required; but in Brazil, they are always scarce." In a footnote, the Azeredo Coutinho adds: "If there were a great number of workmen in Brazil, ships might be built there at a very low price, owing to the abundance of materials. The expence of freight would then become trifling, the colonial products would become cheaper in the mother country, and better than those of foreign nations." The author also devotes several chapters to the Amerindians of Brazil, especially those from his home region of Ouetacazes. These Indians he describes as "the bravest and most faithful allies of the Portuguese." Azeredo Coutinho argues that "the Indians of Brazil are, by nature, fit subjects to follow a seafaring life." He maintains that "the Indians of Brazil are peculiarly clever, in learning all those things, which are acquired by imitation." The author is not as sympathetic toward those of African heritage: "The blacks, whose hands are more fitted, by nature, for continual labour, in the burning heat of the sun, than on the cold water, and who were hitherto employed in navigation, will, if used in husbandry, effect a considerable increase in the products of the fields." And, he adds in a footnote, "it would even be useful to lay a tax on every black, who is a fisherman or a sailor, and, on the other hand, to confer a bounty on every owner of a net or ship, whose servants are all native Indians." Azeredo Coutinho advocates the abolition of the Crown salt monopoly and argues that Portugal should reverse her colonial policy: "The more Portugal owes her settlements abroad, the closer it must unite them with her, and the more dependent they must become on the mother country."

[689] George W. Robinson, ed. *Brazil and Portugal in 1809. Manuscript Marginalia on a Copy of the English Translation of Bishop Jozé Joaquim da Cunha de Azeredo Coutinho's Ensaio Economico sobre o Comercio de Portugal e suas Colonias.* Cambridge, Massachusetts, 1913. 83 pp.

In this useful publication Robinson provides a biographical sketch of Azeredo Coutinho, a detailed description of the *Ensaio*, an examination of the English translation, and a discussion of the manuscript marginalia which he claims "were written in 1809, by some American or British merchant, trader, supercargo, traveller, or possibly naval officer." The notes were written in a copy of the 1808 edition of the English translation of the *Ensaio*. The marginalia are reproduced on pp. 35–70. There are two indices: a general one and another of authors cited in the notes.

[690] Thomas Ashe. *A Commercial View, and Geographical Sketch, of the Brasils in South America, and of the Island of Madeira.* London: Allen & Co., 1812. 160 pp.

Interesting guide to the consumer wants and needs of Brazilians. Billed as "a guide to the commercial world," this book encourages English merchants to fill the void in Brazilian trade caused by the disruptions of the Napoleonic wars. Ashe describes Portuguese needs vis-à-vis each important manufacturing town in England: For example, Birmingham: jewelry; Sheffield: cutlery; Manchester: soft goods; Stockport: hats; Leeds: woolen goods; Northampton: bone lace and fine thread; Nottingham: stockings, both silk and cotton; Coventry: silk; Gloucester: pin trade, etc. He foresaw the possibilities for a thriving market in hats: "The clerical hats alone must now rise to an enormous demand. There are not less than 40,000 Churchmen of every description now in Madeira and the Brazils." But he warned his fellow merchants that "there is no greater error than that of thinking that any rubbish of goods suits the South American market. I know from the most ample experience, that the best articles will sell there well, and at the best possible prices." The English merchants, according to Ashe, had other factors in their favor: "Notwithstanding the charms of the climate, there is something in it which consumes the energies, and disposes the mind to a love of supineness and a state of indolence, completely adverse to the pursuits of business, and the activity and zeal required in every branch of fabric and manufacture." The author concludes with a description of each of the captaincies of Brazil. Though the information is useful, it is sadly out of date, since he still has Salvador as capital of Brazil, a position it relinquished to Rio de Janeiro in 1763—fifty years before Ashe published his account.

XVII. Urban Development [Nos. 691–698]

There is a growing literature on the development of towns in colonial Brazil. Pierre Deffontaines **[691]** discusses the origin and growth of the Brazilian network of towns. Richard M. Morse **[692]** and **[693]** traces the evolution of urban development, as does José Arthur Rios **[694]**. The latter concludes that during most of the colonial period "the role of the city was marginal, dependent on the rural environment." Gerald F. Pyle **[695]** briefly discusses some geographical aspects of colonial urban development. Roberta Marx Delson **[696]** discusses detailed regulations for city-building in colonial Brazil with an emphasis on the eighteenth century. The same author **[697]** also examines the influence of the Enlightenment on urban planning. Donald Ramos **[559]** studies the demography of Ouro Preto at the end of the colonial period. Preston E. James **[698]** compares the development of Ouro Preto (founded in 1698) with that of Belo Horizonte (founded in 1896).

[691] Pierre Deffontaines. "The Origin and Growth of the Brazilian Network of Towns," *The Geographical Review* 28:3 (July 1938), pp. 379–399.

Argues that "Brazil does not seem to be naturally oriented toward urban settlement, and its rural population . . . is essentially a dispersed population." Deffontaines then examines attempts to establish "settlement groups, which developed into towns," the first five and the last playing a role in the colonial period: 1) Reductions and *aldeias* founded by missionaries to more easily convert the Amerindian; 2) agglomerations of military origins for defense purposes—most of them on the coast; 3) the mining towns; 4) road towns—centers for Brazil's large transportation network; 5) towns of the waterways; 6) railroad-station towns; 7) railhead towns; 8) "Sunday Towns"; 9) *patrimonio* towns. The author examines the evolution and composition of this last-mentioned type of town whose origin was a gift of land—a *patrimonio*—given for religious or secular purposes. He concludes with a section on the instability of Brazil's urban network arguing that "the towns of Brazil do not have the permanence of the old cities of Europe. Many of them are in eclipse, and the number of defunct towns is abnormal for a country where the town form has been in existence for less than three hundred years." Based primarily on the author's field research and printed sources. 17 illus. 10 notes.

[692] Richard M. Morse. "Brazil's Urban Development: Colony and Empire," in A. J. R. Russell-Wood, ed., *From Colony to Nation* **[88]**, pp. 155–181.

Useful review of the evolution of urban development in Brazil from the time the first town council was established in 1532 at São Vicente through the nineteenth century. Morse points out that from 1532 to 1650 "some thirty-seven *vilas* and *cidades* were founded, only seven or so by the crown and the remainder by the donataries of the captaincies." He also claims that "early colonial Brazil had only the rudiments of administrative structure. For the most part the colony was a loose assemblage of *vilas* that exercised sweeping powers by default." He examines the controversy over the differences between Spanish and Portuguese urban planning and solutions and observes that "urban development in colonial Venezuela . . . is more analagous to the Brazilian than to the central Mexican or Peruvian pattern." He concludes that "one might argue that the distinction between Spanish and Portuguese town planning in America was not so much a commitment to different principles as a differing pace of evolution." In discussing the Brazilian town councils, Morse shows that "the decline of the *câmaras* power after the mid-seventeenth century coincided with commerical development and royal centralization." However, "expansion of settlement and of informal rural command systems in the eighteenth century challenged governmental efforts at centralization." Based on printed primary and secondary materials. 3 tables. 78 notes.

[693] Richard M. Morse. "Brazil's Urban Development: Colony and Empire," *Journal of Urban History* 1:1 (November 1974), pp. 39–72.

Earlier version of **[692]**.

[694] José Arthur Rios. "The Cities of Brazil," in Smith and Marchant, eds., *Brazil* **[83]**, pp. 188–208.

Most of this article deals with the colonial period. Rios discusses the evolution of cities in Portuguese America from dyewood *feitorias* (factories) having crude buildings surrounded by stockades, a tower for defense, and possibly a few small houses of wattle and daub to the mid-sixteenth century towns, the "first nucleus of public administration," with their living quarters, council house and jail, church and *pelourinho*. The author describes the building of Salvador in Bahia founded in 1549, which could boast of a hundred houses three months after its founding. Slightly more than a half century later, Bahia "possessed three fortresses, the cathedral, and four monasteries of different orders." The development of São Paulo, which had a century after its founding "150 houses, 4 churches, and 1,500 souls," is also traced. Rio de Janeiro and Olinda, the two other "principal nuclei of settlement at the end of the sixteenth century," are also discussed. The author discusses the "urban colonization of the Dutch" in the Northeast, the role of Indian missionary *aldeias* as nuclei of future Brazilian towns, and the needs of defense, the latter leading to numerous towns "born from military encampments produced by the long struggle with Spain." Rios also studies the ephemeral character of many towns in the mining regions and the effect of the transfer of the Portuguese court to Brazil on the development of Rio de Janeiro. He concludes that during most of the colonial period "the role of the city was marginal, dependent on the rural environment." Based on printed primary and secondary sources. 10 notes.

[695] Gerald F. Pyle. "Some Geographical Aspects Basic to Understanding Brazilian Urbanization," *Revista Geográfica* 73 (December 1970), pp. 5–27.

More than a third of the article deals with colonial Brazil. The author discusses various models of colonial cities, the Portuguese heritage, the early Brazilian cities, the late colonial settlement, and urban growth after independence. Based mostly on printed secondary materials. The text contains 6 figures (3—1a,b,c—focus on the colonial period). The appendix contains 5 tables, all on contemporary Brazilian cities. Bibliographical references are found on pp. 22–23.

[696] Roberta Marx Delson. "Town Planning in Colonial Brazil," (Ph.D. Dissertation: Columbia University, 1975). 394 pp.

Points to the existence of detailed regulations for city-building in colonial Brazil, especially in the eighteenth century. The discovery of gold in the 1690s stimulated town planning in the interior. Military engineers supervised construction of towns and cities where Portuguese justice and administration could be effectively wielded. From 1716, the town prototype used was based on Renaissance and Baroque designs, having straight streets, delineated plazas and uniformity of facade. Town planning was equated with royal control and order. Later these designs were used in the renovation of older coastal cities and also in the reconstruction of Lisbon after the 1755 earthquake.
DAI 36/03-A (p. 1750).

[697] Roberta M. Delson. "Planners and Reformers: Urban Architects of Late Eighteenth-Century Brazil," *Eighteenth Century Studies* 10:1 (Fall 1976), pp. 40–51.

Studies the influence of the Enlightenment on urban planning in Brazil during the last half of the eighteenth century. The author analyzes the efforts of three Portuguese-born administrators—José Xavier Machado Monteiro (Porto Seguro), Luis Antônio de Sousa (São Paulo), and Luis da Cunha Menezes (Goiás)—to build towns and cities characterized by carefully regulated physical layouts of aligned streets and buildings with uniform facades and use them as instruments of social control. Fearing that "unplanned communities might deteriorate into a general chaos" and equating "street pattern regularity with regularity of behavior," these administrators, supported by the Portuguese Crown, attempted to use regulated urban planning both to Europeanize the Indians and discipline Portuguese colonists in Brazil. Based chiefly on printed primary sources. 24 notes. 9 illus.

[698] Preston E. James. "Bello Horizonte and Ouro Preto: A Comparative Study of Two Brazilian Cities," in *Papers of the Michigan Academy of Science Arts and Letters* (Ann Arbor: University of Michigan Press, 1933), 18 (1932), pp. 239–258.

Views Ouro Preto (founded in 1698) and Belo Horizonte (founded in 1896) as "representative of two distinct phases of Brazilian settlement." On the one hand, "Ouro Preto is old; its buildings, its narrow, irregular, cobble-paved streets, its layout, and the less tangible 'atmosphere' of the place which these material forms combine to create, are all relics of the eighteenth century. Ouro Preto had its origins as a gold-mining camp, one of the richest of the state of Minas Geraes." On the other hand, Belo Horizonte "is a new city; unencumbered by history or tradition, since about every man-made feature of this urban center is less than forty years old [in the early 1930s], this city belongs to the future." James points out that in mining towns like Ouro Preto "the mine is the *functional nucleus*. . . . A focal location with easy accessibility to the surrounding territory, or even a favorable terrain on which to place the streets and buildings, is a matter of minor importance." The author examines the terrain of Ouro Preto, its urban morphology, and its relationship to the larger region. Based on field research and printed sources. 6 maps (two of which are of special value to students of colonial Brazil); 10 photos (five of Ouro Preto); and 18 notes.

XVIII. Social History [Nos. 699–716]

The starting point for the study of colonial Brazil's social history is Gilberto Freyre's classic, *The Masters and the Slaves* **[699]**. Freyre also provides overviews of social developments in **[702]** and **[703]**. In "The Patriarchal Basis of Brazilian Society," Freyre **[704]** stresses the importance of "the family, its patriarchal structure, and this family arrangement as a special economic system" for understanding Brazilian history. Antônio Cândido **[705]** also examines the role of the family and its influence on the development of colonial Brazil. Recent studies are beginning to challenge some of Freyre's views, especially for the late colonial period and in the southern part of Brazil. See, for example, those of Elizabeth Kuznesof **[543]**, Donald Ramos **[558]** and **[559]**, and A. J. R. Russell-Wood **[288]** and **[456]**. Mitchell Gurfield **[706]** discusses class structure and political power and Fernando Uricoechea **[707]** traces the evolution of bureaucratic patrimonialism. Francis A. Dutra **[297]** and **[475]** analyzes the role of nobility and membership in the military orders. The military, nobility and the search for status are also studied by Ross Bardwell **[279]** and David Tengwall **[289]**. Alan K. Manchester **[708]** describes the development of the Brazilian aristocracy. Stuart B. Schwartz **[284]** and **[602]** and A. J. R. Russell-Wood **[300]** provide good descriptions of Bahian society during much of the colonial period. The Bahian elites, 1750–1822, are studied by John N. Kennedy **[606]**. The Bahian military in the early nineteenth century and their social pretensions are discussed by F. W. O. Morton **[607]**. Elizabeth Kuznesof **[543]** describes the development of society in São Paulo, 1765 to 1836, with her study of household composition and the economy in that captaincy. Social differentiation in areas of the captaincy of São Paulo specializing in agriculture and cattle raising in 1822 and 1824 is studied by Emílio Willems **[545]**. Donald Ramos **[556]** analyzes the social history of Ouro Preto, 1695–1726 and then focuses on marriage and the family **[558]** and the composition of the population **[559]** in early nineteenth-century Vila Rica. Lawrence Nielsen **[557]** also studied Minas Gerais with his discussion of gentry, peasants and slaves in the rural society of Sabará. Billy Chandler **[623]** performs a similar service for Ceará, while Jeremiah Slade **[523]** and Gregory Brown **[522]** study southern Brazil in the late eighteenth and early nineteenth century. David Grant Smith **[598]** provides a collective biography of merchants in Lisbon and Bahia in the seventeenth century, with Charles Boxer **[599]** contributing a note on the commercial records of one such merchant. Rae Flory **[600]** studies Bahian society in the mid-colonial period and along with David Grant Smith **[601]** analyzes the role of Bahian merchants, planters and artisans in the seventeenth and eighteenth century. Susan Soeiro **[332]**, **[33]**, **[334]** studies Bahian nuns and their convent and society.

Stuart B. Schwartz focuses on the question of elite politics and the growth of a peasantry in late colonial Brazil **[709]**. Harry Bernstein **[710]** studies the white artisan in Brazil during the eighteenth century and the first half of the nineteenth. Using late sixteenth- and early seventeenth-century Inquisition records, Patricia Aufderheide **[711]** studies social attitudes and analyzes the role of guilt and shame in enforcing society's rules. In her dissertation **[712]**, she studies "Order and Violence: Social Deviance and Social Control in Brazil, 1780–1840." Dauril Alden **[713]** surveys the population of Brazil in the late eighteenth century.

[699] Gilberto Freyre. *The Masters and the Slaves. A Study in the Development of Brazilian Civilization.* Translated from the Portuguese of the Fourth and Definitive Edition by Samuel Putnam. New York: Alfred A. Knopf, 1946. lxxi, 537 pp. xliv.
[*Casa Grande e Senzala* was first published in Rio de Janeiro by José Olympio in 1933.]

"This essay is the first of a series in which I have undertaken to study the formation and disintegration of patriarchal society in Brazil, a society that grew up around the first sugar mills or sugar plantations established by Europeans in our country, in the sixteenth century." With these words, the Brazilian anthropologist and social historian Gilberto Freyre describes his pioneering panoramic approach to the history of Portuguese America's plantation society. The author begins his study by discussing the process of colonization in Brazil, pointing to the "mobility, miscibility, and acclimability" of the Portuguese in explaining their success as colonizers. He also looks at the role of race, food, climate and disease on the development of the Brazilian people. With this background Freyre then devotes a section to each of the three major racial components that made up the population of colonial Brazil: The Amerindian native, the Portuguese colonizer, and the African slave. The author discusses the role of miscegenation and the interaction of these three races: "Every Brazilian, even the light-skinned fair haired one, carries about with him on his soul, when not on soul and body alike . . . the shadow, or at least the birthmark, of the aborigine or the Negro." This book is a vast storehouse of information—much of it still needing to be digested and evaluated by scholars. Some of Freyre's premises have been convincingly challenged—for example, that long contact with "dark-skinned" Moslems in the Iberian Peninsula of the Middle Ages predisposed the Portuguese for interracial mixture. He also has been validly criticized for his tendency to generalize on the basis of an analysis of one group—e.g., household slaves—or time period—e.g., nineteenth-century Pernambucan society—for all slaves in Brazil and for the entire colonial period. The book is wordy and, at times, poorly organized. Yet, despite these shortcomings, *The Masters and the Slaves* is a major study and a monumental achievement that deserves several readings. No study on plantation society in colonial Brazil or race relations in Portuguese America can be complete without coming to grips with the information Freyre provides or the problems he poses. Samuel Putnam did an excellent job in translating this demanding book. *The Masters and the Slaves* is extensively documented. The footnotes alone provide an enormous amount of information. There is a glossary (pp. 477–500). The bibliography (pp. 501–537) also contains works cited by the translator. There are plans showing the Big House of the Noruega Plantation.

[700] Gilberto Freyre. *The Masters and the Slaves. A Study in the Development of Brazilian Civilization.* Translated from the Portuguese by Samuel Putnam. Second English-Language Edition, Revised. New York: Alfred A. Knopf, 1956. lxxi, 537 pp. xliv.

Everything is identical to that of the first English-language edition except that Freyre has written a new preface to replace the translations of the prefaces to the first four Brazilian editions. As Freyre expresses it: "Rather than preserve here all the prefaces written for the several Portuguese editions of *Casa Grande & Senzala*, I have decided to keep only the Preface written especially for the First English-Language Edition, and to fuse the others into this single synthetic Preface."

[701] Gilberto Freyre. *The Masters and the Slaves. A Study in the Development of Brazilian Civilization.* Translated from the Portuguese by Samuel Putnam. Abridged from the Second English-Language Edition, Revised. New York: Alfred A. Knopf, 1964. 432 pp.

This abridged, paperbound edition of **[701]** omits all the footnotes, the bibliography, the plans showing the Casa Grande of the Noruega Plantation, and the index of the first and second English-language editions. It also leaves out the preface to the first English-language edition and abridges pages xxvii-xliv of Freyre's preface to the second English-language edition, calling it "Author's Introduction" (pp. 3–11 of the paperbound edition). However, this abridged edition does include the glossary and the main divisions of the original English translation, though it leaves out portions of the text.

[702] Gilberto Freyre. "Some Aspects of the Social Development of Portuguese America," in Griffin, ed., *Concerning Latin American Culture* **[96]**, pp. 79–103.

Provides a synthesis of many of the ideas that appeared in *The Masters and the Slaves* **[699]**. This wide-ranging essay covers both the Portuguese and the Brazilian backgrounds. Freyre analyzes the role of the Iberian peninsula's Moslem and Jewish heritage and quotes approvingly the remark of Angel Ganivet that "Portugal separated from Spain, not because the two were too different, but because they were too similar." As for Brazil, the author argues that "through sexual irregularities the best Portuguese mixed with the best Indian blood and the best African blood brought to America." He discusses the value of the Inquisition records and those of the religious brotherhoods for social history. Freyre also details some of the problems encountered in the researching and writing of social history in Brazil. The great scarcity of personal papers, the author believes, is due to Brazil's climate and the fact that Brazilian Catholics told their problems and sins to their confessors while Protestants (in New England, for example) wrote the intimate details of their lives in diaries. When discussing the role of the religious brotherhoods in Portuguese America, he points out that "much of the work that was done by the government or by the church authorities in Spanish America was done in Brazil by those religious brotherhoods: that is, by private enterprise and not by official initiative; by laymen, and not by bishops nor the clergy." Freyre concludes his essay with a lengthy discussion of the role of women in Colonial Brazil. No notes.

[703] Gilberto Freyre. *Brazil: An Interpretation.* New York: Alfred A. Knopf, 1945. vi. 179 pp.

These Patten Foundation Lectures, given at Indiana University in 1944–1945, contain a wide-ranging analysis of Brazilian life and culture with frequent references to the colonial period. However, only one chapter, "The European Background of Brazilian History" (pp. 1–34), focuses specifically on the preindependence period. In these early pages, Freyre captures the essence of his earlier section on the Portuguese colonizer in *The Masters and the Slaves* **[699]**. Chapter two, "Frontier and Plantation in Brazil" (pp. 35–65), also includes some useful material on the colonial period, though it deals mostly with the nineteenth century. Throughout the book, but especially in the first two chapters, Freyre makes frequent comparisons between the Brazilian Northeast and the U. S. South.

[704] Gilberto Freyre. "The Patriarchal Basis of Brazilian Society," in Joseph Maier and Richard W. Weatherhead, eds. *Politics of Change in Latin America* (New York: Frederick A. Praeger, 1964), pp. 155–173.

Freyre argues that "the public image of an age does not reveal its private substance. Rather, it is the private or 'intimate' history that makes us see the true meaning of public history." He further stresses the importance of "the family, its patriarchal structure, and this familial arrangement as a special economic system" for understanding Brazilian history. Though each region in Brazil "had its own special traits," emphasizing either cacao, coffee, cotton, cattle, or rubber, they were never at great variance with the original pattern of the northeast "where sugar, the Portuguese, the African slave, the Indian half-breed, and the horse and the ox were dominant from the sixteenth until the nineteenth century." Freyre traces the development of sugar production in Brazil in the sixteenth century, the role of the Jesuits in colonial society, miscegenation, and family life and organization. He concludes that Brazil's European character would not have lasted "if the Portuguese patriarchal family structure had not been at the root of social formation in Brazil." More than three-fourths of the article deals with the colonial period. No notes.

[705] Antônio Cândido. "The Brazilian Family," in Smith and Marchant, ed., *Brazil* **[83]**, pp. 291–312.

This study deals mostly with the colonial period and the examples refer principally to the central and southern parts of Brazil. The author points out the conservatism of Brazilian society since "probably most of the Portuguese colonists who occupied Brazil and directed its affairs from the sixteenth century on came from the rural zones and from the middle and lower strata of society." Because of the scarcity of white women, "Portuguese familial organization did not find a favorable environment in the colony." The author also stresses that "racial intermixture occured principally through irregular unions." Though Antônio Cândido emphasizes the pervasiveness of paternal authority, he points out that writers have probably "exaggerated the complete submission of the woman." He argues that "perhaps the problem of woman's status in the Brazilian family is better understood if it is viewed as the product of a dual social and cultural situation; in this case the woman appears as carrying on a specific type of cultural participation and a social function, different from those of the husband, and therefore not to be compared with his except with great caution. They are two complementary spheres, each with its ethos more or less differentiated from that of the other, often in conflict, but generally supporting each other in the maintenance of a considerable sociological balance." The role of illegitimate children is discussed. The author concludes his discussion of the colonial period by arguing that the influence of the latifundia economy and of the patriarchal family structure was modified by the evolution of Brazil's economy after the transfer of the Portuguese Court to America in 1808. The "opening of the ports to friendly nations (1808) enriched the social life with a much greater number of possibilities." 23 numbered and 8 unnumbered notes. The former contain bibliographical references.

[706] Mitchell Gurfield. "Class Structure and Political Power in Colonial Brazil: An Interpretative Essay in Historical Sociology," (Ph.D. Dissertation: New School for Social Research, 1975). 296 pp.

A synthesis and, in part, a reinterpretation of class structure and political power in colonial Brazil. Based on secondary sources, it reaffirms previous historical findings, for example, that the class structure was largely determined by the import of slaves and a system of land distribution and that the lower classes were atomized. Also, and in particular, it demonstrates the numerical marginality of the peasantry and puts forth an in-depth synthesis of class structure and political power. The structure of colonial Brazil was found to be unique and cannot be called feudal or capitalistic, nor put into any other traditional classification.
DAI 36/05-A (pp. 3141–3142).

[707] Fernando Uricoechea. "The Patrimonial Foundations of the Brazilian Bureaucratic State: Landlords, Prince and Militias in the XIXth Century," (Ph.D. Dissertation: University of California, Berkeley, 1976). 406 pp.

Discusses how patrimonialism developed in Brazil through land policy and other means during the colonial period, particularly at the local level. Bureaucratic development of the state increased greatly in the second quarter of the nineteenth century. At the same time, however, the Brazilian state began "the most comprehensive and systematic program of patrimonial administration of local government that any Ibero-American country has ever experienced." Local poor freemen were involved through the *Guarda Nacional*, "a status association of freemen in charge of justice and police functions." This patrimonial-bureaucratic experiment lasted for over two generations. The author discusses its successes and failures and explains why it did not develop fully.
DAI 38/02-A (pp. 966–967).

[708] Alan K. Manchester. "The Rise of the Brazilian Aristocracy," *The Hispanic American Historical Review* 11:2 (May 1931), pp. 145–168.

Attempts to trace the development of "a distinct and powerful group in the colony which identified itself with Brazil in preference to Portugal." The author argues that by 1700 "aided by the rural character of the population and by the system of militia employed in Brazil, this class of colonists had created an aristocracy which was based economically on land and legally on the right to vote in the elections for the *câmaras* (town councils). Jealous of its position, this colonial aristocracy forced new arrivals into commercial and mechanical pursuits with the result that there developed a Portuguese class which cherished antipathy for the Brazilian aristocrat." Includes valuable descriptions both of social classes, their acquisition of land and wealth as well as town councils and their composition and function. Recent archival research, however, continues to modify or qualify a number of Manchester's generalizations. Relies very heavily on Rocha Pombo's *Historia do Brasil* and, to a lesser extent, on Pereira da Silva's *História da Fundação do Imperio Brazileiro* as well as printed primary sources. 78 notes.

[709] Stuart B. Schwartz. "Elite Politics and the Growth of a Peasantry in Late Colonial Brazil," in Russell-Wood, ed., *From Colony to Nation* **[88]**, pp. 133–154.

After sketching the historiography of the late colonial and early independence periods and analyzing the social and economic structure of Brazil and the tensions it created, the author focuses on the peasantry [defined as rural workers "whose productive activities are influenced, shaped, or determined to a significant extent by powerful outsiders"], especially those from the northeastern captaincies of Pernambuco and Bahia, and describes the racial characteristics and the material life of these *moradores* and *lavradores* and their relationships to the oligarchy. Based mostly on printed primary and secondary sources. 64 notes.

[710] Harry Bernstein. "The White Working Man in Brazil from Pedro I Through the Regency," *Revista do Instituto Hist*órico e Geográfico Brasileiro 307 (abril–junho 1975), pp. 234–253.

Pioneering work on white artisans in Brazil in the eighteenth and the first half of the nineteenth centuries. The author discusses the role of the *juiz do povo* and the guild corporations in Bahia, Recife and Rio de Janeiro and compares them with those in Portugal. The guilds in Brazil lost much of their power to the various *senados da câmara* [municipal councils] (who favored paid slave artisans) and were eventually abolished by Pedro I in 1824. [Those in Portugal were abolished a decade later by the same monarch.] The author also discusses the role of white immigration during the first four decades of the nineteenth century. Based on printed primary and secondary sources. 16 notes.

[711] Patricia Aufderheide. "True Confessions: The Inquisition and Social Attitudes in Brazil at the Turn of the XVII Century," *Luso-Brazilian Review* 10:2 (December 1973), pp. 208–240.

Uses records of the confessions made to the Inquisition during two of its visitations to Brazil (Pernambuco, 1594–1595 and Bahia, 1618) in an attempt to see patterns of social control based on age, sex, color and wealth. The author also analyzes the role of guilt and shame on enforcing society's rule. Based on printed primary and secondary sources. 84 notes. 2 tables.

[712] Patricia Ann Aufderheide. "Order and Violence: Social Deviance and Social Control in Brazil, 1780–1840," (Ph.D. Dissertation: University of Minnesota, 1976). 436 pp.

Describes social patterns and institutions that served to maintain Brazil's seigneurial society during an era of social and political unrest. Two kinds of social problems are analyzed: Those of marginality, which challenged the social order (e.g., vagrancy), and those of "social deviance" (interpersonal conflict between settled members of society usually in the same peer group), that helped perpetuate the order. Competition among peers lessened intergroup hostility and provided security for the individual even as it reduced social mobility and opportunity. Matching the two kinds of social problems were two institutional changes. A national guard, co-opting local elites, repressed marginality in rural areas, while police did the same in the cities. This represented a switch from private control to one sponsored and administered by the state. Social deviance, itself a guard against social change, did not need such innovations but the times required a more efficient means to deal with personal conflict. Liberals effected reforms in the criminal procedure. Only those that were more efficient in processing cases, without disturbing the judicial role (and informal social alliances), were successful.
DAI 37/10-A (p. 6694).

[713] Dauril Alden. "The Population of Brazil in the Late Eighteenth Century: A Preliminary Survey," *The Hispanic American Historical Review* 43:2 (May 1963), pp. 173–205.

After describing the methods, classifications, and problems involved in census-taking in Brazil during the last quarter of the eighteenth century, the author discusses the different demographic sources for each captaincy and makes adjustments when such accounts are incomplete. Based mostly on archival (mainly Brazilian with some English and Portuguese transcriptions or microfilm) and printed primary sources. 81 notes. 7 tables; 1 map; appendix ("Bibliography of Demographic Sources").

A. The Literature of Social Protest [Nos. 714–716]

The most famous of the social satirists in colonial Brazil is Gregório de Matos. The best analysis is that of Margaret J. Bates **[714]**. Daniel Reedy **[715]** compares the life and poetry of Matos with that of Quevedo. Stuart Schwartz **[284]** uses Matos's satire in his study of *Sovereignty and Society in Colonial Brazil.* Nola Kortner Aiex **[716]** also discusses the seventeenth-century poet along with such other examples of Brazilian satire as that of Tomás Antônio Gonzaga and his *Cartas Chilenas.*

[714] Margaret J. Bates. "A Poet of Seventeenth Century Brazil: Gregório de Matos," *The Americas* 4:1 (July 1947), pp. 83–99.

The author convincingly challenges the view that Matos was a literary great and argues that those who view the poet as an important social reformer attribute to him intentions he did not have. Though he attacked corruption, Matos had little sympathy for Blacks, Mulattoes and Indians. 97 notes.

[715] Daniel R. Reedy. "Gregório de Matos: The Quevedo of Brazil," *Comparative Literature Studies* 2:3 (1965), pp. 241–247.

Discusses the parallels in both the lives and the poetry of the Spaniard Don Francisco de Quevedo and the Bahian-born Gregório de Matos (1633–1696). Mentions people and incidents in Bahia satirized by Matos that should be of interest to historians. 8 notes.

[716] Nola Kortner Aiex. "Social Satire in Brazilian Literature: Seventeenth-Nineteenth Century," (Ph.D. Dissertation: University of Illinois at Urbana-Champaign, 1977). 151 pp.

Contains chapters on Gregório de Matos and his poetry, Tomás Antônio Gonzaga and *As Cartas Chilenas*, Luis Carlos Martins Pena and his plays, and Manuel Antônio de Almeida and the *Memórias de um Sargento de Milicias.*
DAI 38/06-A (p. 3532).

XIX. The Pombaline Era and Its Aftermath, 1750–1808

[Nos. 717–729]

The best overview to date of the Pombaline era and its aftermath is by Kenneth Maxwell **[719]**. Dauril Alden **[274]** and Charles R. Boxer **[42]** also provide valuable observations on the Pombaline dictatorship. Marcus Cheke **[717]** has contributed a biography of Pombal, which, unfortunately, has relatively little on Brazil. Kenneth Maxwell **[718]** has written a fine article on "Pombal and the Nationalization of the Luso-Brazilian Economy."

[717] Marcus Cheke. *Dictator of Portugal. A Life of the Marquis of Pombal, 1699–1782*. London: Sidgwick & Jackson, 1938. viii, 315 pp. [Reprinted by Books for Libraries Press, Freeport, New York.]

There are relatively few references to Brazil in this biography of Pombal. Cheke is more concerned with the Portuguese minister's personal life and how he obtained and kept power. The author particularly emphasizes events in Portugal, with special attention paid to Pombal's efforts in the aftermath of the Lisbon earthquake of 1755, the minister's economic reforms and relations with the English, and the suppression of the Jesuits. Cheke shows how Pombal was feared and hated. As the Austrian envoy to Portugal—a man who was on good terms with Pombal—wrote in 1776: "This nation crushed by the weight of the despotic government exercised by the Marquis of Pombal, the King's friend, favourite, and Prime Minister, believes that only the death of the monarch can deliver the people from a yoke which they regard as tyrannical and intolerable." There is a bibliography on pp. 305–306.

[718] Kenneth Maxwell. "Pombal and the Nationalization of the Luso-Brazilian Economy," *The Hispanic American Historical Review* 48:4 (November 1968), pp. 608–631.

After analyzing the origins and early development of the economic policies of Sebastião José Carvalho de Mello (later Marquis of Pombal) and his attitudes towards Portuguese itinerant traders in Brazil, English universal traders based in Lisbon, established Portuguese merchants, and the Jesuits, the author discusses Pombal's efforts to protect Brazilian commerce and production and make Portugal less dependent on England and English trade by founding the Company of Grão Pará and Maranhão and the Pernambuco Company. Maxwell argues that Pombal's actions were "not characterized by negative phobias but by a pragmatic and positive plan of action." Based on archival and printed primary sources as well as secondary materials. 80 notes.

A. Conflicts and Conspiracies, 1750–1822 [Nos. 719–729]

The best overview of this period is Kenneth Maxwell's fine study with the same title **[719]**. He also contributed an excellent study on the effects of the conspiracies in Minas Gerais and Bahia and makes interesting comparisons between the two **[722]**. Samuel Putnam **[721]** describes the influence of the North American revolution for independence on the intellectuals of Minas Gerais and Thomas Jefferson's meeting with José Joaquim da Maia in Montpellier, France. The Inconfidência Mineira or Minas Conspiracy of 1788–1789 is described by Alexander Marchant **[723]** and Manoel Cardozo **[725]**. Ernesto Ennes **[724]** discusses the trial of the ecclesiastics involved in the conspiracy. Donald Ramos **[726]** examines the Bahian conspiracy of 1798.

Jane Herrick **[727]** and Alfred Hower **[728]** have contributed studies of Hipólito da Costa, who went into exile in England and published the *Correio Braziliense* from 1808 to 1822. Charles Dorenkott, Jr. **[729]** discusses Hipólito da Costa's visit to the United States in 1798 and 1799.

The 1817 revolt in Pernambuco is discussed by Mary Kahler **[878]**.

[719] Kenneth R. Maxwell. *Conflicts and Conspiracies: Brazil and Portugal, 1750–1808*. Cambridge: At the University Press, 1973. xix, 289 pp.

Important analysis of Portuguese and Brazilian history during the Pombaline period (1750–1777) and its aftermath. The author studies the Luso-Brazilian commercial system and the influence of British trade on the Portuguese world. He then examines the privileged trading companies for northeastern and northern Brazil founded by Pombal, that minister's expulsion of the Jesuits in 1759, and his efforts to "nationalize" the Luso-Brazilian economy. Maxwell also describes the efforts of Pombal and his successors to involve Brazilians in the administration of Brazil as well as Pombal's attempts to create a national bourgeoisie in Portugal and encourage manufactures. The author then turns his attention to Minas Gerais and the events leading up to the Minas Conspiracy, 1788–1789, and provides the most extensive treatment in English of this abortive revolt. He concludes by examining the reaction of the Crown and proposals for reform—especially those of Rodrigo de Sousa Coutinho, future Count of Linhares. 5 maps. There is a valuable statistical appendix showing revenues from Minas Gerais, trade between England and Portugal, slave imports to Brazil, sugar prices, statistics for the Company of Grão Pará and Maranhão to 1770 and the Company of Pernambuco and Paraiba to 1777, Brazilian contracts held by the Quintellas, Franco-Portuguese commerce, and the population of Minas Gerais. There is also a useful bibliography (pp. 267–276).

[720] Kenneth Robert Maxwell. "Conflicts and Conspiracies: Brazil and Portugal, 1750–1807," (Ph.D. Dissertation: Princeton University, 1970). 551 pp.

Earlier version of **[719]**. Maxwell explores the influence merchant industrialist groups in Portugal—grown powerful under Pombal—exerted on Brazilian attitudes and actions concerning independence. The metropolitan entrepreneurs' rigid neomercantilism was a factor in provoking the abortive Minas Gerais conspiracy of 1789 and later (after the 1798 Bahian mulatto uprising which frightened whites) in obstructing an accommodation between the metropolis and the Brazilian elites until 1807.
DAI 31/04-A (p. 1713).

[721] Samuel Putnam. "Jefferson and the Young Brazilians in France," *Science and Society* 10:2 (Spring 1946), pp. 185–192.

After discussing Herbert E. Bolton's appeal for a broader treatment of American history, the author attempts to show the influence of the North American revolution of 1776 on the intellectuals from Minas Gerais involved in the 1788–1789 Inconfidência Mineira or Minas Conspiracy. Putnam discusses the encounter between Thomas Jefferson and José Joaquim da Maia at Nîmes, France in 1787 and ties the abortive Minas episode with a series of revolutionary outbreaks in Brazil through the 1840s. Based entirely on printed materials. 10 notes.

[722] Kenneth R. Maxwell. "The Generation of the 1790s and the Idea of a Luso-Brazilian Empire," in Alden, ed., *Colonial Roots* **[87]**, pp. 107–144.

Analyzes and compares the two major independence movements and their participants in late eighteenth-century Brazil—the Minas Conspiracy [*Inconfidência Mineira*] of 1788–1789 and the Bahian Conspiracy of 1798. The former, encouraged by the example of the United States and its achievement of independence, was fomented by such middle-aged members of the elite of Minas Gerais as lawyers, magistrates and clergymen; the latter, inspired by the French revolution and an "amalgam of social resentments [and] high food prices," was promoted by several dozen embittered, young, poor people of color from Bahia. Though there had been earlier uprisings in Brazil, "no previous plot had possessed motivations so fundamentally anti-colonial and so consciously nationalistic. Members of an important segment of that group in society on whom the metropolitan government most relied for the exercise of power at the local level, in one of Brazil's most important, most populous, and most strategically placed captaincies, had dared to think that they might live without Portugal." On the other hand, as Maxwell points out, "the Bahian affair revealed the politicization of levels of society barely concerned with the Minas conspiracy." The conspirators from Bahia "welcomed social turmoil, proposed the overthrow of existing structures, and sought an egalitarian and democratic society where differences of race would be no impediment to employment and social mobility." The author also describes the role during the 1790s and early 1800s of the influential Portuguese minister, Dom Rodrigo de Sousa Coutinho, the future Count of Linhares. Sousa Coutinho "planned 'wise and enlightened reforms, executed by intelligent men, capable of forming well-organized systems, the utility of which would be recognized by all.'" Dom Rodrigo realized the importance of Brazil. In 1798 he "asserted that 'the dominions in Europe do not form any longer the capital and center of the Portuguese Empire. Portugal reduced to herself would within a very brief period be a province of Spain.' He advised that the empire be regarded as being composed 'of provinces of the monarchy, all possessing the same honors and privileges, all reunited with the same administration and all contributing to the mutual and reciprocal defense of the monarchy.'" Maxwell concludes his excellent discussion of late eighteenth- and early nineteenth-century Brazil by praising "the perspicacity of the generation of the 1790s, who brought reason to the analysis of colonial problems, and with optimistic faith projected a grandiose concept of Luso-Brazilian empire." Based chiefly on archival and printed primary materials. 131 notes.

[723] Alexander Marchant. "Tiradentes in the Conspiracy of Minas," *The Hispanic American Historical Review* 21:2 (May 1941), pp. 239–257.

Describes the events surrounding the Inconfidência Mineira and discusses Tiradentes's role, giving countless examples of how he made "no secret of the conspiracy nor sought to bind his hearers to secrecy," with the result that some thought he was crazy. The author further shows that Tiradentes continually fabricated stories of outside aid for and interest in the revolution and failed to make plans for what would happen after the revolt. Based mostly on the printed records of the Crown's investigation. 85 notes.

[724] Ernesto Ennes. "The Trial of the Ecclesiastics in the Inconfidência Mineira," *The Americas* 7:2 (October 1950), pp. 183–213.

Reviews the events leading up to the abortive 1789 revolt in Minas Gerais and discusses the trial and sentences of the twenty-nine laymen involved in the conspiracy. With the aid of previously unpublished documentation in private hands (especially the "autos crimes contra os reus eclesiasticos"), the author clears up much of the mystery and many of the errors surrounding the five priests who were also defendants in the case. The text of two letters by Maria I regarding the judicial proceeding and the commutation of the sentences is published in English. The author concludes by evaluating the importance of the Inconfidência Mineira in Brazilian history. Based mostly on printed sources. 31 notes.

[725] Manoel Cardozo, ed. "Another Document on the Inconfidência Mineira," *The Hispanic American Historical Review* 32:4 (November 1952), pp. 540–551.

Useful and succinct summary of the events surrounding the Minas conspiracy of 1789 as well as a valuable introduction to a previously unpublished, unsigned and undated manuscript from the Biblioteca Publica e Arquivo Distrital of Évora penned by a contemporary living in Portugal but very knowledgeable regarding conditions in Minas Gerais. The anonymous author charged that the betrayer of the conspiracy acted not out of patriotism but in the hope of being forgiven his debt to the Royal Exchequer and attacked the methods of obtaining evidence, criticized the severity of the initial sentences and argued that the trail was used by those conducting it as a means of furthering their own careers. Professor Cardozo concludes that "the Inconfidência Mineira has no real antecedents in Brazilian history." Based mostly on archival and printed primary sources. 46 notes. The document itself is Portuguese.

[726] Donald Ramos. "Social Revolution Frustrated: The Conspiracy of the Tailors in Bahia, 1798," *Luso-Brazilian Review* 13:1 (Summer 1976), pp. 74–90.

Discusses the social and racial background of the thirty-six people who were tried for their part in the stillborn 1798 Bahian revolt. One of the conspirators was a university graduate, another a member of the nobility, two were junior officers and eight were enlisted men in the army, ten were tailors and the remaining fourteen were self-employed artisans or slaves. Almost all were native-born Brazilians. Racially, the group was composed of twenty-four mulattoes, one black and eleven whites. Eleven currently were slaves and three had been born slaves. The author also describes how the social, economic and political atmosphere of the former Brazilian capital was charged with the rhetoric of the French Revolution. A sugar and cotton boom had taken acreage away from subsistence crops, thus causing food shortages and raising the prices of necessary foodstuffs. Mulattoes felt themselves socially and politically restricted. Soldiers resented low pay and strict discipline. Almost all the plotters wanted more equality of opportunity. Ramos shows how the plot developed. He delineates the views of the conspirators on such questions as organized religion, the economy—especially free trade—and independence. Of the thirty-six accused, seventeen were eventually absolved, eight were exiled to Africa, and four poor, uneducated mulattoes were hanged. However, the people of importance who were involved "received relatively lenient penalties or none at all." Ramos argues that: "Faced with the impossibility of keeping control by armed force, the Crown had to appeal to the local elite for support, or at least, neutrality. Thus the government's punitive policy can be seen as a function of this need: 'selective violence' was applied." Based entirely on printed primary and secondary sources. 51 notes.

[727] Jane Herrick. "The Reluctant Revolutionist. A Study of the Political Ideas of Hipólito da Costa (1774–1823)," *The Americas* 7:2 (October 1950), pp. 171–181.

Concludes that Hipólito da Costa, the publisher of the London-based, monthly journal *Correio Braziliense* (June 1808 to December 1822), was not a revolutionist in the generally accepted sense of the term but an admirer of the English system of government who wanted gradual reform and felt that "revolutions are not the way of producing improvements in the government of any country whatsoever." Hipólito demanded that governments act properly and that the governed be virtuous and responsible. He believed that the form of government should be determined by the needs of the people, by their traditions and customs. Based chiefly on the *Correio Braziliense.* 38 notes.

[728] Alfred Hower. "Hipólito da Costa and Luso-Brazilian Journalism in Exile, London, 1808–1822," (Ph.D. Dissertation: Harvard University, 1954).

[729] Charles Dorenkott, Jr. "A Portuguese View of Eighteenth Century America: The Costa Pereira Mission," *Records of the American Catholic Historical Society of Philadelphia* 85: 1-2 (March, June 1974), pp. 70–87.

Describes the reactions of Brazilian-born, University of Coimbra-educated Hipólito da Costa Pereira to the political, social and cultural life of the United States in 1798–1799 during more than a year's stay in North America. (He arrived in Philadephia in December of 1798 and returned to Lisbon sometime in 1800). Hipólito da Costa was sent from Portugal to the United States to make a systematic study of North American agricultural practices and to collect seeds and specimens. Though he visited from the Carolinas to Vermont (and even into Canada), many of his comments are about his stays in Philadelphia (about which he says a great deal), New York, Boston, Providence and Newport. Later in life, Hipólito da Costa would be editor of the London-based *Correio Braziliense*, which championed Brazilian independence for Portugal. Based on Hipólito da Costa's published journal and correspondence. 37 notes.

XX. *The Enlightenment* [Nos. 730–742]

Good overviews of the enlightenment in Brazil are found in two studies by E. Bradford Burns **[730]** and **[731]**. The Portuguese background is ably discussed by Manoel Cardozo **[732]**, who also critically examines the ideas of both Portuguese and Brazilians who doctrinairely accepted European ideas **[733]**. Azeredo Coutinho, the famed bishop of Pernambuco in the 1790s and early 1800s, is studied from two different perspectives by Burns **[734]** and Cardozo **[735]**. A pioneering work that examines the Brazilian "academies" and the libraries of two conspirators in Minas Gerais in 1789 is that of Alexander Marchant **[736]**. E. Bradford Burns **[737]** studies two additional colonial Brazilian libraries, both of which were also in Minas Gerais. Antônia Fernanda Pacca de Almeida Wright **[738]** studies the influence of the American Revolution on Rio de Janeiro and São Paulo. Other aspects of the enlightenment are discussed in section XVIII, A.

[730] E. Bradford Burns. "Concerning the Transmission and Dissemination of the Enlightenment in Brazil," in Aldridge, ed., *The Ibero-American Enlightenment* **[101]**, pp. 256–281.

Quickly surveys the effects of the Enlightenment on eighteenth-century Portugal and demonstrates the relative insignificance of the cultural lag between metropolis and colony. The author discusses how Portuguese, Brazilians who had visited Europe for their education, and foreigners (especially those from France and England) introduced the new ideas to Portuguese America. The role of books and the more important libraries in colonial Brazil, various "academies" that temporarily flourished there, the reformation of education in Portuguese

America after the expulsion of the Jesuits in 1759, and the introduction of the printing press to Rio de Janeiro in 1808 and Bahia in 1811 are all discussed. The essay concludes with a discussion of the Enlightenment's effect on Brazil. Based on archival (Brazilian) and printed primary sources as well as secondary materials. 64 notes.

[731] E. Bradford Burns. "The Intellectuals as Agents of Change and the Independence of Brazil, 1724–1822," in Russell-Wood, ed., *From Colony to Nation* **[88]**, pp. 211–246.

After surveying Brazilian urban growth and the development of a secular intellectual infrastructure during the eighteenth century, the author describes the many changes brought about during the fifteen years following the transfer of the Bragança Court to Brazil. Burns examines public and private libraries, newspapers, the various academies and educational institutions, and private gatherings, salons, and clubs and discusses their role in debating new concepts and the diffusion of ideas. Based largely on printed materials. 147 notes.

[732] Manoel Cardozo. "The Internationalism of the Portuguese Enlightenment: The Role of the Estrangeirado, c. 1700–c. 1750," in Aldridge, ed., *The Ibero-American Enlightenment* **[101]**, pp. 141–207.

After giving examples of some of the exaggerated, contrived and malicious charges that foreigners made against Portugal and its cultural heritage in the eighteenth century, the author argues that, despite various restrictions, the intellectual was able to make his influence felt. To back up his argument, Cardozo discusses the role of such cosmopolitan and internationally minded Portuguese as Dom Luis da Cunha, Dom Rafael Bluteau, Manuel de Azevedo Fortes, Francisco Xavier Leitão, Jacob de Castro Sarmento, Francisco Xavier de Oliveira, Antônio Nunes Ribeiro Sanches, Padre Luis António Vernei and such Brazilian-born figures as Bartolomeu Lourenço de Gusmão and his brother Alexandre de Gusmão, and Teresa Margarida Silva e Orta and her brother, Matias Aires Ramos da Silva de Eça. Based on manuscript and printed primary and secondary materials. 211 notes.

[733] Manoel [da Silveira] Cardozo. "The Modernization of Portugal and the Independence of Brazil," in Russell-Wood, ed., *From Colony to Nation* **[88]**, pp. 185–210.

Quoting extensively from letters, pamphlets and books written in the eighteenth and early nineteenth centuries, the author contrasts Portugal's and Brazil's humanistic and baroque religious and social heritage with the Enlightenment's emphasis on laissez-faire liberalism, modernization, and constitutionalism and concludes that "the independence of Brazil was an inevitable result of the breakup of the Portuguese baroque structures.... [I]ndependence would not have been achieved so readily if the old regime had been vital and strong, if it had not been torn apart by the modernization of Portugal." Focusing on the suppression of the Jesuits and the demise of the other religious orders, the crisis of the nobility, and changes in education during the Pombaline dictatorship, Cardozo charges that "those who, with no solutions of their own to the problems that faced them, looked abroad for guidance and deliverance had a devastating effect upon the larger Portuguese society." Based on some archival but mostly printed primary materials. 93 notes.

[734] E. Bradford Burns. "The Role of Azeredo Coutinho in the Enlightenment of Brazil," *The Hispanic American Historical Review* 44:2 (May 1964), pp. 145–160.

After providing a brief biographical sketch of the Brazilian-born prelate, the author discusses Azeredo Coutinho's three most important economic studies as well as his role in founding the seminary of Olinda and concludes: "Knowingly or, what is more probably, unconsciously, through his essays and through his school, Azeredo Coutinho became one of the most active agents in the transference of the Enlightenment from Europe to Brazil." Based largely on secondary sources. 47 notes.

[735] Manoel Cardozo. "Azeredo Coutinho and the Intellectual Ferment of His Times," in Keith and Edwards, ed., *Conflict and Continuity* **[84]**, pp. 72–103.

Convincingly challenges the view that Azeredo Coutinho (1742–1821), the Brazilian-born bishop of Olinda and later the last Grand Inquisitor of the Holy Office in Portugal, "had something special to do with the Enlightenment in Brazil and that he contributed in some way, through his writings and activities, to the independence of Brazil." The author compares Azeredo Coutinho's educational reforms in Olinda with the earlier ones of the Franciscans in Rio de Janeiro and describes the prelate's views on such topics as popular sovereignty, agriculture, mining, slavery and the slave trade, and the education of women. Cardozo argues that Azeredo Coutinho's ideas were "neither seminal nor revolutionary" and that he was "very much a product of the Portuguese eighteenth century, with all its contradictions, and in a special way of the reformed University of Coimbra." Based mainly on archival and printed sources. 136 notes. E. Bradford Burns's commentary (pp. 104–112) reviews possibilities for further research on the Enlightenment in Brazil. 11 notes.

[736] Alexander Marchant. "Aspects of the Enlightenment in Brazil," in Arthur P. Whitaker, ed., *Latin America and the Enlightenment.* 2nd ed. Ithaca, New York: Cornell University Press, 1961, pp. 95–118.

Provides brief sketches of six Brazilian academies or learned societies founded during the years 1724–1786 as well as analyses of two Brazilian libraries at the end of the 1780s—those of Claudio Manuel da Costa and Canon Luis Vieira da Silva, both from Vila Rica in Minas Gerais and both involved in the Inconfidência Mineira. Based on printed primary and secondary sources. 18 notes. Bibliography. [The first edition was published in 1941.]

[737] E. Bradford Burns. "The Enlightenment in Two Colonial Brazilian Libraries," *The Journal of the History of Ideas* 25:3 (July-September 1964), pp. 430–438.

Examination of the libraries of the José Resende da Costa family (both father and son had been involved in the Minas Conspiracy of 1789) and of Batista Caetano de Almeida ("an outspoken liberal" and republican), inhabitants of Minas Gerais in the late eighteenth and early nineteenth centuries, whose books have become part of the municipal library of São João del-Rei. 21 notes.

[738] Antônia Fernanda Pacca de Almeida Wright. "The Impact of the American Revolution in Two Brazilian Cities: Rio de Janeiro and São Paulo," in Joseph S. Tulchin, ed. *Hemispheric Perspectives on the United States. Papers from the New World Conference.* (Westport, Connecticut: Greenwood Press, 1978), pp. 56–69.

More than half the article focuses on the period to 1822. The author examines a number of newspapers edited by Brazilians and argues that "the writers possessed information about . . . activities in the United

States since independence." She discusses the writings of both North Americans and Brazilians on the "idea of 'federating' metropolis and colony." She concludes that in the various debates leading to independence and during the reign of Pedro I and the regency "the admirers of the United States spoke in moderation, for the most part." Based on printed sources, especially newspapers. 42 notes. The article was translated into English by Maria A. Leal.

A. Science, Technology, and Scientific Expeditions

[Nos. 739–742]

Francisco Venâncio Filho **[739]** and Fernando de Azevedo **[743]** contribute brief histories of science in Brazil, with several references to the colonial period. There is no one study in English on science and technology in colonial Brazil, but there are references to technological developments in mining and agriculture in the works cited in Section XVI. William Joel Simon **[740]** provides a useful discussion of scientific expeditions into Portuguese America and Africa, 1783–1808. He discusses in particular the role of the Brazilian team led by Dr. Alexandre Rodrigues Ferreira, who travelled to the captaincies of Grão Pará, Rio Negro, Mato Grosso and Cuiabá **[742]**. Roderick J. Barman **[741]** studies the Russian imperial scientific expedition to Brazil, headed by Georg Heinrich Langsdorff, 1821–1829.

[739] Francisco Venâncio Filho. "Science," in Hill, ed., *Brazil* **[82]**, pp. 153–180.

Less than a third of this chapter deals with colonial Brazil. The Jesuits are praised "as excellent and painstaking observers of nature." The scientific contributions of the Dutch who accompanied Prince Maurice of Nassau to Brazil are analyzed. There is a brief discussion of "the first successful aerostatic experiment" by the Brazilian-born priest Bartolomeu Lourenço de Gusmão at the court of João V in 1709. Venâncio Filho concludes his discussion of the colonial period with a short description of Rodrigues Ferreira's scientific mission and the contributions of José Bonifácio de Andrada e Silva in the field of mineralogy and geology.

[740] William Joel Simon. "Scientific Expeditions in the Portuguese Overseas Territories, 1783–1808; The Role of Lisbon in the Intellectual-Scientific Community of the Late Eighteenth Century," (Ph.D. Dissertation: The City University of New York, 1974). 403 pages.

Describes three late eighteenth-century Portuguese expeditions—to Brazil, Angola, and Mozambique—which collected specimens for the Natural History Museum and the Botanical Gardens (both in Lisbon) and recorded details of flora and fauna, minerals, and native inhabitants of each area visited. The Brazilian team, led by Dr. Alexandre Rodrigues Ferreira, travelled to Pará, São José do Rio Negro, Cuiabá and Mato Grosso with success despite hazards of tropical fevers. The Crown sponsored such scientific discoveries in order to keep Portugal abreast of new technological developments and discoveries of natural resources. Domingos Vandelli, professor of natural history and chemistry at the University of Coimbra, a sponsor of the three expeditions, exchanged classified specimens with scientists of Western Europe.
DAI 35/04-A (pp. 2195–2196)

[741] Roderick J. Barman. "The Forgotten Journey: Georg Heinrich Langsdorff and the Russian Imperial Scientific Expedition to Brazil, 1821–1829," *Terrae Incognitae* 3 (1971), pp. 67–96.

Discusses the career of the German-born doctor and surgeon Georg Heinrich Langsdorff (1774–1852), who accompanied Prince Christian of Waldeck to Portugal in 1797, served as a botanist on the first Russian voyage around the world, 1803–1808, held the post of Consul-General for Russia in Rio de Janeiro from 1813 to 1830, and from 1821 to 1829 organized and led the Russian scientific expedition to explore Brazil. This latter project also included the Prussian botanist Louis Riedel, the Russian astronomer-geologist Nestor Gavrilovich Rubstov, the French artist Hercules Florence, the Bavarian artist Johann Moritz Rugendas and the French zoologist Edouard Charles Ménétriès, the last two being replaced in 1825 by the artist Aimé Adrien Taunay, whose father Nicolas Antoine was a painter who came to Brazil in 1816, and the Prussian zoologist Christian Friedrich Hasse. In 1822, Langsdorff and his group studied the province of Rio de Janeiro as far as the town of Novo Friburgo. The major portion of the scientific journey, however, did not begin until early May of 1824. Little was published on the results of this expedition, whose value lay "in the anthropological information and the specimens it collected." One hundred and forty years later, the Russian Academy of Sciences was reported to be preparing the documents of the expedition for publication. Barman also traces the post-1830 careers of the major participants. Based heavily on Russian printed sources and Brazilian archival materials (especially those from the Arquivo Histórico do Itamaratí). 1 map. 112 notes.

1. Contemporary Narratives, 1775–1822 [No. 742]

A beautiful facsimile edition of some of the drawings, maps, and plans of the Portuguese scientific expedition of Alexandre Rodrigues Ferreira **[742]** has been published in a Portuguese/English edition. The famous naturalist Prince Maximilian of Wied-Neuwied **[851]** left a description of his scientific expedition of 1815–1817. Part of the account of the travels by Johann Baptist von Spix and Karl Friedrich Philipp von Martius **[546]** has been translated into English.

[742] Alexandre Rodrigues Ferreira. *Viagem Filosófica às Capitanias do Grão Pará, Rio Negro, Mato Grosso e Cuiabá* [*A Scientific Expedition to the Captaincies of Grão Pará, Rio Negro, Mato Grosso and Cuiabá*]. Ed. Edgard de Cerqueira Falcão. São Paulo: Gráficos Brunner, 1970. 192 pp.

In August of 1783, Alexandre Rodrigues Ferreira, a Brazilian-born graduate of the University of Coimbra, left Lisbon for Belém to lead a scientific expedition (inspired by Domingos Vandelli) to study the economic potential of the Amazon region. Almost a year was spent exploring the environs of Belém and the island of Marajó. Ferreira then moved on the the Rio Negro, set up a base at Vila de Barcelos, and remained in that area two years. After receiving new orders from Lisbon, he left Barcelos for Vila Bela, capital of Mato Grosso, via the Madeira, Mamoré, and Guaporé Rivers. Ferreira spent more than a year-and-a-half exploring Cuiabá and the neighboring region. He returned to Belém in January of 1792 and arrived in Lisbon a year later. Ferreira was accompanied by two draftsmen, Joaquim José Codina and José Joaquim Freire, and the botanist Agostinho José do Cabo. Seventy-three of the expedition's drawings—many of them in color—are included in this collection. They are of great value to historians and those interested in art and architecture: A Panoramic View of the City of Santa Maria do Belém do Pará (1784); Plan of the Old City of Pará; Plaza of the Pelourinho and the Departure of an Armed Brigantine; A Prospect of the New Praça das Mercês and the Church of the Order of Nossa Senhora das Mercês; Residence of the Captain-General of Pará; A Hydraulic Machine for Grinding Sugar Cane; A Cotton Gin; a Boat, the Nossa Senhora do Pilar, Built in Pará to Patrol the Amazon and its

Tributaries; Construction of Canoes Indian-Style; Militia Uniforms of Belém; Afro-Brazilian Musical Instruments; Prospect of the Vila de Monforte on the Ilha Grande de Joannes (Marajó); View of the Vila de Cameta and the Arrival of the Governor and Captain-General Martinho de Sousa e Albuquerque (1784); A House in Vila de Oeiras; View of Vila de Monte Alegre, its Church, the Houses of Indians, and Textile Looms Used by the Amerindians; View of the Vila de Barcelos; Barracks of Troops Stationed in Vila de Barcelos; Fort Near the Rio Ixíe Waterfall; Fortress and Village of São José de Marebitenas; Communal House of the Curutus Indians; and the Fortress of São Joaquim do Rio Branco. The editor includes some biographical information on two draftsmen responsible for many of the drawings. Clarival Valladares devotes a page to Antonio Giuseppe Landi, the Italian-born architect who resided in Brazil from 1753 to his death in 1791, a number of whose sketches are also included in this collection. Both the introduction and the titles of the plates are in Portuguese and English. 31 notes.

XXI. Culture in Colonial Brazil [Nos. 743–812]

A. General Accounts [No. 743]

Though there are some excellent studies in English on individual aspects of colonial Brazilian art, architecture and literature, few attempts have been made in English to synthesize the history of the many facets of colonial Brazilian culture. A pioneering effort at such a synthesis—from a sociological perspective—by a Brazilian has been translated into English.

[743] Fernando de Azevedo. *Brazilian Culture. An Introduction to the Study of Culture in Brazil.* Trans. William Rex Crawford. New York: Macmillan, 1950. xxix, 562 pp.

Almost encyclopedic in its coverage, this massive study by the famed Brazilian sociologist Fernando de Azevedo discusses Brazil's physical environment, the interaction between Amerindian, African, and European, the country's economic cycles, the development of urban life, the evolution of the social and political heritage of Portuguese America, and the psychology of the Brazilian people. Part II is devoted specifically to Brazilian culture with chapters on religious institutions and beliefs, the intellectual life and the liberal professions, and literature, science and art. Part III focuses on the transmission of culture and studies the history of education in Brazil. More than half of the book deals with the colonial period. Each chapter is annotated and has a bibliography. There are 418 black and white photographs.

B. Art [Nos. 744–804]

1. The Luso-Brazilian Heritage: An Overview [Nos. 744–750]

As Mario de Andrade **[752]** has perceptively pointed out, during the colonial period "it may be said that only one art existed—architecture—and that all others were dependent on it." Because of this, it is often difficult to categorize art in colonial Brazil and there is frequent overlapping since, as Andrade has shown, "one man might be both architect, woodcarver and sculptor." There are a number of useful surveys in English on Luso-Brazilian art and architecture. George Kubler and Martin Soria **[744]** view the art and architecture of Portugal and Brazil within an Iberian and Ibero-American context. Robert C. Smith **[745]** has synthesized the history of the many aspects of Portuguese art, 1500–1800, while making references to Brazilian developments. The same author **[746]** also reviews a number of major studies on the art and architecture of Portugal and her overseas empire prior to the nineteenth century. John Bury **[747]** relates Luso-Brazilian architecture to its European background. Yves Bottineau **[748]** studies Portugal and Brazil from within the context of the baroque period. Leopoldo Castedo **[749]** emphasizes Brazilian art and architecture but makes references to Portuguese developments. He also views colonial Brazil's artistic achievements within a Latin American context. The same is true of Paul Kelemen's **[750]** study.

[744] George Kubler and Martin Soria. *Art and Architecture in Spain and Portugal and their American Dominions, 1500–1800.* Baltimore: Penguin Books, 1959. xxviii, 445 pp.

In chapter 6 (pp. 101–119), which covers architecture in Portugal and Brazil, George Kubler discusses Manueline and purist styles (1500–1580), Italian and Netherlandish contributions (1580–1640), and "Unified Naves and Cellular Envelopes (1640–1720)." In the same chapter there are special subsections devoted to eighteenth-century Portugal and Brazil. Martin Soria (pp. 183–196) discusses sculpture in Portugal and Brazil (chapter 10) with subsections on the sixteenth century and the trend from Baroque to Neo-Classicism. In chapter 18 (pp. 328–348), Soria describes painting in Portugal, but devotes less than a page to colonial Brazil (p. 348). Well documented. There are useful maps and numerous floor plans. The notes are on pages 351–401. The bibliography is found on pages 403–416. There are 192 pages of plates.

[745] Robert C. Smith. *The Art of Portugal. 1500–1800.* London: Weidenfeld and Nicolson, 1968. xii, 320 pp.

Useful, lavishly illustrated account of three centuries of Portuguese architecture, gilt wood church interiors, sculpture, painting, ceramics, silver, furniture and textiles. It contains 16 color plates, 264 black and white photographs, a map showing important artistic sites, and 9 plans. Smith focuses his greatest attention on Portugal's architecture (pp. 22–126). In his introduction, the author points out that the reigns of Manuel I (1495–1521) and João V (1706–1750) were ones of great prosperity. Not surprisingly, "the two kings who presided over the golden eras, Dom Manuel in the sixteenth century and Dom João V in the eighteenth, were lavish spenders in the realm of art. Both invested hugh sums in palaces and churches, both created princely monasteries and endowed the countryside with costly works of art, setting a royal precedent for bishops and noblemen to follow. Thus the riches of the Indies and Brazil gave Portugal a body of monuments far out of scale with the modest resources of men and money that such a small nation intrinsically could provide." The pages of Smith's history are a testimonial to the artistic activity of these two reigns. In addition to providing a general background for understanding the art and architecture of colonial Brazil, Smith makes a number of specific references to Brazilian art and architecture. Documented. A bibliography follows the notes for each chapter.

[746] Robert C. Smith. "Recent Publications on the Fine Arts of Portugal and Brazil," *The Art Bulletin* 26:2 (June 1944), pp. 124–128.

A useful review of a number of major studies on the art and architecture of Portugal and her overseas empire prior to the nineteenth century. In Part I of his essay, Professor Smith provides an appreciative analysis of several interpretative essays by the eminent Portuguese art historian, Reynaldo dos Santos. One emphasizes the strong Romanesque tradition in Portugal, the lack of acceptance of the conventional European Gothic style, and the importance of the early sixteenth-century Manueline style which "liberated Portuguese architecture from an unwilling subservience to unsympathetic forms and permitted a return to the robust proportions and the naturalism of the Romanesque." A second study describes Portuguese painting in the seventeenth century. Though Portuguese art in the first four decades suffered because of the existence of the Court in Madrid, the portraits of Domingos Vieira (active 1630–1640) and others reveal "a number of well-trained, sincere and engaging portraitists at work in Portugal in the 1600s." A third study by Reynaldo dos Santos makes interesting comparisons between Goya and the Portuguese painter, Domingos António de Sequeira (1768–1837). Part II deals with Portuguese architecture in the Atlantic islands, Africa and Asia, with a special emphasis on the great Jesuit church in Macau of the Madre de Deus or São Paulo as it was sometimes called. The facade, constructed between 1601–1640, provides an excellent example of how the Jesuits combined Italianate forms with Portuguese architecture. This was also true in Goa, India, as well as Luanda, Angola. Part III concentrates on Brazil, where the eighteenth-century church of Nossa Senhora da Gloria do Outeiro in Rio de Janeiro is carefully described as is the Jesuit college and church of Santo Alexandre in Belém do Pará (begun in 1718). There is also a discussion of some seventeenth- and eighteenth-century paintings from Rio de Janeiro. 19 notes.

[747] John Bury. "Portuguese and Brazilian Architecture of the 17th and 18th Centuries: Relation of Exceptional Monuments to Their European Architectural Background," in Marchant, ed., *Proceedings* **[90]**, pp. 119–121.

Points out that "a fundamental characteristic of the architecture of the Lusitanian world was its conservatism. There was the utmost reluctance to accept new forms and formulae, and, once accepted, they were retained long after their abandonment elsewhere. Paradoxically, however, some of the most remarkable and original buildings of their times, from a European point of view, were erected in Portugal and its dependencies." Bury argues that "the churches of the former Jesuit Colleges at Oporto, Coimbra, Salvador da Bahia, and Belém do Pará require additional study in the light of contemporary European architecture." The author gives special emphasis to the early 18th-century Third Order Franciscan Church in Salvador. He describes its facade as "the unique exteriorization in stone of contemporary interior woodcarving" and claims that "it is clearly unnecessary to assume Spanish churrigueresque origins." Bury concludes with a discussion of the late 18th-century churches of Minas Gerais. Though these buildings have "close parallels and precedents" with the architecture of Northern Portugal, "the most striking features of all (the elliptical nave and circular chancel of São Pedro at Mariana and of the Rosário church at Ouro Preto; and the cylindrical towers of the Rosário and of the churches associated with Aleijadinho) have no Portuguese equivalents." No notes.

[748] Yves Bottineau. *Iberian-American Baroque.* Trans. Kenneth Martin Leake. Photographs by Yvan Butler. New York: Grosset & Dunlap, 1970. 188 pp.

Information on Brazil is interspersed throughout this study with separate sections on Portugal and Brazil in four of the chapters. There are also excellent photographs and floor plans, especially on pp. 13–41. Though mentioning other Luso-Brazilian buildings, Bottineau focuses on the Portuguese pilgrim church of Bom Jesus do Monte in Braga, the palace-monastery at Mafra, the Brazilian Third Order Church of São Francisco in Ouro Preto, and the Benedictine Church of São Bento in Rio de Janeiro. The author argues that the Portuguese tradition of "simple, compactly planned buildings" was modified by Spanish and Italian influences and that central and southern Portugal seemed more interested in structure, while "the interest of the North was centered on ornament." This contrast was carried to Brazil, where coastal churches resemble those of central and southern Portugal and the churches of Minas Gerais are similar to those in northern Portugal. In Portugal, "baroque decorations did not flow from interiors to façades." Also, vast areas are covered by *azulejos* or by carved, gilded and polychromed wood. The same was true for Brazil, whose "most original contribution to baroque decoration lies in the work of Aleijadinho." Bottineau compares the pilgrimage sanctuary of Bom Jesus do Monte in Portugal with that of Bom Jesus de Matosinhos (Congonhas do Campo) in Brazil. In the latter are found Aleijadinho's prophets and figures for the Via Crucis. In the debate over the meaning of the term "baroque," the author points out that "experts on Luso-Brazilian architecture prefer to associate it with Mannerism, Classicism and Rococo rather than with Baroque." Though this book contains useful maps, a chronological table, a glossary and a bibliography, there are no notes and no index.

[749] Leopoldo Castedo. *A History of Latin American Art and Architecture. From Pre-Columbian Times to the Present.* Trans. and ed. Phyllis Freeman. London: Pall Mall Press, 1969. 320 pp.

Useful, succinct account. The author points out that although "the Portuguese colonists in Brazil did not find an indigenous labor force with an artistic tradition" like the Spaniards did in Mexico and Peru, the heavy imports of Blacks gave Brazil a strong African heritage that influenced the art of Portuguese America during the colonial period. Initially, Jesuit-style architecture—its chief model being that of the Church of São Roque in Lisbon—played a major role in Brazil. However, even on the Brazilian coast there were exceptions to the Jesuit's rectangular ground plan—the two most notable being the Church of São Pedro dos Clérigos in Recife and the Church of Nossa Senhora do Outeiro in Rio de Janeiro. There were also exceptions to the sober facades of Jesuit churches, the best example being the Third Order Church of São Francisco da Penitência in Salvador, designed by the Bahian-born Manuel Gabriel Ribeiro. The author argues that "this surprisingly complex facade could well be classed as a retable-facade." Though the coastal churches tend to be rather plain on the outside, many of them have "splendidly flamboyant interiors." Some examples of this enthusiasm for interior ornamentation can be found in Pernambuco (e.g., the golden chapel of the Third Order Church of São Francisco in Recife), Bahia (e.g., the Jesuit Collegiate Church [now the Cathedral] and the Church of São Francisco); and Rio de Janeiro (e.g., the Church of São Bento). In Minas Gerais the first churches were small chapels—one with an oriental influence being the Church of Nossa Senhora do O in Sabará. With the resultant prosperity from the gold boom, elaborate churches eventually replaced the small chapels. The use of cylindrical towers became common. In his discussion of sculpture and painting, the author points out how the two worked together—one of the best examples being that of Manuel da Costa Ataíde (the painter) and Aleijadinho (the sculptor) on the figures for the Via Crucis at Congonhas do Campo. Other important painters include: the Olinda-born João de Deus Sepulveda, noted for his frescoes in Recife's churches; José Joaquim da Rocha, Verisimo de Sousa Freitas, Antônio Joaquim Franco Velasco, and Frei José Teófilo de Jesus in Bahia; Frei Ricardo do Pilar, José de Oliveira and Caetano Costa Coelho in Rio de Janeiro. Manuel da Costa Ataíde's paintings "are justly acclaimed as the most original and most valuable colonial paintings in Brazil." Excellent examples of wood carving exist in many of Brazil's colonial churches. Combining sculpture and architecture was Aleijadinho. Castedo argues that "as an architect, Aleijadinho's most enduring works are the pediments of the Carmelite churches in Sabará and Ouro Preto and of the parish churches in Tiradentes and Morro Grande, and, above all, the plans and the façade of São Francisco de Assis da Penitência in Ouro Preto." The author considers Aleijadinho's greatest achievement as a sculptor to be the Sanctuary of Bom Jesus de Matozinhos in Congonhas do Campo with its stone prophets and its wooden figures in the scenes from Christ's passion. 17 illus. No notes.

[750] Pal Kelemen. *Baroque and Rococo in Latin America.* New York: The Macmillan Company, 1951. xii, 302 pp.

Chapter 14, "Rococo in Brazil" (pp. 239–255), provides a good overview of art and architecture in Portuguese America with extensive comments on colonial history. Kelemen argues that "the lack of native craftsmen with a high indigenous artistic culture and the indifference of Portugal toward her colony in the sixteenth century are mainly responsible for the simple, unadorned buildings of the early epoch." Thus, as the author points out, "little attempt was made to transplant here Portugal's ornate Manueline Gothic style, as the Spaniards had done with their contemporary architecture in Santo Domingo." The Portuguese in America used windows more than their Spanish counterparts, but they usually ignored domes and vaults, which, because of Portugal's many earthquakes, were uncommon in the mother country. Kelemen briefly sketches colonial Brazil's coastal architecture. He describes the Franciscan complex in Bahia—the Third Order Church built in 1703, the monastery, and the Church of São Francisco, the latter completed in 1710. He then turns to Belem and the Jesuit church of Santo Alexandre built in 1718 with its "dwelling-house type of facade that was common on the coast of Brazil but most unusual in the Spanish colonies." In Recife, the Church of São Pedro dos Clerigos, designed by Ferreira Jacome, displays many of the characteristics of what Kelemen calls "coastal Baroque." The author argues that "in the general design of its façade, this church reminds one of that in Oporto, Portugal, dedicated to the same saint and built in 1732–1748 by the Italian Nicolo Mazzoni." Kelemen compares three other churches in Recife—Rosário, Santo Antônio, and that of the Carmelite Third Order—before turning to the topic of the heavily ornamented interiors of a number of the churches in coastal Brazil. He describes three examples of this type decoration: São Bento in Rio de Janeiro, the Jesuit church (now the Cathedral) in Bahia and that of São Francisco in the same city—the latter church "lined with wood carving and stucco ornaments gilded and polychromed." The author also briefly reports on a number of churches in Paraiba, north of Pernambuco, "that exemplify an early and lavish Baroque." Examples of carved woodwork are also discussed, before Kelemen turns his attention to the eighteenth-century architecture of Minas Gerais. Since "both monasteries and nunneries were excluded [in the mining region] white and Negro lay societies competed with one another in erecting and adorning their churches. . . . Because of an abundance of superlatively hard wood for beams, few of these churches were vaulted." He describes the combined town hall and prison in Ouro Preto, the only edifice in Minas Gerais "constructed entirely of masonry and without a covering of plaster." He then focuses on the captaincy's churches, especially those on which Aleijadinho worked, paying special attention to the church of São Francisco in Ouro Preto as "an outstanding example of Minas Rococo." He also describes four churches in Minas Gerais "that show variations on the same theme" as São Francisco in Ouro Preto. Two are in Mariana: The Church of São Francisco, begun in 1763 and finished in 1794 by José Pereira Arouca, and that of the Carmelites, begun in 1784 by Domingos Moreira de Oliveira, who worked under Aleijadinho in Ouro Preto. Another, also a Carmelite church, is located in Sabará. The fourth is that of São Francisco in São João d'El Rei. Kelemen also describes the parish church at Tiradentes (formerly São José) and concludes with a discussion of several Portuguese Baroque or Rococo pilgrim churches which strongly influenced similar type churches in Brazil—the most famous of the latter being Bom Jesus do Matosinhos near Congonhas do Campo. The ten bibliographical notes are found on pp. 292–293. Pages 161–173 provide the illustrations for the chapter on Brazil.

2. Architecture [Nos. 751–784]

a. THE PORTUGUESE BACKGROUND [No. 751]

George Kubler **[751]** provides an excellent survey of Jesuit-style architecture in Portugal. Kubler also discusses Portuguese architecture in **[744]**. Robert C. Smith **[745]** gives a lengthy treatment to architecture in his comprehensive history of Portuguese art, 1500–1800. Shorter, but useful, accounts are an earlier effort by Smith **[746]** and the study of Yves Bottineau **[748]**.

[751] George Kubler. *Portuguese Plain Architecture. Between Spices and Diamonds, 1521–1706.* Middletown, Connecticut: Wesleyan University Press, 1972. xvi, 315 pp.

Though this richly illustrated work deals entirely with Portugal, it provides much material for better understanding Jesuit-style architecture (which is intimately related to, if not at times synonymous with, Portuguese Plain architecture) in Brazil. Kubler focuses on both religious and civil architecture under such chapter headings as: Cellular Compositions; Hall Churches; Some Palladian Reductions and Derivations; "Plain Style" and Flemish Ornament; Portuguese Taste and Italian Suggestions; Albert of Austria in Lisbon and Brussels; The Joyeuse Entrée at Lisbon in 1619; New Directions before 1640; After the Restoration. There are 37 figures and 127 black-and-white plates. The bibliography is on pp. 299–308.

b. PORTUGUESE AMERICA: AN OVERVIEW [Nos. 752–764]
Brief accounts of the architecture of colonial Brazil are found in Robert C. Smith **[745]**, George Kubler **[744]**, and Yves Bottineau **[748]**. Leopoldo Castedo **[749]** and Pal Kelemen **[750]** view the architecture of Portuguese America within the general context of Ibero-American architecture. Mário de Andrade **[752]** provides a good summary of colonial Brazilian architecture as does Joaquim de Sousa-Leão **[755]** and Philip L. Goodwin **[756]**. Robert C. Smith **[753]** provides a useful survey. Marinobel Smith **[754]** presents a short photographic essay on the topic. Robert C. Smith **[757]** discusses the periodization of Brazilian art and architecture and divides the colonial period into three eras: 1549 to the mid-seventeenth-century; 1654 to 1750; and 1750-1816. Smith **[758]** also surveys the colonial churches of Portuguese America. John B. Bury **[759]** discusses Jesuit-style architecture in Brazil. Robert C. Smith **[760]**, Sylvio de Vasconcellos **[761]**, Leopoldo Castedo **[762]**, and Sacheverell Sitwell **[763]** emphasize the baroque aspects of colonial Brazilian architecture. Mário Barata **[764]** surveys art and architecture in Brazil, 1750–1850.

[752] Mário de Andrade. "Art," in Hill, ed., *Brazil* **[82]**, pp. 181–194.

The author sees three phases in the development of plastic arts in Brazil: 1) The colonial period and the first half of the nineteenth century when "all art forms bear the stamp of Portuguese culture." 2) 1850–1920, a "period of confusion of styles caused by the influx of European culture which overpowered the Portuguese influence." 3) 1920 to the present, characterized by a search "for a national culture based on universal modern techniques." In the colonial period, according to Andrade, "it may be said that only one art existed—architecture—and that all others were dependent on it. As a result there was little specialization. One man might be architect, woodcarver and sculptor." After pointing out that early in the colonial period, "defense against Indians and pirates determined the planning and architectural designs of towns," the author describes the materials used in construction and construction techniques both for the *casa grande* or plantation house and ecclesiastical architecture. He also discusses some of the most beautiful churches built during the colonial period and such architects and artists as Aleijadinho (Antônio Francisco Lisboa), the sculptors Manuel Inácio da Costa of Bahia, Mestre Valentim and Pedro da Cunha of Rio de Janeiro, and the Benedictine friar Agostinho de Jesus; and painters like José Teófilo de Jesus, of Bahia, Manuel da Cunha, of Rio de Janeiro, and Manuel da Costa Ataíde, of Minas Gerais. "Civil administrative architecture was slow to develop," however, the best examples being found in Bahia and Minas Gerais. There was little adornment of interiors. In 1816, a group of French artists arrived in Rio de Janeiro. With the exception of the architect Grandjean de Montigny, who is credited with designing "some of the most impressive buildings of Rio," they "imposed no permanent Gallic influence on fine arts." More than half of the chapter deals with the colonial period.

[753] Robert C. Smith. "Brazilian Art," in Griffin, ed., *Concerning Latin American Culture* **[96]**, pp. 181–196.

Most of this chapter focuses on the period before independence. Smith uses the paintings of the Dutch artist Frans Post, who spent the years 1637–1644 in northeastern Brazil, to illustrate the development of church architecture in late sixteenth- and early seventeenth-century Portuguese America. One watercolor, for example, depicts "a crude building of wattle walls with roof of palm thatch." Another painting reveals a more permanent church—that of Sts. Cosmas and Damian in Iguarassú. The building "is equipped with a roof of tiles, the walls are covered with plaster, there are stone supports at the angles and about the door, and a single rose window has been opened in the façade." Even more important architectural developments can be seen in the ruins of the Olinda "Basilica." The author also shows how the paintings of Post and those of his companion Albert Eckhout can be used as social documents: Post because of his landscapes portraying life on sugar plantations; Eckhout in his portraits of Blacks, Mulattoes and Amerindians. Smith also describes the architecture of the eighteenth century which varied from Belem's "severe Italianate cathedral, one of the largest buildings in Brazil," to such outstanding examples of Brazilian baroque as the round- and oval-contoured Third Order Franciscan and Carmelite churches in Ouro Preto and São João d'El Rei, both in Minas Gerais. The author concludes his discussion of the colonial period with some comparisons between Spanish and Portuguese American religious architecture: "The round and oval towers and the church plans of Minas Geraes stand out as distinct innovations in colonial American building. On the other hand, the Portuguese-Brazilian architects neglected the structure of their buildings. With rare exceptions they preferred flat wooden ceilings to the cupolas and vaults of their Spanish American colleagues. Nor were their churches so solidly constructed. Nowhere in Brazil is there a structure with the massive proportions of a typical colonial church or convent building in Mexico, Cuba, Peru, or Colombia." No notes.

[754] Marinobel Smith. "The Colonial Period in Brazilian Art," *Think* 9:1 (January 1943), pp. 20, 43–44.

This photographic essay contains twelve illustrations.

[755] Joaquim de Sousa-Leão. "Brazilian Colonial Architecture," *The Studio* 126:607 (October 1943), pp. 113–118.

The Franciscan complex of buildings in Salvador is described as "perhaps the finest architectural group in South America. Nowhere else does one see such display of intricate carving, covering like a gold brocade the whole of the internal structure, otherwise marked by a great purity of proportion." Sousa-Leão claims that Portugal had two great periods of architecture: The Manueline (in the early sixteenth century) and the João V (first half of the eighteenth century). Brazil was founded too early to share in the first great period. She did, however, participate in the second. The author argues that Brazilian baroque owes much to two men: Mestre Valentim and "Aleijadinho." Mestre Valentim, born in Minas Gerais and educated in Lisbon, worked in Rio de Janeiro. Some of his best artistic activity is found in the interior of São Francisco de Paula and Santa Cruz dos Militares and the sacristy and font of the Carmelite church. Aleijadinho, born in Ouro Preto in Minas Gerais, made his great contributions to the art and architecture of his native captaincy—especially in Ouro Preto and Congonhas do Campo. Both artists were born in the 1730s and died in the early nineteenth century. 11 illus. No notes.

[756] Philip L. Goodwin. *Brazil Builds. Architecture New and Old 1652–1942.* Photographs by G. E. Kidder Smith. New York: The Museum of Modern Art, 1943. 198 pp.

Excellent pictorial essay on Brazilian architecture from the mid-seventeenth to the mid-twentieth century. There is a general introduction on pages 17–25. Pages 26–79 cover Brazilian architecture prior to the twentieth century. Each photograph is described and, when known, the date of construction is given. Several illustrations of art work are also included. Some of the more important examples of colonial art and architecture covered are: The Church and Monastery of São Bento and the stairway of the Church of Santo Antônio in Rio de Janeiro; the Church of São Miguel in Rio Grande do Sul; the Church of Nosso Senhor do Bom Jesus de Matosinhos and views of Congonhas do Campo in Minas Gerais; the Church of Nossa Senhora do Carmo, the

Chapel of São José, the Church of São Francisco de Assis, the Church of Rosário dos Pretos, all in Ouro Preto, Minas Gerais; Forts Santa Maria and Montserrat, the Church of São Francisco de Assis, the Franciscan Monastery, and the Church of the Third Order along with the parish church of Nossa Senhora do Pilar in Salvador; the ruins of the church and convent of Paraguassú in Bahia; a colonial church in Guia, Paraiba; the Jaqueira chapel and the Church of São Pedro dos Clerigos in Recife; the Churches of São Bento and São Francisco and a late-seventeenth century house in Olinda; and the Church of Santo Alexandre and a *solar* in Belem. Pages 13–15 contain a listing of the buildings shown in the text. The list is divided into early (17th to 19th centuries) and modern buildings. The former is grouped by states, the latter by type. Though there are a few errors in the accompanying text (mostly dates), this is a book well worth reading.

[757] Robert C. Smith. "The Seventeenth- and Eighteenth-Century Architecture of Brazil," in Marchant, ed., *Proceedings* **[90]**, pp. 109–116.

The author divides architecture in Portuguese America into three periods: 1) 1549 (the arrival of Tomé de Sousa as first governor-general of Brazil) to the middle of the seventeenth century, during which time Brazilian churches were frequently modeled after "the unvaulted chapels of the Portuguese countryside," this renaissance feature being a prime example of "the intensely conservative character of Brazilian colonial architecture"; 2) after 1654, when the Dutch were ousted from Brazil, to the death of João V in 1750, a time span when many of the buildings were characterized by Felippi Terzi's Mannerist designs (cf., Lisbon's São Vicente de Fora) and the influence of Portuguese baroque was also evident; 3) the reigns of José I of Portugal (1750–1777) and Maria I (1777–1816), "the first of which is marked by the domination of the rococo and the second by the flowering of neo-Palladian tendencies, which lead eventually to neo-classicism." In Minas Gerais there is an emphasis on rococo woodcarving, and the towers and facades in that captaincy in the style of Aleijadinho are praised as "the most original expression of Brazilian colonial architecture." No documentation. There is a short resume in Portuguese.

[758] Robert C. Smith, Jr. "The Colonial Churches of Brazil," *Bulletin of the Pan American Union* 72:1 (January 1938), pp. 1–8.

Succinct survey of the major trends in church architecture in seventeenth- and eighteenth-century Brazil. The author points out how seventeenth-century Brazilian churches frequently shared the

Counter-Reformation Italian style as practiced by Juan de Herrera in Spain and Filippi Terzi at Lisbon. In the following century churches in northern and northeastern Brazil used plans identical with many contemporary Portuguese churches—almost all having the two-tower facades made popular by the building in Mafra (1716). Finally, Minas Gerais, the center of the eighteenth-century mining boom, often followed the style evolving in northern Portugal, though native artists and architects made typically Brazilian contributions. 3 notes. 9 illus. The author's historical sketch of sixteenth-century Brazil has a number of errors.

[759] J. B. Bury. "Jesuit Architecture in Brazil," *The Month*. New Series. 4:6 (December 1950), pp. 385–408.

After briefly describing early Jesuit missionary and teaching activity in Brazil, the author discusses the *Estilo Jesuitico* [Jesuit-style architecture] and its relationship to Mannerism. Since many of the sixteenth-century Jesuit churches in Brazil have been destroyed or altered, the author studies early Jesuit buildings in Portugal, India and China as well as Vignola's Gesu in Rome and Terzi's São Vicente de Fora in Lisbon to provide the reader with some idea of early Jesuit-style architecture. Bury then focuses on late seventeenth- and early eighteenth-century architecture in Brazil—especially the Jesuit church in Salvador da Bahia (1672) and the one in Belém do Pará (1719), which he considers to be "the two finest Jesuit monuments in Brazil" and among the most important in the Portuguese world for the period under discussion. The influence of the *Estilo Jesuitico* on early colonial architecture in Minas Gerais (despite the fact that the Jesuits and other religious orders were not initially permitted into the gold regions) and the characteristics of the interior decoration of Jesuit churches are also touched on. To help explain why the Jesuits erected no buildings in colonial Brazil in the baroque style, the author argues that "the Jesuits adopted the architecture of Mannerism and introduced it far afield when it was still a revolutionary new style to the Portuguese. The Fathers could thus regard it as their personal style and might, as such, be understandably reluctant to abandon it." 8 plates. 19 notes (noncontinuous).

[760] Robert C. Smith. "Baroque Architecture," in H. V. Livermore, ed., *Portugal and Brazil* **[81]**, pp. 349–384.

Divides the history of colonial architecture in Brazil into three periods: 1) Early—from the establishment of the governor-generalship at Bahia in 1549 to the middle of the seventeenth century; 2) The Middle Period, ca. 1655 to 1750, dominated by Salvador, the capital of Brazil, and characterized by "a more metropolitan kind of building, inspired directly by models from Lisbon"; 3) Late, ca. 1750–1821, marked by "Pombaline" architecture on the coast and the flourishing of baroque in Minas Gerais. During the early phase of architecture in colonial Brazil, shelter often had precedence over style. The most primitive examples of colonial architecture still existing in Brazil are built of plastered rubble and roofed in wood. The church at Reritiba (completed in 1610) in the state of Espirito Santo, and that at Aldeia de São Pedro, in the state of Rio de Janeiro, have "the three-aisled ground plan of many Portuguese sixteenth-century parish churches, with a rectangular apse followed by a sacristy." They share many of the characteristics of the smaller Renaissance churches of Portugal. In short, both religious and civil architecture of this first period "was of sober, utilitarian, small-scale construction." The most important building constructed during the middle period was Salvador's Jesuit church, now the cathedral, built between 1657 and 1672. "In plan and elevation it shows late Renaissance, sometimes called Mannerist, formulas in vogue in Portugal at the close of the sixteenth century." Smith lists the aisleless nave, the division of the facade into two tiers of pilasters, and the emphasis upon verticality and many rectilinear divisions—all characteristics of so-called Jesuit architecture. According to the author, this middle period shows "how alien was baroque thinking to the Portuguese mind of the time, and how unprepared the Luso-Brazilian builders were to put aside the rectilinear tradition of the late Renaissance and utilize the curve consistently and effectively as the point of departure for a properly integrated design." Smith also describes several town houses in Salvador "built on the model of the old palaces of the Alfama region of Lisbon, where the principal apartments are on the top floor." The third or late period was characterized by two trends. The first is "the Pombaline style of Lisbon," influenced by neo-Palladianism "together with a lingering devotion to small-scale Roman baroque ornament." The best examples of this approach are found in Belem and Rio de Janeiro. The second owes much to northern Portugal, which saw "an abundant use of dark granite trim vigorously carved in flamboyant baroque and rococo designs against a background of glistening white plaster." It is considered to be "the most original architectural achievement since the coming of the Renaissance to Portugal." This style of northern Portugal is associated with Minas Gerais, 1750–1822, and the author discusses the role Aleijadinho played in combining these European influences with his own style. As the colonial period in Brazil drew to a close, there was a trend toward neoclassicism. Smith sees three chief influences on Brazilian neoclassicism: "the limited classicism of the

Portuguese royal architects"; the "English influence which had long existed in Oporto"; and the arrival of the French artistic mission of 1816, which included the architect Auguste-Henri Grandjean de Montigny (1776–1850), "who designed a number of official buildings in the empire style of Percier and Fontaine."

Though the title of Smith's chapter is "Baroque Architecture," he has some valuable comments on painting in colonial Brazil, woodworking and sculpture. The author distinguishes three chronological styles in Brazilian painting: 1) sets of painted panels in Jesuit-type churches of the sixteenth and seventeenth centuries; 2) ceiling panels fitted with "polygonal strips of canvas painted with the images of saints" (early eighteenth century); 3) the abandoning of divisions and painting directly on the ceiling boards. The earliest of the third type is found in Rio de Janeiro in 1737, though Salvador soon became the center for this kind of decoration. In Minas Gerais, Manuel da Costa Ataíde (1762–1837) is considered the foremost exponent of this approach. According to Smith, "the ceilings of the third phase are among the most successful efforts of colonial Brazilian craftsmen to achieve the unified dynamic organization which is one of the principal objectives of true baroque decoration." The author also includes a discussion of gilded wood retables and gilded interiors. He concludes: "It is wrong to speak of Brazilian colonial art, as is sometimes done, as an art inspired by the contemporary models of Portugal and then developed independently under local influences. Everything, and especially the monuments themselves, indicates the contrary. These churches, convents, houses, public buildings, ceilings, and retables prove in undeniable fashion that the Portuguese were able to maintain abroad for 300 years, with a minimum of variation, the continuing tradition of the art and architecture of the mother country." There is a bibliography (pp. 365–366). The book itself includes eleven plates on the art of colonial Brazil. 84 notes.

[761] Sylvio de Vasconcellos. "The Baroque in Brazil," *Américas* 26:6–7 (June–July 1974), pp. S–1 to S–16.

Argues that "the Baroque was always basically concerned with the idea of making appearance prevail over reality, the aggregate whole over details, complexity over clarity." The author attempts to explain the religious context of Baroque architecture, pointing out that "when the Protestants and the Anglicans excluded themselves from the Catholic context, they excluded themselves also from the Baroque." After describing religious architecture in Portugal, the author traces architectural styles in Brazil—all of which he sees as manifestations of the Baroque—dividing their history into four periods: 1500–1650; 1650–1750; 1750–1800; and the Nineteenth Century. Vasconcellos concludes that "the Baroque is, in effect, the cornerstone of Brazilian culture—as it is the fountainhead of all Latin American civilization." Unfortunately, the author confuses the reader by using the concept of "baroque" for the entire colonial period rather than making the distinction between Mannerism and Jesuit-style architecture on the one hand, and Baroque, on the other, as such authorities as Robert Smith and John Bury do. However, the illustrations and their explanatory notes are excellent, presenting the viewer with some of the great masterpieces of Brazilian Baroque art and architecture. 1 map, 26 illus., 4 notes.

[762] Leopoldo Castedo. *The Baroque Prevalence in Brazilian Art.* New York: Charles Frank Publications, 1964. 151 pp.

The author offers three approaches to the Baroque: "Consideration of the Baroque as a historical period; evaluation of the Baroque as the final stage in the evolution of a stylistic period; identification of the supposed baroque spirit with certain specific national predispositions or traits, particularly among the Germans, Bohemians, Portuguese, Spanish and, above all, the Ibero-Americans." Though Castedo discusses the second approach, he is more interested in listing and describing the chief attributes of the Baroque ("Dynamism and delight in the curve, theatricality and the breaking up of symmetry, unfettered imagination, lyricism, sensuality") and arguing that "universality, an intimacy with the divine, sensuality and audacity—national characteristics of the Brazilian people—are distinguishing traits of the Baroque as well." To prove his thesis, the author devotes two chapters to Aleijadinho's life and a careful analysis of two of his masterpieces: The Twelve Prophets and the Scenes from the Passion of Christ, both at Congonhas do Campo. In another chapter, Castedo describes the Baroque influence on a number of churches in such port cities as those of Salvador, Rio de Janeiro and Recife. He concludes that the art and architecture of the recently constructed new capital of Brazil, Brasilia, are also part of Brazil's Baroque heritage. There are 94 illustrations—75 of which deal with the colonial period and are excellent. 76 notes. Bibliography.

[763] Sacheverell Sitwell. *Southern Baroque Revisited.* London: Weidenfeld & Nicholson, 1967. xiii, 306 pp.

Chapter 8, "'Je suis Bresilien, j'ai de l'or,'" covers Brazil (pp. 198–223). "I have at least visited and seen most of the Colonial cities of the Latins, excepting Goa and Manila, and it is all to some degree time wasted, apart from Mexico. . . . Mexico excepted, there is little more to say. The late architecture of the Latins flowered best at its own fountain-heads and on its own roots, which are in Europe, whether in Italy or Spain." With these words from his preface or "Preludio," Sitwell sets the mood for his highly opinionated comments about architecture in colonial Brazil. He was not impressed with the churches of Rio de Janeiro. He describes Nossa Senhora da Gloria do Outeiro "of elegant and elongated oval interior, with pretty blue and white azulejos of obvious import from Portugal the mother country, but quite truthfully of no more importance architecturally than fifty or a hundred churches in villages or small towns in Portugal. It is pretty, and prettily sited, but little more than that." He quickly dismisses the churches of São Bento, Santo Antônio and the Penitência. In Minas Gerais, the author observed that it was important "before we see more of 'O Aleijadinho' to keep our heads and not give in to the indiscriminate praise now lavished on him in compensation for his sufferings." Sitwell was not overly impressed with Aleijadinho's doorway and frontispiece to São Francisco de Assis at São João d'El Rei: "Certainly it is a finely carved and worked ornamental doorway of green soapstone, of a type to be admired, with less fuss made about it, in Northern Portugal." Nor did Aleijadinho's sculpture at Congonhas do Campo rate high marks. The author found the stone statues—which he calls Apostles instead of Prophets (though they are correctly identified in the accompanying plates)—and the wooden statues of the Via Crucis "difficult . . . to admire." Sitwell, however, was fascinated with the church at Tiradentes which he found to be "the authentic 'joyau de l'art baroque en tout Bresil.'" In Bahia, the church of São Francisco, according to the author, could not compare with that of the same name or that of Santa Clara, both in the northern Portuguese city of Oporto. Though he was impressed with the workmanship in jacaranda wood in many of Salvador's churches and sacristies, he felt that "of the other churches in the town not much more need be said." Sitwell found Recife and its architecture more to his liking "than any other town in Brazil." He especially liked the Carmelite Third Order church and the Rosário. Furthermore, "the gilded interiors of at least three or four of the churches of Recife qualify for their inclusion among the *capelas douradas* of all Portugal." 11 plates, one of which is in color. Documented.

[764] Mario Barata. "The Art of Brazil. Research in the Period 1750–1850," in Raymond S. Sayers, ed., *Portugal and Brazil in Transition* (Minneapolis: University of Minnesota Press, 1968), pp. 289–299.

Barata points out that the early part of the eighteenth century "was an age of transcendental esthetic creation in Brazil." In the second half of the century there was a "transition to the rococo and neoclassic in architecture and in wood sculpture. Great urban development became typical; among the Minas Gerais artists, the figure of 'Aleijadinho' or Antônio Francisco Lisboa began to stand out; ceiling painting and other kinds of painting became general in Minas, Bahia, Rio de Janeiro, and Pernambuco. . . . The study of military architecture was renewed, and in 1800, 'drawing and figure study' began officially." The author examines the most studied aspects of the period and argues that "the French Mission cannot be blamed for having ended the baroque in Brazil. That was brought about through the force of historical circumstance, and neoclassicism, which arrived here before the French artists, would have developed in the nineteenth century even if they had not come." Barata concludes with a discussion of the priorities for research in the history of Brazilian art, 1750–1850. 3 plates. 5 notes.

c. COASTAL BRAZIL [Nos. 765–772]
Eighteenth-century Jesuit buildings in coastal Brazil are studied by Robert C. Smith **[765]**. Tom Maia **[766]** contributes pen-and-ink drawings of some of the important colonial landmarks in Recife and Olinda. The art and architecture of colonial Bahia are examined in a large collection of photographs by Edgard de Cerqueira Falcão **[767]**. Elísio de Carvalho Lisboa **[768]** also surveys religious art and architecture in Bahia. The famed Brazilian novelist, José Lins do Rego **[769]** provides an appreciation of Bahia's architecture. The church of Nossa Senhora da Conceição da Praia, which was transported block by block from Portugal, is studied by Robert C. Smith **[770]**, who also analyzes the importance of the Joanine style in eighteenth-century Brazil. Tasso da Silveira **[771]** describes the Benedictine monastery in Rio de Janeiro. Augusto Carlos da Silva Telles **[772]** examines Rio's church of Nossa Senhora da Gloria.

[765] Robert C. Smith. "Jesuit Buildings in Brazil," *The Art Bulletin* 30:3 (September 1948), pp. 187–213.

Based on eighteenth-century architectural drawings from the Arquivo Militar in Rio de Janeiro, this article studies the designs and histories of five former Jesuit buildings in colonial Brazil that were remodeled and put to other uses after the expulsion of that order in 1759: 1) The Seminary of Nossa Senhora da Conceição in Salvador (Bahia), built shortly after mid-century for poor students who did not wish to become Jesuits, was one of the first Jesuit buildings in Brazil designed by military engineers rather than members of that order. Smith carefully describes the structure and lists some of the major expenses involved in its construction. 2) The Church of Salvador and the adjoining Real Colégio das Artes was one of the most impressive structures in colonial Brazil. As the author points out, "eighteenth-century visitors were unanimous in their praise of the magnificence of the church and its decorations. They admired especially the great sacristy with its marble altars and floors, its walls of tile, the furniture inlaid with tortoise shell and the painted ceiling representing heroes of the Company of Jesus." Only the church—which, with some changes became Salvador's cathedral—has survived. The college, after several reconstructions, was destroyed by fire in 1905. Therefore, the 1782 plans and elevations of the military architect and engineer José Antônio Caldas are of importance for understanding the pre-1759 state of this beautiful Jesuit complex and the use to which it was put after the Order's expulsion. 3) The Seminary of Nossa Senhora de Belém near Cachoeira, located inland across the bay from Salvador, was "one of the principal foundations of the Society of Jesus in Brazil." The seminary educated boys between the ages of twelve and nineteen from the Recôncavo and the interior of Bahia, a number of them later becoming Jesuits. Smith describes its history, architecture and its post-1759 disposition. 4) The House of São Cristóvão or Quinta do Tanque in Salvador, a former country house, was used in the seventeenth century by Jesuits and their students as a place of rest and retreat. Padre Antônio Vieira spent seventeen years there and had it rebuilt. Its lands supplied food for the Jesuits of Salvador and served as the site of agricultural experiments—especially with cinnamon from Ceylon and Malabar pepper. A leper hospital was later installed in the remodelled former Jesuit country house. 5) The surviving plan of the Jesuit church and college of São Miguel at Santos, now the principal port for São Paulo, shows the building in ruin. All of the eighteenth-century drawings reveal the conservative character of Jesuit architecture—many of the facades being "essentially a restatement of the style first practiced in Portugal in the second half of the sixteenth century." There are two valuable appendices: I. Portuguese Military Engineers in Brazil; II. José Antônio Caldas. The first traces the educational background of military engineers in colonial Brazil and their role in the history of Brazilian architecture. The second appendix provides a biographical sketch of the author of the valuable detailed account of Bahia in the mid-eighteenth century, *Noticia geral de toda esta capitania da Bahia desde o seu descobrimento até o presente anno de 1759*. According to Smith, "the life of José Antônio Caldas may be considered typical of that of the Portuguese military engineer in colonial Brazil for these reasons. He studied at a military Aula [or engineering school] and later taught his profession there; he spent his whole career at a single post, traveling considerably and suffering hardships and perils; he rose to the rank of major, held municipal office, and distinguished himself as an able draughtsman." Based largely on archival and primary printed materials. 13 illus. 256 notes.

[766] Tom Maia. *Recife and Olinda.* Captions by Thereza Regina de Camargo Maia. Text by Gilberto Freyre. São Paulo, 1978. 178 pp.

Seventy pen-and-ink drawings by Tom Maia, many of them illustrating Pernambuco's colonial history. There is an introductory essay by Gilberto Freyre. Each of the illustrations have descriptive captions. The text and explanatory comments are in Portuguese, Spanish, French and English. Though, to date, there are four other collections of pen-and-ink drawings by Maia, only this volume and the one on Minas Gerais **[771]** have descriptive captions in English. The other three—on Paraty; the Brazilian coast from Rio de Janeiro to Santos; and the Paraiba Valley—have only a resume of the text in English.

[767] Edgard de Cerqueira Falcão. *Relíquias da Bahia* [Relics of Bahia]. São Paulo, 1941. xxxvi, 254 pp.

Magnificent collection of 508 black-and-white-photographs depicting the art, architecture, painting, and sculpture of Bahia. Most of it deals with the colonial period. There is a brief general introduction to the photographs and a one-line description in English for each plate.

[768] Elísio de Carvalho Lisboa. "Colonial Art in Bahia," *Bulletin of the Pan American Union* 80:1 (January 1946), pp. 1–11.

Well-illustrated survey of religious art and architecture in the former capital of Brazil, which briefly describes the church of the Jesuit College, that of the Third Order of St. Francis, the church of São Francisco, that of the Carmelites, the Joanine church of Nossa Senhora da Conceição da Praia and Nossa Senhora do Pilar. Particular attention is paid to the Franciscan monastery, its tiled cloister and the elaborate woodwork of its sacristy and library. Construction on the church of São Francisco was begun in 1708 and completed in 1723, though the interior was not finished until 1750. It is famous for its gilded altar of St. Anthony, the carved wooden statues of the Bahian artist Manuel Inácio da Costa, and the woodwork of the Franciscan Frei Luis de Jesus. 11 illus. No notes.

[769] José Lins do Rego. "Bahia," *Travel in Brazil* 2:2 (1942), pp. 1–11.

An appreciation of the former capital of Portuguese America by the famed author of the regionalistic "Sugar Cane Cycle" novels. Of special interest are the sixteen photographs of Bahia, eleven of which deal with the colonial period. Four show the exterior, interior, library and sacristy of the church and monastery of São Francisco and two the vestry and ceiling of the Carmelite church. No notes.

[770] Robert C. Smith. "Nossa Senhora da Conceição da Praia and the Joanine Style in Brazil," *Journal of the Society of Architectural Historians* 15:3 (October 1956), pp. 16–23.

This basilica is considered to be "the largest and richest example of a colonial building for which all of the stone was cut in Portugal before shipment to America. It is also the first and finest example in Brazil of the style of John V of Portugal, called the *estilo joanino* or Joanine style, which introduced the rise of Roman full-baroque ornament to Portugal and its empire." The Joanine style with its "arched lintels and curved hoods, flared pediments and bombé steeples" was, in turn, heavily influenced by Francesco Borromini **[781]**. The author discusses the Church's architect (the Portuguese military engineer Manuel Cardoso de Saldanha) and the history of its construction and describes its high altar ("one of the masterpieces of Italianate baroque art in Brazil") and the huge ceiling painting of its nave (the Virgin of the Immaculate Conception of José Joaquim da Rocha in 1773). From a quarry outside Lisbon *pedra lioz*, a cream-colored pseudo-marble with veins of rose, was cut according to the church plan and shipped to Bahia. Building was begun in 1739. In 1765, the church, though still unfinished, was consecrated by the Archbishop of Bahia. The basilica was finally completed in 1850. The importation of stone from Lisbon was not unusual. According to the author, the first church to be so constructed was the Jesuit one in Bahia (now the cathedral), 1657–1672, done in Mannerist style. Earlier efforts at introducing the Joanine style to Brazil often resulted in the "extreme simplification of a highly refined metropolitan style." Conceição da Praia is a very close approximation to Portuguese design and is the most complex religious building of its time in Brazil. To a certain degree it played "the role of a way station in the importation of new ideas in architecture, sculpture and painting from Europe to the interior of Brazil." Based on archival as well as printed sources. 12 illus. 60 notes.

[771] Tasso da Silveira. "São Bento Monastery," *Travel in Brazil* 1:1 (1941), pp. 22–25.

The construction of this Benedictine church in Rio de Janeiro began in 1641. The monastery, which is at the side of the church, was begun in 1652. Eighty years later the monastery was destroyed by fire and had to be rebuilt. The author describes both the church and the monastery in detail. Many of the paintings on the ceiling and walls of the church were done by the great Benedictine artist Frei Donato de Pilar. The seventeenth-century woodcarvings of "the frontispiece, the pulpit, and the images in the main chapel" were done by the sculptor Frei Domingos da Conceição. Tasso da Silveira claims that the "chapel is one of the architectural jewels of the continent." No notes. 3 illus.

[772] Augusto Carlos da Silva Telles. *Nossa Senhora da Gloria do Outeiro.* Photographs by Pierre Garnotel. Rio de Janeiro: Libraria Agir Editora, 1969. 98 pp.

Contains excellent black and white as well as color photographs of this important eighteenth-century church and landmark in Rio de Janeiro. There is a brief resumé in English.

d. MINAS GERAIS [Nos. 773–784]

Robert C. Smith **[773]** probably provides the best overall survey of colonial architecture in Minas Gerais. Edgard de Cerqueira Falcão **[774]** lists the most important towns in colonial Minas Gerais and their artistic treasures. Joaquim de Sousa-Leão **[775]**, Mark Bence-Jones **[776]** and Manuel Bandeira **[777]** present short photographic essays on the architecture of Ouro Preto (formerly Vila Rica). Tom Maia **[778]** presents drawings of the artistic treasures of São João del Rei and Tiradentes. John B. Bury **[779]** and Leon Kochnitzky **[780]** study Aleijadinho's architectural style and his influence on Minas Gerais. They also make comparisons with the art and architecture of parts of Spanish America. John B. Bury **[781]**, in a major article on the late eighteenth-century "Borrominesque" churches in Minas Gerais, points out the Italian influence of Francesco Borromini. Edgard de Cerqueira Falcão **[782]** describes the origins of the Shrine at Congonhas do Campo. Lourival Gomes Machado **[783]** discusses the restoration of the church of Bom Jesus at Congonhas along with its Prophets and "Via Crucis." A. J. R. Russell-Wood **[784]** provides a biographical sketch of the Portuguese architect and builder, Manuel Francisco de Lisboa, and his activity in Minas Gerais. Though a skilled craftsman, Manuel Francisco is often better known as the father of Aleijadinho. Antonio Francisco Lisboa (Aleijadinho), though perhaps more famous as a sculptor, was also an important architect—some say the greatest—in colonial Minas Gerais. Studies on his work are covered in Section XXI, B, 3 [Nos. 791–797].

[773] Robert C. Smith, Jr. "The Colonial Architecture of Minas Gerais in Brazil," *The Art Bulletin* 21:2 (June 1939), pp. 110–159.

Masterful survey of the architecture of Brazil's chief mining region in the eighteenth century. The author argues that "of all the former European colonies in the New World it was Brazil that most faithfully and consistently reflected and preserved the architecture of the mother country." There were two main currents in eighteenth-century Portuguese architecture: 1) "a foreign tradition built up by generations of imported Italian architects which was to culminate in the reign of Dom João V [1706–1750]"; 2) a native, rural Portuguese tradition found in the north of Portugal "where the cities of Oporto, Braga, Viseu, Guimarães, Lamego and Viana do Castelo maintained local schools of architecture in varying degrees of regional independence." In Brazil, the court tradition had its greatest influence in coastal towns, while the northern rural Portuguese tradition flourished in Minas Gerais where many of the eighteenth century immigrants were from that part of Portugal. In Minas Gerais, this native Portuguese tradition was influenced by the architecture of Bahia, another important source of immigrants to the mines. Added to these two elements was a remarkable indigenous influence best exemplified by Antônio Francisco Lisboa (O Aleijadinho). Smith divides the religious architecture of colonial Minas Gerais into three periods: 1) the provisory structures, 1698–ca. 1705; 2) the primitive chapels, "which are derived from those of the north of Portugal," 1705–1730; 3) the great construction, 1730–1820. He then describes their characteristics and gives examples from each group. The author also includes a partial chronology of the principal eighteenth-century churches in Minas Gerais with the names of their known builders. In addition, he includes a discussion of the captaincy's civil architecture. As to be expected, the early housing of the prospectors was "like the first Mineiro chapels, crude construction of mud and straw." The second stage "consisted of the transformation of the original cabins into plaster-covered rubble constructions and the substitution of the earlier thatch roofs by tile." A third style, dating from about the mid-eighteenth century, saw "the gradual introduction of stone masonry" and the second story. Smith also describes such public buildings as the house of the governor and the combination town-hall prison (both in Ouro Preto) and the Aljube or ecclesiastical prison in Marianna. He explores the design and chief characteristics of some of the captaincy's bridges and fountains. Smith concludes this major study by pointing out that although the architecture of Minas Gerais was not always first-rate, there were sufficient "innovations of real distinction" to prove that "the builders of Minas Gerais were no mere imitators of their Portuguese colleagues in the mother-country and along the Brazilian coast." These *mineiro* architects did much to make "the colonial architecture of Minas Gerais a distinguished accomplishment in the history of American building during the eighteenth century." 45 illus. 161 notes.

[774] Edgard de Cerqueira Falcão. *Nas Paragens do Aleijadinho (Guia das Minas Gerais)* [In the Footsteps of Aleijadinho (Guide to Minas Gerais)] Ill. J. Wasth Rodrigues. São Paulo, 1955. 199 pp.

The author lists the principal towns of Minas Gerais and describes their most important artistic and architectural treasures. The towns included are: Mariana, Ouro Preto, Sabará, São João del Rei. Tiradentes (formerly São José do Rio das Mortes, and, later, São José del Rei) and Congonhas do Campo. The comments on the artistic treasures of the old mining district are accompanied by 18 pen and ink illustrations by J. Wasth Rodrigues. There is also a list in Portuguese with brief biographical data of the chief colonial *mineiro* artists (pp. 59–79). An English translation of the main text is found on pp. 139–167.

[775] Joaquim de Sousa-Leão. "Ouro Preto, Brazil," *Bulletin of the Pan American Union* 72:8 (August 1938), pp. 456–462.

Briefly sketches the history and points out the most famous examples of the art and architecture of Ouro Preto, formerly Villa Rica, the famous gold-rush town of eighteenth century Minas Gerais. The author also discusses some of the contributions of Antônio Francisco Lisboa (Aleijadinho), Colonial Brazil's greatest architect and sculptor, and his collaborator Manoel da Costa Ataíde, "the most notable painter born in Brazil during colonial times." 2 notes. 6 illus.

[776] Mark Bence-Jones. "A Baroque Boom Town. Ouro Preto, Brazil," *Country Life* 148: 3837 (December 17–24, 1970), pp. 1180–1183.

Sketches the founding and development of the town of Ouro Preto (formerly Vila Rica) and concludes his account with a few words on the Minas Conspiracy of the late 1780s. Bence-Jones lists the town's most important buildings and describes their architecture: The Governor's Palace, designed by the *sargento-mor* José Fernandes Pinto de Alpoim and built in 1740; the Town Hall, begun in 1784; the adjoining Carmo church on which both Aleijadinho and his father labored; the church of São Francisco de Assis, one of Aleijadinho's most famous works, completed in 1812; the single-towered church of São José and the twin-towered one of São Francisco de Paula (the latter begun in 1804), both on the same hill; the Casa dos Contos, with its rococo street facade built in the 1780s by João Rodrigues de Macedo and, also on the same street, the church of Nossa Senhora do Pilar with its "Central European flavour"; and, on the outskirts of town, also reminiscent of Franconian baroque, the church of the Rosário, supported during the colonial period by the town's Blacks. The author also discusses several of Ouro Preto's sixteen baroque fountains. There are 9 excellent black-and-white photographs illustrating the above-mentioned materials. No notes.

[777] Manuel Bandeira. "Ouro-Preto, the Old Villa Rica," *Travel in Brazil* 1:4 (1941), pp. 1–13.

The author briefly discusses the brilliant civilization that developed in the mining region of Vila Rica, mentioning its chief artists: Antônio Francisco Lisboa (Aleijadinho), the sculptor and architect; Manuel da Costa Ataíde, the painter; and the group of poets who make up the so-called "Minas School." The article provides the background for better understanding the 22 excellent black-and-white photographs that accompany it. Most of the illustrations are of such churches as those of São Francisco (to which Aleijadinho contributed so much), Santa Efigência (whose construction is tied to the tradition of "Chico Rei," which the author recounts), Rosário ("whose frontispiece and gables were designed by Manuel Francisco de Araujo"), Carmo (planned by Aleijadinho's father), Pilar, and the parish church founded by Antônio Dias. In addition, there are pictures of a pulpit and a holy water font carved by Aleijadinho. Also included are photographs of the governor's palace (dating from the administration of the Count of Bobadella), the Museu da Inconfidência (honoring those involved in the Minas Conspiracy of 1789), formerly the town hall, and several baroque water fountains. Bandeira also describes in some detail the interior of the former Casa dos Contos. No notes.

[778] Tom Maia. *São João del Rei e Tiradentes.* Captions by Thereza Regina de Camargo Maia. Text by Afonso Arinos. São Paulo: Companhia Editora Nacional, 1978. 169 pp.

Sixty pen-and-ink drawings by Tom Maia with descriptive captions illustrating important works of art and architecture in the two important mining towns of São João del Rei and Tiradentes (formerly São José del Rei). The captions and resumes of the text are in Portuguese, Spanish, French and English.

[779] J. B. Bury. "*Estilo Aleijadinho* and the Churches of Eighteenth Century Brazil," *The Architectural Review* CXI:662 (February 1952), pp. 92–100.

After raising several speculative questions on why Portuguese and Brazilian architecture differed from that of Spain and Spanish America, the author discusses the role of the style developed by Aleijadinho (the nickname of the crippled mulatto, Antônio Francisco Lisboa). Before 1760, Jesuit-style architecture had characterized parish churches in Minas Gerais. With Aleijadinho's rise to prominence, however, a number of Mannerist aspects are modified or abandoned. For example, some towers became "cylindrical in shape, surmounted by balustrades and capped by elegant semi-oval cupolas which in turn are crowned by obelisks" and "the use of external sculptured ornament in high relief" is featured, the latter facilitated by the abundance in Minas Gerais of soapstone, so soft that it could be worked like wood. Bury traces the development of this new style, a "transition from the local Mannerism to Rococo," discussing the churches of the Carmelite Third Order at Sabará, Ouro Preto, Mariana, and São João d'El Rei and the culmination of this new style in the Church of St. Francis in the last-mentioned town. Despite its brilliance, the *estilo aleijadinho* was relatively short-lived, limited more or less to the last quarter of the eighteenth-century and the early part of the nineteenth, and confined mostly to the major urban centers of Ouro Preto and neighboring Mariana and São João d'El Rei. The only important work of Aleijadinho outside these centers is the forecourt of the sanctuary church of Congonhas do Campo. After trying to trace European influences in Aleijadinho's style, the author concludes that "the Portuguese have displayed their native architectural originality in decorative rather than in structural form." The development of the rococo style named after Aleijadinho is evidence of this Portuguese characteristic. 21 illus. 25 notes.

[780] Leon Kochnitzky. "Black Gold of Brazil's Baroque," *Art News* 40:19 (January 15-31, 1942), pp. 22–24, 32.

Argues that of the three major centers of Baroque art in the Americas—Mexico, Peru and Brazil—it was in the latter that "one finds the widest disparity between the European and the American." The author, focusing on Minas Gerais and examining about eighty churches and chapels, "two splendid palaces and many other unique civil edifices and over a dozen elaborately sculptured public fountains," offers several reasons for his assertion: 1) the strong African ethnic factor (though the framework was European, the ornamentation owed much to mulatto and black artists and artisans; 2) towns in the gold-mining regions were founded by Brazilians, while the Portuguese American port cities of Salvador, Recife, and Rio de Janeiro were founded by Europeans. After briefly discussing Aleijadinho's background, Kochnitzky points to the crippled mulatto's uncle's skills as a metalist and argues that "Aleijadinho's technique is closer to that of the engraver than to the sculptor." The author concludes by claiming that Aleijadinho "achieved the first genuinely American artistic creation since pre-Columbian times that was not an imitation or even an interpretation of the art of the Old World." 7 illus. No notes.

[781] John B. Bury. "The 'Borrominesque' Churches of Colonial Brazil," *The Art Bulletin* 37:1 (March 1955), pp. 27–53.

A critical analysis of a small group of late eighteenth-century "Borrominesque" churches in Minas Gerais. "Borrominesque," as coined by the author, designates those buildings which possess the curved ground plans and interest in spatial composition introduced into European Baroque architecture in the seventeenth century by Francesco Borromini. Stylistic antecedents of the monuments are examined. The article includes 11 photographs and 26 diagrams of facades and floor plans.

[782] Edgard de Cerqueira Falcão. *A Basilica do Senhor Bom Jesus de Congonhas do Campo.* São Paulo, 1962. 335 pp.

Though the text is in Portuguese, there is a useful summary in English on pp. 325–328. The author describes the origins of the devotion to a mutilated statue of Christ (the left arm was missing), supposedly found near the mouth of the Douro river in northern Portugal in 124 A.D. Eventually the statue was enshrined at Matosinhos (Braga), also in northern Portugal. Devotion to the Senhor-de-Matosinhos spread to Minas Gerais and the shrine of Bom Jesus was established at Congonhas do Campo. Many of the great *mineiro* artists, sculptors and architects of the late colonial period contributed their talents to the shrine. The church of Senhor Bom Jesus de Congonhas do Campo was raised to the status of a basilica in 1957. There are 66 black and white plates. A few are of the shrine in Portugal, but most of them illustrate various aspects of the architecture, painting and sculpture at Congonhas do Campo, including the prophets carved by Aleijadinho.

[783] Lourival Gomes Machado. *Reconquista de Congonhas/The Reconquest of Congonhas.* Trans. by Guttorm Hanssen. Photographs by Eduardo Ayrosa (Rio de Janeiro: Instituto Nacional do Livro, 1960).

The "reconquest" refers to the restoration that began early in 1957 under the auspices of the Diretoria do Patrimônio Histórico e Artístico Nacional. The author discusses some of the problems faced in restoring the church of Bom Jesus at Congonhas as well as its accompanying sixty-six statues in six chapels. This restoration reveals that the painting and statuary at Congonhas was not the work of simple, ignorant mulatto artisans. In rejecting the sentimentalized legend that he feels has surrounded Aleijadinho, the author shows how great the *mineiro* sculptor's reputation was among his contemporaries by quoting a member of the town council of Mariana in Minas Gerais who in 1790 stated that the genius of Aleijadinho was "superior to them all in sculpture, whether figures or in relief and in design and irregular decorations in the best French style." Gomes Machado also argues that there are many valuable expressions of artistic genius at Congonhas besides Aleijadinho's famed prophets. The author describes the interior of the church of Bom Jesus, its chiselled altars and its paintings—all done by some of that captaincy's leading artists in the second half of the eighteenth century. He gives a detailed description of the ceiling over the aisle painted about 1769 or 1770 by João Nepomuceno Correia e Castro and how it was restored. As for the life-sized statues that made up the scenes from Christ's Way of the Cross, once the several coats of paint that had been liberally added over the space of more than a century and half had been removed and the beauty of the statues restored, the true genius of Aleijadinho, who personally carved some of them and supervised the others, and of Manuel da Costa Ataíde and Francisco Xavier Carneiro, who originally painted them, could be properly appreciated. Gomes Machado concludes that "once the original paint of the statues had been reestablished and the ensembles reorganized, it became evident that only a group of first class artists, highly inspired, highly trained and mainly conscious of their aesthetic function could achieve such team work." The English introduction and text are on pages 73–103. Following page 108 there is an English translation of the legends accompanying the 71 plates.

[784] A. J. R. Russell-Wood. *Manuel Francisco de Lisboa*. Belo Horizonte: Universidade Federal de Minas Gerais, 1968.

This biography of the father of Aleijadinho, the famed sculptor and architect of Minas Gerais, is appropriately subtitled: "A Craftsman of the Golden Age of Brazil." Though the study is in Portuguese, there is a several-page resume in English on the life of this important Portuguese architect and builder who migrated to Minas Gerais.

3. Sculpture and the Decorative Arts [Nos. 785–803]

Much of Fabrice Polderman's article on sculpture in Brazil **[785]** deals with the colonial period, as does that of A. C. Callado **[786]**. Stanislaw Herstal **[787]** provides an excellent survey of religious images in colonial Brazil. Frederico Borghini **[78]** discusses statuary in Bahia's new museum located in a former Benedictine monastery. José Valladares **[789]** describes some of the major pieces of both religious and secular art in colonial Bahia. Carl Ziegler **[790]** does the same for the items housed in Rio de Janeiro's Solar de Monjope.

The most famous sculptor in Brazilian history was Antônio Francisco Lisboa, nicknamed Aleijadinho. There are numerous accounts of his life and work in English. One of the best is that by John Bury **[791]**. Bury **[792]** also analyzes Aleijadinho's twelve prophets at Congonhas do Campo as do Hans and Graciela Mann **[793]** in their photographic essay. Other accounts of Aleijadinho's achievements are found in Irene Diggs **[794]** and **[795]**, Angel Guido **[796]**, and Tendai Mutunha **[797]**.

Robert C. Smith **[798]** describes gilt wood retables in Portugal and Brazil. Joaquim de Sousa-Leão **[799]** and **[800]** explains the importance of Portuguese tiles in Brazilian architecture. Grace Hardendorff Burr **[801]** and Paul Eckhardt and I. G. Labastille **[802]** describe furniture in colonial Brazil. Robert C. Smith **[803]** discusses the importance of silver-making in Portuguese America.

[785] Fabrice Polderman. "Sculpture in Brazil," *Gazette des Beaux-Arts* 30 (October–December 1946), pp. 345–360.

More than sixty percent of this article deals with the period prior to independence. The author focuses on four Brazilian sculptors of the colonial period: Chagas and Manoel Ignácio da Costa (ca. 1759–1849) in Bahia; Antônio Francisco Lisboa, nicknamed "O Aleijadinho" (1730?–1814), in Minas Gerais; and Valentim da Fonseca e Silva, better known as "Mestre Valentim" (1745?–1813), in Rio de Janeiro. By the mid-eighteenth century, Chagas's art work adorned such Bahian churches as those of the Third Order of the Carmelites and Santa Anna. Manoel Ignácio carved outstanding bas-reliefs as well as various figures of Christ and statues of the saints. Aleijadinho's masterpiece,

The Twelve Prophets at Congonhas do Campo, is considered the greatest work of sculpture in colonial Brazil. Other works of importance include the four bas-reliefs of the pulpits in the church of St. Francis of Assisi at Vila Rica and the sixty-six life-sized statues of cedar wood which depict various scenes in the passion and death of Christ. Mestre Valentim's decoration of the Church of the Military Cross in Rio de Janeiro is considered to be the high-water mark of colonial art in the Brazilian capital. The author concludes his section on sculpture before 1822 by arguing that the influence of the French artists who came to Brazil in 1816 was limited to Rio de Janeiro and did not "deflect the Brazilian artistic current from its natural evolution." 14 illus. (5 of them dealing with Aleijadinho). 3 notes.

[786] A. C. Callado. "Brazilian Sculpture," *The Studio* 126:607 (October 1943), pp. 132–134.

Though Callado praises the work of Aleijadinho in Minas Gerais and Valentim da Fonseca e Silva (Mestre Valentim) in Rio de Janeiro, he argues that "the real beginning of the arts in Brazil dates from the arrival of the French Mission of Artists in 1816." The author sees Augusto Taunay and Marco Ferrez, especially the former, as founders of sculpture in Brazil. 5 illus. Undocumented.

[787] Stanislaw Herstal. *Imagens Religiosas do Brasil/Religious Images of Brazil.* Trans. by Elisa Schoffman and Pontes de Paula-Lima. São Paulo: Grafica Technica Ltda., 1956.

Emphasizes religious statuary that might be termed popular because often it was made by humble carvers or sculptors. Many of these images were intended for private homes rather than churches. With few exceptions the extant statues of the colonial period, whether of wood, clay, soapstone or even ivory, are polychromed. Some are also gilded. The author argues that São Paulo, Rio de Janeiro and Rio Grande do Sul were least affected by foreign influence, while Minas Gerais and, especially, Bahia and Pernambuco were most affected. In turn, images from the Brazilian Northeast influenced those of other regions of Portuguese America. Herstal divides image-making into periods. During the sixteenth and seventeenth century Pernambuco and São Paulo were the most active centers of production. Statuary of the seventeenth century was characterized by simplicity of composition, static figures, and monotonous, perpendicular pleating of the robes. In the eighteenth century, the art of imagery remained stagnant in São Paulo, while developing rapidly in the Brazilian Northeast and in Minas Gerais. Images of the eighteenth century are often dynamic figures, of rich composition with flowing robes, but characterized by artificiality. Decline began toward the end of the eighteenth century when art became commercialized. The vast majority of the statues were made of wood, usually cedar; clay was the second choice, especially in São Paulo or coastal Rio de Janeiro; the third choice was ivory, mostly in eighteenth-century Bahia; while soapstone was used in Minas Gerais and Bahia. The author discusses the variety of ways the Blessed Virgin and Christ were depicted. Saints probably had the widest range of poses. Statues frequently were accompanied by such adornments as crowns, crosses, palms, staves, quills, etc. In Minas Gerais black statues of saints existed. Herstal concludes with a discussion of superstition—the punishing (frequently by mutilation) of statues of saints when prayers were not answered. The text is illustrated by 33 figures. In addition, there are 11 color and 304 black-and-white plates depicting religious statuary. The study contains three useful indices: one by region and material, another by saint, and a third by collection. There are 95 pages of text in English and Portuguese on alternate pages.

[788] Federico Borghini. "Treasury of Sacred Art. New Museum in Bahian Monastery," *Américas* 15:4 (April 1963), pp. 8–12.

This article, though describing a new museum of sacred art in the Benedictine monastery of Santa Tereza in Bahia, is useful for its illustrations, classification of statuary, and discussion of such problems as determining the region or country of the work's origin, the identification of the local workshops and the names of the master carvers and other biographical data, and the comparison of the works to better understand regional schools and influences. 5 illus. No notes.

[789] José Valladares. "Bahia and its Museum," *Bulletin of the Pan American Union* 82:8 (August 1948), pp. 449–458.

The author, who is also the director of the Museum, sketches the history of colonial Bahia and discusses the Portuguese, Amerindian, African, Oriental and Spanish American influences on the city's art during the period before independence. Valladares then describes some of Bahia's artistic treasures housed in the museum. Included are Portuguese glazed tiles from the Carmelite convent and the Unhão house; a bronze bell, dating from 1615, from the building in which Bahia's town council held its meetings; paintings, including an oil by

Franco Velasco (1818) for a side altar in the Bomfim church; beds, chairs, sofas, and a combination chest of drawers and an oratory; and gold and silver necklaces worn by Bahian Blacks in the eighteenth and nineteenth centuries. 10 illus. No notes.

[790] Carl A. Ziegler. "The Colonial Architecture of Brazil," *Bulletin of the Pan American Union* 65:5 (May 1931), pp. 499–504.

Provides a brief summary of the history of sixteenth-century Brazil and describes his visit to Solar de Monjope, a house in Rio de Janeiro built by Dr. José Marianno Filho, the former director of the Escola Nacional de Bellas Artes, Rio de Janeiro. The design of the Solar de Monjope was based on "Jesuit Baroque." The building used "fine old wood carving, tile, stonework, etc. from demolished churches and other buildings" in its construction. It also housed many examples of furniture and silver dating from the colonial period. 5 illustrations (four of the Solar de Monjope and one of a colonial Brazilian coffeepot). Undocumented.

[791] John Bury. "The Aleijadinho," *The Cornhill Magazine* 164:979 (Summer 1949), pp. 69–80.

A biographical sketch of O Aleijadinho (the little cripple), the nickname of the mulatto Antônio Francisco Lisboa (1738–1814), Brazil's most famous sculptor, son of a Portuguese architect and a slave. The author concentrates mostly on Aleijadinho's personal life and relies heavily on the sculptor's nineteenth-century biographer, Rodrigo José Ferreira Brêtas. 3 notes. 8 plates.

[792] J. B. Bury. "The Twelve Prophets at Congonhas do Campo," *The Month* New Series, 2:3 (September 1949), pp. 152–171.

Careful examination and description of the statues of each of the twelve prophets sculptured by Aleijadinho: Jonah, Amos, Obadiah, Isaiah, Baruch, Daniel, Jeremiah, Ezekiel, Hosea, Joel, Nahum and Habakkuk. The author discusses the comments of nineteenth-century visitors to Minas Gerais on Aleijadinho's work and compares the statues with such European efforts on similar themes as those of Klaus Sluter, Donatello, Lorenzo Lotti, Bernini, and the Lombardi and the Della Porta brothers. 1 figure. illus.

[793] Hans Mann and Graciela Mann. *The 12 Prophets of Aleijadinho.* Austin, Texas: University of Texas Press, 1967. 131 pp.

Pictorial essay with 96 excellent black-and-white photographs of the town of Congonhas do Campo, its Sanctuary of Bom Jesus, the statues that make up the Calvary collection and the twelve prophets that grace the Sanctuary's atrium. There are also photographs of the Carmelite churches in Ouro Preto and Sabará, the church of São Francisco in Ouro Preto and several statues from the Museu da Inconfidência. The photographs are accompanied by a biographical sketch of Antônio Francisco Lisboa (O Aleijadinho), who was in charge of carving the Calvary figures and the prophets, a short account of the history of the Sanctuary of Bom Jesus, and an appreciation of Aleijadinho's prophets. The latter was written by Carlos Drummond de Andrade, while Graciela Mann was responsible for the remainder of the text. There is a one-page bibliography.

[794] Irene Diggs. "Antônio Francisco Lisboa, Called Aleijadinho," *Magazine of Art* 44:3 (March 1951), pp. 93–96.

Relies heavily on Aleijadinho's first biographer, Ferreira Brêtas, whose account was published in the *Correio Oficial de Minas* in 1858, only forty-four years after Lisboa's death. The author argues that Aleijadinho's "carvings, statuary, pulpits, fountains, [and] panels" carry "the stamp of his undisciplined individualism, his rebellion against slavish copying of Portuguese art, his resentment of caste and slavery, and the unidentified torturing disease which transformed him into the legendary Aleijadinho ('The Little Cripple')." 8 illus. No notes.

[795] Irene Diggs. "O Aleijadinho," *Américas* 2:9 (September 1950), pp. 24–27, 44.

Brief survey of the life of Antônio Francisco Lisboa and his art with a special emphasis on the artist's twelve prophets and the sixty-six life-sized statues depicting the Last Supper and the chief episodes of Christ's suffering and death—both projects gracing the terrace and church gardens at Congonhas do Campo in Minas Gerais. The author claims that Aleijadinho "inaugurated the emancipation of Brazilian art." 9 illus. No notes.

[796] Angel Guido. "O Aleijadinho, the Little Cripple of Minas Geraes," *Bulletin of the Pan American Union* 65:8 (August 1931), pp. 813–822. Translated from an article in *La Prensa*, Buenos Aires, 11 January 1931.

Biographical sketch of Brazil's most famous sculptor, Antônio Francisco Lisboa (1730–1814), nicknamed O Aleijadinho (the cripple). Quickly examining Aleijadinho's most famous works, the author concentrates on the artist's personal life, his relationship with his slaves and apprentices, and the nature of the disease that crippled him at the age of 47 but did not prevent him from continuing his artistic career. Relies heavily on the *Ephemerides Mineiras* and the writings of José Mariano. 4 notes. 8 illus.

[797] Tendai Mutunha. "Antonio Francisco Lisboa: Afro-Brazilian Architect and Sculptor," *Negro History Bulletin* 38:7 (October/November 1975), pp. 460–463.

Mutunha points out that "it was in the field of visual arts that the African arts were transmitted to Brazil in all their magnificent splendor and beauty." He further argues that "Brazilian society, because of the diffusion of African and Portuguese cultures, produced many great black artists, one of the greatest being Antonio Francisco Lisboa." The son of Manuel Francisco de Lisboa **[784]**, a "prominent and prosperous architect," and Isabel "his attractive and beautiful slave woman," Aleijadinho (as he was later called) was given his freedom at Baptism. The author provides a brief sketch of Aleijadinho's life and characterizes his architectural works "as outstanding and impressive in the rococo both for their inventiveness and harmony as well as majestic greatness and sophistication." In addition, the *mineiro's* sculpture "always enhanced and enriched as well as harmonized with his architecture." Based on printed secondary sources. 4 illus. 8 numbered and 2 unnumbered notes. There is a "Selected Bibliography."

[798] Robert C. Smith. "The Gilt Wood Retable in Portugal and Brazil," in *Latin American Art, and the Baroque Period in Europe. Studies in Western Art. Acts of the Twentieth International Congress of the History of Art, Princeton, New Jersey, 1961.* Princeton, New Jersey: Princeton University Press, 1963, III, 165–172.

Points out the importance of wood sculpture to the churches of Portugal and Brazil: "Polychromed and gilded, wood was used for every aspect of the interior fitting—for the altars and their numerous accessories, for the pulpits and picture frames, for the railings of the chancel and for the columns of the choir loft at the entrance to the nave." The author divides the history of the flowering of the gilt-wood altar retable into four periods: 1) a Renaissance phase, ca. 1520–1680; 2) an Early Baroque phase, which Smith defines as the National Style, ca. 1680–1725; 3) a full Baroque period, also called the Joanine style, ca. 1720–1750; 4) a Rococo phase, ca. 1740–1800. The retable (ca. 1625) of the high altar of São Roque, the former Jesuit Church in Lisbon, inspired a number of similar ones like that of the destroyed Jesuit Church in Rio de Janeiro as well as the former church of that order in Salvador. The National Style, which is associated with a church or chapel done entirely in gilt woodwork, can be found in the Franciscan Third Order chapel in Recife, the Benedictine Church in Rio de Janeiro, and the interior of the Franciscan Church at Salvador. Joanine-style retables can be found in the church of São Francisco da Penitência in Rio de Janeiro and that of Nossa Senhora da Conceição da Praia in Salvador **[692]**. The most famous of the rococo retables were done by Aleijadinho in Minas Gerais, especially the Third Order Franciscan Church at São João d'El Rei and the chancel of the same order's church at Ouro Preto. 15 illus. 2 notes.

[799] Joaquim de Sousa-Leão. "Portuguese Tiles in Brazilian Architecture," *The Burlington Magazine* 84:493 (April 1944), pp. 83–87.

Points out that "the use of wall tiles has been one of the most popular and successful forms of decoration of buildings, both internally and externally specially in hot sunny climates, where there is an abundance of clay." Both rich and poor Portuguese used tiles "decorating their rooms much in the same way as the Italians used frescoes or the Northern Europeans tapestries." The author traces the development of these five- or six-inch square tiles or *azulejos* in Portugal, discusses Moorish influences on their design, and shows why these wall tiles were so popular in colonial Brazil. The richest designs in Portuguese America were found in the Northeast. Sousa-Leão points to the Franciscan cloister in Paraiba and the Carmelite cloister in Olinda as examples of classic arabesque. Dating from the late 1730s are the beautiful tiles of the Franciscan convent in Bahia. These *azulejos,* a present of Dom João V, are "counted among the finest *azulejos* in Brazil." Portuguese-manufactured tiles graced the Church of the Rosario as well as many private houses in Salvador. These *azulejos* are rarer in Rio de Janeiro—though there are some beautiful ones in the sacristy of the Penitência—and almost nonexistent in the gold-mining regions, "where the absence of monasteries, forbidden there by the king, removed the scope for this type of decoration requiring continuous wall space." 8 illus. No notes.

[800] Joaquim de Sousa-Leão. "Decorative Art: The Azulejo," in Livermore, ed., *Portugal and Brazil* **[81]**, pp. 385–394.

Traces the evolution of the making and the use of tiles among the Moslems and later the Italians. About the mid-seventeenth century "a new style then emerges that is genuinely Portuguese—the blue and white pictorial compositions—framed by baroque caryatids, dolphins, and cherubim, a transition accelerated by Chinese influence." The seventeenth and the first half of the eighteenth century were ones of great popularity for tiles. According to the author, during the reign of João V (1706–1750), "the pictorial azulejo outgrows the baroque formality of the seventeenth century. Swags and garlands, gorgeous draperies and capricious shells overflow tumultuously from picture-frames no longer respecting the claims of the pictures themselves." However, after the death of João V, the popularity of tiles diminished. Production was also hurt by the Lisbon earthquake five years later. Sousa-Leão shows how the use of these Portuguese-made tiles caught on in Brazil. The Franciscans and Jesuits used them extensively in decorating their churches, colleges and convents. Some of the early Franciscan tiles were destroyed by the Dutch invasion in the 1630s. Other beautiful tiles have been lost through the ravages of time or unfortunate restorations. The author lists many of the buildings famous for tile-work—especially in the Northeast. Tiles were rarer in Rio de Janeiro and almost nonexistent in Minas Gerais.

[801] Grace Hardendorff Burr. *Hispanic Furniture. From the Fifteenth through the Eighteenth Century*. 2nd ed. New York: The Archive Press, 1964. xix, 231 pp.
[The first edition was published in New York (1941) by the Hispanic Society of America with the title: *Hispanic Furniture. With Examples in the Collection of the Hispanic Society of America.*]

Chapter V, "Spanish and Portuguese Colonial Furniture" (pp. 102–120), contains information on Indo-Portuguese furniture from Goa as well as a brief description of furniture from Brazil. The latter is illustrated by four plates: a seventeenth-century table and three eighteenth-century pieces—a secretary, writing desk and table. The author points out that "although many fine pieces made in Brazil compare favorably with Portuguese palace furniture, a tendency toward heaviness and exaggeration of proportion may usually be seen." Portuguese furniture is discussed earlier in the study. The text is accompanied by some interesting plates showing Portuguese arm chairs, side chairs, beds, etc.

[802] Paul Eckhardt and I. G. Labastille. "Some Eighteenth-Century Brazilian Furniture," *Antiques* 19:5 (May 1931), pp. 362–364.

The frontier atmosphere of sixteenth-century Brazil plus the climate help explain why no known colonial Brazilian furniture that antedates 1600 has survived. During the seventeenth century—and even into the early 1700s—there was a strong Dutch influence on Brazilian furniture. By the eighteenth century, however, it was largely replaced by a French-Portuguese style. The eve of independence saw English furniture designs begin to gain popularity. The authors points out that "Brazilian craftsmen continued to imitate styles already out of fashion in Europe, but modified in keeping with the native rustic taste for solid, massive lines and over-ornamentation." The massiveness of some of the eighteenth-century pieces of furniture was due "to the intractable nature of Brazilian hard woods." In addition, some of the pieces—it is argued—were made by slaves "who never completely grasped the fine points of cabinet construction." The Brazilian "resting bed" took the place of the European sofa. Chests were used in place of the wardrobe—especially by those less well-to-do. "House altars in the form of chests of drawers with tops similar to those of the old North American secretaries were widely in use." Very popular in Brazil was the sedan chair. The six photographs that accompany the article are excellent and show a Brazilian "resting bed," a wall table, a bishop's chair (imported from Portugal), a sedan chair, a Bahia bed—all from the eighteenth century—and a wall table dating from the early nineteenth century. No notes.

[803] Robert Smith. "Brazilian Popular Silver," *School Arts* 47:8 (April 1948), pp. 277–280.

In spite of periodical prohibitions against silver making in colonial Brazil—"it took trade away from the craftsmen at home in Lisbon and Oporto and was also thought to be a temptation to the counterfeiting of money"—silversmiths were important and fairly numerous. Not only did these skilled craftsmen fashion silver for the wealthy and liturgical items for churchmen, but they also produced popular objects. Two of the latter were ornaments for crucifixes and medallions or badges for members of religious brotherhoods. The author provides photographs of these ornaments—all dating from the eighteenth or nineteenth centuries—and describes them. Smith also discusses such nineteenth-century silver work as riding whip handles and charm-like ornaments or balangandans. Many of the latter were made or worn by those of African heritage. The author concludes that "the balangandans as a whole are more naturalistic than other kinds of Brazilian popular silver. Great care was taken to make them look exactly like the objects they represent. As a result, they possess neither the distinction of extraordinarily fine craftsmanship nor the arresting character of primitive conceptions." 5 illus. No notes.

4. Painting [No. 804]

Little has been written in English on painting in colonial Brazil. Fortunately, a number of useful studies are beginning to appear in Portuguese to fill this void in the history of art. A helpful survey is provided by Paschoal Carlos Magno **[804]**. Brief treatments in English are found in Martin Soria **[744]**, Robert C. Smith **[746]**, and Mário Barata **[764]**. Tasso da Silveira **[771]** briefly discusses some of the paintings by the Benedictine artist Frei Donato de Pilar, especially those on the ceilings and walls of the church of São Bento in Rio de Janeiro. Lourival Gomes Machado **[783]** describes the discovery and renovation of some of the paintings at Congonhas do Campo.

[804] Paschoal Carlos Magno. "Brazilian Painting," *The Studio* 126:606 (September 1943), pp. 98–105.

Though most of the article deals with the nineteenth century, there are some useful comments on the colonial period. The author argues that the first European painters to depict Brazilian life were Franz Post, Albert Eckhout, and Zacharias Wagner—all of whom accompanied Prince Maurice of Nassau to America during the Dutch occupation of northeastern Brazil. Paschoal Carlos Magno then briefly describes the artistry of José Joaquim da Rocha, "who studied in Portugal and specialized in mural paintings, chiefly the ceilings of churches"; Friar Eusébio da Soledade who left "a series of sixteen small pictures painted on copper panels representing the life of the Virgin" in the Cathedral of Bahia; the Benedictine, Frei Ricardo do Pilar, who died in Brazil in 1700 and who "painted panels of religious subjects for various churches in the style of the early Italians"; José de Oliveira, who, along with his pupils Muggi and João de Sousa, provided paintings for many of Brazil's chapels and cloisters; and Manuel da Cunha, an ex-slave, who became "the most sought-after artist of his time—a master of a large and solid style—and undertook the decoration of churches and the painting of the great people of the period." The author concludes that "no school was formed during our Colonial phase. The artists were timid and humble, many of them former slaves, and their art was an improvization." 28 illus.

C. Literature [Nos. 805–810]

The easiest-to-read survey of colonial Brazilian literature is found in Samuel Putnam's *Marvelous Journey* **[805]**. Issac Goldberg **[806]** devotes two useful chapters to the colonial period. Manuel Bandeira **[807]** and Erico Verissimo **[808]** give a chapter to each of the three centuries of the colonial period, with Verissimo also devoting part of a fourth to the early nineteenth century. Afrânio Coutinho **[809]** includes a lengthy chapter, "From Baroque to Rococo," on the colonial period in his survey of Brazilian literature. A perceptive article on nativism in the eighteenth and nineteenth century is found in Antônio Cândido **[810]**. A discussion of aspects of Brazilian literature are found in Section XI, A, 2, a (the Jesuits), especially **[307]**, **[308]**, and **[318]**, and in Section XVIII, A (The Literature of Social Protest), **[714]**, **[715]** and **[716]**.

[805] Samuel Putnam. *Marvelous Journey. A Survey of Four Centuries of Brazilian Writing.* New York: Alfred A. Knopf, 1948. xvi, 269 pp.

In this well-written and easy to read survey, Putnam devotes six-and-a-half chapters to the colonial period. He frequently quotes appropriate passages from colonial writers and translates them into English. In "Legacy of the Tropical Forest," he discusses the role the Amerindian and African heritages have played in colonial Brazilian literature. The chapter, "Priests, Planters, Travelers, and the Birth of a Literature," analyzes sixteenth-century accounts about Brazil. When discussing the early seventeenth century, Putnam focuses on two writers from the sugar regions of the Northeast—Bento Teixeira and Ambrósio Fernandes Brandão—and quotes extensively from the latter's *Dialogues on the Resources of Brazil.* In "Bohemia in the Wilderness," the author quotes extensively the satiric verse of Gregório de Matos **[714]** and **[715]**. "Music of Parnassus" includes discussions of the writings of such seventeenth- and eighteenth-century prose writers as Padre Antônio Vieira **[315]**, Sebastião da Rocha Pitta, Nuno Marques Pereira and the plays of the Brazilian-born Jew, Antônio José da Silva **[344]**. The poets from Minas Gerais and their role in the Inconfidência Mineira are analyzed in "Arcady and the Rights of Man." Notes.

[806] Isaac Goldberg. *Brazilian Literature.* New York: Alfred A. Knopf, 1922. xiv, 303 pp.

Two chapters are devoted to the colonial period. The "Period of Formation (1500–1750)" discusses Jesuit influence, seventeenth-century nativism, the satires of Gregório de Matos **[714]** and **[715]**, Rocha Pitta, and Antônio José da Silva **[344]**. The "Period of Autonomous Development (1750–1830)" focuses on the epic poems *O Uruguay* by Basílio da Gama and *Caramurú* by Santa Rita Durão, as well as the lyric poems of the *mineiros* Claudio da Costa, Tomás Antônio Gonzaga, José Inácio de Alvarenga Peixoto, and Manoel Inácio da Silva Alvarenga. This chapter also discusses the political satire of the *Cartas Chilenas*, as well as the writings of the "patriarch of Brazilian independence," José Bonifácio de Andrada e Silva. Notes. Selections from Brazilian authors are translated into English.

[807] Manuel Bandeira. *A Brief History of Brazilian Literature.* Trans. Ralph Edward Dimmick. Washington, D. C.: Pan American Union, 1958. 188 pp.
[Reprinted. New York: Charles Frank, 1964.]

Manuel Bandeira introduces his brief history with a discussion of Brazil's ethnic elements. He then devotes a chapter to each of the three centuries of the colonial period. In his study of the sixteenth century, the author singles out Pero de Magalhaes de Gândavo **[186]**, the Jesuit Fernão Cardim **[207]**, Gabriel Soares de Sousa, and Ambrósio Fernandes Brandão, the latter writing his *Dialogues on the Resources of Brazil* in 1618. Bandeira concludes his chapter with a discussion of the Jesuit writings. The seventeenth century's chief writers were the Brazilian-born Franciscan historian, Frei Vicente do Salvador, and the Bahian satirist, Gregório de Matos **[714]** and **[715]**. Brazil's various, but short-lived, "academies" are discussed in the chapter on the eighteenth century. The six *mineiro* poets—Claudio Manuel da Costa, Tomás Antônio Gonzaga, Basílio da Gama, Santa Rita Durão, Alvarenga Peixoto, and Silva Alvarenga—are also carefully studied. Notes. The Portuguese selections are translated.

[808] Erico Verissimo. *Brazilian Literature. An Outline.* New York: The Macmillan Company, 1945. ix, 184 pp.

Chatty, humorous sketch of Brazilian literature. Verissimo discusses the ethnic elements that have influenced Brazilian literature. He then briefly surveys—in general terms without attempting to catalogue authors—the literary history of the seventeenth and eighteenth centuries. No notes.

[809] Afrânio Coutinho. *An Introduction to Literature in Brazil.* Trans. Gregory Rabassa. New York and London: Columbia University Press, 1969. xii, 326 pp.

The colonial period is studied in a lengthy chapter entitled "From Baroque to Rococo (pp. 66–118). Part of the chapter discusses and distinguishes between Renaissance and Baroque. The author briefly surveys the chief writers and trends of the period. Notes.

[810] Antônio Cândido. "Literature and the Rise of Brazilian National Self-Identity," *Luso-Brazilian Review* 5:1 (Summer 1968), pp. 27–43.

Useful discussion of nativism and changes in attitude toward the Brazilian Indian during the eighteenth and nineteenth centuries. No notes.

D. Music [Nos. 811–812]

Little has been written to date in English on the music of colonial Brazil. Two introductory essays, however, are provided by Ann Livermore **[811]** and Gerrit de Jong **[812]**.

[811] Ann Livermore. "Music," in Livermore, ed., *Portugal and Brazil* **[81]**, pp. 394–403.

Describes the role of wind and percussion instruments in Amerindian and African music and argues that "in spite of the overwhelming vitality of these African rhythms, the roots of Brazilian music are Portuguese." Portuguese influence was not only from Minho and other parts of northern Portugal but from Beira and central Portugal as well. After mentioning the use of music by missionaries in their proselytization efforts, she shows the strong religious influence in Brazilian music until independence—especially in processions and in the liturgy. Livermore recounts the role of *cheganças* as "surviving parts of a forgotten tradition, the Jesuit tragicomedy or sacred opera," and the *desafio* or challenge in improvised verse and song. The author concludes the colonial portion of her essay with some comments on the great Brazilian mulatto composer, Padre José Mauricio Nunes Garcia (1767–1830). Undocumented.

[812] Gerrit de Jong, Jr. "Brazilian Music and Art," in Smith and Marchant, eds., *Brazil* **[83]**, pp. 423–448.

De Jong discusses various racial and cultural ingredients that help make up Brazilian folk music. He then looks at the role of music in Jesuit efforts at conversion and argues that "the Church furnished the strongest impetus for the development of music in Brazil during the colonial period." He lists a number of important colonial musicians, the most significant being the mulatto Padre José Mauricio Nunes Garcia (1767–1830), who is said to have "amassed the largest and best music library in all of Brazil" and who composed more than 300 works, including the requiem mass for Maria I in 1816. The author also discusses the role of the Portuguese composer, Marcos Portugal, and Segismund Neukomm, a student of Haydn's, both of whom spent time in Rio de Janeiro during the early nineteenth century. In addition, he describes the musical accomplishments of Pedro I, who composed the Hymn of Independence of Brazil. The remainder of the section on music focuses on the nineteenth and twentieth centuries. Professor Gerrit de Jong devotes several pages to art in colonial Brazil, giving a special emphasis to schools of painting in Bahia and Rio de Janeiro, the French artistic mission of 1816, and Aleijadinho. A list of suggested readings, mostly in Portuguese, is appended (pp. 447–448).

XXII. The Portuguese Court in Brazil, 1808–1821

[Nos. 813–863]

A. General Accounts and Special Aspects [Nos. 813–821]

George Woodcock **[813]** and Clarence H. Haring **[814]** discuss the years 1808–1821 within the context of eight decades of monarchy in Brazil. Bertita Harding **[815]** covers the same period with a focus on its three monarchs: D. João VI, D. Pedro I, and D. Pedro II. Manoel Cardozo **[816]** contributes a fine essay entitled, "The Transition, 1808–1840." A nineteenth-century visitor, John Armitage **[817]**, discusses in detail the events surrounding the Court's stay in Rio in the early part of his history of Brazil, 1808–1831. Norman Holub **[818]** discusses the rise of liberalism. Carlos Manuel Peláez **[819]** examines the establishment of banking institutions in Brazil. Stephen Ferguson **[820]** describes the publication in Portuguese America of Brazil's first legal code. George P. Browne **[821]** traces early nineteenth-century efforts to attract immigrants to Brazil.

[813] George Woodcock. "The Brazilian Empire. An Experiment in Liberal Monarchy," *History Today* 6:5 (June 1956), pp. 404–413.

Though this well-illustrated article gives an overview of the eight decades Brazil was the seat of a monarchy, a third of the survey deals with the period before 1822. After outlining several of the sixteenth-, seventeenth-, and eighteenth-century plans for transferring the Portuguese court to Brazil and/or setting up a separate kingdom in Portuguese America, the author discusses the arrival of the Prince Regent João in Rio de Janeiro, the events leading up to independence, and the early difficulties that Pedro I encountered as the first emperor of Brazil. 7 illus. No notes.

[814] Clarence Henry Haring. *Empire in Brazil. A New World Experiment with Monarchy.* Cambridge, Massachusetts: Harvard University Press, 1958. 182 pp.

The first twenty pages of this survey of the monarchy in Brazil trace the forces at work in Portuguese America leading to independence, the removal of the Portuguese Court to Rio de Janeiro in 1808, the effects of this change on all of Brazil, but especially Rio de Janeiro, the rivalry between Brazilian- and Portuguese-born, the influence of race, the international problems in the Plata region, the Pernambucan revolt of 1817, the events leading to João VI's departure in 1821 and the proclamation of independence by Pedro, his son and heir, in 1822, and a sketch of the character of Brazil's first emperor. The author leans heavily on the work of Manuel de Oliveira Lima **[921]**. Based largely on printed secondary materials. There are footnotes and a bibliography (pp. 173–176).

[815] Bertita Harding. *Amazon Throne. The Story of the Braganzas of Brazil.* Indianapolis and New York: The Bobbs-Merrill Company, 1941. 353 pp.
[A later edition was published in Garden City, New York: Blue Ribbon Books, 1943. 335 pp.]

Popularized biographies of João VI ("The Emigrant"), Pedro I ("The Immigrant"), and Pedro II ("The Native Son") that sometimes lapse into historical novels. Though gossipy and entertaining, Harding's account often fails to distinguish between rumor and fact. The author is also fond of creating dialogue for the major figures of her story. However, she does translate and quote extensively from the correspondence of the Empress Leopoldina and that of Dom Pedro I and his mistress, the Marquesa dos Santos. The book is divided into three parts, each devoted to one of the Braganças mentioned above. There is a bibliography (pp. 329–335) and 33 illustrations. The main texts of both editions have the same pagination. However, the 1943 edition has only eight illustrations.

[816] Manoel Cardozo. "The Transition, 1808–1840," in Hill, ed., *Brazil* **[82]**, pp. 15–34.

"As in most revolutions, the intelligent group of men who fought for independence found support not so much in the people, who were generally apathetic, as in the unsettled conditions of the times." With these words Cardozo sets the stage for his review of three momentous decades in Brazilian history. He devotes a little more than a third of this chapter to a survey of the thirteen-year reign of João VI in Brazil (1808–1821)—which he considers to have been basically enlightened—and the events leading to independence. Cardozo pays special attention to the role of freemasonry, both in Portugal and Brazil, during the early nineteenth century. A selected bibliography is found on page 371. No notes.

[817] John Armitage. *The History of Brazil, from the Period of the Arrival of the Braganza Family in 1808, to the Abdication of Don Pedro the First in 1831.* 2 v. London: Smith, Elder and Co., 1836. xv, 371 pp. viii, 297 pp.

A hundred pages (six-and-a-half chapters) of volume I deal with the period before independence. The first chapter presents an interesting, but very brief (21 pages), survey of Brazil on the eve of the "revolt in Portugal, in favour of a Constitutional government." Though many of Armitage's comments focus on the revolts in Minas Gerais (1789), Bahia, and Pernambuco (1817), he does describe law, administration, the military, the Church, population, education, and the inflation of honors. The events leading to independence are examined in detail: Acceptance of the Portuguese Constitution, departure of D. João VI for Portugal, measures adopted by the Cortes of Lisbon, incorporation of the Banda Oriental in 1821, various manifestations in support of D. Pedro and Pedro's declaration of independence, election of D. Pedro as Emperor, the Andrada ministry, and the coronation of D. Pedro on 1 December 1822. See **[920]**.

[818] Norman Holub. "The Liberal Movement in Brazil, 1808–1854," (Ph.D. Dissertation: New York University, 1968). 364 pp.

Analyzes the rise of liberalism in Brazil during the first half of the nineteenth century, examining the important political figures, the rise of new institutions and the role of several important revolutions. The interpretation presented is that of Teófilo Ottoni and the ideological liberals of the moderate faction. The author argues that the conciliation government of the Marquis of Parana marked the end of the liberal movement.
DAI 29/11A (pp. 3934–3935).

[819] Carlos Manel Peláez. "The Establishment of Banking Institutions in a Backward Economy: Brazil, 1800–1851," *Business History Review* 49:4 (Winter 1975), pp. 446–472.

Between 1808 and 1851 banking in Brazil went through three phases: 1) The First Bank of Brazil, 1808–1829; 2) the economy without banking, 1830–1838; 3) establishment of the first banks of issue, 1839–1851. Founded soon after the arrival of the royal court to Portuguese America, the First Bank of Brazil had a monopoly on banking services. The two decades of its existence were characterized by rapid inflation and, according to the author, "bank credit simply financed government consumption instead of contributing to truly productive economic activities." In contrast, the banks of issue, 1839–1851, "provided the required credit for the new economic activity that first brought modernization to Brazil—coffee exports—and rapid growth of the export sector was attained with relative price stability." The first period was characterized by unfavorable trade conditions, while the third period was one of rapid development of trade. The author argues that the system of banks of issue "was probably one of the best financial structures available to the country—or, at least, better than a perfect monopoly of the credit market by an official bank." There is a useful sketch of the history of the First Bank of Brazil. Based on printed primary and secondary materials. 1 chart; 5 tables. Appendix (2 tables). 48 notes.

[820] Stephen Ferguson. "The *Codigo Brasiliense*: Brazil's First Official Legal Code," *Revista Interamericana de Bibliografia/Inter-American Review of Bibliography* 24:2 (April–June 1974), pp. 129–134.

In 1603, the Portuguese laws Philip II had systematized into a code of five books were published. During the next two centuries, this code was never radically changed, though, beginning in 1761, new laws and royal decrees were collected and published every five years. When the Court was forced to flee to Brazil in 1807, it established a royal press in May of the following year. In 1811, this press published the first volume of the *Codigo Brasiliense*—a collection of new laws and royal decrees enacted in Brazil, but similar in format to those published in Portugal every five years since 1761. The author discusses and gives bibliographical descriptions of copies of Brazil's first legal code not described in Alfredo do Valle Cabral's study of the royal press in Brazil, 1808–1822. 6 notes. Appendix.

[821] George P. Browne. "Government Immigration Policy in Imperial Brazil, 1822–1870," (Ph.D. Dissertation, The Catholic University of America, 1972). 391 pp.

The author argues that when independence was proclaimed in 1822 there was a long "tradition of government sponsorship of immigration" that would be developed and continued during the remaining years of the Empire. The first three chapters deal with the colonial period, with a special emphasis on Portuguese attempts to attract Swiss immigrants after 1808. The next two chapters discuss the recruitment of mercenary troops "under the guise of immigrants" and the use of immigrants to establish strategic settlements in southern Brazil—both of which took place in the 1820s. The remainder of Browne's study deals with the post-1826 period. Relies heavily on printed Imperial legislative records and the official correspondence of the Brazilian agent in Hamburg, Jorge de Antônio de Schaeffer (1823–1828).
DAI 33/02-A (p. 688).

B. Rio de Janeiro, 1808–1822 [Nos. 822–863]

Alan K. Manchester **[822]** provides an excellent study of the transfer of the Portuguese Court to Rio de Janeiro in 1808. Herbert Heaton **[823]** also discusses the transfer of the Court, but paints an unsympathetic portrait of the Prince Regent João. Manchester **[824]** traces the growth of bureaucracy in Brazil, 1808–1821. Maria Odila Silva Dias **[825]** shows how the establishment of the Court in Rio de Janeiro helped unify Brazil. Anyda Marchant **[826]** describes the beginnings of Rio's Botanical Gardens. Manoel Cardozo **[827]** does the same for the National Library, the nucleus of which was brought to Brazil by the future João VI. Sérgio Correa da Costa **[828]** and **[829]** provides biographical sketches of Dom Pedro I. Pedro's first wife, the Empress Leopoldina of Austria, finds a biographer in Emmi Baum **[830]**. Marcus Cheke **[831]** and Loretta Sharon Wyatt **[832]** discuss the role of Carlota Joaquina, wife of João VI. Arnold Burgess Clayton **[833]** examines the life of Tomás Antônio de Vilanova Portugal and his career in Brazil while the Court was in Rio. Additional insights into the social and architectural history of Rio de Janeiro during the years 1808–1821 have been provided by a number of foreigners who left paintings and drawings of their impressions of the new capital of the Portuguese empire. Gilberto Ferrez **[834]** has published 29 watercolors of the English Richard Bate. Michael Teague **[835]** describes the work of John Johnston, an English architect in Brazil. Michel Benisovich **[836]** discusses the French artistic mission of 1816. Jean-Baptist Debret has left hundreds of watercolors depicting daily life in Rio de Janeiro. In addition, he **[837]** painted landscapes of São Paulo, Paraná, and Santa Catarina. Two Austrians—one an amateur (Franz Frühbeck) **[838]**; the other a professional painter of watercolors (Thomas Ender) **[839]** and **[840]**—have depicted places and events in Rio de Janeiro, 1817–1818.

[822] Alan K. Manchester. "The Transfer of the Portuguese Court to Rio de Janeiro," in Keith and Edwards, eds., *Conflict and Continuity* **[84]**, pp. 148–183.

Important description and analysis of the events leading up to the decision of Prince Regent João to move the Court to Rio de Janeiro—an action that successfully thwarted Napoleon's plans to dethrone the House of Bragança and eventually led to the raising of Brazil to the status of co-kingdom in 1815. The author argues convincingly that the transfer was a planned and effective maneuver and discusses how the machinery of government was transported and established in America in an orderly manner. Based largely on archival and primary printed sources. 114 notes. Richard Graham's commentary (pp. 184–190) discusses how Professor Manchester's chapter "contributes to the revisionism launched almost sixty years ago by Oliveira Lima and carried forward in Brazil by Tarquinho de Sousa but still hardly noted in this country." 18 notes.

[823] Herbert Heaton. "When a Royal Family Came to America," *The Canadian Historical Association Report of the Annual Meeting Held at Montreal May 25-26, 1939*. Toronto: The University of Toronto Press, 1939, pp. 48–60.

Unsympathetic view of both the Prince Regent João and the Brazilians, especially those residing in Rio de Janeiro. The author overstresses England's role in the transference of the Court to Brazil and spends about half of the article on English commercial efforts in Portuguese America. Heaton's study is marred by numerous misstatements of fact. 1 note.

[824] Alan K. Manchester. "The Growth of Bureaucracy in Brazil, 1808–1821," *Journal of Latin American Studies* 4:1 (May 1972), pp. 77–83.

Describes and gives examples of the types of bureaucrats who accompanied the Court to Brazil as well as the Portuguese émigrés who came later and analyzes the use of patronage by the Prince Regent (later D. João VI). The author then discusses some of the many new jobs created not only at the Court in Rio de Janeiro but throughout the remainder of Brazil. Manchester concludes: "The creation of the mechanism of a sovereign state in Brazil, parallel to and co-equal with the prototype in Lisbon, produed a centralized, national bureaucracy which looked to Rio de Janeiro as the source of authority. . . . This bureaucracy, both national and provincial, provided a ready made administrative structure with experienced personnel for an independent Brazil." Based on archival (Arquivo Histórico Ultramarino, Lisbon) and printed primary sources. 19 notes.

[825] Maria Odila Silva Dias. "The Establishment of the Royal Court in Brazil," in Russell-Wood, ed., *From Colony to Nation* **[88]**, pp. 89–108. [This is a revised translation of "A Interiorização de metrópole (1808–1853)," in Carlos G. Mota, ed., *1822: Dimensões.* São Paulo, 1972, pp. 160–184.]

After analyzing Brazil's chief social and economic realities on the eve of independence, the author effectively argues that "the seed of 'nationality' had absolutely no revolutionary content. The monarchy and the continuation of the status quo were the major preoccupations of the men forging the transition to empire." Shows how the establishment of the Court at Rio de Janeiro provided the inspiration for the consolidation, integration, and centralization which proved to be "one of the prime moulding forces in politics during the empire"—though often at the expense of the Northeast. Based on printed primary and secondary sources. 69 notes.

[826] Anyda Marchant. "Dom João's Botanical Garden," *The Hispanic American Historical Review* 41:2 (May 1961), pp. 259–274.

Briefly recounting the circumstances surrounding the transfer of the Portuguese Court to Brazil in 1808, the author traces the early beginnings (1808–1829) of "one of the most renowned botanical gardens of the world," located in Rio de Janeiro at the Lagôa Rodrigo de Freitas.

Based entirely on printed sources with a special emphasis on travellers' accounts. 44 notes.

[827] Manoel S. Cardozo. "The National Library of Brazil," *The Hispanic American Historical Review* 26:4 (November 1946), pp. 618–624.

Traces the history of Brazil's national library from the time the Court was transferred to Rio de Janeiro in 1808. Its nucleus was the private library of the royal family organized by José I (1750–1777) after the earlier one was destroyed by the Lisbon earthquake of 1755. It included the books collected by the famous eighteenth-century Portuguese bibliographer Diogo Barbosa Machado. There is a useful discussion of some of the major collections purchased by the library prior to 1854, as well as its important publications. Based on printed sources. 7 notes.

[828] Sérgio Correa da Costa. *Every Inch a King. A Biography of Dom Pedro I, First Emperor of Brazil*, trans. by Samuel Putnam. New York: The Macmillan Company, 1950. 230 pp. front.

Popularized biography of Pedro I with frequent quotations from the writings of Pedro, his wife Leopoldina, and various diplomats and travellers. The author emphasizes the personal characteristics of Pedro's parents (João VI and Carlota Joaquina) and those with whom he came in contact. Stresses Pedro's "intimacy with street urchins," involvement in tavern brawls, horsemanship, and physical stamina. Correa da Costa describes how Pedro was "very frisky with the ladies" and examines his marriage to the daughter of Francis I of Austria, Leopoldina (who "with her wholesome red cheeks and heavy unattractive gait . . . resembled a plump and rosy country maiden") and his lengthy affair with Domitila de Castro, who bore him a number of royal bastards. Amidst these details, the author intersperses bits of the history of Brazil during the first three decades of the nineteenth century. There is some documentation and a bibliography. Translated and adapted from *As Quatro Coroas de Pedro I* [The Four Crowns of Pedro I], Rio de Janeiro, 1941.

[829] Sérgio Correa da Costa. "New World Emperor," *Américas* 1:5 (July 1949), pp. 16–19, 34.

Biographical sketch of the training of Dom Pedro I, the first emperor of Brazil, with some insights into his personality, character, and abilities. The introductory note erroneously states that this article is a chapter from Samuel Putnam's translation of Correa da Costa's biography of Pedro I (*Every Inch a King*) **[828]**. Though part of the article is based on the chapter "The Education of a Prince," much of it contains scattered excerpts from other parts of the biography of the New World emperor. 12 illus. No notes.

[830] Emmi Baum. "Empress Leopoldina: Her Role in the Development of Brazil, 1817–1826," (Ph.D. Dissertation: New York University, 1965). 310 pp.

Sympathetic analysis of Leopoldina, former Austrian Archduchess and first Empress of Brazil, and her accomplishments in smoothing the way for Brazilian independence. Her efforts to attract German immigrants to the newly independent nation and her achievements in bringing a scientific mission to study and record information about nineteenth-century Brazil are also examined.
DAI 26/11-A (p. 6668)

[831] Marcus Cheke. *Carlota Joaquina. Queen of Portugal.* London: Sidgwick and Jackson, 1947. 212 pp.

This biography provides a sequel to his earlier volume on Pombal **[717]**. Half of this account covers the period to 1822. Cheke is sympathetic to the Spanish Carlota and unsympathetic to João VI, the Portuguese and their religious practices. He challenges many of the charges leveled against Carlota and her scandalous sex life and argues that "many of these allegations were doubtless invented at a later date, and spring from political enmity. Nor can the serious historian substantiate them by solid proof." Relying heavily on the accounts of English travellers and diplomats, Cheke surveys events in Portugal and Brazil during the early nineteenth century with a special emphasis on the transfer of the Court to Brazil, Carlota's intrigues regarding the Plata region, and the queen's reactions to the various constitutionalist movements in Spain, Brazil and Portugal. There is a lengthy sketch of Pedro de Sousa, the future Duke of Palmella. The author is disdainful of the lower classes of Portugal and Brazil, regardless of race. Speaking of Brazil, he comments: "The negroes lived a simple life not very different to the existence of savages, but it must not be supposed that they were unhappy." Based entirely on printed sources. There is a brief bibliography on p. 205.

[832] Loretta Sharon Wyatt. "D. Carlota and the Regency Affair," (Ph.D. Dissertation: University of Florida, 1969).

[833] Arnold Burgess Clayton. "The Life of Tomás Antônio de Vilanova Portugal: A Study in the Government of Portugal and Brazil, 1781–1821," (Ph.D. Dissertation: Columbia University, 1977). 377 pp.

Analyzes a turbulent period in the government of Portugal by studying the life of Tomás Antônio de Vilanova Portugal, a government official who served at several levels and in various aspects of administration. Beginning as a local administrator in Portugal, he gained the favor or Dom João VI and became a judge and counselor to the Prince. Influential in transferring the Court to Rio de Janeiro, he served in Brazil, first as *chancelor-mor*, then as the dominant minister in the cabinet. Involved in acting on such important issues of the time as the Pernambuco revolt, the occupation of Uruguay, the institution of the Bank of Brazil, and relations with European powers, he regarded the development of a powerful monarchy in Brazil as his top priority. He advised João to remain in Brazil and refuse to compromise with the constitutionalists. After the *pronunciamento* of February 26, 1821, he resigned from the government. Returning to Europe with the Court, he lived in poverty and obscurity until his death in 1839.
DAI 38/05-A (pp. 2971–2972).

[834] Gilberto Ferrez. *Aquarelas de Richard Bate: O Rio de Janeiro de 1808–1848* [*Watercolors of Richard Bate: Rio de Janeiro, 1808–1848*]. English version by Mary Jessop Dodd Ferrez. Rio de Janeiro: Galeria Brasiliana, 1965. 95 pp.

Twenty-nine watercolors of the amateur artist and British merchant, Richard Bate (1775–1856), are reproduced in color and described in detail. Bate arrived in Brazil in either November or December of 1807 and remained in Rio de Janeiro until 1821. Between that date and his death in England in 1856, he travelled back and forth between the two countries on numerous occasions. Bate had a "Shop of Nautical, Optical, Mathematical and Surgical Instruments and Glasses" on Rua Direita and lived in the fashionable Gloria district. The paintings, which cover the years 1808–1848, were part of the collection (now at Cornell University) of Colonel Francis Reginald Hull **[68]**, a British engineer who spent much of his life in Northeastern Brazil in the late nineteenth and early twentieth century. According to Ferrez, the chief value of the collection "is the emphasis given by Richard Bate to the more characteristic aspects of the town as shown in his paintings of whole streets with their two or three storied houses with their balconies and architectural details portrayed for the first time, in contrast to what mostly attracted other painters, such as fine houses, fortresses, churches and fountains. Bate's is the earliest group of Rio water colours known to us. Shown are nearly the whole of Direita Street, part of Ouvidor Street and of the Matacavalos district (now Riachuelo) and all the shoreline of São Christóvão, Gamboa, Santa Luzia, Passeio Publico, Lapa, Gloria and Flamengo." Almost half of the paintings deal with the period prior to 1826. For these most interesting and valuable watercolors there is an abridged introduction in English on pp. 15–20 and a detailed and carefully documented description of each plate on pp. 81–94. There is also a city plan of Rio de Janeiro in 1831.

[835] Michael Teague. "An English Architect in Brazil," *Country Life* 128:3311 (August 18, 1960), pp. 320–322.

The architect referred to in the title of the article was John Johnston. The young Englishman was sent to Brazil by the Duke of Northumberland to set up a gate copied from a gateway at Syon House, Northumberland's seat in Middlesex, England, which the Duke was presenting as a gift to the Prince Regent, the future João VI. It was set up at the Quinta da Boa Vista at São Cristóvão in Rio de Janeiro. Originally this country estate—with its maginificent view of the city and bay—belonged to a wealthy planter. Upon the Portuguese Court's arrival in Rio de Janeiro in 1808, it was offered to the Prince. Though there had been some reconstruction before that of Johnston, it was the English architect who made substantial changes. "Out of the long colonnaded verandah, which ran the length of the front, he made a 'Gothic Gallery' and placed a great horseshoe sweep of stairs to lead up to the central *patio de honra* where the royal family used to appear on state occasions. Above the main portico he set the royal arms, which had been made by Coade and Co. in London to his designs. He then began to enlarge the palace with four corner pavilions." However, he and the Crown seem to have run out of funds for its completion and only one pavilion was built. Johnston also remodeled two other royal country estates—one at Joaninha, the other at Engenho Velho near São Cristóvão. There are plans—probably by the English architect—in Brazilian archives for renovating the royal palace of Santa Cruz near Rio de Janeiro. In 1818, his appointment as architect to the Court was confirmed. He also designed the English church in Rio de Janeiro, "the first Protestant Church allowed in South America," which was built in 1820. 7 illustrations, one of which by Jean Baptiste Debret includes four stages of the Quinta da Boa Vista in 1808, 1816, 1822 and 1831. No notes.

[836] Michel Benisovich. "Brazil's Early Painters: The French in Rio 125 Years Ago," *Art News* 40:19 (January 15–31, 1942) pp. 25–26, 35.

In the aftermath of Napoleon's defeat at Waterloo, a number of French artists and their families agreed to come to Brazil—among them Joachim Lebreton, the two Taunay brothers (the painter Nicolas Antoine and the sculptor Auguste), and the historical painter Jean-Baptiste Debret. The author discusses their influence on the Brazilian art of the nineteenth century and describes several of their paintings including Nicolas-Antoine Taunay's "The Beach of Botafogo," "Portrait of Jeanneton," the Breton servant who accompanied the Taunay family to the New World, and "Portrait of My Son." The latter, Felix-Emile, was twenty when the group arrived in Brazil. He later became professor of landscapes at the Academie des Beaux-Arts in Rio de Janeiro. One of his paintings, "The Production of Charcoal," is described, as are two of Jean-Baptiste Debret's watercolors: "The Landing of Leopoldina of Hapsburg, Wife of the Crown Prince D. Pedro" and "Portrait of D. João VI." The abovementioned paintings provide the article's six illustrations. No documentation.

[837] J. B. Debret. *Quarenta Paisagens Inéditas do Rio de Janeiro, São Paulo Paraná e Santa Catarina* [*Forty Unedited Landscapes of Rio de Janeiro, São Paulo, Paraná and Santa Catarina*]. Edited by J. F. de Almeida Prado. Notes by Newton Carneiro (São Paulo: Companhia Editora Nacional, 1970). xiii, 148 pp.

Jean-Baptiste Debret, cousin, friend, and student of Louis David, was one of the painters selected by Napoleon to do a series of battle portraits. When the Emperor fell from power, Debret accepted an invitation to go to Brazil as part of the French artistic mission led by Lebreton. He arrived in Portuguese America on 26 March 1816. Debret helped with the decorations for Pedro's marriage to Leopoldina and for João VI's coronation. He also taught at the Academy of Beaux Arts. The author discusses some of the problems Debret and other members of the mission encountered in Brazil. These difficulties included rivalries with Portuguese painters who felt that they should have the professorships in the Academy. There were also rumors that the Frenchmen were plotting to rescue the exiled Napoleon from Santa Helena and that the group harbored potential regicides. The departure of João VI and his court in 1821 and independence in 1822 improved matters for the mission. In 1827 Debret was able to travel in southern Brazil. This previously unpublished collection includes sketches made during his trip by land to Rio Grande do Sul. In 1831, shortly after Pedro I's abdication, Debret returned to France. He died in Paris in 1848 at the age of eighty. Paintings from his 1827 travels include a general view of São Paulo, the governor's palace and the Carmelite convent of that city, the iron works of São João de Ipanema, three leagues from Sorocaba, the falls of Tietê and Porto Feliz, seen from the west bank of the Tietê. There are views of a number of towns: Castro (Iapó), Guaratuba, Parati, Curitiba, Sorocaba, São Carlos (today Campinas), São Pedro, Paranaguá, Itapocoroí and Ubatuba. There are also views of the Ilha de São Sebastião and Ilha Grande along with the scenes of daily life in the four southern provinces. Though most of the text is in Portuguese, there is a good summary in English on pages 49–51. The plates are on pages 61–140. There are several helpful indices.

[838] Robert C. Smith and Gilberto Ferrez. *Franz Frühbeck's Brazilian Journey. A Study of Some Paintings and Drawings Made in the Years 1817 and 1818 and Now in the Possession of the Hispanic Society of America.* Philadelphia: University of Pennsylvania Press, 1960. 128 pp. 16 plates, port., map (on lining papers). Bibliographical references included in "Notes."

The Viennese Franz Josef Frühbeck (b. 1795) was an amateur painter who accompanied the Archduchess Leopoldina of Austria, the future empress of Brazil [she had been married by proxy to the heir to the throne, D. Pedro], on her journey from Europe to Portuguese America. This study contains reproductions and descriptions of twelve previously unpublished gouaches, including six views of Rio de Janeiro, Leopoldina's departure from Leghorn, Tuscany, her festive arrival in Rio de Janeiro, and several portraying life aboard the Portuguese military vessel D. João VI, one of the two ships that brought Leopoldina and her entourage to Brazil. This study contains a description of the Archduchess's journey, a short account of Frühbeck's life and work, and a discussion of the artist's views of Rio de Janeiro. Also included are four pencil sketches and a facsimile edition of the rare German account of his impressions of the voyage [*Skizze meiner Reise nach Brasilien in Sud-Amerika*].

[839] Gilberto Ferrez. *O Velho Rio de Janeiro Atraves das Gravuras de Thomas Ender* [*Rio de Janeiro of Old as Seen in the Paintings of Thomas Ender.*] São Paulo, n.d. 172 pp.

When a scientific expedition to Brazil was being organized to accompany Princess Leopoldina, the Austrian Thomas Ender (1795–1875) was appointed landscape painter and accompanied, among others,

Johann Baptist Spix, the zoologist, and Karl Friedrich von Martius, the botanist **[671]**. Twenty-three years old, Ender arrived in Brazil on 14 July 1817. Because of illness he remained there less than a year, leaving for Austria on 1 June 1818 with six hundred drawings and watercolors. As Ferrez writes: "Some had been finished, others were merely outlined, but all expressed spontaneity, and an absolute fidelity where perspective was concerned. Nothing escaped Ender's sense of observation. Landscapes, panoramas, streets, houses, churches, fountains, human types, white, black, Chinese, mulatto people from São Paulo and Minas, rich, poor, soldiers, the interior of private houses, a whole world was depicted in Ender's paintings. Thus they represent a rich collection of Brazilian iconography, wonderful both in quantity and in quality." The author's sixteen-page introduction in Portuguese has an English version on pp. 33–36. There are 146 plates of Ender's, 32 in color. There are an additional 35 paintings of life in Rio that were included with Ender's paintings but not by him. The frontispiece is a lithograph of the artist in 1834. Bibliography.

[840] Thomas Ender. *Aquarelas Brasileiras* [*Brazilian Watercolors*]. Edited by Lygia da Fonseca Fernandes da Cunha. Rio de Janeiro: Livraria Kosmos Editora, 1967. n.p.

Thomas Ender (1793–1875) was considered one of the outstanding Austrian painters of watercolors in the nineteenth century. He studied at the Fine Arts Academy of Vienna and was appointed by Prince Metternich as the landscape painter on the Austrian Scientific Mission which accompanied the Empress Leopoldina to Brazil in 1817. He returned to Vienna in June of the following year. The editor of this collection describes some of Ender's experiences during the scientific mission. The thirteen watercolors collected here include a painting of Rio de Janeiro's Hospital of the Misericordia, the Franciscan convent of Santo Antônio, a street scene (Rua do Piolho, now Rua Carioca), the aqueduct seen from Santa Teresa, a view of the entrance to the Bay of Guanabara, plus others of such outlying districts of Rio de Janeiro as Catumbi and Laranjeiras. There are also views of São Paulo, Vila Rica (Ouro Preto) and the Serra das Figuras in Goiás. The editor includes a bibliography.

1. Contemporary Narratives [Nos. 841–863]

Thomas O'Neil **[841]** describes the departure of the royal court from Lisbon and their voyage to America. Ralph Rylance **[842]** and Edward James Lingham **[843]** engage in polemics over the transfer of the Portuguese court to Brazil and England's role. John Luccock **[844]**, an English merchant who spent almost ten years in Brazil, 1808–1818, writes perceptively of his experiences in Rio de Janeiro. Henri Sidney **[845]** visited Rio and Bahia, after the court's arrival in Brazil. The North American, George Little **[846]**, was mistaken for a French spy and spent two days in prison in Rio de Janeiro in May of 1810. In his account of the new Portuguese capital he focuses almost exclusively on prison life. Sir William Ouseley **[847]** and James Morier **[848]** spent ten days in Rio in September of 1810 on their way to the Middle East. James Prior **[849]** visited Rio de Janeiro in October of 1813. John Shillibeer **[850]** spent a little more than a week in Rio during the latter part of March 1814. The famed naturalist, Prince Maximilian of Wied-Neuwied **[851]**, visited Rio de Janeiro and travelled to Cabo Frio, Espirito Santo and Porto Seguro. A. P. D. G. **[852]** is uncomplimentary to both Portuguese and Africans in his account of Rio and its slaves. John Mc Leod **[853]**, Henry Ellis **[854]**, and Clarke Abel **[855]** were part of Lord Jeffrey Amherst's embassy to China and spent a week-and-a-half in Rio in March of 1816. A Protestant missionary, William Ellis **[856]**, on his way to the South Pacific, visited Rio de Janeiro in March and April of 1816. H. M. Brackenridge **[857]**, one of the United States observers sent to inspect conditions in South America, spent the latter part of January and early February in Rio. Jacques Arago **[858]**, a member of the French Freycinet scientific expedition, published 19 letters he wrote about Rio which he visited in December of 1817 and January of 1818. A lieutenant in the British Royal Artillery, Henry Chamberlain **[859]** published 36 colored engravings of Rio de Janeiro, 1819–1820, with descriptive explanations. Alexander Caldcleugh **[860]** was part of the entourage of Edward Thornton, British minister at the Portuguese court in Brazil. He spent more than 15 months in the capital of the Portuguese world between 1819 and 1821. He also visited Minas Gerais in 1821 and wrote a perceptive account of his stay in Brazil. Thaddeus Bellingshausen **[861]** visited Rio de Janeiro twice—1819 and 1821—on his voyage to the Antarctic for Russia. Gilbert Farquhar Mathison **[862]** devoted six chapters to his experiences in Rio and its environs in 1821. The North American, Thomas H. Bennett **[863]**, also stopped at Rio de Janeiro in 1821.

[841] Thomas O'Neil. *A Concise and Accurate Account of the Proceeding of the Squadron under the Command of Rear Admiral Sir Will. Sidney Smith, K.C. in Effecting the Escape, and Escorting the Royal Family of Portugal to the Brazils, on the 29th of November, 1807. and also the Sufferings of the Royal Fugitives during Their Voyage from Lisbon to Rio de Janeiro with a Variety of Other Interesting and Authentic Facts.* London: R. Edwards, 1809, lvi, 79 pp.

Thomas O'Neil was lieutenant of the Royal Marines aboard the *London*, one of the English ships escorting the Prince Regent João, Carlota Joaquina, and the demented Queen Maria I to Brazil in the aftermath of the Napoleonic invasion of Portugal. In addition to describing the voyage, O'Neil provides a description of Rio de Janeiro and Salvador. There was a second edition published in 1810 with some slight changes in the title. Both editions are very rare.

[842] Ralph Rylance. *Sketch of the Causes and Consequences of the Late Emigration to the Brazils.* London: Longman, Hurst, 1808. iv, 78 pp.

Anti-Portuguese and anti-Brazilian pamphlet regarding the move of the Portuguese Court to Brazil. According to Borba de Moraes **[20]**, II, 222, "it appears to have been written by a member of the British opposition." The same authority points out that "it presents the history of the negotiations between Canning and Strangford, and the debates in Parliament" concerning the transference of the Portuguese Court to America. It was refuted by Edward James Lingham **[843]**.

[843] Edward James Lingham. *Vindiciae Lusitanae, or an Answer to a Pamphlet Entitled "The Causes and Consequences of the Late Emigration to the Brazils."* London: J. Budd, 1808. 67 pp.

Refutation of the pamphlet by Ralph Rylance **[842]**.

[844] John Luccock. *Notes on Rio de Janeiro and the Southern Parts of Brazil: Taken during a Residence of Ten Years in that Country, from 1808–1818.* London: Samuel Leigh, 1820. viii, 639 pp.

In June of 1808, John Luccock (1770–1826), a Yorkshire merchant representing his in-law's commercial interests, arrived in Rio de Janeiro. With the exception of two rapid trips back to England in 1809 and 1816, he spent the next ten years in Brazil. His notes on what he saw and experienced are considered to be one of the best accounts of early nineteenth-century Portuguese America. Chapters two, three and four provide a detailed description of Rio de Janeiro's public buildings, institutions and society in 1808. Though somewhat critical of Brazil and the Portuguese, Luccock is sympathetic to the Prince Regent, the future João VI, who "has often been accused of apathy; to me he appeared to possess more feeling and energy of character than friends, as well as accusers, usually attribute to him. He was placed in new and singularly trying circumstances, and submitted to them with patience; when roused, he acted with vigour and promptness." Chapter four, "Ranks—Employment—Manners—Character," is especially interesting as Luccock examines social gradations in Rio de Janeiro from the Prince Regent to the lowliest slave. The English merchant felt that justice in Brazil was weighted toward the white minority. "Few of that class had," Luccock wrote, "been recently apprehended for crimes, except those committed against the State, and Mulattoes enjoyed like exemptions, in proportion as their colour approached the dingy or fair." The author also had perceptive comments about the role of women in Brazil. In Rio he found that "women of the higher and middle classes, especially the younger part of them, are much more secluded than in our own country." The most common female employment was "the spinning of cotton, chiefly performed by women of colour, but not quite laid aside by others, even in the city." In addition, "many women, white as well as black, employ themselves in making lace." However, "in every superior family plain sewing is done by the slaves, for this is an employment which fashion, here as elsewhere, has very absurdly marked as a degradation to a lady's fingers." Between 1808 and 1813 Luccock spent time in Uruguay, Paraná and Rio Grande do Sul and devoted three chapters to his experiences there (pp. 138–243). He found that "in this part of the continent there is more than the common proportion of pretty young women and girls; the elder are frank and chatty; none of them go much abroad, though less retrained than in the capital and its neighborhood, more regarded as companions and friends, and more freely admitted into society." He returned to Rio de Janeiro in 1813 and noticed a great deal of change during the years of his absence. Luccock devotes two chapters to his visits to the environs of the Brazilian capital in 1813 and another chapter to his trip around the bay of Rio de Janeiro in 1816. Four lengthy and valuable chapters (pp. 367–515) discuss his visit to Minas Gerais in 1817. He was particularly impressed with Vila Rica, which "is, perhaps, one of the most singularly situated places on the face of the earth; nothing less powerful than the love of Gold could have raised a large town on such a spot. Yet are its streets respectable in their appearance, and more particularly so in their pavement. One of them stretches across several projections of the mountain in a straight line, and is nearly two miles in length. Of two thousand houses, which the place contains, one-fifth, perhaps, are good ones; the rest are slightly built. All of them are white-washed externally; a circumstance, which marks the prevalence of lime in the neighbourhood. The bridges are numerous, and some of them well built; crossing streams, which flow rapidly down from the mountains. The public fountains, fourteen in number, are scattered through the town; they are, in general, noble structures, and supplied with an abundance of pure water." Luccock returned to Rio de Janeiro in 1818, further impressed with the changes that had taken place in the capital city. He provides an interesting discussion of the reaction there to the Pernambucan revolt of 1817. While not advocating slavery, Luccock argued that "slavery is not always a heavy yoke in Brazil" and stated that the laws "respecting Slavery are peculiarly mild." In the appendix are some useful commercial tables describing shipping to and from Brazil (pp. 605–628). There is also a glossary of Tupi words (pp. 629–639).

[845] Henri Sidney. *The Travels and Extraordinary Adventures of Henri Sidney in Brazil, and the Interior Regions of South America in the Years 1809, 1810, 1811, and 1812*. London: J. Fergusson, 1815. 159 pp.

According to Borba de Moraes **[20]**, II, 253, this book is rare. Sidney describes Rio de Janeiro and Bahia.

[846] George Little. *Life on the Ocean; or Twenty Years at Sea: Being the Personal Adventures of the Author*. 12th edition. Boston: Waite, Peirce and Company, 1846. 395 pp.

In April of 1810, the author sailed on the *Baltic* from Boston to Rio de Janeiro. On 15 May the ship arrived at its destination. But because a similar American vessel had "passengers on board who were supposed to be French spies," Little and his companions were arrested and imprisoned. Though the author was to remain in Rio de Janeiro for more than six months, his only description of the capital of the Portuguese empire is the prison where he spent the first two days of his stay. After dark, armed soldiers took the author and the others aboard the *Baltic* "to a loathsome prison appropriated for felons. There we were thrust in with as little ceremony as we had been taken out of the ship, and then left to reflect upon our most unenviable situation. In one corner of this wretched prison were about thirty negroes, chained in pairs; in another were as many more squalid, miserable-looking white men, whose very appearance denoted crime of the deepest dye. These, as I afterwards learned, were imprisoned for deeds of the most horrid character. Indeed, the whole interior of the prison was a mass of filth and vermin. The stench was so horrible, that it was impossible for any of us to close our eyes during the night, and we gave some of those miserable wretches a few pieces of silver to let us stand on a bench that was near to a window secured with large iron bars, so that we might inhale the fresh air. In this way we passed a sleepless night, in the deepest suspense, being wholly ignorant of the cause of this outrage. We were conscious that none of their lives had been violated by us, and that all the ship's papers, and our passports, were correct, and in strict compliance with their laws. With these reflections, therefore, we felt assured that, so soon as our minister was apprized of our condition, he would immediately get us released. This, however, was not so easy a matter, for two reasons,—the first and most prominent of which was, that the American minister had not much influence at the court of Brazil, and secondly, because of the many forms necessary to pass through before it could be effected." Through the intercession of some merchants from the United States, Little and his companions were freed. The Portuguese were apologetic and the author observed that for the remainder of his stay "the Americans were treated with the greatest respect." He remained in the capital as a clerk in an American commercial house which gave him command "of a fine brig to run between Rio, Montevideo, and Buenos Ayres." Little made five successful voyages and a considerable amount of money before his ship was repossessed in Buenos Ayres because the commercial house he worked for had failed. Salvaging only five hundred dollars from his two years' stay in Rio de Janeiro and the Plata region, the author "took passage in the ship *Scioto,* bound for Baltimore."

[847] Sir William Ouseley. *Travels in Various Countries of the East; More Particularly Persia. A Work Wherein the Author Has Described, as far as His Own Observations Extended, the State of Those Countries in 1810, 1811, and 1812.* 3 vols.; London: Rodwell and Martin, 1819.
[Only Volume I (xxvi, 455 pp.) treats of Brazil.]

The author, a noted Orientalist, accompanied his brother, Sir Gore Ouseley, Ambassador extraordinary and Minister plenipotentiary to Persia, and spent ten days in Rio de Janeiro in September of 1810 on his voyage to the Middle East. Sir William was favorably impressed with the city, which he found to be "large and populous" containing "many well-stored shops, particularly druggists, and some warehouses filled with English goods." He was introduced at Court to the Prince Regent and his son and visited several convents and churches where he heard "some fine sacred musick, the vocal parts being admirably performed." Most of his account, however, deals with slavery. He was "shocked, at the appearance of many wretched Africans employed in drawing water near the landing places. Some were chained in pairs by the wrists; others five or six together, by locks attached to heavy iron collars." Many had their backs and shoulders scarred by the lash. He also visited the slave market where he observed "several Africans exposed for sale, whose squalid and sickly aspect offered but few temptatiocs to a purchaser." On the other hand, he wrote "that of the slaves occasionally seen in the streets, many evinced by their looks that they were well fed and kindly treated." Ouseley felt that "reports which accuse several Portuguese of extreme cruelty towards their blacks" were exaggerated and that British treatment of the blacks in the West Indian islands was worse. Ouseley also describes an Amerindian woman who had admitted practicing cannibalism, "whose husband was chief of the Botecudo tribe," and who had been brought to Rio to be civilized. Rio de Janeiro is covered on pages 10–20. Volume I contains several interesting plates: one of the house where he was a guest during his stay; another of the Brazilian cannibal "queen." See also Morier **[848]**.

[848] James Morier. *A Second Journey through Persia, Armenia, and Asia Minor, to Constantinople, between the Years 1810 and 1816. With a Journal of the Voyage by the Brazils and Bombay to the Persian Gulf.* London: Longman, Hurst, Rees, Ormes, and Brown, 1818. xix, 435 pp.

James Morier was part of an entourage that included Sir Gore Ouseley, the English Minister Plenipotentiary to Persia, Mirza Abul Hassan, head of a Persian diplomatic mission that had visited England the previous year, and Sir William Ouseley **[847]**. The ships made Cabo Frio on 11 September 1810 and left Rio de Janeiro on 26 September, though because of light winds, it took almost three days "in getting fairly to sea." Morier found Rio de Janeiro "large, and well built for a colonial town, possessing several handsome churches and large monasteries." However, he was particularly interested in Rio's slaves: "A visit to the slave market impressed us more with the iniquity of this traffic, than anything that could be said or written on the subject. On each side of the street where the market was held, were large rooms, in which the negroes were kept; and, during the day, they were seen in melancholy groupes, waiting to be delivered from the hands of the trader." He added: "It is not infrequent that slaves escape to the woods, where they are almost as frequently retaken. When this is the case, they have an iron collar put about their necks, with a long hooked arm extending from it to impede their progress through the woods, in case they should abscond a second time. Yet, amidst all this misery, it was pleasing to observe the many negroes who frequented the churches; and to see them, in form and profession at least, making a part of a Christian congregation." Morier also describes his audience with the Prince Regent. There is a wood engraving of a black with an iron collar around his neck.

[849] James Prior. *Voyage Along the Eastern Coast of Africa, to Mosambique, Johanna, and Quiloa; to St. Helena; to Rio de Janeiro, Bahia, and Pernambuco in Brazil, in the Nisus Frigate.* London: Richard Phillips, 1819. v, 114 pp.

Prior arrived in Rio de Janeiro on 16 October 1813. He was not favorably impressed with the Brazilian capital and was dismayed at the "general neglect apparent in the houses." He waspishly commented that "it might be conjectured that some of the dirt had been imported along with many of the people from Lisbon." The royal palace he described as "shabby-genteel." As for the Prince-Regent (the future João VI), Prior remarked: "The royal tenant, who is as homely in ideas as appearance, has neither pride nor pomp in any way; he is often without guards, equipages, or attendants of state. His Court, like his house, is plain; ceremony, the current coin of such places, is dispensed with as often as possible by himself." The author is very antislavery. He concludes his description of Rio with the comment: "There is no question among those who best know the country, that, but for the timely arrival of the government, Brazil would have followed, if not preceded, the efforts of the Spanish colonies for independence." After a five-week voyage from Rio de Janeiro, Prior arrived in Salvador toward the end of November. In the former capital of Brazil, he also found "a strong bias towards independence." However, he was not impressed with the city itself. Between the upper and lower parts of Salvador "are several zig-zag or winding paths and streets, scarcely one of which is practicable to a wheeled carriage. Palanquins, therefore, are principally used by those who do not ascend and descend on foot: besides, these avenues are generally narrow and dirty, the habitations mean, the people seemingly poor and squallid objects, peeping their heads through broken panes and disjointed lattices, females of easy access, throwing out their lures to the unwary, and sometimes half-clad children supplicating charity. The summit of the bank alone is the region of fashion; equipages, fine houses, gay people, handsome churches, and some good streets. The beach, or lower town, is the depository of commerce and filth; there the Portuguese seem to make inseparable companions." The city's population was estimated by Prior at "80,000, though commonly estimated higher; some even make it exceed 100,000, but this is much over-rated; the number of whites and mulattoes may be 18,000." The author was least impressed with Recife, where his ship cast anchor on Christmas day: "We saw very little to admire, except a busy, populous place, not at all deficient in dirt, a variety of shops, people bustling to and fro, and boys hawking innumberable parrots through the streets, which are regularly offerred to every Englishman for sale." Despite his misplaced modifier and squeamishness over dirt, Prior provides several useful, brief descriptions of Brazil's three largest towns. He concludes with a short survey of Brazil with considerable attention paid to the Amerindian.

[850] John Shillibeer. *A Narrative of the Briton's Voyage, to Pitcairn's Island; Including an Interesting Sketch of the Present State of the Brazils and of Spanish South America.* 3rd edition. London: Law and Whittaker, 1818. vii, 180 pp.
[The second edition has the same pagination for the chapter on Brazil. It is entitled: *A Narrative of the Briton's Voyage, to Pitcairn's Island.* Taunton: Law and Whittaker, 1817. iii, 179 pp.]

On this voyage Shillibeer visited Brazil, and encountered the survivors of the *Bounty* on Pitcairn's Island. He arrived in Rio de Janeiro on 20 March 1814 and stayed a little more than a week. He was not sympathetic to the Portuguese nor was he overly impressed with the town itself: "The houses are generally well built, some of the streets are good, and all exceedingly filthy. The shops are well supplied with British as well as other wares, and whether the vendor be English or Portuguese, he is equally unconscionable in his demand. Most of the streets are designated by the traders which occupy them." The inhabitants of Rio de Janeiro are "idolaters to fifthiness and not less slaves to it than to superstition." Furthermore, "the laws of this place seem to be very deficient; without money it is impossible to obtain justice, and with it you can prevent its being administered. The murder of a lay-subject is scarcely ever punished; the least insult to the church most rigorously." Shillibeer was outraged by the slave trade and devoted almost half the chapter on Rio to the subject, concluding that "the cruelties these unhappy people are subjected to, is more calculated to fill a volume, than to be brought within the narrow compass of so small a work as this." During his stay, he inquired "the cause of so many slaves lying dead in the streets, and was assured, that when they were ill and thought past recovery, they were disowned by their masters, to evade the expenses of a funeral, and thrown out of doors, where their miserable lives were soon brought to as miserable a termination." The book has sixteen illustrations, two of which deal with Rio de Janeiro. The most important of the latter is "A View of the City of San Sebastian and Isl[d] of Cobrus [sic] Rio de Janeiro." In the upper right hand corner is an insert: "A View of the Aqueduct Rio Janeiro from the Sea." The other illustration drawn by Shillibeer is entitled "A View of Tajuca [sic] Waterfall."

[851] Prince Maximilian of Wied-Neuwied. *Travels in Brazil in the Years 1815, 1816, 1817.* London: Henry Colburn & Co., 1820. x, 335, map, 6 plates. There was also another edition published in the same year by Richard Phillips.
[Translated from *Reise nach Brasilien in den Jahren 1815 bis 1817.* Frankfurt, 1820. 2 vols.]

Maximilian Alexander Philipp, Prinz von Wied-Neuwied, was one of the most famous and thorough of the naturalists to visit Brazil before Independence. This volume (the only one to be translated into English) traces his journey by land along coastal Brazil from Rio de Janeiro northward to Cabo Frio, then through the former captaincy of Paraiba do Sul, northward through the captaincy of Espirito Santo to that of Porto Seguro. As to be expected, most of the book contains detailed descriptions of the flora and fauna of the regions he visited. However, he also gives lengthy and accurate accounts of the many Indians he encountered—especially the Purís and the Botocudos. Also useful for the historian are his descriptions of the towns, churches, economic activities, military preparedness, race relations, fashions, dietary habits, diseases and remedies he observed in the regions he visited—all of which are usually interspersed between his descriptions of plants and animals. Maximilian was one of the few travellers to write about this section of Brazil and there are few scholarly works in English on this part of Portuguese America during the colonial period.

[852] A. P. D. G. *Sketches of Portuguese Life, Manners, Costume, and Character.* London: Geo. B. Whittaker, 1826. xxv, 364 pp.

Though most of the book deals with Portugal, part of chapter XVII (pages 297–307) describes slavery in Brazil during the years João VI was there. The author focuses on Rio de Janeiro and, from an anti-Portuguese, anti-African point of view, discusses the sale and treatment of slaves, crimes committed by them and the punishments they received, and their efforts at manumission. The chapter includes a sketch in color of a Minas merchant bargaining at a slave shop in Rio.

[853] John McLeod. *Narrative of a Voyage, in His Majesty's Late Ship Alceste, to the Yellow Sea, along the Coast of Corea, and through its Numerous Hitherto Undiscovered Islands, to the Island of Lewchew; with an Account of his Shipwreck in the Straits of Gaspar.* London: John Murray, 1817. 288 pp. plates.
There is a recent facsimile edition with an introduction by Shannon McCune and entitled *The Voyage of the Alceste to the Ryukyus and Southeast Asia.* Rutland, Vermont, and Tokyo, Japan: Charles E. Tuttle, 1963.
Borba de Moraes **[20]** feels that the second edition, *Voyage of His Majesty's Ship Alceste, along the Coast of Corea, to the Island of Lewchew,* published in 1818, is the best, though the pagination for Brazil is the same in both editions.

John McLeod, the surgeon of the *Alceste*, a frigate of 46 guns and part of the expedition escorting the British Embassy under the leadership of Lord Jeffrey Amherst to the Court of Peking, spent the last week and a half of March 1816 in Rio de Janeiro. Though most favorably impressed with the natural beauty of the Brazilian capital, he found little to praise during the remainder of his stay. He was of the opinion that the government of Brazil "was perfectly despotic," and wrote that it was "painful to see even Englishmen lose the natural freedom of their character under such dominion." Furthermore, the inhabitants of Rio de Janeiro seemed to be indolent and were "said still to possess their characteristic contempt of all reading." McLeod felt that the slaves in Brazil were "the ugliest race of negroes that can be collected from the African coast." Brazilian males were not much better, being "a squalid, hysterical, grim-looking set; but the ladies, though generally little, and dark-coloured, are not deficient in beauty or expression of countenance." Having arrived in Rio the day after the eighty-two-year-old Maria I had died—a time when "the prices of all black articles felt a sudden and enormous increase"—McLeod was in a good position to describe the state funeral and does. He also made the following perceptive comment on the future of colonial Brazil: "The return of the court to the mother country, it is thought, would be the signal of revolt; for it is not probable the Brazils would long remain in their present fettered state, whilst colonies in all directions around them are freeing themselves from the oppression of the mother country." See also **[854]** and **[855]**.

[854] Henry Ellis. *Journal of the Proceedings of the Late Embassy to China.* London: John Murray, 1817. vii, 526 pp.

Henry Ellis was third commissioner of Lord Amherst's embassy to China, which left England in 1816. The voyagers visited Rio de Janeiro in March of 1816. They arrived on the 21st, the day after Maria I's death, and departed on the last day of the month. Henry Ellis provides interesting information on the events surrounding Maria's death: "The death of the Queen of Portugal, which occurred yesterday, has communicated a character of noisy and luminous melancholy to the harbour and environs of the town; for whilst guns are fired every five minutes from the ships and batteries, the convents and churches are illuminated. Her majesty had an attack of illness six weeks since, from which period she gradually sunk under the infirmities of age. The king [the former Prince Regent, João] was much attached to her, and, notwithstanding her unfortunate derangement, never omitted the daily domestic demonstrations of respect and regard. Her insanity was not uninterrupted, and it is said that her remarks during her lucid intervals displayed ability, and probably produced the greater effect from the peculiar circumstances under which they were made. . . . The body of the Queen of Portugal was deposited on the 23d in the convent of Ajuda. Great expectations had been raised respecting the funeral procession, which certainly were not realised; the only remarkable circumstance was the dress of the chief mourners, described as being the ancient mourning costume of the Portuguese nobility: they were eight in number, and each was accompanied by a servant in rich livery, bearing his armorial shield; the dress, from the distance at which I observed it, resembled that of priests." In general, Ellis was unimpressed with Rio de Janeiro: "St. Sebastian, although at present the residence of a court, and within seven weeks sail of Europe, is in many degrees inferior, in all that contributes to the comforts of civilised life, to the English settlements in India. The state of literature is sufficiently marked by the total impossibility of purchasing books, either of amusement or science; there is, indeed, a public library in the city, but as ill supplied as it is unfrequented." The commissioner found that "articles of living are dear, and of inferior quality, arising entirely from the want of encouragement on the part of the wealthier inhabitants; coarse in their own diet, consisting principally of beef and a very thick vegetable soup, the richest Brazilian Portuguese are either too indolent or too parsimonious to secure improvement in supplies for the table, by giving a larger price for articles of superior quality." Furthermore, "the refinements of social intercourse are little cultivated by the higher orders, who are behind corresponding classes in Europe in the habits and acquirements of civilised life; they neither like nor encourage communication with foreigners; court etiquette, and the superstitious observances of the Catholic religion are their chief occupations." See also **[853]** and **[855]**.

[855] Clarke Abel. *Narrative of a Journey in the Interior of China, and of a Voyage to and from That Country in the Years 1816 and 1817; Containing an Account of the Most Interesting Transactions of Lord Amherst's Embassy to the Court of Pekin, and Observations on the Countries Which It Visited.* London: Longman, Hurst, Rees, Orme, and Brown, 1818. xvi, 420 pp.
[Reprinted by Arno Press & The New York Times, 1971. (The Physician Travelers Series. Edited by Robert M. Goldwyn, M.D.).]

Clarke Abel, the Chief Medical Officer and naturalist to Lord Amherst's mission to China, arrived in Rio de Janeiro in March of 1816, shortly after the death of Maria I. Chapter I (pp. 8–23) describes some of his experiences during his short stay in the Brazilian capital. He had mixed emotions about his visit to Rio de Janeiro: "The strongest efforts of the imagination cannot picture any thing so heavenly as the country, or so disgusting as the town." Abel was especially disturbed by "the fish and vegetable market at the southern extremity of the town, every sense I possessed became disagreeably impressed. My hearing, by the jargon of the different languages used by the slaves who were bartering for their masters, and by the old women who were endeavouring to obtain the highest price for their articles of sale. My sense of sight and of smell, by a horrible combination of every sort of filth, which sent forth the most sickening effluvia that ever exhaled from the corruption of a charnel-house. The very air tasted of putridity, and my clothes felt unctuous to the touch from accidental contamination. Some of my companions who were old travellers felt disposed to joke at my squeamishness." Abel was amazed by the large number of slaves in Rio de Janeiro: "It is affirmed that three-fourths of the population of St. Sebastian are blacks; and, indeed, their visible number is so great, that a stranger unacquainted with the slave-trade, and visiting this city, might imagine that the slaves were its proper inhabitants, and their masters its casual dwellers." On 31 March 1816, he and his companions on the *Alceste* left Rio de Janeiro for the Cape of Good Hope. See also **[853]** and **[854]**.

[856] William Ellis. *Polynesian Researches, During a Residence of Nearly Six Years in the South Sea Islands.* 2 vols. London: Fischer, Son, & Jackson, 1829. xvi, 536 pp.; vii, 576 pp.
[A facsimile edition was published in London by Dawsons of Pall Mall in 1967.]

William Ellis, his wife, and Reverend and Mrs. Threlkeld sailed from Portsmouth in January of 1816 for the Georgian and Society Islands in the South Pacific to undertake missionary work for the London Missionary Society. En route they stopped at Rio de Janeiro, arriving there on 20 March 1816 and remaining for more than six weeks. The early part of William Ellis's stay coincided with that of the Lord Amherst Embassy to China, **[853]**, **[854]**, and **[855]**. Slavery and religion are the chief topics of his six-and-a-half-page account of his visit to Brazil. The author describes the human cargo of "what appeared to be a slave ship returning from the coast of Africa." Later he observed that although "there are, perhaps, few places where the slaves meet with milder treatment, . . . it was most distressing, on passing the slave market, to observe the wretched captives there bought and sold like cattle; or to see two or three interesting looking youths, wearing a thin dress, and having a new red cotton handkerchief round their heads, led through the streets by a slave dealer, who, entering the different houses or workshops, as he passed along, offered the young negroes for sale." In addition, Ellis observed that "in the English or Portuguese families with which we had any opportunities of becoming acquainted, although the domestic slaves did not appear to be treated with that unkindness which the slaves in the field often experience, yet, even here, the whip was frequently employed in a manner, and under circumstances, revolting to every feeling of humanity." As to be expected of a Protestant missionary visiting a Catholic country, "the moral and religious state of the people was the subject of greatest interest." According to Ellis, "ignorance, and disregard of all religious principle, or the substitution of ceremony in its place, appeared everywhere prevalent. To the freedom of the press, and liberty of conscience, the inhabitants were perfect strangers. No book, we were informed, was allowed to be printed or imported for circulation, without the inspection of individuals appointed for this duty, whose censorship, it appeared, was such as to extinguish every source of light, and perpetuate the darkness of the people. Popery is the religion of the country; and we had an opportunity of beholding it in its own element." Ellis visited the royal chapel and reported that "the rich gilding and numerous paintings, the images, massy silver candlesticks, and other costly ornaments of the building; the novel habits and sonorous voices of the priests; and, above all, the music mixed with many of their rites, were certainly adapted to produce a powerful impression upon the feelings of the majority of those who resorted thither; the greater part of whom had perhaps never seen a Bible!" Ellis's description of Rio de Janeiro is found on pp. 10–16 of Volume I.

[857] H. M. Brackenridge. *Voyage to South America, Performed by Order of the American Government, in the Years 1817 and 1818, in the Frigate Congress.* Baltimore, 1819. 2 vols.
[Only Volume I (pages 111–265) treats of Brazil and the Banda Oriental.]

H. M. Brackenridge was secretary to the friendship and fact-finding mission of Caesar A. Rodney, John Graham and Theodore Bland sent by President Monroe to the Plata region. They stopped at Rio de Janeiro at the end of January of 1818 and departed on 9 February, being there for the coronation of João VI three days earlier. The author had "a high opinion of the commercial importance of the city," remarking that "the harbor of New York alone can bear any comparison to this place." In general, Brackenridge enjoyed the food, though he complained about the "wretched inns of the city" and "the narrow and dirty streets without sidewalks." He was amazed at the large number of people he "saw in the street with decorations of one kind or other," but disturbed by the frequent sight of "pairs of lazy lounging soldiers, who it seems are constantly walking in the streets with their bayonets, for the purpose of preventing disturbance." He felt that "their insolent and insulting deportment to the lower classes of people, gave the most certain indications of a despotic government." Like many other travellers, he was impressed by the aqueduct. He marvelled at the general health of the population: "The residents of the city appear to be, especially in the lower classes, extremely lively, active, and cheerful; but from the facilities of gaining a livelihood, and the frequent occurence of their holidays, the greater part of their time is spent in amusements. Few beggars are to be seen, and all except the wretched brutalized slaves, are decently clad. The streets swarm with children." Brackenridge was also astonished by the large numbers of people of color: "All the mechanics are either negroes or mulattoes; and indeed, almost every business which requires attention, and assiduity, is pursued by colored people, a great proportion of whom are free." He added that "the prejudice with respect to complexion, did not appear to me as strong as in the United States. This may be owing to the great number of persons of color, who own large fortunes, and possess wealth and consequence. I remarked several mulatto priests, and in one instance a negro." Brackenridge was also an astute political observer, if not a prophet, remarking that "it would be utterly impossible to reduce the Brazils once more to the colonial state, after having once enjoyed an exemption from the colonial restrictions." He provides a very good survey of the political and economic as well as the geographical characteristics of Portuguese America (including Montevideo and the Banda Oriental): "The only empires that can be compared to the Brazil, in point of magnitude, are those of China, Russia, and the

United States; and although at present the least in point of population, the day will come, when it will be the greatest. Brazil is, in fact, the body and heart of South America; although covering a less extent than the part which belongs to Spain, it possesses great superiority in being more compact, and possessing greater facilities of internal communication. It may seem premature at this day to institute a comparison between the Brazils and our country; but the time will come, when such a comparison will appear natural, and even unavoidable."

[858] Jacques Arago. *Narrative of a Voyage Round the World in the Uranie and Physicienne Corvettes Commanded by Captain Freycinet during the Years 1817, 1818, 1819, 1820.* London: Treuttel and Wurtz, Treuttel, Jun. and Richter, 1823. vi, xxvii, 297.

Arago was a draftsman on the French Freycinet scientific expedition which visited Rio de Janeiro early in December of 1817 and most of January of 1818. He described the entire voyage in a series of 164 letters, of which 19 refer to Brazil. His letters are enjoyable to read: amusing, caustic, and, at times, perceptive. He covers almost all aspects of life in Rio de Janeiro. Arago attacks the indolence of the inhabitants and points out that the city "contains one hundred and twenty thousand souls, five sixths of whom are purchased slaves. Fifty vessels are engaged in the slave trade." Several of his letters are devoted to the topics of slavery and the slave trade. He liked the outside appearance of most of Rio's houses, but felt that "the arrangement of the interior is tasteless." Arago was not very impressed by Rio's public buildings: "As to remarkable buildings, they are extremely rare. The Benedictine convent is the only one that is at all conspicuous. I was shown the royal palace, and I had to seek it again: it may be compared to most of the houses of tradesmen in the rue St. Honoré." The streets were reduced to quagmires in wet weather. But "officious negroes post themselves on such occasions at the corners of the streets, and for the *moderate* sum of eight or ten sous, carry you across in their arms, which are as black with mud as with their natural colour, and set you down on the other side. Sometimes, too, they pretend to slip, drop you in the midst of the mire, and laugh among themselves at your consequent embarrassment." The monks in Rio he described as "an ignorant and debauched crew, sufficiently powerful to place themselves out of the reach of the law, but still too weak to seize the supreme authority; a scandalous troop of sluggards and libertines." Arago also felt Portuguese honors had been debased: "The right of wearing the order of Christ without having deserved it now costs more than four hundred piastres, which are paid into the exchequer at Rio. It has cost the first *castrato* more than that."

[859] Henry Chamberlain. *Views and Costumes of the City and Neighbourhood of Rio de Janiero, Brazil, from Drawings Taken by Lieutenant Chamberlain, Royal Artillery, During the Years 1819 and 1820, with Descriptive Explanations.* London: Thomas M'Lean, 1822.

[Chamberlain's 36 colored engravings plus additional illustrations and the original English text were reprinted in Rubens Borba de Moraes, ed. *Vistas e Costumes da Cidade e Arredores do Rio de Janeiro em 1819–1820 Segundo Desenhos Feitos pelo T.*[te] *Chamberlain, da Artilharia Real durante os Anos de 1819 a 1820 com Descriçoes.* Rio de Janeiro and São Paulo: Livraria Kosmos Editora, 1943. 234 pp.]

Important for the social and architectural history of Rio de Janeiro and its environs. Drawings and descriptions (most of the latter at least a page long) include the church of Nossa Senhora da Gloria, a view of the city of Rio de Janeiro from the anchorage, a Brazilian family, a chaise and *cadeira*, the Largo da Gloria, slaves carrying a woman in a hammock, the western side of the harbor of Rio de Janeiro, Brazilians celebrating the feast of Espirito Santo or Pentecost, the palace, the eastern side of the harbor of Rio de Janeiro, muleteers, Botafogo bay, a peddler and his slave, Brazilians Gossiping, a market stall, the waterfall of Tijuca, the lake called "Lagoa de Freitas," the chapel of Nossa Senhora da Boa Viagem, the estate of Sir Sidney Smith ("Bragança"), a cart drawn by oxen, views of the city of Rio de Janeiro, the Tijuca mountains, Fort Santa Cruz, the "Lazaretto," formerly a hospital for lepers, the slave market, black porters, sick Blacks, galley slaves, food being carried to the prison, and a funeral procession for Blacks.

[860] Alexander Caldcleugh. *Travels in South America during the Years 1819–20–21 Containing an Account of the Present State of Brazil, Buenos Ayres, and Chile.* 2 vols. London: John Murray, 1825. xii, 373 pp.; viii, 380 pp.

Caldcleugh was part of the entourage of Edward Thornton, the British Minister at the Court of Rio de Janeiro. He sailed to America on the *Superb* with a small squadron under the command of Sir Thomas Hardy and arrived in Rio de Janeiro on 23 October 1819. He remained at the Portuguese capital until 18 January 1821 when he sailed for Buenos Aires. He returned again to Brazil on 18 July 1821, after a six-month absence. Caldcleugh was an excellent observer. On the whole, he liked Rio de Janeiro, commenting that "however soured the European may sometimes be with the want of comfort, or the heat, yet he will generally acknowledge, that this spot has not been surpassed, if equalled, by any other that has fallen under his observation." He describes slavery in some detail was well as the slave trade, pointing out that "one of the streets is filled with the warehouses for slaves, where the unhappy negro is prepared for sale. It is crowded with planters and merchants, soon after the arrival of any slave ship." He admired several of Rio's churches and monasteries. "The opera . . .was not conducted in that way which an European audience would have demanded. No great attention to cleanliness was paid, and it cannot be denied that some of the Venuses of the ballet were not exactly of an European tint, but in their climate, great allowances must be made, and the first theatre in South America must not be too severely criticized. The performances were alternately Portuguese and Italian." As to be expected from an Englishman who wished to promote trade with Brazil, Caldcleugh had comments on the topic of manufactures, which he felt "in this part of Brazil are scarcely worthy of notice. Some very coarse cottons and hammocks, and some articles of saddlery come from the interior." But changes were taking place: "The colonial system which was strictly preserved until the arrival of the court, kept the country in a state of ignorance of many of those beautiful articles of English manufacture, now so greedily purchased by all." Though the early part of the first volume described his experiences in Rio de Janeiro, the latter part of the second contained an account of his experiences in Minas Gerais. In Vila Rica, he found "few buildings worthy of note. The churches about fourteen in number, many of which were erected by the vast wealth and piety of the first miners, have little to recommend them. The houses are generally built of stone, with tiled roofs, and of two stories, with heavy wooden balconies. Very little glass is used, owing, perhaps, to the difficulty of conveyance. The streets are well but roughly paved; and as it is impossible to proceed in any direction without ascending or descending, they become excessively fatiguing to the feet. The usual common trades, such as shoemakers, tailors, and saddlers abound; but almost every manufactured article is brought from Rio de Janeiro, eighty leagues distant, two or three times a week. In exchange for which, gold, precious stones, cotton of inferior quality, and coarse cotton cloths, cheese, bacon, and a few other articles, are sent down to the coast."

[861] Thaddeus Bellingshausen. *The Voyage of Captain Bellingshausen to the Antarctic Seas 1819–1821.* Translated from the Russian. Edited by Frank Debenham. London: Hakluyt Society, 1945. 2 v. xxx. 474 pp. [Hakluyt Society, 2nd series, nos. 91–92. Reprinted by Kraus Reprint Limited.]

In the account of his expedition to Antarctica in the early nineteenth century, Captain Thaddeus Bellingshausen described two visits to Rio de Janeiro, a city which he felt "in general presents a disgustingly dirty appearance." The first, in November of 1819, lasted three weeks, during which time he obtained fresh provisions and rest for his crew. Bellingshausen was particularly impressed with the slave market which he describes in some detail as well as his audience with João VI (I, 68–76). On his way back to Russia, at the end of February 1821, he again stopped in Rio de Janeiro, this time for repairs. He provides an interesting account of the stormy days that city experienced before the departure of João VI for Portugal. He also describes his meeting with Pedro, the Prince Regent, and his consort Leopoldina of Austria, discusses the high cost of living in Brazil, and gives a brief sketch of the general economy and trade of Portuguese America. With the exception of the derogatory remark about Rio's cleanliness, he speaks well of his visits to Brazil (II, 440–456). Leaving Rio near the end of April, Bellingshausen sailed for Portugal where he arrived several days before the Portuguese Court did. He spent from 17 June to 6 July in Portugal and recounts the actions of the Portuguese Cortes and the reception João VI received upon his arrival in Lisbon (II, 460–464). 38 plates. Maps.

[862] Gilbert Farquhar Mathison. *Narrative of a Visit to Brazil, Chile, Peru, and the Sandwich Islands, during the Years 1821 and 1822.* London: Charles Knight, 1825. xii, 478 pp.

Mathison sailed from Lisbon on 27 May 1821 on the *Vasco da Gama*, an 800-ton Indiaman, bound to Rio de Janeiro, Manila and Macao. Seven chapters are devoted to Brazil. Chapter one describes his voyage to and his first impressions of Rio de Janeiro. The next three chapters describe his excursions to the environs of the Brazilian capital: Novo Friburgo, Canta Gallo, Aldea da Pedra and São Fidele. Chapters five and six recount his experiences returning to Rio de Janeiro and his visits to Praia Grande and Santa Cruz. Chapter seven (pp. 125–170) contains a general survey of Brazilian History. Mathison describes church processions thusly: "Ladies gladly seize the opportunity, which gruff papas and jealous husbands seldom otherwise afford, of showing themselves in public; and gratifying their vanity by displaying a numerous retinue of female slaves, who follow them in file along the streets."

[863] Thomas H. Bennett. *A Voyage from the United States to South America, Performed during the Years 1821, 1822 & 1823. Embracing a Description of the City of Rio de Janeiro, in Brazil; of Every Port of Importance in Chili; of Several in Lower Peru.* Newburyport, Massachusetts, 1823. 86 pp.

XXIII. Diplomacy [Nos. 864–890]

A. Great Britain [Nos. 864–868]

Though other writers have commented on special aspects of Great Britain's diplomatic activity in the early nineteenth-century Portugal and Brazil, the best general survey on the subject is Alan K. Manchester's *British Preeminence in Brazil* **[864]**, which focuses on the years 1808 through independence.

[864] Alan K. Manchester. *British Preeminence in Brazil. Its Rise and Decline.* Chapel Hill: The University of North Carolina Press, 1933. xi, 371 pp.
[Reprinted: New York: Octagon Books, 1964.]

Manchester reviews the Anglo-Portuguese treaties of 1642–1654–1661 and the Methuen treaty of 1703 before focusing on the nineteenth century and England's role in the transfer of the Portuguese Court to Brazil. He analyzes the treaty of 1810, discusses Portuguese designs on the Banda Oriental and describes British reaction to Brazil's influence in the Plata region. Manchester recounts English efforts to abolish the Portuguese slave trade, 1808–1822, and her role in the recognition of Brazilian independence. Based on archival as well as printed primary materials.

[865] Alan Krebs Manchester. "The Foundation of British Pre-Eminence in Brazil," Ph.D. Dissertation: Duke University, 1930.

Earlier version of **[864]**.

1. Contemporary Documents, 1807–1822 [Nos. 866–868]

Charles K. Webster **[866]** has published an excellent collection of documents on independence, a number of them covering Brazil, 1812–1822. Edward Howard **[867]** has organized the memoirs of Sir William Sidney Smith, Britain's Commander-in-Chief of its South American Naval Station, 1807–1809. Gerald S. Graham and Robin A. Humphreys **[868]** have published some of the most important correspondence of the commanders-in-chief of Britain's South American Naval Station for the years 1807–1823.

[866] Charles K. Webster. *Britain and the Independence of Latin America, 1812–1830. Select Documents from the Foreign Office Archives.* 2 vols. London: Oxford University Press, 1938. xx, 560 pp.; xv, 573 pp.

Excellent collection of documents from the British Foreign Office. Volume I contains a useful introduction (pp. 3–79) and correspondence with Latin America. Brazil is covered on pp. 165–326 and includes all or part of 96 documents, 39 of which cover the years 1812–1822, inclusive. Volume II contains communications with European States and the United States regarding Latin American independence. Although volume II includes material on Brazil, it is nowhere as extensive as that in volume I. The correspondence on Brazil includes information on the proposal to annex Argentina, the invasion and occupation of the Banda Oriental (Uruguay), blockades, commerce, internal affairs in Brazil, and the slave trade.

[867] Edward Howard. *Memoirs of Admiral Sir Sidney Smith. K.C.B., &c.* 2 vols. London: Richard Bentley, 1839. vii, 400 pp.; vii, 411 pp.

Chapters six through ten of volume II cover Sir William Sidney Smith's Luso-Brazilian career. On 27 October 1807, Smith was appointed commander-in-chief of a squadron sent to the coast of Portugal where, after assisting in the departure of the Portuguese Court to Brazil, he declared "the Tagus in a state of blockade." Howard criticizes the Portuguese Court for leaving Portugal: "Much, very much, of turgid eloquence has been displayed, and many the attempts made upon our feelings to excite sentiments of admiration in our bosoms at the sublime and solemn spectacle of the Prince and most of the magnates of the land nobly expatriating themselves, rather than see the land of their fathers overrun by the invader and the oppressor. If the land had been so dear to them, the fugitives should have staid and consecrated their attachment to it by the enriching the soil with their blood." But, Howard continued, "by flying, Portugal, for a time, became a province of

France, and the South American colonies did *not* fall into the possession of England. . . . The Portuguese dynasty was preserved, and England lost a most favourable opportunity of turning the channels of South American commerce towards our own shores exclusively. They must have fallen under our protection, had not the Portuguese family gone to them and encumbered them with an European court, and disgusted them by European prejudices." On 15 January 1808, Sir Sidney Smith was replaced by Sir Charles Cotton. After almost two months of preparations, Smith proceeded to Brazil as commander-in-chief of Britain's South American station and arrived in Rio de Janeiro on 17 May 1808. Though decorated by Prince Regent João, Smith soon took up the cause of Carlota Joaquina. As his biographer phrased it, "almost from the very beginning of Sir Sidney Smith's command, the court of the Brazils had split into two distinct parties,—that of the Prince, and that of the Princess. Sir Sidney was considered to be the leader of the latter, the chief political object of which was to place the Princess at the head of an independent government, (under the name and representing the authority of her brother, Ferdinand VII.,) to be established in the provinces of La Plata." But, as Howard points out, "this project was discountenanced by the British government, and was also very distasteful to the Prince of Brazil, and, consequently, Sir Sidney's position at the court ceased to be so agreeable to him as might have been expected from all that previously occurred before our hero became mixed up with politics." On 7 August 1809, Sir Sidney was back in England. A little less than a year later, he was promoted to the rank of Vice-Admiral. Both excerpts as well as entire transcripts of Smith's correspondence are found in these five chapters. The compilation and the commentary was done by Howard, author of *Rattlin the Reefer.*

[868] Gerald S. Graham and Robin A. Humphreys, eds. *The Navy and South America, 1807–1823. Correspondence of the Commanders-in-Chief on the South American Station.* London: Printed for the Navy Records Society, 1962. xxxiv, 394 pp.

Throughout this correspondence there are references to Brazil. The British admirals frequently were based in Rio de Janeiro and included information on what was happening at the Portuguese Court there. Portugal's intentions vis-à-vis the Plata region were often the cause of concern. The Pernambucan revolt of 1817 received mention. There is also a great deal of information on the events of 1821 and 1822, leading to the return to Portugal of João VI in the former year and Brazilian independence under Pedro I in the latter. The correspondence is well annotated.

B. United States [Nos. 869–882]

Dauril Alden **[869]** provides an interesting note on Pombal's support of Galloway's Plan of Union (1774). Raul d'Eça **[870]** conjectures that Jefferson's meeting with Brazilians interested in independence **[721]** might have been responsible for Portugal's failure to ratify its 1786 treaty with the United States. Raul d'Eça **[871]** examines the role of colonial Brazil in U. S.-Portuguese diplomacy in the late eighteenth and early nineteenth centuries. An early study of the relations of the United States with the Portuguese Court in Brazil is by Joseph Agan **[872]**, who focuses on the neutrality question. The standard survey of U. S.-Brazilian relations in the nineteenth century is that by Lawrence Hill **[873]**. Though dealing more with the period after independence, Charles L. Chandler **[874]** makes several references to U. S.-Brazilian relations. Phil Brian Johnson **[875]** contributes a devastating evaluation of a "diplomatic dullard," Thomas Sumter, the first U. S. minister to the Portuguese Court at Rio de Janeiro. Joseph Agan **[876]** and Martin I. J. Griffin **[877]** provide studies of Abbé José Francisco Corrêa de Serra, the Portuguese minister to the United States, 1816–1820. In her doctoral dissertation, Mary Ellis Kahler **[878]** discusses relations between Brazil and the United States, 1815–1825, with a special reference to the revolutions of 1817 and 1824. Stanley Hilton **[879]** in his study of Brazilian independence argues that the United States and Brazil had little in common. In his dissertation, William L. Cumiford **[880]** studies political ideology in U.S.-Brazilian relations during the nineteenth century. Richard C. Froehlich **[881]** studies the role of the United States Navy in U. S.-Brazilian relations, 1822–1871.

[869] Dauril Alden. "The Marquis of Pombal and the American Revolution," *The Americas* 17:4 (April 1961), pp. 369–376.

Discusses Pombal's support of the Galloway Plan of Union which called for a subordinate parliament in Anglo America. The author argues that the reason behind Pombal's interest in North America was his fear that hostilities there would jeopardize British support for Portugal's impending war in South America. Based largely on archival and printed sources. 29 notes.

[870] Raul d'Eça. "A Little-Known Episode in the Early Negotiations Between the United States and Portugal for a Treaty of Commerce—Was Brazil the Cause for the Failure of the 1786 Treaty?," in Costa, ed., *Actas* **[92]**, II, 209–217.

Conjectures that the meeting at Nîmes, France, between José Joaquim da Maia, the young Brazilian trying to promote the independence of Brazil, and Thomas Jefferson might have been the reason for Portugal's failure to ratify the treaty of 1786 which had been signed by the Portuguese envoy and the American plenipotentiaries in London—especially since Portugal earlier had ordered her vessels to protect U. S. shipping against the Barbary pirates. Based mainly on records of the Continental Congress and the Adams and Jefferson papers. 12 notes.

[871] Raul d'Eça. "Colonial Brazil As an Element in the Early Diplomatic Negotiations Between the United States and Portugal, 1776–1808," in A. Curtis Wilgus, ed., *Colonial Hispanic America* (Washington, D. C.: The George Washington Press, 1936), pp. 551–558.

Because of the outbreak of hostilities in Anglo-America, Portugal, on 5 July 1776, prohibited North American ships from entering Portuguese ports. Though officially Portugal proclaimed itself neutral during the American Revolution, its "neutrality continued to be weakly enforced in favor of British ships." In 1783, the 1776 prohibitions were repealed and U. S. independence recognized. The author discusses efforts of the United States to negotiate a treaty of commerce with Portugal. Though John Adams and Thomas Jefferson wanted American ships admitted into Brazilian ports, the Portuguese desired to sell Brazilian products via Portugal. A treaty was finally signed in 1786, but without concessions on Brazilian trade. It was never ratified by Portugal. However, U. S. interests in Brazil continued to grow, though, as Secretary Pickering wrote in 1800, "unless Portugal would permit a commercial intercourse with her American colony, the Brazils, a treaty would seem to be of no great moment." Based extensively on printed primary materials and State Department archives. 26 notes.

[872] Joseph Agan. *The Diplomatic Relations of the United States and Brazil.* Vol. I. *The Portuguese Court at Rio de Janeiro.* Paris: Jouve, 1926. 146 pp.

Discusses the actions of the United States minister Thomas Sumter **[875]** at the Portuguese Court in Rio de Janeiro. Most of this study deals with the question of neutrality—an important concern for the United States because of Napoleon's actions in Europe, the events leading up to the War of 1812, and the hostilities themselves. Portugal with her activity in the Rio de la Plata region also had an interest in the subject of neutrality, since, among other things, the Uruguayan patriot José Artigas had been commissioning privateers to harass Portuguese shipping. A number of these privateers were based in Baltimore. The remaining four volumes of this projected five-volume study were never published. There is a bibliography on pp. 139–146.

[873] Lawrence F. Hill. *Diplomatic Relations Between the United States and Brazil.* Durham, North Carolina: Duke University Press, 1932. x, 322 pp.

Good account of U. S.-Brazilian relations based mostly on U. S. State Department documents. Hill gives a detailed description of the attitudes of the United States and its officials (both home and abroad) toward the Portuguese Court in Brazil, Brazilian independence, and the reign of Pedro I. Through the eyes and actions of such Americans as the merchant Henry Hill and Thomas Sumter, Jr. **[875]**, respectively the first consul and the first minister to João's court in Brazil, Sumter's replacement, John Graham, the consul and later chargé, Condy Raguet, and his successor, William Tudor, the former American consul at Lima, Peru, the author describes a number of problems the two countries encountered. Hill also discusses some of the difficulties the Brazilian envoy José Rebello faced in the United States. There is a bibliography on pages 306–316.

[874] Charles Lyon Chandler. *Inter-American Acquaintances.* 2nd ed. Sewanee, Tennessee: The University Press, 1917. vii, 187 pp.

A series of essays that include such scattered information on Brazil-United States relations as presidential instructions to Colonel David Humphreys, U. S. minister to Portugal, regarding possible trade between the United States and Brazil; trade between Salem, Massachusetts, and Brazil during the first half of the nineteenth century, and the early U. S. ministers and charges d'affaires to Brazil. The remainder of the book deals with postindependence relations. There is an excellent chronological table on pages 179–187. Unfortunately, there is no index.

[875] Phil Brian Johnson. "Diplomatic Dullard: The Career of Thomas Sumter, Jr. and Diplomatic Relations of the United States with the Portuguese Court in Brazil, 1809–1821," [in *Dependency Unbends: Case Studies in Inter-American Relations*], *West Georgia College Studies in the Social Sciences* 17 (June 1978), pp. 21–35.

Sumter's own words—"Mr. Madison has spoiled a . . . cotton planter and only made a clumsy courtier of me"—provide a good description of the South Carolinian's diplomatic career, especially the ten years he spent in Brazil as Minister Plenipotentiary to the Portuguese Court. According to Johnson, Thomas Sumter, Jr., "the man selected by the Department of State for its first major diplomatic appointment in Latin America," was "a dismal choice, inept, contentious, boorish, barely literate, and only mildly interested in the post." After describing Sumter's poor start in diplomatic service as secretary of legation in Paris in 1802, Johnson shows how Sumter's "bumptious and quarellsome nature" also hindered his work as a diplomat in Brazil. The South Carolinian's chief job in Brazil was threefold: 1) to secure a commercial agreement with the Portuguese Court in Brazil; 2) furnish the Department of State with information on Brazil's commercial resources; 3) obtain intelligence on Spanish American revolutionary movements. Because of strong English influence in Brazil, Sumter failed to gain a satisfactory trade treaty. He also failed to provide his superiors in Washington with data on Brazil. Secretary of State John Quincy Adams later wrote that "information possessed at this Department is so slight and imperfect, that it is not possible to found upon it any precise instructions." Sumter probably best accomplished his third task—that of providing the State Department with information on the activities of revolutionaries in Argentina, Chile and Peru. The most controversial problem Sumter had to face was that of neutral rights—a question that severely strained U. S.-Portuguese relations. Portugal appears to have been the chief offender from 1812–1816 and the United States from 1816–1820. In the War of 1812, Portugal's sympathies were clearly with Britain. Though Portugal and Portuguese America were officially neutral, their neutrality was "limited almost exclusively to prohibitions forbidding the disposition of prizes in her ports." Portugal, the author points out, "violated the spirit of neutrality and displayed official favoritism toward Great Britain and antipathy for the United States." However, during the years 1816–1820, the United States did little to prevent American privateers from seizing Portuguese shipping and later refused to pay reparations for damages inflicted. In 1820, the Portuguese minister to Washington, the Abbe Corrêa da Serra **[876]** and **[877]**, estimated these damages at 65 ships and 81 million dollars. There were also problems regarding United States' attitudes toward the Pernambucan revolt of 1817. Perhaps John Quincy Adams best summed up Sumter's stay in Brazil: "Our relations with Portugal and Brazil have not been well cultivated. Their importance has not been duly estimated. The Minister, who has been there these ten years, was not a fortunate choice. His own temper is not happy. He has been repeatedly involved in quarrels of personal punctilio, even with members of the royal family. He is excessively argumentative, and spins out everything into endless discussions without ever bringing anything to a close." Based on archival as well as printed primary and secondary materials. 27 notes.

[876] Joseph Eugene Agan. "Corrêa da Serra," *The Pennsylvania Magazine of History and Biography* 49:1 (1925), pp. 1–43.

Good biographical sketch of José Francisco Corrêa da Serra (1750–1823), "Minister Plenipotentiary, scientist, historian, philosopher, knight of the Orders of Nossa Senhora da Conceição, and of Christ (successor to the Templars in Portugal), councillor to the king, economist, politician, one-time priest, and member of most of the learned societies of his time," including the American Philosophical Society. A frequent exile because of his liberal tendencies, this renowned botanist twice visited the United States. The first time he came to America (1797–1798), Corrêa da Serra served as Kosciusko's chaplain. He quickly won admittance into the best circles and eventually became friends with four American presidents: Jefferson, Madison, Monroe and John Quincy Adams. Jefferson found Corrêa da Serra to be "the greatest collection, and the best digest of science in books, men, and things that I have ever met with and with these the most amiable and engaging character." In 1816, in the middle of his second sojourn in America (1812–1820), he was appointed the Portuguese minister in Washington by the Prince Regent, the future João VI. Upon hearing the news of his friend's appointment, Jefferson remarked: "This I hope, will give him to us for life. Nor will it interfere with his botanical rambles or journeys. The government of Portugal is so peaceable and inoffensive, that it never has any altercations with its friends. If their minister abroad writes them once a quarter that all is well, they desire no more." Unfortunately for Corrêa da Serra, because of João VI's invasion of the Banda Oriental in June of 1816, the issue of neutrality became a bone of contention between Portugal and the United States and occupied his attention for the next four years. Artigas of Uruguay had recourse to privateers, a number of whom were based in Baltimore. Corrêa da Serra put constant pressure on U. S. officials to promulgate stricter neutrality laws and to punish those involved in privateering operations. He also sought indemnities for Portugal. In addition, Corrêa da Serra had to contend with U. S. reaction to what was to be the short-lived Pernambucan republican revolt of 1817. These controversies injured his earlier friendships with a number of Americans. When he left the United States to accept an appointment in João VI's council, Corrêa da Serra was a changed man. As Robert Walsh explained it to Jefferson: "All the happiness of Mr. Corrêa was destroyed by his appointment as minister. He became fretful, suspicious, valetudinary, and has been more or less wretched ever since." Based chiefly on printed primary sources. 178 notes. An appendix lists Corrêa da Serra's chief scientific and historical works.

[877] Martin I. J. Griffin. "Sketch of the Abbé Joseph Francis Corrêa de Serra," *Records of the American Catholic Historical Society of Philadelphia* 14:2 (June 1903), pp. 129–140.

Pioneering study of the Portuguese-born and Italian-educated priest and botanist who represented Portugal as its Minister to the United States, 1816–1820. Perpetual secretary and one of the founders of The Royal Academy of Sciences at Lisbon, Corrêa da Serra achieved international renown for his scientific studies. He was highly esteemed in the United States. In 1817, H. M. Brackenridge **[857]** dedicated his *Views of Louisiana* to Corrêa da Serra, calling him "the most enlightened foreigner that has ever visited the United States." The author quotes at length from other comments made about Corrêa da Serra by Thomas Jefferson, Francis Walker Gilmer, Fanny Wright, the Rev. William Kinsey, Robert Walsh and Mathew Carey. Based on printed sources. 1 illus. 3 notes.

[878] Mary Ellis Kahler. "Relations Between Brazil and the United States, 1815–1825, with Special Reference to the Revolutions of 1817 and 1824," (Ph.D. Dissertation: The American University, 1968). 334 pp.

Examines relations between Brazil and the United States during the crucial decade 1815–1825. The Pernambucan Revolt of 1817 stimulated interest in Brazil, even as the Portuguese minister to Washington, José Francisco Corrêa da Serra, strained United States/Portuguese relations with his diplomatic blundering. The Confederation of the Equator, 1824, did not attract official United States government attention, but it did involve several citizens of the United States in a private capacity. Commerce between Brazil and the United States grew in spite of British mercantile privileges and was another stimulus to Brazil/United States association. Sources include diplomatic and consular archival materials and printed primary sources.
DAI 29/04-A (p. 1194).

[879] Stanley E. Hilton. "The United States and Brazilian Independence," in Russell-Wood, ed., *From Colony to Nation* **[88]**, pp. 109–129.

Though the United States was the first country to recognize the independence of Brazil, the author argues that "the United States and Brazil had practically nothing in common other than their geographic location in the Western Hemisphere, and that their political intercourse was therefore characterized more by friction and divergence than by mutual understanding." U. S. prejudices towards Brazil's Catholicism and monarchical form of government were perhaps best summed up by Consul Henry Hill in Rio de Janeiro in 1821 who wrote that Brazilians were "immoral, ignorant and superstitious" and "wholly incapable of self-Government." Based mostly on archival and printed primary materials. 55 notes.

[880] William Lloyd Cumiford. "Political Ideology in United States-Brazilian Relations, 1808–1894," (Ph.D. Dissertation: Texas Tech University, 1977). 206 pp.

Studies the influence of political ideas in the diplomatic relations of the United States and Brazil from 1808 to 1894. Special emphasis is given to the period of Brazilian independence (1821–1824), the Rebello Mission to Washington (1824–1830), Brazilian reaction to American Manifest Destiny (1831–1860), and the Brazilian Naval Revolt. Principal sources used were American and Brazilian diplomatic dispatches, instructions, consular notes and legation reports, newspapers, the works of travellers and statesmen, and important secondary studies.
DAI 38/08-A (p. 4999).

[881] Richard Carl Froehlich. "The United States Navy and Diplomatic Relations with Brazil, 1822–1871," (Ph.D. Dissertation: Kent State University, 1971). 564 pp.

Argues that the Brazilian Squadron of the United States Navy "consistently sought to lay the foundations for mutually satisfactory relations between the two nations." It also "managed to successfully resolve much of the acrimony caused by American diplomats," not only in Brazil but in the Plata region. The early chapters discuss events leading up to independence as well as Brazil's war with Argentina over the Banda Oriental.
DAI 32/09-A (p. 5131).

1. Contemporary Documents, 1807–1822 [No. 882]

William R. Manning **[882]** has gathered the diplomatic correspondence of the United States with Latin America regarding the latter's efforts at independence. A number of the documents deal with Brazil.

[882] William R. Manning. *Diplomatic Correspondence of the United States Concerning the Independence of the Latin American Nations.* 3 vols. New York: Oxford University Press, 1925. xxxii, xxx, xxxii, 2228 pp. [Volume I contains pp. 1–666; Volume II, pages 667–1428; Volume III, 1429–2189.]

Volume I (pp. 1–315) contains communications to Latin America from the United States. Of the 112 documents which cover the period to the end of 1822, 8 deal with Brazil. Five of these are addressed to Thomas Sumter **[875]**, U. S. minister to Brazil: nos. 3, 39, 43, 47, 65. Another (44) is to Rodney, Graham and Bland, Special Commissioners to South America; there are also letters to Sumter's successor, John Graham (78), and John James Appleton, U. S. Charge d'Affaires at Rio de Janeiro (94). Also included in volume I is a letter to the Portuguese Minister to the United States (no. 38) the Abbé José Corrêa de Serra **[876]** and **[877]**. Volume II includes Part III—Communications from Brazil to the United States, 1810–1829 (pp. 667–868). Of the 109 documents from Brazil, 57 cover the period prior to the end of 1822. Eighteen letters are from P. Sartoris, Acting Consul of the United States at Rio de Janeiro, sixteen are from Thomas Sumter **[875]**, the U. S. Minister to Brazil, and seven from Woodbridge Odlin, U. S. Consul at Bahia. Because of Portuguese and Brazilian activity in the Banda Oriental, there is also some useful correspondence in Volume III, especially Part XIV—Communications from Uruguay. Six of the eight documents in this section (pp. 2173–2189) deal with the period before 1822. There is an index at the end of volume III for all three volumes.

C. Russia [Nos. 883–888]

Lewis A. Tambs **[883]** describes an eighteenth-century Russian attempt to gain a foothold in Brazil. Russell H. Bartley **[884]** and **[885]** surveys the role of Russia regarding Latin American independence and then focuses on **[886]** the inception of Russo-Brazilian relations, 1808–1828. Francesca Miller **[887]** and **[888]** also discusses early Russo-Brazilian relations.

[883] Lewis A. Tambs. "Anglo-Russian Enterprises against Hispanic South America: 1732–1737," *The Slavonic and East European Review* 48:112 (July 1970), pp. 357–372.

Traces the attempts by English merchant adventurers and the Russian government of Anna Ivanovna to gain a foothold near Lagoa dos Patos in present-day Rio Grande do Sul. "Dissension, doubledealing and lack of official support" frustrated private English efforts, and court intrigue, the Russo-Turkish war and the opposition of the British government resulted in the eventual failure of the Russian enterprise. Through almost the entire scheme were woven the shady dealings of the Portuguese slaver and shipmaster Antônio da Costa, who had established himself in London during the 1730s. Based on some archival but mostly printed sources. 68 notes.

[884] Russell Howard Bartley. "Russian and Latin American Independence, 1808–1826," (Ph.D. Dissertation: Stanford University, 1971). 349 pp.

Examines Russian responses to the independence movements in Latin America during the early decades of the nineteenth century, with a special emphasis on Brazil. Analyzes the social, economic and geopolitical motives of Russia's American policy. Russia's demand for tropical products was facilitated when the Portuguese Court moved to Brazil. Rio de Janeiro became a frequent port of call for Russian fleets of exploration and supply destined for the Pacific basin. After Napoleon's defeat, Russia supported the Royalist cause in America, hoping to further her own interests in that way. By 1818 that policy was seen to be impractical and Russia gave Spain and Portugal little more than moral support in their quarrels with their colonies. Meanwhile, Russia dealt with the newly independent Americans whenever it furthered her interests.
DAI 32/10-A (pp. 5699–5700).

[885] Russell H. Bartley. *Imperial Russia and the Struggle for Latin American Independence, 1808–1828*. Austin: University of Texas Press, 1978. xv, 236 pp.

This book, a revision of the author's doctoral dissertation **[884]**, contains a number of scattered references to Brazil. Since few of these points on Russo-Brazilian relations are developed in more than one or two pages, those interested solely in Brazil should consult Bartley's article on that topic **[886]**. *Imperial Russia* is well documented and based on archival research in Russia, Portugal, Brazil, Spain and the United States. There is a useful bibliography on pp. 203–223. There are seven illustrations and a number of valuable tables on Russian, Portuguese and Brazilian trade and shipping.

[886] Russell H. Bartley. "The Inception of Russo-Brazilian Relations (1808–1828)," *The Hispanic American Historical Review* 56:2 (May 1976), pp. 217–240.

After the first Russian circumnavigation of the globe in the early nineteenth century, Brazil was seen as an important source of supplies for ships sailing around Cape Horn. At the same time, there was a growing demand in Russia for such Brazilian products as sugar, cotton, coffee, indigo, cacao, tapioca, vanilla, cinnamon, clove, pepper, rum, tropical woods and other commodities. Soon direct trade between Brazil and Russia was attempted by Russian as well as Portuguese merchant vessels and encouraged by such Portuguese trading firms as that of Dionizio Pedro Lopes and Russian merchants as Ivan Kremer, both stationed in St. Petersburg. Though the 1798 Russo-Portuguese trade treaty was extended in 1815, such efforts to facilitate commerce were short-lived. In 1816, the tsar abandoned bilateral trade agreements and direct Russo-Brazilian trade rapidly declined. The author also discusses the controversies surrounding the Russian envoy P. F. Balk-Polev, the role of Langsdorff, the consul-general, in promoting Russian ties in Brazil and organizing a major scientific expedition to Portuguese America, and Russia's refusal to recognize Brazilian independence until 1828, when F. F. Borel was appointed ambassador to the Brazilian Court. This excellent article is based largely on Spanish, Portuguese and Brazilian archival materials and Russian sources. 1 table. 103 notes.

[887] Francesca Miller. "Brazil's Relations with Russia, 1808–1840: A Study in the Formation of Foreign Policy," (Ph.D. Dissertation: University of California, Davis, 1977). 279 pp.

Studies the formation of Brazil's foreign policy as a newly independent nation by examining her relations with Russia during the period from the arrival of the Portuguese Court to 1840. Focuses on Georg Heinrich von Langsdorff (1774–1852) and Henri Jules de Wallenstein (1790–1843), successive Russian consuls-general in Rio from 1812 to 1843, whose writings provide an account of Russian interest in the area.

Though Brazil had internal problems, she was able to establish herself in the community of nations because she achieved an early consensus and continuity in foreign policy. The elites believed that successful diplomatic relations were a means of realizing Brazil's potential and also were "a measure of its realization."
DAI 38/06-A (pp. 3674–3675).

[888] Francesca Miller. "Russo-Brazilian Relations, Early National Period: 1813–1841," *Revista do Instituto Histórico e Geografico Brasileiro* 307 (abril–junho 1975), pp. 226–232. [The footnotes and the appendix are found only in the Portuguese translation of the article, pp. 217–225.]

Briefly examines the careers of three Russians who, during the three decades, 1813–1843, served in Brazil as representatives of the Russian Court: The scholarly scientist, Baron G. H. von Langsdorff, consul-general for most of the period, 1813–1830, who established formal Brazilian relations at the ministerial level; Baron G. H. de Lowenstern, a Russian subject who served in Brazil as an envoy of the Danish Court from 1827–1829; and Baron H. J. de Wallenstein, well known in diplomatic and literary circles, who arrived in Rio de Janeiro in 1832 and served as consul-general until his death in 1843. The author gives examples of how these three men interacted with the Portuguese and, later, the Brazilian elites. Based largely on travel and Brazilian newspaper accounts. 17 notes.

D. France and Austria [Nos. 889–890]

Eugene Fair **[899]** provides a brief treatment of French diplomacy in pre-1822 Brazil. Ezekiel Ramirez **[890]** does the same—but in greater detail—for Austria. In the aftermath of the Congress of Vienna, Austria took a greater interest in Brazil—especially after the marriage of Dona Leopoldina, the Emperor Franz Joseph's daughter, to Prince Pedro.

[889] Eugene Robert Fair. "Anglo-French Relations Concerning Spain and Portugal and the American Colonies, 1822–1827," (Ph.D. Dissertation: University of Iowa, 1938). vi, 279 pp.

Though chapter IV, "Portugal and Brazil. 1822 to 1827" (pp. 189–253), covers the period prior to 1825, there is little material on the pre-independence period.

[890] Ezekiel Stanley Ramirez. "The Diplomatic Relations Between Austria and Brazil, 1815–1889," (Ph.D. Dissertation: Stanford University, 1952).

XXIV. The Independence of Brazil [Nos. 891–895]

A. J. R. Russell-Wood **[891]** and Emília Viotti da Costa **[892]** discuss events leading to independence, with Viotti da Costa focusing more on the period 1807–1822 and Russell-Wood devoting a substantial part of his study to the eighteenth century. Harry Bernstein **[893]** stresses the increased political role of Lisbon's *juiz do povo* during the years the Portuguese court was in Brazil. George C. A. Boehrer **[894]** examines the flight of the Brazilian deputies from the Cortes Gerais in Lisbon in 1822. Anyda Merchant **[895]** provides a biographical sketch of Maria Graham **[628]** who visited Brazil three times during the crucial years, 1821–1825.

[891] A. J. R. Russell-Wood. "Preconditions and Precipitants of the Independence Movement in Portuguese America," in Russell-Wood, ed., *From Colony to Nation* **[88]**, pp. 3–40.

Russell-Wood argues that "there was no single stereotyped path towards independence in the Americas." He reviews the first two centuries of Portuguese American history and then focuses on the eighteenth century, the "age of regalism and nationalism." The author points out that "it was a bitter irony that the absolutist and centralizing policies of the brilliant minister of Dom José, the marquis of Pombal (so zealous in his efforts to preserve Luso-Brazilian commercial ties), unwittingly sowed the seeds of the future independence movement in Brazil." Russell-Wood discusses the colonial response to Portuguese policy in the eighteenth century and then sketches the events directly leading to independence after the arrival of the Court to Brazil in 1808. Undocumented.

[892] Emília Viotti da Costa. "The Political Emancipation of Brazil," in Russell-Wood, ed., *From Colony to Nation* **[88]**, pp. 43–88.

[This is a revised translation of "Introdução ao estudo da emancipação politica do Brazil," which appeared in *Brasil em Perspectiva*. São Paulo: Difusão Europeia do Livro, 1968.]

The author challenges the traditional interpretations of Brazilian independence. She then examines colonial criticism of the Portuguese monopolistic system, and concludes that "enlightenment criticism of absolutism in Brazil became, in essence, criticism of the colonial regime." Viotti da Costa analyzes the effects the transference of the Portuguese Court to Rio de Janeiro had on Brazil and points out that although "the laws passed by Dom João did contribute to undermining the colonial system, they were not sufficiently broad to restructure it completely, nor was this their purpose. Privileges and monopolies continued to exist." The author attempts to identify the ideological assumptions of the independence movement and discusses the limits of liberalism in Brazil. She concludes with a study of "Portuguese" vs. "Brazilian" points of view and an examination of the policy of the Portuguese Cortes to Brazil. Based largely on archival and printed primary materials. 95 notes.

[893] Harry Bernstein. "The Lisbon *Juiz do Povo* and the Independence of Brazil, 1750–1822: An Essay on Luso-Brazilian Populism," in Keith and Edwards, eds., *Conflict and Continuity* **[84]**, pp. 191–226.

Traces the history of the little-studied post of *juiz do povo*, the head of the artisan guilds and an elected member of the *senado da câmara* or municipal council in both Portugal and Brazil, with a special emphasis on the Lisbon *juiz* and the years 1750 to 1822. During this latter period there seems to have been an increase in power for both the guilds and the *juiz* even though rivalry grew with the Junta do Comércio over the questions of industrialization and the competition of British manufactures. The author stresses the increased political role of Lisbon's *juiz do povo* during the years the Court was transferred to Portuguese America, his attitude toward Brazil as the new center of the Portuguese empire and the various Portuguese revolts leading to the proclamation of the Constitution of 1820, and his demise in 1834 when constitutional liberalism nationalized the religious and guild corporations. No notes. Bibliography.
In his commentary, George E. Carl (pp. 227–230) after analyzing the duties and prerogatives of the *juiz do povo*, challenges the view that he was a popular leader. Bibliography.

[894] George C. A. Boehrer. "The Flight of the Brazilian Deputies from the Cortes Gerais of Lisbon, 1822," *The Hispanic American Historical Review* 40:4 (November 1960), pp. 497–512.

After detailing the actions of the seven Brazilians during the Cortes' debates and the reactions of the Portuguese deputies and the behavior of the gallery, the author describes not only how the seven left Lisbon illegally on the Falmouth packet to England and eventually returned to Brazil but also the repercussions in Portugal and Madeira. Boehrer argues that the relative unconcern by the Cortes "is further evidence that the Portuguese were on the point of recognizing both the inevitability of Brazilian independence and their own impotence in preventing it." Based on extensive use of archival and printed primary sources. 58 notes.

[895] Anyda Marchant. "The Captain's Widow: Maria Graham and the Independence of South America," *The Americas* 20:2 (October 1963), pp. 127–142.

Short biographical sketch of the Englishwoman Maria Graham (1785–1842) who made three visits to Portuguese America: 1821–1822; 1823; and 1824–1825. She was a friend of Lord Cochrane and the Brazilian Empress Leopoldina and published in 1824 accounts of her experiences in Chile and Brazil, the latter being entitled *Journal of a Voyage to Brazil and Residence there during part of the Years 1821, 1822, 1823*. See Graham **[628]**. Marchant's article is based mostly on her journals. 33 notes.

XXV. Brazil and the Western Hemisphere: Comparative Studies [Nos. 896–905]

Manoel de Oliveira Lima's pioneering study **[896]** suggests a number of topics that deserve further attention by scholars. Alexander Marchant **[114]** in explaining the unity of Brazilian history compares Portuguese and Spanish America. Vianna Moog **[897]** contrasts Brazil with the United States and blames Brazilian problems on the "unstable, predatory style of the *bandeira.*" Stuart B. Schwartz **[898]** discusses similarities and differences between sixteenth-century Mexico City and Salvador, Bahia. Richard Beeman **[899]** focuses on northeastern Brazil and Virginia during the first century of colonization. Sidney Greenfield contrasts the plantation society of Brazil with those in the Caribbean **[900]**. African slavery and sugar plantations in Vera Cruz, Mexico, and Pernambuco, Brazil, during the mid-sixteenth to the late seventeenth century are studied by Geraldo da Silva Cardoso **[901]**. A. J. R. Russell-Wood **[902]** compares the Black family in the Americas. The gold rushes in Minas Gerais and California are discussed by Percy Alvin Martin **[903]**. Robert C. Smith **[904]** compares towns in colonial Spanish and Portuguese America. George Hawrylyshyn **[905]** discusses the United States and Portuguese America in 1776. The comparative aspects of art and architecture are studied in Section XXI, especially part B, 1.

[896] Manoel de Oliveira Lima. *The Evolution of Brazil Compared with that of Spanish and Anglo-Saxon America.* Edited with introduction and notes by Percy Alvin Martin. New York: Russell & Russell, 1966. 159 pp. [This study was originally published in 1914 by Stanford University.]

A collection of six lectures delivered by Oliveira Lima at Stanford University in the Autumn of 1912. The author gives a strong emphasis to Portuguese, Spanish and English attitudes to Africans, Amerindians, the enslavement of people of color, and the topic of interracial mixture. He also discusses and compares town councils, administrative centralization, education, social assistance, the role of the church, and independence movements. Most of Oliveira Lima's study deals with the independence and preindependence periods. Though documented by Percy Alvin Martin as well as Oliveira Lima, this comparative history has no bibliography and no index.

[897] Vianna Moog. *Bandeirantes and Pioneers.* Trans. L. L. Barrett. New York: George Braziller, 1964. 316 pp.
[Translation of *Bandeirantes e Pioneiros.* Porto Alegre: Editôra Globo, 1954.]

Provocative essay comparing the history and national character of Brazil and the United States. The author blames many of Brazil's problems on the "unstable, predatory style of the *bandeira*." He claims that "apparently, in one way or another, in Amazonia, the Northeast, São Paulo, Rio Grande do Sul, Rio de Janeiro, North and South and East and West, in all the islands of the Brazilian cultural archipelago, the mark of the *bandeira* is still, and always, to be found. . . . there is no sector in which residues of the *bandeirante*'s way of life and the trade of the *bandeira* may not be found." Moog sees Aleijadinho, the great eighteenth-century sculptor from Minas Gerais, as one who overcame the cult of the *bandeirante*—"avidity for money and, as soon as it is obtained, in the worship of the good life"—and who through his initiative, technique, teamwork, and adaptation to reality has provided an example for those who wish to make Brazil great. Notes. There is a bibliography on pp. 295–301.

[898] Stuart B. Schwartz. "Cities of Empire: Mexico and Bahia in the Sixteenth Century," *Journal of Inter-American Studies and World Affairs* 11:4 (October 1969), pp. 616–637.

Ambitious effort to compare two capital cities—Salvador in Bahia, Brazil, and Mexico City in New Spain—during the sixteenth century. The author examines functions and social organization. He believes that even though the Spaniards encountered very different demographic and geographical conditions than the Portuguese and settled Mexico City several decades earlier than the Portuguese established Bahia, "the social structures of both reflected similar solutions to the common problem of integrating newly-created groups into an already structured society." Schwartz points out that Mexico City was founded to impose Spanish control over a large Amerindian population and Bahia was established as a royal bulwark against local and proprietary interests. By 1600 Bahia had only one-tenth of Mexico City's 100,000 people. Furthermore, it had no university, no printing press, and no central plaza like the capital of New Spain. Yet both cities played important roles in bringing centralized administration to their respective regions. Based chiefly on printed primary and secondary materials. 82 notes.

[899] Richard R. Beeman. "Labor Forces and Race Relations: A Comparative View of the Colonization of Brazil and Virginia," *Political Science Quarterly* 85:4 (December 1971), pp. 609–636.

An attempt to discover and explain similarities and differences between English and Portuguese efforts in organizing their colonies during the first century of their respective presences in America. Based largely on secondary materials with some useful quotations from coeval printed sources. 71 notes.

[900] Sidney M. Greenfield. "Slavery and the Plantation in the New World. The Development and Diffusion of a Social Form," *Journal of Inter-American Studies and World Affairs* 11:1 (January 1969), pp. 44–57.

Compares the development of a plantation society based on the production of sugar in the Portuguese Atlantic Islands and Brazil with that influenced by the English and the Dutch in Barbados in the Caribbean. The former, the author argues, is characterized by an extended household, "the fundamental unit of Portuguese social organization," and the *município*, based on the Roman municipality; the latter is delineated by a small nuclear domestic group and the "special purpose associations." Greenfield concludes that the development of the abovementioned sets of institutions in America helps explain the "significant sociological differences between the slave plantation systems of the peoples of the Iberian peninsula and northwest Europe." Based entirely on printed materials, the great majority of them secondary sources. 41 notes.

[901] Geraldo da Silva Cardoso. "Negro Slavery in the Sugar Plantations of Vera Cruz and Pernambuco, 1550–1680. A Comparative Study," (Ph.D. Dissertation: The University of Nebraska—Lincoln, 1975). 331 pp.

Compares sugar plantations, their economy and society, in Vera Cruz, Mexico, and Pernambuco, Brazil, during the last half of the sixteenth century and most of the seventeenth. The author studies the role of African slaves, the many hardships they suffered, and their reaction to enslavement. He also discusses the ostentatious life-style of the sugar elite. Cardoso compares the treatment of domestic slaves with field or mill hands and argues that close ties between master and slave—when they existed—were due more to the slave's capacity to imitate European ways than any flexibility or racial tolerance on the part of the Ibero-American slaveowner. Though there were differences in the slave systems of Vera Cruz and Pernambuco, they were due mainly to varying local conditions. In general, similarities outweighed differences. In both cases, according to the author, slavery "gloried in the elevation of an unproductive and useless aristocracy, while reducing the Negro to the level of a beast."
DAI 36/12-A (p. 8249).

[902] A. J. R. Russell-Wood. "The Black Family in the Americas," *Societas* 8:1 (Winter 1978), pp. 1–38.

Argues that Herbert Gutman's study on Afro-American history, *The Black Family in Slavery and Freedom, 1750–1925*, is important not only for better understanding the history of the United States but that of the rest of the Americas as well. Gutman challenged many of the conventional views regarding Afro-American family life in the United States. Russell-Wood examines and criticizes Gutman's conclusions and compares them with the experiences of black families in Spanish and Portuguese America. The author concludes that "it is ironical that a definitive history of slavery, let alone of the black family, has yet to be written for any region of colonial Spanish or Portuguese America, or for the republics of Latin America. Certainly domestic arrangements and adherence to values and practices which bore on the life of the black family in English North America had parallels in the Spanish and Portuguese American empires." Based on printed sources. 50 notes.

[903] Percy Alvin Martin. "Minas Geraes and California: A Comparison of Certain Phases of Their Historical and Social Evolution," in *Annaes do Congresso Internacional de História da America* (Rio de Janeiro, 1925–1930), I, 250–270.

Martin discusses some of the similarities between the two gold rushes. In Brazil when word was received that gold had been discovered "fazendas were abandoned; shops in the cities were deserted; crews in the harbors left their ships; even government officials, infected with the contagion, neglected their duties." The same was true in California. The author describes the civil war between Paulistas and outsiders and points out that "although California, even at the height of the gold rush, offered no spectacle of armed conflict comparable to the pitched battles between the Paulistas and the Emboabas, on several occasions national jealousies and racial prejudices threatened to precipitate hostilities in the mining regions." The discovery of gold in both Minas Gerais and California resulted in great influxes of population. Martin concludes that "as regards the effect of the gold discovery on the social evolution to California conditions *mutatis mutandis* were not so dissimilar to those existing in Minas Gerais."

[904] Robert C. Smith. "Colonial Towns of Spanish and Portuguese America," *Journal of the Society of Architectural Historians* 14:4 (December 1955), pp. 3–12.

Contrasts the Spanish approach to town-building with that in Portuguese America. After 1523, the Spaniards used the gridiron plan for all their American settlements, generally on level inland sites, in conformity with the Laws of the Indies, but "at no time did the Portuguese, who discovered the country in 1500 and held it until 1822, provide a code of rules for urban development." After discussing urban-planning or the lack of it in Lisbon (until after the 1755 earthquake) and making comparisons with Portuguese overseas cities like Luanda, Macao, Goa and Mocambique, the author describes and discusses such Brazilian towns as Salvador, São Paulo, Rio de Janeiro, Cachoeira and Ouro Preto. By the mid-eighteenth century, there is evidence of the gridiron approach for such Brazilian towns as Mariana and, in the early nineteenth century, for Linhares (in Espirito Santo) and Vila Real da Praia Grande (Niteroi). These, the author maintains, were exceptions. Smith concludes that urban development in Portuguese America was the opposite of that in Spanish America. "Settlements [in Brazil] were made in rugged coastal areas. They developed without formal plans in strip formation at several levels, with narrow steep streets that rendered any communication difficult. The resulting plans are all different, disordered but picturesque." Based on archival as well as printed sources. 9 illus. 33 notes.

[905] George Hawrylyshyn. "A Perspective on Development. Brazil and the United States, 1776," *Américas* 29:5 (May 1977), pp. 12–13.

Relying heavily on Moniz Bandeira's *Presença dos Estados Unidos do Brasil* (The Presence of the United States in Brazil) and quoting from Hipólito da Costa's correspondence **[729]** about his visit to the United States at the end of the eighteenth century, the author argues that two hundred years ago the population and land size of Portuguese America and the value of her exports were greater than those of the United States and that Brazil had the potential to soon be a major industrial nation. The opposite occurred. The author cites Moniz Bandeira's argument that Brazil was prevented from maintaining the advantage she had in 1775 by the Royal Letter of 30 July 1776, which forbade manufacturing in Brazil. Though this thesis deserves further study, some of the data used in this article is erroneous and misleading. No notes.

XXVI. The Historiography of Colonial Brazil, 1500–1822 [Nos. 906–939]

A. Colonial Chroniclers and Historians [Nos. 906–914]

Manoel Cardozo **[906]** contributed an excellent introduction for a study of colonial chroniclers and historians with his study of the idea of history in the Portuguese chroniclers of the age of discovery. E. Bradford Burns **[907]** provides a most useful survey of the major chroniclers and historians of colonial Brazil in his fine collection of articles on Brazilian historiography. A. Curtis Wilgus **[908]** falls short in his attempt to provide biographical sketches of the colonial writers who recounted the early events of Brazilian history. However, he **[909]** is more successful in his survey of writers who spent time in the Plata region in the sixteenth century. Herbert Baldus **[910]** surveys the chief observers of the Brazilian Indians. Cardozo **[911]** provides a useful study of André Thevet, the French Franciscan who visited Brazil in the mid-sixteenth century. Alan K. Manchester **[912]** provides useful information on several eighteenth-century historians who wrote about the regions of São Paulo and São Vicente. Manchester's study is complemented by Stanley Stein's **[913]** review of eighteenth and nineteenth century accounts of the history of São Paulo and its *bandeirantes.* Charles Boxer **[914]** provides an excellent survey of eighteenth century writings on Brazil of value to historians.

[906] Manoel Cardozo. "The Idea of History in the Portuguese Chroniclers of the Age of Discovery," *The Catholic Historical Review* 49:1 (April 1963), pp. 1–19.

Analyzes and discusses the philosophy of history of the Portuguese chroniclers of the fifteenth and sixteenth centuries with extensive quotations from their writings. Based chiefly on printed primary sources. 81 notes.

[907] E. Bradford Burns. "Introduction," in Burns, ed., *Perspectives* **[85]**, pp. 1–20.

Useful and succinct survey of the major chroniclers and historians who were born or lived in colonial Brazil and wrote about Portuguese America before the beginning of the nineteenth century. Based on printed primary and secondary materials. 33 notes.

[908] A. Curtis Wilgus. *The Historiography of Latin America: A Guide to Historical Writing, 1500–1800.* Metuchen, New Jersey: The Scarecrow Press, Inc., 1975.

An attempt to give short biographical sketches of the major historical writers who lived in and wrote about colonial Latin America. Sixteenth-century Brazil is covered on pp. 89–101; seventeenth-century Brazil on pp. 177–188 and eighteenth-century Brazil on pp. 270–276. Marred by numerous errors.

[909] A. Curtis Wilgus. "Some Sixteenth Century Histories and Historians of America (Part VIII)," *Bulletin of the Pan American Union* 74:5 (May 1940), pp. 392–397.

This installment includes short biographical sketches of four officials or adventurers who spent time in the region of the Rio de la Plata (including present-day Argentina, Uruguay, Paraguay and Brazil) and left accounts of their travels and experiences. Alvar Nuñez Cabeza de Vaca **[182]** was appointed governor of La Plata in 1540 by Charles V and, in the following year, visited the island of Santa Catarina in southern Brazil, marching overland from there to Asunción, Paraguay. In 1555 he published an account of his South American experiences with the title *La relación y comentarios del governador Alvar Núñez Cabeça de Vaca,* which, according to Wilgus, is "of first class historical importance." A contrary view to that of Cabeza de Vaca is found in the account of his enemy, Ulrich Schmidel **[182]**, published in German in 1567. In 1552 Schmidel journeyed overland from Paraguay to São Vicente in Brazil on his way back to Europe. Another German, Hans Staden **[181]**, probably arrived for the first time in Brazil in 1548, when he aided Pernambucan settlers in their fight with hostile Indians. He returned to Portugal the same year before sailing from Seville to La Plata in 1549. Staden arrived at Santa Catarina Bay in Brazil and then went northward to São Vicente, where he served as a gunner at Bertioga. Captured by cannibalistic Indians, he managed to escape before being eaten, and sailed to France on a French ship in 1555. Though his book "contains some exaggerations, it is thrilling, and the essential facts are true." The fourth account dealing with the Plata region is by the Italian Antonio Pigafetta **[160]**, who accompanied Magellan on his trip around the world and returned to Spain in 1522. He, too, wrote an account of his adventures, making mention of Brazil. All four works are available in English translation. 2 illus. No notes.

[910] Herbert Baldus. *Bibliografia Crítica da Etnologia Brasileira* [Critical Bibliography of Brazilian Ethnology]. São Paulo, 1954. 859 pp.

The Introduction provides an excellent survey of the chief observers and writers on the Brazilian Indians from Pero Vaz de Caminha **[163]** and **[164]** in 1500 to the present. Baldus describes some of the chief problems faced by the white observer, examines pitfalls in the study of Brazilian ethnology, and suggests tasks for the future. The Introduction is in both Portuguese and English, the latter on pp. 25–41. There is also an excellent annotated bibliography containing 1785 items. The annotations, however, are in Portuguese.

[911] Manoel Cardozo. "Some Remarks Concerning André Thevet," *The Americas* 1:1 (July 1944), pp. 15–36.

Useful study of the French Franciscan friar who spent a short time in Brazil in the middle of the sixteenth century and who was one of the chroniclers of the unsuccessful attempt by Villegagnon to found a French settlement in what is now Rio de Janeiro. In addition, the author evaluates Thevet's writings on Brazil. Based on printed sources. 112 notes.

[912] Alan K. Manchester. "Some Brazilian Colonial Historians," *Bulletin of the Pan American Union* 68 (September and October 1934), pp. 634–647 and 698–707.

After surveying the work of the most important chroniclers of sixteenth-, seventeenth-, and the first half of eighteenth-century Brazil, the author devotes the remaining pages of Part I to sketching the tragedy-plagued life of Pedro Taques de Almeida Paes Leme (1714–1777), the Brazilian-born [São Paulo] author of *Informação sôbre as Minas de São Paulo* [Information on the Mines of São Paulo], *História da Capitania de São Vicente* [History of the Captaincy of São Vicente], *Nobiliarchia Paulistana Histórica e Genealogica* [Historical and Genealogical Register of the Nobility of São Paulo], *Noticia Histórica da Expulsão dos Jesuitas de São Paulo em 1640* [Historical Account of the Expulsion of the Jesuits from São Paulo in 1640] and other works that have not survived. Manchester concludes by evaluating Pedro Taques as a historian and praises him for his careful series of biographies, the documentary basis of his research and writing, and his emphasis on the personal lives of his subjects. Part II provides a biographical sketch of the Benedictine Frei Gaspar da Madre de Deus (1715–1800), author of such studies as *Memorias para a História de Capitania de São Vicente* [Notes for the History of the Captaincy of São Vicente], *Notícia dos Anos em que se Descobriu o Brasil e das Entradas das Religiões e suas Fundações* [Account of the Years in which Brazil Was Discovered and of the Arrival of the Religious Orders and their Foundations], *Relação dos Capitães Loco-Tenentes da Capitania de São Vicente* [Report of the Lieutenant Captains of the Captaincy of São Vicente], *Notas Avulsas sobre a Historia de São Paulo* [Scattered Notes on the History of São Paulo] and many manuscripts that have not been preserved. After discussing some of the criticisms made against the Brazilian-born monk, the author argues that Frei Gaspar was "one of the very few colonial historians of Brazil who based his work so fully and accurately on archive material." 20 notes [of editor, not author]. 10 illus.

[913] Stanley J. Stein. "Biblioteca Historica Paulista," *The Hispanic American Historical Review* 34:4 (November 1954), pp. 493–501.

Useful description and analysis of the thirteen-volume collection—*Biblioteca Historica Paulista* (published, 1952–1954)—which provides important primary source materials for the history of São Paulo. Stein divides the publications into three groups: 1) those accounts dealing with the *bandeirantes* and their search for gold and the mining discoveries in Minas Gerais, Mato Grosso, and Goiás, namely Pedro Taques's information on the mines of São Paulo and the documents on the Minas gold discoveries and those on the annual expeditions (monções) from São Paulo to Mato Grosso; 2) those narratives written at the end of the eighteenth century when the boom had ended—accounts like Frei Gaspar da Madre de Deus's history of the captaincy of São Vicente and Pedro Taques's register of Paulista nobility, which "constitute a valedictory to the era of *sertanistas* and miners"; 3) nineteenth-century travel accounts, two of which deal with the period prior to 1825: the narrative of the military engineer Luis D'Alincourt's journey from the port of Santos to Cuiabá and that of the observant and insightful French naturalist Augustin de Saint-Hilaire, who during the turbulent first five months of 1822 travelled from Rio de Janeiro to Minas Gerais to São Paulo and back to Rio. 1 note.

[914] C. R. Boxer. *Some Literary Sources for the History of Brazil in the Eighteenth Century.* Oxford: At the Clarendon Press, 1967. 36 pp.

Divides eighteenth-century literary sources into six categories and then briefly describes and evaluates the major works: 1) histories and chronicles, both secular and religious; 2) descriptive accounts by residents of long standing; 3) pamphlets, panegyrics, sermons, and descriptions of religious and other celebrations; 4) works reflecting a growing humanitarian and antislavery sentiment; 5) poetry—especially that from Minas Gerais; 6) accounts of visiting foreigners, 1699–1792. Some of the more important works discussed are Rocha Pitta's *História da America Portuguesa* (1730), which Boxer defends against attacks by Southey **[70]** and others; Antonil's *Cultura e Opulencia do Brazil por suas drogas e minas* (1711) ["roughly Englished as 'The exploitation of the agricultural and mineral wealth of Brazil'"], which gives us an unrivalled survey of Brazil at the beginning of the eighteenth century"; *Recopilação de noticias Soteropolitanas e Brasilicas contidas em XX Cartas,* by the Regius Professor of Greek at Salvador, Luis dos Santos Vilhena, which provides an excellent view of Portuguese America at the end of the eighteenth century; the *Triunfo Eucharistico,* which describes religious festivities in Ouro Preto [both the celebrations and the publication of the book were financed by Blacks in Minas Gerais]; *Nova e Curiosa Relação* (1764), a dialogue **[562]** between a Lisbon lawyer and a gold miner from Brazil and "a devastating indictment of Negro Slavery in Brazil"; Jorge Benci's *Economia Christãa dos Senhores no governo dos escravos* (1700), a collection of sermons to sugar planters admonishing them to treat their slaves better; Manuel Ribeiro Rocha's *Ethiope Resgatado, empenhado, sustentado, corregido, instruido, e liberto* (1758), which "besides denouncing the mistreatment of slaves by their masters . . . criticized both explicitly and implicitly the institution of slavery itself"; *Cartas Chilenas* by the Oporto-born Tomas Antonio Gonzaga, "whose verses constitute a violent attack on the person and the governorship of D. Luis da Cunha Meneses, Governor of Minas Gerais in 1783–8, who is satirized under the name of Fanfarrao Minezio, the captaincy being transparently disguised as Chile"; and Staunton's *An Authentic Account of an Embassy from the King of Great Britain to the Emperor of China* **[588]**, which includes a description of Rio de Janeiro in 1792. There are three appendices of extracts from the accounts of Woodes Rogers, John Sargent and Lord Macartney. The text has fifty notes. The appendices have eleven.

B. Nineteenth-Century Historians and Their Interpretation of Brazil's Colonial Past [Nos. 915–921]

Stuart B. Schwartz **[915]** examines the career and writings of Francisco Adolfo de Varnhagen. João Capistrano de Abreu **[916]** provides a critique of Varnhagen's *História Geral.* Robert Conrad **[917]**, Katherine Fringer **[918]** and José Honório Rodrigues **[919]**, examine the contributions of João Capistrano de Abreu. Roberta Marx Delson **[920]** appraises John Armitage's history of early nineteenth-century Brazil. Manoel Cardozo **[921]** evaluates the writing of Oliveira Lima.

[915] Stuart B. Schwartz. "Francisco Adolfo de Varnhagen: Diplomat, Patriot, Historian," *The Hispanic American Historical Review* 47:2 (May 1967), pp. 185–202.

Following a resumé of Varnhagen's life is a discussion of the nineteenth-century historian's attitudes toward Indians, Africans and Portuguese, the role of the Jesuits, centralization, monarchy, progress, Europeanization and the various colonial revolts. Concludes that "no matter what its faults may be, Varnhagen's *História Geral* is still the great history of colonial Brazil." Based on printed sources. 84 notes.

[916] João Capistrano de Abreu. "A Critique of Francisco Adolfo Varnhagen," in Burns, ed., *Perspectives* **[85]**, pp. 142–155.

A translation of "Appenso sobre o Visconde de Porto Seguro (Francisco Adolfo de Varnhagen)." This essay praises Varnhagen's search for and discovery of new documents (especially those of the sixteenth century), but argues that his writings on the seventeenth (the history of the Dutch War) and eighteenth centuries "were not overly important," though his yet-to-be-published study of independence showed much promise. Capistrano de Abreu faults Varnhagen on a lack of synthesis and artistry and a failure "to give some design to his work, and show the interrelation of the various elements of Brazilian history." After offering his own suggestions for the periodization of Brazilian history, Capistrano de Abreu concludes that "Varnhagen's *História Geral* is inferior to Southey's *History of Brazil* **[70]** in form, conception, and intuition, but it is inferior only to that work. No Brazilian can actually be compared to Varnhagen." 23 notes [on pp. 226–227].

[917] Robert Conrad. "João Capistrano de Abreu, Brazilian Historian," *Revista de Historia de America* 59 (January–June 1965), pp. 149–164.

After analyzing the influence of positivism on the historical writings of Capistrano de Abreu (1853–1927), the author discusses the lifelong ambitions of Capistrano to write "a general history of Brazil solidly based upon archival materials" and to unearth and publicize sources for such an account. Viewing him as "a historian's historian," Conrad concludes that Capistrano de Abreu's real accomplishment was in his influence on future historians rather than "his own scant and fragmentary historical writings." Based on printed sources. 42 notes. Bibliography.

[918] Katherine Fringer. "The Contribution of Capistrano de Abreu to Brazilian Historiography," *Journal of Inter-American Studies and World Affairs* 13:2 (April 1971), pp. 258–278.

Views Capistrano de Abreu (1853–1927) as one who dramatically changed the course of Brazilian historiography by focusing on the frontier with its greater socioeconomic mobility and opportunities for evading Portuguese control rather than on Brazil's origins, the development of coastal urban and administrative centers, and their ties with Portugal. Discusses how Capistrano gave a new emphasis to geography, ethnography, linguistics and folklore and developed a new periodization for Brazilian history. Based on printed sources. 66 notes.

[919] José Honório Rodrigues. "Capistrano de Abreu and Brazilian Historiography," in Burns, *Perspectives* **[85]**, 156–180.

Rodrigues traces Capistrano de Abreu's career and points out that "he was the first to suggest new interpretations that so modified our historical understanding, such as studying the *bandeiras*, the mines, the explorations, and cattle raising, all of which was unrecognized until then." In addition, "the problems that he indicated needed greater study were the history of the *sesmarias*, municipalities, *bandeirantes*, Jesuits and the mines. They all have since experienced a great expansion of perspective and understanding." Rodrigues concludes this laudatory essay by calling Capistrano de Abreu "the most lucid conscience of Brazilian historiography." No notes.

[920] Roberta Marx Delson. "John Armitage: An English Historian's Interpretation of Early Nineteenth-Century Brazil," in Andrew W. Cordier, ed., *Columbia Essays in International Affairs. The Dean's Papers, 1969.* New York: Columbia University Press, 1970, V, 137–153.

Analyzes Armitage's **[817]** motivation for writing his *History of Brazil* (1808–1831) (to provide information for his fellow countrymen), his techniques (he relied heavily on newspaper articles and private conversations with eminent Brazilian political figures), and his claim to objectivity (he was pro-Brazilian, pro-English, and anti-Portuguese). The author also discusses the major themes stressed by Armitage: 1) poor administration and rivalry between Portuguese and Brazilians; 2) distrust of a created titled nobility which he feels is anachronistic; and 3) failure of Pedro I, primarily because of his pro-Portuguese attitudes. Delson argues that it "is Armitage's perceptive view of the Empire that makes the *History of Brazil* more than just a routine compilation of events." Based on printed materials. 22 notes.

[921] Manoel Cardozo. "Oliveira Lima and the Writing of History," *Revista Interamericana de Bibliografia* 4:1-2 (1954), pp. 43–51.

A bio-bibliographical sketch of Oliveira Lima (1867–1928), the Pernambucan-born, Lisbon-educated diplomat, essayist, bibliophile, and historian who, after spending the last years of his life writing and lecturing in the United States, donated his important library to The Catholic University of America. Though Oliveira Lima's great contribution to Brazilian historiography was his studies on the nineteenth century, especially those on D. João VI and the Brazilian empire, he was at his best writing about diplomatic history. One of the first Brazilian historians "to devote any serious attention to social history and economics," Oliveira Lima also used more foreign archives over a longer period of time than any other Brazilian historian with the possible exception of Varnhagen. After briefly discussing Lima's approach to questions of a historical nature, the author concludes: "Future scholars will no doubt be able, through further study, to throw new light on many of the subjects that Lima treated, but it is not likely that they will be able to supersede him in honesty, method, tolerance, and understanding." Based mostly on the printed works of Oliveira Lima. illus. 25 notes.

C. How the History of Brazil Should Be Written
[Nos. 922–928]

An early and important statement on which directions Brazilian historiography should follow was penned by the German naturalist Karl Friedrich Philipp von Martius **[922]** in 1844. Other suggestions of note are those by José Honório Rodrigues **[923]** and **[924]** and Charles R. Boxer **[925]** and **[926]**. Robert C. Smith **[927]** offers recommendations for research into the history of architecture in 17th- and 18th-century Brazil and Portugal. George C. A. Boehrer **[928]** discusses some lacunae in Brazilian historical bibliography.

[922] Karl Friedrich Philipp von Martius. "How the History of Brazil Should Be Written," in Burns, ed., *Perspectives* **[85]**, pp. 21–41.

Translated from "Como se Deve Escrever a Historia do Brasil" in the *Revista do Instituto Histórico e Geográfico Brasileiro*, VI (1844), pp. 381–403. Argues that a history of Brazil must emphasize the contributions and interaction of Amerindians, Africans and Portuguese and take into consideration the country's regional diversities. Contains perceptive questions historians of Brazil should ask of their material. 13 notes.

[923] José Honório Rodrigues. "Problems in Brazilian History and Historiography," in Burns, ed., *Perspectives* **[85]**, pp. 102–113.

Translated from part of Chapter I of *Teoria da História do Brasil* (1957), I, 9–28. Describes some of the characteristics of the historiography of Brazil—especially regarding the colonial period—and discusses reasons for the greater emphasis by Brazilian historians on the years prior to independence. The author argues that "the study of contemporary history is one of the principal duties of Brazilian historiography" and that Brazil "must deal with topics that will aid it in confronting present problems." 17 notes.

[924] José Honório Rodrigues. "The Periodization of Brazilian History," in Burns, ed., *Perspectives* **[85]**, pp. 114–138.
[This essay is a translation of chapter V, "A Periodização da Historia do Brasil," in *Teoria da História do Brasil.* São Paulo: Companhia Editora Nacional, 1957.]

A good review of nineteenth- and twentieth-century efforts by historians to synthesize and organize Brazilian history. Included in his chapter are comments on the suggestions of Martius **[922]**, Varnhagen **[915]**, Capistrano de Abreu **[917]**, **[918]**, and **[919]**, Oliveira Lima **[921]** and Gilberto Freyre **[699]**. 55 notes.

[925] Charles R. Boxer. "Some Considerations on Portuguese Colonial Historiography," in Marchant, ed., *Proceedings* **[90]**, pp. 169–180.

Very useful and informed survey of important contributions and *desiderata* regarding the Portuguese presence in Asia, Africa and Brazil. The author discusses archival as well as printed primary and secondary materials. In his section on Brazil, Boxer points out the need for more studies similar to that of João Lucio de Azevedo on the Jesuits of Grão Pará, histories of captaincies like Minas Gerais, full-length and adequately documented biographies of provincial governors, analyses of the activities of emissaries of the Inquisition who visited Brazil in the late-sixteenth and early-seventeenth centuries, and an account of the important seventeenth-century institution—the Brazil Company. 45 notes. There is a short resume in Portuguese.

[926] Charles R. Boxer. "Some Reflections on the Historiography of Colonial Brazil, 1950–1970," in Alden, ed., *Colonial Roots* **[87]**, pp. 3–15.

Reviews the chief characteristics of recent scholarship on colonial Brazil. Brings up to date his earlier comments on the subject **[925]**. Boxer calls for additional studies of governors of Brazil as well as other powerful figures during the colonial period. He also suggests that the use of archival records from Portuguese America's *misericordias*, third orders, and lay brotherhoods will provide material for much-needed biographies of what might be called middle-class figures. Other *desiderata* include research into the history of the interior captaincies, studies of the various religious orders in Portuguese America comparable to Serafim Leite's ten-volume history of the Jesuits, monographs on the social and economic aspects of Brazilian life, and biographical sketches of merchants, tax farmers and crown contractors. 11 notes.

[927] Robert C. Smith. "Recommendations for Research and Research Aids in the History of the 17th- and 18th-Century Architecture of Portugal and Brazil," in Marchant, ed., *Proceedings* **[90]**, pp. 126–130.

Stresses the need for careful research on Portuguese architecture at the end of the sixteenth century and during the reign of João V (1706–1750), along with the architects involved in the Pombaline rebuilding of

Lisbon after the 1755 earthquake and those responsible for the flourishing of the baroque in northern Portugal from 1740 to the end of the eighteenth century—all of which will provide a better understanding of Brazilian architectural developments during the colonial period. For Brazil itself, the author suggests that the stylistic variations of buildings constructed by the Jesuit, Benedictine, Franciscan and Carmelite Orders be analyzed and that the architects responsible for designing such churches and monasteries be identified and discussed. Smith concludes by recommending the publication of more research tools such as inventories, plans of principal buildings, and rare books of source material and emphasizing the importance of gathering information regarding design and construction from local church archives. 10 notes. Includes short resumé in Portuguese.

[928] George C. A. Boehrer. "Brazilian Historical Bibliography; Some Lacunae and Suggestions," *Revista Interamericana de Bibliografia/Inter-American Review of Bibliography* 11:2 (April–June 1961), pp. 137–144.

Discusses the accomplishments—with special praise for Rubens Borba de Moraes's *Bibliographia Brasiliana* **[20]**—and the needs regarding bibliographies for Brazilian history in general and for the colonial and national periods in particular. The author argues that "unfortunately, the entire colonial field also lacks one comprehensive bibliographical tool." The same holds true for the period 1808–1822. Boehrer also calls for the publication of more catalogues of the Brazilian holdings of U. S. libraries as well as those of Portuguese and Brazilian archival and manuscript collections. There are a number of useful bibliographical references in his footnotes. 34 notes.

D. Recent Scholarship [Nos. 929–939]

There have been a number of important reviews of scholarship and historians dealing with colonial Brazil from a twentieth-century perspective. Sérgio Buarque de Holanda **[929]** reviews historical thought in twentieth-century Brazil. Pedro Moacyr Campos **[930]** devotes attention to twentieth-century historians, though most of his article deals with those of the nineteenth century. Lewis Hanke **[931]** studies Gilberto Freyre's early career as a social historian, while Samuel

Putnam **[932]** views Freyre more from a personal perspective. A. Teixeira Soares **[933]** lists some of the more prominent historians practicing their craft in Brazil during the first four decades of the twentieth century. Stuart B. Schwartz **[934]** examines the scholarship that has appeared on colonial Brazil since World War II. Russell H. Bartley **[935]** reviews a decade of Soviet historical writing on colonial Brazil, 1958–1968. William C. Atkinson **[936]** describes some of the British contributions to Portuguese and Brazilian studies. Mary Lombardi **[937]** discusses the influence of the concept of frontier on Brazilian historiography. Stanley J. Stein **[938]** critically examines studies on the monarchy in Orazil that have appeared during the years 1920–1960. Rollie E. Poppino **[939]** reviews the *Revista do Instituto Histórico e Geográfico Brasileiro* for the period, 1839–1938, and describes trends in Brazilian historical writing.

[929] Sérgio Buarque de Holanda. "Historical Thought in Twentieth Century Brazil," in Burns, ed., *Perspectives* **[85]**, pp. 181–196.

Though most of the works discussed herein are not available in English, this essay, first published in 1951, gives the reader a feel for the type of historical research that has occupied Brazilian historians during the first half of the twentieth century. No notes.

[930] Pedro Moacyr Campos. "An Outline of Brazilian Historiography in the Nineteenth and Twentieth Centuries," in Burns, ed., *Perspectives* **[85]**, pp. 42–89.

This outline contains a good appreciation of Southey's history of Brazil **[70]**, the writings of Martius **[922]** and the research of Varnhagen **[915]** and Capistrano de Abreu **[917]**, **[918]** and **[919]** as well as some of the more recent historians of Brazil. The major portion of this study deals with nineteenth-century historians. 183 notes.

[931] Lewis Hanke. "Gilberto Freyre: Brazilian Social Historian," *The Quarterly Journal of Inter-American Relations* 1:3 (July 1939), pp. 24–44.

Sketches Freyre's career through 1938 and discusses his efforts at "integrating Brazilian life according to a regional concept rather than by the artificial, state system set up by the first republican constitution." The author then focuses on Freyre's interpretation of the role of race mixture in Brazilian history and concludes with an analysis of *Casa Grande e Senzala* (later published in English as *The Masters and the Slaves*) **[699]** and *Sobrados e Mocambos* (*The Mansions and the Shanties*). 46 notes.

[932] Samuel Putnam. "Gilberto Freyre. Stormy Hermit of Apipucos," *Americas* 1:3 (May 1949), pp. 8–11, 43.

An intimate look at the author of *The Masters and the Slaves* **[699]** by his translator. Apipucos is the suburb of Recife where Freyre has his own *casa grande*. 13 illustrations, 12 of which are caricatures drawn by Freyre himself. No notes.

[933] A. Teixeira Soares. "Brazilian Historians," *Bulletin of the Pan American Union* 72:8 (August 1938), pp. 456–462.

An address delivered at The Catholic University of America, Washington, D. C., on 27 May 1938. It is seldom more than a list of four dozen or so Brazilian historians and other writers dating from the eighteenth century to the 1930s. 2 notes. 3 illus.

[934] Stuart B. Schwartz. "Brazil: The Colonial Period," in Roberto Esquenazi-Mayo and Michael C. Meyer, eds., *Latin American Scholarship Since World War II*. Lincoln, Nebraska: University of Nebraska Press, 1971, pp. 23–49.

Useful and perceptive summary of a quarter of a century of historical writing on Portuguese America before independence. Schwartz reviews 194 books and articles, most of which appeared from the end of World War II to the mid- and late-1960s. Special attention is paid to the bibliographical and historiographical contributions of José Honório Rodrigues; a variety of critical editions of sixteenth-, seventeenth-, and eighteenth-century writings; series of colonial documents; general surveys of colonial Brazil; such categories of economic studies as trade patterns, monographs on particular products, and syntheses of economic history; the role of the frontier and the *bandeirantes*; the Dutch in seventeenth-century Brazil; urban history; religious brotherhoods; and slavery, resistance, manumission and race relations. 10 notes. Bibliography.

[935] Russell H. Bartley. "A Decade of Soviet Scholarship in Brazilian History: 1958–1968," *The Hispanic American Historical Review* 50:3 (August 1970), pp. 445–466.

Serious Soviet scholarship on colonial Brazil dates mostly from the end of World War II. Although a number of studies have been published on late eighteenth- and early nineteenth-century Russian-Brazilian contacts, most of the recent scholarship has tended to focus on socioeconomic tensions during Brazil's colonial and post-Independence periods. Soviet historians have largely ignored the Portuguese background of expansion into Brazil, preferring to study slavery and such related topics as the kingdom of Palmares. There has also been much interest in conflicts between Brazilian planters and Portuguese merchants and/or between creoles and the Portuguese-controlled trading monopolies. The development of Brazilian nationalism has gained much attention. There has also been a strong emphasis on the Inconfidência Mineira and subsequent separatist uprisings such as those of Bahia in the late 1790s and the early nineteenth century, the 1817 Pernambucan revolt and those in Rio de Janeiro and São Paulo in 1821. Not surprisingly, given the importance of the Minas Conspiracy in Russian scholarship, the only book-length biography on the colonial period in the decade being surveyed is entitled *Tiradentes*. 109 notes.

[936] William C. Atkinson. *British Contributions to Portuguese and Brazilian Studies.* rev. ed. London: The British Council, 1974. 47 pp. [An earlier edition appeared in 1945.]

Most of the material deals with the period after independence, but there is a useful discussion of Robert Southey's three-volume history of colonial Brazil and its continuation by John Armitage. Mention is also given to some of the more recent writings by Englishmen on Portuguese America. The earlier section on Portuguese studies—especially the part entitled "Pombal and Napoleon"—has additional information on Southey and his interest in Portuguese and Brazilian history. 1 map. 15 illus. No notes.

[937] Mary Lombardi. "The Frontier in Brazilian History: An Historiographical Essay," *Pacific Historical Review* 44:4 (November 1975), pp. 437–457.

After summarizing the frontier thesis of the U. S. historian, Frederick Jackson Turner (1861–1932), the author surveys the writings of preindependence as well as nineteenth- and twentieth-century historians and commentators and compares and contrasts Turner's ideas with those found in Brazilian frontier historiography. Lombardi concludes: "Current research is more interested in precisely defining the individual and specific processes and dynamics of frontier history than in proposing broad interpretations of the frontier's general significance." Based entirely on printed sources. 70 notes.

[938] Stanley J. Stein. "The Historiography of Brazil, 1808–1889," *The Hispanic American Historical Review* 40:2 (May 1960), pp. 234–278.

Excellent overview and analysis of the most important studies on nineteenth-century Brazil published during the years 1920–1960. Of particular value is Stein's comparison of the earlier studies hy Armitage **[817]**, Varnhagen, and Oliveira Lima with those by Tobias Monteiro and Octávio Tarquínio de Sousa. The first three decades of the nineteenth century are covered on pages 234–248. The writings of Armitage are discussed by Delson **[920]**, those of Varnhagen by Schwartz **[915]** and those of Oliveira Lima by Cardozo **[921]**.

[939] Rollie E. Poppino. "A Century of the *Revista do Instituto Histórico e Geográfico Brasileiro*," *The Hispanic American Historical Review* 33:2 (May 1953), pp. 307–323.

According to the author, "this review of one hundred years of the publication of the *Revista do Instituto Histórico e Geográfico Brasileiro* has a twofold purpose. In the first place, it attempts in a general way to indicate the contributions made to the study of the social sciences in Brazil by the members of one of the most outstanding scholarly bodies of that nation. Secondly, it attempts to describe in general the trends and developments of historical writing in Brazil for the period 1839–1938, as reflected in the pages of the *Revista*." Poppino divides Brazil's history into nine periods, six of which cover the years prior to independence in 1822, and gives the percentage of articles on history published on those periods: Pre–1500 (1%); 1500–1580 (7%); 1580–1654 (9%); 1654–1750 (10%); 1750–1808 (13%); 1808–1823 (12%); 1823–1845 (14%); 1840–1889 (14%); 1889–1938 (6%); unclassified (14%). He also divides the types of history into five classifications: political, social, religious, military and economic. By 1938, social history was in the ascendancy and political history in decline. Overall, however, social history had only a slight lead. Political history was followed by that on religious topics, the economy and the military. More than half of the articles that appeared in the *Revista* dealt with the colonial period. Poppino examines the background of the major contributors and discusses the large number of documents published in this important journal. He concludes that although "the historian now has a wide range of Brazilian publications to consult, . . . he cannot pretend to do thorough research in either colonial or modern history of Brazil without relying heavily upon the volumes of the *Revista do Instituto Histórico e Geográfico Brasileiro*." 6 tables. 18 notes.

Portuguese Currency, Weights and Measures

Currency

real (pl. reis)	1/20 of a vintem	
vintem (pl. vintens)	20 reis	
tostão (pl. tostões)	100 reis	
pataca	320 reis	
cruzado	400 reis	
milreis	1000 reis,	or 1$000, or 1U
oitava	1600 reis,	or 1$600

Weights and Measures

(Most of these weights and measures and many others varied from region to region and from century to century.)

pipa: a liquid measure equal to about 126.6 gallons
arroba: a dry weight equal to approximately 32 lbs.
quintal: 4 arrobas
vara: a unit of measurement equal to about 43 inches

Glossary

A

Adelantado: frontier governor

Administrador: Administrator; in the case of Rio de Janeiro, a prelate with jurisdiction over ecclesiastical matters during part of the sixteenth and seventeenth centuries until Rio was raised to the status of a bishopric in 1676

Agreste: transitional zone between the moist *mata* (q.v.) along the Atlantic coast and the dry *sertao* (q.v.)

Alcaide-mor: commander of a stronghold or district; warden; bailiff

Aldeia: a village settlement. The term is usually applied to settlements of Indians supervised by missionaries or—under the Directorate—by laymen.

Aleijadinho: nickname of the mineiro sculptor and architect, Antônio Francisco Lisboa; literally, "the little cripple"

Almoxarife: customs official

Almud(e): dry or liquid measure, varying widely in capacity from country to country and from century to century

Alvará: a royal decree

Arraial: encampment; applies to both military and mining encampments

Arroba: a measure of dry weight equivalent to approximately 32 lbs. or 14.75 kilograms

Auto: 1) a religious or, at times, secular type of drama similar to the mystery plays of the Middle Ages; 2) an affidavit in an official investigation, law suit or trial

Azulejos: ceramic tiles

B

Banda Oriental: name given to the region on the east bank of the Rio de la Plata

Bandeira: slave-raiding party

Bandeirante: explorers and frontiersmen, usually, but not necessarily, from São Paulo. Mineral wealth or Indians to be enslaved frequently attracted the *bandeirante* to the interior

Batata: potato

Brejos: moist areas; fertile lands where nearby rivers have overflowed

C

Caatinga: drought-resistant scrub vegetation of the interior of northeastern Brazil. It is often considered part of the *sertao*

Cabildo: Spanish for town council

Caboclo: a backwoods farmer, usually of mixed blood, who lives at the subsistence level

Cachaça: sugarcane brandy

Cachoeira(s): waterfalls; cascades

Câmara (*Senado da Câmara*)**:** municipal or town council; the administrative and legislative body of a *vila* (q.v.)

Caminho: road, route

Capela dourada: a chapel whose interior—especially the wood on the walls and ceilings—has been covered with gold

Capitan[i]a: flagship

Capitão-mor: In the sixteenth and seventeenth centuries, the term usually referred to the governor of a captaincy. Since almost without exception, governors in Brazil were also military men, one person usually held the title of governor and *capitão-mor* simultaneously. In the eighteenth century the term *capitão-mor* was also given to governors of unincorporated areas. In addition, *capitão-mor* could also refer to a naval officer in an armada. It was also a rank in Brazil's second-line militia *(ordenança)*.

Carta: letter

Carta régia: royal provision, permanent in nature. This type of royal decree was directed to a particular official or administrative body.

Casa grande: literally, the "big house," or the main dwelling or seat of a plantation, where the master usually resided

Casa de moeda: mint

Cheganças: a type of dance

Cidade: city

Cofradia(s): lay brotherhood in Spain and Spanish America

Colateral: title given to a high official in the Jesuit Order

Comarca: administrative or judicial district

Conselho: council

Conselho de Estado: Council of State

Conselho da Fazenda: Council of the Treasury

Conselho de Guerra: Council of War

Conselho Ultramarino: Overseas Council

Consulta: usually a memorandum incorporating the recommendations of one of the king's councils, after the council has deliberated

Corografia: systematic description of a country or region

Cortes: the Portuguese Parliament

Cristão-Novo: literally, a "New Christian"; a crypto-Jew

Cruzado: a monetary unit equivalent to 400 *reis*

Custos: a superior in the Franciscan Order

D

Degredado: exile

Desafio: musical duel between two singers

Desembargador: crown judge or magistrate

Devassa: a judicial investigation

Dízimo: the tithe; a 10 percent tax collected by the crown in Brazil

Doação, Carta de: royal grant

Donatário: lord-proprietor

E

Emboaba: a perjorative term used by Paulistas to denote an outsider—especially in reference to the mining areas

Engenho: a mill; in sixteenth- and seventeenth-century Brazil, it usually referred to a sugar mill; sometimes refers to the entire plantation

Ensaio: essay

Entrada: an expedition into the interior of Brazil accompanied by military force. *Entradas* often had an official character.

Estância: cattle ranch

Estilo aleijadinho: artistic style named after Antônio Francisco Lisboa, "O Aleijadinho"

Estilo Jesuitico: Jesuit-style architecture

Estilo joanino: literally, "Joanine style"; architectural style common during the reign of João V of Portugal (1706–1750), who encouraged its development

Estrangeirado: frequently refers to Portuguese enlightenment figures of the eighteenth century who were influenced by foreign scientific and/or cultural ideas

F

Fabricantes: manufacturers, producers

Fazenda: 1) treasury; 2) ranch or farm; usually a large estate

Fazenda Real: Royal Treasury

Fazendeiro: owner of a ranch or farm

Feitoria: factory or trading post

Festa: celebration; feast

Fidalgo: nobleman or gentleman

Flota: fleet, especially one accompanied by an armed convoy

Foral (plural: **Forais):** charter

Foro militar: charter of military privileges and exemptions

Freguesia: parish

G

Garimpeiro: an illicit diamond prospector

Gaucho: a native of Rio Grande do Sul

Governador-Geral: governor-general; beginning in 1549, the chief civil and military official in Brazil. The term combines both civil (governor) and military (*capitão-geral* or captain-general) responsibilities. In the eighteenth century, the governor-general was replaced by the viceroy who had similar powers.

Grito: cry, shout

Guarda Nacional: National Guard

Guerra: war

H

Habito: literally, "habit"; the symbol of membership in one of the Portuguese military orders of Christ, Santiago or Avis

I

Inconfidência Mineira: a conspiracy for independence that was hatched in Minas Gerais in 1788–1789

Ingenio: see *Engenho*

Irmandades: religious brotherhoods or confraternities composed of laymen

J

Juiz: judge

Juiz-de-fora: a judicial officer who was expected to look after the crown's interests

Juiz ordinario: a locally elected judicial official who was a member of a town council

Juiz do povo: spokesman for the guilds

Junta do Comércio: Board of Trade, located in Lisbon

L

Lavrador: farmer. Although the term is often used for a sharecropper or one working the land of another, it has a broad range of meanings and can include independent farmers.

Lavrador de cana (pl. **lavradores de cana):** cane growers

Lavras: "washings"; mining deposits where the mineral is obtained by washing earth, etc.

Limpeza de sangue: literally "purity of blood"; those free from the "stain" of Jewish or Moslem ancestors; sometimes—but never officially—applied to those of African heritage

Livro copiador: copy book

M

Madeiras da Lei: timber belonging exculsively to the crown

Mamaluc[o]s: Mamelukes; in Brazil, persons descended from both Amerindians and Europeans

Mascate: peddler

Massape: heavy, clayey soils used for growing sugarcane

Mata: forest; also refers to a region with moist and fertile soil

Meia: one-half

Mercê: a reward by the crown for meritorious services

Mesa da Consciência e Ordens: Board of the King's Conscience and the Military Orders

Mestiço: mixed blood; usually part Amerindian, part European

Mestre do Campo: commander of an infantry regiment

Metropole: mother country; in the case of Brazil, Portugal

Milreis: 1000 *reis* or 400 *cruzados*

Minas Gerais: literally, "General Mines"; the important region of eighteenth- and early nineteenth-century Brazil

Mineiro: 1) miner; 2) a native of the captaincy of Minas Gerais

Misericorida, Santa Casa de: literally, "Holy House of Mercy"; a charitable, religious brotherhood composed of laymen emphasizing the corporal works of mercy

Morador (pl. **moradores**): 1) settler, inhabitant; 2) head of household

Morgado: entailed estate

Município: an administrative division roughly equal to a country in the United States

N

Nau: a large ship

Naufrágio: shipwreck. Also refers to accounts of shipwrecks. Narratives of such disasters were popular in the sixteenth and seventeenth centuries.

Negro de ganho: slave who earned daily or weekly wages

O

Ordenanças: the second-line militia; those who did not qualify for the first-line militia (**auxiliários**)

Ouvidor: a royal judge; the highest judicial official in a **comarca**

Ouvidor-geral: the chief crown judge in Brazil before the arrival of the **Relação**

Padroado Real: literally, "royal patronage"; authority given by the popes to the kings of Portugal as masters and governors of the Order of Christ over all church affairs in the Portuguese overseas empire with the exception of those dealing with faith or morals. In exchange, the Portuguese kings (as masters and governors of the Order of Christ) were to convert the heathen and infidel and promote Christianity.

Palmares: literally, "palm trees." Located in Alagoas, it was the most famous of the runaway slave centers. See also **Quilombos.**

Pardo: person of color; a mulatto

Patrão-mor da Ribeira: waterfront superintendent

Patronato Real: Spanish version of the **Padroado Real** (q.v.), but granted directly to the kings and queens of Spain by Pope Julius II in 1508

Paulista: 1) inhabitant of the province of São Paulo; 2) **bandeirantes** from São Paulo

Pelourinho: stone pillar with the royal coat of arms; usually located in the main square of a town or settlement, it was often used for a whipping post

Plano: as used in item no. 608, it means plan or project

Praça: 1) town square; 2) fortified place

Presidio: garrison; fort

Provedor: comptroller; treasury official

Provedor da Fazenda: Superintendent of the Treasury

Q

Quilombos: a community of runaway slaves

Quinto: the Royal Fifth; a tax of approximately 20 percent—though at times it was lower—on gold and diamonds. Later in the colonial period the tax also applied to hides.

R

Rancho: rude hut often used by herdsmen and travellers

Reais Cortes: royal logging operations

Real (pl. **reis**): Portuguese coin

Recôncavo: the sugar- and tobacco-growing region around the Bay of All Saints (Bahia de todos os Santos)

Regimento: standing orders; instructions

Relação: High Court of Appeals

Revista: journal

S

Sambaquí (s): literally, "a pile of waste shells"

Santa Casa da Misericordia: See **Misericordia.**

Sargento-Mor: a military officer in charge of the military defense of a captaincy, but subordinate to the governor and *capitão-mor*

Senado da Câmara: See *Câmara.*

Senhor de Engenho: owner of a sugar mill

Senhorio: seignory

Senzala: slave quarters

Serra(s): mountain(s)

Sertanejo(s): inhabitant(s) of the dry interior of northeast Brazil; those who live in the *sertão* (q.v.) or backlands

Sertanista: one with first-hand knowledge of the *sertão* (q.v.)

Sertão (pl. sertões): the interior; the back country; backlands

Sesmarias: landgrants made by the crown or its officials

Solar: manor house

T

Terço: infantry regiment

Tiradentes: literally "toothpuller"; the nickname of Joaquim José da Silva Xavier, a conspirator in the *Inconfidência Mineira* (q.v.)

Trapiche: primitive sugar mill

Tropeiro: muleteer

V

Várzea: flood plain; alluvial lands

Vereador: member of the town council (*câmara*)

Vila: town

Vintem (pl. vintens): coin worth 20 *reis*

Index of Authors, Editors, Translators, and Illustrators

[Numbers refer to Items]

A

B

C

N

O

P

Z

Nineteenth- and Twentieth-Century Authors Cited in the Text But Not Abstracted

[*Earlier authors are included in the Biographical Index*]

Biographical Index

[*Italicized numbers refer to entries where the name of the biographee is included in the title of the book or article.*]

A

D

E

F

I

J

K

L

T

V

W

Z